SURVIVORS AND EXILES

SURVIVORS AND EXILES

YIDDISH CULTURE AFTER THE HOLOCAUST

Jan Schwarz

Wayne State University Press
Detroit

© 2015 by Wayne State University Press, Detroit, Michigan 48201. First paperback edition © 2021. All rights reserved. No part of this book may be reproduced without formal permission.

Library of Congress Cataloging Number: 2015934520
ISBN 978-0-8143-4883-3 (paperback)
ISBN 978-0-8143-3905-3 (jacketed cloth)
ISBN 978-0-8143-3906-0 (ebook)

Designed and typeset by Andrew Katz
Composed in Adobe Caslon Pro

Wayne State University Press
Leonard N. Simons Building
4809 Woodward Avenue
Detroit, Michigan 48201-1309

Visit us online at wsupress.wayne.edu

Wayne State University Press rests on Waawiyaataanong, also referred to as Detroit, the ancestral and contemporary homeland of the Three Fires Confederacy. These sovereign lands were granted by the Ojibwe, Odawa, Potawatomi, and Wyandot nations, in 1807, through the Treaty of Detroit. Wayne State University Press affirms Indigenous sovereignty and honors all tribes with a connection to Detroit. With our Native neighbors, the press works to advance educational equity and promote a better future for the earth and all people.

CONTENTS

	Preface and Acknowledgments	vii
	Introduction	1

I. GROUND ZERO

1.	Vilna: Avrom Sutzkever	15
2.	Lodz: Chava Rosenfarb	44
3.	Minsk-Mazowiecki: Leib Rochman	67

II. TRANSNATIONAL ASHKENAZ

4.	*Dos poylishe yidntum:* A Library of Hope and Destruction	92
5.	1953–54: A Year in Yiddish Literature	118

III. YIDDISH LETTERS IN NEW YORK

6.	A Poetics of Retrieval and Loss: Aaron Zeitlin and Yankev Glatshteyn	143
7.	Performing Yiddish Poetry at the 92nd Street Y	181
8.	Prose of the Ashkenazi World: Chaim Grade and Yitskhok Bashevis (I. B. Singer)	210
	Conclusion	238
	Appendix 1. List of Publications: *Dos poylishe yidntum* (Polish Jewry, Buenos Aires, 1946–66)	253
	Appendix 2. Transliteration of Yiddish Texts According to the YIVO System	269
	Notes	291
	Bibliography	325
	Index	339

PREFACE AND ACKNOWLEDGMENTS

As I work on this book, I am frequently asked whether it will be published in Yiddish. Usually I shrug apologetically and reply that a contemporary Yiddish readership would be miniscule for such a work. The question does indicate, however, that there remains a deep memory of a vibrant, secular Yiddish-speaking world that still existed in its final bloom only one generation ago. The shift in the Jewish world from a Yiddish cultural system that catered to hundreds of thousands of people to today's bifurcated English- and Hebrew-speaking world of the Diaspora and Israeli communities (including many other languages) indicates the radical transformation of the Ashkenazi civilization after 1945. This book focuses on the latest chapter of this civilization, following its destruction in Central and Eastern Europe in the Holocaust.

Yiddish culture after the Holocaust provides a case study of the continuation, reconfiguration, and closure of an autonomous transnational network, and its transformation into a culture of remembrance. This shift from a future-oriented Yiddish culture—*di klasikers*, modernism, and mass media—to a culture sustained by past-oriented retrieval and memory occurred during the postwar period's dramatic geopolitical changes. These included the creation of the State of Israel, the growing centrality of the North American Jewish community, and the Iron Curtain's division of Europe. In the first two contexts and behind the Iron Curtain, Yiddish did continue to flourish in a combination of its vernacular setting, translation, academia, and post-vernacular culture.

Like most contemporary Yiddish scholarship, this book is addressed to a readership that is mostly unfamiliar with the basic tenets of Yiddish culture. As a result, I have combined the roles of a participant observer and guide for outsiders to Yiddish culture. The question of what constitutes authenticity hovers over Yiddish scholarship in its pursuit of knowledge and reconstruction of cultural landscapes that have almost completely ceased to exist. Like the Yiddish writers and performers who were forced to confront a radically changed world and set of challenges after the Holocaust, today's Yiddish scholar is faced with the question of how to delineate a culture that has been relegated to memory. The postwar Yiddish writers and performers continued to do their work in their mother tongue for a decimated but still vibrant transnational network of Yiddish speakers. Today's Yiddish scholar, in contrast, functions more like an archaeologist, stripping layer after layer of memory formations and critical methodologies that partly have distorted our understanding of the internal processes that shaped Yiddish culture after the Holocaust.

I have been guided by a set of values rooted in Yiddish culture. The most important is that *mame-loshn*, the Yiddish mother tongue, is given visibility not only in translation and transliteration but in its original Hebrew letters, as remains the case for most Yiddish print and performance culture. To include the vernacular content in the layout of this book is a choice that sets it apart from most other scholarly works in English. In this modest way, I have tried to respond affirmatively, at least symbolically, to the question of whether the book would be published in Yiddish.

The increasing availability of Yiddish source material on the internet has greatly enhanced access to Yiddish culture. The fact that it is possible to download and listen to a story or a song in Yiddish instantaneously on the internet has significantly changed the ways in which Yiddish culture is produced, circulated, and received. Particularly, the book's inclusion of Yiddish cultural performance (lectures, interviews, public readings) has benefited from the increasing online proliferation of Yiddish sources. Without the tireless efforts of Yiddish cultural organizations such as the National Yiddish Book Center (NYBC), and of journals and individuals who have initiated Yiddish blogs, list-serves, Facebook pages, and YouTube videos, this study would have missed a crucial feature of early twenty-first-century Yiddish culture.

***

Without the support and guidance of a cadre of scholars from the inception of this book more than a decade ago, this work would have been much more difficult if not impossible to write. It is the pleasure of exchange and feedback in an international network of colleagues that turns it into a true collaborative effort. Of course, all faults and mistakes are my responsibility alone. Unless otherwise noted in the citations, all translations from the Yiddish are mine.

I would like to thank Professors David G. Roskies, Seth Wolitz, Abraham Nowersztern, Rosemary Horowitz, Hana Wirth-Nesher, Alan Rosen, Jerold Frakes, Monika Adamczyk-Garbowska, Alan Astro, Kathryn Hellerstein,

Mikhail Krutikov, Gennady Estraykh, Anita Norich, Samuel Kassow, Cecile Kuznitz, Michael Steinlauf, Jeffrey Shandler, Dan Miron, Janet Hadda, and Miriam Isaacs for their support, inspiration, and help during the work on the book. Thanks to Ron Finegold, the former archivist of the Jewish Public Library in Montreal, who made the Avrom Tabatshnik interviews available in the form of tape recordings (now digitized on the NYBC website). Thanks to Steve Siegel, the former archivist at the 92nd Street Y in New York City, who generously gave me access to the archive and recordings of the Yiddish poetry readings that took place at the 92nd Street Y in the 1960s. Thanks to the staff at the Harry Ransom Center at the University of Texas for helping me navigate the I. B. Singer archive.

Joseph Sherman z"l organized a conference on Yiddish after the Holocaust at the Oxford Centre for Hebrew and Jewish Studies, Yarnton Manor, August 26–28, 2003, which resulted in one of the first English-language books about Yiddish culture after the Holocaust and included an early version of chapter 5. Thanks to my co-editors, the Jewish historians Antony Polonsky, Gabriel Finder, and Natalia Aleksiun, with whom I edited volume 20 of *POLIN: Making Holocaust Memory* (2008), which included a version of chapter 4. Thanks to Professor Eric Selinger, DePaul University, with whom I organized a conference about American Jewish multilingual literature at the University of Chicago in October 2007, whose papers were published as a special issue of *Prooftexts* (2010), which included chapter 7. Thanks to Professor Shlomo Berger (Amsterdam) and Professor Marion Aptroot (Dusseldorf), with whom I organized the European Yiddish workshop "Yiddish Culture in the 20th Century," in October 2012, at Lund University; and the Centre de Recherches Historiques in Paris, which in June 2014 organized the symposium "Writing the Destruction in the Polish-Jewish World from the End of World War II to the Late 1960s: Productions, Trajectories, Networks."

A sheynem dank to Professor Solon Beinfeld for his thorough reading of the Yiddish quotes in the original and transliteration, and to Professor Abraham Nowersztern for his incisive comments on an early draft of the manuscript. Professor Yechiel Szeintuch's (Hebrew University) work on Yiddish and Hebrew Holocaust literature has been an inspiration for the conception of the book. Thanks to doctoral candidate Malena Chinski (Buenos Aires), who graciously provided additional items to the list of books in appendix 1. I am particularly grateful to Kathryn Wildfong, editor-in-chief of Wayne State University Press, for enabling me to create a beautiful book that adheres to the highest scholarly standards; and to copyeditor Mindy Brown for her meticulous corrections of the final manuscript in English and Yiddish.

Thanks to the daughters of several Yiddish writers for their generous permission to use photographs of their parents: Goldie Morgentaler, Leah Strigler, Rivka Miriam. Thanks to Arnold Chekow, whose photographs of Yiddish writers at the 92nd Street Y in the 1960s grace the book. Thanks to the photographer Chuck Fishman, who generously gave me permission to use his photograph of I. B. Singer. *A hartsdikn dank* to the painter Samuel Bak, who created the cover illustration for the book and provided a photograph of himself as a boy on the lap of Avrom Sutzkever in Vilna, July 1944.

Earlier versions of the book chapters have been published in various journals and books. I thank their publishers and editors for giving permission to reprint this material:

Chapter 1: "After the Destruction of Jewish Vilna: Abraham Sutzkever's Poetry, Testimony and Cultural Rescue Work, 1944–1946," *East European Jewish Affairs* 35, no. 2, ed. John Klier (December 2005): 209–25.

Chapter 3: "Blood Ties: Leib Rochman's Yiddish War Diary," in *The Memorial Books of Eastern European Jewry*, ed. Rosemary Horowitz (Jefferson, NC: McFarland Press, 2010), 163–82.

Chapter 4: "A Library of Hope and Destruction: The Yiddish Book Series *Dos poylishe yidntum*, 1946–1966," and "Appendix: List of 175 Volumes of *Dos poylishe yidntum*," *POLIN 20: Studies in Polish Jewry* (2008): 173–96.

Chapter 5: "1953/1954—A Year in Yiddish Literature," *Studies in Contemporary Jewry* 23, ed. Ezra Mendelsohn (2008): 185–201.

Chapter 6: "The Voice of the Yiddish Poet: Avrom Ber Tabatshnik's Interview with Yankev Glatshteyn in New York, 1955," in *Yiddish after the Holocaust*, ed. Joseph Sherman (Oxford: Boulevard/Oxford Centre for Hebrew and Jewish Studies, 2004), 74–91.

"Encounters with German Language and Literature in Yankev Glatshteyn's Work," in *Between Two Worlds: Yiddish-German Encounters*, ed. Jeremy Dauber and Jerold Frakes, *Studia Rosenthaliana* 41 (Amsterdam: Peeters, 2009), 197–212.

Chapter 7: "Glatshteyn, Singer, Howe and Ozick: Performing Yiddish Poetry at the 92 Street Y, 1963–1969," *Prooftexts: A Journal of Jewish Literary History* 30, no. 1 (2010): 61–96.

Chapter 8: "Confrontation and Elegy in the Novels of Chaim Grade," in *The Multiple Voices of Modern Yiddish Culture*, ed. Shlomo Berger, *Studia Rosenthaliana* (Amsterdam: Menasseh Ben Israel Institute, 2007), 30–55.

"'Nothing but a Bundle of Paper': Isaac Bashevis Singer's Literary Career in America," in *Leket: Jiddistik heute* (Yiddish Studies Today/Yidishe shtudyes haynt), ed. Marion Aptroot, Efrat Gal-Ed, Roland Gruschka, and Simon Neuberg (Dusseldorf: Dusseldorf University Press, 2012), 189–207.

Conclusion: "The Holocaust and Postwar Yiddish Literature," in *Literature of the Holocaust*, ed. Alan Rosen (Cambridge: Cambridge University Press, 2013), 102–17.

As with everything I write in English, it has been a true pleasure to have my wife, Rabbi Rebecca Lillian, apply her outstanding editing skills to my work on the book.

The book is dedicated to my father, Hersh Shmiel (Henning) Schwarz (born 1927), *biz hundert tsvantsik,* and the memory of my uncles Moyshe Arn (Moniek) Schwarz (1924–2013) z"l and Dovid (David) Schwarz (1928–2008) z"l—three survivors of the *kehile kedoyshe* (holy community) of Piotrkow Trybunalski, Poland.

INTRODUCTION

In 1948 a thirty-five-year-old Yiddish poet, a survivor of the Vilna Ghetto who arrives in the Land of Israel as an *ole khadash* (new immigrant), writes a poem titled "*Yiddish*." The poem consists of one sustained argument by "my poetry brother with whiskers," who questions the future of Yiddish. The survivor poet confronts the attitudes of his poetry brother that have been enshrined in the newly established Jewish state; views that marginalize and even excise the very existence of Yiddish language and culture. Only via folk song and jokes—such as the folksy lullaby "*Rozhinkes mit mandlen*" (Raisins and Almonds)—is Yiddish visible in the Jewish state founded on biblical soil and language. This negation of the Jewish Diaspora becomes a negation of Yiddish, the Jewish Diaspora language par excellence.

The poet's response is an outcry, a refusal to be rendered invisible and sidelined by history. With his authority as a survivor and resistance fighter from Vilna, the Jerusalem of Lithuania, he rhetorically asks where the rich cultural inheritance of Yiddish will go to die. If their destruction is to take place at the Western Wall in Jerusalem, the only remnant of the Second Temple, then this survivor of *der driter khurbn* (the Third Holocaust following the destructions of the first and second temples in Jerusalem) will use the full potential of his poetry to create fiery, potent verse that will keep the memory of Yiddish alive throughout the ages.

זאָל איך אָנהייבן פֿון אָנהייב?
זאָל איך ווי אברהם
אויס ברודערשאַפֿט צעהאַקן אַלע געצן?
זאָל איך זיך אַ לעבעדיקן לאָזן איבערזעצן?
זאָל איך איינפֿלאַנצן מײַן צונג
און וואַרטן ביז זי פֿאַרוואַנדלען
וועט זי זיך אין אָבותדיקע
ראָזשינקעס מיט מאַנדלען?
וואָס פֿאַר אַ קאַטאָוועסדיקע
וויצן,
דרשנט מײַן פּאָעזיע־ברודער מיט די באַקנבאָרדן
אַז מײַן מאַמע־לשון גייט באַלד אונטער?

מיר װילן נאָך אין הונדערט יאָר אַרום דאָ קענטיק זיצן
און פֿירן די דיסקוסיע בײַ דעם ירדן.
וױיל אַ שאלה נאָגט און נאָגלט:
אױב ער װייסט גענױ װוּ
די תּפֿילה פֿון בערדיטשעװער,
יהואָשעס ליד,
און קולבאַקס
װאָגלט
צו דער אונטערגאַנג—
טאָ זאָל ער מיר אַ שטײגער,
אָנװײַזן װוּהין די שפּראַך גייט אונטער?
אפֿשר בײַ דער כּותל מערבֿי?
אױב אַזױ, װעל איך דאָרט קומען, קומען,
עפֿענען דאָס מױל
און װי אַ לײב
אַנגעטאָן אין פֿײַערדיקן צונטער,
אײַנשלינגען דעם לשון װאָס גייט אונטער,
אײַנשלינגען, און אַלע דורות װעקן מיט מײַן ברומען!

Shall I start from the beginning?
Shall I, a brother,
Like Abraham
Smash all the idols?
Shall I let myself be translated alive?
Shall I plant my tongue
And wait
Till it transforms
Into our forefathers'
Raisins and almonds?
What kind of joke
Preaches
My poetry brother with whiskers,
That soon, my mother tongue will set forever?
A hundred years from now, we still may sit here
On the Jordan, and carry on this argument.
For a question
Gnaws and paws at me:
If he knows exactly in what regions
Levi Yitskhok's prayer,

Yehoash's poem,
Kulbak's song
Are straying to their sunset—
Could he please show me
Where the language will go down?
Maybe at the Western Wall?
If so, I shall come there, come,
Open my mouth,
And like a lion
Garbed in fiery scarlet,
I shall swallow the language as it sets.
And wake all the generations with my roar!
Avrom Sutzkever, "Yiddish" (1948)[1]

Avrom Sutzkever's poem poses the essential questions raised in this book: What is the role of Yiddish language and culture after the near-complete destruction of its European centers in the Holocaust? How does a Yiddish writer negotiate the radically new circumstances after the Holocaust and the establishment of the Jewish state? How do the treasures of Yiddish language and culture maintain their relevance in the original and translation?

Post-Holocaust Yiddish culture has received much less critical attention than would be expected. The dominant discourse of Jewish culture after the Holocaust as it evolved in its main languages—English, Hebrew, German, and Russian—was not hospitable to Yiddish for various political, ideological, and cultural reasons. Yiddish embodied the Ashkenazi civilization in Eastern and Central Europe which had ceased to exist except for crumbling old books that nobody outside the Yiddish world was able to read. Only the presence of Yiddish writers (survivors and the old guard) and a still significant Yiddish readership ensured the visibility of the language in the Jewish cultural centers of the United States, Israel, and the Soviet Union. Yiddish was viewed as a remnant of the past, tragically eradicated in its prime. Yet during the first two and a half decades following the Holocaust, the Yiddish cultural world was in constant, dynamic flux, maintaining a staggering level of activity in the form of publications, cultural performances, collections of archival and historical materials, and the launching of young literary talents.

This book will tell this generally unknown story and present a multifaceted picture of a transnational Yiddish culture. The book offers a portrait of the 1945 generation of Yiddish writers, trailblazers of the last blossoming of secular Yiddish culture, which consisted of many and varied cultural, political, and literary organizations. These offered a wide range of publications, daily and periodical press, and other media. The ways into this globally dispersed culture will be presented through the works of seven major Yiddish writers who typify the trajectory of this generation's journey from the Old World to the New, through the crucible of the ghettos and concentration camps or by witnessing the Holocaust from New York, Montreal, Tel Aviv, Buenos Aires, and Moscow.

At the United States Holocaust Memorial Museum (USHMM), one encounters the gruesome details of the annihilation of the six million Jews in the exhibit area, workshops, and interviews with the rapidly shrinking group of survivors. However, with the exception of a few Yiddish poems displayed at the end of the permanent exhibit, there are almost no visible signs of the culture and language of the majority of Jews murdered in the Holocaust. Behind locked glass cases flanking the entrance to the USHMM library, a complete set of *Yizker* books, the Yiddish and Hebrew memorial books edited and published by the *landsmanshaftn* (hometown organizations) of Eastern European Jewish towns, is displayed like *sforim* (holy books) in a *beys medresh* (house of study).[2] Characteristically, the *Yizker* books are exhibited as iconic artifacts in the museum but are relatively seldom utilized in Holocaust studies.[3] The reasons for the occlusion of Yiddish culture and language in Holocaust museums, scholarship, and education are multifaceted and complex.[4] The fact remains, however, that until recently the intersection between Yiddish and Holocaust studies has been limited in English-language scholarship.[5] Like most post-1945 Yiddish writing, the works of surviving Jewish historians and literary scholars from Eastern Europe—such as Nakhmen Blumenthal, Philip Friedman, Bernard Mark, Mark Dworzecki, and Joseph Kermish—who began collecting and systematically analyzing Yiddish testimonies and artistic works immediately after the war, have been largely invisible in English.[6] Recently, three books have appeared that locate Yiddish writings at the center of the field of Holocaust studies as a paradigmatic and continuous body of work written by Jews during and after the Holocaust.[7] This book contributes to this renewal of scholarly engagement between Holocaust and Yiddish studies which, as Jewish historian Cecile Kuznitz points out, has a lot to offer: "A closer relationship between Yiddish studies and Holocaust scholarship has much to contribute to our understanding of the catastrophe, placing it in its Jewish context and giving long-overdue attention to the most heroic chapter of Yiddish cultural creativity."[8]

David G. Roskies has argued that post-1945 Yiddish culture has continuously and systematically placed the Holocaust at its center. Particularly between 1945 and the Eichmann trial in 1961, Yiddish culture was arguably the most significant site of critical and artistic engagement with the Holocaust, secondary in importance only to the war years' prolific output of Jewish writings from the ghettos and the camps, and from hiding places on the Aryan side. The heart of this book examines the Yiddish cultural projects and literary works that were implemented by individuals and organizations after 1945. To enter this world is to confront a vastly different set of Jewish attitudes and responses to the Holocaust than the ones usually presented in English. The Yiddish world was claustrophobic, narrow, and divisive, continuing to wage contentious debates about politics and the arts that originated in a pre-Holocaust "Yiddishland" in Poland, the Soviet Union, and the United States. In Roskies's apt words: "Yiddish—the language of the meek, the passive and the pious—became in the wake of the Holocaust the repository of uncensored, unyielding, politically incorrect Jewish rage."[9]

Regardless of the reasons for the occlusion of Yiddish voices from the field of Holocaust studies, and in the broader public arena, the result has been the absurd claim "that the wartime and communal phases of Holocaust memory didn't exist at all."[10] This claim has been vigorously rejected in recent studies, but a concrete mapping of the post-1945 Yiddish world has been slow in coming. This book is the first attempt to present a description and analysis of Yiddish culture after 1945. It focuses particularly on the period through the 1960s, during which the survivors' accounts and points of view were generally invisible outside the Hebrew and Yiddish cultural networks.

As Benjamin Harshav makes clear, there were two Holocausts: the systematic murder of the European Jews and the Germans' attempt to obliterate Jewish culture, language, and history.[11] It is the former that has drawn the most attention, the focal point of the most acclaimed accounts of the concentration camps that remains at the center of Holocaust studies. There has been a strong tendency to highlight the works of writers who wrote during the war under desperate circumstances. Most of this writing was lost, and only a small portion was published posthumously after the war. An even smaller number of texts were rescued and edited by the few surviving writers themselves. The other group of writers whose first works were published before the Holocaust, and whose artistic mastery and world views had been fully formed prior to the war, has received much less attention. Particularly important is the delineation of the Yiddish critical discourse that was developed by historians and critics in order to examine the main tenets of testimonial and literary representation of the Holocaust. As documented throughout this book, the Yiddish critical terminology about such topics as

Holocaust representation, trauma, and commemoration precedes the rise of Holocaust Studies and Memory Studies as academic disciplines by several decades. Current methodologies in these fields will be utilized and compared with the vastly different sets of critical concerns of Yiddish writers and critics during the first quarter-century after the Holocaust.

In his introduction to the bibliography *Essential Yiddish Books: 1000 Great Works from the Collection of the National Yiddish Book Center* (2004), Zachary M. Baker points out that "Yiddish literary activity during the postwar decades is a somewhat underappreciated phenomenon, and this collection implicitly supports the contention that the quarter century following the end of World War II was a 'Silver Age' of the Yiddish book."[12] This "silver age" has not yet been delineated as a full-blown cultural manifestation and final blossoming of Ashkenazi culture in transnational, interconnected Yiddish-speaking communities. This study is an attempt to mark out the parameters of such a cultural mapping by sketching a contradictory picture of rupture and continuity, decline and revival. These terms more accurately describe the development of Yiddish culture and the accomplishment of Yiddish writers after 1945. The regrouping of writers and cultural resources in transnational Yiddish centers was invigorated by the arrival of young survivors whose work would address very different aesthetic, thematic, and ideological concerns from the ones that had defined Yiddish culture in interwar Jewish Eastern Europe, the United States, and the Soviet Union.

The biographical trajectory of this generation of Yiddish writers represents a movement from Europe to the Americas, except for small groups of Yiddish writers who remained behind the Iron Curtain and a group of writers who relocated to the State of Israel. The 1945 generation accumulated intimate knowledge of one or both world wars, the Bolshevik revolution, the Soviet Union, the Holocaust, the chaotic conditions in Europe in the aftermath of the Holocaust, emigration, and starting new lives overseas. These writers grew up in the shadow of (and in some cases experienced) totalitarianism, war, and genocide. The allure of Soviet communism, Zionism, Yiddishism, and assimilation informed their work. Their lives and artistic careers spanned multiple ruptures and movements, from the densely populated Ashkenazic communities of Eastern Europe to the more recently established Yiddish centers overseas. Their artistic, essayistic, and journalistic work articulated a deep sense of continuity (*hemshekh*) that replaced the center, a vibrant Yiddish mass culture in Eastern Europe, with a network of overseas centers. A main condition for this cultural continuity was the existence of a transnational Yiddish infrastructure whose main pillars were the press, cultural organizations, and publishers, and a globally dispersed readership whose biographical profile mirrored that of the writers.

"Post-vernacular Yiddish" in American and Israeli popular culture has become the main focus of current scholarship about Yiddish culture. Jeffrey Shandler, who coined the term, has analyzed the reception, performance, and translation of Yiddish culture in the second half of twentieth-century America as separate from the considerations of the specifics of Yiddish culture defined by its own cultural and linguistic parameters. In contrast, this book offers a selective "inventory or chronicle of Yiddish activities of the past six decades," focusing on the period 1945–71.[13] Mostly, scholars have viewed this period as a waning epilogue to the golden age of Yiddish culture in Warsaw, New York City, and Moscow, spanning the trailblazing works of *di klasikers* in the late nineteenth century through the surge of Yiddish modernism and mass culture in the first four decades of the twentieth century, which was terminated by the outbreak of World War II. As a rule, Yiddish culture after 1945 has been associated with cataclysm and dislocation. Generalizations such as "the end of a language" and "a literary system poised on the edge of complete annihilation" have painted a picture of irreversible decline and extinction.[14] The main argument of this book, in contrast, is that a transnational Yiddish culture after 1945 evolved with a whole new set of priorities. Yiddish writers and cultural leaders emphasized consolidation and continuity, driven by a strong sense of being the last of a generation (*di letste fun a dor*) and thus responsible for completing the historical and cultural projects that in some cases had been initiated during the war.

Yiddish writers after 1945 ended up far from their Ashkenazi homelands; there they reenacted the political battles, passionate debates, and party loyalties that had defined their first exposure to the world of Yiddish letters in Eastern and Central Europe. Their passage through various historical time zones, landscapes, and political minefields continued to serve as their inner map of the world. Particularly important was the writers' confrontation with Soviet communism. Avrom Sutzkever, for example, stood apart from the writers' group Yung-Vilne's socialist leanings in the 1930s and spent 1944–46 in Moscow before his immigration to Palestine via Paris. In Moscow he befriended the Soviet Yiddish writers and witnessed how the Soviet authorities tightened their noose around the writers' necks. Sutzkever became a celebrated poet-partisan in the claustrophobic politicized environment of Yiddish culture in Stalin's Soviet Union. In postwar Moscow, his Yiddishist poetics and beliefs clashed with the political strictures and self-censorship of Soviet Yiddish writers (see chapter 1). During the immediate postwar period, the two Soviet Yiddish prose writers Der Nister and Dovid Bergelson wrote some of their most powerful stories about Jewish martyrdom; these were in some cases published overseas, where they reached a worldwide Yiddish readership. Yitskhok Bashevis, another case in point, stood out as one of the few neoconservatives in Tlomatske 13, the Yiddish Writers Union in Warsaw, which was dominated by communist fellow travelers in the 1930s. The antagonism toward Soviet communism of Sutzkever and Singer—two of this book's key figures—informed their life-long loyalties to poetry and storytelling rooted in the Ashkenazi Jews' historical and cultural heritage (*yerushe*).

The last cultural flowering of Soviet Yiddish culture, in the immediate aftermath of the war (1944–47), was crushed when the USSR executed the leading cadre of Soviet Yiddish writers on August 12, 1952.[15] Not until the early 1960s were Yiddish cultural institutions again allowed to function in the Soviet Union, albeit at a much lower level than before 1947. During the 1940s and early 1950s, the world map of Yiddish culture was in a fluid state, due to the migration of Jewish Displaced Persons from Germany. This included Yiddish writers Chaim Grade, Sutzkever, Leib Rochman, and Mordechai Strigler, who each settled briefly in Paris, an important hub on the way to their destinations overseas. Under the tutelage of the Vilna poet Avrom Sutzkever, who came to Palestine in 1947, the literary group Yung Yisroel (Young Israel), comprised of newly arrived Yiddish writers in Israel, began to make contributions to Yiddish literature in the 1950s.[16]

The communal memory characterizing Yiddish culture after the Holocaust tapped into age-old collective Jewish responses to catastrophe.[17] A group of modernist iconoclasts in New York, including Yankev Glatshteyn, Aaron Zeitlin, and Kadya Molodovsky, infused their poetry with religious imagery, conventional rhymes, and neoclassical forms. They turned to collective forms of commemoration, eschewing their previous individualistic modernism. Glatshteyn even expressed the desire for his poetic lamentation to be included anonymously in a future *sider*, or Jewish prayer book. Without returning to the synagogue, Glatshteyn returned to Jewish religious archetypes in his Holocaust poetry, as in the poem "*Nisht di meysim loybn got*" (The Dead Don't Praise God), echoing the Psalms:

די תּורה האָבן מיר מקבל געווען בײַם סיני,
און אין לובלין האָבן מיר זי אָפּגעגעבן.
נישט די מתים לויבן גאָט,
די תּורה איז געגעבן געוואָרן צום לעבן.

We accepted the Torah at Sinai
And in Lublin we gave it back.
The Dead do not praise God,
The Torah was given for Life.[18]

Yiddish poets such as Glatshteyn, Sutzkever, Zeitlin, and Molodovsky were staunchly secular writers who utilized religious imagery, tropes, and genres to suit their artistic purposes. They downplayed their previous modernist poetics after 1945. Their poetry was instead refracted through testimonial and commemorative modes of expression. There were indeed exceptions, such as Sutzkever's surrealist prose poems "*Griner akvarium*" (Green Aquarium, 1953–54), *Dortn vu es nekhtikn di shtern* (Where the Stars Spend the Night, 1975–77), and *Di nevue fun shvartsapln* (The Prophecy of the Pupils, 1975–89), which stand as the apotheosis of modernism in Yiddish postwar literature.

Religious Yiddish writers, a minority within a minority, did not view their new *goles* (diaspora) after 1945 as qualitatively different from the earlier European one.[19] For them, the true return would come at the end of days, with the arrival of the Messiah and the ingathering of the exiles in the Land of Israel. After escaping Nazi Germany in 1939, Abraham Joshua Heschel began to publish theological, religious, and philosophical works in multiple languages (English, Yiddish, German, and Hebrew). As with Yitskhok Bashevis, Chaim Grade, Aaron Zeitlin, and Leib Rochman, Heschel's work was steeped in the traditional Hebrew-Yiddish bilingualism of Ashkenaz, which he sought to reconceptualize in English adaptation for American-born readers. Heschel wrote his final book (a biography of the Kotzker Rebbe) in Yiddish in the style of the Hasidic homily. In it, the Kotzker Rebbe articulates a traditional interpretation of the religious use of poetry and language as redemptive comfort in response to collective catastrophe and loss:

ווען ירמיה הנביא האָט באַקלאָגט דעם חורבן בית-המקדש און אָנגעשריבן מגילת איכה, האָט ער זייַנע ווערטער מסדר געווען לויט אַלף-בית. פֿרעגט זיך: וואָס אַ שייכות האָבן די קינות מיט אַלף-בית? ענטפֿערט ר׳ מענדל: ווען דער נביא האָט געזען דעם מוראדיקן בראָך, וואָס מען האָט אַלץ צוגענומען פֿון אונדז: דאָס בית-המקדש איז חרוב, די השפּעה פֿון הייליקייט וואָס פֿלעגט דערגיין צו אונדז האָט אויפֿגעהערט, איז ער אַרייַנגעפֿאַלן אין ייאוש, און מורא געהאַט, אַז ייִדן און די וועלט בכלל וועלט קיין קיום נישט האָבן, חס ושלום. ביז ער האָט אײַנגעזען, אַז דער אַלף-בית איז געבליבן. האָט ער דערין געפֿונען אַ טרייסט, דער אַלף-בית איז דער טרייסט. דערפֿאַר הייסט דער חודש ווען עס פֿאַלט אויס תשעה באָב מנחם אָב, א״ב איז דער טרייסט.

> When the Prophet Jeremiah lamented the destruction of the Temple and wrote the Lamentations, he put the words in alphabetical order. The question is: What is the relationship between the dirges and the alphabet? The Kotzker Rebbe answers: When the prophet saw the frightening rupture that everything had been taken from us—the Temple is destroyed, the influence of holiness which used to reach us had disappeared—he fell into despair, fearing that Jews and the whole world would cease to exist, God forbid. Until he realized that the alphabet remained. So he found comfort therein, for the alphabet is the comfort. Therefore the month in which Tisha B'Av falls is called *menakhem av,* the *alef* and the *beys* are the comfort.[20]

Tisha B'Av, the fast day on which Jews mourn the destruction of the two temples in Jerusalem, falls on the ninth day of the month of Av. Av is spelled with the two first letters of the alphabet, *alef* and *beys* (the name of the Hebrew and Yiddish alphabet is *alefbeys.*) The Kotzker's *drash* (interpretation) uses this language pun for his eschatological vision of redemption through the symbolic act of linking together letters and words. The day is called *menakhem av,* the comfort of the month of Av, signifying the comfort of the Hebrew alphabet as well.

Transplanted and displaced in their new countries, Yiddish writers erected artistic replicas in the form of life-writing, artistic works, and testimonies in order to memorialize Ashkenaz, the Eastern European Jewish world. Long before the World Wide Web, they created a virtual web of images, figures, narratives, and language folklore. Their unceasing commitment to building a virtual Ashkenaz in writing, images, song, and performance is the model for this study's examination of selected examples of post-Holocaust Yiddish culture, and how they were transmitted in various ideological contexts in the Americas (New York City, Montreal and Buenos Aires), behind the Iron Curtain (Warsaw and Moscow), and in Israel (Tel Aviv).

A recurrent trope in post-Holocaust Yiddish literature presents the Yiddish writer as being among the last survivors of Ashkenaz civilization. Each of his or her words bears the stamp of Ashkenaz as a synecdoche of a civilization that has ceased to exist. Yitskhok Bashevis's last demon in the story "*Mayse Tishevitz*" (The Last Demon, 1959) has survived the cataclysm in a small town in Poland, where it spends the time counting letters and creating children's rhymes. As long as the Hebrew alphabet can be mined for Yiddish rhymes, the last demon keeps busy in his isolation on a hayloft in a *Judenrein* Polish town. His power to lure people to do evil has vanished, as not a single

Jew remains to be tempted. What remains, however, is the formulaic scheme of good and evil, as performed by the demon storyteller with a yeshiva education. The tales he spins are suffused with elegiac melancholy. As in the Kotzker's parable, the Hebrew alphabet in an old Yiddish storybook is all that comforts the demon and keeps him alive:

אָן אַ ייִדיש אות—
איז אַ שד אַ ייִד—אויס . . .

When the last letter is gone,
The last of the demons is done.[21]

The Yiddish storyteller bears witness to Ashkenaz in the form of meticulously crafted artistic replicas of a bygone age in which individuals argue and debate as if there were no tomorrow. In "The Last Demon" time is frozen in present-tense snapshots of a historical community that is vibrantly alive in the speech and thoughts of demonic characters. (On Singer, see chapter 8.)

Similarly, the novella "My Quarrel with Hersh Rasseyner" (1953) by Chaim Grade, another key figure, articulates the strong sense of continuity that motivated the Yiddish writers who had managed to escape the Nazi genocide and Soviet totalitarianism. It is set in Paris in the spring of 1948 and inhabits a pre-Holocaust map of Ashkenazi Europe that excludes Zionism, Israel, and New York, where Grade settled in 1950. The novella focuses entirely on the repercussions of the Holocaust for survivors of Ashkenaz. Grade's novella depicts a daylong argument between the secular Yiddish writer Chaim Vilner and his opponent, Hersh Rasseyner, an ultra-Orthodox follower of the *muser* movement. Although they discuss the implications of the Holocaust for Jewish life in the Diaspora, neither Zionism and Israel nor America is mentioned in the story. The two protagonists enact a two-decades-long argument originating in their hometown of Vilna. The debate is about the commitment to ultra-Orthodox faith, secularism, and the fate of *klal-yisroel* (the Jewish people) as practiced by displaced *ost-Juden* in the cultural capital of the West. (On Grade, see chapter 8.)

Like Singer's demon hiding in the attic, Yiddish survivor writers such as Grade, Sutzkever, and Zeitlin became portable archives and encyclopedias of Ashkenazi culture, spending their most productive years in exile in their new homes. They made the Yiddish language their lifeline to the six-hundred-year-old Ashkenazi civilization after the complete destruction of its material and social infrastructure. The Yiddish writers remained in perpetual exile, with zero illusions of ever returning home. As the last representatives of their culture, the surviving Yiddish writers continued to create works premised on the existence of Ashkenaz as a Diaspora culture (*goles kultur*). Regardless of their religious or political persuasion, Yiddish writers created works that "retained a collective memory, vision, or myth about their original homeland—its physical location, history, achievements, and, often enough, sufferings."[22] In their new homes the Yiddish writers struggled to survive as a distinct Yiddish cultural entity, a minority within a Jewish minority or, in the case of Israel, within the Jewish majority population.

The Yiddish writers spearheaded the ingathering of Yiddish cultural treasures, or *kinus*, which took place in multiple venues: cultural rescue work in Europe, book series such as *Dos poylishe yidntum* (Polish Jewry), journals, anthologies, and the large-scale project of *Yizker* books, memorial books of the destroyed Jewish communities of Eastern Europe. The approximately one thousand *Yizker* books that have been published to date, written almost entirely in Yiddish and Hebrew by the survivors of Eastern European Jewish communities—in some cases under the editorship and supervision of professional historians—resulted in the collection of an invaluable treasure trove of historical, folkloristic, genealogical, and literary materials.

Dos poylishe yidntum and the *Yizker* books chronicle the religious and cultural histories of Jewish communities, document Jewish spiritual and physical resistance to the Final Solution, and highlight the tenacity and heroism of the *sheyres hapleyte* (the saved remnants—the Yiddish term for "Holocaust survivors"). *Yizker* books created a virtual encyclopedia of hundreds of Jewish communities in Central and Eastern Europe, from the smallest towns and villages to the provincial and governmental centers. Originally composed, edited, and published by a collective of writers associated with the local *landsmanshaft*, the *Yizker* books have transcended their initial internal Jewish context. They have become important source material in a larger public and academic setting. *Dos poylishe yidntum*, a series of 175 books published in Buenos Aires between 1946 and 1966, pointed to the existence of a transcontinental Yiddish cadre of writers and a mass readership. It became a cultural matrix for Yiddish readers' continued engagement with Ashkenazi history and culture and the promulgation of young Yiddish literary talents. These two large-scale collective book projects encapsulate the fundamental tenor of post-1945 Yiddish culture by affirming a fundamental humanist belief in progress and justice. (On *Dos poylishe yidntum*, see chapter 4.)

In the chapters that follow, the contradictory development of continuity and rupture that characterizes the works and careers of Yiddish writers after

1945 will be illustrated through close readings of both poetry and prose, and by examining cultural-historical phenomena and reader reception, including publication venues and critical discourse. The innovation of post-1945 Yiddish culture will be highlighted and situated in the context of institutional and ideological infrastructures in some cases established prior to the war. By focusing on the careers and works of seven major Yiddish writers, we are able to see how the part came to stand in for the whole. The scope and variety of Yiddish culture after 1945 were, in the main, due to the heroic efforts of a small group of survivor writers who relocated to overseas centers which they sought to transform in their own image.

Chava Rosenfarb's literary career began in the Lodz Ghetto, where she began to write poetry that was lost when she was sent to Auschwitz. Rosenfarb's post-Holocaust life story, which took her from Bergen-Belsen to Montreal via Brussels, typifies the westward trajectory of the 1945 generation. Rosenfarb's work as poet, novelist, storyteller, and essayist is paradigmatic for the commitment to Yiddish literature through the early twenty-first century. (On Rosenfarb, see chapter 2.) Some Yiddish writers modeled their personal accounts of survival on the *Yizker* book by fusing historical documentation, commemoration, and novelistic techniques. This was the case for Leib Rochman's war diary, *Un in dayn blut zolstu lebn* (And in Your Blood Shall You Live, 1949). The diary was an actual account of five Jews' survival in hiding, in a hayloft in a small village near Minsk-Mazowiecki, twenty-five miles from Warsaw. They hid there from the winter of 1943 until they were liberated by the Red Army in August 1944. The original diary (located in the Yad Vashem archive), which Rochman kept while in hiding, was reworked in the aftermath of the Holocaust and published in 1949 by the *landsmanshaft* of Minsk-Mazowiecki in Paris. It included an epilogue in the manner of the *Yizker* book, consisting of historical and commemorative sources about the Jewish community in the town. Rochman's Zionist beliefs informed his artistically crafted diary and propelled him, like Sutzkever, to Israel, where he became a correspondent for the New York daily the *Forverts*. (On Rochman and Mordechai Strigler, see chapter 3.)

New York City became the main Yiddish center after the Holocaust, while minor Yiddish centers continued to develop in Buenos Aires, Montreal, Tel Aviv, Warsaw, and Moscow. The Yiddish poet and critic Avrom Tabatshnik's project *Di shtim fun yidishn poet* (The Voice of the Yiddish Poet) in the mid-1950s, consisting of audio recordings of interviews with and readings by the leading Yiddish poets in New York City, bore witness to Yiddish artistic creativity in the past and the present. Similarly, initiated by the poet

Yankev Glatshteyn and William Kolodney (the 92nd Street Y's director of education at the Poetry Center), a series of more than forty Yiddish poetry readings with thirty Yiddish poets and fiction writers at the 92nd Street Y in Manhattan from 1963 to 1969 (including bilingual Hebrew-Yiddish poets) formed part of the cultural stock-taking and ingathering of cultural treasures after 1945. (On Yiddish culture in New York City, see chapters 5 through 8.)

This book's methodology is embedded in a global view of post-1945 Yiddish culture. It maps the culture as consisting of multiple distinctive centers in various national contexts, which were ideologically divided among the centers behind the Iron Curtain and in Israel and the Americas. The centrifugal forces of geographical, political, and cultural fragmentation were counteracted by centripetal forces that joined Yiddish writers and readers together in a transnational network united by common purposes: to commemorate and bear witness to the destruction of Ashkenaz, and to continue to develop a modern Yiddish culture. These conflicting trends of fragmentation and globalization provided the overall context for the creation of artistic works of great originality. Ultimately, this is what distinguishes the 1945 generation as creating a new chapter in the development of modern Yiddish culture.

PART I: GROUND ZERO

1

VILNA

Avrom Sutzkever

When the Yiddish poet Abraham (Avrom) Sutzkever (1913–2010) was imprisoned, along with the remaining one-third of his community, within the walls of the Vilna Ghetto, he imagined the day of liberation as a joyless, anticlimactic moment. In a poem he wrote on February 14, 1943, in the Vilna Ghetto, "*Vi azoy?*" (How?), Sutzkever envisioned liberation as a continued enslavement to the past, its joy erased by "the dark scream of your past-in-chains" ("*dayn fargangenkeyts fintstere shrayung*"). He subtly used the Yiddish word *fargangenheyt* (past) to coin a neologism *fargangenkeyt* (past-in-chains), indicating that the survivor's experiences would forever bind him in the chains of traumatized memories. Similarly, the Polish Jewish writer Henryk Grynberg concluded his memoir *The Victory* (1969), about his experiences as a survivor in Lodz in late 1944: "The war was over, but who had won?"[1]

ווי אַזוי און מיט וואָס וועסטו פֿילן
דיַין בעכער אין טאָג פֿון באַפֿרייונג?
ביסטו גרייט אין דיַין פֿרייד צו דערפֿילן
דיַין פֿאַרגאַנגענקייטס פֿינצערע שריַיונג
ווו עס גליווערן שאַרבנס פֿון טעג
אין אַ תּהום אָן אַ גרונט, אָן אַ דעק?

דו וועסט זוכן אַ שליסל צו פּאַסן
פֿאַר דיַינע פֿאַרהאַקטע שלעסער.
ווי ברויט וועסטו בייסן די גאַסן

און טראַכטן: דער פֿריִער איז בעסער.
און די צײַט וועט דיך עגבערן שטיל
ווי אין פֿויסט אַ געפֿאַנגענע גריל.

און ס׳וועט זײַן דײַן זכּרון געגליכן
צו אַן אַלטער פֿאַרשאָטענער שטאָט.
און דײַן דרויסיקער בליק וועט דאָרט קריכן
ווי אַ קראָט, ווי אַ קראָט—

How and with what will you fill
Your goblet on the day of Liberation?
In your joy, are you ready to feel
The dark scream of your past-in-chains
Where skulls of days congeal
In a bottomless pit?

You will look for a key to fit
Your jammed locks.
Like bread you will bite the streets
And think: better the past.
And time will drill you quietly
Like a cricket caught in a fist.

And your memory will be like
An old buried city.
Your eternal gaze will crawl
Like a mole, like a mole—[2]

The decisive years in Sutzkever's life between 1941 and 1947 can be described by his inner poetic "trial" during and after the catastrophe, and by his public activities, which included cultural rescue work, publication of his Holocaust testimony, and his appearance as a witness before the Nuremberg Tribunal in February 1946.

When Sutzkever passed away at ninety-six in 2010, eulogies in the United States and Israel lamented his invisibility outside the Yiddish-speaking community. Although his work has been translated into thirty languages, including English, Hebrew, Polish, and German, the greatest Yiddish poet of the post-Holocaust period remains marginal outside the Yiddish cultural world, in which he was a tireless advocate for the continuation of high-quality Yiddish literature and editor of the influential journal *Di goldene keyt* (The Golden Chain) from 1949 to 1995. Sutzkever is a prime example of one poet's herculean effort to resuscitate and expand—for more than half a century after the Holocaust—the creative spark and critical discourse of Yiddish culture.

Even among the abundant larger-than-life figures that populate the world of Yiddish culture, Sutzkever is exceptional. His dramatic life story included exile to Siberia as a child during World War I; incarceration in the Vilna Ghetto from 1941 to 1943; sojourn among Soviet Yiddish writers from 1944 to 1946; and immigration to the Land of Israel in 1947. His childhood in Siberia, where he lived until age nine, informed his pantheistic-inspired poetry published in Vilna in 1937 and 1940. In the 1930s he corresponded with the poet Aaron Leyeles in New York, and published his poems in the *Inzikhist* journal and other New York Yiddish publications. The next stage of his life, the Vilna Ghetto period, during which he became a central figure in the Jewish cultural resistance, was followed by his active participation in the Soviet-led partisan groups that organized in the woods outside Vilna. The rescue of Avrom Sutzkever and his wife, Freydke, by a Soviet military plane in the Lake Narocz woods in March 1944, brought him to Moscow and saved the couple from the anti-Semitic perils faced by Jews in Soviet-led partisan groups. During his two-year sojourn in Moscow, he befriended the leading Soviet Yiddish writers, whom he later recorded in a series of portraits of their predicament before the beginning of the liquidation of Jewish culture in the Soviet Union in early 1947.

In February 1946, Sutzkever bore witness before the Nuremberg Tribunal, as a Soviet citizen and representative of the Soviet delegation. After returning to Poland, where he composed his farewell poem *"Tsu Poyln"* (To Poland), he arrived in Palestine in 1947. Two years later, after persuading the Histadrut (General Labor Union in Israel) to publish a Yiddish literary journal called *Di goldene keyt*, Sutzkever brought out its first issue in 1949, during the Israeli War of Independence. The final segment of the poet's life spanned half a century of prolific, groundbreaking poetic work in the Jewish state, where he remained largely invisible outside Yiddish circles and small groups of Israeli literati.

In a eulogy published on January 28, 2010, in the Israeli newspaper *Haaretz*, the poet and translator Dory Manor summed up the cultural and ideological obstacles to Sutzkever's ever becoming visible in Israeli society, despite the excellent Hebrew translators of his work: "It is very hard to separate his poetry from what people think of Yiddish and *Yiddishkeit*. There's some kind of prejudice, and it's a mission impossible to uproot it from people. They think that Yiddish is connected to some kind of shtetl schmaltz, to defeatism and an exile mentality. Sutzkever's poetry is not that at all. There's no connection between it and saccharine folklore."[3]

In contrast to the few Yiddish writers of a popular bent, such as Yitskhok Bashevis and the poet Itsik Manger, Sutzkever, Leyeles, Yankev Glatshteyn, and Aaron Zeitlin found that their modernist works were unable to breach the deeply ingrained prejudice of the Jewish reading public in the United States and Israel, who typically viewed Yiddish as shtetl kitsch, schmaltz (sentimentality), and folklore, as popularized in the musical *Fiddler on the Roof* (1965). As expressed in the poem "*Yiddish*" (see Introduction, pages 1–3), this distortion and rejection of modernist Yiddish culture would become its main public face to the larger Jewish world.

This chapter delineates Sutzkever's achievement as a poet in the Vilna Ghetto and in the aftermath of its destruction, followed by his unique position among the Soviet Yiddish literati before their liquidation in 1947. During the dramatic period that began with the German invasion of the Soviet Union on June 21, 1941, through his illegal immigration to Palestine in 1947, Sutzkever's wanderings from Moscow via Vilna, Lodz, and Paris to Palestine—and his poetic output from those places and times—are emblematic of the transient nature of post-1945 Yiddish culture. Sutzkever's great achievement as a poet was his ability to remain prolific during the German genocide of the Jewish population of Vilna (1941–44) and amid the repressive political climate of the Soviet Union of 1944–46. His unceasing work on behalf of Yiddish as a poet, an editor, and a cultural worker continued in Israel, despite being "ghettoized" and marginalized. The starting point for the examination of Sutzkever's poetry and cultural work during the period 1941–47 is the attack of the German army on the Soviet Union on June 21, 1941, which represented the death knell for Vilna, "the Jerusalem of Lithuania."

The genocide of Eastern European Jewry destroyed more than 90 percent of its population. Lithuanian Jewry suffered the greatest losses. Moreover, as Dina Porat points out, the German killing squads (*Einsatzgruppen*) had already murdered about 75 percent of the Jewish population in Lithuania by the end of 1941, during the first six months of the German occupation: "By the summer of 1944, fully 95 percent of the country's Jewish population was gone. Nowhere else in Europe were the scope and speed of the killing so overwhelming."[4] The liberation of Vilna by the Red Army on July 13, 1944, marked the end of three years of German occupation, which had left the

Jewish section of the city utterly destroyed and most of its Jewish population murdered. After fighting as partisans, the poets Shmerke Kaczerginski, Avrom Sutzkever, and Abba Kovner returned to Vilna in July 1944. They were forced to confront the magnitude of the devastation. During the following months they threw themselves into the enormous task of rescuing cultural treasures, creating self-help organizations, and building a social infrastructure for the Jewish survivors. They also began the vital process of bearing witness to the German atrocities by recording and collecting eyewitness accounts, all of which were eventually included in their Holocaust memoirs.[5]

For Kovner and Sutzkever, liberated Vilna was a way station toward their final destination, *Eretz Yisroel* (the Land of Israel). As a member of the Zionist youth movement Hashomer Hatzair (the Young Guard), the Hebrew poet Kovner had made the first Jewish call for armed resistance in Nazi-occupied Europe among his Zionist comrades in the Vilna Ghetto on January 1, 1942. Sutzkever was not directly involved in Kovner's group, but his ghetto experience led him inexorably to the same conclusion: nothing but a future Jewish state could provide the necessary protection for the surviving remnants of European Jews. As one of the few surviving Yiddish poets from *Lite* (the Jewish areas of Lithuania, White Russia, and northeastern Poland), he set out on a mission to transfer Yiddish culture to the YIVO Institute for Jewish Research in New York City, which had replaced Vilna as the main YIVO branch in 1940.

Avrom Sutzkever's multifaceted work between 1941 and 1947 consisted of three related activities that continued the cultural resistance he had started in the Vilna Ghetto. First, he collected material for the prosecution of war criminals in his memoir *Fun vilner geto* (From the Vilna Ghetto), written in the summer of 1944 and published the following year under the imprint Melukhe Farlag "Der Emes" (The State Publisher "The Truth") in Moscow. This activity culminated in his testimony as a member of the Soviet delegation to the International Military Tribunal at Nuremberg on February 27, 1946.

Second, Sutzkever collected the ghetto poems that he had started writing immediately following the German invasion of Vilna on June 24, 1941, and some of which he published in his 1945 collection *Di festung: Lider un poemes, geshribn in vilner geto un in vald, 1941–1944* (The Fortress: Poems Written in the Vilna Ghetto and in the Forest, 1941–1944). Third, together with his friend Shmerke Kaczerginski, Sutzkever, as mentioned earlier, rescued Jewish cultural treasures in Vilna, most of which had been hidden by members of the "Paper Brigade" (see below), and shipped part of them to the YIVO headquarters in New York City.

Sutzkever wrote a large number of remarkable poems prior to fleeing the ghetto in September 1943. His *poeme* (epic poem) "*Kol Nidre, dertseylt fun a geblibenem*" (Kol Nidre, Told by a Survivor; dated February 6, 1943) was smuggled into Moscow in the spring of 1944, and it instantaneously made him a poet-partisan celebrity, thanks to the Soviet Jewish writer Ilya Ehrenburg. As Abraham Nowersztern points out, this epic poem reflected historical events in a way that differed from most other ghetto poems, in which the historical reality was transformed and sublimated to the extent that it became almost unrecognizable.[6]

The poem is set during the German *Aktionen* on Yom Kippur, 1941. The Germans forced about four thousand Jews into a large prison in Vilna, then sent them directly to the killing fields in the recreational forest area of Ponar, on the outskirts of Vilna. From the prison courtyard, the narrator recounts the story of his eldest son, who had left Vilna twenty years earlier to join the Red Army. The narrator recognizes his son (but not vice versa), who has been captured by the Germans. With the red star insignia gracing his uniform, the son is gathered with other Jews in the prison yard. A German officer eyes the Red Army soldier and his father, and orders the father (the narrator) to kill his son. The biblical *akeyde*—the binding of Isaac (Genesis 22:1–14), in which God commands Abraham to kill his son Isaac—is reenacted with the German officer in the role of God. The narrator kills his last remaining male heir after his four other sons have been murdered in Ponar. The poem's tragic end is very different from "*Dos keyver kind*" (The Graveyard Child), written almost a year earlier, in which the birth of a child in the cemetery signals renewal in the Valley of Death. In "*Kol Nidre*," Sutzkever subverts and mocks the biblical *akeyde:*

און גאָט אַליין האָט ניט געהערט מײַן תּפֿילה,
ער האָט געשלאָסן שותּפֿות מיטן קאַט.
מיט דעם װיל ער זיך אָפּפֿאַסטן נאָך נעילה,
מיט זײַנע זין די פֿיר איז ער ניט זאַט.
און מיט אײן שפּרונג האָב איך דאָס בלאַנקע אײַזן
מײַן לעצטן זון אַרײַנגעזעצט אין ברוסט:
אַזוינס קען טאָן דײַן טאַטע און באַװײַזן
פֿאַר דעם, װאָס האָט דיך פֿײַניקן געגלוסט.

And even God did not hear my prayer,
He joined company with the executioner.

Thus he will end his fast after Neila*
He is not satisfied with my four sons.
And in one jump I pierced my last son's
Breast with the blank iron:
That's what your father is capable of
Against those who wanted to torture you.⁷

Based on a core biblical text and the liturgy of Yom Kippur (the Day of Repentance), the poem reveals just how insufficient, even empty, are Jewish religious laws in confronting the enormity of the German genocide. In addition to the historical epic and rhyme scheme of the poem (not rendered in my translation), two other features set "*Kol Nidre*" apart from Sutzkever's ghetto poems: the vivid depiction of the German perpetrator who, as a rule, is absent from the poet's oeuvre, and the heroic portrait of the soldier who started a new life in the Soviet Union, "forgot that I was once called a kike" ("*fargesn hob ikh, az me ruft mikh zhid*"), and fought the Germans in the Red Army.

In the winter of 1943/1944, writing from his position with the Markov brigade—the Soviet-led partisan group that Sutzkever and his wife, Freydke, joined after fleeing the ghetto on September 12—Sutzkever enclosed a letter, dated December 15, 1943, and addressed to *khaver leyener* (Comrade Reader) in Moscow, along with a copy of "*Kol Nidre.*" In the letter the poet states that the poem contains "a truth that is perhaps too overwhelming to become literature, and if it succeeds in becoming literature—then art can be much stronger than death."⁸ Sutzkever's belief that poetry protects him from death because it serves as an imaginary refuge and as a tool of liberation is again articulated in the letter. Its wording and the choice of "*Kol Nidre*" (rather than his more exemplary ghetto poems) bear witness to Sutzkever's political savvy, which later would stand him in good stead in Moscow and Tel Aviv. He wanted to reach the Soviet cultural leaders with an image of himself as a Soviet partisan and national poet of the Jewish people's tragedy during the war. "*Kol Nidre*" was atypical among his ghetto poems, which usually refracted suffering and destruction in modernist tonalities and dirgelike commemoration; they called for spiritual resistance in the Vilna Ghetto, where some poems were read aloud and set to music. In contrast, the epic form and tragic content of "*Kol Nidre*" spoke directly to the sensibilities of the Soviet

---

*The final prayer of Yom Kippur, the Day of Atonement.

commissars and the Jewish Anti-Fascist Committee.[9] As such, "*Kol Nidre*" was appropriated in support of Stalin's war against Hitler, and reflected the Soviet regime's short-lived license allowing for the artistic expression of the Jews' particular suffering and fate during the war.

In March 1944 the Soviet government rescued the Sutzkevers from the woods surrounding Vilna. For the next two years, Moscow was their primary residence; from there he traveled regularly to Vilna. Sutzkever's close friendship with Ilya Ehrenburg and the Yiddish actor and director Shloyme Mikhoels gave him a certain political protection. Ehrenburg was an extremely popular war correspondent whose bulletins about German atrocities and developments on the front were widely read in the Soviet Union. Moreover, as a member of the Jewish Anti-Fascist Committee, Ehrenburg was actively involved in collecting testimonies, including witness accounts about the atrocities committed against the Jewish population. Ehrenburg recruited Sutzkever to submit a piece about the extermination of Vilna Jewry for *The Black Book*, a documentary anthology about German war crimes against Jews in the occupied territories of the Soviet Union. Its publication was ultimately blocked by the Soviet authorities; the first complete edition was published, in Russian, in Israel in 1980.[10]

After the arrival of Sutzkever and his wife in Moscow, Ehrenburg published an article about the poet in *Pravda* titled "The Triumph of a Human Being" (April 29, 1944), praising the heroism of the poet-partisan. Sutzkever later described his friendship with Ehrenburg: "With the exception of Mikhoels, I considered Ehrenburg my closest friend [in Moscow]. The friendship, I must say, was mutual, active. And it continued under different forms, mostly in heartfelt exchanges of regards, until half a year before his death."[11] This friendship benefited both parties. Sutzkever, the Jewish poet-partisan, fit the mold of the Soviet ideology, with the Great Fatherland War as a united front that included various Soviet ethnic minorities in the fight against German fascism. Sutzkever's Jewish nationalism was especially useful to the Jewish Anti-Fascist Committee as long as it could be subsumed under the communist banner during the short-lived, less oppressive political climate of 1941–46, until Stalin shut down the committee in 1948. For Sutzkever, the friendships with Ehrenburg and Mikhoels made it possible for him to maneuver relatively freely between Moscow and Vilna. This enabled him to rescue material from the warehouse in Vilna (where it had been stored after the complete destruction of the YIVO building) and transfer it to New York, or at least to protect it from immediately being discarded by the Soviet authorities in the chaotic months following the liberation of Vilna.

During the period 1944–46, Sutzkever's work exemplified the upsurge in Jewish writing and the collection of testimonies about German atrocities against the Jewish population that was initiated by the Central Jewish Historical Commission in Poland in the fall of 1944 and by Polish Jewish refugees overseas (see chapters 3 and 4). Sutzkever's activities during this crucial period highlight the central issues facing Jewish survivors of Vilna, most of whom had decided to leave the "Jerusalem of Lithuania." Sutzkever's deep sense of national mission in closing the chapter of Jewish cultural life in Vilna was intrinsically linked to his Yiddishist beliefs in the importance of integrating Vilna's spiritual and cultural heritage into the fabric of postwar Jewish life by way of YIVO in New York and *Di goldene keyt* in Tel Aviv. As Sutzkever characterized this period: "In those years of destruction, I always felt I was a witness to an immense earthly and cosmic play. I felt a divine sense of messianic mission; those were the most elevated moments of my life."[12]

As a member of the Paper Brigade, which consisted of around forty Jewish writers, scholars, and intellectuals tasked by the Germans with selecting Judaica in the YIVO Institute for Jewish Research building, Sutzkever had managed to rescue important material between 1942 and 1943. The purpose of this special Nazi task force, headed by Nazi Germany's chief ideologue, Alfred Rosenberg, was "to ransack and round up Judaica collections throughout Europe and arrange for their shipment to Germany, to the *Institut zur Erforschung der Judenfrage* (Institute for the Study of the Jewish Question)."[13] Between 1934 and 1936 one of the institute's staff members, Dr. Johannes Pohl, had even been sent by the Nazi Party to Hebrew University in Jerusalem to study Judaica and establish a new discipline that Pohl called *Judenforschung ohne Juden* (Jewish Research Without Jews). The Paper Brigade organized a systematic rescue of Jewish archives, books, and art objects in response to the orders of *Einsatzstab des Reichsleiter* Rosenberg. A major part of the Paper Brigade's work, however, was devoted to smuggling valuable books and archival material into the ghetto, located a mere fifteen minutes' walk from the YIVO building. Much of this material was destroyed (first by the Germans and what remained, later, by the Soviets), but part of it was retrieved by Sutzkever and Kaczerginski after the war and sent to YIVO in New York City.

During unobserved moments while working in the Paper Brigade, Sutzkever composed his ghetto poems.[14] In his 1985 address at YIVO's sixtieth anniversary gathering in New York City, Sutzkever recalled that "a significant part of my poetry written between the years 1941–43, which were signed Vilna Ghetto and the date at which they saw the destruction [*khurbn*], I wrote or rattled out [*oysgekhorkhlt*] in its sinking temple. Perhaps even in the Weinreich Room. The divine presence [*shkhine*] of Yiddish did not stray from me. It protected me and poetisized me [*bashiremt*]."¹⁵ This remarkable quote encapsulates several important aspects of the artistic and cultural context in which Sutzkever wrote his ghetto poems. The use of religious imagery in comparing YIVO to a temple (*a heykhl*) and *di shkhine fun yidish* (the divine presence of Yiddish) reveals Sutzkever's belief in the mission of YIVO as a secular replacement for the Jerusalem Temple (*beysamigdesh*). It also expresses a common theme of Sutzkever's: the Yiddish language is endowed with divine powers and capable of saving him from death.¹⁶ This religious fervor and imagery are good examples of the continuity between *Yiddishkeit* (Jewishness) in its *veltlekhe* (secular) and *frume* (religious) forms, as is evident in Sutzkever's tribute to the secular ideology of YIVO and Yiddishism in his 1985 speech. Sutzkever uses the following parable to convey his inner state while writing his poetry in the YIVO building:

אַלטע װילנער געדענקען דעם שטאָט־משוגענעם איסערסאָן. האָט מען אַ מאָל געזען אַזאַ סצענע: אַ מאָליער שטייט אויף אַ לייטער אין אַ שולכל אויפן שולהויף, טונקט דעם פּענדזל אין אַן עמערל קאַלך װאָס הענגט אויבן ביים העכסטן שטאַפּל, און מאַליעװעט מיט אים אַהין און אַהער דעם באַלקן. פּלוצעם דערנענטערט זיך איסערסאָן און שרײַט צו אים אַרויף: האַלט זיך אָן אָן פּענדזל, װייַל איך נעם צו דעם לייטער.

איך בין געװען געגליכן, בין געװאָרן פֿאַרװאַנדעלט אין יענעם שולכל־מאָליער. דער לייטער אונטער מיר איז טאַקע אַװעקגעריסן געװאָרן, אָבער כ׳האָב זיך אָנגעהאַלטן אָן פּענדזל, װאָס האָט שױן ניט געהאַט אַפֿילו קיין באַלקן, און װוּנדער: כ׳בין יעמאָלט ניט אַראָפּגעפֿאַלן.

און דאָס עמערל איז געהאַנגען צװישן ערד און הימל און זײַן קאַלך איז ניט װײַס געװען.

Old people from Vilna remember the village idiot by the name Iserson. Once we saw the following scene: A painter stands on a ladder in a little courtyard next to a synagogue. He dips the paintbrush in a bucket of lime hanging on the highest step, and paints back and forth on the beam. Suddenly, Iserson appears and screams up to him: Hold on to the paintbrush because I am taking away the ladder. I can be compared to and was in fact transformed into that synagogue painter. The ladder had actually been taken out from under me, but I held on to the paintbrush that did not even reach a beam. And a miracle occurred: At that time, I did not fall down. And the bucket hung between heaven and earth, and the lime was not white.¹⁷

To create while hanging in midair brings to mind the work of Sutzkever's friend of many years, the painter Marc Chagall. Like Chagall's airborne figures floating over the Jewish shtetl, Sutzkever's ghetto poems belong to a universe that reflects the mindset of inspired madness touched by a feeble relationship to the sacred space of Judaism, the synagogue. The Yiddish poet in the ghetto is quite literally without foundation, and without hope of ever reaching a reader.

Critical perspectives on Sutzkever's ghetto poems have been divided between appreciating their exceptional character, having been created under extreme circumstances, and a more detached perspective seeking to place them as part of Sutzkever's total poetic oeuvre. Particularly perceptive is the American Yiddish poet Yankev Glatshteyn's observation: "He is the only Yiddish poet who returned with poems from the vale of tears. Some wrote screaming exclamations [*oysgeshreyen*], some wrote dirges, but Sutzkever had a mission, a cursed mission, to play the poems of the greatest destruction [*khurbn*] of our time on his magical flute."[18]

Although belonging to the poets' group Yung-Vilne (Young Vilna) in the 1930s, Sutzkever stood apart from its members due to his esoteric withdrawal from social and political issues and his almost ecstatic relationship with nature and immersion in his craft. He modeled poems on old Yiddish literary forms and styles and started to render the sixteenth-century old Yiddish classic, Eliohu Bokher's *Bove Bukh*, into modern Yiddish. He maintained a close affinity with and published in the journals of the New York *Inzikhistn* (Introspectivists), as is evident in *Lider* (Poems, 1937) and *Valdiks* (Of the Forest, 1940).[19] That such a poetic credo might provide a more resilient response to the unfolding tragedy of Jewish Vilna is already suggested in the fifth of his ghetto poems, "*Penimer in zumpn*" (Faces in the Swamps). Sutzkever fine-tunes his *inzikhist* credo to the radically new circumstances confronting him while hiding in a chimney above his apartment in July 1941, right after the German invasion of Vilna:

באַלד וועט עס געשען!
די שוואַרצע רינגען
ווערן ענג און ענגער אַרום האַלדז!
אומפֿערזענלעך, ווי אַ שטיין אין ברוק
וועל איך בלײַבן ליגן אונטער טלאָען
אויסגעלייזט פֿון וועלט;
נאָר אין מײַן טיף

וועלן בלײַבן וואָגלען דרײַ מוראַשקעס:
אײנע,
אונטער לאָרבער פֿון מײַן קינדשאַפֿט,
וועט זיך אומקערן אין כּישוף-וואַלד.
צווייטע,
אונטער פּאַנצער פֿון מײַן חלום,
וועט זיך אומקערן אין חלום-לאַנד;
און די דריטע
די וואָס טראָגט מײַן וואָרט,
וועט קיין וועג ניט האָבן,
ווײַל פֿאַרפּעסטיקט
איז דאָס לאַנד פֿון גלייבנדיקע ווערטער,
וועט זי וואַכן אינעם טאָל פֿון שאָטנס
איין און עלנט
איבער מײַן געביין.

Soon it will happen!
The black hoops
Grow tighter and tighter around my neck!
Impersonally, like a stone on the pavement,
I shall remain lying under hooves,
Redeemed from the world.
But inside me—
Three ants still stray:
One,
Under the laurel of my childhood—
Will return to magic land.
The second,
Under the armor of my dream—
Will return to dreamland.
The third,
The one who carries my word—
Will have no path,
For the land of believing words
Is covered with plague.
In the valley of shadows, it will watch,
Alone and solitary,
Over my bones.[20]

What occurs is the result of an impersonal force that strangles the "I" and forces him to withdraw from the world. The external pressure—irreversible in its instinctual destructiveness—is neither concretized nor given a name. The focus is instead on the "I"'s poetic response to the murderous assault in the form of creative word engineering, similar to the three ants building an anthill. This diligent work consists of penetrating the glorified truths of childhood, the protective armor of dreams, and, most important, carrying those words of the poet that truly express his inner reality. The enemy is visible only indirectly in "the land of believing words / . . . covered with plague." By steering clear of this totalitarian vision of the mass ideologies of the day—Nazism and communism—poetry can become a truthful testimony to the plight of the individual alone in "the valley of shadows," echoing Psalm 23. Caught in the Nazi death trap, Sutzkever rejects his earlier sense of security and belief in a better future: "Devour us! We were cursed by overconfidence, / Devour us with our children, with our flags!"—as he exclaims in the first poem he wrote after the German invasion of Vilna.[21]

Unlike Paul Celan's German poetry in the language of his people's murderers, forced "to pass through the thousand darknesses of death-bringing speech,"[22] Sutzkever's creates a poetic vehicle perfectly suited to convey his particular Jewish experience during the Holocaust. He draws on biblical models for Jewish responses to catastrophe: "Then God said to Moses: 'Inscribe this in a document as a reminder, and read it aloud to Joshua: I will utterly blot out the memory of Amalek from under heaven'" (Exod. 17:14); "Remember what Amalek did to you on your journey, after you left Egypt . . . you shall blot out the memory of Amalek from under heaven. Do not forget!" (Deut. 25:17, 19).

Amalek is the name of the biblical people who repeatedly sought to annihilate the Israelites. A similar approach to remember what "Amalek did to you" while eradicating Amalek's name is reflected in Sutzkever's ghetto poems. As Michael Bernard-Donals points out in an article informed by Cathy Caruth's trauma theory: "the Hebrew word for 'blot out' means literally to erase, to un-write. So what is commanded is to remember to un-remember, to create and inscribe a memory that at the same time blots out or un-writes what lies at the core of the memory. This is the point Caruth makes about the relation of traumatic memory to testimony: the event is blotted out, making testimony's relation to the event troubled at best and tenuous at worst."[23]

In *Fun vilner geto,* Sutzkever did not adhere to the biblical exhortation to "eradicate the names of Amalek" simply because he intended the book to be a tool for the prosecution of Nazi war criminals. The memoir is chilling in its dry, precise depictions of how the Germans systematically slaughtered Vilna's Jews. At the same time, the emotional and spiritual aspects of Sutzkever's experiences are nearly effaced in his memoir. This is particularly evident in the detached description of how his newborn child was murdered by a German officer in the ghetto hospital, followed by a brief, factual description in the half-page chapter "My Mother's Death" (p. 76). In contrast, the poem that Sutzkever wrote in the ghetto, "*Mayn mame*" (My Mother), dated October 1942, exemplifies the way in which his ghetto poetry attempts to "create and inscribe a memory that at the same time blots out or un-writes what lies at the core of the memory." This poem expresses his combination of self-loathing and guilt at not being able to defend his mother, and likens his poetic vision to the barking of dogs—unworthy ersatz poetry following her murder:

אוּן וווּ בין איך געווען,
בעת אונטער צימבלען
האָט מען דיך געשלעפּט צום עשאַפֿאָט?
אין הינטישער בודע פֿאַרגראָבן ס׳געביין,
מיט הינטישער פֿרייד וואָס פֿאַרשילט זיך אַליין,

Where was I,
When cymbals crashed
And they dragged you to the scaffold?
In a dog's kennel; I buried my bones,
With a dog's joy that curses itself,[24]

The poet returns to his mother's abandoned apartment in the ghetto, as did the poet Chaim Grade in his memoir *Der mames shabosim* (My Mother's Sabbath Days, 1955), finding the domestic remains of her previous life, and finally donning her shirt:

ס׳איז מער ניט קיין העמד, ס׳איז דיין ליכטיקע הויט,
ס׳איז דיין קאַלטער, דיין איבערגעבליבענער טויט.

No longer a shirt—your shining skin,
Your cold, your everlasting death.[25]

In the final strophe the poet creates a cosmological universe of poetic renewal, thereby regenerating his mother as a force of nature; the poet again articulates art's power to defy death, like the plum pit's potential to create a tree:

אַז דו ביסט פֿאַראַן,
בין איך דאָ סײַ-ווי-סײַ
ווי דער יאָדער אין פֿלוים
פֿאַרמאָגט שוין דעם בוים
און די נעסט און דעם פֿויגל
און אַלץ וואָס דערבײַ

If you are still here,
Then I exist too,
As the pit in a plum
Bears in it the tree
And the nest and the bird
And the chirp and the coo.[26]

The ghetto poems about his personal tragedy articulate Sutzkever's internal emotional, artistic, and spiritual states as interwoven in a poetics of resistance that almost completely eradicates the name of Amalek. An exception is the slim 1979 collection *Di ershte nakht in geto* (The First Night in Ghetto), which gives vent to feelings of anger, despair, and harsh self-criticism. The poem "*Der tsirk*" (The Circus), written in hiding in July 1941, is based on an actual event that Sutzkever depicts in his memoir. This incident was summarized in his testimony before the Nuremberg Tribunal:

> In the first days of July 1941, a German [soldier] seized me in the Dokumenskaia Street. I was then going to visit my mother. The German said to me: "Come with me, you will act in the circus." As I went along I saw that another German was driving along an old Jew, the old rabbi of the street, Kassel, and a third German was holding a young boy. When we reached the ancient synagogue, I saw that wood was piled up there in the shape of a pyramid. A German drew out his revolver and told us to take off our clothes. When we were naked, he lit a match and set fire to this stack of wood. Then another German brought out of the synagogue three scrolls of the

Torah, gave them to us, and told us to dance around this bonfire and sing Russian songs. Behind us stood the three Germans; with their bayonets they forced us toward the fire and laughed. When we were almost unconscious, they left."²⁷

Sutzkever chose to wait thirty-eight years to publish "*Der tsirk*" in the collection *Di ershte nakht in geto*. The poem played on emotional registers of anger, despair, and self-pity which violated the poetics of resistance that he sought to cultivate in his poetic response to the Holocaust:

און איך וואָס בין געווען דער לץ אין שענדלעכן ספּעקטאַקל
האָב ניט געהאַט קיין מוטוויל צו אַרויסשטאַמלען אַ קללה
און ניט צו מאָל דעם כּוח זיך אַ וואָרף צו טאָן אין טויט,
ווי מײַנע ברידער אין דער צײַט פֿון אַדריאַן דעם רוימער,
בשעת דער גלויבן האָט דערשטיקט אין קערפּער די יסורים
(כאָטש אַלץ איינס איז דורכגעסמט מיט קוילנגלי מײַן האַרץ
און די אויגן פֿון מײַן גײַסט מיט רויך אַדורכגעשטאָכן).
נאָר מערער נאָך: איך האָב געקניט אַ נאַקעטער פֿאַר דעם
וואָס האָט געשענדט מײַן טאַטן אין זײַן קבֿר
און מיט טרערן ווי מיט שוואַרצע פּאָקן
געבעטן גנאָד.

And I, who was the clown in that disgraceful spectacle
Had no courage to stammer a curse
No strength to throw myself into the death,
As did my brothers in the time of Hadrian the Roman
When faith stifled in their body all the pain
(Though my heart is poisoned with coal glow
And the eyes of my spirit are speared with smoke).
Worse: I knelt naked before him,
Who defiled my father in his grave,
And with tears like black pox,
I begged for mercy.²⁸

Kloles (curses), the verbal expression of rage and revenge, and an important feature of Yiddish literary semiotics (from Sholem Aleichem to Yitskhok Bashevis), would have jeopardized Sutzkever's survival. As a means of poetic expression it would also have undercut Sutzkever's strategy of effacing the perpetrator and blotting out the memory of Amalek. Instead, he turns the curse against himself for his inability to defy this humiliation and join the golden chain of Jewish martyrdom, *kidesh-hashem* (dying for the sanctification of God's name). His punishment is the separation from his brothers and the age-old Jewish commandment to give one's life in sanctification of God's name. The grand pathos of martyrdom and partaking in a Jewish trans-historical collective has been replaced by the deeply humiliating personal experience of being forced to perform in a perverted kind of circus:

איז דאָס דיַין שטראָף צו זשיפען האַלב געטייט
און פרעסן גסיסה-כאָרכל פֿון די ברידער.
ווייל דו האָסט ניט פֿאַרדינט די לעצטע פֿרייד
פֿון ווערן אויס—דאָס מיינט: פֿון ווערן ווידער.

This is your punishment: to gasp half dead,
Gulping death rattles of your brothers, insane.
For you have not deserved the last bread
Of joy: being naught—which means: becoming again.[29]

In a preface in *Di goldene keyt* (1979), Sutzkever explains the complex reasons for his reluctance to publish this and other poems in the collection *Di ershte nakht in geto*: "Why I didn't publish these poems earlier—is a particularly complicated psychological matter. Perhaps they were too raw, too painful, too truthful."[30] However, the same episode was the topic of the poem "*Erev mayn farbrenung*" (Before My Burning), published in the collection *Di karsh fun dermonung* (The Cherry of Remembrance, 1949). Except for four lines, this poem does not depict the event in a concrete, personal way, as in "*Der tsirk.*" Rather, the evocation of the biblical *anokhi* ("I am here," uttered by Abraham, Jacob, and Moses in response to God), which glows from the burning Torah scroll during the dance the poet was forced to participate in, becomes a way of reconnecting the "I" to "the golden chain" and of subsuming trauma and humiliation in the form of a religiously inspired poetics.[31] The process of poetic sublimation in order to "[blot] out or [un-write] what lies at the core of the memory" enables Sutzkever to overcome the traumatic event. It likely propelled him to exclude "*Der tsirk*" and similar poems from his collected Holocaust poetry, *Lider fun yam-hamoves* (Poems from the Sea of Death, 1968). Heather Valencia summarizes the centrality of these two poems in Sutzkever's oeuvre: "The two poems, considered together, are the first example in Sutzkever's work of a process which was to continue throughout his creative life: the constant poetic reworking and transfiguration of the *khurbn* within his monumental oeuvre. They are a confirmation of the transformative power of the poetic word itself. From the agony and guilt of the poem written just after the ordeal itself, Sutzkever is able to change the experience into a source of inspiration for his creative life."[32]

A remarkable feature of the Vilna Ghetto was its rich cultural life, which developed in January 1942 following a momentary break in the German *Aktionen* among the surviving twenty thousand Jews. A significant portion of Sutzkever's ghetto poems was written specifically for cultural events during which they were read aloud. Two poems, "*Di lererin Mire*" (The Teacher Mire) and "*A vogn shikh*" (A Wagon of Shoes), were most likely never read aloud in the ghetto but became the most beloved of Sutzkever's ghetto poems after the war. In a haunting rhythm like a military march, which is stressed in Sutzkever's own recorded reading of "*A vogn shikh*,"[33] a variety of shoes stolen from the murdered Jews and then shipped to Berlin becomes a metonymic image of the annihilation of the Jews, similar to the piles of clothing, shoes, and gold teeth exhibited in the Auschwitz museum. The first and final stanzas are as follows:

די רעדער יאָגן, יאָגן,
וואָס ברענגען זיי מיט זיך?
זיי ברענגען מיר אַ וואָגן
מיט צאַפּלענדיקע שיך

. . .

און ס'קלאַפּן די אָפּצאַסן:
וווּהין, וווּהין, וווּהין?
פֿון אַלטער ווילנער גאַסן
מע טרײַבט אונדז קיין בערלין.

The wheels they drag and drag on,
What do they bring, and whose?
They bring along a wagon
Filled with throbbing shoes

. . .

The heels tap with no malice:
Where do they pull us in?
From ancient Vilna alleys,
They drive us to Berlin.[34]

Repetition of words and verses creates a cyclical sense of continuous movement. The force behind the transport of the shoes from Vilna to Berlin is anonymous, relentless, irreversible. The dialogue between the empty shoes and the "I" is presented as a didactic lesson in the horror of absence. The "I"'s naive expectation of a joyous wedding is turned into a death dance until the climactic moment when he recognizes his mother's shoes.[35] In his testimony before the Nuremberg Tribunal, Sutzkever related the murder of his newborn child, the disappearance of his mother, who was executed at Ponar, and German Commandant Murer's "gift" to the ghetto in the form of a carload of shoes: "In the last of days of December 1941, Murer gave a present to the ghetto. A carload of shoes belonging to the Jews executed at Ponar was brought into the ghetto. He sent these old shoes as a gift to the ghetto. Among them I recognized my mother's."[36] Poetry's ability to recreate through metonymy and synecdoche what has been lost in reality is displayed here for the first time in Sutzkever's work. This is crystallized in the complex meditation on poetry, loss, and trauma in *"Farbrente perl"* (Burned Pearls), dated July 28, 1943. Here poetry is likened to the charred pearls, the only remains of a woman burned to death. The extremity of violence and sheer scope of annihilation turn poetry into a metonymic trope, a signifier of what remains after the conflagration. From the fire Sutzkever has extracted a poem about burned pearls with only a very tenuous relationship to what happened to the owner of the pearls. From the ashes of trauma and loss arises a poetic phoenix of musicality and wholeness:

. . . ווײַל דײַנע קלאַנגען גלימצערן
װי פֿאַרברענטע פּערל
נאָך אַן אויסגעצאַנקטן שײַטער,
און קיינער—אויך ניט איך—דורך טעג צעריבענער,
דערקענט שוין ניט די פֿרוי אין פֿלאַם געוואַשן,
וואָס פֿון אַלע פֿריידן איז געבליבן איר
גראָ-געברענטע פּערל אין די אַשן—

   . . . because your sounds glimmer
   Like burned pearls
   After a burned out fire,
   And no one—not even I—scraped dead by days,
   Can still recognize the woman washed in flame
   For whom, all of her joys
   Grey-burnt pearls in ashes are the sum of what remains.[37]

Sutzkever's ghetto poems must be viewed as an inseparable part of his oeuvre, a particularly strong poetic response to the Holocaust. Without changing his *inzikhist* poetics, he sharpened and refined his poetic medium between 1941 and 1944. His creative impulse became his lifeboat during the chaotic circumstances that ensued after the Nazis occupied Vilna. Sutzkever's ghetto poems enabled him to resist the demoralizing and traumatic effects of losing his mother, child, and, in the end, most of his community. After the destruction, the mysterious life-giving force of nature and words were beautifully captured in the poem "*Farfroyrene yidn*" (Frozen Jews), dated July 10, 1944 (Moscow), and included in the collection *Di festung* (The Fortress, 1944). As pointed out by David Roskies, this is "Ezekiel's vision of the dry bones rewritten for the icy climate of the north."[38]

האָסטו געזען איבער פֿעלדער מיט שניי
פֿאַרפֿרוירענע ייִדן, אַ ריי נאָך אַ ריי?

זיי ליגן אָן אָטעם, פֿאַרמירמלט און בלאָ,
נאָר טויט איז אין זייערע קערפער ניטאָ.

ווייל ס׳פֿינקלט אויך ערגעץ פֿאַרפֿרוירן דער גייסט,
ווי אַ גילדענער פֿיש, אין אַ כוואַליע פֿאַרייזט.

Did you ever see in fields of snow
Frozen Jews, in row upon row?

Breathless they lie, marbled and blue.
Of death in their bodies, no hint and no clue.

Somewhere their spirit is frozen and saved
Like a golden fish in a frozen wave.[39]

Sutzkever and Kaczerginski enjoyed a short period of reprieve in Soviet-ruled Vilna during which they continued the cultural rescue work of Jewish books, archives, and art. But their efforts ran into trouble with the Soviet and Lithuanian authorities from the beginning. According to the historian David E. Fishman, by September 1944, only three months after the Soviet liberation of Vilna, Sutzkever returned to Moscow with "Kruk's diary and other materials in his bag. He sensed that Soviet Vilnius, as the city was now called, was not a safe place for Jewish treasures. With the help of a

FIGURE 1.1. The ten-year-old Samuel Bak on the lap of Avrom Sutzkever in liberated Vilna, July 1944. (Courtesy Samuel Bak)

foreign correspondent, he sent off his first package of materials to YIVO in New York."[40]

Sutzkever documented his friendships with the leading Soviet Jewish writers Peretz Markish, Ilya Ehrenburg, Shmuel Halkin, and Shloyme Mikhoels in a series of portraits that he published in the 1960s. He emphasized their vulnerable position in the transitional period between the end of the "Great Patriotic War" and the onset of Stalin's reign of anti-Semitic terror in 1947. A moving expression of Sutzkever's state of mind during the Nuremberg trials can be found in his diary notes *"Mayn eydes-zogn farn nirnberger tribunal"* (My Testimony at the Nuremberg Tribunal), first published in 1966. The four official languages at the trials were English, German, Russian, and French, which excluded the possibility of Sutzkever testifying in Yiddish. However, he was promised by Ehrenburg and the Russian prosecutor Colonel L. N. Smirnov that he would be able to speak in Yiddish.[41] Nevertheless, until almost two days prior to Sutzkever's appearance, it remained unclear if he would be allowed to testify at all. Then, on February 25, 1946, Colonel Smirnov informed him that he would testify the next day, but in Russian. Sutzkever's diary entry, written immediately after his testimony, summed up the experience:

> I spoke for thirty-eight minutes (including the questions of the prosecutor Colonel Smirnov). . . . Providence put Russian in my mouth. I didn't know that I could express my feelings and thought in that language. It is still difficult to sort out my feelings. Which is

stronger, the feeling of sadness, or the feeling of revenge? It seems that stronger than both is the enormous illuminating feeling that our people lives, has survived its hangmen—and no kind of dark force can ever destroy us.[42]

A meeting in Moscow on April 2, 1946, organized by the Jewish Anti-Fascist Committee and featuring Sutzkever's report on his participation at the Nuremberg trials, was abruptly terminated when he expressed Zionist sympathies. The audience's reaction to this public statement of solidarity with Jewish national aspirations in the Soviet Union was, according to Sutzkever, "fear, joy, and surprise." In his retrospective account from 1962, Sutzkever emphasized his commitment to the Zionist vision as the only lasting expression of revenge. This is what propelled him to leave the Soviet Union once his mission to bear witness and publish his Holocaust memoirs and ghetto poetry had been completed: "Dear friend Mikhoels, you said in your introduction that with my testimony in Nuremberg I have taken the greatest revenge on the worst murderers of our people. But what kind of pleasure can I get from revenge when my mother was burned in Ponar, and Jerusalem of Lithuania is without Jews. Therefore I believe that I will, that we all will, take the greatest revenge on the worst murderers of our people, when we will fight to liberate our own free Jerusalem."[43]

Two political developments reinforced Sutzkever's decision to leave Vilna forever: One was the increasing Soviet control of the city, which made the revival of a Jewish community impossible by subsuming all ethnic diversity under the communist banner. The other was the murderous brutality of Polish anti-Semitism in the aftermath of the Holocaust. The Kielce pogrom in July 1946, which killed forty-two Jewish Holocaust survivors (disarmed by the Polish police the day before), triggered a mass exodus of Jews from Poland. In a few months this reduced the quarter-million-strong Jewish community to approximately 80,000 in the spring of 1947. In his long poem "*Tsu poyln*" (To Poland), written in Poland between July and September 1946, Sutzkever addressed the question of Polish-Jewish coexistence on a broad historical canvas in the aftermath of the Kielce pogrom.

This long poem, written in a rhymed style similar to that of the poem "*Geheymshtot*" (Clandestine City, 1945–47), is a powerful indictment of Polish anti-Semitism. The Romantic vision of a golden age of Poles and Jews living in peace, side by side, their songs and languages harmoniously intertwined in a polyphonic chorus, has been shattered. This is graphically expressed at the end of each of the first four parts of the poem, in which Sutzkever includes the Polish title of a classical poem "*Smutno mi, Boze*" by the Romantic poet Juliusz Slowacki (1809–49), a contemporary of Adam Mickiewicz and Cyprian Norwid:

טאָ װאָס איז געשען מיט זײַן אייניקל, װאָס זשע?
Smutno mi, Boze![44]

> So what happened to his grandchild, what happened?
> I am so sad, my God!

The contrast between the Hebrew letters and the Polish underlines both the incompatibility of Jewish and Polish cultures and the necessity of bridging these differences by focusing on the two peoples' similar struggles for national independence. In the fifth and last part of the poem, Sutzkever replaces this Polish refrain with a quote from Peretz's play *Di goldene keyt* (The Golden Chain). This apotheosis becomes a tribute to Peretz's *Ohel* (grave monument) in the Jewish Cemetery in Warsaw, inside which a ghetto Jew supposedly hid during the war. In the final lines of the poem, Sutzkever takes leave of Poland with the melody of Peretz's poetic words on his lips:

אָט אַזוי גייען מיר,
די נשמות פֿלאַקערן!

> And so we stride,
> the souls—ablaze![45]

The poem ends with the poet's departure from Poland, carrying the portable Jewish words and melodies embodied in the heritage of Peretz. The relocation of Eastern European Yiddish culture to Israel after the destruction of Vilna was encapsulated in Sutzkever's choosing the title of Peretz's play *Di goldene keyt* as the name of the Yiddish journal he started in 1949 in Tel Aviv.[46]

In the poem "*Di blayene platn fun roms drukeray*" (The Lead Plates at Romm's Press), Sutzkever created a powerful poetic myth of Jewish resistance. The famous Romm's Press in Vilna had been the most venerable Jewish printing press in Eastern Europe since the early nineteenth century. In the poem Sutzkever imagines how Jewish resistance fighters broke into the press "and melt down, for our bullets, the spirit of the lead." This reversal of Isaiah's prophecy of the end of days, when "the swords will be beaten into ploughshares," becomes a new archetype of national rebirth. The event never actually took place, which makes Sutzkever's poetic achievement even more impressive.[47] Sutzkever retroactively dated the poem September 12, 1943, the day he escaped the Vilna Ghetto for the forest, where he wrote it. The poem negates the powerlessness of the Jewish Diaspora with the image of the fighting soldier, modeled on the Maccabees, and the rededication of the Temple. Sutzkever's work as poet, autobiographer, and witness for the prosecution of German war criminals was informed by the gnawing questions related to his "past-in-chains" as well as his glorious vision of a Jewish national rebirth.

The poem "*Di froy fun mirml afn Per-lashez*" (The Woman of Marble in Pere Lachaise, signed Paris, 1947) is about the Pere Lachaise cemetery in Paris, where Sutzkever stopped for a short time on the way to the Land of Israel. In it the poet contemplates what homeland and exile mean for the Yiddish poet after the destruction of his hometown, Vilna. Chopin, his world-renowned Polish compatriot, who lived most of his life in Parisian exile, wanted his heart to be removed and buried in Warsaw while his tombstone in Pere Lachaise would remain a site of pilgrimage for music lovers. In contrast, the Yiddish poet has lost his Polish Jewish homeland forever, and the thought of erecting a memorial to him in Poland seems ridiculously misplaced:

געבליבן בין איך אויפֿן פּער-לאַשעז
געליימט. אָן לשון:
כּדאי געווען צו זאַמלען אויף מײַן קאַנטע
דרײַסיק יאָר,
פֿאַרלירן אַלע נאָנטע,
בלײַבן הענגען אויף אַ האָר,
אַרויסגיין פֿונעם קאַלכאויוון
מיט ניט-פֿאַרברענטע טרערן,
אַז איך זאָל איצט, אויף פּער-לאַשעז דערהערן,
אַז מײַן אַלמאַכטיק די ארץ איז ווערט אַ פּיים.
און אויב איך וועל מיר אַ צוואה מאַכן
מע זאָל שפּעטער ברענגען עס אַהיים—
וועט גאָר דאָס טרויעריקע וועלטפֿאָלק—לאַכן.

I turned numb in Pere Lachaise,
speechless:
Was it worth it to count up
some thirty years,

losing those dear to me,
hanging by a hair,
emerging from the ovens
with unburnt tears
only to hear just now at Pere Lachaise
that my strong heart isn't even worth a sou?
And if I were to make a will
so someone should bring my heart home—
the entire Diaspora,
                the sad Diaspora—
                              will laugh.[48]

Although Sutzkever became a mentor for the poets of Yung Yisroel, a Yiddish poetry group in Israel in the 1950s, and wrote poetry about the Land of Israel, it is his Holocaust poetry, prose poems, and metaphysical *Lider fun togbukh* (Poems from a Diary, 1974–85) that exemplify his unique artistic gift and make him the premier Yiddish poet after the Holocaust. With a few exceptions, such as the epic poetry he wrote in the Vilna Ghetto and *Di ershte nakht in geto,* Sutzkever stood apart from the normative response to Jewish collective catastrophe represented by Haym Nahman Bialik's "*In shkhite-shtot*" (In the City of Slaughter, 1904) and Peretz Markish's "*Di kupe*" (The Heap, 1922). The former, written in response to the Kishenev pogroms of 1904, and the latter, in response to the pogroms in the Ukraine after World War I, were "screaming" expressionist poems that sought to shock their readers out of passivity and into political action. Sutzkever, on the other hand, cultivated an individual, introspective, and cosmological poetics that sought to use the full range of the poetic medium to bypass and escape the violence of the historical moment. This Romantic idea of the Poet and of Poetry as redemption and eternal life sources with the potential to stave off the powers of death is programmatically articulated in Sutzkever's introduction to his collected Holocaust poetry, *Lider fun yam-hamoves:* "When it seems as if the sun itself is transformed into ash—I believe with complete faith [*be-emune shleyme*]: as long as the poem does not abandon me, the lead will not kill me; as long as I will live poetically in the dead-suffused world, I will be redeemed and my sufferings will be raised to a higher level [*a tikn bakumen*]."[49]

As an example of this poetic credo, Sutzkever relates that after being beaten by soldiers in July 1941, he escaped to a pit filled with diluted lime. His wounds were burning like fire, and suddenly he saw that the blood from his wounds "mix[ed] with the gluey whiteness and paint[ed] in the lime a wonderful sunset." He forgot the pain, and the fear of being discovered; he allowed himself to be inspired to write a poem, astounded by the fact that his body was able to emulate a sunset, and that the poetic vision can redeem his pain and sadness: "almost everything that I wrote in the ghetto was the result of such a sunset, and I prayed that the poems would not disappear."[50]

For Sutzkever, the artistic word was a source of redemption and hope of continuity; his life's mission after the Holocaust was driven by a strongly held belief in the "resurrection of the murdered Yiddish word."[51] In the sonnet *"Fun beymer makht men vunderlekh papir"* (Trees Are Made into Wonderful Paper), the poet becomes a godlike creator of the world. Unlike Aaron Zeitlin, another Yiddish poet of the 1945 generation, who despaired over the insufficiency of the written word in response to the catastrophe (see chapter 6), Sutzkever fervently believed in the transcendent power of poetry to re-create and animate the world. In the sonnet the Yiddish word becomes "a tree of life" (*der boym fun lebn*), similar to the title of Chava Rosenfarb's almost two-thousand-page novel about the Lodz Ghetto (see chapter 2), derived from the religious and Hebrew designation of the Torah as *ets khayim* (Tree of Life). The sonnet's hymn to the Yiddish word becomes a poetically realized vision of human resiliency and cosmic consciousness:

פֿון ביימער מאַכט מען ווונדערלעך פּאַפּיר. און איך—ס׳פֿאַרקערטע:
פּאַפּיר פֿאַרוואַנדל איך אין ביימער, אין דעם בוים פֿון לעבן.
איך וועל זיך צוּוואָרצלען צו אים, ביז וואַנען עס וועט אויפֿגיין
ס׳געזאַנג פֿון זײַנע פֿייגל.

זיי וועלן זיך צעבליען און ארויסבּלאָזן די ערשטע
געבענטשטע קלאַנגען; אומפֿאַרבײַטעלעך, אײניציק איז מײַן שליחות:
פֿאַרוואַנדלען די פֿאַרוואַנדלונגען אין זײער ערשטן מקור,
פֿאַרוואַנדלען זיך אַליין אין פּראָטאָפּלאַזם פֿון מײַן חלום.

פֿאַרוואַנדלען וועל איך גרודעס ליים אין זייער מענטשלעך פּנים,
פֿאַרוואַנדלען אײדלשטיינער אין אַ לעבעדיקן גאַלדשמיד,
און סודות אָפּגעזונדערטע און מײַלן-ווײַט פֿון ווערטער,
פֿאַרוואַנדלען וועל איך אין אַ שטראַלונג ביזן דנאָ פֿון טרערן.

איך טונק אין זון מײַן זיגלרינג און שטעל אים אין דער פֿינצטער
צו היטן די פֿאַרוואַנדלונגען. מײַן קומעדיקער יורש,
דער קאָסמישער פּאָעט, זאָל קאָנען זוכן און געפֿינען,
און מײַן געבײן זאָל שמייכלען.

Trees are made into wonderful paper. And I—the reverse:
I transform paper into a tree, the tree of life.
I'll graft myself onto its roots—till the dawn
Of its birdsong.

The birds will blossom. They'll flourish the first
Blessed sounds. Unique, inevitable, my mission:
Transform the transformations back to their source,
Transform myself into the protoplasm of my dream.

Transform the clumps of clay into their human face,
The precious jewels into a living jeweler.
Transform the isolated mysteries, miles away from words,
Into rays that reach the depths of tears.

I dip my seal ring in the sun and stand it in the dark
To watch the transformations. My future heir,
The cosmic poet, will seek and find them.
And my bones will smile.[52]

Following the Holocaust, Yiddish writers took on themselves a nearly impossible burden: to resurrect and reimagine a world that was no more. The creation of imaginary verbal replicas of communities that have ceased to exist affords their work a distinct pathos and a heroic quality. This is fundamentally different from what we have come to value as Holocaust literature (mostly in English), informed by Adorno's famous dictum that "to write poetry after Auschwitz is barbaric." In the 1960s Adorno revised this notion (first published in the early 1950s) when he argued that literature must "resist precisely this verdict" and that "perennial suffering has as much right to expression as a tortured man has to scream."[53] For Adorno, as a German Jewish exile in America whose thinking was rooted in the German philosophical and modernist tradition, mutilation and violence during the Nazi era precluded any artistic autonomy after Auschwitz.

For Sutzkever, a Yiddish poet who came perilously close to perishing in the Vilna Ghetto, who witnessed the murder of his mother and his child and watched as his community was completely annihilated, writing poetry during and after the Holocaust became not only a life necessity but the "vaccine" that would redeem traumas and loss, inscribing the Yiddish word as forever unsilenced. As Ruth R. Wisse points out, Sutzkever insisted that poetry had not been, as Adorno stated, irreversibly mutilated by Nazi Germany's crimes and corruption of language: "Governed by an autonomous standard, impervious to the Germans' depravity or any corruption, poetry was for Sutzkever not another casualty but rather the antidote to Auschwitz."[54] However, the cracks in this Romanticist idea of Poetry and the Poet were already visible in the poems that Sutzkever wrote during the first weeks of the German occupation of Vilna in July 1941, which took him almost forty years to publish. The "inner" poetic trial continued after the war was reflected in the ways Sutzkever revised some of his ghetto poems and withheld others from publication. As Abraham Nowersztern points out in his 1983 biography of the poet: "Sutzkever viewed them [the ghetto poems] not only as documents from those days but as an integral part of his work, which began earlier and continued after the Liberation. He revised them with the same thorough sense of high artistic standard as was his usual approach: he erased and polished the poems and refrained for many years to publish a part of them. None of his published books includes a complete collection of his ghetto poems and to this day there are poems that have never been published."[55]

Sutzkever did not allow the German genocide of the Jews to define the poetic work he wrote in the midst of the terrifying events that engulfed him during the war. However, the Holocaust continued to inform the poet's inner world throughout his career, as exemplified by the sonnet "*A grezl fun Ponar*" (A Blade of Grass from Ponar, 1981), from *Poems from a Diary*, which is a meditation on the survivor poet's craft, trauma, and loss:

איך האָב אַ בריוו אַ דערהאַלטן פֿון מײַן היימשטאָט אין דער ליטע
פֿון אײנער וואָס איר יוגנט־חן האָט ערגעץ נאָך אַ שליטה.
אַרײַנגעלייגט האָט זי אין אים איר ליבשאַפֿט און איר צער:
אַ גרעזל פֿון פּאָנאַר.

דאָס גרעזל מיט אַ צאַנקענדיקן וואָלקנדל, אַ גוסס,
האָט אָנגעצונדן אות נאָך אות די פּנימער פֿון אותיות
און איבער אותיות־פּנימער אין מורמלענדיקן זשאַר:
דאָס גרעזל פֿון פּאָנאַר.

דאָס גרעזל איז אַצינד מײַן וועלט, מײַן היימיש־מיניאַטורע,
וווּ קינדער שפּילן פֿידל אין אַ ברענענדיקער שורה.
זײ שפּילן פֿידל און דער דיריגענט איז לעגענדאַר:
דאָס גרעזל פֿון פּאָנאַר.

איך וועל זיך מיטן גרעזל פֿון דער היימשטאָט ניט צעשיידן,
מײַן אויסגעבענקטע גוטע ערד וועט מאַכן אָרט פֿאַר ביידן.
און יעמאָלט וועל איך ברענגען אַ מתּנה פֿאַרן האַר:
דאָס גרעזל פֿון פּאָנאַר.

A letter arrived from the town of my birth
From one still sustained by the grace of her youth.
Enclosed between torment and fondness she pressed
   A blade of grass from Ponar.

This grass and moribund cloud with its flicker
once kindled the alphabet, letter by letter.
And on the face of the letters, in murmuring ash,
   The blade of grass from Ponar.

This grass is my doll's house, my snug little world
Where children play fiddles in rows as they burn.
The maestro's a legend, they lift up their bows
   For the blade of grass from Ponar.

I won't part with this stemlet that yields up my home.
The good earth I long for makes room for us both.
And I'll bring to the Lord my oblation at last:
   the blade of grass from Ponar.[56]

The poet looks back to his origins in "my home town in Jewish Lithuania" (*lite*), from where he receives a letter from a still young friend with "a blade of grass from Ponar." Grass is a crucial metaphor in Sutzkever's poetry, associated with the life force of greenness in the long prose poem "Green Aquarium" (1953–54). The blade of grass triggers the act of recall, fueling the memory of his hometown that "kindled the alphabet, letter by letter." The surrealistic image of "children play[ing] fiddles in rows as they burn" comprises the finality of Ponar: the murderous erasure of his hometown and its future. Like "a blade of grass from Ponar," the sonnet becomes a present to the Lord, a "*heymish-minyature*" (a homey miniature). What remains are an undiscernible trace, a withered blade of grass, and a Yiddish sonnet.

2

LODZ

Chava Rosenfarb

גאָט האָט אונדז אויך מיט מילדער האַנט
געשענקט אַ צווילינג
אַ טויטן-גירוש מיט אַ פֿרילינג—
דער גאָרטן בליט, די זון לייכט
און דער שוחט—שאַכט . . .

With a Mild Hand God
Gave us Twins Moreover
A Death-Expulsion and a Spring—
The Garden Blossoms, the Suns Illuminates
And the Slaughterer—Slaughters . . .

Simkhe-Bunim Shayevitsh, *Friling 1942* (Spring 1942)[1]

In Yiddish culture after 1945, a central distinction was made between the survivors (*sheyres hapleyte*, "the saved remnant," or *lebnsgeblibene*, "survivors") and the non-survivors—between those who had lived through the entire war in Nazi-occupied Europe and the Soviet Union, and those who were kept safe in North and South America, Great Britain, Australia, South Africa, the Soviet Union, and other locations. The small group of Yiddish writers with firsthand knowledge of the *khurbn* (literally, "the destruction"; the Yiddish term for the Holocaust) based on their experiences in concentration camps, ghettos, or in hiding included Mordechai Strigler, Isaiah Shpiegl, Leib Rochman, Avrom Sutzkever, and Chava Rosenfarb. What sustained their creative work during the war was their deep sense of connection to a transnational Yiddish network. After the war they wrote and published prolifically, supported by Yiddish cultural organizations, even as they meticulously honed their artistic craft. After six years of war, they were free to build Yiddish literature and culture anew, a mission they fully embraced. Yet memories of their colleagues who had been murdered haunted them like ghosts during the postwar period's rush toward regeneration and renewal.

After World War II the city of Lodz became one of the short-lived Jewish cultural centers for refugees from the Soviet Union and survivors around Eastern Europe. With some of the leading Yiddish scholars, writers, composers, and film directors settling briefly in postwar Lodz, the city experienced a minor Jewish cultural renaissance: "Among them were the historians Philip Friedman, Bernard Mark and Joseph Kermish, the writers Chaim Grade, Binem Heller, Isaac Ianansovich, Shmerke Kac[z]erginski, Abraham Sutzkever and Rachel Korn, the journalist Leon Leneman, the composer Shaul Berezovski, and the filmmaker Natan Gross."[2]

Undzere kinder, directed by the twenty-eight-year-old Natan Gross in 1948, was the last Yiddish feature film made in Poland. It features the comedians Shimen Dzigan and Yisroel Schumacher as they visit the Jewish orphanage Helenowek near Lodz. This film was made possible as the result of a veritable Yiddish theater boom in postwar Lodz. Between August and December 1946, eight Yiddish plays were produced there; in 1947, 28,000 tickets to the Yiddish theater were sold in Lodz. Dzigan and Schumacher, along with the renowned Ida Kaminska, were the most beloved Jewish actors in Lodz: "Dzigan and Schumacher's performances in postwar Lodz were tremendously successful. The crowd at the first program, *Abi men zet zikh* (We meet again), was huge. The reunion between the Yiddish-speaking audience and the popular Yiddish comedians after years of suffering and loss was a highly emotional one. Both audience and actors stood facing each other for a few moments, and cried."[3]

Undzere kinder was a tribute to Dzigan and Schumacher, who returned to Lodz in 1947 after surviving the war years in the Soviet Union, including a brief period in a labor camp. Their theatrical performances, which play a central role in the film, are framed by documentary footage of Jews being herded into cattle cars, documentary-style Holocaust testimonies performed by the orphanage children, and the duo's performance of Sholem Aleichem's *A sreyfe in Kasrilevke* (A Fire in Kasrilevke), including musical and dance routines. Dzigan and Schumacher's comedy routines contrast sharply with the film's main theme, which is the representation of the Holocaust testimonies and traumas of the children in the orphanage. Critical reception of the film has focused on the three survival stories the young orphans enact in the middle of the night, in the privacy of their rooms in Helenowek. These stories are presented in the last third of the film, following Dzigan and Schumacher's two performances—one for a large audience in Lodz and a later one for the orphanage children. *Undzere kinder* is the only postwar Yiddish feature film to address the trauma of orphaned Jewish children. It represents the children's traumatic experiences by embedding them in a distinctly inward-looking world of Yiddish cultural entertainment—one that is far removed from the Jewish issues of postwar Poland, such as Jewish mass emigration following the Kielce pogrom in the summer of 1946 and other forms of anti-Semitic assaults on Jews and their property.[4] *Undzere kinder*, in contrast, focuses on the prewar Jewish Polish world. The film thus frames the representation of the children's traumatic war experiences without addressing the radically new conditions for Jewish life in postwar Lodz.

In his 1974 memoir *Der koyekh fun yidishn humor* (The Power of Jewish Humor), Dzigan gives a description of the duo's performances throughout Poland in 1947–48 without mentioning *Undzere kinder:*

> In the meantime, we traveled to the Polish cities to perform. There in the theaters sat the remnants of my previous audience. It seemed to me that I performed for the perished. My postwar monologues sounded very sad. I was stripped of any shred of joy. The sadness permeated the audience and the stage. I attempted to bring a little bit of cheerfulness and it came out of my mouth as if it were a Kaddish. The more I wanted to joke about the present, I returned to our past. The longing toward the past choked both the audience and the actors. Against our will, we returned through our performances to the world that had been obliterated. Once again the Yiddish word, the Yiddish song, reminded everyone of the past environment, of their relatives, their best years. The surviving remnant reeking of death was joined again in the homes of their mothers and fathers, brothers, sisters, friends and loved ones. Every song opened pages of happy times. Every joke recalled a close neighbor. Suddenly, it seemed like nothing had happened; that all of it had been a nightmare. Here Schumacher and I spoke with one another in the Lodz dialect. Here we revived Balut [a poor Jewish area of Lodz] with our language, melody, and flexibility. The audience in the theater laughs, they enjoy the familiar sound of words tickling their ears . . . here . . . no . . . no . . . no . . . they are no more, the Jews. They will never be again. I told jokes, and everything inside me wept.[5]

This is the context in which *Undzere kinder* was filmed in 1948 and edited the following year. Dzigan and Schumacher's comedy routines, including lyrics and dialogues by Avrom Goldfaden and Sholem Aleichem, were intended to comfort and unite the survivor audience. The film delineates an iconoclastic version of Polish Yiddish culture as a source and a resource for a particular postwar Jewish audience, while representing documentary cinematography for survivor testimonies.

The film begins with a theatrical performance similar to those that were performed in postwar Lodz. They are introduced by the play's director with these words: "We have set ourselves the task to help Jews forget their sorrows and to console and encourage the building of a new life. But we must not forget the tragic experiences of the recent past." Following this introduction, Dzigan and Schumacher perform "The Ghetto Singers," featuring the duo's comedic performance style. Schumacher delivers a schmaltzy song about his mother's cooking, and Dzigan comments with comedic shtick. The act is accompanied by a klezmer band, Dzigan's Cossack dance, and a *badkhn* (wedding jester)-like rhymed declamation. The children interrupt the act, which they dismiss as escapist entertainment that does not reflect their ghetto experiences.

The duo's nearly eight-minute-long performance of *A Fire in Kasrilevke* highlights the myth of fire and destruction that Dan Miron characterizes as an important feature of the literary image of the shtetl.[6] The fire in Kasrilevke represents the destruction of the House of Israel, which in turn stands in for the destroyed Temple in Jerusalem. The duo's performance is not based on a particular Sholem Aleichem story but rather creates a montage of theatrical and choreographic gestures, facial expressions, and Yiddish language play derived from his storytelling universe. The film creates a mythologized space, utilizing abstract stage design to represent the traditional Jewish life of Kasrilevke, the quintessential fictional shtetl in Sholem Aleichem's work.

The image of the fire contrasts starkly with the real-life fire the children experienced in the Warsaw Ghetto. The formulaic choreography of the duo's performance highlights body language and Yiddish wordplay, the DNA of the Yiddish theater. Dzigan and Schumacher impersonate stock figures, such as the stuttering Kuni Leml (derived from Avrom Goldfaden's play *Di tsvey Kuni-Lemls*), Tevye the Dairyman, the fiddler, the water carrier, the gossipy *yentes*, and the rabbi. They create a shtetl universe of song, dance, and dialogue similar to the one in *Fiddler on the Roof*. Crucial to their performance is the duo's Lodz dialect, which is used to emphasize the distinctly regional form of traditional Polish Jewish life. At the end of the act, the camera focuses on the children's laughter and ovations, followed by the duo's asking whether the children had ever seen a real fire. Several of the children declare that they watched the Warsaw Ghetto go up in flames.

This moment articulates how the duo passes the torch to the young creators of the postwar Yiddish culture: the youthful survivors who experienced the actual fires of the ghettos and camps. At the center of this culture are the testimonial performances about survival. The duo's fairytale-like Sholem Aleichem universe creates a short-lived cultural arena and a performative vocabulary for the young survivors. This allows the children to reconnect with the past through the nostalgia of the Lodz Yiddish dialect, body gestures, and literary stock figures. Forged in the cauldron of cataclysm, the children are initiating a new chapter in Yiddish cultural history by subverting the past achievements of Sholem Aleichem and Avrom Goldfaden.

In the final part of the film, the children enact three survival stories in the privacy of their rooms in the orphanage while Dzigan and Schumacher watch them through a keyhole. We, the viewers of the film, like the two comedians, are given access to the secret world of the children's Holocaust traumas. Dzigan characterizes their skits as a House of Nightmares and wants to flee the orphanage in the middle of the night because he cannot stand the horror of the children's war stories. Such survivor testimonies were shocking glimpses into an unprecedented reign of terror that was until then unknown to Jews who, like Dzigan and Schumacher, had fled to the Soviet Union.

As the historian Gabriel Finder points out, "[T]he Jewish political and cultural elites of the entire ideological spectrum perceived Jewish children as the 'physical and spiritual body,' thanks to which the Jewish community might be 'reborn' after the devastating destruction."[7] Moreover, "the filmmakers meant *Undzere kinder* to be a tribute to the resilience and courage of children who survived the Holocaust."[8] The artistic creators of *Undzere kinder* included the director Natan Gross and producer Shaul Goskind (who produced several Yiddish feature films in 1930s Poland); Rokhl Oyerbakh, a survivor of the Warsaw Ghetto, a member of Ringelblum's Oyneg Shabes archive, and an important figure in the creation of Yad Vashem; and the poet Binem Heller, who had returned from the Soviet Union. As documented by historian Shimen Redlich and Polish Jewish writer Henryk Grynberg, both formerly residents of the Helenowek orphanage who were child actors in the film, "at no children's home including Helenowek, did the children speak Yiddish, the language of all the characters, including the children, in *Undzere kinder*."[9]

The ultimate conceit of *Undzere kinder* was the proposition that the surviving children would restart and continue Polish Yiddish culture. Finder sums up the film's characteristics: "In *Undzere kinder*, the voices of the children—their language, not to mention their memories, recreated from the imagination—clearly belonged to the filmmakers, who essentially ventriloquized the children—children, who irrespective of the belief of contemporary pedagogues and psychologists that child survivors should tell their stories, in reality preferred to keep silent."[10]

The film's final sequence takes place on the morning after the children's nocturnal play-acting. The duo meet "normal," "healthy" children playing in the sandbox, poking fun at the duo's performance of *The Fire in Kasrilevke*. This utopian vision of comedy as a building block for a new postwar Yiddish culture turned out to be a dead end. The film was not approved by the censors after it had been completed and made ready for distribution. Its distinctly Jewish style was ideologically unacceptable to the Polish authorities in the country's shift to communist rule in 1948–49. The film was shown a few times for a specially invited audience in Poland, then smuggled out of the country and shown a few times in the newly created Jewish state in 1951. Then it disappeared until it was restored and released by the Jewish film center at Brandeis University in 1991. *Undzere kinder* never reached its primary audience of survivors in Poland and elsewhere.[11]

In his collection of jokes and feuilletons from Jewish life in postwar Poland, *Gelekhter durkh trern* (Laughter through Tears), M. Nudelman, a well-known Yiddish humorist in interwar Jewish Poland, imagined what would happen "if Sholem Aleichem were alive today." *Gelekhter durkh trern* appeared as volume 10 in the Yiddish book series *Dos poylishe yidntum* published in Buenos Aires, one of only a handful of volumes in the 175-book series that was devoted solely to Jewish humor (see chapter 4). Arriving in postwar Lodz, Sholem Aleichem, like everybody else, is registered by the Jewish Committee as a returning repatriate and receives half a kilo of kasha, 10 grams of fat, 10 grams of sugar, and 10 grams of imitation milk. His main character, Menakhem Mendl, the quintessential *luftmensch*, has been declared the class enemy by the Central Committee, and *Tevye der milkhiger* continues to hide out using Aryan papers. The most popular reading materials are the column "We Seek Relatives" in the Lodz weekly *Dos naye lebn* (The New Life), and Sholem Aleichem's plays *Nokhn mabl* (After the Flood) and *Navenad* (Refugee). After attending the Jewish theater, Sholem Aleichem cannot recognize his own play.

Similarly, by situating Sholem Aleichem at the center of Dzigan and Schumacher's comedy, Natan Gross made a cinematographic tribute to Polish Yiddish culture as it had flourished prior to the Holocaust. All of the Yiddish filmmakers, actors, and other contributors to *Undzere kinder* in Poland left for Israel or North America within a few years' time. Sholem Aleichem served as a link to prewar Jewish Polish culture, an important identity marker during the tumultuous transformation of postwar Poland. The film managed to represent a combination of the survivors' longing for the old Jewish world and their deep need to bear witness; it depicted rebirth after the war, expressed in comedy mixed with sadness and loss—in short, laughter through tears.

* * *

Chava Rosenfarb's career as Holocaust novelist, poet, and essayist was predicated on her authenticity as a witness and survivor of the Lodz Ghetto. Her novel trilogy, *Der boym fun lebn* (The Tree of Life, 1972), belongs to an influential kind of Holocaust literature: the survivors' chronicles. Canonical examples of such works are Primo Levi's and Elie Wiesel's memoirs of survival in Auschwitz. Like the dénouement of the few surviving characters at the end of *Der boym fun lebn*, Levi's and Wiesel's memoirs focus on their stories of survival, through which the subjective experience of dehumanization is delineated, examined, and negated by the act of writing. Fictional survivor accounts are rare in Yiddish and have primarily appeared as short fiction, such as Isaiah Shpiegl's stories written in the Lodz Ghetto and Avrom Sutzkever's prose poems about the Vilna Ghetto. Full-length novels about the ghetto and concentration camp experiences are exceptional in any language.[12]

Der boym fun lebn is the first Holocaust novel written in Yiddish. The two-thousand-page work of fiction in the form of a trilogy holds a unique position among Jewish Holocaust narratives. It received the prestigious Itsik Manger Prize for Yiddish literature in 1979. *The Tree of Life: A Novel about Life in the Lodz Ghetto* was the title of the trilogy when it was published in English translation in 1985 in Australia, and republished by the University of Wisconsin Press in 2005–6. Widely praised by Yiddish critics, the work in English has been almost completely overlooked outside Canada. Rosenfarb's novel is a remarkable exception among Yiddish post-1945 works, and more so because the trilogy was written by a woman. Modern Yiddish literature can claim very few novels authored by women, who generally excelled as poets and short story writers and, to a lesser degree, memoirists.

On May 8, 1945, Victory in Europe Day, Chava Rosenfarb recorded in her Bergen-Belsen diary her tangled emotional state of being haunted by a ghostlike past, feeling the obligation to bear witness and continue Yiddish artistic creativity, and mourning the loss of family and friends:

פֿלעדערמײַז פֿליִען פֿאַרבײַ פֿענצטער.
פֿליגלען פֿלאַטערן אויס דעם טאַנץ פֿון געשפֿענסטער . . .
מײַן אומפֿאַרענדיקטע געטאָ-ליד לאָזט מיך ניט רוען. עס האָט מיך באַגלייט אין מײַן געפֿאַנגענשאַפֿט, מיט אים אויף די ליפּן האָב איך אין די װינטער פֿאַרטאָגן געדרעפּטשעט דורך שנייען צו דער אַרבעט. איך האָב עס מיר אויפֿגעשריבן מיט אַ בלײַ איבער מײַן פּריטשע און װײַטער געװעבט אַ פּאָר שורות. אָבער עס מאָנט עס נאָך כּסדר. עס נאָגט.
איך הער דורכן פֿענצטער די שטים פֿון מעגאַפֿאָן. הײַנט איז די קריג אָפֿיציעל געענדיקט. װו ביסטו טאַטע, אַז כ׳זאָל דיך קענען אַרומנעמען?

Bats fly by the window
Wings flutter like the dance of ghosts . . .

My incomplete ghetto-poem does not let me rest. It accompanied me in my incarceration, with the poem on my lips I hobbled to work through the snow on winter mornings. I wrote with a pencil over my bunk and continued to weave a couple of lines. But it constantly demands its dues. It nags.

I hear through the window the voice of the megaphone. Today, the war officially ended. Where are you my father so I can embrace you?[13]

The first two lines of this quote are part of a ghetto poem recreated after liberation. Its final two lines are excluded from the diary but recalled almost thirty years later in a speech Rosenfarb gave at the Jewish Public Library in Montreal on May 27, 1973, to celebrate the publication of *Der boym fun lebn*:

פֿלעדערמײַז פֿליִען פֿאַרבײַ פֿענצטער,
פֿליגלען פֿלאַטערן אויס דעם טאַנץ פֿון געשפֿענסטער.
נאָמענלאָז פֿאַרגייט דער טאָג דער לעצטער.
מיר קומען אום . . . מיר קומען אום.

Bats fly by the window,
Wings flutter like the dance of ghosts.
Without a name the last days die out.
We are dying . . . we are dying.[14]

Rosenfarb points out that the last line contains the words of the Lodz Ghetto poet Simkhe-Bunim Shayevitsh (1907–44), which he used to hum in a haunting melody that angered her:

מיר קומען אום . . . נאָמענלאָז . . . תּיקונלאָז . . .

We are dying . . . without names . . . without redress.[15]

Ill with typhus in Bergen-Belsen on Victory in Europe Day in May 1945, Rosenfarb is visited by a feverish vision of Shayevitsh and her father. They demand that she never forget them and that she take up her pen to make the Lodz Ghetto live on in the memory of the next generation.[16] As with Sutzkever, poetry is the raison d'être of Rosenfarb's survival during and after the war. Rosenfarb becomes part of a diverse group of survivors and exiles who continue to use Yiddish as an artistic medium after the Holocaust. Their postwar perspective is fundamentally different from that of writers who perished in the Holocaust, leaving behind an archive of posthumously published writings.

Chava Rosenfarb's essay "*Simkhe-Bunim Shayevitsh: Dermonungen*" (Simkhe-Bunim Shayevitsh: Reminiscences; published in English as "The Last Poet of Lodz") discusses the author of the epic poems *Lekh lekho* (Go Forth) and *Friling 1942* (Spring 1942), published posthumously in Lodz in 1946; she analyzes her troubled emotions in attempting to depict her mentor and friend. Shayevitsh is the "ghetto poet par excellence" who captured the inner moral and emotional life of the ghetto-Jew.[17] She acknowledges the poet's influence on her life and work while stressing her "discomfort and frustration"[18] in writing about him. Although Rosenfarb created a complex portrait of Shayevitsh in the character of Simkhe-Bunim Berkovitch in the *Der boym fun lebn* trilogy, she concludes that some essential part of the poet is still missing, "because fiction distorts and disguises [*tsekrimt un farshtelt*], it embellishes, it disfigures [*farkriplt*] to serve its own goals."[19] Like Shayevitsh, Rosenfarb belonged to Miriam Ulinover's group of Yiddish poets who met regularly in the Lodz Ghetto:

> All kinds of discussion and self-education groups appeared, and there was a kind of writing epidemic. Anyone who could hold a pen in his hand wrote so as to maintain his moral existence and leave a trace for posterity in order to bear witness about the cataclysm they experienced on their own bodies. The Lodz Ghetto began to swarm

with writers, poets, journalists, and memoirists. The circle of recognized Yiddish writers met in the home of Miriam Ulinover, the author of *Der bobes oytser* [The Grandmother's Treasure].[20]

The nineteen-year-old Rosenfarb met Shayevitsh in the Lodz Ghetto following the deportation of the poet's wife, daughter, and newborn baby during the so-called *Sperre* in September 1942.[21] During her visits to him, she listened to the poet read aloud from the epic poem he never completed. Although she had a strong desire to memorize her own ghetto poetry, Shayevitsh's poems "made me upset and totally depressed so I tried to erase them from memory after I had heard them. I was young. I wanted to live. I was concerned about writing my own ghetto poems. To absorb his much more shocking poems was more than I could bear."[22] Rosenfarb pointed out that Shayevitsh came closest to capturing the Lodz Ghetto's "shocking reality," which seemed out of reach for her as a surviving writer.

FIGURE 2.1. *From left:* Saul Bellow, Rokhl Korn, an unidentified woman, and Chava Rosenfarb, Montreal, November 9, 1968. (Jewish Public Library Archives, Montreal)

After immigrating to Montreal in 1950, Rosenfarb was embraced by a community of Yiddish writers and cultural organizations that supported her artistic work during the next half-century.[23] The event at the Jewish Public Library in Montreal on May 27, 1973, was sponsored by the Workmen's Circle and the Bund, and exemplified the reverence for the Yiddish writer as cultural hero in her own cultural context after 1945.[24] During this event the Montreal Yiddish fiction writer and survivor Yehuda Elberg repeatedly referred to Rosenfarb's trilogy as a *seyfer* (a holy book).[25] Elberg took on the role of the *gabbai* (beadle) in the *shul* (synagogue) by introducing Rosenfarb's remarks as if he were calling her up to read from the Torah, breaking with the Orthodox practice of not allowing a woman to do so in public. By honoring a female Yiddish writer in this way, Elberg transformed a traditional religious act into a secular-humanist event. Elberg described Rosenfarb's thirteen years of work on the trilogy as her "*farknasung tsu der toyre*" (engagement to the Torah).

The trope of Yiddish literature as sacred text—a new Torah for the surviving remnant—is a defining feature of Yiddish culture after 1945. The fact that Rosenfarb's trilogy was published in three massive volumes, and not initially serialized in the Yiddish press, as was common for novels and memoirs, indicates that she wanted to present the novels as standing apart from the daily Yiddish press. They were perceived as sacred books (*sforim*) that sought to keep alive the memory of the martyrs, the *kedoyshim* who had perished in *der driter khurbn* (the Holocaust). The novel's title, *Der boym fun lebn*, is a Yiddish translation of the Hebrew *ets khayim* (the Tree of Life), a traditional metaphor for the Torah. The three novelistic *pinkosim* (chronicles) are similar to *Yizker bikher* (memorial books) and the *Dos poylishe yidntum* (Polish Jewry) book series in that they were published as hardcover volumes and printed on the best paper, signifying their function as "substitute gravestones" for the nameless victims, none of whom were afforded a proper burial according to Jewish religious law.[26] After 1945, indeed, Yiddish writers endowed secular literature with sacred attributes.

In her 1989 essay "*Paul Celan un zayne goyrl brider*" (Paul Celan and His Brothers of Destiny), Rosenfarb reflects on the fact that several important Jewish Holocaust writers took their own lives: Jerzy Kosinski, Romain Gary, Adolf Rudnitsky, Paul Celan, Piotr Rawicz, and Primo Levi. What they have in common, according to Rosenfarb, is that they wrote in non-Jewish languages and must be considered "*shraybers yidn*" (writers who happen to be Jews) and not "*yidishe shraybers*" (Jewish writers).[27] Unlike the Yiddish writer, who could depend on having a huge Jewish readership and being celebrated as a cultural hero among her own people, the Jewish survivor writing in a non-Jewish language was isolated and consequently exposed to her own inner demons. Despite being honored and praised as witnesses to the Holocaust by their respective national (non-Jewish) readerships, and to a certain extent able to "liberate themselves from silence and grief," they nonetheless committed suicide. The main reason, according to Rosenfarb, was that they lacked "the inner immunity which would have helped them continue to live, carrying the existential malady of the survivors which can never be healed."[28]

The Yiddish cultural world, in contrast, provided the "vaccine" that enabled survivor writers to acquire "the inner immunity" and continue their mission as witnesses to the Holocaust. After 1945 the Yiddish cultural milieu supported Yiddish writers sufficiently to sustain long careers, which resulted in masterpieces such as Sutzkever's poetry and Leib Rochman's prose works. Elie Wiesel initially wrote his first memoir of Auschwitz in Yiddish; it was published as volume 117 in the Yiddish book series *Dos poylishe yidntum* in 1956. This book series published Mordechai Strigler's documentary fiction about Majdanek and slave labor camps, and Ka-Tzetnik's fiction, with its lurid sado-masochist entanglements of perpetrator and victim, giving a worldwide Yiddish readership the opportunity to experience through this genre what it meant to be a Jew under Nazi rule.

Unlike poetry, life-writing, short fiction, and essays, the novel was not a form that was utilized by the ghetto writers. Writing a successful novel requires perspective and ample time, and neither commodity was available in the ghettos. Yet as early as her first days after liberation in Bergen-Belsen (May–August 1945), Rosenfarb's diary fragments reveal that she was already envisioning a grand prose work in which she would portray her four-and-a-half-year ghetto experience:

> That I might be committing an act of rebellion by breaking with the female tradition of writing exclusively poetry or short prose hardly occurred to me. The subject matter imposed the form on me. What I wanted to say was impossible to sing. The brutal reality of the ghetto demanded the dry precision of words. Not that I wanted to ban the poet within me. On the contrary, I wanted her to stand by me, but I wanted her to creep with me through the maze of ghetto streets as low to the ground as possible.[29]

That a woman wrote the first *khurbn roman* in Yiddish can be viewed as an act of transgression against the gendered division between poetry and prose as, respectively, female and male domains in Yiddish literature. Although Rosenfarb continued to write and publish poetry, it would be as a novelist and short story writer that she would succeed in conveying the reality of the Lodz Ghetto and the survivors' "postscript" in Canada.[30]

In the novel's prologue, *Erev veg* (On the Eve of the Journey), which was left out of the English translation, Rosenfarb's alter ego, Rachel Eibeschutz (the name means "eternal protection"), describes her decision to write the novel.[31] Rachel resides in a house in Brussels during the first spring after the war, in 1946. From her window she can see a cherry tree and the local train lines, which remind her of the cattle cars that took her and her family to Auschwitz. The conductor makes Rachel think of the poet Shayevitsh, with whom she begins an inner dialogue. Rachel is pregnant and wants to forget about the war in anticipation of the new life she is carrying. But the poet's voice demands that she recall her ghetto experience and convey it in artistic form. Although Rachel feels that her artistic talent is insufficient, she is persuaded by the poet's voice to start writing the novel. In a Proustian fashion, the blossoming cherry tree triggers Rachel's recollection of a similar tree in the Lodz Ghetto. In addition to its religious associations, the "tree of life" refers to the renewal of the natural cycle that inspires Rosenfarb to depict the inner beauty, resilience, and spiritual resistance of the ghetto Jews.

Der boym fun lebn is an artistic compromise crafted to balance the demands of Rachel's postwar renewal; the obligation to commemorate the tragedy and loss; and "the shocking reality" of the Lodz Ghetto. It was this "Kafka-like kingdom of 'Khayem the First'" (referring to Chaim Rumkowski, the head of the Lodz *Judenrat*) that Shayevitsh captured in his poetry: "the atmosphere of the abnormal, surreal otherworldly ghetto life for which no words exist that could describe it."[32] The years during the war had been "*di shenste yorn*" (the most beautiful years), as Rosenfarb put it at the 1973 event at the Jewish Public Library. In the trilogy Rosenfarb set out to depict life in the Lodz Ghetto as "*a leyter fun derhoybung*" (a ladder of elevation), a uniquely rich material of human existence *in extremis* that was characterized by heroism, spiritual values, and transcendence.[33] Rosenfarb reiterated on several occasions that artistic creation is a life-affirming activity, even when it addresses the most inhumane subject matter, including mass starvation, genocide, and Jewish collaboration with the Germans. Similarly, Isaiah Shpiegl's short stories of the Lodz Ghetto focus on the inner moral strength of the ghetto Jews to overcome their bodily and material degradation, encapsulated by the titles of his short story collections *Shtern ibern geto* (Stars over the Ghetto, 1947) and *Likht funem opgrunt* (Light from the Abyss, 1952).

Sutzkever's prose poems in *"Griner akvarium"* (Green Aquarium, 1953), about the Vilna Ghetto, also uses the regenerative image of the life-giving sap of nature symbolized by the greenness of the grass to transform and elevate the forces of death in a surreal, symbolist poetics.

Reminiscent of the I. J. Singer novel *Di brider ashkenazi* (The Brothers Ashkenazi, 1936), about the rise of the Jewish clothing industry in Lodz in the late nineteenth century, Rosenfarb's trilogy opens with a portrait of the industrialist Samuel Zuckerman, a Polish patriot descended from a long-standing Lodz Jewish family who sets out to chronicle the history of the Jews of Lodz. *Der boym fun lebn* becomes such a chronicle, meticulously recording the collective story of the Lodz Jewish community from the eve of the war in 1939, during the ghetto period of 1940–44, through its final liquidation in August 1944, with the deportation of the last contingent of Lodz Jews to Auschwitz. Rosenfarb depicts ten characters from various social, cultural, and political backgrounds, tracing their interpersonal relationships and inner struggles. The *minyan* of ten, the basic unit of the Jewish prayer quorum, is the indestructible part that stands in for the whole, similar to Sutzkever's poetic portrait of ten characters who survive in the sewers under the Vilna Ghetto in the epic poem *"Geheymshtot"* (Secret City, 1947). Recounted by an omniscient narrator, the novel is interspersed with diary notes by David, a young teenager from a Bundist background, and unsent letters written by the physician Michal to his lover Mira in Paris. The head of the *Judenrat*, Chaim Rumkowski, Simkhe-Bunim Berkovitch (based on Shayevitsh), and Rachel Eibeschutz (Rosenfarb's alter ego) are the only characters directly modeled on historical figures. Like the inhabitants of the Lodz Ghetto, the ten main characters seem to be ignorant of the death camps Chelmno and Auschwitz, to which the Lodz Jews are deported and then gassed on arrival. The destiny of the final group of Lodz Ghetto Jews to be deported to Auschwitz—including Rachel, Berkovitch, Michal, David, and Rumkowski—is indicated by six blank pages prefaced by the following lines: "Chapter twenty-nine . . . Thirty . . . Thirty-one . . . ad infinitum. Auschwitz. Words cease, stripped naked, their meaning, their sense shaven off. Letters expire in the smoke of the crematorium's chimney . . ."[34]

By the time the trilogy was published in 1972, several accounts of the death camps, including Elie Wiesel's . . . *Un di velt hot geshvign* (1956; translated as *Night*, 1960) and Primo Levi's *Survival in Auschwitz* (1960), had already appeared. Rosenfarb's six blank pages, then, commemorate the six million Jews while signaling that this novel would not depict Auschwitz. Rosenfarb would eventually write harrowingly in her 1992 novel, *Briv tsu*

Abrashn (Letters to Abrasha), about the character Miriam's incarceration in Auschwitz, Sasel, and Bergen-Belsen concentration camps. Following the six blank pages, a brief epilogue, "After the Journey," presents the correspondence between two of the novel's surviving characters, Rachel and Junio. They have begun new lives in Canada and on a kibbutz in Israel, respectively.

Der boym fun lebn is narrated from the perspective of the characters themselves rather than from retrospective or nonrealist points of view. This style, influenced by Victor Hugo and Romain Rolland, keeps the novelistic prose, in Rosenfarb's own words, "as low to the ground as possible."[35] A characteristic example of Rosenfarb's style is the dramatic moment when Simkhe-Bunim Berkovitch returns with food for his family during the *Sperre* in September 1942. The English translation is by Rosenfarb, in collaboration with her daughter Goldie Morgentaler:

> The street was dead. Bunim ran over it with tangling steps. *A huge truck filled with colors wailed* as it passed him by. Through the gate beneath the bridge rows of empty trucks came rushing in. Bunim entered his backyard. It was black with people swaying, circling *in a vertiginous maddening dance.* Women were tearing the hair from their heads, knocking themselves against the walls; they lay prostrated on the *dzialkas* (plot of land). *The whole backyard was united in one howl.*
>
> Blinded, bent under the load on his back, he dashed to the hut. The lock was broken. The sack slid from his shoulder; the potatoes rolled over the floor. The loaf of bread fell from his hand. He entered the other room. Miriam's bed was empty. He opened the wardrobe and with the hands of a blind man tapped at the emptiness between Miriam's dresses. The drawer of the dresser where the baby had been hidden stood open. The shutters on the windows were torn off. Through them the morning had come in to find its reflection in the mirror of the open wardrobe door. The room was full of light. The sun, a yellow cat, lay stretched out on the creased cover of Miriam's bed. The bed was still warm and smelled of Miriam. As he lay on it, he embraced the room with dry eyes. On the floor near the door lay Lily the doll, staring at him with her glass eyes.[36] (italics added)

The first paragraph employs literary flourishes and metaphors designed to recreate the atmosphere of panic and chaos (the phrases I've placed in italics). The second paragraph consists of short, breathless sentences that register the details of material objects, and the absence of Bunim's wife and two children is encapsulated in the metaphoric phrase, "On the floor . . . lay Lily the doll, staring at him with her glass eyes."[37] Rosenfarb competently employs the artistic resources of literary realism and mimesis, recreating the dramatic moment when Bunim faces the loss of his spouse and children, arguably the most traumatic experience of the inhabitants of the Lodz Ghetto. Bunim's unexpected possession of more food than the usual hunger ration is juxtaposed with the absence of his wife, daughter, and newborn son. The dramatic event is narrated in a prose style that seeks to convey how Bunim experienced this extreme moment of emotional chaos, panic, and loss.

In yene koshmarne teg (In Those Terrible Days), the journalist Josef Zelkowicz's diary written in the Lodz Ghetto, which he planned to publish after the war, presents a very different account of the *Sperre*.[38] Zelkowicz also contributed to *The Chronicle of the Lodz Ghetto*, written in Polish and German by a group of Jewish intellectuals (and first published in English in 1984). This chronicle is a monumental work consisting "of about 1,000 bulletins ranging in size from half a page to ten or even more in length."[39] Recorded daily by a team of professional journalists and writers in the Lodz Ghetto, it documents the weather, births and deaths, social and cultural conditions, German decrees, deportations, and the orders and speeches of the "Eldest of the Lodz Ghetto," Chaim Rumkowski. A document of crucial importance for the historical record of the Lodz Ghetto, the chronicle is constrained by its loyalty to Rumkowski's regime. Its carefully chosen euphemisms indicate the extent to which the chroniclers sought to preempt censorship from both the Germans and the internal Jewish monitors. Zelkowicz's private Yiddish writing, on the other hand, penned immediately following the events of the *Sperre*, focuses on the abnormality of the ghetto population's response to the loss of almost fifteen thousand family members:

> It would seem that the events of recent days would have immersed the entire population of the ghetto in mourning for a long time to come, and yet, right after the incidents, and even during the resettlement action, the populace was obsessed with everyday concerns—getting bread rations, and so forth—and often went from immediate personal tragedy right back into daily life. Is this some sort of numbing of the nerves, and indifference, or a symptom of an illness that manifests itself in atrophied emotional reactions? After losing those nearest to them, people talk constantly about rations, potatoes, soup, etc.! It is beyond comprehension! Why this lack of warmth

toward those they loved? Naturally, here and there, there are some mothers weeping in a corner for a child or children shipped from the ghetto, but, as a whole, the mood of the ghetto does not reflect last week's terrible ordeal. Sad but true!⁴⁰

Zelkowicz's account addresses the *Sperre* from the perspective of a reporter and participant observer who is stunned by the breakdown of human empathy and compassion. Like the contributors to Emanuel Ringelblum's Oyneg Shabes archive in the Warsaw Ghetto, Zelkowicz wants to get at the truth of the event regardless of its damaging view of the ghetto Jews.

In comparing the Yale video interviews of Holocaust survivors and the (literary) memoirs of their experiences during the Holocaust, Lawrence Langer points to the almost insurmountable difficulty of retrospectively depicting the abnormality of the events of the Holocaust in written form. Langer suggests that video interviews might provide more direct access to the recalled past in the interviewee's recounting (and reliving) of the events in front of the video camera. Langer's interpretation of the Yale video interviews, like Zelkowicz's report of the *Sperre*—highlighting the difficulty of conveying the ghetto population's abnormal response to the event—emphasizes that "one of the most powerful themes on these tapes is thus the difficulty of narrating, from the context of normality now, the nature of the abnormality then, an abnormality that still surges into the present to remind us of its potent influence."⁴¹

Zelkowicz's contemporary reporting was an eyewitness account of the increasing dehumanization of the ghetto population, which he records with a meticulous commitment to journalistic truth. Like the Yale video interviews of survivors, Zelkowicz's report is shot through with the horror of human behavior *in extremis*. In contrast, Rosenfarb's realist prose highlights the inner experience of an individual responding to violence, trauma, and loss. Rosenfarb wants to reclaim the character's humanity so that we, the readers, sympathize and identify with him. Drawing on her recollections and conversations with Shayevitsh in the Lodz Ghetto, Rosenfarb uses a fictional documentary style that reconceives the abnormality in a recognizable, realistic frame.

Rosenfarb employs the realist, historical novel in order to uphold "the trinity of event, character, and plot which still provided the staple both of the nineteenth-century realist novel and of that historiography from which nineteenth-century literature derived its model of realism."⁴² As Hayden White points out, modernist art dissolves this trinity, particularly "the dissolution of the event as a basic unit of temporal occurrence and building block of history," challenging and subverting the very distinction between fact and fiction, realistic and imaginary discourse.[43] For White, the Holocaust is the paradigmatic modernist event in Western European history, and this "event is of such a kind as to escape the grasp of *any* language even to describe it and of *any* medium—verbal, visual, oral, or gestural—to represent it, much less of any merely historical account adequately to explain it."[44] The primary concern in artistic representation of the Holocaust is the danger of "aestheticization of this event" to the extent that the actions of the actors—perpetrator, bystander, and victim—are familiarized and fetishized. As a result, White suggests that modernist artistic approaches are better suited to represent the events of the Holocaust: "Modernist techniques of representation provide the possibility of defetishizing both events and the fantasy accounts of them which deny the threat they pose in the very process of pretending to represent them realistically and clear the way for the process of mourning which alone can relieve the burden of history."[45]

Bogdan Wojdowski's Polish Jewish novel *Bread for the Departed* (1971), based on his experiences as a child in the Warsaw Ghetto, is such a modernist novel which, through stream of consciousness, multiple voices, and various stylized usages of multiple languages (Polish, Yiddish, Hebrew, and German), presents a fragmented, polyphonic kaleidoscope of the ghetto experience. *Bread for the Departed*'s fundamental difference from Rosenfarb's ghetto novel indicates that artistic style and narrative form, particularly the difference between modernist and realist aesthetics, are as important as—if not more important than—the choice of Jewish versus non-Jewish languages in representing the events of the Holocaust.[46]

In the Lodz Ghetto, writers and painters discussed how to depict its unprecedented abnormality—"the shocking reality," in Rosenfarb's apt phrase; how to commemorate the human losses; how to aesthetically represent the destruction of the Lodz Jewish community. In Rosenfarb's *Fragments of a Diary*, kept in the three months following her liberation in Bergen-Belsen (May–August 1945), she reflects on the aesthetic challenges in writing about her ghetto experiences:

איך טראכט צי וועלן מיר אַמאָל דעם אָבן אַ קינסטלעריש, אַרומנעמענדיק ווערק וועגן דעם פאַרגאַנגענעם. איך צווייפל דערין. איך דערמאָן זיך מײַנע שמועסן מיט שאַיעוויטשן אין געטאָ. ער האָט געשריבן די גרויסע פּאָעמע.

איך האָב אים געזאָגט: אַזאַ עפּאָפּייע דאַרף מען שרײַבן פון פּערספּעקטיוו, נאָך אַ צײַט. ער האָט דעמאָלט נישט געוווּסט ווי זײַן פּאָעמע וועט זיך ענדיקן, אַז זי וועט

בלײַבן אומפֿאַרענדיקט. ער האָט מיר געזאָגט:—פֿון אונדזער לעבן מוז מען שרײַבן אַזוי. װאָס טו איך דען? איך לאָז טריפֿן אונדזערע טעג פֿון מײַן פּעדער. מער דאַרף מען נישט.—המצנט װײַס איך, אַז אַנדערש קען מען נישט די פּערספּעקטיװו װעט װאַקסן, זיך אויסציען. װערטשע װעט קענען ברענגען דעם ציטער פֿון יענע געטאָ-טעג? פֿון אַזעלכע טעג קאָן מען נאָר שרײַבן אין די הײסע שעהן פֿון זײער דויערן. מיט אַ קורצן, אָפּגעריסענעם אָטעם; װי עס האָבן עס געטאָן די שרײַבער און מאָלער פֿון געטאָ, װען מען האָט דיסטאַנס קאָן מען נאָר געבן דעם שאַרבן פֿון גאַנצקײט, אָבער אָן פּולס פֿון צאַפּלענדיקע-צעפֿיבערטע בלוטן.

צי קענען דען פּאַסן די אָנגענומענע קינסטלערישע פֿאָרמען פֿאַר אַ בוך פֿון געטאָ? איז עס נישט קײן מאַסקע אויף דער רויקײט און אוממיטלבאַרקײט מיט װעלכער מען דאַרף זיך צורירן צו דער טעמע? איז די פֿאָרם פֿון אַ קינסטלערישן ראָמאַן נישט צו עלעגאַנט, צו שלומדיק, צו רויק און גמיטלעך? איך פֿיל דערין אַ באַלײדיקונג פֿאַר מײַנע טײַערע און פֿאַר מיר אַלײן.

I ponder if we will ever have an artistic, comprehensive work about the past events. I doubt it. I remember my conversations with Shayevitsh in the ghetto. He wrote the grand poem.

I told him: Such an epic work needs the distance of perspective, the passing of time. At that moment, he didn't know that his poem would never be completed, that it would remain unfinished. He told me:—One must write about our life in this way. How do I do it? I let our days seep through my pen. That is what is required.—Today I know that it can't be done otherwise. The distance of perspective will grow, stretch out. Who will be able to convey the shiver of those ghetto-days? Those days can only be conveyed in the immediate hour of their passage. With a brief, staccato breath; like the way the writers and painters did it in the ghetto. When there is a distance of perspective only the shell of wholeness can be conveyed, without the pulse of squirming-feverish blood.

Do the conventional artistic forms suffice for a book about the ghetto? Is it not a mask covering the rawness and directness that are required to approach this theme? Is the genre of an artistic novel too elegant, too peaceful, too calm and comfortable? I feel that it would be an insult to my dear ones and myself. (Diary entry, June 30, 1945)[47]

These metapoetic ruminations are based on an aesthetic and cultural hierarchy: The core of Holocaust literature consists of works penned by ghetto writers who eventually perished there, which were created in the midst of the actual suffering. These are the most truthful accounts, the Urtexts that never will be superseded and can only be approximated in quality and authenticity by the next rank in the hierarchy, the works of the survivor writer. What characterizes Shayevitsh's grand poem that was left incomplete and never retrieved after the war? Rosenfarb does not describe the content of his poem in any detail, other than that it had "cadences of the Jewish religious writing" and that "a biblical atmosphere permeated the entire text." For Shayevitsh the text was not "mere literature," it was a sacred text that did not permit any criticism. Particularly striking is Rosenfarb's recollection of her reception of Shayevitsh's reading of the poem in his room in the Lodz Ghetto: "For my part, I was so troubled and frightened by what I heard that I wanted to escape that gloomy room as soon as I could. I wanted to blot out the lines and rhythms that haunted me. I wanted to erase them from my memory." On one of the few occasions that Shayevitsh read from his poem to the group of writers in Ulinover's apartment, his work was met with stunned silence and despair. Rosenfarb sums up the power of the poem: a "Jeremiah-like *cri du coeur* to reach us 'from the other side.'"[48]

Like other (artistic) texts written in the ghettos, in the camps, and in hiding during the Holocaust, Shayevitsh's ghetto poems' aesthetic status and reception were radically transformed after the war:

> The rich and unique body of wartime writing that had survived by dint of extraordinary collective and clandestine effort, and sometimes just by chance, was rooted in different times, places, and circumstances, which often required decoding. Simply put, its natural audience had perished or was too scattered to stand up and be counted. As long as the postwar ruins were divided between East and West and Left and Right, wartime writing—the bedrock of Holocaust memory, the source for everything that followed—languished in obscurity. What followed, therefore, had to be reinvented.[49]

The foremost challenge for surviving Yiddish writers was how to negotiate the vastly changed cultural and political landscape after 1945. The situation was light-years away from anything that even vaguely resembled what they had known prior to and during the war. In addition to serving as the embodiment of continuity and hope for the future of Yiddish culture, these writers felt a strong obligation to give voice to the nameless dead, particularly to their perished writer colleagues in the ghettos and camps. Shayevitsh, Ulinover, and Zelkowicz's original ghetto readership had been annihilated, and the surviving remnant was too scattered and powerless to reclaim their posthumous writings as the Urtexts in a canon of Holocaust literature. Typically, the publications of the ghetto writings from Warsaw, Lodz, and Vilna appeared in small Yiddish editions in Poland, and only decades later were a small portion of them translated into major languages.[50] It was only the efforts of the surviving Jewish writers and critics to reclaim and reference a few of the perished writers' works from the ghettos that ensured the latter's literary afterlife which, for decades, existed only in Yiddish and Hebrew. After the war the perished writers' posthumous works were reconceived, reframed, and removed from their original readership and cultural and political contexts. Fictional portraits of Shayevitsh appeared in Rosenfarb's novels and essays; of the Polish Jewish writer Bruno Schulz in Cynthia Ozick's *The Messiah of Stockholm* (1987) and David Grossman's *See: Under Love* (1986); of the contributors to the Ringelblum archive in John Hersey's *The Wall* (1950); and most recently of Chaim Rumkowski and a host of (fictional and historical) characters from the Lodz Ghetto in the Swedish author Steve Sem-Sandberg's novel *The Emperor of Lies* (2009). Thus the historical ghetto figures regained a lease on a literary afterlife by being removed from their original historical and cultural contexts, and reconceived for a very different readership.

Rosenfarb's short story collection *Survivors* (2004), a compilation of works originally published in *Di goldene keyt* in the 1980s and 1990s, depicts Holocaust survivors in Canada, "the Land of the Postscript." The stories focus on rootless refugees who, despite their outward success, are plagued by survivor guilt and live a shadow existence. The novella "Edgia's Revenge" is a confession narrated by the Jewish *kapo*, Rella. The relationship between Rella and Edgia as it develops over decades in Montreal is the main focus of the story. Both women belong to a small circle of Holocaust survivors who participate in the cultural riches of the Canadian metropolis. Rella's one and only act of human empathy as a Jewish *kapo* was to save Edgia from a selection for the gas chamber. Over decades of upward social mobility and business success as a designer in Montreal, Rella is haunted by the fear that Edgia will reveal her past as a *kapo*. It turns out that the survival of this group has been bought at a high price. Rella's sexual favors to a German overseer in the camp secured her a privileged status; Lolek, a survivor from Lithuania who claims to have been a Jewish partisan, actually survived unheroically in hiding.

Unlike Isaac Bashevis Singer's survivors in the novels *Shadows on the Hudson* (1991) and *Enemies: A Love Story* (1972), who are deeply rooted in Judaism and Jewish culture, Rosenfarb's survivors make a deliberate effort to distance themselves from their Jewish roots. They speak Polish or English among themselves, and Edgia is drawn to the Christian cross at the top of Mount Royal, a particular landmark in Montreal. Rella's only reason to go on living is her friendship with Edgia, the sole witness to Rella's humanity in the camps. When Edgia terminates their friendship, Rella decides to take her own life. The sleeping pills she has been hoarding from the day of liberation serve as replacement for her family, community, and identity by offering the alluring promise of death: "These pills were the only possessions that I brought with me to Canada from the European continent. They took the place of my parents, my grandparents, my sixteen-year-old brother and my ten-year-old sister; my darling Maniusha. They took the place of all my aunts, uncles, and cousins, of my hometown, my childhood, early adolescence, and my first and only love. Sleeping pills became my life—and my death. And now they have become my only road back to innocence."[51]

Uniting the suicide Rella with her perished community, Rosenfarb has come full circle: from her apprenticeship as a Yiddish writer in the Lodz Ghetto, to her postwar rebirth, followed by decades as an acclaimed novelist, poet, and essayist on behalf of Yiddish culture in Montreal. Rosenfarb crossed the bridge to postwar affluence from "the other side"—in the Lodz Ghetto, in the Auschwitz, Sasel, and Bergen-Belsen concentration camps—and became a prolific Yiddish writer adored and supported by a vibrant Yiddish cultural network in Montreal. Although Rosenfarb spent a significant part of her career writing novels, it was in her short fiction and essays that she most astutely captured the nightmarish desolation of the Jews from "the other side." As she had already intuited in her Bergen-Belsen diary, the novelistic form allowed her to be expansive; to utilize multiple perspectives and chronological frames while threatening to become "a mask that covered the rawness and directness" of the Lodz Ghetto experience.[52] The immediate experiences of the Jews trapped in the ghetto had found their most authentic and precise expression in the poems of Shayevitsh. Like most Lodz Ghetto Jews, Shayevitsh was largely unaware of the destiny of the deportees, a blindness that seeped into his poetry as a daily torture of doom and death premonitions. Having survived Auschwitz, Rosenfarb would never be able to return to that tangled emotional state of living in a community on death row. Instead, like other Yiddish survivor writers, Rosenfarb erected literary monuments that faithfully documented the inner historical, social, and cultural trajectories of a centuries-old Polish Jewish community in its final death throes. It was this strong impulse to commemorate and mourn that compelled Rosenfarb to select six white pages to represent the six million Jewish victims as a wordless memorial at the end of the trilogy. As Rosenfarb feared in her Bergen-Belsen diary, the prose style and narrative of a realist, historical novel risked serving as a mask covering the truth of a community under siege, thereby becoming "an insult to my dear ones and myself." Instead, the trilogy received almost no critical attention in English translation outside Canada, while being acclaimed but rarely reviewed in Yiddish.

In Rosenfarb's essay "The Last Poet of Lodz," the context of writing and performing Yiddish poetry in the ghetto is brought to life in a devastating portrait of Shayevitsh that allows the reader to gauge the tragic magnificence of his life and poems:

> the reading of this one [the unfinished poem] was transformed into a sort of morbid ritual. It would take place on the day when he had picked up his food and firewood or peat ration. He always wore one of his washed shirts for the occasion. His hair was combed. He would light not one but two candles, seat himself on the floor, and begin to recite the chapter of his work in a hasty slurping voice, as if he were a pious Jew rushing through a prayer. He often broke into sobs, and his hoarse voice began to crack. As he raced through the lines, his torso bent lower over the sheets of paper on his knees, and his entire body, like Laocoön's, seemed to writhe with pain. It was torture to watch and listen to him.[53]

The images used here to depict Shayevitsh's poetic performance combine the traditional Jewish Kaddish, recited after the death of a relative and on the anniversary of their death, readings from Lamentations during Tisha B'Av (while sitting on the floor), and the tragedy of the Roman poet Laocoön, who predicted the invasion of the Spartans, was blinded, and lost his two sons in battle. It is in this portrait that Rosenfarb comes closest to capturing the tragic dimensions of Shayevitsh, the man and the poet. That Shayevitsh's two poems were found in a garbage heap in the Lodz Ghetto after the war and "made their way into print and are thus imperishable" is finally a solace to the surviving writer.[54]

3

MINSK-MAZOWIECKI

Leib Rochman

We, the very few left of Eastern European Jewry, are mostly people who have no graves left behind. Everything has been completely destroyed. We seek them constantly on the earth. Wherever we are, we step on and are pulled to a source. As if we were still bound to the graves. Everywhere, we are propelled to visit our ancestors' graves from our old lives.

Leib Rochman, "*Af keyver-oves*"
(Visiting the Ancestors' Graves, 1976)[1]

In a 1976 article, the Yiddish writer Leib Rochman described his visit to the graves of Yiddish writers at the Workmen's Circle cemetery in Queens on the sixtieth anniversary of the great Yiddish writer Sholem Aleichem's death. Although Yiddish writers still lived and worked in New York, they seemed like anachronisms belonging to a past era. In Rochman's view, the young generation of American-born Jews, by contrast, was removed from the past, indifferent and ignorant about their roots in Ashkenaz: "The works of modern and classical Yiddish writers fall down from the shelves. The sons and daughters don't want to know about them. Many are already absorbed in other cultures. They marry outside the faith. Their children don't know about their own ancestry. That is also the destiny of the great majority of the luminaries of Yiddish literature."[2] The group visiting the cemetery consisted of Rochman, Rochman's wife, Esther (they were both visiting New York from their home in Jerusalem), the sociolinguist Joshua Fishman and his wife, Gele, and the widow and daughter of the Yiddish poet Yankev Friedman. The rain poured down like a *mabl* (flood), which Rochman associated with the flood that destroyed the world in the biblical story of Noah.[3] To the visiting group the cemetery seemed desolate and abandoned. When they finally reached the graves of the Yiddish writers, Rochman was overwhelmed by their sheer numbers. It seemed impossible to pay tribute to each and every one who had touched his life since childhood. After seeing the graves of the Yiddish writers, many of whom had spent the main part of their careers in the United States, the group finally reached Sholem Aleichem's grave, where together they read his epitaph, his poem *"Do ligt a yid a posheter"* (Here Lies a Simple Jew), which was engraved on his tombstone. The poem became their Kaddish (a prayer said in remembrance of a deceased person) for Yiddish literature.

More than thirty years earlier, in the immediate aftermath of the Holocaust, Rochman and other surviving Yiddish writers, driven by a zeal to bear witness to the German crimes against the Jewish people, produced a huge record of Yiddish testimonies, memoirs, autobiographical fiction, diaries, novels, short stories, and poems. In this chapter I will delineate the main features of the Yiddish cultural world, in the aftermath of the Holocaust, that welcomed and encouraged the survivor writers to publish their Holocaust memoirs. This testimonial literature became the cornerstone of the silver age of Yiddish culture, which lasted for a quarter of a century after the Holocaust. Moreover, this time marked the beginning of contentious debates in the Yiddish world, starting from 1945 onward, about how the Holocaust should be depicted, remembered, and passed on to the next generation. Political and ideological differences surfaced and played a significant role in how the various Yiddish centers and writers engaged in creating a culture of remembrance after the Holocaust.

The shapers of Jewish memory of the Holocaust were primarily Jewish writers who had survived in Poland, Lithuania, and the Soviet Union. After the war, they began writing and publishing their wartime diaries, poetry, memoirs, and songs. The transformation of the diaries and chronicles into public testimonies took place in DP camps, courtrooms, historical commissions, commemorations of the *landsmanshaftn* (organizations of immigrants from the same region), and the Jewish mass media.[4] The Yiddish press in New York, Paris, and Buenos Aires were particularly important in disseminating testimonies and diaries written during the war and, for those who survived, reworked in its aftermath. What set Yiddish literary testimonies apart from testimonies in non-Jewish languages was the existence of a worldwide Yiddish mass media and readership that commissioned, published, and discussed witness accounts from the war. Yiddish mass media continued to make *belles-lettres* and testimonies about the Holocaust a centerpiece of Yiddish culture. This took several forms, such as journalistic accounts of trips to the destroyed Jewish communities in Eastern Europe; serialized novels and memoirs, some of which were based on diaries kept during the war; *Yizker* books about Jewish towns and cities; and publications of historical and personal documents written in the ghettos, in camps, and in hiding.

Yiddish testimonies gave voice to Jewish survivors, many of whom became consumers of and contributors to Yiddish mass media worldwide. More important, they addressed a Yiddish readership eager to learn about what had happened. Historical and literary issues related to the publication of original Jewish documents written during the war were hotly debated in the Yiddish press. In addition to young Yiddish literary talents, some of whom came of age in the ghettos, in hiding, and in the concentration camps, historians and editorial boards of *Yizker* books sponsored by *landsmanshaftn* compiled the history of destroyed Jewish towns. Rescued material from the ghettos, such as the Ringelblum archive, and diaries of cultural and political figures and ordinary people, were edited for publication in the Yiddish book series *Dos poylishe yidntum* in Buenos Aires (see chapter 4). The diary, in particular, became a template that authenticated the testimonial account of a specific time and place. For surviving writers, the act of addressing a specific readership and shaping public memory determined how they transformed their wartime diaries into testimonial literature.

Mordechai Strigler, who chronicled his survival in multiple concentration and labor camps, including Majdanek, published prolifically in Yiddish almost immediately after his liberation in Buchenwald by the US army on April 11, 1945. He edited and wrote for the first DP journal, *Tkhies hamesim* (Resurrection of the Dead), which was published for the first time on May 4, 1945, in Buchenwald, in a handwritten format. His pamphlet "To You Liberated Sisters and Brothers: Post-War Problems of the Jewish People," completed at the end of May 1945 in Buchenwald and revised in Paris the following month, was published by the New York Workmen's Circle branch of his hometown, Zamosz, in 1945. In it, Strigler presented the first coherent program in any language for the resurrection of Jewish culture after the Holocaust.

Strigler begins his pamphlet by stating that the *sheyres hapleyte* (Jewish survivors) or Displaced Persons (DPs), as they were called, must liberate themselves from self-hatred, the result of almost six years of wartime experiences of being hunted and tortured as racially inferior beings. They must reclaim their pride as heirs to the long history of the Yiddish language and culture. For Strigler, the *sheyres hapleyte* were the seeds of the regeneration of the Jewish people after the Holocaust, the young builders of a new culture on the ruins of the destroyed communities:

דענקט אָבער נישט, אַז בלויז איר זענט לעבן געבליבן. איר זענט נישט קיין צעבראָכענע מצבֿות איבער די אומבאַקאַנטע קבֿרים, נאָר די יונגע זאָמען אויף אַ פֿעלד, פֿון וועלכע ס׳מוז צוריק אויפֿשטיין אַ נײַ פֿאָלק.

> Don't think that you are only survivors. You are not broken gravestones on the unknown graves, but the young seeds in the field in which a new people will be resurrected.[5]

The *sheyres hapleyte* are not the last remnant of Ashkenaz but integral parts of transcontinental Yiddish-speaking communities with which they must reconnect after being cut off and isolated during almost six years of war:

די גרויסע צענטערן פֿון ייִדן אין אַמעריקע, ראַטנפֿאַרבאַנד און ארץ-ישׂראל ווייזן אונדז, אַז מיר זײַנען נישט קיין געגצלעך-פֿאַרלאָזטער שבט אין דער אייראָפעישער פֿעלקער-משפחה. נאָך זײַנען די מיליאָנען ייִדיש-רעדנדיקע און ייִדיש-טראַכטנדיקע מיט אונדז!

> The great Jewish centers in America, the Soviet Union and Land of Israel show us that we are not an entirely abandoned tribe in the family of European nations. Millions of Yiddish-speaking and Jewish-thinking people are still behind us.[6]

After Buchenwald, Strigler lived in Paris from 1946 to 1953. He made contact with the Yiddish world in New York through the Yiddish poet H. Leivick, and published letters and poems in the New York journal *Di tsukunft*. Simultaneously, he created a body of Holocaust memoirs whose scope and quality are exceptional in Jewish letters and which, with a few exceptions, have never been translated into English.[7] In four works of Holocaust memoirs of a total of approximately fifteen hundred pages, he bore witness to his eighteen-month incarceration in Majdanek and in the ammunition factory Verk C, in the slave labor camp Skarzysko-Kamienna in the Radom district of central Poland.[8] Strigler's output in the book series *Dos poylishe yidntum* was breathtaking. Between 1947 and 1955, he published his four memoirs in the book series about his experiences in German labor and extermination camps as well as one historical novel: *Maydanek* (vol. 20, 1947), *In di fabrikn fun toyt* (In the Factories of Death, vol. 32, 1948), *Verk "Tse"* (Work "C," vols. 64–65,

1950), *Goyroles* (Destinies, vols. 85–86, 1952), and *Georemt mit vint* (Embraced by Wind, vols. 108–9, 1955). In an introduction to the memoir *Maydanek*, from May 1946, one of the first works about an extermination camp, Strigler presented his program for Yiddish literature:

אַלץ, וואָס ס׳איז וועגן אונדזער תקופֿה געשריבן געוואָרן, איז בלויז געווען אַן אַרומגיין
אַרום דעם פּינטל. דאָס סאַמע עיקרדיקע האָט מען צוליב דעם נישט אַרויסגעזען. און
עפּעס דאַרף דאָך דערצײלט ווערן וועגן דעם אינערלעכן ווײ, דעם טיפֿן פּסיכאָלאָגישן
געראַנגל און אַזוי מענטשלעכן וויטיק פֿון אַ דור אין שוידערלעכן פֿאַרגיין . . . די וועלט,
אַפֿילו די יִידישע, ווייסט גאָר נישט פֿון דעם, וואָס איז פֿאַקטיש פֿאָרגעקומען. און זי מוז
עס וויסן! מיט אַלע פּינטעלעך . . .

What has been written about our historical period has only touched the surface. The essence has not yet been disclosed. And something must be told about the internal pain, the deep psychological struggle, and essential human sadness of a generation's terrifying death. . . . The world, even the Jewish world, *doesn't know what really happened! And they must know! To the last detail.*[9]

During his sojourn in Paris from 1946 to 1953, he wrote for the Labor Zionist weekly *Undzer vort* and conducted a voluminous correspondence with Jewish cultural leaders and Yiddish writers all over the world.[10] H. Leivick, a central Yiddish cultural figure in America, introduced Strigler's first publication in *Di tsukunft* in August 1945: two letters and a poem, "*Der letser yid in geto*" (The Last Jew in the Ghetto). In 1912 Leivick had escaped his Siberian exile after serving four years of hard labor for publicly criticizing the tsarist regime and arrived in New York in 1913 after a grueling four-month march in a column of chained convicts. This personal experience of suffering for his political beliefs gave Leivick an unchallenged moral stature in New York's Yiddish circles. On the front page of his 1945 poetry collection, *In treblinke bin ikh nit geven (1940–1945)* (I Was Not in Treblinka), Leivick included a motto expressing his guilt over having the privilege to write poetry in New York during the Holocaust:

אָ ווער וועט אויף שליאדן פֿון טרעבלינקע-גאַנג,
פֿאַרגעבן דיר די שולדן פֿון געזאַנג?

Oh, who will on the path of Treblinka-march,
Forgive you the guilt of singing?[11]

Leivick's deep identification with the victims of the Holocaust is evident in the book's title poem, "*Treblinke kandidat*" (Candidate for Treblinka):

אין טרעבלינקע בין איך ניט געווען
אויך ניט אין מײַדאַנעק,
אָבער איך שטיי אויף זייער שוועל
און אויף זייער גאַנעק.
שוועל—גאָטס גרויסע וועלט
מיט אַ יענע-וועלט-ווערַאַנדע,
שטיי איך און איך וואַרט,
גרויסע וועלט, אויף דײַן קאָמאַנדע:
ייִדן-קאָפּ, אין גאַז-קאַמער אַרײַן!¹²

I was not in Treblinka,
Also not in Majdanek,
But I stand on their threshold
And on their porch.
Threshold—God's great world
With the world-to-come veranda,
I stand and I wait,
Great World, on your command
Juden-head, inside the gas-chamber!

The rhyme *Maydanek/ganek* ("porch") illuminates the gulf that separates Leivick and the victims of the Holocaust, opposing his domestic life in the safety of New York with that of the victims of the death camps. It was Leivick's reputation in the Yiddish world of New York that propelled Strigler to send his two letters from Buchenwald to *Di tsukunft* in New York. In an introduction to Strigler's letters published in 1945 in *Di tsukunft*, Leivick emphasized the importance of opening Yiddish American journals for the testimonies of the *sheyres hapleyte:* "We must open our whole heart to the bitter Treblinka, Buchenwald revelations. We must prepare ourselves for more and more [material], we must be ready to receive it."¹³ Leivick wrote introductions to several works of Holocaust testimonies and a collection of Yiddish songs from the ghettos and camps compiled by the Vilna partisan-poet Shmerke Kaczerginski. In May 1946 Leivick went on a six-week visit to Jewish DP camps in the American zone in Germany, which he described in the form of a diary.¹⁴

In Strigler's two published letters in *Di tsukunft*, he articulated his sense of ambivalence in regard to Yiddish culture in America. It would take several years before he would make up his mind about where to go next, to Israel or to New York, where he finally settled in 1953: "Also there [in America], the Hebrew and Yiddish word encounters obstacles in the business-oriented, assimilated American labyrinth . . . but there is plenty in which to submerge oneself; there are millions of Jews who have not lived through the catastrophic cataclysm, and whose psychic foundations have not been shaken to the ground."[15]

Strigler's poem, dated April 1943 and written in conventional rhyme and meter, presented a harrowing account of the brutal murder of the last Jew of Zamosz, a baker by the name of Moshe Rapaport. After being forced by the SS to have sexual intercourse with a Jewish girl, the baker and the girl were shot in their genitals and then thrown into the street. This poem, Strigler's debut in an American Yiddish journal, encapsulated the main challenge for the *sheyres hapleyte* in reaching the Yiddish-reading public: how to communicate the unspeakable German crimes to American Jews, even such sympathetic listeners as Leivick. In a lengthy introduction to the second volume in *Oysgebrente likht*, Strigler characterizes the work as a fusion of historical documentation, personal experiences, and *belles-lettres:*

געשריבן ווערט דאָס דאָזיקע ווערק אין אַ האַלב-בעלעטריסטישער פֿאָרם. די אַלע געשעענישן, בילדער און פֿאַסירונגען זענען אָבער געשריבן אויפֿן גרונט פֿון מחברס פערזענלעכע איבערלעבענישן.

צווישן די פֿאַרשידענע לאַגערן אין נאַצי-אָקופּירטן פּוילן און דײַטשלאַנד—האָט דער מחבר געלעבט 15 חדשים אין דער "האַסאַג"-פֿאַבריק פֿון סקאַרזשעסקאַ-קאַמיננאַ, בײַ ראַדאָם. דאָרט האָט ער אין געהיים און סך געשריבן און געזאַמלט אַלע געשעריאַלן, וואָס האָבן נאָר געקענט שפּעטער נוצן פֿאַר אַ גענויער געשיכטע-שרײַבונג פֿון אָט דעם עמק-הבכא. לײדער זענען די אַלע מאַטעריאַלן פֿאַרלוירן געגאַנגען—פּונקט ווי דעם מחברס אַנדערע ווערק—אין רעזולטאַט פֿון געשלעפּט ווערן פֿון איין לאַגער אין צווייטן. דאָס דאָזיקע בוך ווערט דערפֿאַר געשריבן לויט זכרון און איז בלויז אַ ברוכטייל פֿון דעם פֿאַקטיש-פֿאָרגעקומענעם.

This work is written in a half-literary form. All the events, pictures, and happenings have been chronicled based on the author's personal experiences. Between the different camps in Nazi-occupied Poland and Germany, the author lived fifteen months in the HASAG factory in Skarzysko-Kamienna, near Radom. There he wrote a lot in secret and collected material which later could be utilized for a precise historical documentation of this Vale of Tears. Unfortunately, all the material was lost—like the author's other work—as a result of being dragged from camp to camp. This book has been written based on my memory and is only a fragment of what actually took place.[16]

The introduction to the book combines its various generic features of historical document, eyewitness accounts, personal reminiscences, and imaginative sections about the inner life of the camp inmates. Surviving Yiddish writers, like Strigler in his *Oysgebrente likht*, utilized a variety of literary styles and genres to reach a readership with the full force of their chronicles of survival. As long as the author anchored the narrative in a specific locale and at a specific point in the German extermination process, the Yiddish readership was willing to accept a great deal of poetic license. Yiddish testimonies were typically less concerned with who had done what to whom than with employing the full range of literary techniques to recreate the inner experience of Jewish life under Nazi rule. In his review of Yehuda Elberg's first book of short stories from the war, *Unter kuperne himlen* (Under Copper Skies, 1951), the Yiddish critic Shmuel Niger pointed out that "like Mordechai Strigler, Elberg is not concerned with telling us exactly what happened to Hitler's victims. He touches the deep dimension (and the main dimension) of their tragic experiences."[17] *Maydanek*, the first volume of Strigler's *Oysgebrente likht*, prompted the Yiddish critic Y. Rapoport in Melbourne, Australia, to reflect on the thorny issues related to creating art about the extermination camps. Many of the concerns raised in his review would be rehashed several decades later in the field of Holocaust Studies. Rapoport states that "because the human language has no words for what took place in Majdanek, its most appropriate expression is perhaps stuttering."[18] Rapoport argues that Strigler's artistic perspective in the aftermath of the war was already fully developed in Majdanek: "Of course, Strigler wrote the book as a free man, but the artistic perspective . . . Strigler [. . .] accomplished in the camp. Otherwise, he wouldn't have been able to convey it with such plasticity and deep psychological feeling."[19]

Leib Rochman kept a diary beginning on February 17, 1942, three months after he went into hiding with his wife, his wife's sister and brother-in-law, and a friend. It ended with their liberation by the Red Army on August 8, 1944. The five Jews survived in hiding with a Polish family, in a village in the vicinity of their hometown, Minsk-Mazowiecki, thirty-five kilometers from Warsaw. In the final months of the war, the group of Jews was hidden with a different Polish family in the same general area. A comparison of the original diary (located in the Yad Vashem archives in Jerusalem), the serialized version of the diary in the New York daily *Der tog* and the Buenos Aires daily *Di yidishe tsaytung*, and the 1949 book sponsored by the Paris *landsmanshaft* of Minsk-Mazowiecki reveals how the original diary was reworked by the author for different publications. The various versions of the diary to date—the diary manuscript, the serialized version in the Yiddish press, the Yiddish book, and the English translation—highlight the cultural transmission that took place, reshaping the book's genre for various readerships.[20] The original title of the manuscript, "*Dos tog-bukh fun tsvantsikstn yorhundert, 1942–1944*" (The Diary of the Twentieth Century, 1942–1944), indicates that Rochman originally conceived the book in universal terms. When the Minsk-Mazowiecki *landsmanshaft* decided to underwrite its publication, the war diary was framed as a *Yizker* book, and the original title was abandoned.[21]

Only two years separate the publication of Anne Frank's Dutch diary in 1947 and Rochman's in 1949, both of them published in minor languages. The English translation of Anne Frank's diary, published in 1952, catapulted it to international bestseller status. Rochman's diary was not published in English translation until 1983, with the assistance of Zachor: Holocaust Remembrance Foundation, which arranged for the "the translation and editing of this neglected classic." Elie Wiesel, who served on the advisory board of the Holocaust Library, noted: "Its purpose is to offer to the reading public authentic material, not readily available, and to preserve the memory of our martyrs and heroes untainted by arbitrary or inadvertent distortions."[22] The English translation was published with an introduction by the Israeli survivor writer Aharon Appelfeld, which highlighted its artistic importance. The English translation changed the title to *The Pit and the Trap*, based on a quote from Isaiah 24:17–18. It is shorter (261 pages) than the Yiddish book (361 pages) and does not include the *Yizker* section of the Yiddish book, which recounts the town's history, ancestry, and destruction. Instead, a map of the Minsk-Mazowiecki area is inserted at the end of the English translation.[23]

It was not only the fact that the book's translation into a major language did not occur until 1983 that made Rochman's diary invisible outside the Yiddish world. Other reasons for its exclusion were that the book was too Jewish (religiously, culturally, and linguistically); it depicted a complex relationship between Poles and Jews while giving a realistic account of widespread Polish anti-Semitism; it described the Holocaust as a local affair, with Germans and Poles collaborating in the killing of Jews at close range by shooting and burning; it depicted the Jewish will to survive in a nonviolent way (passive rather than active resistance); and it offered a Zionist religious vision of Jewish redemption as the main lesson of the war. In short, Rochman's diary goes against the grain of what has been canonized as Holocaust literature in English translation, as exemplified by Anne Frank's *Diary*, Primo Levi's *If This Is a Man*, and Elie Wiesel's *Night*, all of which are either Western European– or Auschwitz-centered. The historian Timothy Snyder points out that "Auschwitz as symbol of the Holocaust excludes those who were at the center of the historical event. The largest group of Holocaust victims—religiously Orthodox and Yiddish-speaking Jews of Poland, or, in the slightly contemptuous German term, *Ostjuden*—were culturally alien from West Europeans, including West Europeans Jews. To some degree, they continue to be marginalized from the memory of the Holocaust."[24] Snyder situates the Nazis' Operation Reinhard, instead of Auschwitz, at the center of the Holocaust. Operation Reinhard led to the creation of the extermination camps Treblinka, Belzec, Majdanek, and Sobibor, where the majority of the victims of the Holocaust—Polish and Soviet Jews—were killed. Approximately 1.5 million Jews were also killed in mass executions, with bullets fired into the victims as they stood at the edges of the death pits.[25] Two-thirds of the Jews killed during the war were already dead by the end of 1942, when the five Jews in Rochman's diary went into hiding.

The focus on childhood and early adolescence that characterizes the self-depictions in Anne Frank's *Diary* and Wiesel's *Night* is very different from the perspective of the young man who narrates Rochman's diary. He is in his mid-twenties and newly married to Esther in the Minsk-Mazowiecki Ghetto in 1942. Rochman belongs to a small group of Yiddish and Hebrew writers who came of age in interwar Poland, survived the war, and continued to write prolifically after 1945. Other surviving Yiddish writers born in the 1910s and 1920s included Chaim Grade, Avrom Sutzkever, and Shmerke Kaczerginski, survivors of the Vilna Ghetto; the Yiddish actor Jonas Turkov, survivor of the Warsaw Ghetto; Isaiah Shpiegl and Chava Rosenfarb, survivors of the Lodz Ghetto; Ka-Tzetnik, survivor of Auschwitz; and Mordechai Strigler, survivor of multiple concentration camps.[26] In contrast to the perspectives of younger Yiddish writers, such as Elie Wiesel (born in 1928), these writers' "approach to art, reality, and history determined their responses to Hitler" and had been crystallized prior to the war.[27] This group of writers has been less favored by Holocaust scholars, who generally have been studying authors who were fundamentally transformed by their wartime experiences.

MINSK-MAZOWIECKI 77

FIGURE 3.1. Leib and Esther Rochman's wedding in the Minsk-Mazowiecki Ghetto, Lag B'Omer 1942. (Courtesy Rivka Miriam)

Rochman's biography can be divided into four phases, demarcating the continuity between his pre- and postwar life:

1. *Prewar Poland:* Rochman first studied with *melamdim* (traditional Hebrew school teachers) and then in a yeshiva (Talmud academy) in Warsaw that combined secular and religious subjects. He became a follower of the Porisover Rebbe in Warsaw and Otvotsk, left the Hasidic environment, and became a journalist for the daily Yiddish newspaper *Varshever radio* (Warsaw Radio).
2. *The war:* He spent the first part of the war in the Minsk-Mazowiecki Ghetto. After it was liquidated in August 1942, he was sent to a nearby labor camp. In November 1942 he went into hiding with his wife and three other Jews, sheltered by a Polish family in a small village near Minsk-Mazowiecki. He survived the final months of the war in hiding with another Polish family in the same area.
3. *Immediate postwar:* He became a contributor to the journal *Dos naye lebn* in Lodz (1944–45), then left Poland for Switzerland at the end of 1945. He published his first book, *Un in dayn blut zolstu lebn* (1949), in Paris, and settled in Israel in 1950.

4. *New life:* Rochman worked in Israel as a journalist for the daily *Forverts* and other publications. He published several books based on his war and postwar experiences, including the 600-plus-page novel, *Mit blinde trit iber der erd* (1968),[28] a grand modernistic work that depicted the aftermath of the Holocaust in various European cities. Rochman was awarded the Itsik Manger Prize in 1975, and died in 1978.

Rochman's artistic biography is typical of the Yiddish writers of his generation who started out in interwar Eastern Europe as young authors and continued to write during the war in the ghetto, in hiding, or in exile in the Soviet Union. After liberation they published literary testimonies in various genres (epic poems, memoirs, and fiction) during their brief sojourns in the Soviet Union, Poland, Switzerland, Germany, and France, and continued to publish prolifically after their immigration to New York City, Tel Aviv, Montreal, and Buenos Aires in the 1940s and early 1950s. During the last phase of their artistic careers, they published works that depicted their experiences of the Holocaust from multiple generic, stylistic, and narrative perspectives. A turn to their childhood and youth in pre-Holocaust Eastern European became a prominent theme of their late work, such as Chaim Grade's and Chava Rosenfarb's novels about interwar Vilna and Lodz.

A section at the end of Rochman's Yiddish diary book from 1949 describes the history and destruction of Minsk-Mazowiecki, the Jewish resistance fighters, and the memorial to the murdered Jews in the Cimetière parisien de Bagneux, the Paris Cemetery of Bagneux. These features—the narrative sequence of before, during, and after the destruction of a particular town, relayed in a commemorative mode—are typical of the *Yizker* book. Indeed, Rochman's diary is presented in the framework of a *Yizker* book, documenting how the Jews of the town were murdered and how fewer than a hundred survived out of the prewar Jewish population of more than five thousand. Moreover, the *Yizker* book's retrospective focus on the collective history of the town creates an interpretive framework for the diary. The final section of the book, "Our Memorials" ("*Undzere denkmeler*"), stresses the diary's commemorative and redemptive qualities:

"בדמיך חיי"—"און אין דמען בלוטו זאָלסטו לעבן"—אַזוי הייסט דאָס בוך פֿון אונדזער לאַנדסמאַן, דעם אָפּגעראַטעוועטן דורך טויזנטער נסים, יונגן שרײַבער, לייב ראָכמאַן, וועלכעס מיר טראָגן דאָ צו דעם לייענער, ווי אַ דענקמאָל נאָך אונדזער שטאָט. בדמיך

חיי—דער אָפּפֿלוס פֿון בלוט וועט אונדזער פֿאָלק שטאַרקן און קרעפֿטיקן צו אַ נײַ לעבן
און צו אַ באַנײַט לעבן!

> "*Bedamayikh hayyi*"—"And in Your Blood Shall You Live"—that's the name of the book by our *landsman* who survived through a thousand miracles, the young writer, Leib Rochman, which we bring to the reader as a memorial of our town. Live in your blood—the outpouring of blood will strengthen our people to a new life and a renewed life![29]

The title of the diary, *And in Your Blood Shall You Live*, is from Ezekiel 16:6–7, in which the prophet admonishes the people of Israel for their transgressions. The Hebrew words "*Bedamayikh hayyi, bedamayikh hayyi!*" (In your blood shall you live) are central to the liturgy of the *bris mile* (Jewish circumcision ceremony), stressing the blood bond between the God of Israel and the newborn Jewish boy entering into His covenant. The confirmation of traditional religious values inscribed in the title highlights its message of renewed life for the survivors in the Jewish state where Rochman and his wife settled in 1950, a year after the book's publication.[30] Moreover, blood signifies a state of impurity resulting from the rejection of God's commandments, as exemplified by the inhabitants of Sodom and Gomorrah referred to in Ezekiel. Jewish ritual laws, such as dietary rules, the separation of men and women, and observance of the Sabbath and holidays, have been abolished among the Jews in hiding so that they may be able to survive. They have no choice but to eat the *treyf* (non-kosher) food served by their Polish helpers; the extremely close quarters behind a screen in the hayloft make modesty impossible to maintain; opportunities to observe Jewish ritual time are rare. However, the impurity of blood that defines the condition under which the five Jews must live is never viewed through the traditionally biblical scheme of reward and punishment. Rather, it is presented by the diarist as an inexplicable curse that has been forced on them. Obviously, blood also refers to the slaughter of the Jews' family and *landsleyt* (member of a *landsmanshaft*) in their hometown, which they witnessed at close range while hiding in the nearby fields before they were taken to their hiding place by an old Polish woman, Auntie. Their relationship with their Polish helpers, Auntie and her brother Felek, becomes a blood tie that binds them together in life and death. The Jews and their Polish helpers are dependent on each other for survival; the latter constantly threatens to denounce the former to the Germans.

At the end of the diary, in an entry from June 25, 1944, Rochman depicts the Polish fields, ripe for a rich harvest of wheat and corn:

מיר קוקן ארויס אויף די ארומיקע פֿעלדער— און טאַקע— אַלץ איז צעוואַקסן און איבערפֿולט. די לאַנגע זאַנגען שווערן זיך אַזש אַראָפּ צו דער ערד, אַנגעדראָלן און אָנגעוויזן קרעפֿטיק. איין גרויס גערעטעניש אויף גאָטס ערד. דער מענטש האָט איר, דער ערד, די לעצטע יאָרן געגעבן אַזוי פֿיל בלוט צו טרינקען— גיט זי אים איצט איר באַלוינונג: פֿעטע תּבֿואות זיך צו שפּײַזן, נישט פֿאַר איין— נאָר פֿאַר עטלעכע יאָר; . . . אונטן, אונטער דער ערד איז אָבער אַ בונט, אַ בונט פֿון בלוט, וואָס קאָן נישט פֿאַרגליווערן, עס ברויזט, זידט, קאָכט און רײַסט זיך און וועט נאָך אויסשיסן ביז צו די הימלען מיט אַ וווּלקאַן, מיט אַן ערדציטערניש, ערגער ווי אין קרחס צײַטן. די ערד און דער מענטש וועלן צוזאַמען צעשטויבט ווערן!

> We looked at the surrounding fields—and indeed—everything is bursting and overripe. The long stalks are bent almost to the ground, heavy with produce. A big riddle on God's earth! Man has giving the earth so much blood to drink—so now they receive its reward: fat stalks will be fed not one but several years . . .
>
> Underneath, under the earth is a rebellion, a rebellion of blood, which cannot congeal, it sparkles, simmers, boils, and tears apart and will yet shoot to the heavens like a volcano, an earthquake, worse than in Korach's times. The earth and man will jointly turn into dust![31]

The "rebellion of blood" (*bunt fun blut*) is a literary trope that encapsulates a primordial universe similar to the biblical Korach's rebellion against the leadership of Moses and Aaron in the desert (Exodus 6:21). The blood simmers under the earth, a sign of the total anarchy that has swallowed the last traces of Jewish existence. This apocalyptic image subverts the seasonal transformation of the Polish landscape, highlighting the irreversible rupture of natural and moral laws that has turned Poland into a blood-soaked land of nameless graves.

Unlike a typical diary written privately by an individual, Rochman's diary is conceived as a collective project, a vehicle for the discussions taking place among the five Jews who live together in hiding. Thus the first person plural is frequently used. In the case when the first person singular appears, it is usually a disguised representation of the collective of five, characterizing the book as an example of Jewish communal memory. Only rarely does Rochman describe the individuality of the four other Jews who are depicted as being part of a common communal entity. As is the case for war diaries in general, the diarist is imagining a future readership, and organizing to hide the manuscript and secure its publication after liberation. These issues are discussed among the Jews in hiding:

"שרײַב אַ טאָג-בוך!" פֿרויִמאַן עצעט מיר, דאָס אָנגעשריבענע אַרײַנצושיקן דורך דער פּאָסט צו אַ באַקאַנטן קריסט, בעטן ער זאָל עס נאָך דער מלחמה איבערגעבן אין ייִדישע הענט. אַזוי אַרום וועל איך מזכּה זײַן די וועלט, נאָך מיר, מיט שילדערונגען, מיט "סענסאַציאָנעל" מאַטעריאַל און אפֿשר—מיט ליטעראַטור.

מורי-ורבותי, מענטשן פֿון נאָך דעם קריג! כ'ווייס, אַז קיין קראַנץ אויף מײַן קבֿר וועט איר נישט ברענגען, אויך וּמילַ בשעת'ן לייענען מײַנע שילדערונגען וועט איר זיצן "על סיר הבשׂר" און בײַנאַכט וועט איר גיין אין טעאַטער, צוריקצושטעלן דעם מוט און—איר וועט ניט וויסן מײַן קבֿר, ווי איך ווייס ניט די קבֿרים פֿון מײַן מוטער, שוועסטער, ברודער און פֿון אַלע בײַ קאַנטע, פֿון גאַנצען פֿאָלק, וואָס מיט זייערע קבֿרים זענען פֿול אַלע פֿעלדער און גערטנער. גראָז וואַקסט שוין, פֿרוכטן בליִען און יונגע פֿאַרלעך, וואָס גלויבן אין יעזוס קריסטוס רעדן פֿרעכע רייד און טוען מיאוסע מעשׂים איבער זיי—איבער די פֿאַרגעסענע פֿון בײַדע וועלטן.

נײן, מיט אַזאַ שרײַבן האָב איך מורא. כ'האָב מורא, אַז איך פֿאַרשוועך חלילה דעם אָנדענק פֿון די פֿאַרגעסענע קדושים, וואָס אין צען, אָדער אין נאָך ווייניקער יאָרן, וועט כּמעט קיין איין מענטש זיי שוין נישט דערמאַנען. נישט זיי און נישט דעם מוראדיקן קאַטאַקליזם. נײן, חבֿר פֿרויִמאַן, כ'וועל עס צו קיין קריסט נישט איבערשיקן! וועט גאָט שענקען לעבן, וועט דאָס אויף זײַן זמן, און אויב, חלילה—זאָל קיינער שפּעטער, פּונקט ווי פֿון מיר, אויך פֿון מײַנע שורות נישט וויסן. זאָלן זיי שפּעטער רויִקער עסן דאָס פֿלייש. צו וואָס צעשטערן דעם הומאָר פֿון די נאָך-מלחמהדיקע פֿאַרלעך—גייט בעסער שפּעטער אין טעאַטער, נישט צוריקצובאַקומען מוט, נאָר בכדי זיך צו וּמעל גלײַך מיט דער גאַנצער וועלט פֿון נאָך דעם קריג. און אײַך, מײַנע אָרעמע שורות, לייען איך דערווײַל פֿאָר פֿאַר מײַנע פֿיר מיטזיצערס, מיט די רויטע העמדעלער.

"Keep a diary!" Froiman [one of the Jews in hiding] advises me to mail what I've written to a Christian acquaintance and ask him to hand it over to Jews after the war. That way I can bequeath to the world, after I'm gone, interesting descriptions, "sensational" material, maybe even literature.

My teachers and friends, people after the war! I know that you will not bring any laurels to my grave, and while reading my account you will be indulging in luxury. At night you will go to the theater in order to regain your courage—you will not know my grave just like I don't know the graves of my mother, sister, brother, and all my relatives and my whole people whose graves fill the fields and gardens.

> Grass already grows there, fruits blossom, and young couples who believe in Jesus Christ are talking indecently and conducting lewd acts on the graves—on the forgotten from both worlds.
>
> No, I am afraid of this kind of writing. I fear that I diminish the memory of the forgotten martyrs, who in ten, or perhaps less than ten years, won't be remembered by anybody, neither they nor the fearful cataclysm. No, my friend Froiman, I won't ask any Christian to hide my writing! If God will grant me life, then my writing will survive, and if not, God forbid—nobody shall know about me and my writing. Let them quietly eat from their fleshpots. Why interrupt the humor of the postwar couples who would rather go to the theater . . . to idle away with the rest of the world after the war. And my poor scribbles, I read them in the meantime to my four friends in hiding, condemned to death.[32]

This remarkable entry from the beginning of the diary (February 1943), written six months after the German annihilation of the diarist's community (in August 1942) and three months after they went into hiding, affords the reader a glimpse into the inner debate that takes place in the diarist's mind and among the five Jews in hiding. For Rochman it is pertinent to maintain his agency in shaping postwar memory of the cataclysm. As a result he vows that only if he stays alive will he publish his diary. Only his survival will enable him to control the way in which the diary is presented to the reading public and avoid being exploited for sensationalist purposes. The survivor's fear of his friends' and teachers' lack of understanding and, in particular, the hostility of the Polish bystanders collaborating in the German genocide of the Jews, are viewed as threats to his agency in creating Jewish memory of the Holocaust. Without his authority as witness and survivor, Rochman fears that his words will be misrepresented. At the same time, the intended readership of "brothers and sisters" in the United States and the *yishuv* in Palestine provides hope for the Jews in hiding:

זיכער איז תּישעה-באָב אין אַלע ייִדישע שטובן אין דער וועלט! אָ, ווי מיר וואָלטן
געוואָלט זען כאָטש אַ ייִדישע צײטונג פֿון דאָרט! ווי פֿאַרביטערט און צאָרנדיק מחמן
זמן די אַרטיקלען פֿון די ייִדישע שרײבערים. ס׳מוח דאָך אַלץ דערשײנען אין אײן גרויסער
ראַם! צי איז נאָך בײַ ייִדן דאָ הומאָר? צי שפּילט נאָך ייִדיש טעאַטער אויף דער וועלט?
אָ, ברידער אונדזערע, ווען איר ווײסט, ווי מיר מאַטערן זיך אין איצטיקן מאָמענט! ווען
איר קאָנט כאָטש אַ בליק געבן צו אונדז! און איר ברידער און שוועסטער אונדזערע אין

ארץ-ישראל, מיר שטעלן זיך פֿאָר אײַער שטילן צער און אײַערע ברויזנדיקע יסורים! צו אײַערע שטרעקן זיך אונדזערע אָרעמס!

> It is for sure Tisha B'Av in every Jewish home in the world! Oh, if we could only see a Yiddish newspaper from over there! How bitter and painful must be the articles by Jewish writers. Everything is surely published in a big black frame. Is there still humor among Jews? Is Yiddish theater still being performed in the world? . . . And you brothers and sisters in the Land of Israel, we imagine your quiet pain and intense sufferings! Our arms reach out to you![33]

Rochman skilfully intertwines two time frames: the sequence of the systematic murder of the Jews of Minsk-Mazowiecki in August 1942, as recollected from Rochman's vantage in hiding, and the group's daily tribulations to stay alive, recorded chronologically from February 1943 to liberation on August 8, 1944. The literary shaping of the diary is particularly visible in the suspenseful dialogue sections, such as the depiction of Rochman's encounter with an SS officer.[34] In his review of the book in *Di goldene keyt*, Avrom Lis compared Rochman's diary to the literary works of Avrom Sutzkever and Yitskhok Katzenelson.[35] Similarly, in *Forverts*, Yitskhok Varshavski (a pen name of Isaac Bashevis Singer) praised the work's excellent language, noting that it reads "like good belletristic."[36] In *Der tog*, Shmuel Niger characterized the book as being "not only a chronicle, not a collection of 'episodes' . . . it is, if you will, a novel."[37]

Like other Jewish diarists during the second half of the war in Eastern Europe (1942–44), Rochman witnessed the systematic murder of his town and had no illusions about the universal scope of the German genocide of the Jewish population. The diarist's accounts of the various phases of mass murder and deportation become a way of confronting his traumatic pain and loss. The diary combines multiple genres—lamentation, memoir, confession, *journal intime*, and witness account—that fashion a memorial to the destruction of a community.[38] The five Jews in hiding are depicted with almost no personal prewar history and only through their responses to German assaults and their daily tribulations. They belong to a new breed of Jews, the survivors, marked by the blood ties of suffering and breakdown of Jewish normative behavior. Their new identities erase their pasts, which appear only sporadically in formulaic ways, such as their reciting of Psalms and the *Shema* in moments of danger.

The social and economic ties connecting the Jews in hiding to their Polish helpers occupy a central part of the diary. The Jews' only bargaining power is in their ability to exchange goods and money, some of which have been entrusted to Polish friends. Their survival is contingent on being able to cash in their belongings (clothing, jewelry, furniture, and the like) by using their Polish helpers to claim their property from their Polish debtors. Their ability to stay alive derives in part from their ingenuity in inventing stories that allow them to put pressure on their Polish debtors. They spread the word that Jewish partisans will take revenge on their Polish debtors if they don't follow through on their word and return the Jews' property. They shrewdly invoke the anti-Semitic stereotypes of the Polish farmers who believe that a Jewish conspiracy controls the Allied forces and the Red Army, which will reward the Jews' Polish helpers after liberation. At the same time, the diary provides ample evidence of the lawlessness and brutality of the Polish population, graphically depicting how Poles exploited Jews and stole their property. Jews were routinely handed over to the Germans. Polish farmers and their families were mostly hostile to the Jews or at best indifferent to their life-and-death struggle. As vividly depicted in the diary, in some cases Poles killed Jews for no apparent reason.

In Aharon Appelfeld's introductory words to the English translation, *The Pit and the Trap*, he notes that "the essence of the book . . . lies in the unwilling dialogue between the old woman who offers protection and the young people who are condemned to death."[39] The Jews' protectors, Auntie, an old whore, and her brother Felek, a small-time criminal, are looking out for their own interests. But Auntie and Felek are also generous and risk their lives to save the Jews, repeatedly invoking the Sixth Commandment. The book's depiction of the bond between these two Polish outcasts who, despite their flaws, are willing to sacrifice their lives to save these Jews, is a tribute to the small number of Polish righteous Gentiles.[40]

From the very beginning of his diary, Rochman expresses the belief that Jewish life in Poland will never be the same again. In a particularly striking depiction of an imagined postwar Poland without Jews, dated February 17, 1943, Rochman presents a catalogue of religious books, objects, and dresses that have been appropriated by the peasants after their original owners have disappeared:

יונגע שיקסעס קליידן זיך אין עלעגאַנטע בלוזקעלעך און ספּודניצעס—איבערגעמאַכט פֿון טליתים; אין קאַפּעלושלעך—פֿון סאַמעטענע היטלען; אין פֿוטערנע קעלנער פֿון נעלקענע און סקונסענע שטרייַמעלעך. פּויערישע טישן זענען באַפּוצט מיט זילבערנע

קידוש-בעכערלעך, בשמים-ביקסלעך, די קאַמאָדעס—מיט עץ החיים׳ס, מיט זילבערנע יד׳ס און שבתדיקע לייכטער.

דער ווינט בלאָזט איצט איבער די דערפֿער מיט טויזנטער בלעטלעך פֿון חומשים, גמרות, מ פרשים, מוסר און חסידישע ספֿרים, צאינה וראינה׳ס, מעשׂה-ביכלעך, ייִדישע קלאַסישע און נײַעסטע ליטעראַטור, וויסנשאַפֿטלעכע און פֿילאָזאָפֿישע ביכער, די קלאַזעטן זענען מיט זיי פֿול. מען פֿאַרקויפֿט מאַקולאַטור אין די געוועלבער אויפֿן פוד, אויפֿן קילאָ. מען וויקלט אין שמות—שפּײַז, חזיר-פֿלייש און הערינג, די לעדערנע טאָוולען ווערן איבערגעאַרבעט אויף נוצלעכע קוישלעך.

Farm girls wear elegant blouses and skirts made out of prayer-shawls; bonnets made of the black velvet hats worn by Hasidim; and fur scarves made out of the Hasidic *shtrayml*. Farmers' tables are set with silver kiddush cups and spice boxes, and their dressers and buffets decorated with silver Torah plates, Torah pointers, and Sabbath candlesticks.

The wind sweeps across the countryside, scattering thousands of pages torn from *Pentateuchs*, the Talmud, commentaries, books of *Musar* (ethics) and Hasidism, the *Tsena Urena*, chapbooks, classical and modern Jewish literature, scientific and philosophical works. These pages are tightly piled in the peasants' outhouses; then sold in the shops as wastepaper by the pound and kilogram; used for wrapping ham, herring, and the like. The leather bindings are worked over into useful items such as handbags and wallets.[41]

Not only has the Jewish religious and culture heritage been eradicated in the war but its artifacts are stolen by the Polish population. Jewish traces remain everywhere in the form of items that look absurdly out of place among the Polish families. Delineating how the Polish robbery of Jewish property begins immediately following the Jews' deportation is part of the diarist's documentation of the greed of his Polish neighbors.[42] Moreover, Rochman conceives his war diary as a *Yizker* book by recollecting the social, cultural, and religious features of his community, whose sudden absence has left a void in the Polish landscape and social fabric. *Un in dayn blut zolstu lebn* demonstrates that the diary, as an eyewitness account of atrocities committed against the Jews, was informed by Rochman's realization that Jewish life in Poland had been terminated. This initiated the diarist's mourning process in the *Yizker* mode which, in the absence of actual gravestones for the gassed, shot, and burned victims, could serve as a symbolic "substitute gravestone." Rochman went beyond Ringelblum's directive to a member of the Oyneg

Shabes archive to document and "collect as much as possible—they can sort it out after the war."⁴³ In addition to Rochman's retrospective recollection of what had happened to his community during and after its annihilation, he recorded his experience of belonging to the last Jews on Polish soil. As a (former) religious Jew writing in Yiddish, Rochman had access to the various biblical archetypes of Jewish responses to catastrophe. In an entry dated May 9, 1944, the diarist addresses *"reboyne shel oylem"* (God of the Universe) in an outpouring of pain and desolation, and quoting from the Psalms. This entry is prefaced by the diarist's brief depiction of the circumstances of his diary writing:

צוויי טעג האָב איך געשריבן. כ׳בין געלעגן אויסגעצויגן אין שטאַל אויף דער ערד, פֿאַר אַ שפּאַרע אונטערן פֿונדאַמענט, און געשריבן. אויבן אויף דער וואַנט האָט מיך אסתּרל פֿאַרטרעטן און געהאַלטן וואַך. זי איז שוין מיד. היינט, פֿינף פֿאַרטאָג, האָב איך ווידער געמוזט פֿאַרנעמען מיין פּאָסטן. איך קוק אַרויס און פֿאַר די אויגן שוועבן מיר נאָך אַלץ די בילדער פֿון יענע טעג.

> I wrote for two days. I lay outstretched in the stall on the ground, under a crack in the foundation, and wrote. Esther stood guard up above. She is already tired. Today, five in the morning, I had to take on my guard duty. I look out and the images from those days float in front of my eyes.⁴⁴

Unlike Jewish diarists writing in non-Jewish languages, who "often kept in their heads the image of an audience of strangers from the outside world reading their diaries,"⁴⁵ Rochman did not picture his readership as strangers. He perceived them as "sisters and brothers," representing the hope for a return to normalcy that would entail resuming reading and writing in his Yiddish mother tongue. The act of rewriting began in the extreme circumstances of hiding during the war, while the diarist was still in mortal danger. On May 19, 1944, the diarist requested that Janek, one of the Poles sheltering the group, retrieve his writings that lie buried in a container in the field. He tells Janek:

"איך דאַרף זיי האָבן עפּעס נאָכצוזען. כ׳וועל זיי אין עטלעכע טעג אַרום אים צוריק געבן". שוין אַ שפּאָר ביסל העפֿטן האָט ער דאָרט געהאַט באַגראָבן. שטענדיק, ווען איך פֿאַרענדיק אַ פֿרישן העפֿט—גיב איך אים און ער באַגראָבט אים צוזאַמען מיט די פֿריערדיקע. איך דערמאָן כּסדרה, אַז ער וועט דערפֿאַר אַמאָל באַלוינט ווערן.

"I need them to look for something. In a few days I will return them to you." He has already buried several notebooks. When I finish a notebook—I give it to him and he buries it with the earlier notebooks. I remind him constantly, that one day he will be rewarded.[46]

Although the Yiddish critics of Rochman's diary stressed the active Polish participation in killing Jews, some also mentioned the book's path-breaking depiction of the Polish farmers. Beyond the anti-Semitic stereotypes of the farmers, Rochman portrays the Polish rescuers Auntie, Felek, Janek, and Szhube in ways that enable the reader to sympathize with the difficult choices these Poles had to make in order to shelter the Jews in hiding. In his 1949 review of the book, Yitskhok Yanosovitsh pointed out that Rochman's realistic depiction of the Polish village is a departure from Yiddish literature in the interwar period. The intimate portrait of the Polish peasant society is made possible by the position of the Jews as *roye veeyne-nire* (they see but are not seen). Yanosovitsh praises Rochman's artistic objectivity, which despite "his despondent Jewish heart does not lead him to rush to quick conclusions."[47] Despite the diary's overwhelming documentation of Polish hostility and murderous desire to get rid of the Jews, Rochman's artistic skill in depicting the mundane details of the daily life of the Polish peasants makes the diary an important historical document: "Particularly interesting from a general human point of view are Auntie and Felek, whom the author paints with deep understanding of the complexity of their characters. A lot could be written about why the Gentile criminal Felek is almost the only representative of humanity and how the human inclinations come to expression in his character. Much could also be written about Auntie and her contradictory character and the same about Szhube and his mix of fear and avarice."[48]

Rochman attempted as objectively as possible to grapple with the complexity of the choices the Poles and Jews had to make during the extremity of the war. Unlike Emanuel Ringelblum, the initiator of the Oyneg Shabes archive, who viewed "history as an antidote to a memory of catastrophe,"[49] Rochman embedded his literary testimonial in Jewish collective memory that drew on age-old religious archetypes as well as Yiddish literary realism. Ringelblum, in the Warsaw Ghetto and in hiding on the Aryan side, fashioned a usable past out of Polish Jewry's death throes, recorded with meticulous commitment to historical objectivity. He did not survive to see the publication of his war writings. Rochman, a Yiddish survivor writer, was able to maintain agency over his war diary, which he reworked for publication after the war by fusing fictional styles, documentary testimony, and scriptural antecedents.

The book is informed by Rochman's immediate postwar experiences in Poland, where he wrote for the Yiddish newspaper *Dos naye lebn* in Lodz, and his retrospective view while rewriting it in Switzerland and Paris. As documented by historian Jan Gross and others, the period right after the war was particularly dangerous for Polish Jews returning to their hometowns and reclaiming their property.[50] The void in Polish social and economic life that resulted from the Germans' annihilation of almost the entire Jewish population contributed to the onset of anti-Semitic murderous attacks on Jews who returned home after the war. This led to the mass emigration of the Polish Jewish survivors following the Kielce pogrom in the summer of 1946. By the spring of 1947, before the consolidation of the new communist regime in Poland the following year, only ninety thousand Jews were left in the country.

Obviously, these dramatic changes in Polish life informed Rochman's editing and rewriting of his diary. It would have been difficult, if not impossible, for him to publish the work in Poland, where the topics of Polish collaboration with the Germans and continued postwar anti-Semitic assaults on Jews were highly contentious issues regulated by communist censorship. Rochman found economic sponsorship from the Paris *landsmanshaft* of his hometown, Minsk-Mazowiecki, to publish the book. This gave him a worldwide Yiddish readership and produced reviews in major Yiddish journals and newspapers. After settling in Israel in 1950, Rochman sought to make the book available in Hebrew translation in 1960, just a year before the Eichmann trial, which for the first time publically put the testimonies of Holocaust survivors front and center on the world stage. As David Roskies mentions, the Hebrew translation of the book was a total failure, and the publisher sustained a considerable loss.[51] In Yiddish, however, Rochman's war diary partook in the collective Jewish effort to create memorials to the destroyed Jewish communities. The Yiddish book doubled as a *Yizker* book until 1977 when, one year before his premature death at the age of sixty, Rochman participated in the publication of *Seyfer Minsk-Mazowiecki: Yizker bukh nokh der khorev-gevorener kehile Minsk-Mazowiecki* (The Book of Minsk-Mazowiecki: Memorial Book after the Destroyed Community of Minsk-Mazowiecki). Like many other Yiddish writers, Rochman contributed to and served as a member of the editorial committee of his hometown's *Yizker* book.[52]

Rochman's short story "*Di levaye*" (The Funeral, 1978) is a remarkable self-portrait of the Holocaust survivor as a middle-aged man. The omniscient

FIGURE 3.2. Leib Rochman in Jerusalem (undated). (Courtesy Rivka Miriam)

narrator refers to him only as *der bagleyter*, the follower. He is the last survivor of his town, and the story opens with him accompanying the mourners at the Jerusalem funeral of "Sh.," who has committed suicide. The funeral is depicted from the perspective of this unnamed town's last survivor, who now lives in Israel. The funeral brings him face to face with himself, as well as with his family and community—all of whom were murdered in 1942, in the cemetery of his hometown. As the funeral procession winds through the streets of Jerusalem, it is portrayed as a surrealistic movement toward the burial site:

פלוצעם איז די לוויה אַרויס אויף אַן אָפֿענער גאַס. אַ שפּאַצירער עולם האָט זיך איצט
געשטופּט. פֿעטערס, וויבעה, מיידלעך— אַלע פֿון זייער שטאָט. די פֿעטערס האָבן
נישט געדענקט די צײַט אַ מענטש זאָל זיך נעמען דאָס לעבן. בײַ זיי אין געטאָ, אין די

מסוכנדיקסטע מינוטן, האָט מען דאָס נישט געטאָן. דער באַגלייטער האָט געקוקט אויף
די פֿעטערס מיט בערד. אין געטאָ זענען זיי שוין געווען עלטערע ייִדן. איצט איז ער אין
זייער עלטער, אָן אַ באָרד, אַ ייִנגל. הײַנט וואָלט ער שוין אויך אפֿשר געהאַט אייניקלעך.

> Suddenly the funeral is on the open street. A considerable group has now moved ahead. Uncles, wives, girls—all from his town. The uncles cannot recall a time when a person would commit suicide. Back in the ghetto, in the most life-threatening of moments, nobody had ever done that. The follower gazed at the uncles with beards. In the ghetto they were not old Jews. Now he is their age, without a beard, a boy. Today, he would perhaps also have had grandchildren.[53]

The follower is associating the unknown people at the funeral with the inhabitants of his childhood town, where he saw everything truthfully, and *"fun demolt on iz alts far im dermonung"* (since then everything for him is memory). All of his fellow townspeople who were murdered by the Germans were deprived of an old age, and the follower is now older than they had been then, with "an eternity" (156). As the only survivor, the nameless follower did not share his townspeople's "blind destiny" (*blinder goyrl*). He tries to imagine what his life might have been like without *dem umkum* (the Holocaust) that has become an inseparable part of his being, a horrifying thought:

פּלוצעם האָט ער דערזען, טיף־באַהאַלטן צווישן זײַנע גייענדיקע חבֿרים—אַ נאָענטן
סילועט. ס'איז אים באַפֿאַלן אַן אומהיימלעכקייט. דאָס גייט דאָרט צווישן זיי, ער אַליין,
זײַן מאַמעס זון. ער איז אַ מאָל צוזאַמען מיט יענע פֿאַרשוווּנדן. ער דאָ איז אַן אַנדערער,
אַ פֿרעמדער. ער האָט זיך געשראָקן צו קוקן אַהין, זיך צו טרעפֿן אויג אויף אויג.

> Suddenly he saw, deeply hidden between the walking friends—a close silhouette. Something uncanny befell him. There he walks between the others, alone, his mother's son. He disappeared once together with them. Here and now, he is another, a foreigner. He was afraid of looking over there, meeting himself eye to eye.[54]

As in Jorge Luis Borges's short story "The Other" (1975), in which the narrator meets and converses with himself as a young man, Rochman's follower gets a glimpse of himself from "the other side," perishing in that old cemetery along with his family and townspeople. The chasm between his younger and older selves, between "the other side" and the Israeli present, has shaped his destiny.[55] Decades later, the funeral of the Jerusalem suicide is the final act of the tragedy in which the follower experiences the final moments of his family and neighbors, just prior to their being shot:

> דער זיידע האָט געפילט, ס׳איז דער סוף! ער האָט געוואָלט בעטן מחילה ביַי ש. איינער
> פֿון די פֿעטערס האָט געשריגן: "ייִדן, מען האָט אונדז שוין איין מאָל אויסגעששאָסן אויף
> בית-עלמינס. איצט איז אָבער אומקום! ייִדן, אַנטלויפֿט!" אלע האָבן געשפאַנט ווי צו
> אַ שעכטהויז, געשלעפט זיך נאָכן זעלבסטמערדער. דער באַגלייטער און דער רבֿ זענען
> נאָכגעגאַנגען נאָך דער מיטה און געזאָגט צידוק-הדין.

> The grandfather felt that this is the end! He wanted to ask forgiveness of Sh. One of the uncles cried: "Jews, we have already once been shot to death in the cemetery. But now it is annihilation! Jews, run away!" They all strode as if toward a slaughterhouse, dragging themselves after the suicide. The follower and the rabbi went after the funeral procession and recited the prayer for the dead.[56]

Rochman's story is a meditation on time, memory, and trauma, as narrated by an Eastern European Jewish town's last survivor, who now resides in Jerusalem. Similar to the visit to the Workmen's Circle cemetery in Queens in 1976, the follower perceives the dead to be more alive than those who are actually living and breathing in the present time. Memories of his childhood and his annihilated community continue to haunt the survivor with moments of violent death.

PART II: TRANSNATIONAL ASHKENAZ

4

DOS POYLISHE YIDNTUM

A Library of Hope and Destruction

> Just as the survivors return to life, so does the Yiddish book. To collect the disposed holy documents, to redeem the homeless letters—that is the demand of the hour.
>
> Asher Pen, "*Naye yidishe bikher in Argentine*" (New Yiddish Book in Argentina; 1946–47)[1]

> [T]he series presents us with one of the most important efforts ever undertaken anywhere in the world to perpetuate and chronicle the history, the lifestyle, the spiritual creativity and the ultimate destruction of Polish Jewry.
>
> Abraham Nowersztern, "*Dos poylishe yidntum*" (1991)[2]

In a 1955 article the Yiddish critic Shmuel Niger mentioned "a series of more than one hundred books which the youngest, most active and productive Yiddish publishing house has published in the last years . . . entitled *Dos poylishe yidntum*."[3] The book series, initiated in 1946 in Buenos Aires by Mark Turkov, a Jewish journalist and political activist in interwar Warsaw, was terminated in 1966 with the publication of its 175th volume.[4] With an average publication rate of almost ten books per year, *Dos poylishe yidntum* became one of the most remarkable memorials to the destroyed Polish Jewish community. The books were published in attractive formats replete with drawings and photographs that reflected the series' "modern approach, youthful touch, and innovative character combined with a rich imagination."[5] An estimated quarter-million books of *Dos poylishe yidntum* had been printed and sold by 1954, which year saw the publication of the hundredth volume, Mark Turkov's *Di letste fun a groysn dor* (The Last of a Great Generation). In 1947 the books were distributed in twenty-two countries, including among survivors of the Holocaust in Poland and in the DP camps.[6] The speed with which the books were published in the first years was quite remarkable. An average of two books per month were published in three-thousand-copy print runs, which were increased to five thousand copies in some cases—a high number for a Yiddish book.[7] Many were boldly marked *oysfarkoyft* (sold out) on the list of publications inserted at the end of each book. Buenos Aires–born Yiddish scholar Abraham Nowersztern recalls: "In hundreds of Jewish homes throughout Argentina one could immediately recognize the shelves of volumes standing back to back in their distinctive black bindings, a modern *Zeykher lekhurbm* [Holocaust memorial]. One can therefore say without exaggeration that the series 'Polish Jewry' is also a milestone which helped to establish Argentina as a central point on the Jewish world map."[8]

The books' raison d'être as vehicles of commemoration, *kinus* (ingathering), and literary entertainment was closely tied to their Yiddish cultural context during the two decades following the Holocaust. They shaped the discourse about Polish Jewry and its destruction that was continued in Yiddish after the Holocaust. *Dos poylishe yidntum* indicates the existence of a vibrant Yiddish book market that empowered Jewish survivors to share their experiences about life before, during, and in the aftermath of the Holocaust.

Yiddish publishing after 1945 did "continue to exert an incontrovertible force and vitality"; however, the irreversible demographic trend of aging writers and readers, and the lack of replenishing by a new generation, led to the creation of several Yiddish publication centers "that functioned on a far more limited scale compared to what came before, centres that emerged suddenly, flourished for a decade or two, and then rapidly declined."[9] *Dos poylishe yidntum* was a typical example of Yiddish publishing after the Holocaust in terms of its prolific output over the course of twenty years and its implementation by one individual who took full advantage of beneficial cultural and economic conditions for Yiddish book publishing. The cost of printing, binding, and paper was, as Zachary Baker points out, "a critical factor determining the emergence or demise of a centre."[10]

Like Avrom Sutzkever, who succeeded in obtaining financial support from the Histadrut (the Israeli Labor union) to publish his literary journal,

Di goldene keyt, Turkov established a partnership with the Central Union of Polish Jews in Argentina at a time when it was relatively easy to raise money for Yiddish publications. A 1947 letter to Turkov from Menashe Unger, a Yiddish writer at the New York daily *Der tog*, described the altered circumstances for the *landsmanshaftn* in the United States in the aftermath of the Holocaust:

> The name of the publishing house [*Dos poylishe yidntum*] is very popular here. People brag about you and your publishing house and you should utilize this sentiment. I don't need to tell you what the *landsmanshaftn* have become in America. They have tons of money. They don't know what to do with it. The towns in whose names they were created have been eradicated and made *Judenrein*. Every *landsmanshaft* wants to erect a monument to their home shtetl, to publish a book by a writer from their home shtetl.[11]

However, as Jewish historians Yankev Shatski and Philip Friedman pointed out, the populous and wealthy American Jewish community was not able to pull off a project like *Dos poylishe yidntum*. The strong commitment to commemoration and Yiddish cultural renewal that Turkov combined in *Dos poylishe yidntum* did not find a place in the much larger and more politically fragmented Yiddish world in the by far largest center of New York City.[12] Moreover, the strong financial support of Yiddish culture among Jewish businesspeople in Buenos Aires was a precondition for the implementation of Turkov's project. In a letter printed in the twenty-fifth jubilee pamphlet of the book series, the directors of Banco Israelita del Rio de La Plata pledged their support to publish volume 26, Leo Finkelstein's *Megiles poyln* (Scrolls of Poland). They emphasized the book series' broader goals to sponsor relief work in Europe and to initiate Yiddish literary renewal: "The 25 volumes published so far are not only a monument to the great history of Polish Jewry, its martyrology, and heroic resistance; they are also an important contribution to Yiddish literature and a documentary source for the future scholar of this tragic era in the history of our people."

In 1957 the head of the Argentine YIVO, the Yiddish cultural leader Shmuel Rozhanski, launched the *Musterverk* (Masterpieces) series, which ran until 1984, after the publication of its one-hundredth volume. This series featured the most important works of Yiddish literature from premodern times through the first half of the twentieth century. They were introduced by Rozhanski, providing modern Yiddish reprints of classical and contemporary works, including glossaries and critical articles that could be used by scholars, study groups, and teacher seminaries. The South African businessman Joseph Lifshitz supported the publication of this impressive Argentine book series, which remains an important tool for Yiddish education and literary studies.[13]

During the same period as *Dos poylishe yidntum*, the Polish state-sponsored Yidish-bukh publishing house in Warsaw issued more than three hundred Yiddish books, including new and classical works.[14] Abraham Mitlberg, secretary and co-editor of *Dos poylishe yidntum*, discussed in a 1947 article the close cooperation between *Dos poylishe yidntum* and the Central Jewish Historical Commission in Poland. This led to the shipment of hundreds of books to survivors in Poland and the DP camps. In some cases titles were simultaneously published in Yiddish and Polish: "The books are published in Polish in Poland and here in Argentina in Yiddish."[15] The international scope of the book series was a significant departure from pre-Holocaust Yiddish publishing in Argentina, which had an almost entirely local character. The ascendance of Buenos Aires as an international center for Yiddish publishing was made possible by a convergence of circumstances: the strong leadership of Turkov and Mitlberg; the worldwide need for Yiddish books about the literature, history, and destruction of Polish Jewry; and, most important, sufficient funds to support the endeavor. Mitlberg summarized: "We feel deeply that we are implementing a historical mission in the Yiddish publishing industry, by elevating the importance of the Yiddish book; by creating an address for Yiddish writers and familiarizing a worldwide Yiddish readership with the tragically terminated chapter of the martyrological history of Polish Jewry."[16]

After a five-week trip to several South American countries, Turkov wrote to Yankev Shatski in 1949: "I must answer approximately 100 letters which arrived while I was away. Most contain suggestions for new books. Even the widow of Leon Kobrin suggests that I publish her husband's plays. She has no other possibility for publishing the plays. Unfortunately I can't take on every request. By the way, Friedman's *Oshvientshim* is now being sent to the printer."[17] *Dos poylishe yidntum* became a magnet for Yiddish writers and acquired a reputation as a commercial success. The reality was very different, as is evident from Turkov's letters to contributors in the series. A typical example: "We have—as usual—limited funds, but we work hard and make plans for the future. The truth is, in the foreseeable future, the whole thing could go down the drain. Basically, we have no more energy to toil and to dupe the printer and the binder. Such is our destiny."[18]

In a 1952 letter Mitlberg complains that it is not financially viable to ship books abroad, but the publishing house will nevertheless publish ten books in "this bad year."[19] Despite repeated complaints about financial worries, the publishers adhered to the highest standards. Books were printed on excellent paper; they were typeset with the best typography; they included illustration, photographs, and indices. Most of the books contained introductions by Yiddish writers and cultural figures, as well as reviews of previous books in the series, an invaluable source for the critical reception of the books. The introductions and reviews turned the series into a portable library for a community of readers who functioned as de facto subscribers. This impression was further emphasized by the books' characteristic black binding and cover illustrations.

In the introduction to the first volume, *Malke Ovshyany dertseylt* (Malke Ovshyany Tells Her Tale, 1946), one of the first published Holocaust testimonies by a woman, the objective of the book series was first presented:[20]

> Under the name "Polish Jewry" the Central Union of Polish Jews in Argentina has decided to publish a series of books and pamphlets whose aim is to bring the Jewish mass readership and the world at large closer to the problems related to the destroyed Jewish life in Poland. Conscious of the great responsibility in implementing this task, the Central Union of Polish Jews in Argentina intends to ensure that Polish Jewry will receive a multifaceted and strictly non-partisan coverage in the books, in all its aspects and in every area of its social, political and cultural creativity. Cities and towns where once a colourful vibrant Jewish life existed and which was eradicated from the face of the earth by the Nazi-destroyers, episodes and events characteristic of the history of the destroyed Jewish community in Poland, memoirs of famous Jewish personalities whose life and creativity were an intrinsic part of Polish Jewry will be the main themes of the published books and pamphlets.[21]

The sponsor of the book series, the Central Union of Polish Jews, was the umbrella organization of most of the *landsmanshaftn* in Argentina and was not prone to the political partisanship that otherwise characterized Yiddish publishing houses, such as those associated with the Bund, right- and left-wing Poalei Zion, anarchists, and communists. As was the case for *Yizker* books published by the *landsmanshaftn*, the goal was to offer broad, nonpartisan coverage of all aspects of Jewish life in Poland prior to and during the Holocaust. Moreover, a note on the title page of the first volume read: "The profits for this book will be donated to the relief work for the benefit of surviving Jewish children who are hospitalized in sanatoriums in Sweden."[22] Thus was born the practice during the first years of *Dos poylishe yidntum* of donating the profits from the sales of books to relief work among the Jewish survivors in Europe.

The Jewish community in Buenos Aires was dominated by the second wave of Polish Jewish immigrants who arrived after World War I. The first wave of Jewish immigrants, mostly Bessarabian Jews who came to Argentina in the 1890s, sponsored by Baron Maurice de Hirsch, was settled primarily on farms in small towns in the provinces. This early immigration was the topic of Mark Turkov's *Oyf yidishe felder* (In Jewish Fields, 1939), in which he depicted his impressions from a journey through the Argentine provinces in the late 1930s. After visits to Argentina in the late 1940s, the Jewish historian Yankev Shatski stressed that Yiddish language and culture remained central to the Argentine-born children of Polish Jewish immigrants arriving in the 1920s who had become successful professionals in Buenos Aires:

> This generation, born in Argentina, reads Yiddish newspapers, visits Yiddish lectures, goes to the Yiddish theater, although they speak Spanish among themselves. Despite limited Jewish religious knowledge, these people are Jews of the national-secular type. In Argentina, Jewish clergy have generally not played the same role as they have in the United States. One does not find Orthodox or Reform rabbis among community leaders. Their Jewishness consists of . . . the Yiddish language and everything connected to it: theater, book, lecture, etc. Because they are strongly secular they fully understand language-nationalism.[23]

Shatski emphasized the central role played by Polish Jews who brought a secular Yiddishist ideal of Jewish nationalism to Buenos Aires: "Their vision was to continue, on the banks of La Plata, the cultural treasures which they had absorbed on the banks of the Vistula. Bundists, Poalei Zion, communists, general Zionists—one ideal united them all: Yiddish culture."[24] Shatski praises the newly created branch of YIVO in Buenos Aires under the leadership of Shmuel Rozhanski, who turned the YIVO library into a repository "for living books which are read so diligently that each book is constantly in circulation." Shatski concludes that the cultural presence of Polish Jews in Argentina was a necessary requirement for the implementation of *Dos poylishe yidntum*.[25]

Only one-and-a-half years after the series had begun, the publication of the twenty-fifth volume was celebrated with a booklet that included brief articles by leading Yiddish cultural figures and writers from all over the world. In his article, "The Idea of the Book Series," Turkov emphasized that the Central Union of Polish Jews both supported relief work among the survivors of the Holocaust—the main obligation of the *landsmanshaftn*—and contributed to the writing of Polish Jewish history. This broader goal of the book series as contributor to economic relief work and cultural revival grew out of a concept of Polish Jewry as a national body:

> The initiators of the project had the privilege of heading the organization that represents the organized Polish Jewry in Argentina. They understood that this organization with more than 30 years' experience of social activity cannot be limited to functioning as a local *landsmanshaft*. It cannot limit itself to relief work—regardless of its importance—but must develop into a broader level of activity that . . . can contribute to the thousand-year history of Polish Jewry. Clearly we were more than a Jewish community. We were a Jewish people on Polish lands—as the well-known Jewish historian Dr. Yankev Shatski correctly has characterized Polish Jewry.[26]

The series included a variety of genres that exemplified the richness and complexity of Jewish life in Poland. A significant number of books were Holocaust memoirs, diaries, and testimonies from the ghettos, camps, and aftermath of the war, such as Hillel Seidman's *Togbukh fun varshever geto* (Diary from Warsaw Ghetto, vol. 15), Shmerke Kaczerginski's *Partizaner geyen!* (Partisans March! vol. 18), Joseph Kermish's *Der oyfshtand in varshever geto* (The Warsaw Ghetto Uprising, vol. 30), and Jonas Turkov's *Azoy iz es geven: Khurbn Varshe* (So It Was: The Destruction of Warsaw, vol. 27). As the series progressed, an increasingly large number of the books were cultural historical studies and memoirs about Polish Jewish life, such as Yankev Shatski's *In shotn fun over* (In the Shadow of the Past, vol. 13) and sociologist Yankev Lestschinsky's articles from the interwar Polish Yiddish press, *Oyfn rand fun opgrunt* (On the Edge of the Abyss, vol. 21) and *Erev khurbn* (On the Eve of Destruction, vol. 77). The series featured poetry by young Yiddish writers such as Rokhl Korn's *Heym un heymlozikeyt* (Home and Homelessness, vol. 39); Chaim Grade's *Pleytim* (Refugees, vol. 17) and *Sheyn fun farloshene shtern* (Light of Extinguished Stars, vol. 66); and Z. Segalovicz's *Gebrente trit* (Burned Steps, vol. 22). It included reprints of classical Yiddish works related to Polish Jewry, such as Yankev Glatshteyn's *Ven Yash iz geforn* (When Yash Set Out, vol. 128), Yehoshue Perle's *Yidn fun a gants yor* (Ordinary Jews, vol. 76), and Sholem Asch's *Farn mabl* trilogy (Before the Deluge, vols. 56–58). Several books about I. L. Peretz and memoirs about the Yiddish PEN Club in Warsaw, Tlomatske Street 13—the main address of Polish Yiddish culture—emphasized the series' secular Yiddishist orientation.

While many of the featured authors had perished in the Holocaust, a talented group of surviving young Yiddish writers published their first or early work in the series. Among them were Chaim Grade, Rokhl Korn, Yehuda Elberg, Mordechai Strigler, and Elie Wiesel, all born in the 1910s and 1920s (only Korn and Grade had made their poetic debuts prior to the war). The series imparted a sense of Yiddish cultural renaissance that paralleled Avrom Sutzkever's editorship of the literary journal *Di goldene keyt* (in Tel Aviv). *Dos poylishe yidntum* recreated the idea of a secular Yiddish culture following the destruction of its heartland in Poland. It signaled a Yiddish cultural rebirth through its consistent output over two decades, coupled with its enthusiastic reception by a worldwide readership.

Although the series included a few works by Jewish historians such as Mayer Balaban, Emanuel Ringelblum, Yankev Shatski, and Max Weinreich, the bulk of the books were memoirs and autobiographical accounts about Polish Jewish life before and during the Holocaust, as well as some fiction. Shmuel Niger characterized the Yiddish book market in the decade after the Holocaust:

> The destruction of the old home has reawakened among us the wish to mourn its passing, to tell its history, to erect a gravestone and memorialize. Since the Holocaust, a sorrowful call has resounded through Yiddish literature: The tree of Jewish life in Europe has been pulled up by its roots. May its genealogical tree live on in literature! Writers cannot stop writing about their family origins. They write in different forms: novels and stories, history and biography, and personal memoirs, ghetto chronicles and more than ever *Yizker* books.[27]

The origin and history of families became a popular genre in Yiddish literature, as evidenced in the many books about Polish Jewish families in the series. These include Elkhonon Zeitlin's *In a literarisher shtub* (In a Literary Home), about his father Hillel Zeitlin's literary salon in Warsaw prior to World War I, and Mark Turkov's *Di letste fun a groysn dor*, personal memoirs and historical episodes about eight prominent Polish Jewish families. Niger used the concept of *kinus* (ingathering) to describe the Yiddish book market as a means of "collecting and preserving anything of worth in the literary past."[28] Central to this effort was the huge amount of life-writing—memoirs and autobiographical accounts—that flooded the Yiddish book market in the aftermath of the Holocaust.[29] In some respects, the series embodied the dominant trend in post-Holocaust Yiddish culture that historian Eli Lederhendler characterizes as "a culture of retrieval": "a culture that was losing its proximity to its Yiddish roots was also losing the possibility of using those roots for cultural innovation. It was, instead, thrown back on mimicry of the past."[30] Although this backward-looking trend in some cases resulted in nostalgia, *Dos poylishe yidntum* mostly adhered to the highest literary quality and included some of the best and worthiest works from the Polish Jewish past and present. The series actually went beyond *kinus* in its effort to publish young Yiddish literary talent, marking a renewal of Yiddish literature.

Approximately 80 percent of the books in the series can be more or less evenly divided into three categories: Holocaust memoirs and scholarship, life-writing, and fiction. The majority of the Holocaust books (48) were memoirs and personal accounts, many of them based on original documents (diaries and testimonies). Books drawing on life-writing (48) consisted mostly of Jewish writers' recollections of Polish Jewish life, particularly accounts of the writer's family background. Holocaust and life-writing were evenly distributed from the beginning to the end of the series. The fiction section (37) overlapped with the Holocaust category in the works of young writers such as Mordechai Strigler, Yehuda Elberg, and Elie Wiesel, who wrote literary memoirs based on their Holocaust experiences. However, discussion of fiction (novels and short stories) began in earnest with Y. Y. Trunk's essay *Di yidishe proze in poyln* (Yiddish Prose in Poland, vol. 52), after which fiction regularly appeared in the series. Folklore (13 works) consisted mostly of Hasidic customs and stories; historical works (8) included *Yizker*-style books as well as scholarly writing (Shatski and Ringelblum). Three collections of first-rate poetry featured Chaim Grade (2 volumes) and Rokhl Korn. Other small categories were literary criticism (2), journalistic essays (3), and two works about Jewish life beyond Poland: the history of the Lithuanian Jewish Haskalah (vol. 70) and a biography of a Russian Jewish intellectual figure (vol. 116).

FIGURE 4.1. Mark Turkov surrounded by his three brothers, Jonas, Zygmunt, and Yitskhok Turkov, in Israel (undated). *First row, from left:* Yitskhok, Mark, Jonas, and Jonas's wife, Diana Blumenfeld. *Second row standing, from left:* Shura Turkov (wife of Yitskhok), Zygmunt Turkov, Roza Turkov (wife of Zygmunt), and Guta Konrad (a relative of Diana Blumenfeld). (Archives of the YIVO Institute for Jewish Research, New York).

The Holocaust was the primary theme of the series, and quantitatively the largest thematic group, as exemplified by literary memoirs and fiction about ghetto life and extermination camps. Although the demand for popular stories and nostalgic accounts of the "old country" was strong and commercially tempting, Mark Turkov held on to his original vision for the series. In a letter to the Yiddish writer Yekhiel Hirshoyt in the late 1940s, Turkov wrote: "People require that we stop printing books about the Holocaust. They don't want to read them anymore; that's the sentiment I encounter from all sides. I am afraid that we won't have funds for our continued work. In that case, I would rather terminate the project because without Holocaust literature I have absolutely no interest in it whatsoever."[31]

Turkov's brother, the Yiddish actor Jonas Turkov, had five books in the series. These are representative of the Holocaust category. In three volumes Jonas Turkov depicted his incarceration in the Warsaw Ghetto, the ghetto uprising, and the aftermath of the war up to his immigration to the United States. In two other volumes, *Farloshene shtern* (Extinguished Stars, vols. 95–96), he sketched mini portraits of a large number of Yiddish actors in

A

B

C

D

FIGURE 4.2 (*left and facing page*). Book covers for the series *Dos poylishe yidntum*. Shtetl and City. (Courtesy Malena Chinski). *A:* Pinkhes Shtaynvaks, *Yidn tsum gedenken* (Jews to Remember), 1955; *B:* Abraham Nahtomi, *In shotn fun doyres: Kindheyt* (In the Shadow of Generations: Childhood), 1948; *C:* Zusman Segalovicz, *Der letster lodzher roman* (The Last Lodz Novel), 1951; *D:* Daniel Charney, *Vilne: Memuarn* (Vilna: Memoirs), 1951; *E:* Abraham Teitelbaum, *Varshever heyf: Mentshn un gesheenishn* (Warsaw Courtyards: People and Happenings), 1947.

E

Poland before and during the Holocaust. Especially remarkable were the meticulously compiled indices to these books, making them vital scholarly sources for anyone studying the histories of Yiddish theater and the Warsaw Ghetto. Based on diaries and original documents from the Warsaw Ghetto that Jonas Turkov managed to hide and retrieve after the war, his books were rightly praised for their objectivity and richness of detail. In his review, Noakh Gris related Jonas Turkov's methodology to the spirit of collecting (*zamler gayst*) that Emanuel Ringelblum had imbued through his Oyneg Shabes archive in the Warsaw Ghetto: "Turkov, the artist, demonstrated a good deal of historical professionalism in preparing and editing his material. Particularly important is the inclusion of an index of approximately [a] thousand names of people mentioned in the book. This is important both from a historical and a personal perspective (for the relatives of people listed in the index)." Gris concluded his review by praising the memoirs' objectivity and high publishing standards: "It is a book of high documentary value, published with unique reverence reflected in the many details, from the cover to the index, from the high paper quality to the careful assemblage of tens of pictures in the text."[32]

The historian Yankev Shatski, who published several volumes in the book series, belonged to a generation of Polish Jewish historians who viewed their work as serving the secular Jewish revival in Eastern Europe.[33] The emphasis on utility for the Jewish masses placed Shatski's historical work in the camp of such YIVO historians as Emanuel Ringelblum, whose selected writings about Jewish life in Poland were featured in the series introduced by Shatski (vols. 91–92, 1953). The new circumstances for Polish Jewish historiography in the aftermath of the Holocaust were reflected in statements by Shatski that encapsulated the volatile zeitgeist among Jewish historians, which swayed from despondence to hope. In a lecture titled "The Confessions of a Jewish Historian," held at the New School for Social Research in New York in 1954, Shatski said: "Instead of national history, history is transformed into a national symbol, a myth. For this you don't need archival material, and obviously not hard facts. For this kind of history, it is perhaps enough to create a grand epic, a poetic convulsion of a gigantic imaginary mind.... The eastern European sector lives on because of the remnants of the great [Polish] Jews whose weekdays were more Jewish than the holidays of American Jews."[34]

The overall composition of the book series' 175 volumes expressed this epic dimension of the everyday life of ordinary Polish Jews, from its early history through its destruction. Most of the books were personal accounts that were written in an intimate manner, without scholarly pretension. The books were perfectly attuned to the needs of the Yiddish readership. They breathed new life into the bones of a bygone era by restoring the Polish Jewish *mentalité* in its primary language, Yiddish.[35] Shatski fully understood the post-Holocaust Jewish demand for "emotional history" and "history written *cum ira et cum studio* (with anger and with bias)."[36] At the same time he warned that this tendency could undermine the professional historian's objectivity: "Never before has the question of a scientific approach in studying Jewish history been more urgent. The horrific years of Nazism and the catastrophic result of the Hitler-era have resulted in a frightening accusatory mindset ... some Jewish intellectuals have begun to demonstrate their pathological antipathy to historical realism."[37] For Shatski, it was crucial to maintain the distinction between the current popular demand—lamentation, commemoration, and *kinus*—and the requirements of historical scholarship. Reviewers of the book series constantly reminded the reader that the historical works would be written later and to a large extent built on the testimonies and memoirs that were being published in such overwhelming numbers. The research director at YIVO in New York, Max Weinreich, echoed this sentiment: "Mark Turkov has ... compiled a series of books that will remain part of our literature for future generations. Despite the fact that the books are not scientific writing, but information, we can rest assured that the scholar must turn to the books in researching the years of destruction."[38]

In his brief introduction, Leibush Lehrer summarized the content of the *Bibliography of Yiddish Books about Destruction and Heroism* published by Yad Vashem in 1962. Of the 1,900 titles included in the bibliography, 83 percent consisted of, in equal parts, documents and descriptions, and fiction and other art forms. Only 274 titles dealt with the Holocaust in an analytical and scholarly manner.[39] It was the books' "emotional history" that made them, like *Dos poylishe yidntum*, a unique and authentic Jewish response to the catastrophe. As Y. Robinson writes in his foreword to the bibliography: "The importance of the Holocaust literature in Yiddish is not predicated on its literary qualities, but on its unmediated depiction of personal experiences."[40] As the historian Philip Friedman made clear, the importance of Holocaust literature in Yiddish was further highlighted by the fact that very little archival and periodical material was available during this period:

> True, it is not easy to write a historical monograph when all archival sources, both the national ones and those belonging to Jewish communities, have been destroyed or remain behind the "Iron Curtain." Even the local periodicals which are so important for the history of the last decade are almost unavailable. As a result, it is necessary to reconstruct the historical past from random pieces, built on oral evidence, and from memoir literature. Jewish historians and editors of *Yizker* books have more than once mentioned these difficulties.[41]

Another important series of memorial books, the *Yizker* books were published by *landsmanshaftn* in limited editions of less than one thousand copies, and primarily addressed to the inner circle of *landslayt* and their families. In contrast *Dos poylishe yidntum* reached a significant readership, and thereby helped to invigorate the Yiddish book market during a time of cultural decline and fragmentation. The book series as a whole can be viewed as a composite of the different parts of the *Yizker* book: history, folklore, literature, life-writing, genealogically based memoirs, and the Holocaust. The editorial choices in the creation of the two book projects were identical. The goal was to commemorate the destruction of Jewish communities in Eastern Europe by enlisting all classes and strata of the surviving Jews to provide testimonies and recollections of the "old country." As pointed out in a 1973 study:

They [the *landsmanshaftn*] felt very deeply that professional historians in their analytic and synthetic research would not be able to encompass the problem in its enormity; meanwhile their contemporaries whose own memories were invaluable sources of rich information would gradually pass away. As a result of this project of commemoration, approximately 400 memorial books for different European communities (mainly in Eastern Europe) were published between 1945 and 1972.[42]

Despite the often questionable historical methodology used in compiling *Yizker* books, they "contain a greater amount of information and data on the life of East European Jewish communities than all other publication in this field that have so far been published."[43] To sift through this material and sort out historical fact from fiction and folklore, however, it is important to delineate the context in which the *Yizker* books were financed, edited, and published.[44] The significance of the approximately more than one thousand *Yizker* books published to date for anthropologists, folklorists, literary scholars, and historians cannot be overestimated. Although Antony Polonsky points to *Yizker* books' particular documentary value for research on the destruction of Polish Jewry, and often as the only sources available about the war years, the books are also important sources for Polish Jewish life before 1939, particularly Jewish folk customs, local Jewish history of cities and towns, genealogy, and Yiddish linguistics.[45] Like *Yizker* books, the volumes in *Dos poylishe yidntum* are repeatedly referred to as *sforim* (sacred books) in contemporary correspondence and reviews. However, to ensure that these two monumental book projects are not buried in a historical "tomb" as "sacred" icons of Polish Jewry, they must be read in the contexts in which they were conceived, studied in Yiddish, and made available in translation. Eleven percent of the books in *Dos poylishe yidntum* have been translated into Polish, English, Hebrew, German, Spanish, and French; the rest are available only in Yiddish, which narrows their utility almost entirely to the scholarly community.[46]

Elie Wiesel published his first book in Yiddish, titled . . . *Un di velt hot geshvign* (And the World Was Silent), in 1956, as volume 117 in *Dos poylishe yidntum*.[47] A condensed translation of the Yiddish book appeared in two different versions and languages two years apart: *La Nuit* (1958) in French and then *Night* (1960), translated from the French into English. The editorial and artistic choices made by Wiesel in the text's passage from Yiddish to French and English touch on key questions related to the themes, narrative structure, style, and audience of this Holocaust memoir as it was originally conceived in the book series. Moreover, the reception and interpretive context of Wiesel's work shifted as it was transformed from a Jewish to a non-Jewish language. Wiesel mentions that he first wrote his "account of the concentration years—in Yiddish" in his cabin on a boat from Marseille to Sao Paulo in 1954: "I wrote feverishly, breathlessly, without rereading. I wrote to testify, to stop the dead from dying, to justify my own survival. I wrote to speak to those who were gone. As long as I spoke to them, they would live on, at least in my memory. My vow of silence would soon be fulfilled; next year would mark the tenth anniversary of my liberation."[48]

In "An Interview Unlike Any Other" (1978), Wiesel refers to his vow not to speak of his concentration camp experiences for at least ten years. He points out that his mistrust of words, and his lack of an approach "to describe the un-describable," made him decide to wait "long enough to see clearly."[49] Wiesel mentions that he was introduced to Mark Turkov, "a Jewish book publisher," on the boat's stopover in Montevideo. Turkov showed interest in Wiesel's manuscript and promised that he would publish it: "In December [1955] I received from Buenos Aires the first copy of my Yiddish testimony 'And the World Was Silent,' which I had finished on the boat to Brazil."[50] Although Wiesel pays tribute to the Jewish ghetto writers in Yiddish and Hebrew—"the great documents on the tragedy had been written in Yiddish and Hebrew"[51]—he does not mention Turkov's book series *Dos poylishe yidntum*, in which his first book appeared, in his memoirs. Instead, the French writer François Mauriac is enshrined as his literary midwife: "He was the first person to read *Night* after I reworked it from the original Yiddish. He submitted it to his own publisher, promising to write a preface for the book, to speak of it in the press, and to support it with all the considerable means at his disposal." Mauriac helped Wiesel negotiate a contract with Jerome Lindon at Editions de Minuit, and he wrote an important foreword to *Night*. This foreword remains an inextricable part of the work and its interpretative context.[52]

Wiesel's debut work as a writer, the novella "*A bagegenish*" (An Encounter), appeared in Paris in 1947.[53] In the following years he contributed short stories, journalistic pieces, reviews, and reportages to Yiddish journals and newspapers in Paris and New York City. His novel *Shtile heldn* (Quiet Heroes) was serialized in the New York journal *Der amerikaner*. In addition to his work as foreign correspondent for the Israeli newspaper *Yediot Ahronot*, he also became a staff member at the Yiddish daily *Forverts* in 1956, and befriended Yiddish writers in New York in the 1950s and 1960s. As Alan Astro points out, Wiesel's childhood in a Hasidic family (born in 1928, he was eleven years old at the outbreak of World War II) in Sighet, in the Carpathians, far from the centers of Yiddish secular culture, meant that "his first significant exposure to secular Yiddish literature and formal Yiddish grammar occurred in the French capital, after the war."[54] Wiesel's subsequent connection with Turkov enabled him to become an author of a Holocaust memoir that was conceived as part of the Yiddish book series with a particular readership and its horizon of expectations. The encouragement and direction Wiesel received from Turkov empowered the young writer a decade after the war to access and express his memories of the war, and his incarceration in Auschwitz. The importance of using his mother tongue as an artistic medium that served as "a bridge" to his childhood is outlined in this quote from Wiesel's 1995 memoir:

> I love Yiddish because it has been with me from the cradle. It was in Yiddish that I spoke my first words and expressed my first fears. It is a bridge to my childhood years.... I need Yiddish to laugh and cry, to celebrate and express regret, to delve into my memories anew. Is there a better language for evoking the past, with all its horror? Without Yiddish the literature of the Holocaust would have no soul. I know that had I not written my first account in Yiddish, I would have written no others.[55]

Ka-Tzetnik's *House of Dolls*, published as vol. 115 in *Dos poylishe yidntum* a few months before ... *Un di velt hot geshvign,* was the author's Yiddish version of his 1953 Hebrew novel about the prostitution of Jewish women by Gestapo. The work also appeared in an English translation in 1955 and was republished in Yiddish in Tel Aviv in 1958. Ka-Tzetnik (a pseudonym for Yekhiel Dinur), a survivor of Auschwitz, was one of the first Israeli authors to write about the Holocaust. A whole generation of Israelis learned about the Holocaust primarily through his books, including *Salamandra* (1946), *House of Dolls* (1953), and *The Clock: Stories of the Holocaust* (1960). His books contain detailed descriptions of the horrors of Auschwitz, including torture, cannibalism, and sexual abuse of children. In a review Wiesel praised the author for his courage and artistic originality in depicting human life on the "planet" Auschwitz: "He is a witness in the highest sense of the word, a witness who took a piece of fire with him from the conflagration of the Holocaust."[56] Thus Wiesel's ... *Un di velt hot geshvign* entered a diverse field of Holocaust memoirs and fiction works in the book series that included Ka-Tzetnik's sensationalist and graphic work.

FIGURE 4.3. Book covers for the series *Dos poylishe yidntum*. Death Camps and Martyrology. (Courtesy Malena Chinski). *A:* Mordechai Strigler, *Maydanek* (Majdanek), 1947; *B:* V. Grossman and Y. Viernik, *Treblinke* (Treblinka), 1946; *C:* Noah Gruss, ed., *Kinder-martirologye: Zamlung fun dokumentn* (Children Martyrology: Collection of Documents), 1947.

FIGURE 4.4. Book covers for the series *Dos poylishe yidntum*. Resistance and Partisans. (Courtesy Malena Chinski). *A:* Joseph Kermish, *Der oyfshtand in varshever geto* (The Warsaw Ghetto Uprising), 1948; *B:* Shmerke Kaczerginski, *Partizaner geyen! Fartseykhenungen fun vilner geto* (Partisans March! Notes from the Vilna Ghetto), 1947; *C:* Michal Borwicz, *Arishe papirn* (Aryan Papers), 1955.

At 245 pages, . . . *Un di velt hot geshvign* is twice the length of *Night* (126 pages). From the beginning Elieyzer Wiesel, as his name appears on the Yiddish book's cover, depicts the catastrophe in explicitly Jewish terms, as illustrated by the following comparison:

אויפֿן ה ויף —א מאַר ק: ווערט-זאַכן, טײַערע טעפּיכער, זילבערנע לײַכטער, אַ
חלה-טישטער, אַ בשמים-פּושקעלע, מחזורים, סידורים—אַלץ וואַלגערט זיך אויף דער
שמוציקער ערד, אונטערן צו בלויען הימל. גלײַך זײ וואָלטן קײַנמאָל קײן בעל-הבית נישט
געהאַט, גלײַך עס וואָלט קײן בעל-בית אױף דער וועלט נישט געווען.
לית דין ולית דיין. אַלץ איז הפֿקר, מוראדיק הפֿקר.
ווען דער מענטש איז אויס מענטש, איז די וועלט אויס וועלט.

The yard—a marketplace: valuable things, expensive carpets, silver candelabras, *khale*-covers, spice boxes, holiday prayerbooks, Sabbath prayer books were scattered on the dirty earth, under the too blue heaven. Like they never had a master, like there was no master in the universe. *Without a law and without a judge.* Everything is abandoned, frighteningly abandoned. When a human ceases to be a human, the world ceases to be a world. (. . . *Un di velt*, 30)

Our backyard had become a real marketplace. Household treasures, valuable carpets, silver candelabra, prayerbooks, Bibles, and other religious articles littered the dusty ground beneath a wonderfully blue sky; pathetic objects which looked as though they had never belonged to anyone. (*Night*, 26)

The Hebrew expression "*les din veles dayen*" (without a law and without a judge) encapsulates the narrator's interpretative strategy in viewing the abandoned backyard as representing a godless universe. A few pages later, Wiesel uses the same rhetorical method to describe the abandoned ghetto: "Open rooms everywhere. Doors and windows—wide open, like after a fire, after total destruction. An abandoned world. *Whoever is hungry let him come and eat,* everybody can come and take what they desire" (. . . *Un di velt,* 34). Wiesel employs the Aramaic phrase "*kol dikhfin yeisei veyeykhol*" (let all who are hungry come and eat), which introduces the Passover Seder, to highlight the absurdity of Jewish religious observance in the midst of the evacuation of Jews from the Sighet Ghetto during Passover 1944. This reference situates the description in a religious framework by mocking its sacred meaning in the extreme conditions of the ghetto.

Not only were such Jewish cultural and religious references excluded from *Night*, but so too were the meta-narrative signifiers. Although these signifiers interrupt the narrative flow, they add a distinct moral perspective and emotional pathos to the narrator's voice. Two typical examples not included in *Night:*

. . . און איצט, שרײַבנדיק די דאָזיקע שורות, זע איך אים נאָך אַלץ שטײן אין שאָטן פֿון בלאָק, אָנגעלענט אין אַ האָלצערנעם סלופּ, אײַנגעבױגן איבער מיר. איך זע נאָך אַלץ זײַנע אױגן װאָס האָבן צאָרן־פֿלאַמען געװאָרפֿן אױף דער אַרומיקער װעלט, צאָרן־פֿלאַמען װעלכע װעלן דורך מיר, אײביק דערמאָנען דער װעלט, דער מענטשהײט, אַז צוליב איר שװײַגן, צוליב איר פֿאַרברעכערישער גלײַכגילטיקײט, איז דײַטשלאַנד פֿאַרװאַנדלט געװאָרן אין אַ מזבח פֿאַרן ייִדישן פֿאָלק . . .

And now, writing these lines, I still see him standing in the shadow of the block, leaning on a wooden pole, bent over me. I still see his eyes which threw flames of rage on the surrounding world, flames of rage which, through me, will eternally remind all humanity, that because of its silence, its criminal indifference, Germany was transformed into a sacrificial altar for the Jewish people. (. . . *Un di velt,* 140)

. . . מאָדנע: שרײַבנדיק די דאָזיקע שורות, גלױבט עס זיך עפּעס מיר נישט, מיר אַלײן. ס׳דוכט זיך: איך שרײַב אַ שרעק־ראָמאַן. אַ ראָמאַן װעלכן מ׳דאַרף נישט לײענען בײַנאַכט. ס׳קען זיך נישט גלױבן, אַז דאָס אַלץ װאָס איך שרײַב—איז טאַקע געשען, מיט מיר אַלײן געשען. און—בלױז מיט צען יאָר צוריק!

. . . Strange: writing these lines, I don't believe them. It seems as if I am writing a horror-novel. A novel it is forbidden to read at night. It is impossible to believe that everything that I write—in fact happened to myself. And—only ten years ago. (. . . *Un di velt,* 210)

The meta-narrative signifiers provide a glimpse into the mind of the narrator in the process of narration as well as situate the events in a historical context ("only ten years ago"). They bring the narrator closer to the reader. This is further emphasized by the narrator's frequent address to "the dear reader" and "dear friend." This rhetoric of intimacy between narrator and reader has been a staple of modern Yiddish literature from its inception in the mid-nineteenth century. The flame of rage in his father's eyes in the first quote above obligates Wiesel to remind "the world" of its "criminal indifference" during the Holocaust. The book is dedicated to Wiesel's mother, father, and sister, who were "killed by the Germans murderers." This formula is typically employed in the dedication to Holocaust memoirs in *Dos poylishe yidntum*. In the English version, the dedication is subdued in a fundamentally different formula: "In Memory of My Parents and of My Little Sister Tzipora."

The subtitle of the last section of . . . *Un di velt* is appropriately titled "The End and the Beginning." Wiesel's rejection of "the image of myself after death"[57] brings him back to life. His shattering the mirror at the end of the Yiddish book is followed by his first note-taking for his testimony: "After I got better, I stayed in bed for several days, jotting down notes for the work that you, dear reader, now hold in your hands."[58] Although Wiesel intends his testimony to refute that the "Germans and anti-Semites tell the world that the story of six million Jewish victims is but a myth,"[59] he recognizes the powerlessness of his words to make the world break its silence. By breaking the mirror Wiesel is able to resist succumbing to the image of himself as a corpse. In that sense Wiesel's point, that "had I not written my first account in Yiddish, I would have written no others," indicates that, if not for his defiance of death in the act of bearing witness, he would not have survived. This complex of testimony as a life-saving, creative act that empowered the survivor to return from "the dead" to the world of letters has been excluded from *Night*. By writing the first version of his Holocuast memoir in Yiddish, Wiesel found his artistic voice and gained access to the world of Yiddish letters. Additionally, the translation and rewriting of the work in French and English opened a very different artistic source and readership for the young writer. In the French and English versions, Wiesel decided to un-shatter the mirror to create a fixed image of the survivor as a suffering, isolated victim. For Mauriac, the otherworldly image of the suffering survivor became the embodiment of Jesus Christ.[60]

The original Yiddish text and context of *Night* reveal a set of responses to the Holocaust mostly unknown outside the Yiddish cultural world. They are very different from what has become known as "Holocaust literature," which remains primarily an English-language phenomenon (including works translated into English). Obviously, a work's original language and audience must always be the point of departure for any serious interpretative practice. This is particularly important in cases where the original text has undergone significant editorial reworking in translation. Original responses to the Holocaust in Yiddish and Hebrew in anthologies such as *Anthology of Holocaust Literature* (1968) and *The Literature of Destruction: Jewish Responses to Catastrophe* (1989) can add much to our knowledge of the particular ways in which Jewish survivors drew on their religious, cultural, and literary traditions.[61] This body of Jewish Holocaust memoirs and testimonies is an invaluable source for the original context and literary means of expression originating in the long history of Jewish responses to catastrophe. Moreover, these works significantly revise any notion of the survivors' silence until the Eichmann trial in Jerusalem in 1961. Instead Yiddish testimonies such as those in *Dos poylishe yidntum* indicate the existence of a vibrant Jewish discourse that empowered survivors to express and share their experiences in Yiddish. The surrounding world, Jewish and non-Jewish, was largely unaware of the voluminous creativity in Yiddish that took place in New York City, Buenos Aires, Tel Aviv, and Paris in the late 1940s and 1950s. The issue was not that of "silence" of the survivors; rather, it was the world's inability, indifference, and sometimes even hostility to hearing the survivors' own voices in Yiddish.

In remaking . . . *Un di velt* as *La Nuit*, Wiesel wrote a book with almost no Jewish references, which was stripped of most of its original *cum ira et cum studio*, the main characteristic of the Jewish Holocaust memoir, according to Yankev Shatski. Obviously, the artistic and ideological gains were considerable. By rewriting the Yiddish memoir for a general non-Jewish audience, Wiesel has made *Night* a seminal text of Holocaust literature, due mainly to its aesthetic qualities of condensed storytelling and a powerful indictment of the passivity of God and the world. This great achievement, however, would not have been possible without the Yiddish cultural revival in the late 1940s and 1950s, when Wiesel was starting out as a Yiddish writer. Writers mostly unknown outside the Yiddish and Hebrew literary world, such as Mordechai Strigler, Yekhiel Dinur, Chaim Grade, and Avrom Sutzkever, influenced and empowered Wiesel in his quest to discover his literary voice. They exemplified a vibrant Jewish literary tradition and models for articulating his Holocaust experiences. Moreover, Mark Turkov's interest in Wiesel in 1954 in Montevideo and his subsequent publication of . . . *Un di velt* in *Dos poylishe yidntum* provided the young writer with a Jewish readership. This happened at a time in the mid-1950s when "Holocaust literature" in non-Jewish languages was still a rather marginal phenomenon. Like that of I. B. Singer, Wiesel's bilingual oeuvre exemplifies the fact that only by engaging in translating (and muting) the distinctive Jewishness of their Yiddish work for a non-Jewish audience did they succeed in breaking out of the Yiddish cultural circuit to become writers of world literature.

Of the more than 150 writers whose books are included in *Dos poylishe yidntum*, only Sholem Asch and Wiesel managed to reach a worldwide

FIGURE 4.5. Book covers for the series *Dos poylishe yidntum. Sheyres hapleyte*—The Saved Remnants. (Courtesy Malena Chinski). *A:* H. Shoshkes, *Poyln—1946: Ayndrukn fun a rayze* (Poland—1946: Impressions from a Journey), 1946; *B:* S. Izban, *"Umlegale" yidn shpaltn yamen* ("Illegal" Jews Split the Seas), 1948; *C:* Fryda Zerubavel, *Na venad: Fartseykhenungen fun a pleyte* (Homeless: Notes of a Refugee), 1947.

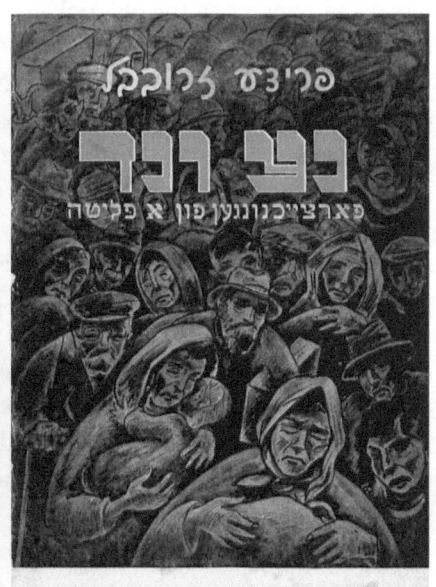

readership in translation. Moreover, . . . *Un di velt hot geshvign* remained mostly invisible outside the Yiddish world until the mid-1980s.⁶² Until then, the English version of *Night* was universally perceived as a translation of a work that had originally been written in French. Naomi Diamant aptly summarizes Wiesel's exceptional role among Jewish survivor writers: "Wiesel alone has attained an international authority based on his victimhood and survival. Through his writing and his persona, Wiesel has rendered the Jewish victim accessible to a Christian audience. He is the archetypical translator figure, a sort of John the Baptist to the Holocaust."⁶³

In the aftermath of the Holocaust, Turkov was confronted with the urgent task of shaping a textual corpus and creating a mini-library that would provide a symbolic lifeline to his destroyed community. *Dos poylishe yidntum* was an impressive achievement, starkly highlighting that what remained of the largest and most vibrant Jewish community in Europe was a library of Yiddish books. This sentiment was summed up by a Yiddish critic of the series: "It is tragic that this type of book series must be published in memory of such a horrific catastrophe. Recalling this catastrophe, it is difficult to be joyful about the series' success. But such is our destiny . . . we continue to build, and draw upon the old, 'golden chain.' That is a great comfort. Yes, it is a comfort, even though it is impossible to be comforted.—[I]n the memorial period for Polish Jewry, there remains only this shelf with a little over eighty books."⁶⁴

The massive effort to write down and collect eyewitness accounts to bear witness to unspeakable crimes perpetrated against Jews was the driving force behind *Dos poylishe yidntum*. However, such testimony was always framed in the broader cultural context of Jewish continuity and renewal. By placing accounts about the destruction of Polish Jewry in the context of a revival of Yiddish book publishing, Turkov and Mitlberg went beyond commemoration and *kinus*. *Dos poylishe yidntum* became a venue of hope for the continued creativity of Yiddish literature as well as a cultural anchor for survivors in DP camps, their relatives, and the Yiddish reading public worldwide. Eastern European Jews had always defined their communities in mythological and religious terms as Jerusalem *shel mayle* (heavenly Jerusalem), a *kehile kedoyshe* (a holy community), and the people of portable books. The name *Dos poylishe yidntum* expressed the sheer *khutspe* with which Turkov and Mitlberg insisted that a Yiddish library of 175 secular books could symbolically replace the "real" Polish Jewry. Despite clear indications that Turkov and Miltberg belonged to the last great generation of Polish Jews (*di letste fun a groysn dor*), the publishers' titanic effort signaled a return to a semblance of normality for survivors and their relatives. *Der driter khurbn* (the third destruction—the Holocaust) began with the Nazi book burnings as a prelude to the burning of people. *Dos poylishe yidntum* proudly announced that the surviving remnant of Polish Jewry—once again publishing, reading, and discussing Yiddish books in their new diasporas in Buenos Aires, New York City, Tel Aviv, and Warsaw—was returning to life.

5

1953–54

A Year in Yiddish Literature

דער ייִדישער שרײַבער פֿון אַמעריקע ווערט נישט שיר געטריבן יעדן טאָג נישט בלויז
צו אַ חשבון-הנפֿש, נאָר צום שטעלן זיך פֿאַרן יום-הדין און צום אונטערציִען מעת-
לעתיק אַ סך-הכּל: ווּ האַלט איך? ווי ווײַט גרייט מײַן וואָרט? וואָס זענען די שאַנסן
אויף אַן עכאָ? ווּ איז דער וואַלד, פֿון וואַנען אַן עכאָ קאָן קאָן קומען?

א. גלאַנץ-לייעלעס (1954)

The Yiddish writer in America is forced not only to make an "account of the soul" but to stand at "Judgment Day." He must continuously confront himself: Where do I stand? How far do my words reach? What are the chances of an echo? Where is the forest from which an echo can come?

A. Glantz-Leyeles, Velt un vort:
Literarishe un andere eseyen (1954)[1]

In 1952, a Yiddish historical journal in Warsaw published "*Khurbn varshe*" (The Destruction of Warsaw), an indictment of most of the Warsaw Jews, including the *Judenrat*, written in 1942 in the Warsaw Ghetto. This led to an exchange of articles between the Yiddish poet H. Leivick in New York City and the Jewish historian Bernard Mark in Warsaw. H. Leivick claimed in his article "*Tsvey dokumentn*" (Two Documents), in the New York daily *Der tog*, that the document must be a falsification. He believed that all Jews, regardless of their roles in the ghettos and camps, shared a common martyrdom. As a result, Leivick considered any attempt to address the various kinds of Jewish collaboration with the Germans among the ghetto police, *Judenrat*, and *kapos* a sacrilege to the sacred memory of the victims. Opposing this view, Bernard Mark documented—with facsimiles of handwritten records rescued from the Warsaw Ghetto—that the divisions and hostility among different strata of the Jewish ghetto population were commonly expressed and recorded by the ghetto's Jews, including historian Emanuel Ringelblum, the organizer of the Oyneg Shabes archive.

Bernard Mark proved without a trace of a doubt that the author of the diatribe against the *Judenrat*'s collaboration with the Germans was none other than the Yiddish novelist Yehoshue Perle (1888–1943).[2] In a lengthy 1953 article, "*Yudenratishe ahaves-Yisroel: An entfer afn bilbl fun H. Leivick*" (*Judenrat* Love of Israel: An Answer to a False Accusation of H. Leivick), Mark labeled Leivick and the members of the Warsaw *Judenrat* "collaborators" whose "love of Israel" was a betrayal of the Jews in the Warsaw Ghetto and of the historical memory of them. The public clash between Mark and Leivick revealed some of the deep-rooted ideological frictions in post-Holocaust Yiddish culture. Leivick articulated the dominant sentiments among Jewish Americans who had registered the aftershocks of the Warsaw Ghetto's death throes from four thousand miles away, and were prone to mythologize the Jewish victims. On the other hand, Mark, a native son of Jewish Warsaw and a communist believer, sought justice based on historical documentation. The confrontation between the mythmaker and the hard-nosed historian took place in a Yiddish cultural context and did not reverberate in the broader Jewish community in New York. As David G. Roskies points out, Mark won the debate, but it turned out to be "a Pyrrhic victory, for the series of Yiddish wartime writings that he [Bernard Mark] managed to publish from 1948 to 1955—novels, short stories, reportage, prose poems, diaries, and a variety of other genres that, even suffering from political censorship, ought to have formed the primary canon of Holocaust literature—was morally inassimilable to their intended audience in the west. They languish in obscurity to this very day."[3]

Since the end of the war, the vexed topic of Jewish collaboration with Nazis in their own destruction had been addressed in historical commissions, legal proceedings, and public discussion among the survivors.[4] The difference in the interpretation of Jewish collaboration in the 1952 debate highlighted the distance—experientially, geographically, and ideologically—between Leivick, who had made a successful career as a Yiddish poet and cultural figure in New York City, and Mark, who had escaped the Nazi onslaught in Poland in 1939 by fleeing to the Soviet Union. Since 1949 Mark had been the director of the Jewish Historical Institute in Warsaw, professor in history

FIGURE 5.1. H. Leivick, Toronto (undated). (Archives of the YIVO Institute for Jewish Research, New York)

at Warsaw University, and scholar of the Jewish resistance in the Warsaw and Bialystok ghettos. He was also a preeminent leader of Yiddish cultural work in communist Poland as director of Warsaw's Yidish-bukh publishing house.[5] Mark's prolific output as historian, editor of anthologies of Yiddish ghetto writing, and participant in the rebuilding of Jewish life in Poland was displayed in Yiddish, Polish, and Hebrew.[6]

Although the debate was resolved in Mark's favor, the real debate about Jewish collaboration never got underway. Leivick's glorification of the Jewish collective as *kedoyshim* (holy martyrs) remained posed against Mark's historical documentation and analysis of Jewish life in Nazi-occupied Poland, informed by his ideological commitment to the Communist Party. The documents Mark retrieved in the Oyneg Shabes archive revealed a complicated picture of internal Jewish factionalization in the ghettos and labor camps. Not until 1962, when debate about the role of the *Judenrat* was initiated by Hannah Arendt's *Eichmann in Jerusalem*, would Jewish American intellectuals begin to address the painful topic of Jewish collaboration during the Holocaust.[7]

What united Mark and Leivick, however, was their commitment to Yiddish culture. As the public faces of Yiddish culture in Warsaw and New York, they continued to build the Yiddish cultural infrastructure, writing and publishing and engaging in scholarly and popular debates. Mark published *Tvishn lebn un toyt* (Between Life and Death) in 1955, an anthology of fictional and autobiographical texts from the Ringelblum archives that included two texts by Yehoshue Perle. In a 1957 study, Mark examined "Jewish Life and Yiddish Literature in Poland, 1937–1957."[8] From the perspective of Jewish political and cultural life in Poland in the 1930s, in which Mark had been involved, he delineated the continuities and ruptures in Polish Yiddish culture before, during, and after the war. Particularly perceptive is Mark's analysis of how the Yiddish writers responded in writing to the radically altered war and postwar conditions. Mark emphasized that Yiddish

FIGURE 5.2. Bernard Mark, Warsaw (undated). (Courtesy Emanuel Ringelblum Jewish Historical Institute, Warsaw)

literary creativity in the ghettos and camps was an integral part of Jewish resistance. The study ended by praising the Polish communist state, which supported the flowering of Yiddish culture and education in postwar Poland, where the Yiddish theater attracted huge audiences. Compared to the main part of Mark's study about the Yiddish mass culture in prewar Poland, what remained in the mid-1950s was a communist-controlled Yiddish culture of limited scope.[9]

Stalwarts of Jewish national pride, such as Avrom Sutzkever and Yankev Glatshteyn, would abandon their sense of objectivity when presented with a compelling account of the last hours of a Gerer Hasid's monologue, ostensibly written in the Warsaw Ghetto on April 28, 1943. The text "*Yosl Rakover redt tsu got*" (Yosl Rakover Speaks to God) was published by Sutzkever in *Di goldene keyt* in 1954 as an authentic historical document. In an article in a French Yiddish journal the following year, the French Jewish writer Michal Borwicz documented that the text was in fact authored by the writer Zvi Kolitz (1912–2002), who had never set his foot in the Warsaw Ghetto, and published in a Buenos Aires Yiddish newspaper, *Di yidishe tsaytung*, on September 25, 1946. As a result, Sutzkever and Glatshteyn retracted their initial enthusiastic support for the document's historical authenticity.[10] As the Wilkomirski affair in the 1990s revealed on a global scale, the temptation to claim the authenticity of fictional texts as authored by "real" Holocaust victims was not always easy to resist. Again, mythology and historical documentation were pitted against each other in the Yiddish cultural leaders' response to how the Jews had confronted their destruction. The temptation to glorify the Jewish victims was strong among Yiddish writers and cultural leaders, often silencing the voices of historical realism originating within the monumental work of Emanuel Ringelblum's Oyneg Shabes archive.

In 1953 in Montreal, the Yiddish poet Melekh Ravitsh published a long poem, "*Di kroynung fun a yungn yidishn dikhter in amerike*" (The Coronation of a Young Yiddish Poet in America). Written in rhymed four-line stanzas and divided into thirteen chapters, the poem depicted the semi-autobiographical narrator's encounter with an American-born Jewish child named Yosef ben Yisroel. The main part of the poem is set in New York during World War II, which provides the background for the narrator and his protégé's vision of the future of world Jewry. Ravitsh made use of Theodor Herzl's renowned statement "If you will it, it is no dream" (*Oyb ir vilt—iz es nisht keyn maysele*) as the book's epigraph, while at the same time acknowledging the paradox of using Herzl's Zionist call to action in a poetic vision concerning the revival of

Yiddish culture in America. The poem insists that the future of world Jewry and the Jewish state are both dependent on the direction taken by the Jews of America, representing half of the world's Jews. American Jews could either turn their backs on their past and "sell their birthright for a pot of lentils" by embracing material comforts and assimilation or else they could revive Yiddish, the language of the martyrs (*loshn kedoyshim yidish*), in a manner similar to the resurrection of Hebrew (*loshn koydesh*) in the land of Israel.[11]

The narrator and his student, Yosef ben Yisroel, are visionaries pointing the way toward Yiddish cultural regeneration. The poem depicts Yosef ben Yisroel's quasi-messianic coronation at a Yiddish cultural event in honor of I. L. Peretz. Ravitsh's poetic alter ego represents the "world Jew" (*velt-Yid*) in America who, in the poem's final chapter, addresses his poet friends from prewar Warsaw: the Zionist Uri Zvi Greenberg in Israel and the communist Peretz Markish in Moscow. The latter, unbeknownst to Ravitsh in 1953, had been executed on Stalin's order the previous year, along with many other Soviet Jewish writers. With the exception of a description of Yosef's childhood in Harlem (where he falls in love with a black girl from the neighborhood) and references to the Lower East Side, the poem seems oddly distant from the city of New York. Even Jewish New York, the locus of the poem's visionary resurrection of the East European Jewish heritage, seems vague and intangible. Written in Montreal (where Ravitsh settled in the 1940s) and in Tel Aviv (during the years 1948 through 1953), "The Coronation of a Young Yiddish Poet in America" was inspired, Ravitsh wrote, by his conversations with two refugees from Vilna, the Yiddish poets Chaim Grade and Avrom Sutzkever.[12] In his epilogue, Ravitsh mentions that he originally intended to publish the poem in a bilingual Yiddish-English version: "The poem should first of all influence those—who do not yet, or not at all, know Yiddish in America."[13] However, Ravitsh did not accomplish this task, which accounts for the poem's invisibility for the vast majority of American Jewish readers. Yet even in English translation the poem's religiously colored language, messianic symbolism, Yiddish diasporism, and references to writers such as Uri Zvi Greenberg, Peretz Markish, and Dovid Edelshtat made it highly obscure to most Jewish Americans in 1953.

Ravitsh's poem, one of many Yiddish literary publications in the year 1953–54,[14] highlights the fact that Yiddish literature after 1945 was invigorated by a new vanguard of writers, almost all of them refugees and recent immigrants to postwar centers of Yiddish culture, particularly New York City. The most important of the Yiddish writers who settled in New York were Yitskhok Bashevis (1904–91; emigrated from Warsaw to New York in

1935), Aaron Zeitlin (1898–1973; emigrated from Warsaw to New York in 1940), Chaim Grade (1910–82; emigrated from Vilna [Vilnius] via Paris to New York, in 1948), Mordechai Strigler (1921–98; emigrated from Paris to New York in 1953), Y. Y. Trunk (1887–1961; emigrated from Warsaw to New York in 1941), and Kadya Molodovsky (1894–1974; emigrated from Warsaw to New York in 1935). These writers would be responsible for the first resurgence of Yiddish literary creativity in the post-Holocaust period. In New York City, the postwar capital of Yiddish letters, an old guard of Yiddish writers, among them H. Leivick, A. Leyeles, Yosef Opatoshu, Sholem Asch, and Yankev Glatshteyn, continued to embody the modernist sophistication of American Yiddish culture.[15] But with the arrival of writers such as Yitskhok Bashevis, Zeitlin, Molodovsky, Strigler, and Grade, a very different set of ideological baggage and literary agendas was brought into play.

As with previous waves of Jewish immigration to the United States, the post-Holocaust influx set the stage for a new phase in Yiddish literary history that reflected the specific worldviews and backgrounds of the émigrés. As noted by Hana Wirth-Nesher and Michael P. Kramer: "The history of the Jews in America is not linear. It unfolds as successive, largely discrete waves of immigration . . . and each produced a literature reflecting both its distinct heritage and its peculiar experience of acculturation."[16] Most of the new arrivals were marked by their experiences in the Nazi ghettos and camps or by the Soviet totalitarian system (or both). In the American Jewish world and the Yiddish community, these recent émigrés were foreign, exotic, and out of step with the zeitgeist of upward social mobility. Yet at the same time, as will be seen, permeable boundaries existed between Yiddish and Anglo-Jewish writing, and the year 1953–54 was distinguished, among other things, by the increased availability of Yiddish literature in English translation.

Nonetheless, the flowering of Yiddish culture in the post-Holocaust period was utterly incompatible with the concerns and goals of the majority of American Jews. According to Jewish historian Arthur Hertzberg, these concerns and goals were encapsulated in the important ideological role that the new Jewish state played for upwardly mobile American Jews. Israel offered a vision of renewal through a rejection of the East European Jewish past:

> But here was another, even deeper connection—hidden and never defined—between the new Israel and the post-war Jewish community in America. The Israelis were giving the Americans something even more precious than vicarious pride; they were offering

forgiveness. Israel was proclaiming that the Jewish past had been a mistake; one could feel proud, and not guilty, of starting a new life in defiance of Jewish memory. In the deep subconscious of American Jews, in mid-century, this message resonated: they, too, had the right to fresh beginnings. In the new land they, too, had the right to fashion their own new lives of success and well-being.[17]

Conversely, in poems, essays, and stories published during 1953–54, Yiddish writers evoked the lost world of their childhood; mourned the destruction of their people and homelands and the decline of their language; voiced their disillusionment with modernism and socialism; and offered their own particular visions of America and Israel. Perhaps the most remarkable feature of Yiddish writing in that year was its sheer scope, variety, and quality. It was almost as if the horrors of what had occurred in Europe had been transcended, as if Yiddish writing was now continuing under "normal circumstances." The past, however, was far from being forgotten or neglected, and in a variety of works published in 1953–54, the transformation of Yiddish culture into a culture of commemoration, past-oriented and inward-looking, was readily apparent.[18]

By the early 1950s, the immigration narrative had become passé as a consequence of the successful integration and upward mobility of second-generation American Jews. Stalin's anti-Semitic campaign of the late 1940s (culminating in the execution of leading Soviet Yiddish writers on August 12, 1952) resulted in a significant defection from the socialist cause among the shrinking group of Yiddish writers who had previously maintained their loyalty to the Soviet Union. Although New York City, as noted, had become the world capital of Yiddish letters following the destruction of the Jewish centers in Warsaw, Lodz, and Vilna, the Yiddish culture that had flourished there from the 1880s through the Depression had already shown signs of decline by the 1930s. In addition, the establishment of the State of Israel in 1948 shifted the focus of American Jews toward Israel and Hebrew. New York had four Yiddish dailies in 1950 (*Der tog, Morgn-Zhurnal, Forverts,* and *Morgn-Frayhayt*) with a total of 238,500 readers, alongside high-quality publishing houses with a stable annual production of Yiddish books and a growing Orthodox Yiddish-speaking population.[19] The infusion of tens of thousands of Holocaust survivors into the greater New York Jewish community added significant numbers of Yiddish speakers. Meanwhile, outside of New York, Yiddish publishing flourished in a number of other centers, notably Buenos Aires and Montreal, and starting in 1954, Tel Aviv, where a cultural infrastructure was in place and publishing costs were low.

Holocaust commemoration and testimony were the ground notes that sounded through Yiddish culture in 1953–54, in sharp contrast to the general lack of interest in discussing the Holocaust within the broader American Jewish community.[20] In a 1954 article in *Commentary*, the Yiddish modernist poet and Anglo-Jewish writer Judd L. Teller addressed the new conditions of the American Yiddish writer after the Holocaust. Teller argued that the American Yiddish writer would be able to reach a new generation of American readers only by confronting the radically new circumstances in all their starkness. Yiddish modernism, as inspired by Ezra Pound, T. S. Eliot, James Joyce, and Moyshe Leib Halpern, had reached a dead end. Replacing the American Yiddish writer's "overlong dalliance in the Lotus Land of non-sectarian *yidishkeyt* and his lack of concern with anything Yiddish but the tongue itself" was a new reality that brought such writers "face to face with the outside world" after the mass extermination of Yiddish-speakers in Eastern Europe. Teller concluded his article by stating:

> Few American Yiddish writers, barring refugees of the Nazi and postwar periods, are now under fifty. Many celebrated their fiftieth birthdays in the last several years and were hailed on these occasions as "young and promising" by elders on either side of sixty. . . . The depressing atmosphere of a convalescent home to which affluent children retire their perfectly healthy but aging parents hovers over American Yiddish letters today. These people, sound of mind and of sturdy constitution, are eager to make themselves useful, but few want their skills.[21]

In fact, this isolation from a readership and from contemporary cultural concerns was—for a brief moment—broken in the 1940s and early 1950s, when Yiddish writers took on a new mission of mourning and bearing witness to the catastrophe. This enabled them to reach American Jews with close ties to the destroyed communities in Europe. Yet these were mostly groups of survivors and their supporters in the Yiddish and Anglophone Jewish world. Among the larger American Jewish community, mainstream organizations adapted quickly to the new Cold War era and, rather than focusing on the six million victims of the Holocaust, oriented their political support and fund-raising efforts to the "free world's" fight against communism and to the support of Israel.[22]

In four articles published in the Yiddish literary journal *Di goldene keyt* in 1953–54, the critic A. Mukdoni summarized the state of Yiddish letters in America as being surprisingly vibrant despite the bleak prognosis for its future.[23] He compared Yiddish literature in America with a mortally ill patient who harbored an enormous will to survive. As Mukdoni pointed out, this was expressed in the variety of newly published Yiddish historical works, criticism, fiction, memorial (*Yizker*) books, and Holocaust memoirs. He was particularly impressed with the high publishing standards of these new works, which stood in sharp contrast to the cheap paper and poor binding typical of Yiddish works published prior to World War II. Despite all this, however, the undeniable fact was that most Yiddish writers were in their fifties and sixties, and there was no young generation in sight. As Mukdoni put it, "*der emigrant iz gekumen keyn Amerike mit zayne shraybers un er vet avek fun der velt mit zey*" (the immigrant came to America with his writers and he will leave the world with them).[24]

One of the books mentioned in Mukdoni's article was Shaye Miller's *In di shvartse pintelekh* (In the World of Letters), a short story collection published in 1953. One of the stories in this collection, "Reb Odem" (Mr. Adam), deals with the predicament of Yiddish writers in New York. This story is an American parallel to Chaim Grade's story "My Quarrel with Hersh Rasseyner," published the same year in English translation in *Commentary* (November 1953). The religious, cultural, and spiritual distance between these two stories—Grade's tale of a postwar encounter between two Vilna-born survivors in Paris, versus Miller's portrayal of two New York writers—is evident in their vastly different perspectives. Grade's characters, both of them ex-yeshiva students, argue about God, art, and the meaning of life in a richly textured Hebraized Yiddish filled with learned references to religious sources. In contrast, Miller's story is sprinkled with English words indicating the characters' close ties to American life. And whereas Grade's characters focus their conversation on the survival of the Jewish people and the collapse of Western civilization, Miller's characters talk about the threat of American consumer culture to their artistic integrity, using the opposition between "high literature" and *shund* (commercialism) as a springboard for the debate about possible artistic responses to the Holocaust.

One of the protagonists in Miller's story, Aron Libson, makes a comfortable living as a journalist who writes for the Yiddish press. He wants to help a writer friend, Shakhne Cohen, and suggests that the latter can make some money by writing Yiddish advertisements for kosher chicken soup. Cohen is suffering from writer's block. He has attempted to write about the

Holocaust, but lacking direct experiences to validate his words, he feels himself a liar; as a result, he has not written anything for six months: "*Sutzkever, Shtrigler, Shpigl, nokh a por, fun di vos zenen geven dortn, zey lignern nit, zey megn shraybn, afile shlekht shraybn megn zey, un lomir dir zogn, eynike fun zey shraybn gut, ober mir do, mir . . .*" (Sutzkever, Strigler, Shpiegl, and a couple of others among those who were there: they don't lie, they are allowed to write, even badly, and let me tell you, some of them write well, but we here, we . . .).[25] According to Cohen, Yiddish writers in America view the Holocaust in stark categories of heroes and villains; in the absence of a direct experiential perspective, their work is devoid of psychological insight and depth. Cohen argues that Yiddish storytelling should address the Holocaust by adding a fourth gift to the "three gifts" (*dray matones*) of I. L. Peretz's classic tale of martyrdom. Peretz's story is steeped in a traditional universe of premodern anti-Semitism that, according to Cohen, is insufficient to address the martyrdom of the Holocaust. However, in order to depict the man he calls "Reb Odem," that is, the human being who was annihilated in Auschwitz, something radically different is required: something even Yiddish survivor writers such as Sutzkever, Shpiegl, and Strigler can only approximate. Libson, passionately defending humanism, has the last word, secretly leaving a twenty-dollar bill for his unemployed friend, yet the story ends with a question mark. In Grade's story, on the other hand, the two protagonists, the secular Yiddish writer and his Orthodox friend from the *muser* yeshiva, embrace one another in a plea for Jewish rapprochement and cultural continuity in the aftermath of the Holocaust.

In 1953 Yankev Glatshteyn published a new collection of poems, *Dem tatns shotn* (My Father's Shadow). Both in style and in content, this collection is vastly different from the poet's previous artistic explorations of his inner self in kaleidoscopically crafted free-verse, in poems from his 1921 collection *Yankev Glatshteyn* through *Yidishtaytshn* (Yiddishmeanings, 1936). As its title indicates, the shadow of his father, who was murdered at Treblinka, now lingers over Glatshteyn's poetic universe. The proudly declared individuality of his first book has been subsumed by the collective task of mourning the destruction of East European Jewry. Glatshteyn's *inzikhist* vision of a Yiddish high modernism and a new secular *Yiddishkeit* has been crushed by history. The poem "Yidishkeyt" from this work of 1953 traces the end of his prophetic dream of a new secular *Yiddishkeit*—a new Great Synagogue—inspired by Peretz's vision of integrating Jewish values and content into a universal modernism. Instead, this dream has been reduced to language folklore, nourishment for old men's nostalgia:

נישט מער ווי אַ משורר ביסטו,
וואָס איז יוצא פֿאַר זיך
מיט אַן אמן אין כאָר פֿון אונטערגאַנג.
מיר האָבן זיך צופֿיל פֿאַרלאָזט אויפֿן זכּרון,
ביז ס'האָט טראָפּנווײַז פֿון אונדז
אַלץ אויסגעדענקט.
איצט זײַנען מיר פֿאַרבענקט
נאָך אַ זמרל, נאָך אַ גראַם,
נאָך אַן אויסגעוועפּטן טעם.
אַרום אונדזערע קעפּ דרייען מיר אַלע
אַ כּפּרה-האָן,
אָבער דער געפֿרעפּלטער תּוכן
גייט אונדז מער ניט אָן.
בענקשאַפֿט-ייִדישקייט איז אַ וויג-ליד פֿאַר זקנים,
וואָס טשקאַיען אײַנגעווייקטע חלה.
זאָלן מיר צושטעלן די ווייכע קרישקעס,
די ווערטער אויסגעלעבטע און הוילע,
מיר וואָס האָבן געחלומט
פֿון אַ נײַער אנשי כּנסת הגדולה?

You're no more than a choirboy,
content with an amen-chime
in a chorus of decline.
We staked too much on memory
till bit by bit it dripped
out of mind.
Now we pine
for a tune, for a rhyme,
for some stale savor.
We whirl the sacrificial hen
around our heads for sin's redress,
but the muttered essence
does not touch us.
Longingkeyt-Yidishkeyt is merely a lullaby for old men
whose gums knead soaked challah.
Should we provide the soft shreds,
the bare, the outlived words,
we who dreamed
of a new Great Convocation?[26]

The Yiddish poet has become an anonymous voice in the chorus of cultural decline (*untergang*). The poetic universe is inscribed in a religious framework of customs and folklore feeding the nostalgia of old men. The poet's role has been reduced to provide the memory shards of Yiddish words to its last surviving speakers. The visionary dream of poetic transformation and reevaluation of all values, Peretz's modernism of the poet's youth, has become yet another nostalgic gesture of a dying culture.

Reviewing Glatshteyn's book in *Di goldene keyt* (1954), the critic Yehoshua Rapoport in Melbourne, Australia, criticized the poet for burdening his poems' musicality and linguistic inventiveness with "moral messages." The exceptions, according to Rapoport, were the *Khurbn* and *Brastlaver* poems that Glatshteyn had introduced in his earlier volumes, *Gedenklider* (1943) and *Shtralndike yidn* (1946). As in Glatshteyn's long poem, *Yosl Loksh fun Khelm* (Yosl Loksh of Chelm), published in *Yidishtaytshn* and reprinted as a separate book in 1944, the persona of the Bratslaver (Nachman of Bratslav, 1772–1810, a Hasidic rabbi and great-grandson of the founder of Hasidism, Bal Shem Tov) enabled Glatshteyn to employ an alter ego from a Hasidic universe. In this voice he could address poetic, spiritual, and religious concerns detached from the destruction of European Jewry. While Hasidic masters had previously been employed as subjects in Yiddish poetry, Glatshteyn was the first to utilize the Bratslaver as a vehicle through which he expressed the soul-searching of modern people. The Bratslaver's colloquial voice conjured up an entire Eastern European Jewish rural world. In his review, Rapoport especially praised the poem *"Faran aza gekekhts vi hunger"* (Such a Dish as Hunger Exists) from the same collection, in which Glatshteyn self-critically exposed his poetry's commitment to collective mourning as a threat to his "hunger" for poetic innovation and renewal:

זינג מיר נישט קיין לידעלעך פֿון הונגער,
זאָג מיר נישט קיין טרויעריקע רייד,
דערצייל מיר נישט קיין מאָראַלישע מעשׂהלעך.
זיי טויגן אַלע אויף טויזנט כּפּרות.
קענסטו דאָס געזאַנג פֿון בויך-גרימעניש,
פֿון ליידיקע קישקעס,
דאָס געזאַנג פֿון דער פֿאַרלעדערטער צונג,
פֿון דעם עיפּושדיקן מויל,
וואָס זינן איינציק קמיעכץ
איז שלינגען אייגן שפּייעכץ.
מוחל, זינג מיר נישט קיין לידער.

> Don't sing me any songs of hunger,
> Speak no sad talk,
> Tell me no moral tales.
> They all are worth a thousand times nothing.
> Do you know the song of colic,
> Of empty intestines,
> The song of the leathery tongue,
> Of the stinking mouth,
> Whose only nourishment,
> Is to swallow its own spit.
> No thanks, don't sing me any songs.[27]

The distance from the actual, lived hunger experienced by Jews in the ghettos and the camps highlights the poet's empty words, his *moralishe mayselekh* (moral tales). The self-ironic approach informing the poet's declared inability to voice the suffering of Jews in the Holocaust serves to tone down the pathos of the best of Glatshteyn's *Khurbn* poems.

Avrom Sutzkever's "*Griner akvarium*" (Green Aquarium), published in 1953–54 in *Di goldene keyt,* bears out Miller's point in "Reb Odem" about the experiential gulf between Holocaust survivors and their American observers. When Sutzkever was in the Vilna Ghetto, he experienced poetry as a means of defying death; he truly believed that it had the power to keep him alive. He would turn this experience into a literary credo that made his life dependent on his ability to create lasting art. Sharing the fate of most Vilna Jews up until their murder in Ponar, however, Sutzkever was caught in the same quandary as the Yiddish writers in New York. Both he and Glatshteyn insisted that their poetry was a means of rescuing the shards of a civilization cut down in its prime. But Sutzkever's experiences in the Vilna Ghetto and partisan groups suffused his poetry with urgency and a richness of metaphor that Glatshteyn's meditation on memory and loss rarely matched.

Irving Howe recalled in his memoir, *A Margin of Hope* (1982), that "one day in 1953" he received a note from the Yiddish poet Eliezer Greenberg, which initiated a partnership "in the editing-and translating-Yiddish business." This collaboration resulted in the publication of six collections of Yiddish prose and poetry in English translation during the next two decades. While working on their first anthology, *A Treasury of Yiddish Stories,* published in 1954, Greenberg showed Howe a story by Yitskhok Bashevis (Isaac Bashevis Singer published his Yiddish stories under this name). Howe then persuaded Saul Bellow, a native Yiddish speaker, to translate the story into

English. During a three- or four-hour session, Bellow translated sentence by sentence while Greenberg read the story in the original. Howe sent Bellow's translation to *Partisan Review* editor Philip Rahv, who had never heard of Yitskhok Bashevis. The story "Gimpel the Fool" was accepted for publication and became Singer's entry into the American literary world. Howe's retrospective account emphasizes the indifference of American Jewish writers "to the presence of a vibrant Yiddish culture that could be found, literally and symbolically, a few blocks away."[28] The invisibility of Yiddish culture in the eyes of New York Jewish writers is similar to the observation made by the Polish poet Czeslaw Milosz in his memoir, *Native Realm* (1968), that, while he participated in Polish cultural life in Vilna in the 1930s, he knew nothing about Yung-Vilne, a cadre of young Yiddish writers in the Jewish part of town. It was only after Milosz immigrated to the United States in the 1950s that he discovered Yiddish literature in Howe and Greenberg's 1954 anthology.

Yiddish literature, as packaged for an American readership in Howe and Greenberg's introduction to *A Treasury of Yiddish Stories*, emphasized the collective ethos of East European Jewry as a means of glorifying the anti-heroic, powerless East European Jew. As in Abraham Joshua Heschel's idealized depiction of "the inner world of the Jews in Eastern Europe," the subtitle of his *The Earth Is the Lord's* (1950), Mark Zborowski and Elizabeth Herzog's anthropological study *Life Is with People* (1952), and Leivick's glorification of the victims of the Holocaust in his debate with Bernard Mark, Howe and Greenberg intended to erect a monument to an organic, otherworldly, and morally superior Jewish community in Eastern Europe. This literary ethos, "characterized by attitudes we should look to with admiration, perhaps even yearning,"[29] was meant to be a utopian alternative to the Americanization and memory loss that characterized second- and third-generation Jewish Americans. To bring this point home, Howe gave vent to this rhetorical outburst: "Because of its own limitations, the world of the East European Jews made impossible the power-hunger, the pretensions to aristocracy, the whole mirage of false values that have blighted Western intellectual life. The virtue of powerlessness, the power of helplessness, the company of the dispossessed, the sanctity of the insulted and the injured—these, finally, are the great themes of Yiddish literature."[30]

Fortunately, the stories selected for the anthology contradict this sanitized image of Yiddish literature. The "power-hunger" is on full display in the stories by Isaac Meir Weissenberg and I. J. Singer; the pretension to aristocracy has a long, distinguished career in Yiddish storytelling, as is evident in the stories of I. L. Peretz, Sholem Asch, and Chaim Grade. "The whole mirage of false values that have blighted Western intellectual life" is a central theme of Sholem Aleichem's, Grade's and Dovid Bergelson's stories, and the list goes on. Finally, "the insulted and the injured," as depicted in Jonah Rosenfeld's "Competitors" and I. B. Singer's "Gimpel the Fool," raise troubling questions about sexual abuse and economical exploitation of Jews by Jews. To their credit, Howe and Greenberg included these and other stories, thereby presenting a literary image of East European Jewry that is much more complex than their own critical introduction.[31]

Language provides a key to understanding the year 1953–54 in Jewish American literature. To write in Yiddish in the 1950s was to address a segment of the Jewish population that was particularly receptive to the Holocaust. In contrast, by writing in English, Jewish writers were mostly signifying their downplaying of Jewish concerns and literary models. This division by language among American Jewish writers was dramatically accentuated during and after the Holocaust.[32] A good example is Saul Bellow's breakthrough novel, *The Adventures of Augie March*, published in 1953. It is an American rags-to-riches story; the famous opening lines state as much: "I am an American, Chicago born—Chicago, that somber city—and go at things as I have taught myself, free-style, and will make a record in my own way: first to knock, first admitted; sometimes an innocent knock, sometimes a not so innocent."[33]

Bellow made the urban environment a central trope of his work. Jewishness became a metaphor, a state of consciousness or a spiritual vantage point from which he would depict his American Jewish roots in Chicago.[34] Bellow's novel was an American *Bildungsroman*, a mid-twentieth-century successor to Mark Twain's *Huckleberry Finn*, in which Augie March and his family were only indirectly characterized by a Jewish sensibility or Jewish cultural references. A brief review of *Augie March* appeared in A. Mukdoni's survey of Yiddish culture in America in *Di goldene keyt* (1953). In a passage that is indicative of Yiddish writers' disparaging attitudes toward Jewish writers in English, Mukdoni concludes: "[The book] presents a gallery of well portrayed Jewish characters, but these characters could as well have been Italians, Greeks etc. . . . I think it is an empty book, a naked book. . . . For the world it is a Jewish book, but like all 'Jewish' books in English, it will disappear in the great ocean of English books and will be listed in the registry of English literature."[35]

In a 2001 interview with Jonathan Rosen, Bellow shed interesting light on the state of his mind while writing *Augie March* in Paris:

> Bellow recalled writing "The Adventures of Augie March"—the grand freewheeling novel that made his reputation—in Paris in the late 1940s. Holocaust survivors were everywhere . . . and, as a Yiddish speaker, he had access to the terrible truths they harbored. But, as Bellow put it, he was not in the mood to listen. "I wanted my seven-layer cake." . . . He did not wish to burden his writing at that early moment in his career with the encumbering weight of Jewish history.[36]

I. B. Singer's breakthrough as an American writer was made possible by the appearance of a new generation of New York writers who redefined American prose in the late 1940s and early 1950s. Thus Singer, the obscure fabulist of dark tales from the forgotten past of Polish Jewry, avoided the not-so-unlikely fate of being reduced to a footnote in the annals of Jewish American literature. Singer first won notice with his chronicle of prewar Polish Jewry, *The Family Moskat* (1950), which was modeled on his older brother I. J. Singer's realist novels such as *The Brothers Ashkenazi* (1936). Then Saul Bellow, as previously recounted, translated his story "*Gimpl tam*," which was published as "Gimpel the Fool" in *Partisan Review* eight years after it had originally appeared in the Yiddish journal *Tsukunft* in 1945. This story catapulted Singer into the mainstream of American letters, appearing as it did at an auspicious time for Jewish American literature.

The 1950s saw the emergence of African-American, Jewish, and Beat writers, all of whom departed from the dominant social realism of the 1930s.[37] Like the "invisible man" in Ralph Ellison's eponymous novel of 1952, Saul Bellow's *Adventures of Augie March*, J. D. Salinger's Holden Caulfield in *Catcher in the Rye* (1951), and Jack Kerouac's Sal Paradise in *On the Road* (1956), Gimpel the Fool was a *shlemiel* and a *luftmentsh* who lived on the margins of society. Like these up-and-coming American writers, I. B. Singer—in colorful, colloquial language—reported from a hitherto unknown world. In his stories of the 1950s, the nihilistic vision of mass psychosis and the triumph of evil that were present in some of his early works, notably *Satan in Goray* (1935; translated into English, 1955), were balanced by humor, compassion, and sometimes even hope. The cuckolded Gimpel leaves behind his life as a baker and head of a household. He becomes a wandering storyteller, abandoning his family's static world for mobility and self-discovery. As with the works by Bellow, Ellison, Salinger, and Kerouac, self-creation in monologue form took precedence over social realism and mimesis.

While joining forces with the American literary vanguard of the 1950s, Singer began tapping the humorous, farcical potential of the classical Yiddish writer Sholem Aleichem. In lifting his stories out of the gloomy realm of shtetl dwellers fighting their collective demons, he suffused them with a postmodern, skeptical sensibility removed from the characters' social-historical conditioning. Gimpel, the "Little Shoemakers," Jacques Kohn in the story "A Friend of Kafka," and Singer's semi-autobiographical characters were direct descendants of the shtetl inhabitants Sholem Aleichem had depicted a generation earlier in his Kasrilevke stories. While most Yiddish writers collectively mourned the murdered European Jews by keeping the memory of them alive in mimetic replicas of a destroyed world, Singer maintained his literary independence and deepened his imaginary vision. As a storyteller and novelist, he created work that was eminently translatable. In contrast, the Yiddish poets Yankev Glatshteyn, Avrom Sutzkever, Aaron Zeitlin, Kadya Molodovsky, and Chaim Grade contributed dirges (*kines*) to the modern Book of Lamentations that to this day remain mostly unknown outside Yiddish circles. And although Grade's stories and novels situated in Vilna were destined to become classic chronicles of the split between secular and religious forces among Lithuanian Jewry, a far larger and broader readership preferred Singer's postmodern tales, whose turbulent plots teemed with the action of postwar America in the grips of radical social, cultural, and spiritual transformation.

In his review of Yankev Pat's *Shmuesn mit yidishe shrayber* (Conversations with Yiddish Writers, 1954), the Yiddish poet A. Leyeles observed that "seven Yiddish writers of the fourteen with whom Pat conducted his interviews (now collected in a book) have left the land of the living. The conversations took place recently.... The seven are: Dovid Ignatoff, Yosef Opatoshu, Mani Leib, Tsivion, Avrom Reisen, Shmuel Niger, H. Royzenblat. That is a huge part of the Yiddish world of letters in America, a massive part of our world literature."[38] The other seven writers included in the book were similarly significant to Yiddish literature: Dovid Einhorn, Yankev Glatshteyn, A. Leyeles, Y. Y. Trunk, H. Leivick, Itsik Manger, and Y. Y. Schwartz. The longest conversation was the one with H. Leivick, who praised the variety and richness of contemporary Yiddish literary works, including those by younger writers saved from the Holocaust (Mordechai Strigler, Rokhl Korn, Avrom Sutzkever, Isaiah Shpiegl). Despite the many new Yiddish titles on his desk, Leivick summarized the Yiddish literary state of affairs as "the sadness of being the last." For Leivick, the year 1953–54 was characterized by a surplus of high-quality Yiddish publications by middle-aged or older writers and a rapid decline in readership. Pat's conversation with Leivick also took stock of Yiddish culture prior to the Holocaust. This retrospective approach is evident as well in Leivick's Walt Whitman–inspired tribute, "*Tsu Amerike*" (To America, 1954), in which he paraphrased his own poem *Yidishe poetn* (Yiddish Poets, 1932–40):

וואָס, נאָך מיט דרײַסיק יאָר צוריק, האָב איך אונטער די הימלען דײַנע
געטרויערט טיף אין זיך, געקלאָגט זיך אַז איך טראָג מײַן ייִדיש ליד
אין אַנגסט, דורך דײַנע גאַסן און דורך דײַנע סקווערן,
פֿאַרקלאַמערט צווישן מײַנע צײן, ווי ס׳טראָגט אַ קאַץ אַן עלנטע
ווי די קעצעלעך אירע, זוכנדיק פֿאַר זיי אַ רו-אָרט אין אַ קעלער ווו;—
אַז ווען איך טראַכט נאָר וועגן מײַנע ברידער—ייִדישע פּאָעטן—
נעמט זייער גורל ווי אַ קלאַמער מיך אַרום, און ס׳ווילט זיך תּפֿילה טאָן פֿאַר זיי,
פֿאַר זייער מזל,— און גראָד דעמאָלט ווערן אַלע ווערטער שטום.
אוודאי איז עס מײַן שולד, און ניט דײַן, אויף הײַנט, ווען נאָכן אָפּגאַנג
פֿון יענע דרײַסיק יאָר טוט טרויערן מײַן האַרץ אויף ס׳נײַ עלעגיש
וואָס הײַנט, נאָך מער ווי ווען עס איז, האָט ס׳בייזע מזל
צעשלײַדערט אַלע ייִדישע פּאָעטן איבער נײַ-סיבירן,
און אונדזער פֿלאַטערדיקע דיכטער-שיף פֿאַריאָגט אין תּהום פֿון שטורעמס,
אין תּהום פֿון שטורעמס אויך אויף דײַנע וואַסערן, אַמעריקע,

    That thirty years ago I mourned under your skies
    Deep inside me, lamented that I carry my Yiddish song
    In fear, through your streets and through your squares,
    Clenched in my teeth, as a forsaken cat might carry
    Her kittens, in search of a cellar, a place of rest;—
    That when I think of my brothers—
       Yiddish poets—their destiny
    Embraces me like a clamp, I want to pray for them,
    For their lot—and then all words grow mute.
    Certainly, it is my fault, not yours, when even now
    After thirty years have passed my heart mourns again,
    An elegy on how, now more than ever, the evil lot
    Has scattered all Yiddish poets over New-Siberias
    And chased our trembling poets' ship into an abyss of storms,
    Into an abyss of storms on your waters too, America,[39]

In his poem *Yidishe poetn*, Leivick had used the metaphor of the mute tongue (*zayn shtume tsung*) to express his sense of alienation, poverty, and disgrace. The muteness originated in the wretched immigrant life of New York, in which the writing of Yiddish poetry was a quixotic activity as insignificant as the fertility of cats. In bearing witness to the "New-Siberias" in his hymn "*Tsu Amerike*," Leivick extends the muteness (*vern ale verter shtum*) to Yiddish writers all over the world in the aftermath of the Holocaust. The poem's Whitmanesque diction and rambling, expanding style indicates the Yiddish poet's debt to America, its landscape, mythology, poetry, and, most important, his sense of safety and distance separated by an ocean from the recent "storms" that had eradicated a third of the Jewish people in Europe.

Staunchly secular Yiddish writers such as Glatshteyn and Molodovsky used religious metaphors in their response to the catastrophe without reclaiming the God of Israel or becoming *bal tshuves* (newly religious). Like the survivor writers, most of who came from traditional religious backgrounds, the New York Yiddish writers employed religious vocabulary and archetypes in a secular manner. Irving Howe summed up Glatshteyn's use of God imagery in his Holocaust poetry: "The God that figures in these poems is hardly the omnipotent one of traditional belief, yet neither is he a mere construct of modern religiosity; he is an indestructible presence in Jewish life beyond acceptance or denial. 'The God of my disbelief is magnificent'— this is as far Glatstein could go in reconciliation."[40]

Mani Leib, a founding member of the early twentieth-century Yiddish poetic group *Di yunge*, wrote Yiddish sonnets during the last twenty years of his life. They were published posthumously a couple of years after his death in 1953. In the poem *A floym* (A Plum), Mani Leib conveys the bliss of an older married couple:

אין קילן אָוונט האָט דער בעל-הבית
פֿון בוים אַ ריפֿע פֿלוים אָראָפּגעריסן
אין איינעם מיטן בלאַט, און אויסגעביסן
די טווייק בלויע הויט. האָט פֿון זײַן שלאַס

דער שלאָפֿעדיקער זאַפֿט געטאָן אַ גאָס
מיט קילן שוים. און צו פֿאַרשליסן
איר גאַנצן זאַפֿט—אַ טראָפּן ניט פֿאַרגיסן—
האָט ער פֿאַמעלעך, ווי מען טראָגט אַ כּוס

מיט װמן, אין ביידע פֿולע הענט די פֿלױמען
געבראכט דער װײב און אײדל צוגעטראָגן
צו אירע ליפּן. האָט זי מיט אַ ליבן

"אַ דאַנק"—פֿון זײנע הענט גענומען נאָגן
די פֿלױמען. ביז אין די הענט איז אים פֿאַרבליבן
די הױט, דאָס ביינדל און צעקלעקטער שױם.

In the cool evening, the good provider plucked
From off a tree a fully ripened plum,
Still with its leaf on, and bit into some
Of its dewy, blue skin. From there, unlocked,

The long-slumbering juice came leaping up,
Foaming and cool. In order to make use
Of every single drop of all that juice,
Slowly, as one walks bearing a full cup

Of wine, he brought a double handful of plum,
To his wife, and gently raised it to her mouth,
Whereupon she could lovingly begin—

"Thanks," she said—to gnaw the plum from out
Of his hands, until those hands held only skin,
And pit, and flecks of overbrimming foam.[41]

William Shakespeare's *Sonnets* had been translated into Yiddish in 1953 by Berl Lapin, and the influence of the English sonnet form is present in *A floym*'s tightly rhymed stanzas. The classical meter and rhyme of the fourteen-line sonnet are employed to convey marital bliss in a utopian paradise. Unlike Adam and Eve, who ate the forbidden fruit and were banished from Eden, the *balebos* (the good provider) picks a ripe plum so full of juice and aroma that it seems like a cup filled with wine. He hands it to his wife, who gratefully thanks him for the plum and eats it until nothing but the last shred and the pit remain. The married couple performs a ritualized sanctification of the wine, the *kidesh*, fulfilling the command to be thankful for eating and drinking but without saying the religiously prescribed blessing. The man and woman in the poem have consecrated the act of eating the plum and drinking its wine in a secularized manner. The rhyme *balebos* in the first line and *kos* in the eighth line in the poem's center—the only words of Hebrew origin in the entire sonnet—highlights the essence of religious observance, which is subverted in the sonnet's secularized form of Jewish ritual. This sonnet exemplifies the pinnacle of Mani Leib's poetic achievement through the fusion of secular and religious modalities in a classical poetic form.

The sonnet was part of the voluminous assortment of life-writing, fiction, and poetry that highlighted the centrality of Peretz's literary heritage for Yiddish culture after the Holocaust. The centrality of Peretz was stressed in Eliezer Greenberg's article *"Di yidishe literatur un di literatur af english,"* appearing in *Di goldene keyt* in 1954, which addressed the growing number of Yiddish works in English translation. Acknowledging the importance of making Yiddish literature available in "the most widely spoken and read language in the world," he ended the article with a quote from Peretz, "whose vision for Yiddish literature today is as relevant as when he first wrote it [in the early twentieth century]."[42] Greenberg paid tribute to Peretz's vision of humanism and socialism as the ideological drive behind Yiddish culture in America.

In a volume published by L. M. Shteyn Farlag in Chicago in 1953, the critic Borekh Rivkin's contribution to Yiddish letters was assessed by a number of leading Yiddish critics.[43] Nakhmen Mayzil presented a succinct evaluation of Rivkin's work (dated July 1953); the former was an accomplished Yiddish critic and previous editor of the prestigious literary journal *Literarishe bleter* in interwar Warsaw. Mayzil pointed out that, except for the two leading critics Bal Makhshoves and Shmuel Niger, Yiddish criticism had been following in the footsteps of Yiddish writers rather than establishing new artistic visions and paradigms. Rivkin (1883–1945) was an exception in his attempt to delineate the main trends and hidden forces at work in shaping Yiddish literature.[44]

Rivkin sought to map the big picture of Yiddish literary creativity in America from a prescriptive point of view by examining what made Yiddish literature different from non-Jewish literature. Rivkin used the critical tools that Peretz had pioneered in the first decade of the twentieth century in his attempt to straddle the Yiddish writer's openness to non-Jewish influences and the excavation of his own cultural and historical heritage. Rivkin based his critical principles on Peretz's belief that *"literatur zol toyre zayn farn folk tsu lebn mit ir"* (literature should be the Torah according to which the people live).[45] As Mayzil noted, Rivkin's critical philosophy paralleled that of Ahad Ha'am's vision for a Hebrew spiritual center in Palestine: "B. Rivkin wanted to turn Yiddish literature into a spiritual center that would replace the physical, material territory."⁴⁶ Rivkin's concept of *kemoy-teritorie* (quasi-territory) was supposed to replace religious law for a new generation of secular Yiddish speakers. In America cultural openness and freedom would make it possible to start from scratch "*fun onheyb on*" at a fundamental distance "*meeyver leyam*" (on the other side of the ocean) from the old-style Yiddishism in Eastern Europe—with its dependence on the traditional religious world—driven by the impulse to "*ibergeshribn dem altn yidishn seyfer*" (rewrite the old Jewish holy book).⁴⁷

One of several inconsistencies in Rivkin's critical thinking, however, was his belief that Yiddish culture in an open, democratic America, whose commercial infrastructure was determined by capitalistic market forces, would be able to further an ideologically driven Yiddish culture under the banner of Peretz. As Rivkin acknowledged in his essay written right before his death in 1945, the gulf between Yiddish literature and the American-born Jewish youth was unbridgeable for the simple reason that the new generation was completely immersed in American culture in English. When American-born Jews sought out Jewish writing, they had to turn to Anglophone works, including Yiddish literature in translation, as typified by Howe and Greenberg's anthology. Peretz's call for the ingathering of spiritual and cultural treasures in a distinctly Jewish mode and written only in Yiddish made sense during his lifetime, when several hundred thousand potential Yiddish readers had recently left traditional observance behind. Rivkin's attempt to resurrect a Peretzian credo for American Jewish readers, on the other hand, was clearly doomed to failure. Yiddishists like Mayzil and others applauded Rivkin's Yiddishist agenda in the aftermath of the Holocaust, lauding it for articulating "*hemshekh*" (continuation) and spiritual resistance in response to the prospect of Yiddish cultural decline. Like Sutzkever and other ghetto writers who rallied for spiritual awakening and resistance during and following the Holocaust, Rivkin and his Yiddishist supporters in America maintained their belief in Peretz's credo. Dan Miron sums up the quixotic agenda of Yiddishism in the early 1950s:

> [T]he assumption, that Yiddish being the language of the folk could become the vehicle for a modern, humanist Jewish culture that would retain its autonomous existence without a territorial basis, both in Eastern Europe and in the centers of Jewish immigration in the West, was clearly undermined by unstoppable historical processes. As much as Yiddishists clung to it, attempting to shore it up by chains of schools with Yiddish as the language of instruc-

tion, political parties, and youth organizations, their upbeat verbiage of self-encouragement sounded more and more like whistling in the dark.[48]

The cultural and ideological distance between Yiddish writers and their American-born sympathizers, such as Irving Howe and Isaac Rosenfeld (who translated Sholem Aleichem for *A Treasury of Yiddish Stories*), was rapidly widening. Yiddish writers pledged their artistic careers to keeping alive the memory of the Eastern European Jewish heritage, while closing ranks with fellow writers in Yiddish centers worldwide. In contrast, the vast majority of Jewish Americans and Israelis were preoccupied with "making it" in the English and Hebrew cultural environments, both of which pushed Yiddish and the Holocaust to the margin. In Israel the Zionist promise of reclaiming the biblical land and reviving Hebrew as a spoken language set the daily agenda. In the United States the remaining educational, racial, and social impediments to Jews' equal participation in the American dream were significantly reduced in the 1950s. The process of fully embracing America as the new homeland was realized in the white suburbia that became home to an increasing number of Jews.[49]

A symposium titled "*Yisroel, der yidisher shrayber, un di yidishe velt*" (Israel, the Yiddish Writer, and the Yiddish World), convened by the organization of Yiddish writers and journalists in Israel, took place in Tel Aviv during Passover 1954. Of the three main speakers—Dovid Pinski, M. Gros-Zimerman, and Avrom Sutzkever—the last one provided a succinct overview of the state of Yiddish culture. Sutzkever emphasized the importance of "*ahaves erets-yisroel un ahaves yidishe literatur*" (love of the Land of Israel and love of Yiddish literature) in the Diaspora.[50] Predicting that the current political repression of Yiddish culture in the Soviet Union would be lifted, resulting in a resurgence of literary talent (which actually occurred in the late 1950s), he conveyed his experience from visiting Yiddish centers in South Africa and Argentina. In those communities Yiddish literature and Israel provided equally important rallying points for Jewish identity and continuity. Absent from Sutzkever's lecture was any mention of New York, the main Yiddish cultural center, indicating the widening gulf between Jewish American culture (particularly in English) and the reconstituted network of Yiddish cultural centers worldwide.

The sense of being the "last of the Mohicans" was deeply ingrained among the small group of Yiddish writers who remained in perpetual exile from their Eastern European Jewish homelands. The new phase in Yiddish literary history after 1945 was primarily shaped by European refugees and immigrants to the Americas and the Land of Israel who brought with them a deep skepticism about political ideologies, modernism, and aestheticism. Writers such as Chaim Grade, Isaac Bashevis Singer, Avrom Sutzkever, and Aaron Zeitlin continued their artistic quest into the collective archetypes and conflicts of Eastern European Jewry while refining and deepening their artistic medium. Yiddish literature in 1953–54 expressed the tension between commemoration of and confrontation with the age-old Ashkenazic civilization in Europe that, even prior to the catastrophe, was rapidly disintegrating as a result of modernity, secularization, and migration. Yiddish writers were coming to terms with the debris of the political, religious, and cultural ideologies of interwar Warsaw and Vilna; for some in Nazi-occupied Europe and the Soviet Union, these had defined their artistic beginnings.

While the prognosis for the future looked grim, because of the abandonment of Yiddish by native-born Israelis and American Jews, a cadre of exceptionally talented writers hailing from Eastern Europe held out promise for the continuation of secular Yiddish culture in the "advanced phase of its decline."[51] A great sense of mission propelled the witnesses to the Nazi and Soviet communist atrocities in the 1930s and 1940s, including a group of Yiddish writers, to sustain the creative flame by contributing to the effort to forge a new link in the Golden Chain. The Silver Age of Yiddish culture post-1945 tended to be more immune from outside influences, more self-reflective and introspective, and therefore more out of touch with the concerns of the larger Jewish worlds than had been the case in Peretz's era. However, Peretz's and Rivkin's cultural agenda still propelled Yiddishists to work tirelessly for the implementation of the Yiddish cultural "quasi-territory." As a whole, Yiddish culture in 1953–54 was alive and well, unanimously addressing the ramifications of the Holocaust and grappling with its consequences.

PART III: YIDDISH LETTERS IN NEW YORK

6

A POETICS OF RETRIEVAL AND LOSS

Aaron Zeitlin and Yankev Glatshteyn

> Can we imagine the tragedy of writers—H. Leyvik, Jacob Glatshteyn, A. Leyeles, others—who felt such a mission of beginning in their own lifetime and stood before the abyss of the end, losing first their readership, then their source, their people in Europe (along with their own parents), and finally the very language that they had made into such a fine instrument?
>
> Benjamin and Barbara Harshav, *American Yiddish Poetry: A Bilingual Anthology* (1986)[1]

During the war and in its immediate aftermath, two mid-career Yiddish poets created powerful verse that responded, urgently and with a raw edge, to the unfolding genocide in Europe. Yankev Glatshteyn, trailblazer of the *inzikhist* movement in New York, where he had resided since 1914, published two books of poetry, *Gedenklider* (Poems of Remembrance, 1943) and *Shtralndike yidn* (Illuminated Jews, 1946). The titles indicate a turn toward the past, commemorating the memory of the martyred Jews. Aaron Zeitlin, a Hebrew and Yiddish poet in interwar Warsaw and a neo-orthodox modernist, wrote a series of poems in Cuba, where he had arrived as a refugee from Poland in 1939. After settling in New York in 1940, he collected the poems he had written during and after the war in the two-volume *Gezamlte lider* (Collected Poems, 1947), and partly revised them in the 1967 *Lider fun khurbn un lider fun gloybn* (Poems of the Holocaust and Poems of Faith).

The works of these two poets indicate the major trend in Yiddish culture during the first years after the *khurbn:* raw, uncensored rage against Germany, the model of Emancipation, Enlightenment, and *Kultur* for several generations of Yiddish writers. Simultaneously, the two poets began the process of mourning and commemoration. This frequently took the form of autobiographical recollection in a move toward a purified, idealized poetics of Yiddish. In this chapter, I will chart these parallel trends in the poetry that Glatshteyn and Zeitlin wrote in the 1940s, and delineate how the commemorative impulse increasingly dominated their poetry in the 1950s, when they contributed to the critic Avrom Tabatshnik's project *Di shtim fun yidishn poet* (The Voice of the Yiddish Poet). As major poets, Glatshteyn and Zeitlin encompassed a wide spectrum of Yiddish culture's secular and religious compass, which continued to refract through their work after the Holocaust.

New York's Jewish world after World War II is vividly portrayed in Abraham Joshua Heschel's 1948 review of Zeitlin's *Gezamlte lider:*

> We still feel the blow to our head. It feels like the heavens above us have fallen in chunks. We have not yet grasped the disaster that has befallen us. We are still before the funeral—still prepared to sit *shiva,* confounded, confused and petrified.
>
> How do we endure this? How do we bear the pain? Are we idiots? Are we base? When I think of my people, burned and cremated in Poland, a shudder courses through my veins. I feel the nails of insanity.
>
> I choke on pain and drive away from myself the picture, the sound, the woe. No, one cannot drive away an ocean, one can bury oneself in a hole, in a pit of forgetfulness.
>
> How worthless is such a life in hiding. The sound of the ocean roars in the distance, there is nowhere to run away. Our misfortune is [as] large as God. We mask the sound of the shudder with cheap noisemakers. Talk is a waste of time, we won't experience any good fortune (and even saying these words is foolish). We have Tisha B'Av all year and yet—we put on Purim plays.[2]

Heschel's poetic diagnosis of the emotional volatility in response to the *khurbn* among the Jews with the closest ties to the annihilated Jewish communities provides a snapshot of the Yiddish zeitgeist in New York, 1948. Heschel (1907–72), a newly arrived refugee in America, used his review of Zeitlin's poetry to highlight his criticism of secular Jewish culture, and what he describes as its worship of European art and literature. The demand of the day, according to Heschel, was for Jews to return to the sources of religious *Yiddishkeit* (Jewishness) of Ashkenaz. Heschel had paid tribute to the latter, in his lecture at the YIVO Institute of Jewish Research in January 1945 titled "*Di mizrekh eyropeisher tkufe in der yidisher geshikhte*" (The Eastern European Period in Jewish History), which was published in an English version as *The Earth Is the Lord's* in 1950. In the review, Heschel characterized Zeitlin as an authentic religious poet, quoting from "*Nokh a kleyne poeme, geshribn 1946: Vegn frau Hilde un Her von Goethe*" (Yet Another Small Poem: About Mrs Hilde and Herr von Goethe, 1946). In the poem, the poet rejects his former glorification of European literature and art, including Goethe, the icon of the German Enlightenment:

איך, ווידעה, בין געוועזן א ליטעראט אין ווארשע,
וואָס האָט געגלויבט אזוי ווי אלע
אין דעם נעמלעכן געטע און אין נאָך אזעלכע געניאלע עגאיסטן.
נישט געוווּסט האָב איך, ווי קליין דער מהלך איז פֿון פֿאוסט ביז פֿויסט,
פֿון געטע'ס איבערמענטש צום אונטערמענטש און צו די היטלעריסטן.
וואָס וואָלט געהיימראט געטע געטאָן אין היטלער'ס צייטן?
וואָלט געסעסן אין ווײמאר און געקוקט פֿונדערווײטן
ווי זײנע דײטשן פֿאַרגאזן מײנע מיליאנען.
ער, וואָס האָט זיך גערעדט פֿון ליטעראטור מיט נאפאלעאנ'ען,
וואָלט צו היטלער'ן גערעדט מן הסתּם
מיט א געשליפֿן-טיפֿזיניקן עפיגראם.
ס'וואָלט אים אפֿילו נישט א צוק געטאָן א ברעם—
קאן דען א געטע מקדש מיין דעם שם?
קאן ער זיך מקריב זײן? אזעלכע קענען נאָר דיכטן,
בעת די היטלערס פֿארניכטן.
אָ, די גרויסע עגאיסטן, וואָס מאכן די ווערטער!
עשו, ווי זע איך אצינד דעם פֿארבינד
צווישן דײנע וואָרט-מענטשן און דײנע מערדער!

As for me, I was a man of letters in Warsaw,
who believed like all the others
in the same Goethe and in other such brilliant egoists.
I did not know how short the distance is between Faust and fist,
From Goethe's "uebermensch" to the "untermensch" and to the Hitlerites.
What would privy councillor Goethe have done in Hitler's time?

> He would have sat in Weimar and looked from a distance
> How his Germans gassed my millions.
> He who spoke of literature with Napoleon,
> Would probably have spoken to Hitler
> With a polished profound epigram.
> Not even an eyebrow would have twitched—
> Can then a Goethe sanctify the Name of God?
> Can he sacrifice himself? Such people can only create poetry,
> While the Hitlerites annihilate.
> Oh, the big egoists, who make the words!
> Esau, how I now see the connection
> Between your wordsmiths and your murderers![3]

Heschel points out that Zeitlin's poetry has national significance as an expression of a new direction in Jewish literature. Being blinded by the light of European civilization, in Heschel's words, "we could not appreciate the value of the small fire of our eternal light."[4] These lines echo Glatshteyn's famous poem, "*A gute nakht, velt*" (Good Night, World), written in 1938, about the return to Jewish sources, "*Fun vagners gets-muzik tsu nign, brumen*" (From Wagner's pagan music to the humming of Hasidic melodies).[5] The Jewish Enlightenment, the Haskalah of the past 150 years, had been a great mistake, which had created only spiritual confusion among Jews by alienating them from the religious sources of Judaism.

During 1945 and 1946, Heschel was in regular contact with the research director at YIVO, Max Weinreich, in connection with his participation in YIVO conferences and publications. Like Heschel, Weinreich and his son Uriel had arrived in the United States in 1940, barely escaping the Nazis. Just as Heschel had left his relatives behind in Warsaw, Weinreich had left his community and his family in Vilna, although he did succeed in rescuing his wife and youngest son, Gabriel, after the outbreak of the war. More than half a century later, Gabriel reflected on his father's state of mind during the critical years after the Holocaust. According to Gabriel, his father's greatest loss was that of his first child—not Uriel, but the Vilna YIVO and its community of supporters and contributors. As a result, he was consumed by hatred of the Germans who had caused the destruction of the Vilna YIVO. Gabriel gives a penetrating portrait—behind the public face of Weinreich, the intellectual and scholar—of his father's emotional turmoil, which he attempted to rein in and exorcise by writing his book-length indictment of Hitler's professors:

כדי צו פֿאַרשטיין דעם טאַטן מוז מען פֿאַרשטיין, אַז דער פֿאַרראַט פֿון היטלערס
פּראָפֿעסאָרן איז געווען פֿאַר אים אַ פּערזענלעכער פֿאַרראַט, וואָס ער האָט געפֿילט.
ומיט זמן סטודיום אין דמטשלאַנד, דאָס וואָס ער האָט געבראַכט מיט זיך פֿון זמן סטודיום
אין דמטשלאַנד, וואָס ער האָט געוואָלט געבן דער ייִדישער וועלט, וואָס ער האָט געמיינט
אַז ער קען זיך אויף דעם פֿאַרלאָזן, דאָס איז מער ניט געווען. און איך ווייס, אַז דאָס האָט
ער ניט געוויזן אַזוי שטאַרק פֿאַר אַנדערע, ווי פֿאַר דער משפּחה . . .
היטלערס פּראָפֿעסאָרן איז געווען דער סימבאָל פֿון דעם וואָס ער האָט פֿאַרלוירן,
צוזאַמען מיט זמן בכור: די אָריענטאַציע פֿון אַ וויסנשאַפֿטלעכן צוגאַנג, וואָס ער האָט אַ
גאַנץ לעבן נאָך דעם געפּרוווט ווידער צוזאַמענצוברענגען.

In order to understand my father, one must understand that the betrayal of Hitler's professors he [Max Weinreich] felt as a personal betrayal. His studies in Germany, and what he brought back from his studies in Germany and wanted to give to the Jewish world, something he thought he could always count on—all that didn't exist anymore. And I know that he didn't show this as strongly to others as he did to his own family. . . . *Hitler's Professors* was a symbol of what he had lost together with his firstborn (YIVO): the orientation of a scientific approach, which he tried to reconstitute the rest of his life.[6]

The contrast between the public and private Weinreich, and his feeling of betrayal by Germany and German science, was, according to Gabriel, poignantly expressed in the late 1960s, when the elder Weinreich was awarded an honorary decree by University of Marburg, where he had completed his doctorate in Yiddish philology in 1923. In response, Weinreich wrote a letter to the university declining the award. Gabriel reminisced about reading this letter in the presence of his father:

אַז איך האָב געלייענט דעם בריוו, וואָס ער האָט געהאַט אָנגעשריבן, האָב איך געשטוינט.
ערשטנס, אויפֿן ערשטן פּלאַץ—פֿון דער עלעגאַנץ פֿון דער דמטשער שפּראַך, וואָס ער
האָט געשריבן. אַ וווּנדערלעכער ליטעראַרישער דמטש, וואָס אַלע ווערבן זמנען געקומען
ערשט אין דריטן פּאַראַגראַף, מיט אַלע העפֿלעכקייטן און אַלע ריכטיקע סטיליסטישע
שטריכן. אָבער דער ענין פֿון בריוו איז געווען: "אַ הייסער פֿאַרשאָלטענער קדחת אמך."

When I read the letter he had written, I was astonished. Firstly, I was impressed by the German language that he had used, a wonderful literary German in which all verbs first appeared in the third paragraph, with all kinds of politeness and the correct stylistic forms. But the essence of the letter was: *A heyser farsholtener kadokhes aykh* (May you be accursed by shivering fever!)[7]

Yet Weinreich's emotional states of anger, hatred, and revenge were absent from his public activity, scholarly writing, and statements on behalf of the newly established main branch of YIVO in New York. In articles and conferences during and shortly after the war, Weinreich rallied his supporters to the idea of reinvigorating YIVO in New York as a way of "Vilnaizing" American Jewish life. He sought to revive the Eastern European Jewish heritage as a counterforce to the immigrant nostalgia of "Hester Street" and the assimilated Reform Jews in America. Informed by their diverse Jewish backgrounds and commitments, Heschel and Weinreich were fighting the same battle against the suppression and rejection of the Ashkenazic heritage among American-born Jews. Weinreich wrote about the indifference of American Jews regarding his plans for the revival of YIVO in a 1947 letter to the Yiddish poet Avrom Sutzkever in Paris: "Here (in New York), everything is terribly old, not in years but in spirit. The general impression of the Yiddish world here is: first and foremost exhaustion; secondly, resignation; thirdly, satisfaction with oneself, that is, a feeling of self protection toward the world, it is not possibly to do better, the maximum has already been achieved."[8]

In these circumstances Weinreich published "*Hitlers profesorn: Der khilek fun der daytsher visnshaft in daytshlands farbrekhns kegn yidishn folk*" (Hitler's Professors: The Role of German Academic Scholarship in Germany's Crimes Against the Jewish People). The study was completed on March 15, 1946, and published in *YIVO-Bleter* in the spring and summer of 1946. An English translation followed in the fall of 1946, and a Yiddish book version came out in 1947. The Nuremberg Tribunal convened by the four victorious Allied powers, which tried twenty-four top Nazi leaders between November 20, 1945, and October 1, 1946, provided the historical context for Weinreich's book. Using thorough documentation, some of which was appended to the end of the book in the original German, Weinreich demonstrated the German scholars' collaboration with the Nazi regime. The English translation was timed to appear at the height of the proceedings of the Nuremberg Tribunal, which was followed closely by the American public in newspaper reports and documentary footage in the fall of 1946.

Weinreich conceptualized the study in strictly scientific and legalistic terms: the book's thesis was persuasively proved by a long list of evidence—mostly books, articles, and statements by German scholars and intellectuals from before and during the Nazi period. The study set out to prove "that German scholars from the beginning to the end of the Hitler era worked hand in glove with the murderers of the Jewish people and that the official indoctrination literature of 1944–1945 which openly proclaimed: 'The Jews must be annihilated wherever we meet him!' repeated to the letter the 'facts' and 'reasons' contained in the scholarly literature. To a degree, this may be said even of the actual orders to kill."[9]

As a social scientist in the fields of youth culture and psychology, and the author of *Der veg tsu undzer yugnt* (The Road to Our Youth) from 1936, Weinreich demonstrated his mastery of the two fields' methodology in the execution of the book's analysis. However, the limits of such an academic approach in confronting the Nazi crimes became clear in the book's conclusion:

> What is to be gained by this recital of agony and crime? No one of our murdered six million will be reawakened to life. But perhaps man is capable of learning from experience. Because of that chance, one is duty bound to rummage the piles of that unsavory [*muktse makhmes mies*] literature of the Nazi era. Because of that chance, one must go through the pain of translating "extinguished" parents, brothers and sisters, and life-long friends, one's people, into impressive comparisons and percentages.[10]

In the study's last lines, Weinreich made its first explicit political statement: "The question of legal responsibility is for a United Nations Tribunal to decide. Before the world's conscience, German scholarship stands convicted."[11] No United Nations tribunal was ever convened, and the German scholars and scholarship never had their day in court.

In her 1946 *Commentary* review of *The Black Book: The Nazi Crime Against the Jewish People* and Weinreich's *Hitler's Professors*, Hannah Arendt praised the latter over the former book by stating that Weinreich's work "constitutes the best guide to the nature of Nazi terror that I have read so far."[12] The main problem with *The Black Book*, according to Arendt, was its lack of conceptual tools to delineate "the reality of politics." In contrast, Weinreich's book provided a survey of German scholars' complicity in the Holocaust, demonstrating in great detail their contribution to Nazi ideology. As was the case for *The Black Book*, however, the main problem with Weinreich's work was its lack of distinction between the German scholars' contribution to anti-Semitic and racist ideology and their active participation in the implementation of the Nazi policies. Arendt ended her review: "But neither science, nor even 'scientificality,' neither scholars nor charlatans, supplied the ideas and techniques that operated the death factories. The ideas came from politicians who took power-politics seriously, and the techniques came from modern mob-men who were not afraid of consistency."[13]

For Arendt the question of legal liability for the genocide lay squarely in the court of the Nazi leadership who had implemented the anti-Semitic policies. German scholars and intellectuals were a sideshow that played only a minor political role. Weinreich, on the other hand, identified fully with the plight of his people, the Yiddish-speaking masses of Eastern Europe who had suffered the greatest losses during the war. In *Hitler's Professors*, Weinreich's agenda was primarily a personal one: to express his deep sense of betrayal by the German scholars and the German scientific tradition in which he had been educated, and which had provided him with the tools to establish YIVO in Vilna. Weinreich's book made a strong case for the scientific quest for truth independent of politics and ideology.

Hitler's Professors marked a new juncture in Weinreich's relationship to German culture and language. In the Yiddish version of the book, the Nazi quotes were rendered in idiomatic Yiddish, while the original German was placed in the book's appendix, including quotes in Gothic letters. This use of German—as a demarcated realm in the appendix or translated into Yiddish—reflected Weinreich's new orientation toward Yiddish as a language of the Way of the Shas (*derekh hashas*, the Mishna, Jewish religious law).[14] Simultaneously, his translation of Nazi German lingo into idiomatic Yiddish indicated the mutual linguistic and literary influences that had characterized the exchange and dialogue between the two languages for centuries. Weinreich's concept of Yiddish as the "language of the Way of the Shas" resembles Glatshteyn's turn to a more authentic Yiddish language in his post-Holocaust poetry, and the seeds of this notion can be found in *Hitler's Professors*. In the words of Jerold Frakes: "It seems almost as if, in developing his 'poetics of authenticity,' the poet [Glatshteyn] attempts to transport back across the interstitial space between German and Yiddish and to jettison that which Yiddish had, over the course of centuries, imported, adapted, and internalized (from German)."[15]

In an article published in the journal *Di yidishe shprakh* in July–August 1942, Weinreich analyzes "*Vos heyst shraybn yidishlekh?*" (What Does It Mean to Write in a Jewish Manner?) in Mendele's Yiddish translation of Leo Pinsker's German treatise "Autoemanzipation" from 1882. This article is a linguistic statement of principles regarding the relationship between Yiddish and German. Weinreich points out that the Jews in the Middle Ages lived in a separate world from their German-speaking neighbors. Despite direct social and cultural contact between Jews and Christians, it was the religious and spiritual separation between the two peoples that was reflected in Yiddish. The language was a product of "powerful spiritual literary movements, but these originated with Tanakh and even more so, the Talmud, Rashi, *musar* books and Shulkhan Orekh."[16] Yiddish was influenced not by humanists such as Locke, Rousseau, Lessing, and Goethe but by the internal bilingualism of Ashkenaz. With the rise of modern Yiddish literature in the middle of the nineteenth century, the primary readership of Mendele's translation was the so-called *beysmedresh intelligents*, those Jews who had left the yeshiva world.

By emphasizing the difference and distance rather than the hybridity and mutual influences between the two languages, Weinreich argues for a move away from German, stylistically and linguistically. which in his view characterized the origin of modern literary Yiddish, as exemplified by Mendele's translation. By the early 1940s, Yiddish had developed to such an extent that it could be used to render the full range of modern German. The so-called *yidishlekh* style of Mendele had become a largely outdated mode of expression. However, Weinreich maintains that the point of departure for the continued development of the Yiddish language is Mendele's literary style of *derekh hashas,* or in his own words: "*Biz hayntikn tog muzn mir geyn tsu im in kheder*" (Today we must study with him in the Jewish elementary school).[17]

Weinreich's *Hitler's Professors* highlights a number of intersecting issues that characterized the Yiddish poets' response to the *khurbn* in the 1940s. The anti-German sentiments that proliferated in the Yiddish poetry and writing of Sutzkever, Glatshteyn, and Zeitlin between 1943 and 1947 disappeared almost completely in the following decades. Sutzkever did not publish "*Mayn eydes-zogn farn nirnberger tribunal: Togbukh-notitsn*" (My Witness Account for the Nuremberg Tribunal: Diary Notes) until 1966. These diary entries articulated a stereotypical, vengeful image of Germany and Germans that was absent from Sutzkever's Holocaust poetry. In the diary Sutzkever describes how he lobbied Ilya Ehrenburg to get permission to present his testimony in Nuremberg in Yiddish:

איך וויל רעדן אויף דער שפּראַך פֿונעם פֿאָלק, וואָס די געמישפּטע האָבן זיך פֿאַרמאָסטן אויסצוראָטן צוזאַמען מיט זײַן שפּראַך. זאָל דערהערט ווערן אונדזער מאַמע-לשון. זאָל

מען דערהערן אונדזער לשון, און זאָל צעפּלאַצט ווערן אַלפֿרעד ראָזענבערג. זאָל מײַן שפּראַך טריומפֿירן אין נירנבערג ווי אַ סימבאָל פֿון אומפֿאַרגייִקייט!

> I wanted to speak in the language of the people whom the convicted set out to murder together with its language. May our mother tongue be heard. May they hear our language, and may Alfred Rosenberg explode. May my language triumph in Nuremberg as a symbol of our indestructability![18]

In the end, Sutzkever had to abide by the rules of the tribunal and present his testimony in Russian, one of the four official languages permitted in the courtroom. (The three others were English, French, and German.) Although Sutzkever appeared before the Nuremberg Tribunal as a member of the Soviet delegation, his *mame-loshn* was just as invisible there as Weinreich's attempt to resurrect YIVO was percieved by a majority of his American Jewish constituency in New York. Behind the public arena of politics, court proceedings, and Weinreich's indictment of Hitler's professors, however, the poetry of Zeitlin, Glatshteyn, and Sutzkever articulated a more complex set of responses to the *khurbn*.

In two poems in *Gedenklider* (Poems of Remembrance, 1943), "*Der rayzeman*" (The Traveling Man) and "*Undzer tsikhtik loshn*" (Our Neat and Tidy Language), Glatshteyn included references to German language and culture. *Der rayzeman*—a *daytshmerism* (the Yiddish word for a traveler is *vegsman*)—has been all over the world and boasts about his experiences in Germanized Yiddish:

שטעלט אים אָפּ אַ דײַטשל אין גאַס
און זאָגט אים: — מאַגע
איך אינען שטעלן אַ פֿראַגע?
זאָגט דער רײַזעמאַן: — אַדעראַגע,
מיט דער גרעסטער פֿאַרגעניגן.
מאַכט דאָס דײַטשל אָט אַזוי:
האָסטו געזען די קופּערנע פֿרוי?
גיט זיך דער רײַזעמאַן בײַ דער באָרד אַ גלעט
און זאָגט מיט אַ שמייכל: כ'מאַך אַ וועט.
אָוואַדע, וואָדען?
אָוואַדע, וואָדען?
אַלץ געזאַן און אַלץ געזען.

אַליין געזען די קופּערנע פֿרױ
װי איך בין אַן אַלטער גױ.

A German on the street
Stops him and asks: "Pardon me,
Would you mind a query?"
"With the greatest pleasure.
You can take my measure."
The German puts his question:
"Have you seen the copper woman?"
The traveling man strokes his beard,
smiles and answers, "You bet I have.
   Of course, what else?
   Of course, what else?
Everything shown, everything seen,
My own eyes saw the copper *froy*,
I swear as I'm a proper *goy*."[19]

The Gentile traveler is unable to experience anything new on his trip because he is locked into a pursuit of "*der tsoyberfas*" (the magic barrel) and "*di kuperne froy*" (the copper lady), archetypical images derived from a mythological map of the world. The static, formulaic character of the *rayzeman*'s trip is associated with the German character of his speech. *Der rayzeman* becomes a Don Quixote figure whose speech exposes, in Janet Hadda's words, "his fakery and essential provincialism." Glatshteyn creates a kind of "hyper-German" in words such as *gezan*, which does not exist in German, and in the word *fargenage*, which combines the Yiddish *fargenign* with the German *Vergnügen*.[20]

"*Undzer tsikhtik loshn*" does not present a creative dialogue with the German component of Yiddish; rather, Glatshteyn's poem exposes a violent clash of incompatible elements. German is no longer a source of inspiration and innovation; the language is demarcated as primitive, ugly, and un-Yiddish. The poet applies the very "rhetoric of ugliness"—with which the *Maskilim* (the proponents of the Haskalah) ridiculed and rejected Yiddish—to German language and culture. In the poem's revisionist history of the Yiddish language, "*di gute yidn fun amol*" (the good Jews from the past) use the Slavic and Hebrew-Aramaic component to refashion the Yiddish language while rejecting German as a cancerous growth on the Yiddish language body. German is characterized as a "*blut-vursht shprakhe*" (blood-sausage language), referring to the murderous character of Germany and its defilement of Jewish dietary laws. Wagner is summoned to express the cultural underpinnings of the death cult in the German onslaught on the Jews. The angry desperation of Glatshteyn's posture is encapsulated in the rhyming of the German "*Sprache*" and "*Rache*" and the Yiddish "*shvakhe*":

נאָר דו אַליין אויף דײַן בלוט-ווורשט שפּראַכע,
קאָנסט אויסרעוועון ווי דו האָסט גענומען,
דײַטשע, משוגענע ראַכע,
פֿון דערשראָקענע, אומבאַשיצטע, שוואַכע.

> Only you alone, in your blood-sausage language,
> Can bellow about how you took
> Insane Germanic revenge
> On the frightened, the defenseless, the weak.[21]

The poem "*Motsart*" from the collection *Shtralndike yidn* (1946) is presented as the record of a dream in which Mozart appears as the crucified Jesus. The separate categories of Jews and Christians are blurred by the introduction of a third imaginary group, "the Mozartians," for whom the poetic "I" becomes an apostle:

ווי וווּנדערלעך איז פֿון געטלעכן מענטש
זײַן מוזיקאַלישער טעסטאַמענט,
ווי דורכגענאָגלט מיט געזאַנג
זײַנען זײַנע ליכטיקע הענט.
אין זײַן גרעסטער נויט,
האָבן בײַם געקרייציקטן זינגער
געלאַכט אַלע פֿינגער.
אין זײַן ווייניקסטן טרויער,
האָט ער נאָך מער ווי זיך אַליין
ליב געהאַט דעם שכנס אויער.

> How marvelous this godly man's
>   musical testament;
>   laughter
> lit the fingers
> of the crucified singer.
> In deepest despair,

In sadness most bitter,
He loved more than himself
The ear of his neighbour.²²

The centrality of the ears as metonymical figures appears repeatedly in Glatshteyn's work. In his autobiographical novel *Ven yash iz geforn* (1938), "*di goldene oyern*" ("golden ears") set Yash apart from the other passengers on the ship to Europe because of their sensitivity to the stylistic musicality of the passengers' voices.²³ Compared to Mozart's musical genius and love of his neighbor's ears, the Sermon on the Mount is inferior: "*Vi orem un vi karg / antkegn motsarts farblayb, / iz di droshe afn barg*" (How meager a thing, how scant, / compared with Mozart's testament / is the Sermon on the Mount). Glatshteyn situates aesthetic pleasure in a nonverbal musical/poetic realm that, in romanticist fashion, is superior to moral and religious categories. Significantly, the poem does not contain any linguistic and literary references to German-Austrian language and literature except for the name Mozart. The Yiddish poet's apostlelike dedication to Mozart's musical testament becomes Glatshteyn's dream fulfilment of his debt to the Western cultural heritage. In the year of the poem's publication, only ruins were left of the German-Austrian culture that gave birth to Mozart. In the aftermath of Nazi totalitarianism and Holocaust, only a delicate link to European culture is articulated in the poem's dreamlike vision.²⁴

To reconcile his poetic ear to the collective task of commemoration, Glatshteyn employed the character Nachman of Bratslav as a poetic mask in a series of poems published between 1943 and 1953. This allowed him to articulate an authentic Hasidic sensibility without sacrificing his poetic musicality. In his more overt commemorative poems, on the other hand, Glatshteyn added his poetic voice to the chorus of "the collective wailing"—a term he coined in a 1947 article: "A whole poetry has become monotonic and mono-thematic. The times have made Jewish monotheism into monothemisms; but precisely in this singing together or, better, wailing together, lies a kernel of light and a promise for tomorrow."²⁵ This new collective purpose that briefly rescued Yiddish poetry from obscurity in the late 1940s, as encapsulated in Judd L. Teller's point that Yiddish poets had been "joined to their generation by the accident of shipwreck," would be harnessed to Glatshteyn's *inzikhist* poetics.²⁶

In March 1945 the I. L. Peretz Shrayber Fareyn (I. L. Peretz Writers Union) in New York published a book titled *Finf un zibetsik yor yidishe prese in Amerike, 1870–1945* (Seventy-five Years Yiddish Press in America,

1870–1945), with contributions from some of the leading Yiddish cultural figures in America. The introductory article, written in the last months of World War II, provides a broader context for Glatshteyn's reorientation in the immediate aftermath of the Holocaust.[27] The article points out that the Yiddish press was the first to document the genocide against the European Jews while "the Jewish tragedy becomes cold lead, on the twentieth page of the foreign newspapers." In a contemporary context, Yiddish writing has become "a fortress and a holy site."[28] The article pays homage to the normative view of *muster* (normative) Yiddish originating with Mendele: "While regards from the other side of the ocean were already carried here in Mendele's . . . living breath of his vibrant Yiddish word, *daytshmerism* tore at the Jewish heart and ears, and blemished the healthy face of our folk language in America."[29] However, "the Yiddish language ceased to be delivered by German," and the Yiddish press became "an academy of our language."[30] The article emphasizes the heroism of the Yiddish-speaking victims and the American Yiddish press as a sanctuary in a hostile world, the last mainstay of Yiddish culture for a million readers.

In the poem from *Shtralndike yidn* (1946), "*Ikh davn a yidish blat in sobvey*" (I Pray from a Yiddish Newspaper in the Subway), Glatshteyn associates reading the Yiddish newspaper with the expression *lernen a blat gemore* (to study a page of Talmud). The act of reading a Yiddish newspaper in the subway is compared to a religious Jew's morning prayer, which is concluded with the *shmone esre* at the end of the poem. Unlike the *goy* who is reading his American newspaper, the Yiddish newspaper-reader points out:

כ׳לייען נישט, ליבער גוי,
דאָס דאַוון איך אַזוי.
כ׳זאָג תפֿילות, קינות.
אינמיטן דעם טומל, דעם סאָבוויי-האַרמידער,
דאַוון איך פֿון מײַן טעגלעכן סידור.

> I don't read, dear Gentile,
> here I pray.
> I say prayers, dirges.
> In the middle of the crowd, the Subway noise,
> I pray from my daily prayer book.[31]

Referring to the Kielce pogrom in the summer of 1946, the news in the Yiddish newspaper focuses on the continued threat to Jewish survivors. The Jew in the subway remains stateless, constantly on guard against outbreaks of a violent anti-Semitism equated with natural disasters, the eruption of volcanic craters. The only reference to Germany is the word "*vilkomen*," associated with the main tenets of Catholicism:

אָבער דו, מײַן טײַערער אינטערנאַציאָנאַלער גוי,
מיטן גאָלדענעם פּאַספּאָרט,
ביסטו אומעטום װילקאָמען,
אין נאָמען פֿון טאַטן, זון און הייליקן גײַסט.

> But you, my dear international Gentile,
> with the golden passport,
> is welcome everywhere,
> in the name of the father, the son, and the holy spirit.

In a particularly angry section of the poem, the forgiving God of Christianity is equated to an idol, while the Jewish God's indifference to Jewish suffering is evident from the recent national catastrophe: "My God holds in his bosom a whole people."[32] At the end of the poem, the Jew in the subway's experience is compared to the Israelites' forty years of wanderings in the desert, the length of time the Jew has spent in America:

מיט אַ דערשראָקענעם פּאַספּאָרט אין קעשענע,
דורך די פֿינצטערע און שװינדלענדיקע פֿענצטער,
װאַרפֿט מען מיר אַרײַן בריװ פֿון טאַטע מאַמע.

> With a fearful passport in the pocket
> through the dark and dizzying windows
> are thrown letters from father and mother.

These letters, signed "from us, your dead father and mother," ask how much longer their son must travel before he reaches America. The words "*alter yid*" (old Jew), applied to the American son, and "*toyter tate, toyte mame*" (dead father, dead mother) are both repeated like a mantra at the end of the poem, emphasizing the American son's identification with his dead parents in Poland. The Jewish immigrant in the New York subway, who has lived forty years next to the Statue of Liberty (part of the Emma Lazarus poem inscribed on the statue is quoted in the poem), is suddenly experiencing the anti-Semitic nightmare of his European parents as a concrete, paranoid vision of vulnerability. The American son uses the Yiddish newspaper as a secularized morning prayer that exposes him to his fellow Americans' anti-Semitic assault. This quasireligious practice underlines the Jewish son's passivity, powerlessness, and inability to Americanize by casting off the yoke of his Polish Jewish parents' fear of the *goyim*.

Both the 1945 article and "*Ikh davn a yidish blat in sobvey*" articulate Glatshteyn's strong identification with the victims of the Holocaust. By sanctifying the Yiddish press in America, the main vehicle of *daytshmerism* and *shund*, Glatshteyn articulated his newfound belief in Yiddish as *loshn hakedoyshim* (the language of the martyrs), regardless of its medium, style, and function. In the immediate aftermath of the Holocaust, all internal distinctions in Yiddish culture had been made obsolete. Now was the time for the Yiddish writer to protect, retrieve, and commemorate what remained of Yiddish culture and its native speakers.

During the mid- to late 1950s, the Yiddish poet and critic Avrom Tabatshnik recorded the voices of seventeen Yiddish poets in New York.[33] The name of the project, "*Di rekodirte antologye: Di shtim fun yidishn poet*" (Recorded Anthology: The Voice of the Yiddish Poet), indicated its multifaceted purpose: to create a recorded anthology of Yiddish poets' voices reading their poetry and answering questions about their work.[34] In his article "*Di shtim fun yidishn poet*" (The Voice of the Yiddish Poet, 1955), Tabatshnik outlined the rationale behind the project. Modern Yiddish poetry articulated an aesthetic approach similar to that of the nineteenth-century English Romantic poets in their stress on the primitive and unconscious aspects of the human mind. Tabatshnik mentions the nineteenth-century English critic William Hazlitt's essay "On the Conversation of Authors" as a model for his project:

אויך אין דעם לייענען פֿון די מאָדערנע ייִדישע פּאָעטן באַזונדערס די "יונגע" הערט מען דעם "סינג-סונג", הערט מען דאָס קול, אָדער דעם ניגון פֿון דעם אורקוואַליקן און אורשטאַמיקן אין דער פּאָעזיע— דאָס קול וואָס מען הערט אַרויס פֿון די לידער פֿון פּרימיטיווע פֿעלקער, וואָס ווילן מיט זייער מאָנאָטאָנעם טאַם-טאַם ריטם, מיט זייער צודרינגלעכן "סינג-סאַנג" דערגרייכן היפּנאָטישע און מאַגישע עפֿעקטן.

Also in the reading of the modern Yiddish poets, particularly *Di yunge*, one hears the "sing-song," the voice, or the wordless melody [*nign*] originating with the source of poetry—the voice heard in poems of primitive people who in monotonous tom-tom rhythm and urgent "sing-song" want to achieve hypnotic and magical effects.³⁵

Di yunge's revolt against the socialist and proletarian poetry of Morris Rosenfeld, Dovid Edelshtat, and Morris Vintshevski paralleled the English Romantic poets' rejection of the "didactic" and "rationalistic" trends in eighteenth-century English poetry. Tabatshnik points out that the ancient origins of Yiddish poetry lie in the oral tradition of the troubadour, followed by *badkhonim* (wedding jesters), Purim *shphilers, di Broder Zinger*, and the Yiddish theater. The last link in this poetic "golden chain" includes Itsik Manger's poetry readings in the Eastern European cities and shtetls in the 1930s. To encapsulate the poetics of *Di yunge*, Tabatshnik quotes from Peretz's story "*Mekubolim*" (Cabbalists): "*a nign, vos zingt gor on a kol*" (a wordless melody which sings without a voice). The "internal *nign*" (*ineveynikster nign*) of modern Yiddish poetry made it "*tsu shtimungsful, tsu din, tsu fartift, tsu delikat nyansirt*" (too spirited, too thin, too deep, to delicately refined) for poetry readings on the Yiddish stage, with its dramatic oratorical style.³⁶ In contrast to the Yiddish theater, which vulgarized the "living word," Tabatshnik was motivated by a longing toward a past era as defined by the founder of high modernism in Yiddish, Peretz:

טראַכטנדיק וועגן די דאָזיקע זאַכן און בענקענדיק נאָכן קול פֿון ייִדישע פּאָעטן, וואָס זײַנען שוין אויף אייביק פֿאַרשטומט געוואָרן, איז מיר אַמנגעפֿאַלן—פֿאַררעקאָרדירן די שטים פֿון ייִדישן פּאָעט. איז דאָך די שטים פֿון אַ פּאָעט, לכל הדעות, ניט ווייניקער וויכטיק פֿאַר די צוקונפֿטיקע דורות, ווי זײַנע פֿאָטאָגראַפֿיעס, ווען ער איז געווען אַ קינד, אַ חתן, אָדער אַ פֿײַער־לעשער, ווי פּרץ.

Contemplating these things and longing toward the voice of the Yiddish poets who already had been silenced forever, it occurred to me to record the voice of the Yiddish poet. The voice of the poet, at any rate, is no less important for future generations than his photographs when he was a child, a groom, or a fire-fighter like Peretz.³⁷

The sound of the poet's voice is a kind of aural photograph, a way of capturing past lives of writers whose work, according to Tabatshnik's Peretzian credo, reflects a transcendent poetic realm. The historical importance of preserving the voice of the Yiddish poet as the cultural pinnacle of his age was the driving force behind Tabatshnik's project. His intent was to leave a record comparable to that of the great American poets' voices stored on tapes in the Library of Congress.³⁸ It is a way of touching "the holy spark" that Peretz sought to capture in his Hasidic tales. Modern Yiddish poets are latter-day bearers of the inspired, sacred tongue that originated with the Hebrew prophetic tradition:

מען וועט אפֿשר אַמאָל וועלן הערן ווי שיין אונדזער מאַמע-לשון האָט געקלונגען אין מויל פֿון די וואָס האָבן עס מיט ליבשאַפֿט געכאָוועט, און געצערטלט. אָבער ניט נאָר ליבהאָבער און גענוסער פֿון ייִדישן ליד, נאָר אויך פֿאָרשער פֿון ייִדישער פֿאָעטיק און פֿאָנעטיק, וואָלטן פֿון די רעקאָרדירונגען געהאַט אַ סך נוצן.

> Someday, it will perhaps be possible to hear how beautiful our mother tongue sounded in the mouth of those who lovingly cultivated and caressed it. But not only aficionados and readers of the Yiddish poem, but also scholars of Yiddish phonetics, would be able to derive a lot of utility from the recordings.³⁹

Glatshteyn characterized Tabatshnik as someone who, "from the stormy verbal warfare in defence of *Di yunge*, became a refined and intelligent Yiddish critic."⁴⁰ Tabatshnik's most succinct critical statement about Yiddish poetry was a lecture he delivered in connection with the Yiddish PEN Club's celebration of Yiddish literature, from 1900 to 1950, in New York on December 16–17, 1950. In this lecture, "*Traditsye un revolt in der yidisher poezye*" (Tradition and Revolt in Yiddish Poetry), Tabatshnik initially emphasized the uniqueness of Yiddish poetry in comparison with other literatures: "Our poetry developed with shortcut speed. In some fifty or sixty years we have had to experience as much as other literatures have in two or three times that time span."⁴¹ Tabatshnik's lecture is a polemic both against the Marxist critics and against an unreflective application of modernist critical categories to Yiddish poetry. Tabatshnik's credo, shaped by his affiliation with *Di yunge*, can be characterized as modernist traditionalism:

> As Yiddish poetry grew more modern, even modernistic, as it grew freer in rhythm, subtler in tonality, more artful and sophisticated in imagery, it also grew more Jewish—I would say more Hasidic, in the Reb Nachman of Bratslav sense of the word. The very first revolt in Yiddish poetry, that of the "Yunge," was expressed in a turning back to the origins—which Peretz called "barely experienced

sources"—to the religious vision of the Jewish people, its sorrow and rapture, its Messianic longing and redemption myth.⁴²

Rather than breaking with the past, *Di yunge*'s "revolt" reaches back and gives voice to the eternal Jewish religious and spiritual quest for redemption and mystical transcendence. Tabatshnik's emphasis on continuity between past and present, religion and secularism, is also apparent in his evaluation of Soviet Yiddish poets as an "important achievement not only in the early period but also in the later years." At the end of the lecture, Tabatshnik warns that recently "the turn toward Jewish spiritual tradition, once so penetrating and fruitful, begins to degenerate into tedium and hollowness, a 'love-of-Israel' committed to nothing."⁴³

FIGURE 6.1. Avrom Tabatshnik, New York (undated). (Archives of the YIVO Institute for Jewish Research, New York)

Tabatshnik's 1955 interview with Yankev Glatshteyn in New York was unique among his recordings of Yiddish poets, such as Aaron Glants-Leyeles, Itsik Manger, Chaim Grade, Aaron Zeitlin, Kadya Molodovsky, and Rokhl Korn. In the case of Glatshteyn, Tabatshnik not only encountered a major Yiddish poet and one of the founders of the *inzikhist* movement; he also faced the leading critic in American Yiddish letters. His tendency in most of the other recordings was to limit the questions to issues related to the poet's own work. This is less pronounced in Glatshteyn's interview, which addressed the contemporary context for Yiddish poetry in the 1950s and reflected on how the project should be used in the future; such reflections are mostly absent from the other recordings.

Tabatshnik adheres to a list of questions that he asks meticulously, in a soft-spoken voice. Glatshteyn's voice, in contrast, is argumentative and energetic; he speaks a rapid Polish Yiddish tinged with a declamatory flourish that reflects a sense of self-importance. At times the exchange of questions and answers breaks down because of voices raised so high, it is nearly impossible to hear the words clearly. However, most of the recording with Glatshteyn is clear except for approximately fifteen minutes, due to technical problems with the microphone. Glatshteyn's readings are considerably longer than that of all other poets in the anthology. The recording is more than ninety minutes long, beginning with recitations of poems from his first collection, *Yankev Glatshteyn,* and ending with a few poems he would later include in *Di freyd fun yidishn vort* (The Joy of the Yiddish Word), published in 1961.[44] At the end of the interview, Tabatshnik asks whether Glatshteyn wants to make a final statement.[45] Following a few words on the importance of the wider Jewish world in the aftermath of the Holocaust and the foundation of Israel for contemporary Yiddish poetry, Glatshteyn comments:

דאָס איז באמת אַ פֿרייד אַז ס׳פֿאַלט אַרײַן אַ דיכטער ווי אײַך צו קומען צו יידישע פּאָעטן, רעקאָרדירן די שטים פֿון דער יידישער פּאָעזיע . . . דאָס איז נישט נאָר די שטים פֿון יידישן פּאָעט, דאָס איז די שטים פֿון יידישן דור, אונדזער דור, דאָס איז פֿאַר מיר אַליין אַ געוואַלדיקע דערמוטיקונג. מען קען אויף דעם אַליין זײַער אַ סך בויען. איך וואָלט געוואָלט אַז סײַ איר און סײַ מיר זאָלן דאָס אויפֿנעמען נישט אין גײַסט פֿון פּינוס, נישט אין גײַסט פֿון אָמנזאָמלען . . .

It is truly a joy that a writer, like you, visits Yiddish poets, records the voice of Yiddish poetry . . . and not only the voice of the Yiddish poet, but the voice of a Jewish generation, our generation. This is a tremendous encouragement. A lot can be built on that foundation. I would hope that both you and I should not receive it in the spirit of *kinus*, the spirit of collecting . . .⁴⁶

Glatshteyn uses the words *kinus* and *aynzamlen* as they were appropriated by YIVO in the interwar period: collecting (*aynzamlen*) as a tool to gather material, from the Jewish folk in the Central and Eastern European shtetls, about all aspects of Jewish life in order to stimulate new cultural creativity and provide "raw material" for scholarly investigation. In contrast Glatshteyn emphasizes the project's potential for inspiring new artistic and critical creativity; he distances himself from collecting as a means of commemoration and historical documentation.

. . . אַ מאָדערנע מאַשין וואָס נעמט אַרונטער דאָס קול, רעקאָרדירט, דאָס איז אַ בלײַבעדיקע זאַך, איר פֿאַרשטייט. דאָס זאָל ווערן אַ כּוח וואָס זאָל סטימולערן צו טאָן נייע זאַכן. איך האַלט אַז מע דאַרף פֿאַרטראַכטן ווי אַזוי דאָס אויסצונוצן . . . צו מאַכן דערפֿון אַ נײַ קאַפּיטל פֿון שעפֿערישקייט, נעמען אויפֿן באַסיס פֿון דעם וואָס ייִדישע שרײַבערס האָבן זיך אַוועקגעזעצט רעדן, און וואָס ייִדישע שרײַבערס האָבן געלייענט זייערע לידער, די לעבעדיקע אַנטאָלאָגיע שפּילן און נאָך אַמאָל שפּילן און איבערשפּילן, פֿאַר מיר איז דאָס גרויסע מוזיק, פֿאַר מיר איז דאָס מער מוזיק ווי קאַרוסאָס אַריעס, נעמען און שפּילן און איבערשפּילן און אויב מען זאָל קענען געפֿינען אַ וועג צו סטימולירן און עפֿענען אַ נײַ קאַפּיטל און איך האַלט אַז מען דאַרף קענען געפֿינען אַ וועג . . .

. . . a modern machine which records the voice is a lasting thing, you understand. This will become a force which should inspire new things. I believe that we all must consider how to utilize it; to develop a new chapter of creativity based on the fact that Yiddish writers sat and talked and read their poems . . . to play and replay the living anthology is for me, great music; greater than Caruso's arias. Play and replay it, and if it is possible, find a way to inspire and open a new chapter. I believe that it is necessary to find a way . . .⁴⁷

The tape recorder's ability to record the song, rhythm, and musical quality of poetry is central to the project. Through the taping of the actual voices, an essential aspect that is lacking on the printed page can be kept alive (*a lebedike antologye*) and made available for future generations. Its lasting significance originates in the possibility of playing and replaying the recordings repeatedly (*shpil un ibershpiln*), just like classical music records.

. . . און דאָס זאָל נישט זײַן בלויז קיין מוזיי זאַך, אַוועקגעגעבן ייִוואָ . . . און אַזוי וויטער אונטערגאַנג, שלוס . . . ניין איך האָב געוואָלט סײַ איר און סײַ מיר, אַז אַלע פּאָעטן זאָלן אַוועק מיטן געדאַנק אַז דאָס איז אַ נײַ אופֿן שעפֿערישקייט.

> . . . and that should not only be a museum thing, a donation to YIVO . . . and so on, decline, the end . . . . No, I would want both you and me and all poets to take with them the idea that it is a new creative form.[48]

Glatshteyn repeats that the recorded anthology should be comprised of more than museum objects and scholarly source material in YIVO, and reiterates its potential as inspiration for new creativity (*sheferishkayt*), the last word in the interview.

Unlike others interviewed for the recorded anthology, Glatshteyn confronts Tabatshnik's first question head on: "*Vos iz di oyfgabe fun a yidishn poet in der hayntiker tsayt?*" (What is the task of a Yiddish poet today?). Glatshteyn points out that the Yiddish poet writes under highly abnormal conditions due to the destruction of European Jewry. He touches on issues of silence versus speech in giving voice to the horrors of the Holocaust, and stresses the responsibility of the Yiddish poet to make a record of the destruction. In response to Tabatshnik's question, "*Tsi vern di yidishe lider banayt haynt?*" (Are Yiddish poems being renewed now?), Glatshteyn says:

> I would say, regrettably no. All contemporary Yiddish poets seem sort of frightened. We have no large audience. We keep hearing the same old story: "Our language is dying." You must understand what it means to keep hounding a creative person, especially a poet, with the information that he's writing in a language that is on the verge of extinction, that may have, indeed, already died. This threatening atmosphere has intimidated all Yiddish poets, frightened them into a huddle like a flock of hens before a storm. And in this frightened state, they have concluded a peace that is, in essence, detrimental to poetry . . .
>
> . . . The modernism of which you speak is impossible today because we all write under the sign of fear. The sign of fear unites us. We have all become classics. [*Mir shraybn ale unter dem tseykhn*

fun shrek. Der tseykhn fun shrek fareynikt undz. Mir zaynen ale gevorn klasikers.]⁴⁹

Glatshteyn argues that, unlike the Yung Yisroel group, which has a future because it is affiliated with a vibrant Hebrew culture in Israel, Yiddish poets in America are paralyzed around a *"fayertop fun shrek"* (caldron of fear).⁵⁰

Glatshteyn's poem *"A zuntik iber nyu york"* (A Sunday over New York), from *Dem tatns shotn* (My Father's Shadow, 1953), addressed the Yiddish writer's situation in New York in the early 1950s.⁵¹ In this poem Glatshteyn conveyed the "collective fear" that he mentioned in the Tabatshnik interview. In its first part, a quiet, sunny autumn Sunday in New York has momentarily disrupted the city's Gold Rush, *"geipesht mit alt-ayzn, gazolin un gelt"* (the stink of old iron, gas, and money), exposing a natural environment of overripe fruits, harvest, and fresh earth. The city has been transformed into small yards, a villagelike space. It has become *"a farvaldikte shtot"* (a forested city), releasing the fine smells of trees, autumnlike frost, and a childish joy. Only a few references to God, suffering, and pogroms interrupt this image of autumn in New York. The windows of the buildings sing like cloister bells:

בלויז קלויסטערכאָרן
קענען זינגען אַזוי רויִק
צו אַ פֿאַרחלשטן גאָט
וואָס האָט אַפֿילו פֿאַרגעבן זײַנע פּײַניקער.

Only church choirs
can sing so calmly
to a swooning God
who even forgives his torturers.⁵²

This is a mocking reference to Jesus and the gospel of Christian love and forgiveness as a highly inadequate response to the recent Jewish suffering in Europe. In the last part of the poem, the "I" is introduced as bearer of a suppressed reality of pogroms, and the city is transformed into an Eastern European shtetl. Its inhabitants are *"gutmutike poyerim"* (good-natured peasants), and the metropolitan synagogue is viewed as the only place of refuge from *"ale mayne geshreyen"* (all my screams). The "I" maintains the silence of a long-visiting guest (*ikh shvayg mit der farlegnkeyt fun a gast*), with his voice sounding like cloister bells. However, the "I"'s inner reality threatens to overwhelm the Sunday quiet of New York:

די קריסטלעכע שטאָט רוט
און מײַנע אַלע אומגליקן דרימלען אומגעדולדיק.
איך קום צוריק צו מײַן איינזאַמער שול.
זי שטייט איצט אויך אײַנגעזונטיקט אין שרעק.

The Christian city rests,
and all my old calamities sleep restlessly.
I return to my lonely synagogue.
It stands now also steeped in Sunday-dread.[53]

Like the synagogue, the "I" has been set aside in a separate Sunday as a time of fear ("*ayngezuntikt*," a typical Glatshteyn neologism). In the final lines the "I" is subsumed in the third-person plural, indicating the collective fear of New York Jews who harbor memories of anti-Semitism from the Old World:

מאָרגן וועלן אונדזערע וווּנדן
ווידער גוואַלדעווען,
אָבער די קולות פֿון דער שטאָט
וועלן זיי אַריבערשרײַען.

Tomorrow our wounds
will cry out again,
but the voices of the city
will outshout them again.[54]

New York, which in his earlier works Glatshteyn depicted with modernist images and jazzlike rhythm, appeared in "*Zuntik iber nuy york*" as yet another *Goles* (Diaspora) space, a hostile, threatening, preindustrial location in the grips of Christian anti-Semitism. The identification with the Jewish victims of the Holocaust made Glatshteyn retreat into a nightmare of "fear of the *goyim*" as the defining characteristic of his existence in New York. This fear is never concretized in specific images; rather, it remains enwrapped in generalities. While Sutzkever's "Green Aquarium" (1953–54) evoked the Vilna Ghetto and its vicinity with great power in a surrealist poetic idiom, Glatshteyn employed a more conventional poetic strategy in witnessing the Holocaust and its aftermath from afar in New York.

As mentioned earlier, in the poem "*Motsart*" (Mozart), the poet envisioned Mozart as a crucified Jesus figure who "*in zayn veynendikstn troyer / hot er nokh mer vi zikh aleyn / lib gehat dem shokhns oyer*" (Through dooms of tears / more than himself he loved / his neighbor's ears).⁵⁵ Thus Glatshteyn stressed the importance of poetry's dialogical and musical qualities in communicating with the listener/reader. In *"Lider fun shtilkeyt"* (Poems of Silence) from *Dem tatns shotn*, Glatshteyn exclaimed:

שאַרפֿע, שנײַדיקע, ווידערשטאַנד, וווּ ביסטו?
יונג-מעסערדיקער צו-להכעיס.
דײַן דור האָט דיר אָנגעטאָן אַ יאַרמעלקע,
וואָס פֿאַלט דיר איבער די אויערן,
און האָט דיר אויסגעלערנט
צו ריידן הייליקע דברים בטלים.

> Sharp, cutting resistance, where are you?
> Young knifelike spite.
> Your generation has dressed you up in a yarmulke,
> Which covers your ears
> And have taught you
> To speak holy idle words.⁵⁶

The voice of resistance and youthful spite had been eliminated by the demands of the poet's generation that poetry become part of a collective task of commemoration. His generation had forced a yarmulke on his head, literally blocking the poet's ears from being used as finely tuned musical organs. The poet's words had become *"heylike dvorim beteylim"* (holy idle words), a sacrilegious use of his poetic voice and a vehicle of didactic and ideological phraseology. This related to Glatshteyn's point in the Tabatshnik interview that the religious and ethical prohibitions of Jewish life made the Bible, not Homer's epic poetry, the prototypical kind of Jewish literature: "Even today, Jews are inclined to read the kind of book that will give them the same spiritual nourishment they derive from a religious work. This may be bad, but it's ours. We cannot depart from it. This is the light I write in; this is the light we all write in."⁵⁷

Glatshteyn introduced a commemorative poetics in the long poem *"Ikh tu dermonen"* (I Keep Recalling), which closes *Shtralndike yidn* (1946) and a volume of Glatshteyn's collected Holocaust poetry from 1967 with the same title.⁵⁸ The poem focuses on Glatshteyn's home town of Lublin as a microcosm of Jewish Eastern Europe. His childhood upbringing in a religious family is depicted as the embodiment of traditional *Yiddishkeit*. As in the Holocaust poetry of Avrom Sutzkever and Chaim Grade, the mother figure appears prominently as a symbolic replacement for a lost civilization. The origins of *mame-loshn*, the mother tongue, are imagined in the image of the poet's dying mother:

מײַן טײַערע מאַמע, מײַן קלוג מויל,

מײַן אייגן מאַמע-לשון, וואָס איז אַזוי

צערטלעך אויפֿגעגאַנגען פֿאַר מיר

אין לובלינער געשעפּטשעטע פֿאַרנאַכטן.

מײַן מאַמע-לשון, מיט דעם וועקסענעם פּנים,

מיט די יסורים-דערשראָקענע,

האַלב-פֿאַרמאַכטע אויגן.

נאָך דאָס מוז איך דערמאָנען.

> My dear mother, my wise mouth,
> My own mother-tongue,
> Who developed so gently for me
> In the whispering twilights of Lublin.
> My mother-tongue, with her waxy face
> And pain-frightened,
> Half closed eyes—
> This too I must recall.[59]

Glatshteyn's previous horizontal engagement with contemporary literary and cultural trends in European and American letters has been replaced by a vertical approach. The birth of the Yiddish artist in Lublin in "I Keep Recalling" takes place in a universe validating Max Weinreich's view of Yiddish as the language of *derekh hashas* (the ways of the Mishna; traditional Judaism), a demarcated Yiddish land untouched by the outside Gentile world. As Christopher Hutton points out, the development of Yiddish as a heritage language was begun by Yiddish linguists and artists in the first half of the twentieth century who viewed "the linguistic system in isolation from the social complexities surrounding its use and its identification to view it in the abstract, to objectify it as an ideal or potentially ideal cultural artefact: *muster yidish* [normative Yiddish]."[60] As Hutton argues, this trend in Yiddish linguistics and literature was an attempt to create an idealized past that could serve as the touchstone for authenticity in the struggle against fragmentation and loss of cultural continuity: "A search for authenticity is by its very nature a conservative, backward-looking one. It is this ideology of authenticity that in the twentieth century has defined Yiddish as existing 'truly' or 'fully' only in the idealized past of an imagined, perfect cultural and personal integration."⁶¹

After the Holocaust, Glatshteyn abandoned to a large extent his earlier commitment to the development of modernist Yiddish poetry in creative dialogue with literary trends in European and American literature. The voluminous output of critical articles, collected in eight books, indicated a reorientation in Glatshteyn's work toward journalistic criticism. Simultaneously, the decline of a mass Yiddish readership reinforced his turn to a more commemorative, backward-looking poetry in the 1950s and 1960s. Although Glatshteyn in his critical articles fought against the irreversible demographic and historical forces that isolated and marginalized Yiddish culture in America, the poet was painfully aware that he was out of touch with the general aspirations of the American Jewish community. In the poem *"Gebentsht zol zayn"* (May It Be Blessed), from the collection *Di freyd fun yidishn vort* (The Joy of the Yiddish Word, 1962), he articulated the gulf that separated him from his children and grandchildren by imagining the *gnize* (genizah, Scriptural writings that have been discarded and hidden, typically in a synagogue) as protection against the defilement (*metame zayn,* making ritually unclean) of the Yiddish language. Thus Glatshteyn defiantly turned his back on a contemporary audience and guarded his obscurity as an artistic virtue, because it enabled him to preserve what he prescribed as the authenticity of Yiddish for future generations of readers:

איז געבענטשט זאָל זײַן אונדזער באָבע ייִדיש.
די ניט-גערעדטע, די ניט-געלייענטע,
אין געראַטעוועטער גניזה
די ניט-פֿאַראומרייניקטע.

מיר, די פּליטים פֿון אונדזערע קינדס-קינדער,
טראָגן אַ געדעכעניש ווי אַ באַשערטן יאָך.
קיין לעפֿצן קאָנען נישט מטמא זײַן
אונדזערע ייִדישע רייד,
פֿון שבת און דער פֿולער וואָך.

Bless grandmother Yiddish,
unspoken, unread;
in secret treasure,
undefiled, intact.

> Refugees from our children's children,
> We lug memory like a fated yoke.
> No lips will pollute
> Our Yiddish speech—
> From Sabbath on, throughout the week.[62]

In the introduction to *Ikh tu dermonen* (1967), Glatshteyn referred to Germany as a latter-day Amalek by quoting the scriptural proof-text partly in Hebrew. Amalek, the name of the biblical tribe that repeatedly sought to annihilate the Israelites, represented the prototype of the enemies of Israel in Jewish tradition: "*Ikh tu dermonen, az yidn torn keynmol nisht fargesn—osher oso lekho germanya*" (I keep recalling that Jews must not forget what *Germany did to you*).[63] The biblical commandment to remember "what Amalek did to you" and at the same time in biblical fashion to "blot out the memory of Amalek from under heaven" became paradigmatic of Glatshteyn's response to the German perpetrators' crimes against his people.[64]

A year after Tabatshnik's interview, Glatshteyn summed up his poetic career in the retrospective collection *Fun mayn gantser mi* (From All My Toil, 1956). Glatshteyn's work as a critic and contributor to the Yiddish press took the front seat in his career only after the Holocaust, as is evident from his eight books of critical articles published between 1947 and 1978 (the two last posthumously). This prolific output made him the leading Yiddish critic in America after 1945. Glatshteyn's tireless efforts on behalf of Yiddish literature in general and his own in particular are evident from his archive in YIVO, which covers the period from the mid-1950s until his death in 1971.[65] In an English letter to a young friend dated December 4, 1963, the sixty-seven-year-old poet delineated his daily workload in detail. As can be deduced from the content and tone of this unpublished letter, its recipient was an outsider to the world of Yiddish letters. However, even "at least half an outsider"[66] such as Howe did not fathom the Yiddish poet's sense of urgency and desperation—that time was running out:

> We passed each other yesterday as you hurled at me, by way of a friendly greeting, the following question: You work very hard, don't you? It was, of course, a joke and it sounded familiar to me, for I heard you ask me this humorous question about a half dozen times. . . .
> Now, as to my "hard" work generally: I write two weekly columns, edit the monthly *Zukunft*, writing editorials and reading manuscripts. I write a literary column every week for the *Kemfer* which

entails, of course, a great deal of reading. In order to meet these deadlines, I have to limit my sleep to about 4 and a half hours a day. I therefore rise about 5 o'clock in the morning to do my extra curricular work. My book of essays which was published only a few weeks ago, is realistically titled "With My Books at Dawn." It is a book of about 600 pages, and—marvels—I actually wrote it, as I wrote my other 19 books of poetry, novels and essays. Add to this that my participation is required in every major Yiddish cultural enterprise which practically keeps me from resting every week-end in the year.

And add to this a little bit of love-life and laughter and you will have an account of a day's work, perhaps not as hard as yours, young man, but adequate for my years, I hope.[67]

This frantic pace of productivity reflected Glatshteyn's burden of being the leading spokesperson of Yiddish culture in America, fighting for the continuation of Yiddish literature against all odds. The zeitgeist in the American Jewish community was forward-looking, as it rallied behind the newly founded Jewish state. English-speaking children of Yiddish speakers were venturing into American society, taking advantage of the unlimited possibilities for upward mobility. Yiddish embodied the "old home" that had so recently come to such a terrible end on European soil. The main response among American Jews was to forget the past and look forward to a brighter future, embodied in the uniquely new American Diaspora and in the first sovereign Jewish state in two thousand years.[68] The New York Yiddish writers reacted by retreating into a self-imposed cultural ghetto, where they mourned the destruction of their communities.

Tabatshnik's 1969 interview with the Yiddish and Hebrew poet Aaron Zeitlin, published in *Di goldene keyt*, exposed the shaky foundation of the post-Holocaust poetics of Glatshteyn and his ilk in their narrow commitment to Yiddish. Like his compatriot and friend Yitskhok Bashevis, Zeitlin stood apart from the New York Yiddish cultural world:

> *Tabatshnik*: I ask my question [*shayle*] out of love of Yiddish literature that you encounter among Yiddish poets; a kind of patriotism of literature that is understandable given our great losses. Do you also feel this love of Yiddish literature, this . . . patriotism?
> *Zeitlin*: It is a bad sign when one begins to speak about a special love and one declares it to the whole world. Why is it necessary to advertise one's love of Yiddish, Yiddish poetry, Yiddish

literature? If it is a natural thing, then why is it necessary all the time to talk about how dearly one loves; how mightily one loves Yiddish literature and how sacred Yiddish poetry is? Are the Gentile writers, for example, patriots of their literatures? And what is literature? A collective thing? No, I have never been a literature patriot.

Tabatshnik: I must say, I don't understand your isolation [*opgezundertkeyt*].⁶⁹

For Zeitlin and Yitskhok Bashevis, any political, ideological, and cultural commitment to Yiddish literature compromised literary creativity, and made it a handmaiden to "external" purposes that were detrimental to the fundamental freedom and individuality of literary creativity. Zeitlin and Yitskhok Bashevis considered it both a dangerous limitation and illusion to infuse their creative work with anything that smacked of collective concerns, including Glatshteyn's attempt to bolster the communal spirit among Yiddish writers in New York or, to paraphrase Tabatshnik's words, "literature patriotism." This caused a rift between, on the one hand, Zeitlin and Yitskhok Bashevis, and, on the other, most other New York Yiddish writers.

Aaron Zeitlin's poem "Warsaw, 1912" belongs to a group of poems titled "*A Bintl Varshe-lider*" (A Bundle of Warsaw Poems) included in *Gezamlte lider* (Collected Poems, 1947). This title brings to mind the popular *Bintl briv* column in the Yiddish daily newspaper *Forverts*, which combined the role of therapist and social worker. Like the highly personal questions to *Bintl briv*'s editor, "Warsaw 1912" ends with a question, quoting the popular Yiddish song "*A brivele der mamen.*" This was one of the most popular songs in both Europe and America during the era of large-scale immigration prior to World War I. It speaks of an old mother left behind in Europe, anxiously awaiting news of her children in the New World. In Zeitlin's version:

אַלע װאָלטן מיר געשריבן
אַ בריוועלע איבער ימ׳ען
אַ בריוועלע דער מאַמען
אָבער—
װוּ איז די מאַמע? . . .

We would all have written
A letter over the ocean,
A letter to mother

But—
Where is my mother? . . . [70]

The contrast between the dramas of Jewish immigration to the United States in 1912 and the poet's question about the fate of his mother in 1945 highlights the radical new circumstances of post-Holocaust Jewish culture. Instead of the immigration era's nostalgia for the Old World, and the *Bintl briv* column's promise of generational continuity, the question opens a void. The absence of the poet's mother is highlighted sharply against a backdrop of public spaces depicted in the poem. Moreover, the mother figure, being derived from a popular Yiddish song, creates a memory shard from the collective consciousness; a stand-in for the loss of mother-tongue, motherland, and the actual

FIGURE 6.2. Aaron Zeitlin, New York (undated). (Archives of the YIVO Institute for Jewish Research, New York)

mother. The father figure in the poem, on the other hand, is split between the image of the Hasidic *rebbe* modeled on the poet's father, Hillel Zeitlin, and Yitskhok Leybush Peretz, the main influences on Aaron Zeitlin's poetry. In a 1932 letter from Warsaw to the literary critic Shmuel Niger in New York, Zeitlin described his credo: "I am not Orthodox, nor am I religiously dogmatic, and my anti-secular views are very far from any proselytizing tendencies. But I am a son of Hillel Zeitlin and a grandson of great-grandfathers . . . the God-experience runs in my blood, and it wouldn't occur to me for one minute to get rid of it, and to exchange ancient gold for quasi-new filth."[71]

Zeitlin's recitation of his poem "*Varshe, 1912*" for Avrom Tabatshnik's anthology, *Di shtim fun yidishn poet,* sounded out the intonations of the Warsaw Yiddish dialect, Yiddish-*taytsh,* and the popular song "*A brivele der mamen.*" Zeitlin's performance of the poem stressed its polyphonic character: Warsaw Yiddish, "*yakh koyf*"; the tall Russian merchant, "*a hoykher katsap,*" who yells out his goods in Russian; *kheder* instruction conducted in the traditional *yidish-taytsh,* "*veyoymer—hot gezogt, adonay—got, al moyshe—tsu moyshen*" (and He said [Hebrew]—said [Yiddish]—God [Yiddish], to Moses [Hebrew]—to Moses [Yiddish]). The poem's final stanza—"*Vu iz di mame?*" (Where is my mother?)—points to a rupture between mother and son, Warsaw and New York, present and past.[72] The poet in New York is an exiled orphan forever severed from his family and his homeland.

The poem contrasts the internal and the external: the dark, boxlike courtyard versus the open summer streets of Warsaw. People move in and out of these two spaces, invoking visual and auditory recollections from a lost time and place. Like Proust's remembrance of the taste of the madeleine, the sound of a gramophone blasting the popular Yiddish song "*A brivele der mamen*" out of the window in a Warsaw courtyard triggers Zeitlin's recollections. The only named figure in the poem is Yitskhok Leybush Peretz, who makes a brief appearance on the street. Like the magician, *der kishef-makher,* a tightrope walker who performs his daring antics in the Warsaw courtyard at the beginning of the poem, Peretz is "*ful mit kishef*" (full of magic) and "*ingantsn kishef*" (completely magical). The repetition of words in this section adds to the charisma and otherworldly character of the Peretz figure.

Like the tightrope walker, Peretz operates in a realm that transcends the laws of nature "*un er—er flit, er flit*" (and he—he flies, he flies). In a manner similar to Peretz's story "*Der kishefmakher*" (The Magician) in *Di folkstimlekhe geshikhtn,* Zeitlin recreates a Peretz figure who embodies redemption through the artistic imagination that crystallizes "*doyres, veltn, klangen*" (generations, worlds, sounds).[73] In Peretz's story, a poor couple is visited at the first Seder by an unexpected guest. He turns out to be a magician who conjures up much-needed food and drink. Similarly, Peretz bursts unexpectedly onto the scene in Zeitlin's poem, conjuring up a world of artistic transcendence. Only once in the poem does Zeitlin use a Hebrew word from Scripture: *shol takhtie*, the underworld, the world of the dead used to describe the Warsaw courtyard. This space, likened to a narrow box (*shmoler kastn*), indicating the deathlike existence of the courtyard's inhabitants longing for a different world—and forecasting their impending ghettoization by the Nazis and murder in Treblinka—is embodied by the tightrope walker in the sky. Death appears a second time in the poem in the form of a horse-drawn hearse that silences the Jewish street musician. Unlike the casket image of the courtyard, the hearse indicates the end of the natural life cycle:

אַזוי לעשט זיך דער בן-אָדם, אַזוי מוז יעדער
גיין נאָכ'ן מלאך-המוות
אַהיים צו די אָבות.

> That's how a human being is extinguished, like anybody must
> Follow the Angel of Death
> On the way home to his ancestors.[74]

This scene is followed by the voices of Jewish boys in the *kheder* reciting *khumesh-taytsh*, continuing the traditional chain of learning. After the brief appearance of the Hasidic *rebbe* invoked by the reference to the Yiddish song "*Sha shtil, makht nit keyn gerider / der rebbe geyt shoyn tantsn vider*" (Shh, hush, don't make any noise / the rebbe will continue to dance), the worldly creative force embodied by Peretz is introduced. The poem's style, themes, and language are embedded in an aesthetic context encapsulated by the long-haired *bokher* (unmarried young man) and the words "*poezye—shafung—muze*" (poetry, creation, muse).[75] Unlike in other parts of Zeitlin's poetry, God is not mentioned at all. In "Warsaw, 1912" Zeitlin drew upon his religious background in a distinctly secular poetic mode.

Like most of his contemporaries in Yiddish literature, Zeitlin took Peretz's neoromantic and modernist work as his point of departure. A huge picture of Peretz hung in Tlomatske 13, *der literatn-fareyn*, the Yiddish Writers Union in Warsaw, which served as the most important social and cultural institution for Jewish writers during the interwar period. Zeitlin was the head of another important cultural institution, the Yiddish PEN club, between 1930 and 1934 and in 1938. Moreover, between 1932 and 1934, Zeitlin and his friend Yitskhok Bashevis edited the monthly literary journal *Globus*. As its name indicated, this publication sought to create the critical foundation for a world spanning Yiddish literature, modeled on Peretz's vision for a cutting-edge, modern literature fused with indigenous Jewish forms, styles, and themes.

Zeitlin was not the only Yiddish writer to pay tribute to Peretz as a cornerstone of Yiddish literature after the Holocaust. Y. Y. Trunk devoted *Perets*, volume 5 of his seven-volume memoir, *Poyln* (1944–53), to describing Peretz's literary salon in Warsaw. Zeitlin wrote the foreword to *In a literarisher shtub* (In a Literary Salon, 1946), his brother's intimate portrait of his father Hillel Zeitlin's literary salon in Warsaw prior to World War I. These memoirs were part of the outpouring of life-writing that highlighted the centrality of Peretz's literary heritage for Yiddish culture after the Holocaust. In 1952 the leading Yiddish critic Shmuel Niger published a five-hundred-page biography of Peretz which, for the first time, delineated the author's life and work in a grand synthetic portrait. Yitskhok Bashevis returned from a seven-year writer's block with an article in *Tsukunft* in 1943, "*Arum der yidisher literatur in Poyln*" (On Yiddish Literature in Poland), which acknowledged Peretz as the only major Jewish writer who had influenced his work. A former secretary of Tlomatske 13, the Yiddish poet Melekh Ravitsh, introduced his three volumes of mini-biographies of Polish Jewish writers, *Mayn leksikon* (My Encyclopedia, 1945), with a fictional introduction by Peretz.[76]

In the poem "*Nokhklang tsu 'bay nakht afn altn mark'*" (Echo of "A Night in the Old Marketplace"), dated February 1945, Zeitlin added a dialogue to Peretz's play *Bay nakht afn altn mark* (A Night in the Old Marketplace). The poet (Peretz's shadow) is hopelessly searching for the various political and religious characters who made up Jewish Poland in the Old Marketplace, in order to continue the play's exploration of modern Jewish existence. The Angel of Death responds to the Peretz figure in the final words of the poem:

אויס בית-עולמס,
אויס תכריכים, אויס קדיש, אויס קבֿר-ישׂראל,
אויס שטילער שווידעה,
אויס כּישוף-פֿלעמל, מתים-געזעמל,
אויס יענע-וועלטיקער ניגון,
יענע-וועלטיקע רו.
אויס בר-מיננס, וואָס לעבן אין פֿיבער-נעכט אויף
אויף דער באַשווערונג פֿון אַזעלכע ווי דו.
קיינער פֿון די דמיניקע נישטאָ—

נישט אַלט, נישט יונג,
נישט פֿרום, נישט אומפֿרום, נישט רעכטע, נישט לינקע.
נישט קיין מלאך בין איך, נאָר אַ לעצטער "אוי"
פֿון אַ ייִד פֿאַרברענט אין טרעבלינקע.

No cemeteries,
No burial shrouds, no *kadish*, no Jewish burial place,
No quiet tremble,
No magic-fire, no cluster of corpses,
No otherworldly melody,
Otherworldly peace.
No dead people, who are revived in a fever night
By your imploring words.
Nobody of your kind any longer—
No old, no young,
No religious, no irreligious, no rightwing, no leftwing.
I am not an angel, but only a last "oy"
Of a Jew burned in Treblinka.[77]

The poem is a *nokhklang*, the fading echo of "A Night in the Old Marketplace" that indicates the end of Peretz's art in Treblinka.[78] This sense of being the last surviving remnants of a great tradition imbues Zeitlin's Holocaust poetry with a note of hopelessness and despair. The poet is left only with words—"*Gornisht oyser verter*" (Nothing Remains but Words), the title of another poem. In the poem "*Mayn foter*" (My Father), Zeitlin pays tribute to his father, Hillel Zeitlin, stressing his own worthlessness as an exiled poet severed from his father and his people:

. . . איך, דײַן זון, האָב גאָרנישט
אויסער ווערטער. צו דעם שד פֿון ווערטער
בין איך פֿאַרקויפֿט און כ׳שלעפּ די בייזע משׂא,
ס׳וויל נישט קוקן אין מײַן זײַט כּביכול,
ווי כ׳וואָלט געווען אַ מקח-טעות.

I, your son, have nothing
Except words. I am sold to the demon of words
And I carry the evil load
And God will not look to my side
As if I were a misunderstanding.[79]

The word "*literaturekhts*" appears often in Zeitlin's correspondence from the interwar period and in his Holocaust poetry. The Slavic suffix *ekhts* changes the meaning of the word "literatur" into an inferior, wasteful activity, a pale imitation of the real thing. Zeitlin used this word to criticize the worldliness and superficiality of Yiddish literature in his interwar correspondence with Shmuel Niger. After the Holocaust, Zeitlin applied this word to his own poetry. Zeitlin's redefinition of Peretz's credo for the post-Holocaust age is tied to his strongly felt sense of personal and artistic inferiority. In the poem "*Zeks shures*" (Six Lines), the Yiddish poet has become the superfluous man:

איך ווייס: קיינער דארף מיך נישט אויף אָט דעם עולם,
מיך, ווערטער-בעטלער אויף דעם יידישן בית-עולם.
ווער דארף א ליד—און נאָך דערצו אויף יידיש?

נאָר בלויז דאָס האָפֿנונגסלאָזע אויף דער ערד איז שיין,
און געטלעך איז נאָר דאָס, וואָס מוז פֿארגיין,
און נאָר הכנעה איז מרידיש.

I know: that in this world nobody needs me,
me, a word-beggar in the Jewish graveyard.
Who needs a poem, especially in Yiddish?

Only what is hopeless on this earth has beauty
and only the ephemeral is godly
and humility is the only true rebellion.[80]

The rhyme "*yidish / meridish*" (Yiddish / rebellion) in the poem's third and sixth lines crystallizes subtly the poet's vision of "*mer (y)idish*" (more Yiddish), as comfort and revolt in the Jewish graveyard post-1945. The Yiddish artistic word not only survives but continues, like Singer's demons, to act out of spite against all odds, turning hopelessness into rebellion against the decline of the Yiddish speech community. Simultaneously, the six lines represent the six million Jewish victims, serving as a commemorative inscription, a simile of a poetic tombstone.

"Warsaw, 1912" presents a highly selective image of Warsaw, formerly the largest Jewish urban center in Eastern Europe. As Hana Wirth-Nesher points out, Jewish fiction and life-writing's creation of imaginary replicas "are not elegies for cities past, as many readers of the novel would have it, nor are they paeans to the city present. They are encoded landscapes of self and place, left to be decoded again and again."⁸¹ Similarly, Zeitlin's poem creates a particular vision of Warsaw's urban space, indebted to Peretz's poetics, while foreshadowing its destruction, implemented by the Nazis less than two and a half years before the poem's creation (in December 1945). In focusing on the Jewish collective way of life—its characters, institutions, and voices—the poem depersonalizes the depiction of Warsaw in 1912 while stressing the formative influence of Hillel Zeitlin and Peretz on the poet's artistic quest. The poem is more than an elegy and a paean to Jewish Warsaw. It is a deeply felt expression of the poet's quest, as a writer and a son of Jewish Warsaw, which has been disrupted but not terminated by the Holocaust.

Aaron Zeitlin came from a religious family and was trained in classical Jewish texts in the *kheder* and yeshiva. Although the poet in a few cases employs scriptural references and models, his works as a whole are embedded in the secular context of the daily Yiddish newspaper where they initially were published. The poem's use of a popular Yiddish song—a genre associated with *shund* and vaudeville—underlines Zeitlin's choice of a stylistic tonality that subverts any divine and redemptive models derived from the Hebrew scriptural tradition. New York as the place of recollection provides the vantage point from which the poet looks back and confronts his Warsaw past.

The Yiddish writer in New York during the war is the prototypical exile whose life, in the words of Edward Said, is "led outside habitual order. It is nomadic, decentered, contrapuntal; but no sooner does one get accustomed to it than its unsettling force erupts anew."⁸² In the few cases in which Zeitlin depicts the urban space of New York, it appears foreign and exotic compared to the culturally specific urban landscape of "Warsaw, 1912." After describing the exoticism of Washington Square Park in Manhattan on a May morning (including a stereotypical portrait of African Americans), Zeitlin ends the 1942 poem "*Zuntik af Vashington skver*" (Sunday in Washington Square):

ס׳איז זונטיק. ס׳איז מײַ.
פֿאַרלעך און פֿייגל אויף וואַשינגטאָן סקווער.
אויך אהרן צייטלין איז דאָ דערבײַ—
ווער ווייס, וואָס מיט אים איז דער מער.
אויך ער איז דאָ דערבײַ—
ווי קומט ער איבערהויפט אהער?
אַ וועלט האָט ער געהאַט, אַ וועלט פֿאַרלוירן.
זמן וועג—פֿאַרהוילן.
עס טאַנצט פֿאַר אים אַ וואָרט,

אַרומגעהילט מיט פֿלאַמען פֿון מאָרד
אַ סיגנאַל, אַן אַקאָרד:
פּוילן.

It is Sunday. It is May.
Couples and birds in Washington Square.
Aaron Zeitlin is also here—
Who knows what's up with him.
He is also around—
How did he end up here?
A world belonged to him, a world lost.
His way—concealed.
A word dances in front of him,
Surrounded by flames of murder,
A signal, a chord,
Poland.[83]

7

PERFORMING YIDDISH POETRY AT THE 92ND STREET Y

Why	Farvos di Vy?
the Y?	Ich reyd
Lectures	ohn freyd
to specters,	un sheydim tantsen derbei,

Cynthia Ozick, "Envy; or, Yiddish in America" (1969)[1]

On November 2, 1966, Yankev Glatshteyn read his dadaist hymn to Yiddish, "Sing Ladino," for an attentive audience at the 92nd Street Y in Manhattan. The recording of the event enables us to hear the poet's voice, in clear diction, reciting his radical performance of Jewish language hybridity, which is impossible to convey in English. This is followed by the audience's appreciation, which is palpable in the silence following the reading. Glatshteyn had asked the audience not to applaud after each poem, so that his listeners would have the opportunity without distraction to immerse themselves fully in the sound, rhythm, and texture of the poetry:

זינג לאַדינאָ

זינג לאַדינאָ, בלאָנדער זענגעה,

אונדזער צויבערזשאַרגאָנינאַ,

אלקאַלירטע רעדעריי,

אַלצעצונגטע שפּראַכבעריי

זונפֿאַרגינאַ, גינאַ-גינאַ,

גינגאַלדיקער אויפֿשטראַל, אויפֿפֿראַל—

אלגעפֿאַרבגעדאַנקעריי,

אלע ברויטן, אלע טויטן,

אלע טייגן, אלע טונדרען,

אַלע װאונדרען אַלקאָלירן,
אַלחרוזין,
אַלאושפּיזין,
אַלע קנויטן, אַלע הויטן,
געלרייט און פּאַלאשינאַ,
פּאַלעסטינאַ דאַבּעַרינאַ,
אונדזער, אונדזער אוניװערסלאַדינאַ,
בּלאָנדער אַלאַדינאַ זינג.

פֿון די טיפֿן און טיפֿערנאָכן,
סלאָװיש, ליבּאױש און טערקאַױש,
ליאַכיש, קאַצאַכיש
יעװאָניש און טעװטאָניש,
קאַװקאַזיש, אשכּנזיש,
קאַרפּאַטיש און אזיאַטיש—
אונזער שפּראַכגעטומל,
אונדזער טרויעריקן אַלגעראומל,
אונדזער רומל, אונדזער שומל,
אונדזער לעטװיש, אונדזער
ליוטװיש,
זשאַרגאַנינאַ,
שלאַנקער דענגער,
בּלאָנדער זענגער,
זינג לאַדין

Zing ladino
Zing ladino, blonder zenger,
undzer tsoyberzshargonino
alkolirte rederay,
altsetsungte shprakheray
zunfargino, gino, gino,
gingoldiker oyfshtral, oyfpral—
algefarbgedankeray,
ale broytn, ale toytn
ale teygn, ale tundren,
ale vundren alkolirn,
alkhroyzn,
alushpizin,
ale knoytn, ale hoytn,

gelroyt un falashino,
palestino daberino,
undzer, undzer universladino,
blonder aladino zing.

Fun di tifn un tifernokhn,
slavish, libavish un terkavish,
liakhish, katsakhish,
yevonish un tevtonish,
kavkazish, ashkenazish,
karpatish un ayzatish—
undzer shprakhgetuml,
undzer troyrikn algeruml,
undzer ruml, undzer shuml,
undzer letvish, undzer
liutvish,
zshargonino
shlanker denger,
blonder zenger,
zing ladino.

Three years later, a Jewish American writer, Cynthia Ozick, used the Yiddish poetry readings at the 92nd Street Y as the main setting for her novella "Envy; or, Yiddish in America." She employed the full range of multilingual strategies—Yinglish, Yiddish, and Hebrew in transliteration, and Yiddish-inflected immigrant English—to portray the state of Jewish letters in America. As the above quote from "Envy" indicates, it was the incompatibility between the Yiddish original and its transposition in various forms of translation and transliteration which Ozick used to chart Jewish multilingualism in America. Irving Howe, the critic and anthologizer of Yiddish literature, and Ozick contributed to the final event of the Yiddish poetry series held in 1969, at which they paid tribute to the Yiddish poets who were still writing, publishing, and performing poetry in New York.

Thanks to the 92nd Street Y's recording of these events, the Yiddish poetry series offers an aural portrait of secular Yiddish culture in America during the 1960s, when most of the great Yiddish poets were still alive. The 92nd Street Y's Poetry Center's Yiddish and Hebrew Poetry Series ran from the 1962–63 through the 1969–70 season, featuring more than thirty Yiddish poets plus a handful who wrote in Hebrew, including Yiddish/Hebrew bilingual poets.³ Most of these writers lived in New York, where they had been working for decades; nevertheless, they remained virtually unknown outside their specific cultural environments in Yiddish and Hebrew. The recorded material features major Yiddish writers such as Yitskhok Bashevis, Yankev Glatshteyn, Avrom Sutzkever, Itsik Manger, Aaron Zeitlin, Chaim Grade, Rokhl Korn, and Kadya Molodovsky as well as the lesser-known Yiddish women poets Chava Rosenfarb, Rosa Gutman, and Rochelle Weprinsky. If we use Glatshteyn as the reference point for discussing the Yiddish poetry series, a wider perspective of intersecting fields of Jewish American writers employing multilingual strategies will come to light. As Lawrence Rosenwald points out: "Because it was Glatshteyn who was reading Auden and [Marianne] Moore and not the reverse, it is Glatshteyn through whom the lines of connection run. From Moore's viewpoint, from Auden's, those lines were invisible. From Glatshteyn's, they are alive and important, and by centering on him we can get a larger view of the still closely knit story."⁴

Unlike Herts Grosbard's popular *vort-kontsertn* (word concerts), which had captivated audiences in Europe and the Americas since the 1920s, the poetry readings at the Y were conducted by the poets themselves, in front of small audiences.⁵ This was a far cry from the celebrity readings by the "classical" Yiddish writers Sholem Aleichem, Mendele Moykher Sforim, and I. L. Peretz in the first decade of the twentieth century in the Pale of Settlement, or Grosbard's readings to huge audiences. However, Itsik Manger and Avrom Sutzkever, both with long, distinguished careers as public readers of their own poetry in Eastern Europe in the 1930s and in the Vilna Ghetto (Sutzkever), infused their reading with the performance style of the wanderings troubadours (Manger) and the Russian poetry declamation of dramatic presentation (Sutzkever). None of the poets who read at the Y in the 1960s approximated the mastery of diction and elocution that characterized Herts Grosbard's word concerts. The public character of the poetry reading was emphasized at the Y, in contrast to the intimate readings of Yiddish poets for Avrom Tabatshnik's project *Di shtim fun yidishn poet* in the mid-1950s. Only a few writers (Yitskhok Bashevis, Greenberg, and Manger) read in their Ukrainian and Polish Yiddish dialects; the rest used a standard Yiddish diction that only rarely was infused with dialectical features.

As the American poet Charles Bernstein points out, "[T]he tendency among critics and scholars to value the written over the performed text, has resulted in a remarkable lack of attention given to the poetry reading as a medium in its own right, a medium that has had a profound impact on twentieth-century poetry, and in particular the poetry of the second half of the century."⁶ In a Jewish context, this tendency to focus on the written over the spoken word has been even more pronounced, despite the widespread consensus among cultural historians of the centrality of spoken-word events in the creation of Jewish public culture.⁷ Like radio or chamber music, the poetry reading is an "oasis of low technology," which requires only a reader and a microphone in front of an audience. The recorded material provides insights into the social and cultural features of the Yiddish poetry series, which supplement published versions of the performed poems and the archival material about the planning and execution of the events. Most important, the recorded material allows us to hear the voices of the poets performing live, in front of an audience, which responds with applause, laughter, questions, and comments. Moreover, all the poetry readings at the Y were introduced by Yiddish poets, a fact that provides important material about the social and cultural significance of the events and their aesthetic and critical framing. The poetry reading contributes to "multifoliate . . . performances of the poem" and is one of multiple copies of the poem in its distribution from poet to readers: "the anti-expressive poetry reading stands out as an oasis of low technology that is among the least spectaclized events in our public culture. Explicit value is placed almost exclusively on the acoustic production of a single unaccompanied speaking voice, with all other theatrical elements being placed, in most cases, out of frame. The solo voice so starkly framed can come to seem virtually disembodied in an uncanny, even hypnotic, way."⁸

This chapter partakes in the renewed interest in multilingual literary expression in America in current scholarship and in writing of American literary history.⁹ Material presented contributes to the mapping of multilingualism in the conception and development of American literature. The Yiddish poets at the 92nd Street Y viewed themselves as part of American literature even as they were conscious of the fact that few outside the Yiddish-speaking world read or even knew about them.¹⁰ As early as the 1920s, Yiddish poets were painfully aware of their invisibility as minority writers in American culture. However they remained confident of their importance for American literature even if very few had heard about them in the Anglophone world. The poet A. Leyeles typified that sentiment in his diagnosis of the monolingual state of American letters in a 1937 article in the journal *Inzikh:* "The pettiest Jewish scribbler in English, the lowest reporter in an English newspaper feels sky high above Yiddish—whether it's the Yiddish press or the demanding, original Yiddish literature. So many years in America, such a fine literature created here, and we remain strangers to our neighbors as if we had lived in Siam or had written in some Eskimo dialect."¹¹

A shift in the reception of Yiddish culture in American society began to occur from the mid-1950s through the 1960s. It was marked by three cultural phenomena: the increasing availability of Yitskhok Bashevis's work in English translation; Irving Howe and Eliezer Greenberg's anthologies *A Treasury of Yiddish Stories* (1954) and *A Treasury of Yiddish Poetry* (1969); and most important, the musical *Fiddler on the Roof* (1964), based on Sholem Aleichem's novel *Tevye the Dairyman*. These English-language adaptations of Yiddish literature indicated a change in attitude toward Yiddish among second- and third-generation American Jews. Rather than viewing Yiddish as the domain of Jewish comedy, a jargon and a primitive immigrant language to be abolished as soon as possible, a younger generation of American Jews turned to Yiddish as an authentic expression of their Eastern European Jewish heritage.[12]

The Yiddish poetry series at the Y encapsulated the various intersecting cultural domains of the two main sectors of Jewish culture, the Anglo-Jewish and the Yiddish. It can serve as a test case for the shifting boundaries between these two cultural areas whose mutual significance in the broader context of American literature was reconceptualized in the 1960s. The Yiddish poetry series at the Y marked the end of a Yiddish literary generation. Most of these writers were in their sixties and seventies, so the series did not initiate a new beginning that would break down the walls of invisibility of Yiddish culture in America. The Y paid tribute to a rich Jewish American poetic tradition that had no literary successors. The generational shift that had taken place in Jewish American literature in the 1940s and 1950s was on full display at the final event in the poetry series in 1969: an aging group of Yiddish poets, such as Glatshteyn, Rokhl Korn, and Kadya Molodovsky, and a younger generation of poet-translators, such as Cynthia Ozick, John Hollander, and Adrienne Rich.

As one of the founders of the *inzikhist* movement during the interwar period, Glatshteyn moved to the center of Yiddish culture in the post-Holocaust period and became the unofficial poet laureate of Yiddish letters in America. In addition to his poetic work, he was the chief representative of Yiddish criticism, exemplified by his weekly column, "*In tokh genumen*" (The Heart of the Matter), in the Labor Zionist journal *Der yidisher kemfer*, collected in eight volumes of literary criticism.[13] Glatshteyn's crucial role in keeping the flame of highbrow Yiddish culture alive propelled him to conceive and organize the poetry series. Glatshteyn viewed it as an opportunity for the still sizable number of active Yiddish writers to receive the long overdue recognition that had thus far eluded them in America.

The storyteller Yitskhok Bashevis—the only performer of prose in the series—read from his work at three different events. Two of them were conducted entirely in English; his were the only readings to be given in English.[14] Singer had received critical accolades and popular success for his work in English translation since the mid-1950s. He saw the future of Yiddish literature as dependent on its ability to reach out to an American audience in translation. Unlike Glatshteyn, Singer made the transposition of his Yiddish work into English his central artistic concern. Glatshteyn advocated fierce loyalty to the Yiddish language, while Singer circumvented the relationship between original and translation, the latter to which he referred as a "second original." The 92nd Street Y poetry series gave Glatshteyn and Singer access to the premier literary podium in the United States, and they used it to articulate their diverging views of Yiddish literature.

Irving Howe, along with the Yiddish poet Eliezer Greenberg, edited several anthologies of Yiddish literature in English translation, a project that culminated in their first anthology of Yiddish poetry in 1969. Organized by Howe, the final event in the poetry series featured the publication of the anthology *A Treasury of Yiddish Poetry*. At this event, Yiddish poets and their translators, young Jewish American poets, appeared together on stage, reading Yiddish poems in the original and in translation. Irving Howe saw his mission as editor and translator in maintaining the modernist seriousness of Yiddish poetic expression. He wanted to normalize the status of Yiddish poetry by demonstrating that it grew out of the major trends in European and American modernism. Howe and Greenberg's anthology contributed to the exchange of poetry between Yiddish and Anglo-Jewish poets through the latter's selection and translation of the former's work. Translation was vital for Anglophone Jewish writers in that it opened up vistas of historical and cultural experiences beyond the horizons of American-born writers: "Through such matchmaking, various voices otherwise inaudible . . . were heard in an increasingly monolingual country."[15]

Cynthia Ozick, a prose writer and translator of Yiddish literature, used the poetry readings as the setting for her novella "Envy; or Yiddish in America" (1969). This was a spoof about two Yiddish writers modeled on Glatshteyn and Singer. It became a turning point in Ozick's literary career, as she acknowledged in a 1972 posthumous tribute to Glatshteyn. After Ozick's first Henry James–inspired novel, *Trust* (1966), her debut as a Jewish writer was "Envy; or, Yiddish in America." The story's turn to Jewish languages and themes corresponded with an assignment as translator of Yiddish poetry for Howe and Greenberg's *A Treasury of Yiddish Poetry*. As she recalled in the

1972 tribute to Yankev Glatshteyn, "It was not until about five years ago that I began to read Yiddish poetry seriously and passionately."[16] Ozick's work in translating Yiddish poetry triggered memories of her father, and as a result of this work, Ozick wrote "Envy; or, Yiddish in America":

> I wrote it as an elegy, a lamentation, a celebration, because six million Yiddish tongues were under the earth of Europe, and because here under American liberty and spaciousness my own generation, in its foolishness, stupidity, and self-disregard had, in an act tantamount to auto-lobotomy, disposed of the literature of its fathers. I thought of my own, now middle-aged, generation of American Jewish writers as unwitting collaborators in the Nazi extirpation of Yiddish.[17]

In response to the story, "a terrible thing happened." Ozick received threatening telephone calls, and she was branded an enemy of Yiddish in the Yiddish press. To her grief, "Glatshteyn was one of those who misunderstood." Two years later, in 1971, with the angry words about her story still reverberating, Ozick decided to write a letter to Glatshteyn "to explain the misunderstanding and the hurt."[18] The next day she read his obituary. More than eight years earlier, Glatshteyn had organized the first event at the 92nd Street Y, which sought to make Yiddish poetry readings an integral part of the cultural offerings at the Y. Ozick was one of the young American Jewish writers who actively participated in the events.

Glatshteyn's conception of the Yiddish poetry series was outlined in the Yiddish daily *Der tog*'s English section on January 12, 1963: "A week earlier," the reviewer S. Margoshes reported, "more than a hundred poetry-hungry men and women jammed the Y.M.Y.W.H.A. on 92nd Street and Lexington Avenue, to listen to a Yiddish poetry reading by Jacob Glatshteyn, the eminent Yiddish poet and essayist." Margoshes pointed out that the Jewish cultural agencies had neglected Yiddish language and literature, which were little known in wide American Jewish circles. The reviewer hoped that "the great attendance at the Yiddish poetry reading [at the Y] will make a breakthrough in the wall of indifference to and neglect of Yiddish literature." Margoshes suggested that "[p]erhaps a bi-lingual cultural evening could be arranged to meet the requirements of those whose knowledge of Yiddish is scanty or non-existent."[19] Only one writer in the series read and took questions in both Yiddish and English, however: Yitskhok Bashevis. Every other reading was conducted in either Yiddish or Hebrew, with a few bilingually in Yiddish and Hebrew. The final event in the series, held on November 2, 1969, featuring some of the Yiddish writers and their translators from *A Treasury of Yiddish Poetry* (1969), was conducted primarily in English.

The Yiddish series was the brainchild of William Kolodney, director of education at the Y's Poetry Center. Repeatedly, the Yiddish presenters paid tribute to Kolodney, who remained a staunch supporter of the readings both financially and logistically. The Y, the largest and oldest continuously operating YM-YWHA in the United States, had created a secular humanist approach to the dissemination of Jewish culture. As Naomi Jackson describes in her study of modern dance at the Y: "within its walls, Jewishness was often defined by constituency, association, and patronage rather than manifestly Jewish content. Although sectarian programming occurred, the emphasis was on general cultural and educational activity. Interest in such programming evolved in line with widespread progressive thinking in arts and adult education circles regarding the cultivation of the individual within an American democracy."[20]

Kolodney also created the Poetry Center, which reflected his view of secular humanism as a replacement for traditional religion. In his 1951 dissertation about the 92nd Street Y, Kolodney pointed out that "[t]he Poetry Center was started to meet the need of the very few persons in New York to whom poetry offers the theological, the ethical and the aesthetic equivalent of traditional religion."[21] Moreover, as he stressed, "poetry, more than any other art, can be a substitute for prayer."[22] By the early 1960s the Poetry Center had become the most venerable and sought-after venue for poetry readings in the United States. The advent of the counterculture, headed by Norman Mailer and Allen Ginsberg, clashed with Kolodney's vision for the Poetry Center, which they viewed as a fortress of establishment culture. As reported in the *New York Times* on February 8, 1961, Kolodney decided to bring down the curtain in the middle of Norman Mailer's reading the previous night: "According to Dr. William Kolodney . . . the action was taken to end 'a recital of raw, obscene images and vocabulary which broke the limits of good taste from any point of view.'"[23] The sixties avant-garde had made their first appearance at the Poetry Center and would continue to dominate the readings at the Y during the 1960s. The Yiddish and Hebrew poetry readings, in contrast, expressed a poetic discourse more in line with Kolodney's vision for the Poetry Center. Unlike most other poetry readings at the Poetry Center, they were focused on the past and removed from the cultural turbulence and transformation of the 1960s.

In his introduction of Yankev Glatshteyn at the first Yiddish poetry reading on January 7, 1963, Zvi Scooler took on the role of the *gabbai* (caretaker) in the synagogue and called up the poet to the *bimah* (lectern in front of the ark), where he would read from the *sedre funem tog* (the Torah reading of the day).[24] Scooler referred to the auditorium in which the reading took place as a *mokem koydesh*, a holy place, and a book of poetry as a *seyfer*, a holy book. Furthermore, the event was described as a "*simkhe far yidish*" (celebration of Yiddish), "*a bashaynung fun yidish*" (an illumination of Yiddish), and the poetry as "*yidish tokh af yidishn loshn*" (Jewish content in a Jewish language).[25] Scooler's equation of Yiddish poetry reading with a religious service, drawing on I. L. Peretz's fusion of secular and religious modalities, was not repeated in the following poetry readings. The performance of Yiddish poetry at the 92nd Street Y in the 1960s articulated an ideal of Yiddish poetry as the embodiment of Jewish national aspirations, or, in the words of the Yiddish critic B. Rivkin, a *kmoy-teritorye* (quasi-territory) for the remnants of the Yiddish-speaking Diaspora.[26] Peretz and Rivkin had developed their humanist Yiddishism, in which Yiddish literature was central, during the heyday of Yiddish culture in, respectively, pre–World War I Poland and interwar United States. This ideal of secular *Yiddishkeit* was an anachronism in 1960s New York, a mostly symbolic retrieval of cultural ideologies of the past at odds with the post-Holocaust era's increasingly open and prosperous American society. However, it was highly significant that Scooler began the poetry series by highlighting the sacred function of Jewish poetry that, in the words of Maeera Schreiber, "[is] . . . a paradigm in which poetry and religion vie for the same social space and function, [and] resonates powerfully with a certain trajectory in the history of Jewish poetics."[27]

The final poem Glatshteyn read at the first Yiddish poetry reading was "*S'yidishe vort*" (The Yiddish Word), originally published in his collection *Gedenklider* (Poems of Remembrance) in 1943. This poem elaborates on the symbolism of the almond branch in the Bible. In Numbers, Aaron's staff sprouted and bore almonds (*shaked*), a miracle that confirmed Moses's leadership in the desert. In Jeremiah, the almond tree becomes a symbol of the prophetic gift of being "a watchman unto Israel." Glatshteyn's poem uses this biblical imagery to create a hymn to the Yiddish word. The physical sensations and tangibility of the Yiddish words—*batamt*/tasty, *shmekn*/smell, *trifn*/dripping, *bazaft*/juicy—are drenched in *bobeshaft* (grandmotherhood), one of Glatshteyn's neologisms in a landscape of past-ness (*amolikeyt*). The wanderer (the *vandrovnik*) in the poem is a lover drawn to his *basherter* (destined one), the Yiddish word, which both is physically present in the sprouting almond branch (smelling of sweet herbs) and articulates hidden potentials expressed in Glatshteyn's neologisms *nishtviserayen* and *farshteytzikher*.

FIGURE 7.1. Yankev Glatshteyn at the podium of the 92nd Street Y, 1969–70 Yiddish Poetry Series. (Courtesy Arnold Chekow)

These "dark perplexities," as Richard Fein translates *nishtviserayen*, achieve clarity in the world of *bobeshaft;* Glatshteyn's neologism brings to mind *landsmanshaft*, with its associations of Jewish communal autonomy and mutual aid societies. In the final lines the wanderer, a stand-in for the poet, praises the sprouting almond trees in "screeched pain" (*veygeshrign*).

Glatshteyn's hymnlike poem praises the Jewish/Yiddish word as associated with a combination of religious biblical references and sensations of smell, touch, and beauty that originate in *bobe-loshn*, the grandmother tongue, once removed from *mame-loshn* (the mother tongue), indicating an inner landscape of a familiar past associated with the communal life of the immigrant generation of Yiddish-speaking Jews from Eastern Europe. The poem combines the *inzikhism* of Glatshteyn's early poetry in the form of playful neologisms with his later work's biblical tonalities and images. Like most of Glatshteyn's poetry, this poem is deeply rooted in the Yiddish language, and draws intimately from Jewish cultural and religious references:

ס'ייִדישע װאָרט בליט אויף אַ מאַנדלשטעקן.
און יעדע ברכה איז באַ׳טעמ׳ט,
יעדע קללה איז געגראַמט,
יעדער װאָרט טוט שמעקן,
יעדער װאָרט טוט טריפֿן,
און יעדער װאָרט איז באַזאַפֿט
מיט באַבעשאַפֿט.
אַ, געטרייע לאַנדשאַפֿט פֿון אַמאָליקייט—
אין אַ זאַמדיקן מדבר.

אין אַ מדבר בליט אַ מאַנדלשטעקן,
און אויף אים שפּראָצן ייִדישע װערטער.
אַ װאַנדראָװניק אויף אַ קעמל
ציט אַהין װי צו זײַן באַשערטער.
און אַרום דעם שטעקן װאַקסן
זיסע קרייַטעכצער,
און עסט מען זיי, עפֿענען רעטענישן
זייערע באַטײַטעכצער,
און אַלע פֿאַרהוילענע נישטװיסערייען
װערן סאַמע קלאָרע פֿאַרשטייטזיכעװע.
און אַלץ װערט כּדאי,
און אַלץ װערט האָפֿט,
אַלץ װערט אָנגעיאָרנט
און אָנגעטרונקען מיט פֿרייד
פֿון באָבעשאַפֿט.

דער װאַנדראָװניק שרייַט אַרייַן אין דער נאַכט
און טוט װעקן—
הוי, װייִגעעשריגן,
אין דער מדבר בליט אַ מאַנדלשטעקן!

> The Yiddish word sprouts on an almond branch:
> every blessing savored,
> every curse crafted,
> every word scented,
> every word succulent,

every word steeped
in essences of Grandma's world.
Oh, the constant landscape of ago—
in a sandy desert.

In a desert sprouts an almond branch,
and on it flower Yiddish words.
A wanderer on a camel
is lured to his intended love.
Around that branch grow
sweet herbs,
and if one feeds on them, riddles
reveal their intimations,
and dark perplexities
turn into certitude.
And all becomes worthy,
and all becomes coherent,
all ferments,
all is drenched
in essences and joy of Grandma's world.

The wanderer shrieks in the night,
stirring things up—
hey, screeched pain,
in the desert sprouts an almond branch.[28]

The next event in the series, Yitskhok Bashevis's reading on October 27, 1963, was conducted entirely in Yiddish, except for the question and answer session. At this time, Singer had become a celebrity who attracted a much younger audience than was captured in the photographs of the Yiddish writers at the Y taken by Arnold Chekow.[29] In his 1965 article, "Singer's Literary Reputation," Glatshteyn described the 1963 Singer reading at the Y:

> In presenting Isaac Bashevis Singer to a recent literary gathering, I observed that he is the most famous Yiddish writer of his time; and indeed his repute is growing from day to day. Introducing Singer was of course a mere formality, since the audience—a predominantly youthful one—well knew whom it had come to hear. But in my brief remarks I speculated aloud on the curious fact that

Singer, who is so deeply rooted in the Yiddish language, should have achieved fame through translations in a dozen languages, particularly in English, by means of which he has acquired for himself a recognized place in American literature.[30]

Glatshteyn confesses that he has "never written before about Singer. My sincere and strong distaste for his stories made it impossible to find any kind of approach to them."[31] The gist of Glatshteyn's critical attack on Singer's work is that Singer "dehumanizes and brutalizes his characters," and "Singer lacks an ear for language as well as a sense of style."[32] This rejection of Singer's work, written in a sloppy style (and marred by a surprising number of typos in the reprint), is very different from Glatshteyn's introductory words at the October 27, 1963, event. In Yiddish, in front of a mixed Yiddish/English-speaking audience, Glatshteyn praised Singer for his artistic nonconformism, and described him as "an original" whose stories are deeply rooted in the Yiddish language. Glatshteyn equated Singer's mastery of the Yiddish language with Sholem Aleichem's, and pointed out that, like the latter in his time, Singer is the most famous Yiddish writer alive. Unlike the work of Sholem Asch, who wrote what "*di kristn hobn gefodert*" (the Christians demanded) and betrayed his Jewishness to please "*di goyim*," Singer's work is suffused with "*yidishn inhalt, yidishe temes, yidishn klang*" (Jewish content, Jewish themes, Jewish sound). Translations of Singer into other languages have made Singer's work widely available without sacrificing its artistic qualities. In short, Glatshteyn basked in Singer's success, using it to promote the poetry series. By giving Singer the second slot in the series and inviting him to return for two more readings, Glatshteyn used Singer's celebrity status to reach out to a younger audience.[33]

Singer's Yiddish stories, according to Glatshteyn, may have been nihilistic and obscene; nonetheless, they were deeply rooted in Yiddish culture. In English, however, the Jewish aspects of his stories were downplayed. What remained, in Glatshteyn's view, was the "naked sadism" that was "cut to the measure of prevailing modes and . . . perfectly adapted to current fashions in world literature."[34] A binary opposition was at play in Glatshteyn's rejection of Singer, originating with a central trope of American Jewish discourse: "This trajectory of associations—which puts the poetic, the religious, and the feminine in opposition to narrative, secularity, and the masculine—has important consequences for Jewish American culture, with its own well-rehearsed legacy and trope of the Jews as effeminate and feminine."[35] For Glatshteyn, poetry was associated with a transcendent, sacred realm, and the

Yiddish poetry series was conceived as a secular replacement of the house of worship. In contrast, as the only performer of prose literature in the series, Singer and his stories expressed a mundane, humorous sensibility that, according to Glatshteyn, fed into American culture's—the *goyim*'s—morbid fascination with sex and death. Moreover, the gendered binary opposites that associated poetry with marginalized and powerless femininity, and storytelling with a masculine domain of cultural significance, placed Glatshteyn's poetry in the women's section, behind the *mekhitse* (the separation between men and women in the synagogue), in a powerless, enclosed domain of Yiddish cultural exchange with no impact on American culture.

At the October 27, 1963, event, in a thirteen-minute introduction, Singer tapped into the widely held view in Anglo-American culture that the sounds, words, and mentality of Yiddish were inherently comical. This perception of Yiddish originated with Yinglish, a mixture of English and Yiddish styles, syntax, and vocabulary. Yinglish became particularly popular in Borscht Belt entertainment acts, in which comedians such as Mickey Katz used Yiddish speech patterns and obscene words in stand-up comedy. Singer's performance at the Y was a balancing act between his contribution to a still-vibrant high culture in Yiddish and his deliberate attempt to reach a younger bilingual audience by employing an entertaining mix of Yiddish and English. Singer's "*araynfir*" (introduction) was an essay about translation that was performed as a stand-up routine. His comparison of English and Yiddish vocabulary in two thematic groups, "poverty" and "craziness," enabled him to skilfully play off Yiddish words such as "*shnorer*" and "*shleper*" that already had entered the American English vocabulary against the neutral "*goyish*" words "pauper" and "poor man." To expound on Yiddish words about "poverty" and "craziness" in front of an affluent, upwardly mobile group of American Jews was a deeply ironic reminder of their parents' and grandparents' immigrant backgrounds and their upper-middle-class obsession with psychoanalysis. (Singer mentions that English synonyms for "crazy" are mostly clinical terms.)[36] Singer satirized YIVO's attempt to normalize Yiddish by inventing new terms for practical purposes, such as repairing a car, as an artificial Esperanto that betrays the authenticity of Yiddish. What is striking about Singer's introduction is his superb command of the multiple components of American Jewish discourse, which included intersecting and incompatible versions of *Yiddishkeit:* high Yiddish culture (the poets in the series); a patois of multiple language elements (Yinglish); Yiddish as medium of humor; and Yiddish as the mythical past of *bobe-mayses* (old wives' tales). To emphasize this last category, the story "*Kleyn un groys*" (Big and Little), which Singer read at the

1963 event, was a grandmother's monologue. Singer's performance at the Y "managed to pull all the pieces together" and, unlike Glatshteyn's contradictory appraisal of Singer, refrained from taking sides in the internecine state of Jewish American culture.[37]

Unlike the other readings, particularly the ones by survivors such as Rokhl Korn, Avrom Sutzkever, Aaron Zeitlin, Chava Rosenfarb, and Joshua Rubenstein, Singer's did not address *der khurbn*. The sophisticated anticommunist and member of the interwar Warsaw Yiddish *literatn fareyn* (PEN Club) had reinvented himself as a grandfather-like fabulist whose strong Yiddish accent reminded the young audience of their immigrant grandparents. Singer's appearance as a Jewish American writer was predicated on an "as if" philosophy. In Irving Howe's words, Singer "wrote about a world destroyed beyond hope of reconstruction . . . as if they were still there, as if the world of the past were still radiantly alive: the Hasidim still dancing, the rabbis still pondering, the children still studying, the poor still starving, and nothing yet in ashes."[38] This deliberate conceit distinguished Singer from the Yiddish poets in the series who stressed elegy and commemoration in their response to the Holocaust.[39]

Kadya Molodovsky read her poem "*Tsind on mayn likht*" (Kindle My Light) at the Y on April 20, 1964. This poem was published in her 1965 collection, *Likht fun dornboym* (Light of the Thornbush). What animated the group of Yiddish poets at the Y in the 1960s was articulated in the poem's anthemlike confirmation of the artistic flame:

דור פֿון תוהו
דור וואָס האָט געזען דעם הימל פֿאַלן.
די זון האָט פֿינצטערניש געזױפט,
און אױפֿן סיני האָט מען אױפֿגעשטעלט די טמא-שטאַלן.
און בײַ דעם טיש אָט דעם צעבראָכענעם, צעקרימט, צעלאָמעט,
צינד אָן דײַן ליכט.
און אױף דער װאָקלדיקער ערד שטעל אױף דײַן עמוד . . . ,
צינד אָן דײַן ליכט.

A generation of chaos,
watched the heavens fall.
The sun extinguished in darkness;
and on Mount Sinai they erected the abomination of stalls.
At that very altar, yes, all bent and wracked and crippled,
kindle your light.

And on that quaking earth, set up your lectern . . .
Kindle your light.[40]

Once again, a Yiddish poet conflates the secular and the religious, crystallized in the word *omed*, which refers to both a lectern and the Torah reader's desk in the synagogue, providing a liturgical context. Despite the destruction of the Holocaust and the aging of the poet, the poem implores the reader/listener to seize the day and to light the poetic fire. The latter is indicated in the biblical prooftext of the "bush that burned but was not consumed," used as the epigram for *Likht fun dornboym*.

Molodovsky edited the Yiddish literary quarterly *Svive* from 1960 until 1973. Reflecting on the significantly reduced Yiddish cultural sphere in America since the journal's first short-lived run in 1943, Molodovsky

FIGURE 7.2. Kadya Molodovsky in her apartment in Manhattan, winter 1970. (Courtesy Arnold Chekow)

emphasized in *Svive*'s first issue in 1960 the need for a small literary journal to maintain the aesthetic standards among the small group of Yiddish writers: "We believe—that Israel is no widower, and there are probably at least a *minyen* Jews who feel the necessity of such a journal" ("*Mir gloybn—loy almen leyisroel, un es zaynen nokh do bay undz, mistome, a minyen yidn vos filn di neytikeyt fun aza oysgabe*").[41] Listing the contributors to the first twenty issues of *Svive*, Moyshe Shtarkman, a Yiddish critic, mentioned that forty-eight Yiddish writers (six of them female) contributed to the journal between 1960 and 1965.[42] Among its various topics, the journal addressed the increased language assimilation of Jews in America. In a brief announcement, "*Mendeles boyd in yugnt-tsenter af der 92ter gas*" (Mendele's Covered Wagon at the 92nd Street Y; *Svive*, December 1964), Molodovsky praised the Yiddish poetry series as a much-needed attempt to challenge the monolingual state of Jewish American life: "Thus the 92nd Street Y has raised itself above the rigid frozen conditions of 'the purity of English' which blossoms with such force in our social life. In Mendele's wagon which enters the Yiddish-Hebrew series will flow a deep-rooted source of authentic Jewish expression."[43]

Glatshteyn's introduction of Eliezer Greenberg on January 5, 1965, used the death of T. S. Eliot on the previous day as the point of departure for a comparison of the two poets. By juxtaposing Eliot's famous lines "This is the way the world ends / Not with a bang but a whimper" with Greenberg's "*Ikh hob shlofn zikh geleygt in tsvantsikstn yorhundert / un oyfgevekt in mir der groyl fun mitlalter*" (I went to sleep in the twentieth century / and the horror of the Middle Ages woke up in me), Glatshteyn situated Greenberg as the "most American of Yiddish poets" even while highlighting the Jewish *khurbn* as the defining quality of Greenberg's poetry. Greenberg's quick, rhythmic reading style, with its distinct dialectical features, articulated an American vision of the metropolis.[44]

On April 28, 1965, S. Margoshes introduced the folk bard and master balladeer Itsik Manger as a representative of the European poetic tradition that had rejected "*der kult fun umfarshtendlekhkeyt*" (the cult of incomprehensibility) in the modernism of T. S. Eliot, Ezra Pound, and James Joyce. With a reference to the deceased H. Leivick, whose name had also been invoked by Zvi Scooler at the first reading in 1963 (the year Leivick died), Margoshes introduced Manger as a neo-romantic poet. According to Margoshes, Manger's use of simple, popular forms such as the ballad, the biblical poem, and a tribute to the Bal Shem Tov, articulated a more accessible poetics at odds with the cutting-edge modernism that characterized the performance of poetry at the Y in the 1960s.

FIGURE 7.3. Joseph Mlotek (*left*) and Yankev Glatshteyn (*center*) among the audience listening to Yiddish poetry, 92nd Street Y, 1969–70 Yiddish Poetry Series. (Courtesy Arnold Chekow)

On November 5, 1967, at the Festive Opening of the new season sponsored by the Y in collaboration with the Workmen's Circle, Joseph Mlotek (educational director of the Workmen's Circle) mentioned that the event was situated "on the margin of the American world." The program featured a choir and a *vort kontsert* with the Yiddish actress Miriam Kressyn, who read poems by H. Leivick, M. Rozenfeld, Zishe Landau, and Yehoash. Yankev Glatshteyn, in his introduction to his poetry reading, reflected on the generation gap between American-born children and their Yiddish-speaking parents: "language lives in the mouths of children, Yiddish poets were the children."[45] In short, Yiddish poetry in America had been and remained a one-generation affair, lacking successors in the next generation.

The climactic 1969 event of the series was discussed in Irving Howe's letter to the administrator at the Y, Galen Williams, in which he laid out how he envisioned the distribution of Yiddish and English readings:

> We do strongly feel that the Yiddish poets—the few still at hand—should be included in the program. They deserve what little honor they can get; after all, they wrote the poems. In addition, a good

part of the audience is likely to be their partisans and want to hear poems in Yiddish. My idea at the moment is that we needn't read every poem in both languages; that we do more in translation than in the original; but that there has to be a consistent strand of poems in the Yiddish.[46]

Four Yiddish poets read at the 1969 event: Eliezer Greenberg, Rokhl Korn, Kadya Molodovsky, and Yankev Glatshteyn. The program was conducted almost entirely in English, and featured translations by Marie Syrkin, John Hollander, Cynthia Ozick, Adrienne Rich, and Stanley Kunitz. Howe introduced the anthology by presenting a pantheon of Yiddish poets, selected because of their representative historical and aesthetic value and their readability in English translation. Except for John Hollander's almost pitch-perfect English rendering of poems by Mani Leib and Moyshe Leib Halpern, most of the translations sounded removed from the *Yiddishkeit* of the originals. With few exceptions, such as Cynthia Ozick and John Hollander, Anglophone writers associated Yiddish literature with a closed chapter of history, sealed in a black box of forgetfulness and destruction. The invisibility of the Yiddish "Other" was expressed by the poet Stanley Kunitz: "the fact that these poets have been writing for years, amid us, and we never knew what they were really writing, is so ironic and even sad."[47] Howe was a fluent Yiddish-speaker and one of the best-informed American-born critics of Yiddish literature. Nevertheless, he decided to publish the poetry anthology in an English-only format. It would take almost twenty years until two comprehensive anthologies of Yiddish poetry were published in bilingual editions. Howe co-edited one of these, the *Penguin Book of Modern Yiddish Verse*, together with Ruth Wisse and Khone Shmeruk, in 1987. Indicative of the invisibility of Yiddish poetry outside Jewish cultural circles, the Y administrator Galen Williams, who had planned the events in the poetry series and attended most of them, mentioned in a letter to Howe: "I have just finished reading the galleys of your beautiful anthology. I am absolutely overwhelmed by the poetry that has now been made available to us who know no Yiddish . . . I had no idea all these years of the Yiddish readings at the Y of the beauty of the living Yiddish poets."[48]

The tendency of American critics to view Yiddish literature, in the words of Anita Norich, as "museum pieces, archeological finds even at their moments of creation" was reflected in the historical approach to the performance and selection of poetry at the 1969 event.[49] Glatshteyn closed the event with his 1938 poem *"A gute nakht velt"* (Good Night, World), followed

FIGURE 7.4. Cynthia Ozick (*left*), Rokhl Korn (*center*), and Adrienne Rich (*right*), at the 92nd Street Y event marking the publication of *A Treasury of Yiddish Poetry,* which featured various performers, November 2, 1969.

by Marie Syrkin's translation. The poem's angry rejection of the promise of Jewish emancipation in Western societies and defiant return to "the small Jewish world" of study and introspection was recontextualized as yet another poetic artifact in the event's (and the anthology's) historical survey of Yiddish poetry in translation. Removed from its original cultural context and political relevance, the poem became a poetic artifact that spoke of and from the past. This historical trajectory of Yiddish literature in Howe and Greenberg's anthology and the 1969 event at the Y encapsulated, as Eli Lederhendler suggests, New York Jewish culture in the 1960s: "Self-validation in the American idiom turned toward the future, while self-validation in the Jewish idiom turned toward the past."[50]

For the Yiddish writers and critics, language remained the lens through which the American literary landscape was mapped. The disparaging attitude that Yiddish writers held toward Anglo-Jewish writers was summed up by the critic Eliyahu Shulman in his 1971 article "*Iz meglekh a yidishe literatur af a nit-yidisher shprakh?*" (Is a Jewish Literature Possible in a Non-Jewish Language?). According to Shulman, the lack of intimacy between writer and reader in a non-Jewish language often led to a self-hating approach to Jewish issues among Anglophone Jewish writers. Shulman pointed to a long tradition of Jewish self-criticism among Yiddish and Hebrew writers, from the Haskalah onward, and emphasized that "these writers were free of self-hatred." For Yiddish writers in America threatened by linguistic assimilation, language remained the dividing line between Jewish and non-Jewish writers. This distinction served to keep the flame alive by rejecting the Anglo-Jewish writers because of their lack of "intimacy and feeling for one's own heritage."[51] In contrast, for the Anglo-Jewish writers, even such "half outsiders" as Irving Howe and Cynthia Ozick, the question of language was less significant in the context of American multiculturalism of the 1960s, in which ethnicity and race defined one's identity. Characteristically, Ozick's plea for a New Yiddish in her article "America: Toward Yavneh" (1970) took as its point of departure an American English that would have to be reshaped liturgically, which she attempted to do in "Envy."

In her 1972 tribute to Glatshteyn, Ozick reflected on the coincidence of her being awarded the B'nai B'rith Book Award for her short story collection *The Pagan Rabbi and Other Stories* together with the posthumous presentation of an award for excellence in literature to Yankev Glatshteyn, who had died the previous year. The event was a rare and highly symbolic moment in Jewish American literary history. Ozick, a new Jewish American literary voice expressing a return to Jewish texts and concerns, paid tribute to the most important Yiddish poet in America. Ozick recalled that, not since 1942, when she went to "the *Forverts* building to witness the presentation of a poetic prize to Yankev Glatshteyn," had she been "in the company of the community of Yiddish writers."[52] This was not entirely true, because Ozick had attended the 1969 event at the Y, where she read her translations of Yiddish poetry for the Howe-Greenberg anthology, and probably other Yiddish events as well.

The key passage in "Envy" is its final section, in which the character Edelshtein confronts the twenty-one-year old Hannah, an American-born Yiddish-speaker and niece of the insane Vorovsky, the author of a bilingual German-English mathematical dictionary that languishes in obscurity. Ozick's rebellious energy and guilt for having abandoned Yiddish culture, so evident in her tribute to Glatshteyn, is mirrored in Edelshtein's angry words to Hannah: "Forget Yiddish!" he screams at her. "Wipe it out of your brain! Extirpate it! Go get a memory operation! You have no right to it, you have no right to an uncle, a grandfather! No one ever came before you, you were never born! A vacuum."[53] Memory loss denoted "paganism," idol worship, which was distinctly different from the kind of Jewish writing Ozick advocated in her essay "America: Toward Yavneh." (1970).[54] The ferocity of Ozick's denunciation in her essay of American writers such as Philip Roth, Norman Mailer, and George Steiner for their betrayal of Jewish peoplehood points to a new creative phase that characterizes the strongest part of Ozick's later work.

The character of Hannah in "Envy" (born in 1945) is depicted as a Jewish representative of the 1960s anti-establishment generation in its rejection of their parents' ghetto past and Jewish suffering. Hannah's exceptional Yiddish proficiency makes her a sought-after translator, and the scapegoat for Edelshtein's fury at her betraying her Yiddish heritage. "Envy" marks a unique point of intersection between Anglo-American and Yiddish culture. Its dense allusions to Yiddish writing, including untranslated Yiddish phrases (such as the epigraph for this chapter), addressed the kind of Jewish reader who attended the Yiddish poetry series and was sufficiently proficient in Yiddish to appreciate the story's satirical reproduction of Yiddish speech patterns and poetry in Yinglish. Glatshteyn and Greenberg resented the story's hostile exposition of their weaknesses and internal squabbles, particularly its reduction of their Yiddish cultural aspirations to low comedic *shtik*. These sentiments were perhaps best articulated in Eliezer Greenberg's response to Howe's "partial defense of the story": "He turned to me with anger and said, 'Some things are more important than writing a good story!' Too late, I agree."[55]

The section of the novella set at the 92nd Street Y is, like the rest of the story, told from Edelshtein's perspective, including his internal monologue and examples of his poems. The reader at the event is Ostrover (modeled on Singer), and the hall is packed with mostly younger people. There is a reference to the golden letters of names of Jewish luminaries (Moses, Einstein, Maimonides, Heine) that are engraved in the main lecture hall at the Y. Edelshtein's thoughts and feelings are conveyed in strings of free associations informed by bilingual puns, such as the play on the Yiddish pronunciation of the Y (*vy*). It sounds similar to the word "why" included in the bilingual poem Edelshtein sings to himself: "Why the Y? *Farvos di Vy?*" (57). Edelshtein has command of both English and Yiddish, unlike the younger members of the audience who are dependent on Ostrover's English

FIGURE 7.5. The Yiddish writer Moyshe Dluznowsky (1903–77) and his wife listening to Yiddish poetry, 92nd Street Y, 1969–70 Yiddish Poetry Series.

translation of his Yiddish stories. Moreover, Edelshtein's inner monologue is peppered with Yiddish quotes with no reference to their sources and without English translation. Edelshtein describes the loneliness and desolation of reading his poetry in suburban Y's with a quote from a well-known poem by the Yiddish poet Dovid Einhorn, "*Geshtorbn der letster bal-tfile*" (The Last Prayer Leader Died), which Ozick translated for *A Treasury of Yiddish Poetry* (1969). Einhorn included this poem in the performance of his poetry in the series on November 19, 1967. The line from the poem in the novella highlights the emptiness and desolation of the Y in the phrase, "*Pust vi di kalte shul mayn harts*" (Empty as the cold synagogue is my heart).

Baumzweig's wife, Paula, refers to Singer as "*der shed*" (the demon), a common word in Singer's demonological stories. In the Yiddish poets' conversation with each other, he is referred to as "washed white pig" (58). The main character of Ostrover's story, which he reads at the Y, is a "Zwrdlian" poet, a fictional language of unpronounceable consonants, and includes references in French and Italian. The language of the story is distinctly different from the previous section in its simple dialogue and narrative development. Ostrover's story depicts a writer who sells his soul to the devil in order to achieve fame in translation. As price for his fame, the devil demands that the poet's creation be burned so it disappears forever.

Ostrover's responses to the audience's questions—which center around the viability of Yiddish in translation—is conducted in stand-up fashion, reminiscent of Singer's performance at the Y: "Q: What do you think of the future of Yiddish? A: What do you think about the Doberman pinscher?"[56] Like characters in an Isaac Bashevis Singer story, the Yiddish poets view themselves as ghosts at the Y event. Their language and inner world have been erased from the public event at the Y. The only performance of Yiddish poetry in the story takes place outside the auditorium, where Edelshtein declaims his Yiddish poems for Ostrover, Vorovsky, Baumzweig, and Hannah. Without the Yiddish originals, Edelshtein's poems are removed from their original cultural and linguistic contexts, similar to the translated poetry in Howe and Greenberg's anthology. Ozick uses her creation of English versions of nonexistent Yiddish poems to represent a version of Edelshtein's poetry as nostalgically and sentimentally infused with Holocaust images.

The envy depicted in the story is determined by multiple things. On the most literal level, it refers to Edelshtein's envy of Ostrovsky's fame, because the latter is able to reach a younger audience in translation. Jeffrey Shandler "retranslates" Edelshtein's poem into Yiddish and shows that "[t]he appeal of these virtual texts lies in their elusiveness, thereby suggesting a complement to Edelshtein's envy of Ostrover's success in translation—namely, the monolingual English reader's envy of those who have access to the abstruse milieu of Yiddish."[57] Shandler views the novella as a prime example of postvernacular Yiddish culture.

The "envy" of the story is also related to a distinctly Ozickian ideational universe. The word "envy" appears several times in Ozick's essay "America: Toward Yavneh" as a criticism of the American Jewish attempt to assimilate by imitating the Gentiles: "Diaspora-flattery is our pustule, culture-envy our infection. Not only do we flatter Gentiles, we crave the flattery of Gentiles. Often in America we receive it."[58] Ozick's article is a manifesto for a new Jewish American literature which, similar to the way Jews turned a Germanic dialect into Yiddish in the Middle Ages, will reshape English into a Jewish, liturgical language. Her cultural diagnosis of the state of American Jewish culture compares its future prescriptively to Spain rather than to Germany, although both "ended in abattoir." The article, like the novella, passionately engages in the debate about the future of Anglophone Jewish culture, which is obsessively occupied with reclaiming and translating Jewish texts: "We translate Yiddish with the fury of lost love, we publish translations of medieval Hebrew documents. We pour *piyyutim* into the air of every household. Even the enviers brood on the propriety of their envy. Even those who crave flattery are disposed to examine their lust. We have a fascination not with what we are, but with what we might become."[59]

For Hannah in Ozick's novella, Yiddish belongs to the past, and its poetic practitioners are ghosts. She is stunned to learn that the poet Edelshtein, whom her long-dead grandfather read many years ago, is not only still living but standing right in front of her. Ozick's story is infused with the rebellious Oedipal energy of dethroning the poetic elders of the tribe, the Yiddish poets of Ozick's father's generation (her uncle was the Hebrew and Yiddish poet Abraham Regelson). Morris Dickstein points to the story's overt hostility, which likely caused Glatshteyn, Greenberg, and other Yiddish writers to react with such fury: "Cynthia Ozick is thought of as some kind of pious traditionalist, but this, her best story, written with ferocious energy and style, is a work that radiates hostility from first to last, reminding the reader of the polemical turn she often takes in her essays."[60]

The Glatshteyn figure represented by Edelshtein in "Envy" belongs to a very different cultural context which, as Naomi Seidman points out, exists "within a coarse, physical, 'Freudian' setting far removed from the literary norms that framed their own subculture. . . . Ozick's story thus 'recovers' these lost Yiddish figures but does not fail to also (inevitably?) mutilate them, in the familiar language and images of Singer himself."[61] Singer's influence, which is stylistically and thematically discernable in the story, has been somewhat of an obstacle to telling a more complex story about the Yiddish poets from their own perspective, and from within their own subculture. The fascinating story of the Yiddish poets at the 92nd Street Y is a far cry from Ozick's mutilated characters, caught in a Freudian Oedipal rebellion, and informed by Singer's idiosyncratic style and images.

By focusing on Yankev Glatshteyn and the other Yiddish poets who performed at the Y, we can conceptualize the issue of translation differently from the all-pervasive Singer-focused approach to Yiddish literature in America. Singer's performance at the Y stood out for his superb use of bilingualism and his celebrity status, a crucial condition for literary success in America. As a result of Singer's mastery in spanning various cultural worlds—American, Yiddish, Old World European—he was able to dance at multiple weddings with relatively little harm to his artistic integrity. As a storyteller and novelist with a straightforward prose style (unlike innovative stylists like Dovid Bergelson and Moyshe Kulbak), Singer created work that was relatively easy to translate. Sutzkever and Glatshteyn, the great Yiddish poets, had no choice but to stay within the boundaries of their linguistic medium and hope that attention to their few works in translation would draw more readers to their Yiddish work.[62]

Glatshteyn's poetic priorities in the 1950s and 1960s can be gauged from his 1956 poem *"Mayn getselt"* (My Tent). Like *"S'yidishe vort,"* the poem is a love song to the Yiddish language, addressed directly to his object of desire—*loshn mayns*/language mine—and compared to a faithful and jealous wife. There is a direct line from Glatshteyn's return to his circumscribed Jewish space in the 1938 poem *"A gute nakht, velt"* and his desire to be confined to "my tent" in *"S'yidishe vort,"* a symbol of biblical Israel's dwellings in the desert. The defiant slamming shut of the door to the world in *"A gute nakht, velt"* is taken one step further in *"Mayn getselt"*: *"loz mikh vern shtum-loshn far der velt / afile in der bester iberzetsung"* (let me be a sign language for the world / even in the best translation) (my translation, which differs from Fein's). The poem indicates that the particularity of poetic language—its sound, meaning, and rhythm—cannot be transmitted into another language. The raison d'être of poetic translation is instead to turn the reader's gaze from its incomplete approximation to the Yiddish poem's linguistic particularity. The poem ends with the image of the *"volkn-zeyl,"* the pillar of cloud by which God guided the Israelites' wanderings in the desert. A beam of light/*a likht-shtral* becomes the Yiddish poet's last trace, his inheritance to his fellow Jews:

נעם מיך אַרום מיט ווערגנדיקער געטרײַשאַפֿט,
לשון מײַנס, ווער מיר אַן אײפֿערזיכטיק ווײַב,
בינד מיך צו צום געצעלט,
לאָז מיך ווערן שטום-לשון פֿאַר דער וועלט,
אַפֿילו אין דער בעסטער איבערזעצונג.
זאָלן זיי מיך פֿאַרטײילן.
פֿאַרקלײן מיך, ביז ניט-דערשעצונג,
מיך אַרט נישט אַז זיי וועלן מיך נישט צײילן,
פֿאַרשוווער מיך, אַ געטרײַען,
צו דיר מיט גורלדיקער באַשערטקייט,
אַז ס׳זאָל מיך קיינער פֿון דײַנע אָרעמס נישט באַפֿרײַען.
אמת, איך וועל נישט זײַן אוניווערסאַל,

אָבער אַז איך וועל אַוועק,
וועל איך ווערן אַ וואָלקן-זײַל
אַ ליכט-שטראַל,
איבער אונדזער קליינעם משכּן.

> Embrace me with choking devotion,
> language mine, like a jealous wife;
> confine me to my tent;
> let the world never grasp what I meant,
> even in the best translation.
> Let them exclude me,
> diminish me, disparage me.
> I don't care if I'm not in their number.
> Summon me, irrevocably,
> to your destiny.
> Let no one coax me from your arms.
> Take my word. I don't want to be universal.
> When I take my leave
> I will become a pillar of cloud,
> a gleam of light,
> above our small sanctuary.[63]

Like Ozick's symbol of the *shofar* in her "Yavne" essay, Glatshteyn chose to stay within his "small tent" and "blow into the narrow end of the shofar."[64] In what is his perhaps most untranslatable book of poetry, *Yidishtaytshn* (translated by Benjamin and Barbara Harshav as *Exegyidish*), in which his poem "Sing Ladino" appeared in 1937, Glatshteyn remained loyal to the unique recourses of his poetic medium and continued to do so during the rest of his literary career. This was due, in part, to his modernist poetic credo, which was based on exploring and utilizing the full register of the Yiddish language. Glatshteyn's defiant return to his "little tent" reflected his strong identification with the murdered Eastern European Jews: "Burrowing into Yiddish, Glatshteyn felt that he was not only closing the door on a potential international public but burying himself in the fate of the most threatened part of the Jewish people.... The more inventively he used the Jewish language, the more Jewish he became. He came to believe that a master craftsman had to experience the fate of his language as his own."[65] In that sense, Glatshteyn can be viewed as the exemplary Jewish American writer who, to paraphrase Ozick, refrained from seeking to represent "Mankind."

The transitional moment of the 1960s transformed the Jewish American cultural landscape. For the Yiddish poets, the Y poetry series was their grand finale; fewer than a dozen important writers continued their creative work beyond the 1960s (including Rosenfarb, Grade, Sutzkever, Katz, Preil, Yitskhok Bashevis, and Molodovsky). The story of Yiddish in America closed with the passing of the immigrant generation who brought Yiddish and Hebrew with them from Eastern Europe. With a few exceptions, no American-born generation of Yiddish and Hebrew writers appeared. For that reason the audio recordings of Yiddish poetry are vital source materials, allowing us to hear the voices of Yiddish poets at the heights of their powers, and to reconstruct a vibrant Yiddish cultural world in 1960s New York. Most important, the audio recording provides a very different view of Jewish American literature than the dominant Anglophone perspective. The Yiddish view from the margins gives us a renewed insight into hitherto lost connections, influences, and permutations between Anglophone and Yiddish writing in America.

8

PROSE OF THE ASHKENAZI WORLD

Chaim Grade and Yitskhok Bashevis (I. B. Singer)

איך האָב אָבער די פֿאַרשוויגענע אַליין-גייער, אָט די פֿון קיינעם ניט-באַמערקטע
בטלנים און למד-וואָוווניקעס, ניט געזוכט צו מאַכן 'אינטערעסאַנטער' דורך
צוטראַכטן אַ שפּאַנענדיקע סיפּור-המעשׂה, וואָס זאָלן זיי צוזאַמענהאַלטן. איך האָב
די באַזונדערע געשטאַלטן און די געשיכטע פֿון זייער לעבן צונויפֿגעוועבט דורכן
פֿאַרטונקלטן שײַן פֿון בין-השמשות, וואָס פֿאַלט אויף זיי אַלעמען גלײַך, בעת זיי
זיצן האַלב-פֿאַרגליווערטע אויפֿן זעלבן גרויען הינטערגרונט פֿון זייער הויף און קלויז.

I did not seek to make the silent loners and the invisible idlers and holy men more interesting by inventing an exciting story which would unite them. Instead, I wove together their separate characters and the history of their lives in the dim twilight which surrounds them, as they sit half congealed against the same grey background of their courtyard and synagogue.

Chaim Grade, "Introduction," *Der shtumer minyen*
(The Silent Minyan, 1976)[1]

I like to write ghost stories and nothing fits a ghost better than a dying language. The more dead the language, the more alive are the ghosts. Ghosts love Yiddish, and as far as I know they all speak it. . . . I am sure that millions of Yiddish-speaking ghosts will rise from their graves one day and their first question will be, "Is there any new book in Yiddish to read?"

Isaac Bashevis Singer: Conversations (1992)[2]

The honorary degree awarded to Chaim Grade by Yeshiva University in 1980 indicated that his work was much appreciated in the Modern Orthodox

FIGURE 8.1. Chaim Grade, New York, 1978. (Archives of the YIVO Institute for Jewish Research, New York)

community. In his speech at that ceremony, the president of Yeshiva University, Norman Lamm, claimed Grade as an antidote to what he viewed as the artistic and moral decay of current literary trends. Lamm particularly disdained the work of I. B. Singer, the other great Yiddish prose writer in post-1945 America and a recipient of the Nobel Prize in literature in 1978. Lamm characterized the contemporary literary scene as "a time when literature, even Yiddish literature, often wallows in the mud of cynicism and frivolity, in the scatological swamp of amorality; when it heralds the fascination with the demonic and with sexual weirdness."[3] According to Lamm and other leaders of the Modern Orthodox community, Grade's work was the most authentic literary representation of the learning, and the ethos, of the *litvaks* (the Lithuanian Jews): a community that had been unjustly occluded by Singer's phantasmagoric Hasidic universe, originating with the "false messiahs" Sabbatai Zevi and Jacob Frank.

Elie Wiesel's 1974 review of *The Agunah* in the *New York Times* similarly praised the authenticity of Grade's work: "Before approaching the book, we should speak, however briefly, of its author, who unfairly has never been accorded proper recognition by the American public at large. And state openly something that those who read him in the original don't hesitate to say in private; namely that the work of Chaim Grade, by its vision and scope, establishes him at the age of 64 as one of the great—if not the greatest—of living Yiddish novelists. Surely he is the most authentic."[4] According to Wiesel, the artistic merit of Grade's work can be fully appreciated only in the Yiddish original. As this quote indicates, negotiating between "private" and "public," the Yiddish original and its English translation, was crucial for the critical reception of Grade's work. As the Yiddish world faced isolation and decline in America, the attempt to create a "life-line" to the broader public by translating Yiddish works into English became increasingly urgent. According to Wiesel and Lamm, Grade's work remained the hidden treasure of Yiddish literature, unknown to the American public due to the lack of English translations, and, to some extent, its inherent untranslatability.

Grade began writing serialized novels and short stories for the Yiddish press after his immigration to New York in 1948. Like other Yiddish writers after 1945, Grade wrote for a worldwide Yiddish readership, and only late in his career (after 1967) did he begin to reach a broader audience in English translation. Like other contemporary Yiddish writers, Grade's work depicted the lost world of Eastern European Jewry. The view of the post-1945 generation among Yiddish critics was expressed by Khayim Bez: "Only the outbreak of fascism and the major disasters which befell our people during the Second World War temporarily severed the connection between Yiddish literature and world literature, its writers and critics. After the ghettos were torn down, a spirit of ghetto and separation remained. But Bashevis, Chaim Grade, Avrom Sutzkever and the novelist Mendel Man have broken through the barriers."[5]

For Yiddish critics and intellectuals, Yiddish literature had always been an integral part of world literature, at once particular and universal in scope. Following a brief isolationist hiatus after the Holocaust, the post-1945 generation of Yiddish writers reemerged and renewed this tradition. For the readership of the limited body of Yiddish literature available in English translation, however, it seemed that Singer was the only Yiddish writer after 1945, or the only Yiddish writer worth reading. This distortion of Yiddish post-1945 literary history, perpetuated by critics without access to the original Yiddish works, has established a skewed perception of "the silver age" of Yiddish letters in New York, Montreal, Buenos Aires, Tel Aviv, Warsaw, Paris (in the late 1940s), and Moscow.

In this chapter I will examine Grade and Yitskhok Bashevis's fiction as representative of the post-1945 generation of Yiddish writers which, despite diverse artistic views and practices, addressed common concerns that set them apart as a distinctly new trend in Yiddish literature. They were acutely aware that they belonged to the last of a great generation of Yiddish writers born and raised in Jewish Eastern Europe. The critical reception of Yiddish works in English translation after 1945 highlighted fundamentally different concerns about their representational value as a reflection of a culture that had been eradicated in the Holocaust. The continued creative vibrancy of the Yiddish cultural world in major and minor centers post-1945 remained a "private" Jewish world that in only a few instances (most prominently with I. B. Singer) came to the attention of the American reading public.

Morris Dickstein, historian of American letters post-1945, noted that literary realism went against the grain of the Jewish American literary renaissance and the literary taste of the American reading public in the 1950s and 1960s:

> Straightforward realism was never an option for Jewish writers in America; it belonged to those who knew their society from within, who had a bird's eye view, an easy grasp of its manners and values. As newcomers dealing with complex questions of identity, Jews instead became specialists in alienation who gravitated toward outrageous or poetic norms of humor, metaphor, and parable—styles they helped establish in American writing after the war. The key to the new writers was partly their exposure to the great modernists—Kafka, Mann, Henry James—but also their purchase on Jews not simply as autobiographical figures in a social drama of rebellion and acculturation but as parables of the human condition.[6]

Yiddish writers after 1945 came with a deep knowledge of their "society from within" and "easy grasp of its manners and values," which they used to great effect in realist novelistic representations of urban and small-town (shtetl) settings in Jewish Eastern Europe. Grade, in particular, brought his great knowledge of *litvak* (*misnagdim*, the opponents of the Hasidim) and *muser* Judaism to bear in novels informed by the great nineteenth-century Russian writers Dostoyevsky and Tolstoy. A typical example can be found at the end of Grade's novel *Der brunem* (The Well, 1958), in a description of the conflict between Muraviov and Mende the Porter. Muraviov, named after a Russian governor of Vilna who, during the Polish uprising in 1865, "had hanged and buried . . . [Polish] grandfathers," is the most feared and prosperous beggar in the synagogue courtyard. Similar to the beggar Rasputin in Grade's autobiographical novel *Der mames shabosim* (My Mother's Sabbath Days, 1955), who leads a gang of seven beggar women, Muraviov's brutality and egotism, associated with the czar, makes him the beggar king of Jewish Vilna. Dressed like a Russian soldier, blind from trachoma, "he snatched contributions angrily, cursing, foam spurting from his mouth, and even when he wasn't begging he would holler and shout as if he were chasing off dogs with his cane."[7] Although Muraviov donates a Hanukkah menorah to the Gravediggers Synagogue in memory of his father, he reserves it for his personal use.

Watching Muraviov's mastery of begging, which has made him rich and allowed him to be in charge of leasing prayer shawls and yarmulkes to visitors, Mende the Porter emulates the beggar in his pursuit of funds to repair the broken well. This turns out to be a complete failure, due to Mende the Porter's physical appearance. Mende looks like a strong, healthy peasant so unlike the decrepit, blind Muraviov who, standing in the back, gloats at Mende's failure as a beggar. At the end of *Der brunem*, Muraviov finances a Torah scroll with his riches and celebrates the completion of the Torah scroll with a procession of musicians. Simultaneously, Mende the Porter and members of the community inaugurate the repaired well, paid for by the contributions Mende has collected. There is no reconciliation between these two celebrations—Muraviov's tribute to himself and Mende the Porter's altruistic contribution to the community.

Grade's knowledge of the Vilna Jewish community, its manners and its values, is here expressed in a subtle depiction of begging as both an institutionalized religious activity and a lucrative profession. Grade's artistic eye penetrates the mindset of the small shopkeepers and ritual slaughterers who, despite their reluctance to give alms to the beggars, nevertheless feel obligated to alleviate the hunger of the endless numbers of poor in Vilna. Grade's description of how this religious value shapes the behavior and mindset of the Jews in the courtyard makes it an important cultural historical document.

Characteristic of Grade's work is its in-depth portrait of rabbis and yeshiva students who are confronted with the lives of ordinary Jews. His main theme is the contrast between "*Di kloyz un di gas*" (The Synagogue and the Street, 1974), which became the title of four novellas from 1974 that were published in English translation in 1983 as *Rabbis and Wives*. A particularly interesting example of the opposition between Jewish clergy and *poshete yidn* (regular Jews) is given in a panoramic scene in the middle of the novel *Der brunem*, when Mende the Porter is collecting money to repair the broken well in the Vilna *shulhoyf* (synagogue courtyard). Mende goes to the rabbinical assembly convening at the Palace Hotel to ask for money. In a novel that consists of argumentative dialogues, and almost no action among the porters, beggars, and storekeepers in the *shulhoyf*, this section stands out for its encounter between Mende the Porter and the rabbinical luminaries of Lithuanian Jewry.

The chapter begins with a description of the theatrical setting for the assembly: the organizer, Yudel Tsofnas, "ordered the decorations of its last dramatic production removed from the stage."[8] Then the main players are introduced: first the young boys and rabbinical students in the back rows, followed by young rabbis "who had inherited town rabbinates from their fathers-in-law or had bought them outright for money."[9] In the front rows sit middle-aged rabbis in their fifties whose wives are angry because of their meager wages and rebellious children. They look worried, facing as they do old age and declining status in their communities. On the stage, described in a seasonal metaphor as "deep winter" (*tifer vinter*), are assembled the oldest and most venerable rabbis of Lithuania, bemoaning the decline of religious commitment among the students.[10] Finally, an empty chair for the Chofets Chaim (1838–1933), the *goen* (scholarly genius) of his generation, awaits his arrival in the next chapter. Also attending is a single Hasidic Rabbi of Slonim, a stranger among the "the stony Lithuanian Misnagdim, the traditional foes of Chasidism."[11] Grade introduces the rabbinical assembly from young to old, starting in the back rows and ending in the limelight on the stage, from hopeful spring to disillusioned winter.

The theatrical setting provides the backdrop for the pantomime of body gestures. The narrator zooms in on a variety of fingers and their movements, which become a synecdoche for the rabbis' life of studying, officiating, and ritual decision-making:

אויסגעאײַידלטע פֿינגער, פֿאַרבלאַסטע, פֿאַרחלשטע, וואָס דרייען זיך אויף רצועות יעדן אינדערפֿרי, בלעטערן ספֿרים, קושן ספֿרי-תורה און טונקען זיך הונדערט מאָל אין טאָג אין וואַסער, נאָכן גיין אויף נקיות, בײַם וואַשן זיך צום עסן און בײַם אָפּגיסן מים-אחרונים; ווייכע פֿינגער מיט פּוכיקע קישעלעך, וואָס גיבן שלום, צעשפּרייטן זיך מיט זײַדישער ליבשאַפֿט אויף קעפּ פֿון אייניקלעך בײַם בענטשן, און צעשפּרייטן זיך כּהנית בײַם דוכנ־ענען; פֿינגער, וואָס טאַפּן מיט צערטלעכער ליבשאַפֿט אתרוגים און לולבֿים, פֿאַרשטעלן זיך די אויגן בײַ קריאת-שמע, האַלטן דעם קידוש-בעכער, דעם הבֿדלה-כּוס, און ברעכן זיך צוזאַמען בײַם שלאָגן זיך אין האַרצן על-חטא; פֿינגער וואָס גיבן זיך אַ דריי מיט אַן

איפּכא-מסתברא, דער פּשט איז פּונקט פֿאַרקערט; געקניפֿלטע דאָפּלטע פֿינגער-קנעכ־
לעך, באַוואַקסן מיט שטעבלקעס, מיט געדראָוועטע האָר, וואָס קראַצן זיך מיט מעשענע
נעגל, קניפּן אויס שטיקער פֿלייש פֿון אייגן לײַב, ווי אַ בייזער מלמד קנײַפּט ייִנגלעך;
פֿינגער וואָס שלעפּן האָר פֿון דער באָרד ביז אַ שווערער סוגיא און קרײַזלען זיך די פּאות;
פֿינגער פֿאַרגעלטע פֿון שמעקן טאַבאַק און פֿון רויכערן טיטון . . . די אַלע פֿינגער באַוועגן
זיך, פּייקלען אין טיש, רעדן צווישן זיך און ברוגזן זיך איינע אויף די אַנדערע . . .

Delicate fingers, grown pale and feeble, that wound phylacteries every morning, thumbed through the pages of holy books, caressed the Scrolls of the Torah, dipped into cleansing water countless times each day; soft fingers with puffy tips that extended in greeting, in loving blessing over the heads of grandchildren, or the stiff reach of the priestly benediction; fingers that handled sacred objects of worship with tender respect, that covered the eyes during the "Hear O Israel" prayer, and broke into a self-castigating fist during the penitential prayers of the Day of Atonement; gnarled fingers that dipped and ascended in exposition of a Talmudic problem; fingers that plucked hair from the beard when confronted with a difficult section of Gemorah; fingers yellowed from nicotine and snuff—these fingers moved, tapped the table, debated, and argued among themselves.[12]

Although the theatrical setting illuminates the public performative role of the rabbis, Grade avoids any hint of satire or symbolism that would detract from their ordinary human qualities. Instead, the poemlike excerpt above enumerates the various rabbinical roles as they are expressed in particular finger movements. Grade's artistic innovation in *Der brunem* is the realist portrayal of the rabbis that has been conspicuously absent from Yiddish fiction. In an introduction to *The Agunah* (The Abandoned Wife, 1961), Grade outlined his departure from the formulaic depictions of the rabbi in Yiddish literature:

לויט מײַן מיינונג, האָט אונדזער ליטעראַטור ליטעראַטור בכלל ניט געגעבן קיין צו-עכטע אָפּשפּיגלונג
פֿון דײנים און מורי-הוראות, וואָס זיינען דורות-לאַנג געווען אונדזערע איינציקע
גײַסטיקע מנהיגים. אָדער מען האָט זיי כאַראַקטעריזירט דורכאויס נעגאַטיוו, אונטער
אַן אַלגעמיינער ביטולדיקער באַצייכענונג "כּלי-קודש"; אָדער מען האָט זיי געשילדערט
בלויז פֿון דרויסן, די בערד, די קאַפֿטאַנס און די העוויות, אָבער ניט אויסגעטיילט קיין
באַזונדערע טיפּן, ווי לויט אַ פֿאָרמולע, אַז "אַלע רבנים האָבן איין פּנים"; אָדער מען האָט
זיי אינגאַנצן אויסגעטאָן פֿון זייער גוף און אויסזען, כּדי זיי פֿאַרצושטעלן ווי סימבאָלן פֿון
מעשׂים-טובֿים און פֿערזאָניפֿיקאַציעס פֿון ריינע אידייען; אָדער זיי זײַנען געוואָרן העלדן
פֿון דער לעגענדע; אָדער טעאַטראַלע פֿיגורן, דעקאָראַטיווע און פּאַטעטישע.

איך ווייס בלויז פֿון אייניציקע אויסנאַמען אין אונדזער ליטעראַטור, ווען קרעאַטיווע
קינסטלערישע האָבן געשילדערט רבנים מענטשלעך-רעאַל, ניט צו-הימליש און ניט
צו-גראָב ערדיש.

> In my opinion, our literature has generally not presented a truthful representation of rabbis who for generations were our only spiritual leaders. They have either been characterized in a completely negative way, under the general, pejorative, label of "clergy"; or they have been described only in terms of externals (the beards, the kaftans and the gestures) but not separated into different types, as though following a formula that "all rabbis have one face"; or they have been removed from their bodies and appearances altogether in order to present them as symbols of good deeds or personification of pure ideas; or they have become legendary heroes; or theatrical figures, decorative and pathetic. I only know a few exceptions in our literature when creative artists have depicted rabbis as truly human, not too heavenly and not too earthy.[13]

In Yiddish literature "*klekoydesh*" (Jewish clergy) have typically been portrayed as symbolic and satirical icons: Peretz's neoromantic glorification of the rebbe in his Hasidic stories or the otherworldly rabbis in An-Ski's *Der dybbuk*. In contrast, Grade seeks to portray the rabbi "as truly human, not too heavenly, and not too earthy." Grade's rabbis belong in the *misnagdish litvak* environment, in contrast to I. B. Singer's Hasidic rebbes. Not only is Grade the quintessential *litvak*, he is also a belated heir to Sholem Yankev Abramovitsh's social realism, stripped of its satirical thrust.[14]

When Mende the Porter makes his way "through the yard, up a narrow staircase"—because he is not allowed to enter through the main doors to the hotel—he suddenly finds himself in a dressing room with costumes, props, and other theatrical paraphernalia: black mustaches for a Russian official and a rabbi's ceremonial marriage robe. For the pious, simple-minded Mende, the scene reminds him of a horror tale about devils "that hoarded the beards of modern Jews who shave their faces."[15] He finally finds his way to the backstage, confused and blinded by "the forest of beard in the hall below." He wonders whose beards he had seen in the dressing room

> [and] was struck by the wild thought that those must have been the beards of rabbis and prominent Jews who pretended to be more pious than they really were. He had often heard Reb Kopl, beadle

of the Seven Witnesses Congregation, shouting at the beadle of the Old-New Synagogue: "Turk! What kind of a Jew are you? You don't even wear a beard!" To which the other usually shouted back: "Better a Jew without a beard than a beard without a Jew . . ." Suddenly Mende shuddered, angry with himself for his fears and unholy thoughts. What he saw in the dressing room was make-believe, masquerade, but the Jews sitting here before his very eyes were real flesh-and-blood rabbis.[16]

In this episode, with its potential for various flights of the imagination—supernatural, comical, satirical—Grade does not depart from his artistic project, which seeks to realistically portray "flesh-and-blood rabbis." Like Mende the Porter, Grade rejects all these "wild thoughts." This loyalty to a realist credo that portrays characters in their authentic Jewish environment, without superimposing models of behavior and a mindset foreign to these figures' collective way of life, epitomizes Grade's novelistic art.

Before settling in New York in 1950, Grade published several collections of poetic lamentations about Vilna and his years of wandering in the Soviet Union.[17] In the 1950s and 1960s, when large Yiddish-speaking communities existed worldwide, Grade traveled to Miami, Chicago, Los Angeles, Johannesburg, and Buenos Aires, lecturing on historical and literary topics.[18] Grade's beginnings as a prose writer were triggered by the enthusiastic reception of what he called "an essay, not fiction," "*Mayn krig mit Hersh Rasseyner*" (My Quarrel with Hersh Rasseyner), at a public event in New York in 1948.[19] "My Quarrel" develops the main themes of Grade's early work, "*Di musernikes*" (1939), a long poem or *poeme* that consists of disputations between Chaim Vilner (Grade's alter ego) and various students in the Novaredoker yeshiva. Grade studied in the Novaredok yeshiva from 1922 to 1932, when he was between the ages of twelve and twenty-two. This religious education provided him with most of the setting, characters, and themes of his work.

The *muser* movement, originally founded by Israel Salanter in mid-nineteenth-century Lithuania, expanded significantly in Poland and in Lithuania during the interwar period. What characterized the Novaredok strand of the *muser* movement were the religious-ethical ideals that Salanter's student Yosef Hurwitz implemented in creating the Novaredok yeshiva in 1896: "His novel contribution was a philosophy of moral extremism. Hurwitz was convinced that the improvement of one's religious-ethical character could be achieved and sustained only through radical and extreme acts, not through gradual moderate change."[20]

Grade's *muser* education shaped his personality from a young age, and is an important biographical backdrop for his novels and short stories, which to a large extent consist of religious arguments and disputes. The model for this discourse of opposing, often extreme positions was the soul-searching and self-introspection that characterized the *muser* yeshiva, where "religious-ethical perfection [was] taking precedence over the mastery of Torah knowledge."[21] Grade cultivated a literary discourse that was energized by the conflict between opposing points of view pitted against each other, and left unresolved at the end of the works. The two antagonists in his first story, "My Quarrel," represent the primary poles of Grade's work: the Novaredoker and the secular Yiddish writer and former *musarist* Chaim Vilner arguing about God, Evil, and the fate of the Jewish people in the aftermath of the Holocaust. The dramatic tension in this work derives from the elaborate verbal ingenuity with which the characters argue their points of view.

This artistic method elaborates on the oral and colloquial qualities that have characterized modern Yiddish fiction since its inception in the early nineteenth century. *The Well* and *The Agunah* each consists of the long, uninterrupted dialogues of characters passionately voicing their opinions. Although the reader is privy to the characters' inner dialogues, presented by the omniscient narrator, these are mostly an extension of the public debate. When the narrator gives a rare depiction of Vilna's urban landscape, it functions primarily as stage direction for the dramatic exchange of points of view. Grade employs a novelistic discourse that recreates a tight theatrical drama through the voices of his characters. These voices, despite their individual differentiation, engage in a collective chorus or contrapuntal opera that elaborates on a particular issue or theme.

"My Quarrel," *The Well*, and *The Agunah* each combines various genres—theatrical drama, the epic poem, and the essay—packed into a novel of social, sexual, and ethical/religious manners. Grade created a new kind of novelistic prose that was perfectly attuned to his turbulent, passionate personality: one trained in religious argument and self-introspection. The historian Lucy Dawidowicz's portrait of Grade, whom she first met during her one-year stay in Vilna in 1938–39, emphasizes these contradictory qualities:

> Short and squarish, his squat build made you think—especially when he was angry—of a bull. But on closer observation you could see that his was not sinewy brawn, but flabby fat. He had a roundish baby face and wore glasses. At twenty-eight, he was already balding, with a receding hairline that made his high forehead look even

higher. He had a rich strong voice, with which he could hold an audience rapt as he recited his own verse.... He was driven by precisely those passions which Navaredok had tried to eradicate—lust and greed for everything the world could offer, vanity and pride, rage and envy. He was still at war with himself. Though he no longer went to shul and no longer studied the religious texts, he was still in many private ways a child of tradition.[22]

Grade's first full-length prose work, *Der mames shabosim* (1955), was an autobiographical novel that featured Grade's mother, Vela Grade. She was the owner of a small fruit stall in Vilna, and Grade depicted her as the embodiment of traditional female virtues. The book's third and final part, *Di zibn geselekh* (The Seven Little Lanes), depicts Grade's 1944 return home to a Vilna in ruins. There he encounters a Jewish female doctor and her son, mirroring the maternal focus of the book's first section. This final part of the book elevates the saintly mother figure—a staple of Grade's work beginning with his first collection of poems, *Yo* (1936), through the elegies written during and after World War II—to an icon of "mother Vilna." This mother figure disappeared from Grade's work after *Der mames shabosim*. It was replaced with the female figures in *The Well* and *The Agunah* which, like the defiant voices of the market women in *Der mames shabosim*, rebel against male authority and God. Moreover, Grade introduces two female figures in *The Agunah* who pose a serious challenge to the maternal integrity and piety of *Der mames shabosim*. The author moves from being the loyal son who glorifies the mother to a man who confronts his masculinity in relationship to female desires and irrational behavior. Merl, the *agunah*, and Rabbi Levi Hurvitz's daughter Tsirl (associated with "*tsirung*," which means "jewelry/ornament" in Yiddish) confront the rabbinical characters with a new set of issues related to sexuality and insanity.

Grade edited a posthumous volume of the Yiddish short-story writer Jonah Rosenfeld's work in 1955. Rosenfeld's work explored the borderlines of insanity and so-called "normality," twisted sexual relationship, and changing gender roles in the Jewish working-class family torn apart by incest and abuse.[23] Less radical than Rosenfeld, Grade followed his artistic path in delineating the breakdown of traditional religious values in the aftermath of war, revolution, and secularization of Jewish society. The backdrop of *The Well* and *The Agunah* is World War I and its loss of life due to combat, hunger and disease. Families suffer from the traumatic aftershocks of war, as exemplified

by the main character the *agunah*, the abandoned wife, and by Reb Bunem
in *The Well*, who is grieving the loss of his children who have died of disease
and starvation. Reb Bunem, traumatized and seeking religious consolation, is
confronted by his wife, who defiantly challenges his religious world view. The
greatest threat to male authority, however, originates with the cases of clinical insanity exemplified by Tsirl in *The Agunah*. She is the daughter of Reb
Levi Hurvitz, the rabbi in charge of implementing the rabbinical decrees
pertaining to the *agunah*. The wife of Reb Levi's antagonist, Reb David
Polotsker, is confined to bed because of a heart condition. Both rabbis are
torn between their obligations to Jewish law (*halakha*) and to the declining
mental and physical conditions of their wives and daughters, engulfing them
in psychological and existential chaos.

Grade's portrait of Merl and Tsirl, unmarried and orphaned young
women, departs from similar female characters in An-Ski's famous play *Der
dybbuk* (1913–1917) and I. B. Singer's *Sotn in Goray* (1935). These two works
belong in a Hasidic universe of romanticism, folklore, and superstition. Their
female main characters become vehicles for transcendental and transgressive
acts, such as *dybbuk* possession and exorcism. In contrast, Merl and Tsirl are
firmly rooted in a Lithuanian Jewish reality that defines their personalities
and behavior. However, like Singer and An-Ski's female characters, Merl and
Tsirl represent the sexual, instinctive, and biological drives that challenge
rabbinical authority. As Grade elaborated on his portraits of his female characters, the gender split between sexuality and law, irrationality and morality
became more pronounced.

Although Grade's novels examine how Jewish law cripples both male
and female characters, they also demonstrate how women pay the heaviest
price by being excluded from Jewish male society. Merl and Tsirl are depicted
as superfluous beings, objects of their own desire in a strictly male universe
ruled by religious law. This is beautifully captured in *The Agunah* where Merl
gazes at herself in the mirror:

דאָס שטיבל איז געווען פֿאַרגאָסן מיט אַ טונקל-בלוי ליכט, און אין האַלבן שפּיגל
איבערן קאַמאָד האָבן אירע אַקסל און בריסט געבלאַנקט ווי אײַז. זי האָט זיך אָפּגערוקט
אַהינטער, כּדי צו זען איר גאַנצע פֿיגור, נאָר פֿון וויַיטן איז איר לייב אין שפּיגל אַמעגנגעגאַנגען
אין דער טיף פֿון געשליפֿענעם גלאָז, ווי איר גוף וואָלט אויפֿגעהערט עקזיסטירן, בעת זי
אַליין לעבט נאָך. מערל האָט זיך דערמאָנט וואָס מען דערציילט אין שטאָט ווי אַזוי דעם
רבס משוגענע טאָכטער איז אַרויסגעשפּרונגען פֿון איר צימער אַ נאַקעטע. מסתּמא האָט
אויך דעם רבס טאָכטער שטאַרק ליב דעם אייגענעם קערפּער. מערל איז צוריק אַרין

אין בעט, איר גוף האָט געגליט און זי האָט געשווידערט פֿון קעלט און שרעק: וואָס קומט מיט איר פֿאָר? זעגנט זי זיך מיטן לעבן? זי האָט זיך אײַנגעהערט, ווי געוואַרט אויף אַן ענטפֿער, און דערהערט פֿון גאַס דאָס געוואָי פֿון ווינט.

A dark blue light filled the apartment, and in the mirror above the chest her shoulders and breast shone like ice. She stepped back in order to see her entire body, but from that distance it blended into the depths of the polished glass, as though her body had ceased to exist and only she herself lived on. Merl remembered the reports about Reb Levi Hurvitz's crazy daughter jumping out of her room naked. The rabbi's daughter probably loved her body, too. Merl returned to bed, her body aflame, shivering with cold and fear. What was happening to her? Was she saying farewell to life? She listened carefully, as though awaiting an answer, and heard the wind moaning outside.[24]

A comparison of this scene and I. B. Singer's short story *Der shpigl* (The Mirror) highlights the particular quality of Grade's novelistic art. Singer's story depicts a beautiful young woman named Tsirl similarly gazing at her naked body in the mirror. It turns into a formulaic monologue of temptation narrated by a demon, modeled on Peretz's 1888 poem "*Monish*." In contrast, Grade creates the mirror image of Merl's female beauty as a disembodied ice statue, disconnected from any social or religious reality represented in the novel. Where Singer crafts his story to expound on his male fantasy about female desire and sexuality, Grade depicts Merl as a tragic figure in a male universe that ultimately drives her to suicide.[25]

Like other survivors, Grade had to confront his guilt over having survived while his family, friends, and community had perished in the Holocaust. Survivor guilt can be at once a powerful motivation and a stumbling block for a writer. The enduring qualities of Elie Wiesel's and Primo Levi's work derive from their unblinking, confessional confrontation with survivor guilt. As in the second and third sections of *Der mames shabosim* and "My Quarrel," Grade addressed his guilt over having survived the Holocaust in his poetry. At the heart of Grade's work is a resistance to go beyond the pale of traditional Judaism, due to a fierce loyalty to the memory of the victims. The complex of survivor guilt and testimonial comes to the fore in the final pages of *The Agunah*, when Reb David realizes that his reinstatement in the rabbinical hierarchy after having almost been excommunicated is due to the tragic suicide of Merl:

—איך בין געוואָרן אַ יחסן. מען צאָלט מיר שכירות ווי אַ שטאָטישן מורה-הוראה, מען
גיט מיר אָפּ כּבֿוד און אַלע פֿילן זיך קעגן מיר שולדיק. אָבער דער אמתער שולדיקער
בין איך. איך האָב ניט באַרעכנט וויפֿל צרות איך וועל ברענגען אויפֿן קאָפּ פֿון דער
געפּלאָגטער פֿרוי דווקא דורך מײַן היתר. די שטאָט זאָל אַריבערגיין אויף מײַן זײַט, האָט
זי זיך באַדאַרפֿט מקריבֿ זײַן. איך בין גרויס געוואָרן, אַ חשובֿ געוואָרן דורך איר אומגליק,
אויסגעוואַקסן אויף איר קבֿר.

> —I have become somebody. They're paying me the wages of a Vilna rabbinic authority; they honor me and everyone feels guilty about their past behavior toward me. But really I am the guilty one. I didn't foresee how much trouble my permission would cause that tormented woman. In order for the city to side with me she had to sacrifice herself. As a result of her tragedy I've become famous and important. I've blossomed on her grave.[26]

The quote refers to Reb David's lenient interpretation of the *agunah* laws that permitted Merl to remarry and thus set in motion the social earthquake in the Jewish community that led to Merl's suicide. When one reads the quote from the perspective of Grade the survivor—"I've blossomed on her grave"—one hears him expressing his guilt toward the dead, whom he has "utilized" as fictional characters in his novels, the stepping stones of his literary career in America.

The canvas of Grade's novels is circumscribed to the inner world of the traditional *litvaks* and its struggle with the interpretation of the Law. The historical specifics of Jewish Vilna in the interwar period—its cultural, political, and religious institutions—are, with a few exceptions, absent from his work. Grade recreated religious rituals and behaviors that had become obsolete among secular Jews, who generally figure as minor characters in his novels. The absence of chronological movement and narrative drive turns the episodes and portraits in Grade's novels into testimonial tableaux. The characters are stuck in dramatic moments, engaged in passionate internal debate about religious laws and behavior. They are unable to change, however, and like Sisyphus, they are condemned to eternal repetition. This inward-looking and past-oriented perspective makes Grade a typical representative of post-1945 Yiddish literature. The decline of Yiddish as a spoken language and culture in America reinforced Grade's artistic orientation as chronicler of prewar Jewish Vilna. Grade's poem *"Der oysgebrenter dorn"* (The Extinguished Bush), in referring to Moses's vision of the burning bush, expresses this predicament:

איך בין דער דיכטער וואָס לעבט מיט זכרון
און פֿיל אויף מײַן צונג ווי עס וויאַנעט מײַן לשון
הלוואי קען איך זאָגן, אז איך בין דער דאָרן,
וואָס ברענט אין דעם מדבר און ווערט ניט פֿאַרלאָשן.

> I am the poet who lives in memory
> And feels on my tongue how my language is withering
> I wish I could say that I am the thorn
> That burns in the desert and is not extinguished.[27]

As a poet, Grade eulogized the lost world of the *litvaks* in verses of lamentation. As a novelist, Grade's philosophical bent shifted the focus from plot development to elaboration on moral and religious issues. Moreover, the autobiographical character of Grade's most accomplished prose works, *Der mames shabosim* and his two-volume *Tsemakh Atlas: Di yeshive* (The Yeshiva, 1967–68), informed their novelistic universe. In these two works and in "My Quarrel," Grade recounted crucial phases of his life story. This autobiographical trilogy can be viewed as a return from Paris in 1948 ("My Quarrel") and Vilna in 1944 (*Di zibn geselekh*), back to the formative years of his childhood and teens in the 1920s *muser yeshiva* (*Tsemakh Atlas*). The return in Grade's prose from a post-Holocaust setting to his childhood in Vilna indicates a deepening engagement with his own autobiography as it was shaped by three role models: his mother, the Hazon Ish, and the *musarists* (Tsemakh Atlas and Hersh Rasseyner).[28] Tsemakh Atlas is the embodiment of *muser*: radical, introspective, and antisocial. Tsemakh (which means "growth" in Hebrew) serves as an ethical religious compass who helps Chaykl Vilner (Grade's alter ego) navigate the world (atlas) by embodying a universal principle of *muser*. This natural force of personal regeneration and growth gives Grade's novels of confrontation a moral urgency and dialogical intensity.

Grade's last novel, *Fun unter der erd* (From under the Earth), was serialized in the *Forverts* (1979–82) but was left unfinished with his sudden death. In it, the main moral principle is embodied by the character Shayke Tshemerinski, a stand-in for the Yiddish poet and partisan Shmerke Kaczerginski, upon his return to Vilna after liberation in 1944.[29] Tshemerinski becomes the director of the Jewish museum, the main repository of Jewish culture in Vilna in the aftermath of the war. He heroically resists the Soviet attempt to eliminate Jewish cultural treasures, books, and archives. Grade's last novel is a historical roman à clef that returns to an almost *judenrein* Vilna, which provides the setting for Tshemerinski's enactment of the moral imperative of saving the Jewish cultural heritage. In depicting the destroyed Jewish Vilna from the perspective of the partisan-poet Tshemerinski, Grade's work has come full circle from his autobiographical lamentations, *Di zibn geselekh*, set in the same time and place but published twenty-five years earlier. The painful futility of Tshemerisnki's endeavor is expressed by a Jewish doctor who returns to Vilna in the novel's first chapter:

"און אז מען וועט באווייליקן פאר דעם מוזיי א פאלאץ אנשטאט די געטאָ־תּפֿיסה;
און אויב אפֿילו די סאוועטישע מלוכה זאל אנשטעלן א גאנצן שטאב צו סארטירן און
רעגיסטרירן די ביכער, די ספֿרים, די אנגעשטאפטע פעק און זעק מיט קארטלעך פון
אלערליי געלערנטע נודניקעס, וואס האבן זיך יארצענדליקער געגרייט צו שרײַבן גרויסע
ווערק, די גרעסטע ווערק—וועט די אויסגעשאכטענע ווילנע אויפֿשטיין תּחית־המתים?
בערג מיט צעפֿליקטע ביכער קענען פֿארבײַטן א שטאט מיט לעבעדיקע ייִדן?"

And if it were a palace instead of this ghetto-prison that was officially designated as a museum; and even if the Soviet state should employ a whole staff to sort out and catalogue the books, the Torah scrolls, and other holy texts, the overflowing bags and boxes with cards by scholarly *nudniks* [bores] who for decades prepared to write important works—would the slaughtered Vilna be resurrected? Can mountains of moldy books replace a city of living and breathing Jews?[30]

Asked by the Yiddish critic Avrom Tabatshnik, in an interview in the early 1950s, to summarize his most important contribution to Yiddish literature, Grade replied that it was to create a memorial to Vilna, the Jerusalem of Lithuania.[31]

Grade's faithfulness as a custodian and archivist of a culture that had been obliterated in its prime gives his novels a high moral purpose. At their best they recall the ethical religious urgency of Dostoyevsky's novels, which also stylistically provided an important influence. The elegiac strand of Grade's novels is most pronounced in the static tableaux of his character portrayal, which the Yiddish poet Avrom Sutzkever perceptively characterized as *Rembrantish* (like Rembrandt).[32] As Wiesel pointed out in his *New York Times* review, Grade's role as chronicler of Vilna Jewry turned his novels into authentic cultural historical documents about the ethos and *mentalité* of the traditional *litvak* world. In contrast, Norman Lamm's praise of Grade and indictment of Singer in his 1980 speech at Yeshiva University blurred the lines between the novelist's virtues and commitments, and his artistic creations. As Cynthia Ozick points out: "If a novel's salient aim is virtue, *I want to throw it against the wall.* It is commonly understood (never mind the bigots' immemorial canards) that to be a Jew is to be a good citizen, to be socially responsible, to be charitable, to feel pity, to be principled, to stand against outrage. To be a novelist is to be the opposite—to seize unrestraint and freedom, even demonic freedom, imagination with its reins cut loose."[33]

Grade's novels are typical of works by the post-1945 generation of Yiddish writers, most of whom came of age in interwar New York, Warsaw, Vilna, and other urban centers. Like them, Grade wrote about the world of Eastern European Jewry before its destruction, rarely venturing beyond these spatial and chronological parameters. Unlike I. B. Singer and Yankev Glatshteyn, who wrote extensively about American themes and settings after 1945, Grade stayed within his *litvak* world of traditional Jews prior to the Holocaust. Like Glatshteyn and Singer, his literary career in America and almost half of his life (1948–82) were predicated on the publication venues and support of the Yiddish cultural circuit. What set him apart from Singer was less the number of works adapted or translated into English than an artistic orientation that placed him outside Yiddish modernism. His social realist portraits of low-class peddlers and shopkeepers, Yeshiva students poring over the Talmud and struggling with the *yeytser-hore* (the Evil Inclination), made Grade a belated example of a previous generation's break with tradition. His work grew out of Jewish Vilna's political and ideological struggle of the 1930s, where Grade briefly flirted with socialism; it seemed anachronistic if not outdated in the post-1945 American literary world. In America, Grade continued to draw on his autobiographical memories about acculturation and struggle with the Jewish tradition; he remained a child of the tradition that he venerated and explored in his work.

Singer, in contrast, started out in mid-1920s Warsaw as a modernist traditionalist who made transgression and border crossing his artistic point of departure in his debut novel *Satan in Goray* (1935) and monologues of the *yeytser-hore* (the Evil Inclination) in the early 1940s. Jewish American writers, and Singer in particular, as Dickstein points out, made their "purchase on Jews not simply as autobiographical figures in a social drama of rebellion and acculturation but as parables of the human condition."[34] This enabled Singer to reach a broad American public not only because of his skills in marketing his work in English translation but because his work in the 1930s and 1940s carved out a subversive new territory of world literature. From his early work onward, Singer transformed a particular Jewish world into universal parables of the human condition. Grade's novels, on the other hand, stayed faithfully close to the inner world of *musarists* and other Orthodox Jews. As such, they have achieved a canonical status as classics of the Jewish literary imagination, ensconced in their particular linguistic, religious, and literary universe.

In 1943 Singer published a reprint of *Satan in Goray* and five new stories.[35] Four of these stories were narrated by the *yeytser-hore* (the Evil Inclination), part of a planned series of monologues titled "The Diary of the Evil One." Singer's talent for storytelling blossomed in these monologues' formulaic battle between Good and Evil among ordinary shtetl Jews who were tempted by the Evil One to perpetrate the most outrageously transgressive acts. Singer turned the monologue into a sustained narrative unit that subverted the progressive humanism of Yiddish writers such as I. L. Peretz and Sh. An-Ski. Peretz's debut work, the epic poem "*Monish*" (1888), is similarly narrated by the Evil One. Monish, the innocent young Talmud scholar, is tempted to perpetrate the ultimate act of heresy: he swears on the Torah that the universe is godless. In "*Monish*" the temptation is embodied by the beautiful voice of Maria, the Gentile daughter of a German businessman, representing the allure of German *kultur*. In contrast, the Sabbataian creed of sexual promiscuity as "redemption through sin" leads Singer's characters to utter desperation and suicide.[36]

Singer graphically outlines, in contrast to Monish's punishment (having his earlobe nailed to a doorpost in the netherworld, a Jewish purgatory), the collective punishment of the sinners in the story "*Der khurbn fun Kreshev*" (The Destruction of Kreshev), included in the 1943 volume. After Lisa is encouraged by her husband to commit adultery with a servant named Leybl Shmayser (Laybl Whip), her husband eventually confesses everything to the town rabbi. The punishment is swiftly carried out with a vengeance. Carted through the town, Lisa becomes the target of verbal and physical abuse from the shtetl's Jews. Again Singer subverts the father of Yiddish literature I. L. Peretz, who in the story "*Dray matones*" (Three Gifts) portrayed a martyred woman's heroism. The woman nailed her clothing to her body with pins in order to maintain her chastity (*tsnies*) during a similar act of public humiliation. The main difference, though, is that in Peretz's story the abusers are anti-Semites cheered on by priests and the mayor of the town, while in Singer's the drama is played out entirely among Jews with almost no reference to the Gentile world. Again, Peretz's martyrological universe, the quintessential sanctum of modern Yiddish culture, has been violently imploded by Singer's chillingly detached depiction of the collective orgy of revenge that descends on the poor sinner Lisa, who eventually commits suicide. Singer closes one of his darkest stories with the complete destruction of Kreshev in a conflagration perpetrated by Leybl Shmayser. The only character to escape the *yeytser-hore*'s evil net is Gimpel, Lisa's father. This namesake of the righteous Gimpel the Fool (*Gimpl tam*, 1945) would reappear under different guises in Singer's stories published after the Holocaust.

The Family Moskat, Singer's first work to be translated into English, became the test case for the standard procedure, after 1950, of trimming and shortening his serialized Yiddish novels that had appeared in the *Forverts*. The correspondence between the publisher Alfred A. Knopf and Singer in 1948–49 indicates that the latter, contrary to the demand of his publisher, initially was against cutting the Yiddish text. Knopf pointed out that his older brother, I. J. Singer, had no issues "in cutting very considerably the Brothers Ashkenazi," the bestselling novel the publisher had made available in English in 1936. The main issue was that the American readership in English was very different from Singer's Yiddish readers: "After all you must remember that we are publishing books in English for American readers to whom you are not as yet even a name." A central part of the editing and translating of Yiddish novels was the question of accessibility that applied to foreign-language writing regardless of the fact that Singer and many other Yiddish writers, like their publishers, lived in New York, where they had a huge, devoted Yiddish readership. Perceptively, Knopf articulated the quality that set Singer's work apart, "which I respect as being a sort of monument to a life that has ceased to exist and will never exist again." Literature as retrospective reconstruction of a lost world would be a central trope of post-1945 Yiddish literature, continuing a trend already evident in the historical novels of the two Singer brothers in the interwar period.[37]

The mutual influence between I. J. Singer and his younger brother has been noticed but not systematically analyzed. Key texts are I. J. Singer's novels *Yoshe Kalb* (1932) and *The Brothers Ashkenazi* (1936), which can be viewed as prototypes against which Singer conceived his early historical novels, *Satan in Goray* (1933), *The Sinful Messiah* (1936), and the *Family Moskhat* (1945–48). An examination of the popularity of the Yiddish historical novel, a staple of the literary supplements in the Yiddish newspaper, will undoubtedly highlight the centrality of I. J. Singer in the development of this genre and its reconceptualization in I. B. Singer's work.[38] Moreover, I. J. Singer became a literary father figure to his younger brother, enlisting him in the world of Yiddish letters in Warsaw (as proofreader of the highbrow journal *Literarishe bleter* in 1923) and in New York (as contributor to the newspaper the *Forverts* in 1935).

Singer debuted as an American Jewish writer in *The Family Moskat* (serialized in *Forverts* in 1945–48, and published as Yiddish and English books in 1950). Then Saul Bellow translated "Gimpel the Fool" in 1953, eight years after the story's publication in Yiddish.[39] A few years prior to the appearance of "Gimpel the Fool" in English, the internal split in post-1945 Yiddish culture—between turning its back on the *goyish* world and Singer's quest to conquer it—was articulated in the pages of the Yiddish literary journal *Di goldene keyt*. A contentious exchange took place about the viability and future of Yiddish literature between *Der lebediker* ("one who is alive," a pseudonym for the humorist Khayim Gutman, 1887–1961) and the Yiddish pedagogue Avrom Golomb.

Der lebediker's article "*Lamdn un amorets in der yidisher literatur*" (Scholar and Ignoramus in Yiddish Literature) presented an iconoclastic attack on the utilitarian tendency in Yiddish literature that sought to further a particular ideological point of view. According to *Der lebediker*, the greatest danger to the renewal of Yiddish literature was "*lamdones*" (scholarship), its attempt to replace aesthetic beauty and entertainment with the values of a *seyfer*, a holy book's ethical and religious qualities. *Der lebediker* characterized this literature as "remaining stuck in its own unartistic domain, which means Sabbath abyss literature."[40] Rejecting this *bal-tshuve* tendency in Yiddish literature, *Der lebediker* summed up his position:

צוריק צום עם-הארץ!—דארף זײַן אונדזער רוף. זאָל למדנות בלײַבן פֿאַר פּובליציסטן און מאמעריסטן. אונדזער שײנע ליטעראַטור מוז זײַן כּכּל-הגוייִמדיק, וועלטלעך און נאָך א מאָל וועלטלעך!

Back to ignorance!—must be our credo. Let scholarship be for publicists and essayists. Our belle-lettres must be similar to non-Jewish literature, worldly and even more worldly.[41]

In the following issue of *Di goldene keyt*, the Yiddish pedagogue Avrom Golomb responded in the article "*Lo zeh haderekh*" (That Is Not the Way), referring to Ahad Ha'am's call for a Jewish spiritual-cultural home in Palestine in the Hebrew journal *Hamelitz* in 1899:

פֿאַר אונדז אַלעמען, גלײב איך, איז דאָס וואָרט "גאָלדענע קייט" ניט סתּם אַ שײנער אויסדרוק, נאָר עס איז אַ גאַנצע פּראָגראַם. אַ פּראָגראַם אין לעבן און אַ פּראָגראַם אין דער ליטעראַטור, אין אונדזער קולטור-שאַפֿונג. דאָס וואָרט מײנט פֿאַר אונדז: המשך,

״קולטור-המשך אָן איבעררײַסן, דאָס כּסדרדיקע און אייביקע . . . ״קיבל-תּורה-ומסורה״
וױַטער און וױַטער פֿון דור צו דור.

> For all of us, I believe, the word "the golden chain" is not simply a beautiful expression but a whole program of life and literature, our cultural creativity. The word means for us: continuity, cultural continuity without rupture, the constant and the eternal—receiving the Torah and the Tradition continuously from generation to generation.[42]

Obviously, *Der lebediker*'s attack on Yiddish literature's self-imposed ghettoization antagonized deeply held convictions in the Yiddish world. According to Golomb, the Yiddish writer was to serve as a guardian of the flock, a national hero; if Yiddish literature turned into *di goyim*'s literature, it meant betrayal: "Today, in 1950, the *goyim* on whom we model ourselves appear in front of me, and I see them as one huge Majdanek."[43]

Der lebediker's position is unexceptional in its advocacy for the independence of aesthetic categories from extra-literary ends. However, five years after the end of World War II, the Yiddish cultural world—having suffered a catastrophic blow in terms of Yiddish speakers and writers murdered in the Holocaust—was in a state of hyperactivity, traumatized and beleaguered. At that time, Singer was not only in search of "God and Love"—the title of the first two volumes of his memoirs *Love and Exile* (1976–82). He was in search of a cultural arena outside the decimated remnants of survivors and the old guard of Yiddishist patriots, and would soon find it in English.

American Jewish intellectuals such as Irving Howe and Philip Rahv were to a certain extent removed from the Holocaust intellectually, culturally, and personally. They did not address publically its ramifications in a more sustained manner until the early 1960s, in the debate over Hannah Arendt's *New Yorker* articles covering the Eichmann trial in Jerusalem.[44] Singer's fables and supernaturalism dressed in postmodern garb was an exotic reminder of the Jewishness that these intellectuals had abandoned in their quest to become fully Americanized. The New York Jewish intellectuals became Singer's ticket to the wider American cultural world via English versions of his work that were backed by their cultural prestige. In return Singer guided some of them back to the "world of our fathers."[45]

Until "Gimpel the Fool" appeared in *Partisan Review* in 1953, Singer was virtually unknown outside the Yiddish world. At almost fifty, Singer had contributed a few original stories and novels that had secured him steady employment as a journalist at the *Forverts*. He had barely made a name for himself as a Yiddish writer and was primarily known as the younger brother of the late I. J. Singer. His meteoric rise to literary fame in America was partly due to his artistic versatility, which he had established during his decade-long apprenticeship as a professional Yiddish writer in Warsaw between 1925 and 1935. During the first decade of his literary career, Singer published literary criticism, short stories, novels, and life-writing, and translated into Yiddish eleven books by writers such as Knut Hamsun, Thomas Mann, Stefan Zweig, and others. His four-volume translation of Mann's *The Magic Mountain* (1929–30) was praised as a major contribution to Yiddish letters. Singer replicated this diversification in the different context of American culture post-1945. He published bread-and-butter journalism, middle-brow novels, and life-writing in the *Forverts* under the pseudonyms Varshavski and Segal; promoted and participated in translating his work into English; and, beginning in the 1960s, became an extremely popular performer, lecturer, and interviewee.[46] Singer's best work was published under the name Yitskhok Bashevis in Yiddish journals and newspapers. For the first time in his career, his prolific output as writer and cultural figure enabled Singer to achieve financial security. He pursued his literary career with a single-minded business zeal, insuring that his literary stock went up by promoting his works at public performances all over North and South America and Israel and publishing prolifically in English.

Singer maintained his artistic independence post-1945, when many Yiddish writers were reclaiming literature as a means to lament and commemorate what had been lost. Even in the novel *Enemies: A Love Story* (1966) and the short story "The Cafeteria" (1969), the Holocaust served merely as backdrop for his grand comedy of human passions and beliefs. Singer clung to the independence of literature from any political, social, and cultural ideology. In a 1955 article the Yiddish critic Shmuel Niger criticized the danger of political correctness for a living and breathing Yiddish literature, echoing *Der lebediker*'s position in *Di goldene keyt*:

אונדזער ליטעראַטור, וואָס איז בעת און באַלד נאָך די יאָרן פֿון קאַטאַקליזם געוואָרן עפּעס
אַ מין כאָר (אמת, אַ כאָר מיט סאָלאָס), הייבט ביסלעכווײַז אָן צו קומען צו זיך און
צוריק ווערן, וואָס אַ ליטעראַטור דאַרף זײַן—אַ וועלט ניט פֿון לויטער ציבור און אויך
ניט פֿון שליחי-ציבור, נאָר פֿון אָריגינעל-שעפֿערישע יחידים, וואָס גראָבן טיפֿער, קוקן
ווײַטער און הייבן זיך אויף העכער פֿונעם קהל און זײַנע מינהגים און מינהיגים.

> Our literature which, during and after the cataclysm, became a chorus (in truth, a chorus with solos), is slowly recovering and returning to what a literature ought to be—not only a world of community and cantors, but original creative individuals who dig deeper, see further, and lift themselves higher than the community with its customs and leaders.[47]

The critical consensus has long been that the three Yiddish volumes of Singer's short fiction originally published in Yiddish newspapers and journals (*Tsukunft, Di goldene keyt, Svive,* and *Forverts*) are his most important contribution to Yiddish letters. The twelve collections of short stories published in English translation, beginning with *Gimpel the Fool and Other Stories* (1957) and ending with *The Death of Methuselah and Other Stories* (1988), established this body of work as the Essential Singer for a worldwide readership. The three-volume Library of America edition of his short stories in English translation published in honor of Singer's centennial in 2004 is the most recent addition to the canonization of Singer as American short story writer.

The indisputable fact remains that Singer is a universally acclaimed writer due to his prominence and visibility in English. This does not detract from his mastery of the Yiddish artistic word nor challenge his place as the last great heir to the Yiddish storytelling tradition that began with Nachman of Bratslav and I. L. Peretz. Any serious critical engagement with Singer's work must begin with the original Yiddish stories while acknowledging that "the spell of Singer" is eminently translatable because of their narrative and stylistic simplicity.[48] The critical attempts to subsume Singer and other post-1945 Yiddish writers in Cynthia Ozick's novella "Envy; or, Yiddish in America" (1969) have tended to overstate Singer's difference from other Yiddish writers. In crucial ways Singer was a remarkably normative Yiddish writer in the post-Holocaust period. His work would have been unthinkable without the classical Yiddish writers as a sounding board against which he could develop his iconoclastic philosophy of protest, sabotaging sacrosanct notions of humanism and modernism. Like the works of Chaim Grade, Leib Rochman, Chava Rosenfarb, and Eli Schechtman, the finest Yiddish prose writers of his generation, Singer's fiction is set in a particular part of Central and Eastern Europe—in his case, the small *shtetlekh* of the Lublin region, including Yanov, Frampol, Tishevitz, Goray, Kreshev, Yosefov: "In his short stories, Bashevis Singer remarkably shows himself as a regionalist in the truest, fullest sense, a writer of genius who, with precision and meticulous care, uses the particular as his chief and best means of reaching the universal."[49]

Singer's urban locus is Krochmalna Street, the poor section of Jewish Warsaw, where his father, a *moyre-horoe* (rabbi authorized to answer ritual questions), conducted his rabbinical court (*bezdn shtub*) prior to World War I, as depicted in the memoir *Mayn tatns bezdn-shtub* (My Father's Court).[50] In family chronicles such as *The Family Moskat* (1950) and *The Manor* (1967), Singer recreated the narrative sweep of multiple generations of Polish Jews prior to the catastrophe. Beginning in the late 1950s, Singer began writing novels and short stories about Jewish life in America, such as *Shadows on the Hudson* (1957–58), *Enemies: A Love Story* (1966), and semi-autobiographical short stories.[51] Singer's America serves as a projection screen for his existential crises and internal struggle, which originated in Jewish Poland. Even in the most American of his novels, *Shadows on the Hudson,* in which the protagonist Hertz Dovid Grein travels to Miami and upstate New York, Singer depicts these locations mostly through the suffocating world of the Holocaust survivors whom Grein runs into in cafeterias and hotels: "The wider America with which Grein came into contact was just as complicated as he was himself. He would never understand it properly. America remained for him the one country in the world where people walked with their heads held high, yet he could see that behind all individual differences the eternal human tragedy remained constant."[52]

Singer's literary career as Jewish American writer embodied continuous change and productivity in his later years, which would open up "a new vein in his work, and really a different style."[53] Singer's late style is characterized by a greater freedom in addressing survivor guilt, suicidal behavior, and his characters' lack of agency. However, even Singer's usual disregard for literary decorum had its limits when it came to allowing the publication of *Shadows on the Hudson* in English translation. In this novel he "lets it all hang out" in an almost exhibitionist exposure of survivors' nihilism, promiscuity, and self-destruction. Singer forbad the publication of this work in English translation until after his death; it appeared forty years after the Yiddish original, in 1998, in a translation by Joseph Sherman.[54]

The reception of the posthumously published novel is indicative of the contradictory critical responses to Singer's work in English. In the *New York Times,* the reviewer applauded the work as revealing "Singer speaking in an unfamiliar raw and brutal voice, the grandfatherly Yiddish writer stripped of the kindly, gentle tone and the flights of the supernatural fantasy that we mostly know him by."[55] The novel is given the highest marks as "a startling, piercing work of fiction, a book with a strong claim to being Singer's masterpiece."[56] In another review in the *New York Times,* the novel is torn to shreds as "chaotic, rambling, repetitive and parochial," so unlike Singer's short stories that, "at their best, are like hard diamonds of perfection." The reviewer perceptively points to the novel's having been written "on demand, and for a very specific audience with very specific intellectual and emotional needs."[57] The Montreal Yiddish poet and fiction writer Chava Rosenfarb agreed with the *New York Times* reviewer's negative assessment, noting that "Bashevis's work which was first published in *Forverts*, was usually shabby and chaotic. Only when they were published in the English version did they achieve their true artistic form."[58] Singer never oversaw the editing of the English version of *Shadows on the Hudson*, which was translated more or less directly from the serialized version. As a result, the novel allows us to enter the uncensored world of Singer's serialized novels in the *Forverts* with a minimum of edits and touchups that otherwise improved his novels in English.

Like Hertz Dovid Grein, most of the characters in the novel arrived in America one or two decades before the Holocaust; a few, such as Anna, have escaped war-torn Europe under dramatic circumstances. In a plot similar to that of *Enemies: A Love Story*, which is a more artistically fulfilled version of the same theme, Grein finds himself entangled with three women at the same time: his loyal wife, his long-time lover, and his most recent infatuation, Boris Makover's daughter, Anna. Its main characters drift aimlessly, sexually and professionally, outwardly successful in America but inwardly suffering desperately over their loss of family and Ashkenazi homeland in the Holocaust. Their pursuit of happiness in America remains unfulfilled, trapping them in serial relationships and get-rich schemes. In a few cases they seek out the certainty of clear-cut solutions to their predicament in Orthodox Judaism (Boris Makover and Grein) and spiritualism (Dr. Margolin). The novel succeeds in delineating the plight of the *sheyres hapleyte*—the traumatized remnants of the Holocaust exiled from their Ashkenazi Jewish homelands—in crass, materialistic, intellectually superficial America. Less successful is the novel's character development, which, as often is the case in Singer's work, tends to turn into caricatures. Singer's particular talent lies in uncovering the deep archetypical battles between Good and Evil, the basic existential choices of modern Jews, rather than in elaborating on the subtle aspects of their social and psychological conditioning.[59]

Singer is a typical representative of the exiled Yiddish writers from Jewish Eastern Europe: refugees before or after the conflagration who lived out their remaining days writing and publishing prolifically in places such as New York, Buenos Aires, Montreal, and Tel Aviv. Singer, like Chaim Grade and Aaron Zeitlin, experienced the survivor guilt of not having had "the

FIGURE 8.2. Isaac Bashevis Singer in his Upper West Side Manhattan apartment a few days before going to Stockholm, Sweden, to receive the Nobel Prize in Literature, December 1978. (Courtesy Chuck Fishman, copyright 1978, 2014)

privilege of going through the Hitler Holocaust," and it suffused his work and sharpened his deliberate exposition of desperate nihilism and self-destructive tendencies.[60] Like the works of other post-1945 Yiddish writers, Singer's writing—his enormous output on the staff of a Yiddish newspaper, continued productivity, and embrace of new genres until a ripe old age—reflected his work's life-affirming character.[61]

Singer's work is intrinsically woven into the web of Yiddish cultural politics, personal relationships, various newspapers and journals from *rekhte* to *linke* (politically right and left) in which the shrinking group of Yiddish writers and *kulturtuers* (cultural activists) fought each other in the uphill battle against assimilation and oblivion. American letters in the postwar period, which provided a fertile ground for younger Jewish writers such as Bellow, Malamud, and Roth, enabled Singer to break out of the increasingly ghettolike character of Yiddish in New York to become a major player on the American literary stage. The post-9/11 era has actualized aspects of Singer's work that highlight moral issues (e.g., "the axis of evil"), nihilism, and the threat of religious and political fundamentalism. The celebration of his centennial in 2004 and the jubilee edition of his short stories by the Library of America, the only Yiddish writer to be so honored, indicate that his literary star is unlikely to dim any time soon.

The 1967 story "My Adventures as an Idealist" is vintage Singer in its bittersweet self-portrait of the artist as a middle-aged man exiled between languages and cultures. The mysterious Sigmund Seltzer, the narrator's sparkling Freudian alter ego, has commissioned the narrator to write his autobiography. Seltzer wants the narrator to provide a Yiddish translation of a German version ghostwritten by somebody else. Like Singer, the narrator has translated Thomas Mann's *The Magic Mountain* into Yiddish. The narrator continues to expand the work into a fictitious autobiography that he is unable to complete (like Singer himself, who also throughout his career continued to publish many volumes of a never-completed autobiography). The meaning of Seltzer's life becomes tied to his quest to get his ghostwritten autobiography published. Visiting the dying Seltzer in the hospital, the narrator closes the story with this prescient observation of literary posterity:

> Our eyes met in silence. His hair had become white and sparse, his forehead higher. An expression of gentleness and wisdom I had never seen before shone in his eyes. He half winked, half smiled, as if to say, I know everything that you know, and a little more in addition. He was no longer the Sigmund Seltzer I had known all these years, but a sage purified by suffering. He stared at me with a look of fatherly affection and murmured, "In the end what remains after us writers? Nothing but a bundle of paper."[62]

The story was originally published with the title *Der mekhaber* (The Author) in *Forverts* in 1965, and not collected in a short story collection. This was probably due to the cartoonlike lack of character development with which it demolishes the myth of the Author, and his Original Creation. Like Seltzer's autobiography, which is pieced together by ghostwriters and translators,

Singer's English oeuvre, which lifted him out of obscurity in America, was the result of an auspicious collaboration of publishers, translators, and editors.[63] Ever the professional writer and son of a Hasidic rebbe in Warsaw, Singer did not harbor any illusions about the Yiddish word's longevity after its severance from Hebrew Scriptures and religious law (*halakha*), as a result of the rise of the Haskalah (Jewish Enlightenment) in nineteenth-century Eastern Europe. In an article in *Algemeyner zhurnal* in 2006, Rabbi William Berkowitz, a close friend of Singer, described how his son approached the writer and asked him to inscribe the book *Shivkhey HaRan*, a Hebrew volume in praise of Nachman of Bratslav: "When Singer took the book his hands were trembling. 'I don't know,' he said, 'I'm not worthy of inscribing anything in this book.' My son insisted and he wrote *This book was written by a great human being. There never has been nor is there anyone like him.*"[64] Singer had internalized the distinction between what was traditionally viewed by his Hasidic father as a *seyfer* (in Hebrew, a holy book) and his own work, *yidishe bikhlekh* (Yiddish secular books).

Singer closed the Yiddish literary canon in the second half of the twentieth century while devising a life raft for his work in English translation. He created a new readership for his work in America without cutting his umbilical cord to the *Forverts* and its readership. Traces of Singer's Old World storytelling, supernaturalism, nihilism, and *sheyres hapleyte* are evident in the work of Jewish American writers such as Saul Bellow, Bernard Malamud, Cynthia Ozick, Steve Stern, Jonathan Safran Foer, Nicole Krauss, Dara Horn, and Jerome Rothenberg, among others.[65] His work remains a vital bridge between the last flowering of Yiddish literature after the Holocaust and the rise of a new Jewish literary center in North America.

CONCLUSION

אין יענער צײַט האָבן זיך געצויגן צו מיר, דעם רעדאַקטאָר פֿון "גאָלדענע קייט", אין מײַן אָפּגעצוימטן ווינקל איבער גראָע אויסגעטראָטענע טרעפּ, צענדליקער פֿון די אַנטרונענע, מיט זייערע כּתבֿים, ווי מוראַשקעס מיט אייערלעך אין מויל; געבראַכט פֿאַרן שאַצקאַמער פֿון דער אייביקייט זכרונות און טאָגביכער פֿון זייערע טויט-איבערלעבונגען, בעת מלחמה און חורבן, וואָס אויב מ'זאָל זיי אַלע אָפּדרוקן, און איינטאָוולען, איז עס אַ ביבליאָטעק פֿון די רײַכסטע וווּנדן.

> In those days [the late 1950s], tens of refugees were drawn to me, the editor of *The Golden Chain*, ascending on worn-out steps to my narrow corner, with their writings like ants full of eggs in their mouths; they brought a treasure of eternity, the memoirs and diaries of their death experiences during the war and the Holocaust. If they were all published between hard covers it would be a library of the richest wounds.
>
> Avrom Sutzkever, "*Zunroyzn*" (Sunflowers, 1987)[1]

After 1945, Yiddish writers were largely occupied with erecting permanent cultural edifices and sustaining their infrastructure, which bore witness to the violent end of Ashkenazi civilization in Europe during six years of war. The Yiddish writers of the 1945 generation did not weaken the sharp edge of their responses to the Holocaust following the end of the war. Instead their aesthetic and ideological reactions grew increasingly radical. These writers continued to struggle with issues that challenged the collective, normative response to the Holocaust in Yiddish culture. Their works plumbed the depths of the survivor's traumatic memory and means of representation. In the late style of Sutzkever's *Nevue fun shvartsaplen,* Rochman's *Der mabl,* Rosenfarb's *Survivors,* and Singer's *Shadows on the Hudson,* the survivor universe remains an open wound, grotesque, supernatural.[2] Like Aaron Zeitlin's poem "*A kholem fun nokh Maydanek*" (A Dream from after Majdanek, 1946), these works employ a wide range of genres, styles, and narratives:

CONCLUSION

אויך דאָס וועט ווערן פֿאַרגעסן, אויך דאָס.
פֿאַרברענט געוואָרן מײַן פֿאָלק,
און ס׳וועט ווערן פֿאַרגעסן אויך דאָס.
וווּ די נאַלעווקעס האָבן געוווישט—
בלאָז פֿון ווינט צווישן גראָז.
ווינט און גראָז.

ביימער זויפֿן זאַפֿט פֿון לעבנס טויטע.
צו אַ זונה אַ זון
זינגט אַ פֿויגל אַ שוטה.

אַ קוימען אָן אַ דאַך,
אַ קוימען אַ בלינדער,
שטאַרצט פֿון מיסט ווי אַן אַלטער צילינדער—
אַ צילינדער אָן אַ קאָפּ.

אויף אַ הויפֿן ציגל
ווי אויף אַ פּיעדעסטאַל
בלמבֿט שטיין, גלמך
נאָפּאָלעאָן בײַ די פּיראַמידן,
אַ גרויסער אומעטיקער שטשור,
קוקט אָן די אַזוי־גערופֿענע נאַטור,
אַ וועלט אָן גאָט און אָן ייִדן.

בײַנאַכט
יאָגט זיך אַ משוגענער נאָך ווילדע קעץ,
ווערט מיד און זעצט זיך אויף די שטיינער קלאָגן:
וווּ איז משיח? וווּ איז דער קץ?

This too will be forgotten, also this.
My nation was burned,
and this too will be forgotten.
Where the Nalevkes rustled—
a gust of wind in the grass,
wind and grass.

Trees guzzle sap from dead lives.
To a whore a sun
sings a bird a fool.

A chimney without a roof,
a blind chimney,
protrudes from the garbage like an old top hat—
a top hat without a head.

On a pile of bricks
Like a pedestal
remains standing, like Napoleon at the pyramids,
a large gloomy rat,
gazes at the so-called nature,
a world without God and without Jews.

At night
a madman chases after wild cats,
becomes tired and sits down on the stones lamenting:
Where is the Messiah? Where is the Redemption?³

Zeitlin's poem opens with the mention of two distinct locations: the Nalevkes and the pyramids. The poet delineates the distance in time and place between pre–World War II Nalewki Street (in Polish) and Nalevkes (in Yiddish, indicating a Jewish section of Warsaw) and the ancient pyramids. In today's Warsaw, the name of the street is Bohaterow Getta (Heroes of the Ghetto), which adds yet another layer of memory. The decimated cityscape is a stage set devoid of human beings, and marked by the chimneys of crematoria. These are the latter-day pyramids erected by slaves, or by the "racially inferior," who were consumed in their fire. This apocalyptic universe is the ultimate Godless and *Judenrein* nightmare. Napoleon, like Hitler, is a gloomy rat whose gaze has turned everything into dust and despair in the quest for world dominance. The Jewish poet is a madman who proclaims his Yiddish lamentations and poses age-old Jewish questions about the coming of the Messiah. In his dream from after Majdanek, the poet/prophet envisions the death factories, destroyed cities, and memories of a Warsaw Jewish neighborhood, all of which he fears will eventually disappear into a black hole of amnesia. In the middle of the poem, a children's ditty lists the Yiddish names of murdered Jewish children:

בלימעשי. טויבעשי. ריוועלע.
לאהניו. פייגעניו. פערעלע.
חאצקעלע. מאטעלע. קיוועלע.
הערשעלע. לייבעלע. בערעלע.

שאיעשי. חיה׳שי. גאָלדעשי.
מענדעלעך. גנענדעלעך. מינדעלעך.
כ׳צייל אין דער נאַכט אין דער שלאָפֿלאָזער
נעמען פֿון ייִדישע קינדערלעך.

. . .

אויס און נישטאָ מער די העשעלעך,
העשעלעך, פּעשעלעך, הינדעלעך.
קלאַנגען, בלויז קלאַנגען, בלויז ליד-קלאַנגען—
נעמען פֿון ייִדישע קינדערלעך.

וווּ איז דײַן פֿיסעלע, זיסעלע?
ציפּעלע, וווּ איז דײַן צעפּעלע?
רויך ביסטו, יענטעלעס הענטעלע!
אַש ביסטו, קאָפּעלעס קעפּעלע!

Blimeshe—Toibeshe—Rivele.
Leahnu—Feigenu—Perele.
Khazkele—Motele—Kivele.
Hershele—Leibele—Berele.

Shayeshi, Kahyeshi, Goldeshi.
Mendelekh, Gnendelekh, Mindelekh.
I count in the sleepless night
names of little Jewish children.

. . .

Gone and not here anymore the Heshelekh,
Heshelekh, Peshelekh, Hindelekh.
Sounds, only sounds, only poetic sounds—
Names of little Jewish children.

Where is your little foot, Zisele?
Zipele, where is your little braid?
You are smoke, Yentele's little hand!
You are ashes, Kopele's little head![4]

Like the Biblical Lamentations (*Eykho*), composed as a Hebrew acrostic one or two generations after the 586 BCE destruction of the First Temple in Jerusalem, the survivor poet of *der driter khurbn* (the third destruction) encrypts his apocalyptic vision into the names, sounds, and rhymes of the Yiddish language, commemorates and collects, while despairing over the raison d'être of his poetic mission and craft.

The 1945 generation gave voice to the experiences of those who survived the Holocaust or Soviet communism or both. These writers became the primary bearers of a transnational culture that came to replace an indigenous culture in its Eastern European territory.[5] This deep sense of belonging to a worldwide network of Yiddish centers is what sustained writers such as Shpiegl, Rosenfarb, Sutzkever, Strigler, and Rochman as they struggled to stay alive in the ghettos, in concentration camps, and in hiding. Their solace was *mame-loshn*, the Yiddish mother tongue that connected them to the Ashkenazi past and present, while providing a modicum of hope for the future. The 1945 generation was born of a primal desire to bear witness and shape their wartime writing so it would reach a postwar readership. As Emanuel Ringelblum predicted, history as the antidote to a memory of catastrophe became marginal in Yiddish culture after 1945:

> Over time [Emanuel] Ringelblum realized more and more clearly that survivor identity would overshadow the prewar past. The "before" would be erased by the "after." As he confronted the unfolding disaster he fought all the harder to preserve the "Now" and the "Before," to keep the a posteriori label of "victim" from effacing who the Jews were before the war. In a very real sense he saw history as an antidote to a memory of catastrophe which, however well intentioned, would subsume what had been into what had been destroyed.[6]

Instead Yiddish writers created a mythological and emotional approach to their experiences during the war years. Although important historians contributed to *Dos poylishe yidntum* and *Yizker* books, these series presented an all-encompassing view of Ashkenaz that subsumed the objectivity of the historian in a grand vision of a Jewish civilization's rise and fall. Yiddish culture offered history as myth and archetype. It incorporated distinctly religious modes while utilizing a wide range of genres, styles, and narrative forms to convey the tragedy and heroism of the Jewish wartime experience.

Beginning in 1945 Yiddish organizations continuously addressed the Holocaust in a collective mode of Jewish response to catastrophe (*Yizker* books), ingathering the Ashkenazic cultural treasures (*Dos poylishe yidntum*), and rallied around their cultural heroes, the survivors and exiles. This worldwide activity, with its on-going publications and performances, involved the participation of hundreds of thousands of Yiddish writers, readers, and activists. The Yiddish language itself became a pillar of continuity, the link to a six-hundred-year-old Ashkenazi civilization that had escaped total annihilation. After 1945 Yiddish continued its daily existence as both a mother tongue and a cultural vehicle for a minority of American, Canadian, South American, Soviet, Polish, and Israeli Jews. However, the overwhelming majority of Jews rejected Yiddish as a relic of a Jewish past that they associated with tragedy, loss, and genocide.

The Yiddish transnational network continued with a significant scope in terms of readership, publication activity, and cultural exchange. This is most evident in the worldwide range of contributors to and readers of the book series *Dos poylishe yidntum* in Buenos Aires, the publishing house Yidishbukh in Warsaw, the literary journals *Sovetish heymland* in Moscow and *Di goldene keyt* in Tel Aviv. The growing Jewish communities in North America and Israel developed their own distinct national identities, increasingly distinguishing themselves from the old Ashkenaz in Europe. In contrast, the Yiddish transnational network continued to embody the Ashkenazi civilization in the form of a virtual "quasi-territory" (*kemoy-teritorye*).[7]

Surviving historians and literary scholars from Eastern Europe, such as Rachel Auerbach, Max Weinreich, Philip Friedman, Joseph Kermish, Nakhmen Blumental, and Bernard Mark, made a major contribution to Holocaust studies, beginning immediately after the end of World War II in May 1945. They published seminal studies and primary sources about the German intellectual elite's participation in the Final Solution, the Warsaw Ghetto uprising, the Auschwitz chronicles, and much more. Their scholarship, however, which should have laid the foundation for the field of Holocaust studies, remained untranslated and invisible outside the Yiddish world. With the publication of Raul Hilberg's seminal *The Destruction of the European Jews* (1961), the focus on the German perpetrators and German sources became emblematic of the first phase of Holocaust studies. Not until the early 1990s, and largely spearheaded by survivors, did the creation of Holocaust museums and academic Holocaust studies programs shift the focus to the Jewish victims. This was followed by the appearance of an increasing number of English translations of Holocaust testimonies and memoirs. In some cases they were translations of works that had originally been published in Yiddish or Hebrew decades earlier. In contrast, beginning in 1945, the Yiddish cultural world saw an unbroken chain of artistic and scholarly activity that recorded, analyzed, and commemorated the Holocaust.

The Holocaust did not signify "the end of Yiddish." Rather, the catastrophe galvanized the commitment to and the use of Yiddish as a means of continuity (*hemshekh*), commemoration, and the retrieval of cultural treasures. Yiddish culture after the Holocaust is an exemplar of the inherent ability of Ashkenaz to regenerate and renew itself in response to the destruction. The myth of "the Holocaust as the end of Yiddish" has, in many ways, been more resilient than "the myth of silence." As argued in this book, Yiddish writers' activities, initiatives, and forward-looking cultural work in response to the Holocaust demonstrate the exact opposite. Indeed, the masses of Yiddish-speaking Jewry in Eastern Europe, along with their cultural infrastructures, had been annihilated by 1945. However, a transnational cadre of Yiddish cultural activists and survivors ensured that the "golden chain" continued.

The myth of "the end of Yiddish" is based on the expectation that the Yiddish cultural world map of 1939, with its almost eleven million Yiddish speakers on three continents, would remain the measure against which the post-1945 period necessarily would fall short. In fact, there was an actual increase in Yiddish cultural activity in the 1940s and 1950s, due to the urgent sense of mission to commemorate and memorialize the people and places that had been destroyed. In many cases, this collective sense of duty overcame the political balkanization of Yiddish culture.

Recent studies of the various post-1945 Yiddish cultural centers (particularly Moscow, Montreal, New York, Buenos Aires, Paris, and Tel Aviv) have enhanced our understanding of the dynamic interchange between the local and the global that has sustained Yiddish culture throughout its modern existence.[8] The transnational network enabled Yiddish survivor writers to maintain their creativity, readership, and support after the Holocaust. Ultimately, this set of networks provided them with escape routes to new locations overseas. After the Holocaust, the far-flung Ashkenazi dispersion made it possible for Yiddish culture to recover some of its previous scope and reach. If one is to gauge the artistic multiplicity and multiculturalism of writers such as Bashevis, Zeitlin, Grade, Rochman, Rosenfarb, Wiesel, Heschel, and Sutzkever, the key is to understand the ways in which they fused two or more Jewish urban identities, both before and after World War II. In the process of migrating from the Ashkenaz territory in Eastern Europe to the New World, they brought with them an inner cultural map of local, geographically dispersed Yiddish centers as part of a transnational Ashkenaz. In the post-1945 period, this map of the world grew increasingly virtual. It became an "imagined community" or "quasi-territory" consisting of Yiddish literary, musical, theatrical, and other artistic works that filled the void left behind after the destruction of Ashkenaz in Central and Eastern Europe. This rich cultural outpouring articulated the collective phantom pain after the Jewish body had been burned to ashes. The ghostly presence of characters inhabiting a world that had ceased to exist resulted in the creation of Yiddish magical realism or supernaturalism in the works of Rochman, Sutzkever, and Yitskhok Bashevis, while novelists Grade, Rosenfarb, and Strigler erected mimetic replicas in search of lost worlds.

A transnational network gave a cadre of major Yiddish writers, and hundreds of minor ones, the support and impetus to create works at the highest artistic level even as vernacular Yiddish was undergoing a rapid decline. The "silver age" of the Yiddish book represents the culmination of the great achievements of a group of literary artists who brought to fruition the cultural agendas, the visions, and the potential that originated in the golden age of Yiddish culture prior to World War II. The artistic triumphs of these writers are independent of the decline of vernacular Yiddish. In fact, the increasingly post-vernacular character of Yiddish, the result of a major decline in Yiddish-language proficiency among second- and third-generation Israeli, American, and Russian Jews, has been detrimental to the ability of scholars to access Yiddish source material. Recently there has been an effort to "challenge the myth of silence," providing a reevaluation of Yiddish culture after 1945:

> Millions of Jews around the world spoke Yiddish as their first language [post-1945]. The existence of the Yiddish-speaking Jewish Diaspora facilitated the rapid translation and distribution of key texts. Scholarship in Yiddish flourished. However, the precipitous decline of Yiddish and the contraction of language competency closed off much of this source material, finally creating the illusion that it had never even existed. Sheer ignorance and linguistic ineptitude, from the 1970s to the 1990s, was more important than prejudice in the 1940s and 1950s.[9]

The artistic treasures of Yiddish culture after 1945 will have a long afterlife, and most of them are available only in Yiddish. A small percentage of Yiddish sources has been published in English translation (estimated by the National Yiddish Book Center as less than 2 percent of all Yiddish books),[10] but many of these are highly questionable in terms of quality and selection: "If, as some maintain, the future of Yiddish is in translation, this will be a much diminished version of a rich culture; it is the responsibility of Yiddish scholars to insist on presenting that culture in all its depth and variety."[11] As a result, the role of the Yiddish scholar has increasingly become that of guide, translator, and purveyor of certain quality standards to a readership with almost no prior knowledge of Jewish languages and cultures. Similarly, this book is an interpretative act of cultural transmission that includes many translated excerpts of Yiddish poems, prose, and discursive writing. It contributes to post-vernacular Yiddish while seeking to draw some readers to the Yiddish primary and secondary sources.

The study of post-vernacular Yiddish is the result of an increasing focus on popular culture and symbolic modes of Yiddish-language use in primarily American English and Israeli Hebrew contexts. Current scholarship in cultural studies applies concepts and methodologies that explore new interdisciplinary areas of Yiddish-land and beyond. The recent generations of scholars at American universities who came of age in the 1990s and early 2000s have steered away from the Holocaust. Informed by postmodern and cultural studies theory, these scholars have viewed the Holocaust with suspicion because of its potential to turn the field into yet another example of "the lachrymose version" of Jewish history. This is evident in the anthology *Choosing Yiddish: New Frontiers of Language and Culture* (2013):

> ... although readers might expect a section on Yiddish and the Holocaust, we have chosen not to create such a rubric. This decision stems from our efforts to rethink the traditional thematic divisions of Jewish studies, and, specifically, to avoid the teleological claim of citing the Holocaust for the end of Yiddish. Thus we have chosen not to pigeonhole this colossal event into an arbitrary category that would also not do justice to the historical trajectory of the language and culture of Yiddish. Instead numerous—if not most—essays throughout the collection address, both directly and indirectly, the impact of the Holocaust on the development and decline of Yiddish as a vernacular language. By the same token, this volume does not feature studies that focus on many of the so-called canonical Yiddish writers. Indeed, the most current scholarship in the field today often directly challenges canonical constructs.[12]

Again the trope of "the Holocaust as the end of Yiddish" is reiterated from the point of view of contemporary scholarly concerns about the predominance of post-vernacular Yiddish, primarily in America and Israel. As this book has argued, Yiddish culture flourished to a certain extent in response to the Holocaust. Deemphasizing this fact diminishes the scope and depth of its multifaceted characteristics post-1945. Moreover, mostly absent from current scholarly concerns is the pivotal role played by the Yiddish culture hero, a concept that originated with *di klasikers,* particularly I. L. Peretz. As Anita Norich points out, the transformation of Yiddish culture in the 1940s was facilitated through the revival of the view of Peretz as culture hero in connection with celebrations to mark the thirtieth *yortsayt* (anniversary) of his death in 1946. Peretz became the role model for survivor and exilic writers in their efforts to revive Yiddish culture. Poets and fiction writers were crucial to the renewal of Yiddish culture after the Holocaust. They were focal points embodying Yiddish culture's highest ethical and spiritual aspirations. Current scholarship tends to pay less attention to such "canonical constructs" of Yiddish cultural production in both past and present, further reducing its scope, conceptual map, and central concerns.

In Jewish literary studies, the dominance of Isaac Bashevis Singer's work in English translation has been partly responsible for occluding other post-1945 Yiddish writers. Singer's centrality in Jewish American literature notwithstanding, his stature in America as the anti-normative Jewish writer par excellence has been detrimental to delineating a more accurate picture of Yiddish culture after World War II. Cynthia Ozick's novella "Envy; or, Yiddish in America" exemplifies the Singer-induced distortion of the Yiddish cultural landscape, which reflected Jewish Americans' rejection of Yiddish culture, even as Singer's more than half-century of weekly contributions to the daily *Forverts* continued to fuel his artistic iconoclasm and bilingualism.

Elieyzer Wiesel, Yankev Glatshteyn, and Yitskhok Bashevis each devised his own solution to the problem of translation. Wiesel wrote his first Holocaust memoir in Yiddish, and worked as a Yiddish journalist during the early part of his career in the 1940s and 1950s. After the early 1960s, he mostly abandoned Yiddish and continued his literary career in French and English. This shift was less a question of betrayal of Yiddish culture than a pragmatic choice based on his self-definition as a Jewish survivor of Auschwitz with a commitment to reach out to the world with a universal message of "never forget."

Glatshteyn and Singer chose fundamentally different approaches to the question of translation. Although both continued to work inside the Yiddish cultural system throughout their careers, Glatshteyn intensified his loyalty to Yiddish in response to the Holocaust. The Holocaust confirmed his rejection of the world at large, and his return to the Jewish "ghetto," as he had proclaimed in his 1938 poem *"A gute nakht velt,"* to embrace Yiddish and secular

Yiddishkeit as both medium and message. Yitskhok Bashevis, in contrast, began a double career after 1950. He continued to contribute to the daily *Forverts* as a critic, journalist, and fiction writer even as he increasingly began to translate and shape his oeuvre into English. Today Yitskhok Bashevis is canonized as the American writer Isaac Bashevis Singer, thanks to his prolific output of short stories and novels in English. His Yiddish persona is virtually unknown outside scholarly circles, and most of his Yiddish works are available only on microfilm and have never been published in book form. In short, translation remains crucial for understanding the transnational and multicultural character of Yiddish culture after 1945, in which writers negotiated their culture's marginality and minority status through adaptation of their works into major languages.

In the aftermath of the Holocaust, Yiddish writers and cultural organizations began to make a concerted effort to reach out to the world at large through translations and cultural events. This is exemplified by the publication of bilingual editions of historical and literary works such as Weinreich's *Hitler's Professors* (1946), Abraham Joshua Heschel's *The Earth Is the Lord's* (1950), the translations of Yiddish literature in anthologies edited by Irving Howe and Eliezer Greenberg, I. B. Singer's American oeuvre, and the 1960s poetry series at the 92nd Street Y. Translation of Yiddish works into English, which practice has recently been viewed by some scholars as the ultimate remedy for Yiddish cultural survival, was a minor concern prior to the 1970s. In the quarter-century after the Holocaust, Yiddish culture thrived inside its own linguistic domain, with a significant number of writers, readers, and cultural organizations that tirelessly promoted its various ideological stripes. A few doomsday voices in the 1950s, such as Judd Teller, Yankev Glatshteyn, and H. Leivick, questioned Yiddish culture's long-term viability. The primary issue of Yiddish culture in the 1940s and 1950s, however, was not the survival of Yiddish as a vernacular language. Rather, the concern was to sustain a high level of cultural activity so as to ensure that the Yiddish transnational network would continue to respond forcefully to the Holocaust.

Recordings of performances of Yiddish poetry in intimate and public settings are important source materials that have been made increasingly available on-line. As discussed in the cases of Rosenfarb, Glatshteyn, Bashevis, and others, poetic and critical works often were initially presented at events at the Jewish Public Library in Montreal, the 92nd Street Y in New York, and other venues. Their lectures, stand-up routines, and poetry readings were often published in Yiddish periodicals or newspapers. The local cultural venues set the "horizon of expectation" for the ways in which the Yiddish writer would deliver and select his or her material for publication.

The various genres employed by Yiddish poets after 1945 derived partly from Hebrew scriptural models, such as Psalms and Lamentations; others from the Russian *poema*, with its epic, declamatory style, such as Sutzkever's poem *"Farfroyrene yidn"* (Frozen Jews), which he performed at the 92nd Street Y in an almost dirgelike rhythm. Influenced by Anglo-American modernism, Glatshteyn sometimes used an understated, self-ironic performance style. In general, Yiddish poets employed a high stylistic register, utilizing a pathos in poetic diction, style, and performance that is foreign to American culture and difficult to convey in English.[13]

In prose fiction, there was a turn toward testimonial realism, eschewing postmodern flights of the imagination. The exceptions, such as Sutzkever's surrealistic short prose and Yitskhok Bashevis's supernatural stories, highlight the normative trend in Yiddish prose fiction after 1945: nineteenth-century realism, reportage, and descriptive prose exemplified by Rosenfarb's trilogy, Strigler's memoirs, Rochman's war diary, and Grade's novels about the Jerusalem of Lithuania. With some important exceptions, the burden of bearing witness and commemorating the collective tragedy precluded postmodernist innovation.

Central to this book's methodology is the division of the postwar period into overlapping historical phases: "the angry 1940s"; before and after the 1961 Eichmann trial; "the silver age" of Yiddish book publishing; and the rise of post-vernacularity. The status, reception, and performance of Yiddish Holocaust literature changed in distinctive ways from the 1940s through the 1970s, often in response to cultural changes in the majority cultures. The angry anti-German poetry of Glatshteyn and Zeitlin, and Weinreich's *Hitler's Professors*, corresponded to the anti-German sentiments in American culture at large during the immediate postwar period. The outpouring of Yiddish publications in response to the Holocaust peaked in the 1940s and 1950s, but the trend in the Anglophone American Jewish community was quite different. The output of Holocaust literature in English during the 1950s was relatively small. The 1961 Eichmann trial, however, opened up a more in-depth public engagement with the Holocaust in America. This was followed by the publication of an increasing number of Holocaust studies, memoirs, and artistic works.[14]

Although Yiddish communist culture behind the Iron Curtain was severely curtailed, it nevertheless enabled a cadre of Jewish communists to continue Yiddish cultural work after the Holocaust. These were significant, and included the three hundred volumes published between 1946 and 1968 by Yidish-bukh in Warsaw, and the literary journal *Sovetish heymland* in Moscow, in publication from 1961 to 1991. Moreover, the politics of Yiddishism compelled the work of cultural leaders such as Mark Turkov, Max Weinreich, Yankev Glatshteyn, and Avrom Sutzkever, all of whom posited the centrality of Yiddish culture and language for Ashkenazi Jews in their new diasporas. Instead of viewing our period as the "post-ideological" phase of Yiddish scholarship, we should perhaps more appropriately understand Yiddishism and other types of ideologies as important driving forces that continue to shape current Yiddish scholarship and cultural work.

The terms *Ashkenaz* and *Ashkenazi Jewry* have been used throughout this study to signify a much broader engagement with Yiddish culture as the defining features of the six-hundred-year Jewish civilization in Europe.[15] The study has been conceived as a journey from old/new Ashkenaz in Vilna and Lodz (with a stop in Moscow) to the Ashkenazi diasporas in the New World, primarily New York, Montreal, Buenos Aires, and Tel Aviv. In these centers, Jewish languages and cultures continued to include English, Polish, German, Russian, French, Spanish, and Hebrew. These languages remained important artistic vehicles for continued engagement with Ashkenazi culture after 1945.[16] This study endeavors not to turn Yiddish literature into an "essence" that is somehow more authentically Jewish than Jewish literature in non-Jewish languages. Rather, the core argument is that Yiddish culture remains a crucial and indispensable means of studying Jewish responses to the Holocaust, and Jewish cultures and literatures after 1945.

The ongoing work of making Yiddish culture, in both print and performance form, available on-line, which began in earnest during my decade-long work on this book, continued the ingathering of Yiddish cultural treasures (*kinus*) initiated by the editors of the *Yizker* books, Tabatshnik's *Voice of the Yiddish Poet*, and the poetry series at the 92nd Street Y. Several of these projects have been made available on-line in the form of full-text and sound archives. This development not only has made Yiddish print culture and performances available for an international group of researchers, it also has further transformed Yiddish into a virtual culture accessible to anyone with a computer. Particularly important for the development of a transnational Yiddish culture has been the beneficial symbiosis of English, the most prestigious and widely used language on the planet, with Yiddish, a tiny minority language with fewer than a million speakers.[17] As exemplified by the small group of influential Jewish intellectuals in New York—such as Irving Howe and Saul Bellow in his seminal translation of "Gimpel the Fool," and various American publishers and editors who promoted the work of I. B. Singer—and starting in the late 1960s with Yiddish translators such as Cynthia Ozick, Adrienne Rich, Benjamin Harshav, Richard Fein, and John Hollander, the transmission of Yiddish culture in English has been an important bridge between the particular and the universal. The iconic example is of course *Fiddler on the Roof*, the 1964 musical that transformed Sholem Aleichem's novel *Tevye the Dairyman* into a fundamentally different cultural matrix for a worldwide audience. Thanks to the status of American Jewish culture, Yiddish words, cultural references, and literary works have been transmitted far beyond their own linguistic borders. Although the post-vernacular use of Yiddish, and in some cases promotion of its culture, has resulted in a watered-down, pale version of the original, it nevertheless has insured that the Yiddish cultural heritage continues to be circulated, reviewed, and accessed in English and in multiple other languages via translations from the English versions.

Today, *mame-loshn* is universally viewed as a viable object of academic research and cultural engagement in various forms of translation and adaptation, and in the original language. The increased use of Yiddish in the Haredi community during the last decades has challenged some of the enshrined notions about the "death of Yiddish" as a spoken language and creative cultural medium. That is a topic for a different book, one about the development of vernacular Yiddish in the twenty-first century. This study has been demarcated by the map of multiple Yiddish-lands originating in the Eastern European territories of Ashkenaz prior to World War II. It staunchly advocates for reading Yiddish texts and performances in their own contexts: the Jewish centers after the Holocaust that continued the transnational trajectory of Ashkenaz.

APPENDIX 1

List of Publications: *Dos poylishe yidntum* (Polish Jewry, Buenos Aires, 1946–66)

Listed below are the 175 volumes in the series *Dos poylishe yidntum* (Polish Jewry), Buenos Aires, 1946–66, noting their original editions and translations from and into other languages.

דאָס פּוילישע יידנטום

1. מאַרק טורקאָוו, מלכּה אָווישיאַני דערציילט . . . כראָניק פון אונדזער צייט

1. Mark Turkov (1904–83), *Malke Ovshyany dertseylt . . . Khronik fun undzer tsayt* (Malkah Ovshyany Tells Her Tale . . . Chronicle from Our Time), 1946. 172 pp.

Spanish edition: *Malka Owsiany relata: Crónica de nuestro tiempo. Memorias recopiladas por Mark Turkow.* Translated by Israel Laubstein. Prologue by Moshé Korin. Buenos Aires: Milá, 2001.

2. ה. ד. נאָמבערג, י. ל. פּרץ

2. Hersh-Dovid Nomberg (1876–1927), *Y. L. Perets* (I. L. Peretz), 1946. 115 pp. Originally published as H. D. Nomberg, *Gezamlte verk,* volume 8. Warsaw: Kultur-lige, 1928.

3. וו. גראָסמאַן, י. ווערניק, טרעבלינקע

3. Vasili Grossman (1905–64) and Yankel Viernik (1889–1972), *Treblinke* (Treblinka), 1946. 124 pp. Translation of Vasili Grossman's Russian-language reportage, "Treblinka Hell" (1944), in *A Writer at War: Vasily Grossman with the Red Army 1941–1945,* ed. Antony Beevor and Luba Vinogradova (New York: Random House, 2005), 280–309; and Yankel Viernik's Polish text, *Rok w Treblince* (A Year in Treblinka, 1944).

Grossman Spanish edition: *El infierno de Treblinka.* Buenos Aires: Ejecutivo Sudamericano del Congreso Judío Mundial, 1968.

Grossman French edition: *L'enfer de Tréblinka.* Paris: Arthaud, 1945.

Grossman German edition: *Di Holle von Treblinka.* Moscow: Verl. für Fremdsprachige Literatur, 1946.

Viernik French edition: *Une année à Treblinka.* Translated by Sara Bouskéla-Schipper. Paris: Éditions Vandémiaires, 2012.

Viernik Spanish edition: *Un año en Treblinka.* Buenos Aires: Ejecutivo Sudamericano del Congreso Judío Mundial, 1973.

4. פּרץ גראַנאַטשטיין, מיין חרוב שטעטל סאָקאָלאָוו: שילדערונגען, בילדער און פּאָרטרעטן פון אַ שטאָט אומגעקומענע יידן

4. Perets Granatshteyn (1907–?), *Mayn khorev shtetl Sokolov: Shilderungen, bilder un portretn fun a shtot umgekumene yidn* (My Destroyed Shtetl Sokolov: Descriptions, Pictures, and Portraits from a Town's Perished Jews), 1946. 188 pp.

5. ישראל טאבאקסבלאט, חורבן-לאָדזש: 6 יאָר נאַצי-גהינום

5. Israel Tabaksblat (1891–1950), *Khurbn-Lodzh: 6 yor natsi-gehenem* (The Destruction of Lodz: 6 Years of Nazi-Hell), 1946. 203 pp.

6. יעקב זרובבל, באַרג חורבן: קאַפּיטלען פּוילן

6. Jacob Zerubavel (1886–1967), *Barg khurbn: Kapitlen Poyln* (Mountainous Destruction: Polish Chapters), 1946. 220 pp.

7. אלחנן צייטלין, אין אַ ליטערארישער שטוב: בילדער, באַגעגענישן, עפּיזאָדן

7. Elkhonon Zeitlin (1900–1942), *In a literarisher shtub: Bilder, bagegenishn, epizodn* (In a Literary Home: Pictures, Encounters, Episodes), 1946. Introduction by S. Niger and Mark Turkov; afterword by Aaron Zeitlin. xxix + 238 pp.

8. חיים שאָשקעס, פּוילן—1946: אײַנדרוקן פֿון אַ רײַזע

8. Henry Shoshkes (1891–1964), *Poyln—1946: Ayndrukn fun a rayze* (Poland—1946: Impressions from a Journey), 1946. 189 pp.

9. ז. סעגאַלאָוויטש, טלאָמאַצקע 13: פֿון פֿאַרברענטן נעכטן

9. Zusman Segalovicz (1884–1949), *Tlomatske 13: Fun farbrentn nekhtn* (Tlomatske 13: From an Extinguished Past), 1946. 255 pp.

10. מ. נודעלמאַן, געלעכטער דורך טרערן: זאַמלונג פֿון הומאָריסטיש-סאַטירישע שאַפֿונגען פֿונעם נאָכמלחמהדיקן לעבן פֿון פּוילישע ייִדן

10. M. Nudelman (1905–67), *Gelekhter durkh trern: Zamlung fun humoristish-satirishe shafungen funem nokh-milhomehdikn lebn fun Poylishe Yidn* (Laughter Through Tears: Collection of Humorous-Satirical Creations of Postwar Life of Polish Jews), 1947. Introduction by Mark Turkov. 238 pp.

11. מאיר באַלאַבאַן, די ייִדן-שטאָט לובלין

11. Mayer Balaban (1877–1943), *Di yidn-shtot Lublin* (The Jewish City Lublin), 1947. Introduction and trans. from the Polish by A. L. Shushaym. 191 pp.

12. ישראל אפרת, היימלאָזע ייִדן: אַ באַזוך אין די ייִדישע לאַגערן אין דײַטשלאַנד

12. Israel Efros (1891–1981), *Heymloze yidn: A bazukh in di Yidishe lagern in Daytshland* (Homeless Jews: A Visit to the Jewish Camps in Germany), 1947. 249 pp. Co-publisher: Sociedade Beneficente dos Israelitas Poloneses en Sao Paulo.

13. יעקב שאַצקי, אין שאָטן פֿון עבר

13. Jacob (Yankev) Shatski (1893–1956), *In shotn fun over* (In the Shadow of the Past), 1947. 239 pp.

14. דוד פֿלינקער, אַ הויז אויף גשיבאוו: ראָמאַן

14. Dovid Flinker (1900–?), *A hoyz oyf Gzshibov: Roman* (A House on Gzhibov: A Novel), 1947. Introduction by Z. Segalovicz. 356 pp.

15. הלל זיידמאַן, טאָג-בוך פֿון וואַרשעווער געטאָ

15. Hillel Seidman (1915–95), *Tog-bukh fun varshever geto* (Diary from the Warsaw Ghetto), 1947. Introduction by Yosef Heftman. 335 pp. Co-publisher: Federatsye fun poylishe yidn in Amerike. Originally published in Hebrew as *Yoman geto Varshah*. Tel Aviv: Umah u-moledet, 1945.

English (US) edition: *The Warsaw Ghetto Diaries*. Translated by Yosef Israel. Southfield, MI: Targum Press, 1997.

French edition: *Du fond de l'abyme: Journal du ghetto de Varsovie.* Edited and translated from Hebrew and Yiddish by Nathan Weinstock. Paris: Plon, 1998.

16. נח גריס, קינדער-מארטיראָלאָגיע: זאַמלונג פֿון דאָקומענטן

16. Noah Gruss (1902–84), ed., *Kinder-martirologye: Zamlung fun dokumentn* (Children Martyrology: Collection of Documents), 1947. 286 pp.

A different version, published in **Polish**: *Dzieci oskarzaja* (The Children Accuse). Ed. M. Hochberg-Marianska and N. Grüss. Warsaw: Central Jewish Historical Commission, 1947.

17. חיים גראַדע, לידער און פּאָעמען געשריבן אין ראַטן-פֿאַרבאַנד אין 1941–1945 פּליטים:

17. Chaim Grade (1910–82), *Pleytim: Lider un poemen geshribn in Ratn-Farband in 1941–1945* (Refugees: Poems and Epic Poems Written in the Soviet Union in 1941–1945), 1947. 188 pp.

18. שמערקע קאטשערגינסקי, פּארטיזאנער גייען!: (פֿארצייכענונגען פון ווילנער געטאָ)

18. Shmerke Kaczerginski (1908–54), *Partizaner geyen! (Fartseykhenungen fun vilner geto)* (Partisans March! Notes from the Vilna Ghetto), 1947. 176 pp.

19. פֿרידע זרובבל, נע- ונד: פֿארצייכענונגען פון א פּליטה

19. Fryda Zerubavel (birth/death dates unknown), *Na venad: Fartseykhenungen fun a pleyte* (Homeless: Notes of a Refugee), 1947. 174 pp.

20. מרדכי שטריגלער, מאַידאַנעק

20. Mordechai Strigler (1921–98), *Maydanek: Oysgebrente likht*, vol. 1. (Majdanek: Extinguished Lights, vol. 1), 1947. Introduction by H. Leivick. 248 pp.

French edition: *Maidanek*. Paris: H. Champion, 1998.

21. יעקב לעשטשינסקי, אויפֿן ראנד פון אפגרונט: פון ייִדישן לעבן אין פּוילן 1927–1933

21. Jacob (Yankev) Lestschinsky (1876–1966), *Oyfn rand fun opgrunt: Fun yidishn lebn in Poyln: 1927–1933* (On the Edge of the Abyss: From Jewish life in Poland, 1927–1933), 1947. 247 pp.

22. סעגאַלאָוויטש זוסמאַן, געברענטע טריט: איינדרוקן און איבערלעבונגען פון א פּליטים-וואַנדערונג

22. Zusman Segalovicz (1884–1949), *Gebrente trit: Ayndrukn un iberlebungen fun a pleytim-vanderung* (Burned Steps: Impressions and Experiences from a Refugee's Wanderings), 1947. 255 pp.

23. אברהם טייטלבוים, וואַרשעווער הייף: מענטשן און געשעענישן

23. Abraham Teitelbaum (1889–1947), *Varshever heyf: Mentshn un gesheenishn* (Warsaw Courtyards: People and Happenings), 1947. 207 pp.

24. טאַניא פֿוקס, א וואַנדערונג איבער אָקופּירטע געביטן

24. Tania Fuks (1896–1950), *A vanderung iber okupirte gebitn* (Wanderings Through Occupied Territories), 1947. 271 pp.

25. שמואל ליב שנײַדערמאַן, צווישן שרעק און האָפֿענונג: א רײַזע איבער דעם נײַעם פּוילן

25. Sh. L. Shnayderman (1906–96), *Tsvishn shrek un hofenung: A rayze iber dem nayem Poyln* (Between Fear and Hope: A Journey in the New Poland), 1947. 367 pp.

English (US) edition: *Between Fear and Hope*, trans. Norbert Guterman. New York: Arco Publishing, 1947.

26. לעאָ פֿינקלשטיין, מגילת פּוילן: תורה, חסידות און שטײגער-קולטור אין ייִדישן פּוילן

26. Leo Finkelstein (1895–1950), *Megiles poyln: Toyre, hasides un shteyger-kultur in Yidishn Poyln* (Scrolls of Poland: Torah, Hasidism, and Cultural Ways of Jewish Poland), 1947. 346 pp.

27. יאָנאַס טורקאָוו, אַזוי איז עס געוועז: חורבן ווארשע

27. Jonas Turkov (1898–1982), *Azoy iz es geven: Khurbn Varshe* (So It Was: The Destruction of Warsaw), 1948. 543 pp.

Hebrew edition: היה היתה וארשה יהיה Translated by Yisrael Zemurah. Tel Aviv: Tarbut vehinukh, 1969.

French edition: *C'était ainsi: 1939–1943*. Translated by Maurice Pfeffer. Paris: Ed. Austral, 1995.

28. שמואל איזבאן, "אומלעגאַלע" ייִדן שפּאַלטן ימען: די געשיכטע פֿון אן אומלעגאַלער רײזע קיין ארץ ישראל

28. Shmuel Izban (1905–?), *"Umlegale" yidn shpaltn yamen: Di geshikhte fun an umlegaler rayze keyn Erets Yisroel* ("Illegal" Jews Split the Seas: The Story of the Illegal Journey to the Land of Israel), 1948. Introduction by Ruth Kliger. 335 pp.

29. יעקב פּאַט, העניעך: אַ ייִדיש קינד וואָס איז ארויס פֿון געטאָ

29. Jacob Pat (1890–1966), *Henekh: A Yidish kind vos iz aroys fun geto* (Henekh: A Jewish Child Who Left the Ghetto), 1948. 159 pp.

Hebrew edition: *Henekh*. Translated by Mosheh Aram. Tel Aviv: Hotsa'at Y.L. Peretz, 1974.

Spanish edition: *Un niño judío salió del ghetto*. Translated by Elías Singer. Buenos Aires: Siglo Veinte, 1951.

30. יוסף קערמיש, דער אויפֿשטאַנד אין ווארשעווער געטאָ: 19-טער אפּריל–16-טער מאי 1943

30. Joseph Kermish (1907–2005), *Der oyfshtand in varshever geto: 19-ter April–16-ter Mai 1943* (The Warsaw Ghetto Uprising: April 19–May 16, 1943). 1948. 159 pp. Translated from the original Polish, by Shloyme Lastik, Powstanie w getcie warszawskim, 19. iv.-16. v.1943. Co-publisher: Jewish Historical Institute, Warsaw, 1946.

Hebrew edition: Itonut-hamahteret hay-yehudut be-warsa/5 desember 1940–mars 1942. Jerusalem: Yad Vashem, 1979.

31. שמחה פּאָליאַקיעוויטש, אַ טאָג אין טרעבלינקע: כראָניק פֿון אַ ייִדיש לעבן

31. Simkhe Polakiewicz (1913–?), *A tog in Treblinke: Khronik fun a yidish lebn* (A Day in Treblinka: Chronicle from a Jewish Life), 1948. Introduction by Mark Turkov. 143 pp. Co-publisher: Landslayt fareynen fun Sokolov-Podlask in Argentine un Urugvay.

32. מרדכי שטריגלער, אין די פֿאַבריקן פֿון טויט

32. Mordechai Strigler (1921–98), *In di fabrikn fun toyt* (In the Factories of Death), 1948. 429 pp.

33. אברהם נחתומי, אין שאָטן פֿון דורות: קינדהייט

33. Abraham Nahtomi (1900–1978), *In shotn fun doyres: Kindheyt* (In the Shadow of Generations: Childhood), 1948. 191 pp.

34. יחיאל לערער, מיין היים

34. Yekhiel Lerer (1910–43), *Mayn heym* (My Home), 1948. 174 pp. Originally published in Warsaw, 1937–1938, as *Mayn heym: Durkh nakht tsum bagin* (no publisher identified).

Spanish edition: *Mi pueblito*. Buenos Aires, Milá, 1990.

35. יוסף וואָלף, לייענענדיק פּרצן

35. Yosef Wolf (1912–74), *Leyenendik peretsn* (Reading Peretz), 1948. 111 pp.

36. צפּורה קאַצענעלסאָן-נאכומאװ, יצחק קאַצענעלסאָן: זײַן לעבן און שאַפֿן

36. Tsipora Katsenelson-Nakhumov (1901–72), *Yitskhok Katsenelson: Zayn lebn un shafn* (Yitskhok Katsenelson: His Life and Work), 1948. 223 pp.

37. יחיאל הירשהויט, פינצטערע נעכט אין פּאַװיאַק: זכרונות, געשטאַלטן, בילדער
37. Julian (Yekhiel) Hirshoyt (1908–83), *Fintstere nekht in Povyak: Zikhroynes, geshtaltn, bilder* (Dark Nights in Povyak: Memoirs, Characters, Pictures), 1948. 239 pp.
   English edition: *Jewish Martyrs of Pawiak.* New York: Holocaust Library, 1982.
   Polish edition: *Ciemne noce Pawiaka.* Translated by Wojciech Spisak, Karolina Spisak, and Michał Jasnowski. Warsaw: Wydaw. Instytut Śląski, 2001.

38. נחום סאָקאָלאָװ, פּערזענלעכקײטן
38. Nahum Sokolow (1859–1936), *Perzenlekhkeytn* (Personalities), 1948. 254 pp. Translated from Hebrew (1911 and 1934) and with an introduction by Moisés Senderey.

39. רחל ה. קאָרן, הײם און הײמלאָזיקײט: לידער
39. Rokhl Korn (1898–1982), *Heym un heymlozikeyt: Lider* (Home and Homelessness), 1948. 256 pp.

40. א. אלמי, מאָמענטן פֿון אַ לעבן: זכרונות, בילדער און עפּיזאָדן
40. A. Almi (1892–1963), *Momentn fun a lebn: Zikhroynes, bilder un epizodn* (Events from a Life: Memoirs, Pictures, and Episodes), 1948. 253 pp.

41. מנשה אונגער, פּשיסכע און קאָצק
41. Menashe Unger (1899–1969), *Pshiskhe un Kotsk* (Pshiskhe and Kotsk), 1949. 301 pp.

42. מ. בורשטין, איבער די חורבֿות פֿון פּלוינע
42. M. Burshtin (1897–1945), *Iber di hurves fun Ployne* (Over the Ruins of Ployne), 1949. 222 pp. Introduction by Jacobo Botoshansky. Originally published in Vilne: B. Kletskin, 1931.

43. מ. קיפּניס, זמרה זעליגפֿעלד און מ. קיפּניסעס קאָנצערט רעפּערטואַר הונדערט פֿאָלקס-לידער: פֿון
43. M. Kipnis (1872–1942), ed. *Hundert folks-lider: Fun Zemirah Zeligfeld un M. Kipnises kontsert-repertuar* (Hundred Folk Songs: From Zemirah Zeligfeld and M. Kipnis's Concert Repertoire), 1949. Introduction by Mark Turkov. 269 pp.

44. ז. סעגאַלאָװיטש, מײַנע זיבן יאָר אין תּל-אָבֿיבֿ
44. Zusman Segalovicz (1884–1949), *Mayne zibn yor in Tel-Aviv* (My Seven Years in Tel-Aviv), 1949. Introduction by B. Shefner. 237 pp.

45. חיים שאָשקעס, אַ װעלט װאָס איז פֿאַרבײַ—: קאַפּיטלעך זכרונות
45. Henry Shoskes (1891–1964), *A velt vos iz farbay: Kapitlekh zikhroynes* (A World That Is Over: Chapters of Memoirs), 1949. 368 pp.

46. שלמה װאַגאַ, חורבן טשענסטאָכאָװ
46. Shloyme Vaga (1900–?), *Khurbn Tshenstokhov* (The Destruction of Tshenstokhov), 1949. 231 pp.
   English edition: *The Destruction of Czenstokov (Częstochowa, Poland).* Translated by Gloria Berkenstat Feund. New York: JewishGen, 2012.

47. אבֿרהם זאַק, יאָרן אין װאַנדער: לידער און פּאָעמען
47. Abraham Zak (1891–1980), *Yorn in vander: Lider un poemen* (Years of Wanderings: Poems), 1949. 244 pp.

48–49. שמואל איזבאַן, פֿאַמיליע קאַרפּ: ראָמאַן
48–49. Shmuel Izban (1905–?), *Familye Karp: Roman* (The Family Karp: Novel), 1949. 2 vols.
   Hebrew edition: *Beit Karp: Roman.* Translated by Abraham Leviush. Tel Aviv: Masada, 1955.

50. א. מוקדוני, מײַנע באגעגענישן: ייִדישע געשטאַלטן, וואָס איך האָב באַגעגנט אין מײַן לעבן
50. A. Mukdoni (1877–1958), *Mayne bagegenishn: Yidishe geshtaltn, vos ikh hob gagegnt in mayn lebn* (My Encounters: Jewish Figures, That I Have Met in My Life), 1949. 303 pp.

51. ה. שושנה קאהאן, אין פֿײַער און פֿלאַמען: טאָגבוך פֿון אַ ייִדישער שוישפּילערן
51. R. Shoshano Kahan (1895–1968), *In fayer un flamen: Togbukh fun a Yidisher shoyshpilerin* (In Fire and Flames: Diary of a Yiddish Actress), 1949. Introduction by F. Bimko. 406 pp.

52. יחיאל ישעיה טרונק, די ייִדישע פּראָזע אין פּוילן: אין דער תקופה צווישן ביידע וועלט-מלחמות
52. Y. Y. Trunk (1887–1961), *Di yidishe proze in poyln: In der tkufe tsvishn beyde velt milkhomes* (Yiddish Prose in Poland: In the Period Between the Two World Wars), 1949. 159 pp.

53. יאָנאס טורקאָוו, אין קאַמף פֿאַרן לעבן
53. Jonas Turkov (1898–1982), *In kamf farn lebn* (In Struggle for Life), 1949. 431 pp.
French edition: *La Lutte pour la vie*. Translated by Maurice Pfeffer. Paris: Champion, 2005.

54. יצחק פּערלאָוו, די מענטשן פֿון "עקזאָדוס 1947": (יציאת איירופע תש"ז): ראָמאַן
54. Yitskhok Perlov (1911–80), *Di mentshn fun "Eksodus 1947": Roman* (People from "Exodus 1947": Novel). 1949. 430 pp.
English edition: *The People of "Exodus": Novel*. Translated by Jeannette E. Shoham. Tel Aviv: Yechiel, 1960.

55. פּנחס ביזבערג, שבת-יום-טובֿדיקע ייִדן: דאָס געזאַנג פֿון אַ דור
55. Pinkhes Bizberg (1898–?), *Shabes-yontefdike yidn: Dos gezang fun a dor* (Sabbath-Holiday Jews: The Song of a Generation), 1949. 190 pp.

56-57-58. שלום אש, פֿאַרן מבול: ראָמאַן
56–57–58. Sholem Asch (1880–1957), *Peterburg: Ershter bukh fun "Farn mabl": Roman* (Petersburg: First Volume of "Before the Deluge": Novel), 1949. 366 pp. *Varshe: Tsveyter teyl fun bukh "Farn mabl": Roman* (Warsaw: Second Volume of "Before the Deluge": Novel), 1949. 380 pp. *Moskve: Driter teyl fun bukh "Farn mabl": Roman* (Moscow: Third Volume of "Before the Deluge": Novel), 1949. 451 pp. First published as *Farn mabl*, 3 vols. Warsaw: Kultur-Lige, 1929, 1930, 1931.
English edition: *Three Cities: A Trilogy*. Translated by Willa and Edwin Muir. New York: G. P. Putnam's Sons, 1933.
Hebrew edition: *Li-fene ha-mabul, roman*. Translated by Y. L. Barukh. Tel Aviv: Devir, 1934.
French edition: *Pétersbourg*. Translated (from the German) by Alexander Vialette. Paris: Mémoire du livre, 2000. *Varsovie*. Translated by Aby Wieviorka. Paris: Mémoire du livre, 2001. *Moscou*. Translated by Rachel Ertel. Paris: Mémoire de livre, 2002.
Spanish edition: *Tres ciudades: San Petersburgo, Varsovia, Moscú: Una trilogyía novelada*. Buenos Aires: Claridad, 1946.

59. פֿיליפּ פֿרידמאַן, אָשוויענטשים
59. Philip Friedman (1901–60), *Oshvyentshim* (Auschwitz), 1950. 223 pp.
English edition: *This Was Oswiecim: The Story of a Murder Camp*. London: United Jewish Relief Appeal, 1946.

60. בער י. ראָזען, טלאָמאצקע 13
60. Ber I. Rozen (1899–1954), *Tlomatske 13* (Tlomatske 13), 1950. 142 pp.

61–62. דוד פֿלינקער, אין שטורעם: ראָמאַן
61–62. Dovid Flinker (1900–?), *In shturem: Roman* (In the Storm: Novel), 1950. 2 vols.

LIST OF PUBLICATIONS: *DOS POYLISHE YIDNTUM* 259

63. יאנוש קאָרטשאַק, משהלעך, יאָסעלעך, ישראליקלעך

63. Janusz Korczak (1878–1942), *Moyshelekh, Yoselekh, Yisroyliklekh*. Originally published in Polish in Warsaw, 1922. Translated from the Polish by Yehoshue Perle, with an introduction by Sholem Asch, Yitskhok Grinboym, and Mark Turkov, 1950. 189 pp.

64–65. מרדכי שטריגלער, װערק "צע"

64–65. Mordechai Strigler (1921–98), *Verk "Tse": Bukh dray fun dem tsikl "Oysgebrente likht,"* 2 vols. (Work "Tse": Third Volume of the Cycle *Extinguished Lights*), 1950. 225 pp. and 252 pp.

66. חיים גראַדע, שײַן פֿון פֿאַרלאָשענע שטערן: לידער און פּאָעמען

66. Chaim Grade (1910–82), *Shayn fun farloshene shtern: Lider un poemen* (Light of Extinguished Stars: Poems), 1950. 192 pp.

67. רבֿקה קװיאַטקאָװסקי-פּנחסיק, פֿון לאַגער אין לאַגער

67. Rifke Kwiatkowski-Pinchasik (birth/death dates unknown), *Fun lager in lager* (From Camp to Camp), 1950. 301 pp.

68. יואל מאַסטבױם, מײַנע שטורמישע יאָרן

68. Joel Mastboym (1884–1957), *Mayne shturmishe yorn* (My Stormy Years), 1950. 175 pp.

69. אליהו טראָצקי, גלות דײַטשלאַנד: אײַנדרוקן פֿון אַ רײַזע

69. Elyahu N. Trotski (1879–1969), *Goles Daytshland: Ayndrukn fun a rayze* (Diaspora Germany: Impressions from a Journey), 1950. 207 pp.

70. יעקב שאַצקי, קולטור־געשיכטע פֿון דער השׂכּלה אין ליטה: פֿון די עלטסטע צײַטן ביז חיבת ציון

70. Yankev Shatski (1893–1956), *Kultur-geshikhte fun der haskole in lite: Fun di eltste tsaytn biz khibes tsien* (Cultural History of the Enlightenment in Lithuania: From the Oldest Times to *Khibes Tsien*), 1950. 231 pp.

71. נחמן מייזיל, געװען אַמאָל אַ לעבן: דאָס ייִדישע קולטור־לעבן אין פּױלן צװישן בײדע װעלט־מלחמות

71. Nakhmen Mayzel (1887–1966), *Geven amol a lebn: Dos yidishe kultur-lebn in Poyln tvishn beyde velt-milhomes* (There Was Once a Life: Yiddish Cultural Life in Poland between Both World Wars), 1951. 399 pp.

72. יחיאל ישעיה טרונק, שׂימכּע פּלאַכטע פֿון נאַרקאָװע: אָדער, דער ייִדישער דאָן קיכאָט

72. Y. Y. Trunk (1887–1961), *Simkhe Plakhte fun Narkove: Oder, Der Yidisher Don Kikhot* (Simkhe Plakhte from Narkove: Or, The Yiddish Don Quixote), 1951. 383 pp.

73. יהודה עלבערג, אונטער קופּערנע הימלען: דערצײלונגען

73. Yehuda Elberg (1912–2003), *Unter kuperne himlen: Dertseylungen* (Under Copper Skies: Stories), 1951. 252 pp.

74. א. מוקדוני, אױסלאַנד: מײַנע באַגעגענישן

74. A. Mukdoni (1877–1958), *Oysland: Mayne bagegenishn* (Abroad: My Encounters), 1951. 340 pp.

75. זיגמונט טורקאָװ, פֿראַגמענטן פֿון מײַן לעבן: זכרונות

75. Zygmunt Turkov (1896–1970), *Fragmentn fun mayn lebn: Zikhroynes* (Fragments of My Life: Memoirs), 1951. 303 pp.

76. יהושע פּערלע, ייִדן פֿון אַ גאַנץ יאָר

76. Yehoshue Perle (1888–1943), *Yidn fun a gants yor* (Ordinary Jews), 1951. 421 pp. Originally published in Warsaw, 1935.

English edition: *Everyday Jews: Scenes from a Vanished Life.* Trans. Maier Deshell and Margaret Birstein; foreword by David G. Roskies. New Haven, CT: Yale University Press, 2007.

Hebrew edition: *Yehudim setam: Roman.* Translated by Yehuda Gur-Arie. Tel Aviv: Kibbutz ha-me'uhad, 1992.

77. יעקב לעשצינסקי, ערב חורבן: פון ייִדישן לעבן אין פוילן 1935–1937

77. Jacob Lestschinsky (1876–1966), *Erev khurbn: Fun Yidishn lebn in Poyln, 1935–1937* (Before the Destruction: From Jewish Life in Poland, 1935–1937), 1951. 255 pp.

78. דניאל טשארני, ווילנע: מעמואַרן

78. Daniel Charney (1888–1959), *Vilne: Memuarn* (Vilna: Memoirs), 1951. 319 pp.

79. זוסמאן סעגאַלאָוויטש, דער לעצטער לאָדזשער ראָמאַן

79. Zusman Segalowicz (1884–1949), *Der letster lodzher roman* (The Last Lodz Novel), 1951. 398 pp.

80. בעלכאטאָװ: יזכור-בוך: געװידמעט דעם אָנדענק פון אַ פֿאַרשװוּנדן ייִדיש שטעטל אין פוילן

80. *Belkhatov: Yizker-bukh: Gevidmet dem ondenk fun a farshvundn yidish shtetl in Poyln* (Belkhatov: Memorial Book: Dedicated to the Remembrance of a Disappeared Jewish Shtetl in Poland), 1951. 511 pp. Edited and with an introduction by Jacob Botoshansky and Pinie Wald, Yizker-bukh committee. Co-publisher: Belkhatover landslayt-fareynen in Argentine, Brazil un Tsofn-Amerike.

81. משה יודל שעליובסקי, אויף אַ פֿולער וואָך: דערציילונגען

81. Moshe Yudl Shelubsky (1893–1974), *Oyf a fuler vokh: Dertseylungen* (In a Full Week: Stories), 1951. 376 pp.

82–83. יצחק פּערלאָװ, דער צוריקגעקומענער: ראָמאַן

82–83. Isaac Perlow (1911–80), *Der tsurikgekumener: Roman* (The Returning Person: Novel), 1952. 2 vols.; 712 pp.

84. יוסף אָקרוטני, דאָס בוך פון די עלנטע

84. Josef Okrutny (1906–91), *Dos bukh fun di elnte* (The Book of the Lonely), 1952. 228 pp.

85–86. מרדכי שטריגלער, גורלות

85–86. Mordechai Strigler (1921–98), *Goyroles* (Destinies), 1952. 2 vols.; 365 pp. and 353 pp.

87. יוסף טענענבוים, גאַליציע, מייַן אַלטע היים

87. Joseph Tenenbaum (1887–1961), *Galitsye, mayn alte heym* (Galicia, My Old Home), 1952. 319 pp.

88. זלמן שזר, שטערן פאַרטאָג: זכרונות, דערציילונגען

88. Zalman Shazar (1889–1974), *Shtern fartog: Zikhroynes, dertseylungen* (Stars at Dawn: Memoirs, Stories). Translated from the Hebrew by Mordechai Strigler, 1952. 270 pp.

89. משה דוד גיסער, דאָס געזאַנג פון אַ לעבן

89. Moses David Giser (1893–1952), *Dos gezang fun a lebn* (The Song of a Life), 1953. Introduction by Baerungs-komitet and Pinkhos Bizberg. 302 pp. Co-publisher: Baerungs-komitet far Moyshe Dovid Giser in Tshile.

90. זלמן יצחק אנכי, ר' אבא: און אַנדערער כתבים

90. Zalman Yitskhok Anokhi (1876–1947), *Reb Aba un andere ksovim* (Mr. Aba and Other Writings), 1953. 301 pp. Originally published in Warsaw: Velt-biblyotek, 1911.

Hebrew edition: *R. Aba: Sipurim u-mahazot.* Introduction by Avraham Kariv. Tel Aviv: Agudat ha-sofrim ha-'Ivrim le-yad Devir, 1960.

91–92. עמנואל רינגעלבלום, קאפיטלען געשיכטע פון אמאליקן יידישן לעבן אין פוילן
91–92. Emanuel Ringelblum (1900–1944), *Kapitlen geshikhte fun amolikn Yidishn lebn in Poyln* (Chapters of History from the Bygone Jewish Life in Poland). 1953. Edited and with biographical introduction by Yankev Shatski. 589 pp.

93. ש. האראנטשיק, אין געroise פון מאשינען
93. Sh. Horontshik (1889–1939), *In geroysh fun mashinen: Roman* (In the Noise of Machines: Novel), 1953. Introduction by Josef Okrutny. 318 pp. Originally published in Warsaw: Kultur-lige, 1930.

94. גרשם באדער, מיינע זכרונות . . .
94. Gershom Bader (1868–1953), *Mayne zikhroynes . . .* (My Memoirs . . .), 1953. 429 pp.

95–96. יאנאס טורקאוו, פארלאשענע שטערן
95–96. Jonas Turkov (1898–1982), *Farloshene shtern* (Extinguished Stars), 1953. 2 vols.; 324 and 308 pp.

97–98. אלטער קאציזנע, שטארקע און שוואכע: ראמאן אין פיר טיילן
97–98. Alter Kacyzne (1885–1941), *Shtarke un shvakhe: Roman in fir teyln* (Strong and Weak: Novel in Four Parts), 1954. Introduction by Melekh Ravitsh. 2 vols.; 334 and 415 pp.

99. פועה ראקאוּוסקי, זכרונות פון אַ יידישער רעוואלוציאנערין
99. Puah Rakovski (1865–1955), *Zikhroynes fun a Yidisher revolutsyonerin* (Memoirs of a Jewish Revolutionary Woman), 1954. Introduction by Rokhl Katsenelson-Shazar. 318 pp. First published in Hebrew as *Lo nikhnati*. Translated and abridged by David Kalai. Tel Aviv: N. Tverski, 1951.
English edition: *My Life as a Radical Jewish Woman: Memoirs of a Zionist Feminist in Poland.* Edited and with an introduction by Paul E. Hyman; translated by Barbara Harshav, with Paula E. Hyman. Bloomington: Indiana University Press, 2002.
French edition: *Mémoire d'une révolutionnaire juive.* Translated and with an introduction by Yitshok Niborski. Paris: Phébus, 2006.

100. מארק טורקאוו, די לעצטע פון א גרויסן דור: געשיכטלעכע עפיזאדן און פערזענלעכע זכרונות וועגן יידישע משפחות אין פוילן
100. Mark Turkov (1904–81), *Di letste fun a groysn dor: Geshikhtlekhe epizodn un perzenlekhe zikhroynes vegn yidishe mishpokhes in Poyln* (The Last of a Great Generation: Historical Episodes and Personal Memoirs about Jewish Families in Poland), 1954. 350 pp.

101. י. הירשהויט, יידישע נאפט-מאגנאטן
101. Julian (Yekhiel) Hirshoyt (1908–83), *Yidishe naft-magnatn* (Jewish Oil Magnates), 1954. 397 pp.

102. משה זאנשיין, יידיש-ווארשע
102. Moses Zonshayn (1906–60), *Yidish-Varshe* (Jewish Warsaw), 1954. 221 pp.

103. פ. מינץ (אלעקסאנדער), די געשיכטע פון א פאלשער אילוזיע: זכרונות
103. P. Mintz (Aleksander) (1895–1962), *Di geshikhte fun a falsher iluzye: Zikhroynes* (The History of a False Illusion: Memoirs), 1954. 381 pp.

104. יחיאל ישעיה טרונק, די וועלט איז פֿול מיט נסים: אָדער, מעשה מגימל אחים
104. Y. Y. Trunk (1887–1961), *Di velt iz ful mit nisim: Oder, mayse megiml okhim* (The World Is Full of Wonders: Or, the Story *Megiml Okhim*), 1955. 333 pp.

105–107. מיכאל באָרוויטש, אַרישע פּאַפּירן
105–107. Michal Borwicz (1911–87), *Arishe papirn* (Aryan Papers), 1955. Introduction by Yankev Pat. 3 vols.; 304, 231, and 298 pp.

108–109. מרדכי שטריגלער, געאָרעמט מיטן ווינט: היסטאָרישער ראָמאַן פֿון ייִדישן לעבן אין פּוילן
108–109. Mordechai Strigler (1921–98), *Georemt mitn vint: Historisher roman fun Yidishn lebn in Poyln* (Embraced by the Wind: Historical Novel of Jewish Life in Poland), 1955. 2 vols.

110–111. א. מוקדוני, אין ווארשע און אין לאָדזש: מײַנע באַגעגענישן
110–111. A. Mukdoni (1877–1958), *In Varshe un in Lodzsh: Mayne bagegenishn* (In Warsaw and Lodz: My Encounters), 1955. 2 vols.; 302 and 298 pp.

112. ברוך האגער, מלכות חסידות
112. Barukh Hager (1898–1985), *Malkhes khsides* (In the Kingdom of Hasidism), 1955. 283 pp.

113. ב. ב. שעפֿנער, נאָוואָליפּיע 7: זכרונות און עסייען
113. B. B. Shefner (1896–1977), *Novolipye 7: Zikhroynes un eseyen* (Novolipye 7: Memoirs and Essays), 1955. 318 pp. Financed by the Conference on Jewish Material Claims Against Germany.

114. פּנחס שטיינוואַקס, ייִדן צום געדענקען
114. Pinkhes Shtaynvaks (1905–77), *Yidn tsum gedenken* (Jews to Remember), 1955. 340 pp. Financed by the Conference on Jewish Material Claims Against Germany.

115. ק. צעטניק, דאָס הויז פֿון די ליאַלקעס
115. K. Tzetnik 135633 (1917–2001), *Dos hoyz fun di lyalkes* (The House of Dolls), 1955. 382 pp. Originally published in Hebrew: *Bet ha-bubot*. Tel Aviv: Devir, 1953. (Numerous translations in various languages worldwide.)

English version: Ka-tzetnik 135633, *House of Dolls*. Translated from the Hebrew by Moshe M. Cohn. New York: Simon and Schuster, 1955. Financed by the Conference on Jewish Material Claims Against Germany.

Spanish version: *La casa de muñecas*. Translated by Estela Canto. Buenos Aires: Israel, 1960.

116. מאַקס וויינרייַך, פֿון ביידע זײַטן פּלויט: דאָס שטורעמדיקע לעבן פֿון אורי קאָוונערן, דעם ניהיליסט
116. Max Weinreich (1894–1969), *Fun beyde zaytn ployt: Dos shturemdike lebn fun Uri Kovnern, dem nihilist* (From Both Sides of the Fence: The Stormy Life of Uri Kovner, the Nihilist), 1955. 254 pp. Financed by the Conference on Jewish Material Claims Against Germany.

117. אליעזר וויזל, . . . און די וועלט האָט געשוויגן
117. Eliezer Wiesel (1928–), *. . . Un di velt hot geshvign* (And the World Was Silent), 1956. 253 pp. Financed by the Conference on Jewish Material Claims Against Germany.

Revised and abridged French edition: *La Nuit*. Introduction by Francois Mauriac. Paris: Editions le Minuit, 1958.

English editions: *Night*. Translated from the French by Stella Rodway. New York: Hill and Wang, 1960.

Night. New translation from the French, by Marion Wiesel. New York: Hill and Wang, 2006.

(The French and English editions have been translated into numerous languages worldwide.)

118. ש. ש. בערלינסקי, ירושה: דערצייילונגען

118. Shloyme S. Berlinski (1900–1959), *Yerushe: Dertseylungen* (Heritage: Stories), 1956. 205 pp.

119. יוסף טענענבוים, צווישן מלחמה און שלום: ייִדן אויף דער שלום-קאָנפֿערענץ נאָך דער ערשטער וועלט-מלחמה

119. Joseph Tenenbaum (1887–1961), *Tsvishn milkhome un sholem: Yidn oyf der sholem-konferents nokh der ershter velt-milkhome* (Between War and Peace: Jews at the Peace Conference after World War I), 1956. 264 pp.

English edition: *Between War and Peace.* Jerusalem, 1960 (no publisher identified).

Hebrew edition: *Ben milhamah ve-shalom: Ha-yehudim be-ve'idat ha-shalom be-motsa'e milhemet ha-olam ha-rishonah.* Jerusalem: Ha-kongres ha-Yehudi ha'olami, senif Yisrael, 1960.

120. יוסף אָקרוטני, סוף קאַפּיטל: ראָמאַן

120. Josef Okrutny (1906–91), *Sof kapitl: Roman* (The End of the Chapter: Novel), 1956. 445 pp. Financed by the Conference on Jewish Material Claims Against Germany.

121. זיגמונט טורקאָו, טעאַטער-זכרונות פֿון אַ שטורמישער צײַט: פֿראַגמענטן פֿון מײַן לעבן

121. Zygmunt Turkov (1896–1970), *Teater-zikhroynes fun a shturmisher tsayt: Fragmentn fun mayn lebn* (Theater Memoirs from a Stormy Time: Fragments of My Life), 1956. 374 pp. Financed by the Conference on Jewish Material Claims Against Germany.

122. בער י. ראָזען, פּאָרטרעטן

122. Ber I. Rozen (1899–1954), *Portretn* (Portraits), 1956. Edited and with an introduction by Pinkhes Shvarts. 238 pp. Financed by the Conference on Jewish Material Claims Against Germany.

123. אברהם טענענבוים, לאָדזש און אירע ייִדן

123. A. Tenenbaum (1883–1970) *Lodzsh un ire Yidn* (Lodz and Its Jews), 1956. 393 pp.

124–125. משה קאַגאַנאָוויטש, די מלחמה פֿון די ייִדישע פּאַרטיזאַנער אין מזרח-אייראָפּע

124–125. Moyshe Kaganovitsh (birth/death dates unknown), *Di milkhome fun di yidishe partizaner in mizrekh eyrope* (The War of Jewish Partisans in Eastern Europe), 1956. 2 vols.; 422 and 421 pp. Prologue by Ben-Tsiyon Dinur. Financed by the Conference on Jewish Material Claims Against Germany. First published in Hebrew as *Milhemat ha-partizanim ha-Yehudim be-Mizrah-Eropah.* Tel Aviv: Ayanot, 1954.

126–127. אברהם זאַק, קנעכט זענען מיר געווען

126–127. Avraham Zak (1891–1980), *Knekht zenen mir geven* (We Were Slaves), 1956. 2 vols.; 366 and 329 pp. Financed by the Conference on Jewish Material Claims Against Germany.

Spanish edition: *Gimen los bosques siberianos.* Translated by A. Rosenblum. Buenos Aires: Candelabro, 1971.

128. יעקב גלאַטשטיין, ווען יאַש איז געפֿאָרן

128. Yankev Glatshteyn (1896–1971), *Ven Yash iz geforn* (When Yash Set Out), 1957. 278 pp. First published in the United States (New York: Farlag "Inzikh," 1938). Reprinted as the first part of *The Glatstein Chronicles,* trans. Norbert Guterman and Maier Deshell. Introduction by Ruth R. Wisse. New Haven, CT: Yale University Press, 2010.

Spanish edition: *A la llegada de Iash.* Translation and introduction by Lázaro Shallman. Buenos Aires: Candelabro, 1960.

Hebrew edition: *Keshe Yash nasa.* Translation and introduction by Dan Miron. Tel Aviv: Ha-Kibuts ha-me'uhad, 1994.

129–130. דוד פֿלינקער, נײַע צײַטן: ראָמאַן פֿון אַמאָליקן ייִדישן לעבן אין פּוילן
129–130. Dovid Flinker (1900–?), *Naye tsaytn: Roman fun amolikn Yidishn lebn in Poyln* (New Times: Novel about Bygone Jewish Life in Poland), 1957. 2 vols.; 372 and 384 pp. Financed by the Conference on Jewish Material Claims Against Germany.

131. משה יודל שעליובסקי, אין דער וועלט אַרײַן: דערצײלונגען
131. Moyshe Y. Shelyuvski (1893–1974), *In der velt arayn: Dertseylungen* (Into the World: Stories), 1957. 350 pp.

132. יצחק שוואַרצבאַרט, צווישן ביידע וועלט-מלחמות: זכרונות וועגן דעם ייִדישן לעבן אין קראָקע אין דער תקופֿה 1919–1935
132. Isaac Schwarzbart (1888–1961), *Tsvishn beyde velt-milkhomes: Zikhroynes vegn dem yidishn lebn in Kroke in der tkufe 1919–1935* (Between Both World Wars: Memoirs about Jewish Life in Crakow in the Period 1919–1935), 1958. 385 pp. Financed by the Conference on Jewish Material Claims Against Germany.

133. לעאָן לענעמאַן, דער חשבון בלײַבט אָפֿן—: וועגן די באַציונגען פֿון פּאָליאַקן צו ייִדן בעת דער היטלער-תקופֿה
133. Leon Leneman (1909–97), *Der kheshbm blaybt ofn—: Vegn di batsiungen fun Polyakn tsu Yidn bes der Hitler tkufe* (The Accounting Remains Open: About the Relationship between Poles and Jews During the Hitler-Era), 1958. 238 pp. Financed by the Conference on Jewish Material Claims Against Germany.

134. שלמה פֿראַנק, טאָגבוך פֿון לאָדזשער געטאָ
134. Salomon (Shloyme) Frank (1902–66), *Togbukh fun Lodzsher geto* (Diary from the Lodz Ghetto), 1958. Introduction by Nakhmen Blumental. 350 pp. Financed by the Conference on Jewish Material Claims Against Germany.

135. מלך באַקאַלטשוק-פֿעלין, זכרונות פֿון אַ ייִדישן פּאַרטיזאַן
135. Melekh Bakaltshuk-Felin (1896–1960), *Zikhroynes fun a yidishn partizan* (Memoirs of a Jewish Partisan), 1958. 310 pp. Financed by the Conference on Jewish Material Claims Against Germany.

136. פּנחס וועלנער, אין יענע טעג
136. Pinkhes Velner (1897–1965), *In yene teg* (In Those Days), 1958. 223 pp. Financed by the Conference on Jewish Material Claims Against Germany.

137. אלימלך ראק, זכרונות פֿון אַ ייִדישן האַנטווערקער-טוער
137. Elimelekh Rak (birth/death dates unknown), *Zikhroynes fun a yidishn hantverker tuer* (Memoirs of an Activist Jewish Craftsman), 1958. Introduction by Mark Turkov and Yankev Kristal. 234 pp. Financed by the Conference on Jewish Material Claims Against Germany.

138. הירש אבראַמאָוויטש, פֿאַרשוווּנדענע געשטאַלטן: זכרונות און סילועטן
138. Hirsh Abramovitsh (1881–1960), *Farshvundene geshtaltn: Zikhroynes un siluetn* (Lost Figures: Memoirs and Silhouettes), 1958. 480 pp. Financed by the Conference on Jewish Material Claims Against Germany.
English edition: *Profiles of a Lost World: Memoirs of East European Jewish Life before World War II*. Translated by Eva Zeitlin Dobkin; introduction by David E. Fishman and Dina Abramovitsh. Detroit, MI: Wayne State University Press, 1999.

139. ב. טערקעל, צווישן שאקאלן: שבעה מדורי "גן־עדן"

139. Betsalel Terkel (1909–61), *Tsvishn shakaln: Shive medorey "gan-eydn"* (Among Jackals: The Seven Circles of "Paradise"), 1959. 361 pp. Financed by the Conference on Jewish Material Claims Against Germany.

140. י. ל. וואלמאן, פוילישע ייִדן: ראמאן פון ייִדישן לעבן אין אמאליקן פוילן

140. I. L. Wohlman (1880–1955), *Poylishe yidn: Roman fun yidishn lebn in amolikn poyln* (Polish Jews: Novel of Jewish Life in the Old Poland), 1959. Introduction by Miriam Shir. 284 pp. Financed by the Conference on Jewish Material Claims Against Germany.

141–142. נ. שמען, דאָס געזאנג פון חסידות: די ראָל פון חסידיזם אין אונדזערע דורות

141–142. Nakhmen Shemen (1912–?), *Dos gezang fun khsides: Di rol fun hasidizm in undzere doyres* (The Song of Hasidism: The Role of Hasidism in Our Generations), 1959. 2 vols.

143–144. צבי כהן, שטורמישע דורות: היסטאָרישער ראָמאן

143–144. Tsvi Kahn (1885–?), *Shturmishe doyres: Historisher roman* (Stormy Generations: Historical Novel), 1959. 2 vols.; 306 and 349 pp.

145. יאָנאס טורקאָוו, נאָך דער באפרײַאונג: זכרונות

145. Jonas Turkov (1898–1982), *Nokh der bafrayung: Zikhroynes* (After Liberation: Memoirs), 1959. 328 pp. Financed by the Conference on Jewish Material Claims Against Germany.

French edition: *En Pologne, après la libération: L'impossible survie des rescapés juifs*. Translated by Maurice Pfeffer. Paris: Calmann-Lévy, 2008.

146. העלענא שערעשעווסקא, צווישן צלם און מזוחה

146. Helena Szereszewska (birth/death dates unknown), *Tsvishn tseylem un mezuzeh* (Between Cross and Mezuzah), 1959. 397 pp. Translated from the Polish, *Krzyż i mezuzah*, by Diana Blumenfeld. Financed by the Conference on Jewish Material Claims Against Germany. Published in Polish in 1993, Warszawa: Czytelnik.

Hebrew edition: *Ben ha-tselav veha-mezuzah*. Translated by Shulamit Frister. Tel Aviv: Moreshet, 1969.

147. פנחס שטיינוואקס, ייִדישע מאמעס צום געדענקען

147. Pinkhes Shtaynvaks (1905–77), *Yidishe mames tsum gedenken* (Jewish Mothers to Remember), 1959. 202 pp. Financed by the Conference on Jewish Material Claims Against Germany.

148. וואָלף מערקור, די וועלט איז כעלעם

148. Volf Merkur (1897–?), *Di velt iz Khelem* (The World Is Chelm), 1960. 278 pp.

149. ראובן בן־שם, פוילן ברענט—

149. Reuven Ben-Shem (birth/death dates unknown), *Poyln brent—* (Poland Burns), 1960. 366 pp. Financed by the Conference on Jewish Material Claims Against Germany.

150. יצחק טורקאָוו־גרודבערג, פנימער און מאסקעס: דערצײלונגען און סקיצן

150. Isaac Turkov-Grudberg (1906–70), *Penimer un maskes: Dertseylungen un skitsn* (Faces and Masks: Stories and Sketches), 1960. 184 pp. Financed by the Conference on Jewish Material Claims Against Germany.

151. שלמה פריזאמענט, בראָדער זינגער

151. Shloyme Prizament (1889–1973), *Broder zinger* (The Broder Singers), 1960. Introduction by Zalmen Hirshfeld and Zigmunt Turkov. 238 pp. Financed by the Conference on Jewish Material Claims Against Germany.

152. דוד לעדערמאַן, פֿון יענער זײַט פֿאָרהאַנג

152. Dovid Lederman, (1892–?), *Fun yener zayt forhang* (From the Other Side of the Curtain), 1960. 397 pp.

153. שײַנע מרים בראָדערזאָן, מײַן לײַדנס-וועג מיט משה בראָדערזאָן

153. Sh. M. Broderzon (birth/death dates unknown), *Mayn laydns-veg mit Moyshe Broderzon: Di milhome hot gedoyert far undz zibetsn yor . . . zikhroynes* (My Road of Suffering with Moshe Broderzon: The War Lasted 17 Years . . . Memoirs), 1960. 182 pp. Financed by the Conference on Jewish Material Claims Against Germany.

154. פּאָלאַ אַפּענשלאַק, יאַנוש קאָרטשאַק: ביאָגראַפֿישער ראָמאַן

154. Pola Apenshlak (birth/death dates unknown), *Yanush Kortshak: Biyografisher roman* (Janusz Korczak: Biographical Novel), 1961. Translated from the Polish by Diana Blumenfeld. 361 pp. Financed by the Conference on Jewish Material Claims Against Germany.

Spanish edition: *Una luz en las tinieblas: Vida y pasión de Janusz Korczak: Novela*. Translated by Luis Kardúner and Abraham Rosenblum. Buenos Aires: Candelabro, 1963.

Hebrew edition: *Ha-Doktor nish'ar: Roman biografi 'al Yanush Korchak*. Jerusalem: Kiryat sefer, 1946.

155. שלמה ברײַנסקי, מענטשן פֿון זשעלעכאָוו

155. Shloyme Brainski (1902–55), *Mentshn fun Zshelekhov* (People from Zshelekhov), 1961. Introduction by Shimon Guberek. 201 pp.

156. זיגמונט טורקאָוו, די איבערגעריסענע תּקופֿה: פֿראַגמענטן פֿון מײַן לעבן

156. Zygmunt Turkov (1896–1970), *Di ibergerisene tkufe: Fragmentn fun mayn lebn* (The Interrupted Period: Fragments from My Life), 1961. 478 pp. Financed by the Conference on Jewish Material Claims Against Germany.

157–158. דוד דאַווידאָוויטש, שולן אין פּוילן

157–158. Dovid Davidovitsh (1905–?), *Shuln in Poyln* (Schools in Poland), 1961. Translated from the Hebrew by Meir Kazshen. 2 vols.; 533 pp. Financed by the Conference on Jewish Material Claims Against Germany.

159. אברהם זאַק (רעד.), א. אלמי בוך: לכּבֿוד א. אלמיס ווערן אַ בן-שבֿעים

159. Abraham Zak (1891–1980), editor, *A. Almi bukh: Lekoved A. Almis vern a ben-shivim, mit a biblyografye tsuzamengeshtelt fun Yefim Yeshurin* (A. Almi Book: In Honor of A. Almi's 70th Birthday, with a Bibliography by Yefim Yeshurin), 1962. 222 pp.

160. יצחק לעווין, ייִדן אין אַלטן פּוילן: היסטאָרישע עסייען

160. Isaac Levin (1906–?), *Yidn in altn Poyln: Historishe eseyen* (Jews in Old Poland: Historical Essays), 1962. 184 pp. Financed by the Conference on Jewish Material Claims Against Germany.

161. מלך ראַוויטש, דאָס מעשה-בוך פֿון מײַן לעבן

161. Melekh Ravitsh (1893–1976), *Dos mayse-bukh fun mayn lebn, bd. 1. Fun di yorn: 1893 biz 1908* (The Storybook of My Life, vol. 1: From the Years 1893 to 1908), 1962. 387 pp.

Hebrew edition: *Sefer ha-ma'asiyot shel hayai'*. Translated by Mosheh Yungman. Tel Aviv: Ha-Hevrah ha-Amerikait-Yisre'elit le-molut, 1976.

162. ישׂראל עמיאָט, פֿאַרדעקטע שפּיגלען: דערצײלונגען און סקיצן

162. Israel Emiot (1909–78), *Fardekte shpiglen: Dertseylungen un skitsn* (Covered Mirrors: Stories and Sketches), 1962. 201 pp. Financed by the Conference on Jewish Material Claims Against Germany.

164–163. הערשל ה. וויינרויך, קאָמיסארן: ראָמאַן

163–164. Hershl H. Vaynroykh (1903–83), *Komisarn: Roman* (Commmisars: Novel), 1962. 2 vols.; 372 and 388 pp. Financed by the Conference on Jewish Material Claims Against Germany.

165. ישעיה טרונק, געשטאַלטן און געשעענישן: היסטאָרישע עסייען

165. Isaiah Trunk (1905–81), *Geshtaltn un gesheenishn: Historishe eseyen* (Figures and Events: Historical Essays), 1962. 286 pp. Financed by the Conference on Jewish Material Claims Against Germany.

166. אברהם זאַק, אין אָנהייב פֿון אַ פֿרילינג: קאַפּיטלעך זכרונות

166. Abraham Zak (1891–1980), *In onheyb fun a friling: Kapitlekh zikhroynes* (In the Beginning of Spring: Chapters of Memoirs), 1962. 329 pp.

167. שלמה שאפּיראַ, זכרונות פֿון אַ מאַראַן: אין דער תקופֿה פֿון דער נאַצי־קאַטאַסטראָפֿע

167. Shloyme Shapiro (birth/death dates unknown), *Zikhroynes fun a maran: In der tkufe fun der Natsi-katastrofe* (Memoirs of a Marrano: During the Period of the Nazi Catastrophe), 1963. 237 pp. Translated from the Hebrew by Z. Olitzky. Introduction by Nakhmen Blumental. Financed by the Conference on Jewish Material Claims Against Germany.

168. בצלאל טערקעל, די זון פֿאַרגייט ביים אמו־דאריא: פֿונעם פּליטים־לעבן אין ראָטנפֿאַרבאַנד

168. Betsalel Terkel (1909–61), *Di zun fargeyt baym Amu-Darya: Funem pleytim-lebn in ratnfarband* (The Sun Disappears at Amu-Darya: From Refugee Life in the Soviet Union), 1963. Introduction by Moyshe Knapheys. 379 pp. Financed by the Conference on Jewish Material Claims Against Germany.

169. ד. זאַקאַליק, אין שטורעם

169. David Zakalik (1905–?), *In shturem* (In the Storm), 1963. 235 pp. Financed by the Conference on Jewish Material Claims Against Germany.

170. נ. קאַנטאָראָוויטש, פֿאַרשוווּנדענע ייִדישע ישובֿים

170. N. Kantorovitsh (1897–1977), *Farshvundene yidishe yishuvim* (Vanished Jewish Communities), 1963. 353 pp. Financed by the Conference on Jewish Material Claims Against Germany.

171. מלך ראַוויטש, דאָס מעשׂה־בוך פֿון מײַן לעבן

171. Melekh Ravitsh (1893–1976), *Dos mayse-bukh fun mayn lebn, 1908–1921*, bd. 2 (The Storybook of My Life, 1908–1921, vol. 2), 1964.

172. קעהאָס קליגער, די שיינע רויז: טעג און נעכט פֿון אַ מיידל

172. Kehos Kliger (1904–85), *Di sheyne royz: Teg un nekht fun a meydl* (The Beautiful Rose: Day and Night of a Girl), 1964. 205 pp. Financed by the Conference on Jewish Material Claims Against Germany.

173. יצחק טורקאָוו־גרודבערג, אויף מײַן וועג: שרײַבער און קינסטלער: דערמאָנונגען און אָפּשאַצונגען

173. Isaac Turkov-Grudberg (1906–70), *Oyf mayn veg: Shrayber un kinstler: Dermonungen un opshatsungen* (On My Way: Writer and Artist: Recollections and Appreciations), 1964, 343 pp. Financed by the Conference on Jewish Material Claims Against Germany.

174. אברהם זאַק, אויף וועגן פֿון גורל: דערציילונגען

174. Abraham Zak (1891–1980), *Oyf vegn fun goyrl: Dertseylungen* (On the Road of Destiny: Stories), 1964. 220 pp. Financed by the Conference on Jewish Material Claims Against Germany.

175. נחמן בלומענטאל, שמועסן וועגן דער ייִדישער ליטעראַטור אונטער דער דײַטשער אָקופּאַציע
175. Nachman Blumental (1905–83), *Shmuesn vegn der yidisher literatur unter der daytsher okupatsye* (Conversations about Yiddish Literature during the German Occupation), 1966. 189 pp. Financed by the Conference on Jewish Material Claims Against Germany and Fundatsye far yidisher kultur.

APPENDIX 2

Transliteration of Yiddish Texts According to the YIVO System

Introduction

pp. 1–2:

Zol ikh onheybn fun onheyb?
zol ikh vi avrom
oys brudershaft tsehakn ale getsn?
Zol ikh zikh a lebedikn lozn iberzetsn?
Zol ikh aynflantsn mayn tsung
Un vartn biz farvandlen
vet zi zikh in ovesdike
rozhinkes mit mandlen?
Vos far a katovesdike
vitsn
Darshnt mayn poezye-bruder mit di baknbardn,
az mayn mame-loshn geyt bald unter?
Mir veln nokh in hundert yor arum do kentik zitsn,
un firn di diskusye bay dem yardn.
Vayl a shayle nogt un noglt:
oyb er veyst genoy vu
di tfile fun Berditshever,
Yehoashes lid
un Kulbaks
voglt
tsu der untergang—
to zol er mir, a shteyger,
onvayzn vuhin di shprakh geyt unter?
Efsher bay dem koysl mayrovi?
Oyb azoy, vel ikh dort kumen, kumen,
efenen dos moyl
un vi a leyb
ongeton in fayerdikn tsunter,
aynshlingen dem loshn vos geyt unter.
Aynshlingen, un ale doyres vekn mit mayn brumen!

p. 8:

Di toyre hobn mir mekabl geven baym sinay
Un in Lublin hobn mir zi opgegebn.

Nisht di meysim loybn got,
Di toyre iz gegebn gevorn tsum lebn.

p. 9:
Ven Yirmeohu hanovi hot baklogt dem khurbn beysamigdesh un ongeshribn megiles eykho hot er zayne verter mesader geven loyt alefbeys. Fregt zikh: vos a shaykhes hobn di kines mit alefbeys? Entfert R' Mendl: Ven der novi hot gezen dem moyredikn brokh, vos men hot alts tsugenumen fun undz: dos beysamigdesh iz khorev, di hashpoe fun heylikeyt vos flegt dergeyn tsu undz hot oyfgehert, iz er arayngefaln in yiesh, un moyre gehat, az yidn un di velt beklal veln keyn kium nisht hobn, khas vesholem. Biz er hot ayngezen, az der alefbeys iz geblibn. Hot er derin gefunen a treyst, der alefbeys iz der treyst. Derfar heyst der khoydesh ven es falt oys tishebov, menakhem ov, alefbeys iz der treyst.

p. 11:
On a yidish os—
iz a shed a yid—oys . . .

Chapter 1

pp. 15–16:
Vi azoy?

Vi azoy un mit vos vestu filn
dayn bekher in tog fun bafrayung?
Bistu greyt in dayn freyd tsu derfiln
dayn fargangenkeyts fintstere shrayung
vu es glivern sharbns fun teg
in a thom on a grunt, on a dek?

Du vest zukhn a shlisl tsu pasn
far dayne farhakte shleser.
Vi broyt vestu baysn di gasn
un trakhtn: der frier iz beser.
Un di tsayt vet dikh egbern shtil
vi in foist a gefangene gril.

Un s'vet zayn dayn zikorn geglikhn
tsu an alter farshotener shtot.
Un dayn droysiker blik vet dort krikhn
vi a krot, vi a krot—

p. 20:
Un got aleyn hot nit gehert mayn tfile
Er hot geshlosn shutfes mitn kat.
Mit dem vil er zikh opfastn nokh nile,
Mit zayne zin di fir iz er nit zat.
Un mit eyn shprung hob ikh dos blanke ayzn
Mayn letstn zun aryangezets in brust:
Azoyns ken ton dayn tate un bavayzn
Far dem, vos hot dikh paynikn geglust.

p. 24:

Alte vilner gedenken dem shtot-meshugenem Iserson. Hot men a mol gezen aza stsene: a molyer shteyt oyf a leyter in a shulkhl oyfn shulhoyf, tunkt dem pendzl in an emerl kalkh vos hengt oybn baym hekhstn shtapl, un malyevet mit im ahin un aher dem balkn. Plutsem dernentert zikh Iserson un shrayt tsu im aroyf: halt zikh on on pendzl, vayl ikh nem tsu dem leyter. Ikh bin geven geglikhn, bin geven farvandlt in yenem shulkhl-molyer. Der leyter unter mir iz take avekgerisn gevorn. Ober kh'hob zikh ongehaltn on pendzl, vos hot shoyn nit gehat afile keyn balkn, un vunder: kh'bin yemolt nit aropgefaln.

Un dos emerl iz gehangen tvishn erd un himl un zayn kalkh iz nit vays geven.

pp. 25–26:

Bald vet es geshen!
Di shvartse ringen
vern eng un enger arum haldz!
Umperzenlekh, vi a shteyn in bruk
vel ikh blaybn lign unter tloen
oysgeleyzt fun velt;
Nor in mayn tif
veln blaybn voglen dray murashkes:
Eyne,
unter lorber fun mayn kindshaft,
vet zikh umkern in kishef-vald.
Tsveyte,
unter pantser fun mayn kholem,
vet zikh umkern in kholem-land;
Un di drite
di vos trogt mayn vort,
vet keyn veg nit hobn,
vayl farpestikt
iz dos land fun gleybndike verter,
vet zi vakhn inem tol fun shotns
eyn un elnt
iber mayn gebeyn.

p. 28:

Un vu bin ikh geven,
Beys unter tsimblen
Hot men dikh geshlept tsum eshafot?
In hintisher bude fargrobn s'gebeyn,
mit hintisher freyd vos farshilt zikh aleyn,

pp. 28–29:

s'iz mer nit keyn hemd, s'iz dayn likhtike hoyt,
S'iz dayn kalter, dayn ibergeblibener toyt.

az du bist faran,
Bin ikh do say-vi-say

Vi der yoder in floym
Farmogt shoyn dem boym
Un di nest un dem foygl
Un alts vos derbay.

p. 30:
Un ikh vos bin geven der lets in shendlekhn spektakl
hob nit gehat keyn mutvil tsu aroysshtamlen a klole
un nit tsu mol dem koyekh zikh a vorf tsu ton in toyt,
vi mayne brider in der tsayt fun Adrian dem roymer,
beshas der gloybn hot dershtikt in kerper di yesurim
(khotsh alts eyns iz durkhgesamt mit koylngli mayn harts
un di oygn fun mayn gayst mit roykh adurkhgeshtokhn).
Nor merer nokh: ikh hob geknit a naketer far dem
vos hot geshendt mayn tatn in zayn keyver
un mit trern vi mit shvartse pokn
gebetn gnod.

p. 31:
Iz dos dayn shtrof tsu zhipen halb geteyt
Un fresn gsise-khorkhl fun di brider.
Vayl du host nit fardint di letse freyd
Fun vern oys—dos meynt: fun vern vider.

p. 32:
Di reder yogn, yogn,
Vos brengen zey mit zikh?
Zey brengen mir a vogn
Mit tsaplendike shikh.
. . .
Un s'klapn di optsasn:
Vuhin, vuhin, vuhin?
Fun alte vilner gasn
Me traybt undz keyn Berlin.

p. 33:
. . . vayl dayne klangen glimtsern
vi farbrente perl
nokh an oysgetsanktn shayter,
un keyner—oykh nit ikh—durkh teg tseribener,
derkent shoyn nit di froy in flam gevashn,
vos fun ale freydn iz geblibn ir
gro-gebrente perl in di ashn—

p. 34:
Hostu gezen iber felder mit shney
farfroyrene yidn, a rey nokh a rey?

Zey lign on otem, farmirmlt un blo,
nor toyt iz in zeyere kerper nito.

Vayl s'finklt oykh ergets farfroyrn der gayst,
vi a gildener fish, in a khvalye farayzt.

p. 37:
To vos iz geshen mit zayn eynikl, vos zhe?

p. 37:
Ot azoy geyen mir,
di neshomes flakern!

p. 38:
Geblibn bin ikh afn Pere Lachaise,
    geleymt. On loshn:
keday geven tsu zamlen oyf mayn konte
draysik yor,
farlirn ale noente,
blaybn hengen oyf a hor,
aroysgeyn funem kalkhoyvn
mit nit-farbrente trern,
az ikh zol itst, oyf Pere Lachaise derhern,
az mayn almakhtik harts iz vert a peym.
Un oyb ikh vel mir a tsavoe makhn
me zol shpeter brengen es aheym—
vet gor dos troyerike veltfolk—lakhn.

p. 40:
Fun beymer makht men vunderlekh papir. Un ikh—s'farkerte:
Papir farvandl ikh in beymer, in dem boym fun lebn.
Ikh vel zikh tsuvortslen tsu im, biz vanen es vet oyfgeyn
S'gezang fun zayne feygl.

Zey veln zikh tseblien un aroysblozn di ershte
Gebentshte klangen: umfarbaytlekh, eyntsik iz mayn shlikhes:
Farvandlen di farvandlungen in zeyer ershte moker,
Farvandlen zikh aleyn in protoplazm fun mayn kholem.

Farvandlen vel ikh grudes leym in zeyer mentshlekh ponem,
Farvandlen eydlshteyner in a lebedikn goldshmid.
Un soydes opgezunderte un mayln-vayt fun verter,
Farvandlen vel ikh in a shtralung bizn dno fun trern

Ikh tunk in zun mayn ziglring un shtel im in der fintster
Tsu hitn di farvandlungen. Mayn kumediker yoyresh,
Der kosmisher poet, zol konen zukhn un gefinen,
Un mayn gebeyn zol shmeykhlen.

pp. 42–43:
Ikh hob a briv derhaltn fun mayn heymshtot in der lite
Fun eyner vos ir yugnt-khen hot ergets nokh a shlite.
Arayngeleygt hot zi in im ir libshaft un ir tsar:
A grezl fun Ponar.

Dos grezl mit a tsankendikn volkndl, a goyses,
Hot ongetsundn os nokh os di penimer fun oysyes.
Un iber oysies-penimer in murmlendikn zshar
Dos grezl fun Ponar.

Dos grezl iz atsind mayn velt, mayn heymish-minyature,
Vu kinder shpiln fidl in a brenendiker shure.
Zey shpiln fidl un der dirigent iz legendar:
Dos grezl fun Ponar.

Ikh vel zikh mitn grezl fun der heymshtot nit tsesheydn,
Mayn oysgebenkte gute erd vet makhn ort far beydn.
Un yemolt vel ikh brengen a matone farn har:
Dos grezl fun Ponar.

Chapter 2

p. 44:
Got hot undz oykh mit milder hant
Geshenkt a tsviling
A toytn-geyresh mit a friling—
Der gortn blit, di zun laykht
Un der shoykhet—shekht . . .

p. 51:
Fleydermeyz flien farbay fentster.
Fliglen flatern oys dem tants fun geshpenster . . .
Mayn umfarendikt geto-lid lozt mikh nit ruen. Es hot mikh bagleyt in mayn gefangenshaft, mit im oyf di lipn hob ikh in di vinter fartogn gedreptshet durkh shneyn tsu der arbet. Ikh hob es mir oyfgeshribn mit a blay iber mayn pritshe un vayter gevebt a por shures. Ober in mir mont es nokh keseyder. Es nogt.

Ikh her durkhn fentster di shtim fun megafon. Haynt iz di krig ofitsyel geendikt. Vu bistu tate az kh'zol dikh kenen arumnemen?

p. 51:
Fleydermayz flien farbay fentster,
fliglen flatern oys dem tants fun geshpenster.
Nomenloze fargeyt der tog der letster,
Mir kumen um . . . mir kumen um.

p. 52:
Mir kumen um . . . nomenloz . . . tiknloz.

pp. 61–62:

Ikh trakht tsi veln mir amol hobn a kinstlerish, arumnemendik verk vegn dem fargangenem. Ikh tsveyfl derin. Ikh dermon zikh mayne shmuesn mit Shayevitshn in geto. Er hot geshribn di groyse poeme.

Ikh hob im gezogt: aza epopeye darf men shraybn fun perspektiv, nokh a tsayt. Er hot demolt nisht gevust vi zayn poeme vet zikh endikn, az zi vet blaybn umfarendikt. Er hot mir gezogt:—fun undzer lebn muz men shraybn azoy. Vos tu ikh den? Ikh loz trifn undzere teg fun mayn feder. Mer darf men nisht.—Haynt veys ikh, az andersh ken men nisht. Di perspektiv vet vaksn, zikh osytsien, verzshe vet kenen brengen dem tsiter fun yene geto-teg? Fun azelkhe teg kon men nor shraybn in di heyse shoen fun zeyer doyern. Mit a kurtsn, opgerisenem otem; vi es hobn es geton di shrayber un moler fun geto, ven men hot distans kon men nor gebn dem sharbn fun gantskeyt, ober on puls fun tsaplendik-tsefiberte blutn.

Tsi kenen den pasn di ongenumene kinstlerishe formen far a bukh fun geto? Iz es nisht keyn maske oyf der roykeyt un ummitelbarkeyt mit velkher men darf zikh tsurirn tsu der teme? Iz di form fun a kinstlerishn roman nisht tsu elegant, tsu sholemdik, tsu ruik un gemitlekh? Ikh fil derin a baleydikung far mayne tayere un far mir aleyn.

Chapter 3

p. 70:

Denkt ober nisht, az bloyz ir zent lebn geblibn. Ir zent nisht keyn tsebrokhene matseyves iber di umbakante kvorim, nor di yunge zomen af a feld, fun velkhe s'muz tsurik oyfshteyn a nay folk.

p. 70:

Di groyse tsentern fun yidn in amerike, ratnfarband un erets-yisroel vayzn undz, az mir zaynen nisht keyn gentslekh-farlozter sheyvet in der eyropeisher felker-mispokhe. Nokh zaynen di milionen yidish-redndike un yidish-trakhtndike mit undz!

p. 71:

Alts, vos s'iz vegn undzer tkufe geshribn gevorn, iz bloyz geven an arumgeyn arum dem pintl. Dos same ikerdike hot men tsulib dem nisht aroysgezen. Un epes darf dokh dertseylt vern vegn dem inerlekhn vey, dem tifn psikhologishn gerangl un azoy mentshlekhn veytik fun a dor in shoyderlekhn fargeyn. . . . Di velt afile di yidishe, **veyst gor nisht fun dem, vos iz faktish forgekumen. Un zi muz es visn! Mit ale pintelekh** *. . .*

p. 71:

*O ver vet af sliadn fun Treblinke-gang,
fargebn dir di shuldn fun gezang?*

p. 72:

*In Treblinke bin ikh nit geven
Oykh nit in Maydanek,
Ober ikh shtey af zeyer shvel
Un af zeyer ganek.
Shvel—gots groyse velt
Mit a yene-velt-verande,
Shtey ikh un ikh vart,*

Groyse velt, af dayn komande:
Yudn-kop, in gaz-kamer arayn!

p. 73:

Geshribn vert dos dozike verk in a halb-beletristisher form. Di ale gesheenishn, bilder un pasirungen zenen ober geshribn afn grunt fun mekhabers perzenlekhe iberlebenishn.

Tvishn di farshidene lagern in natsi-okupirtn Poyln un Daytshland—hot der mekhaber gelebt 15 khadoshim in der "Hasag"-fabrik fun Skarzysko-Kamienna bay Radom. Dort hot er in geheym a sakh geshribn un gezamlt ale materialn, vos hobn nor gekent shpeter nutsn far a genoyer geshikhte-shraybung fun ot dem emeyk-habokhe. Leyder zenen di ale materialn farloyrn gegangen—punkt vi dem mekhabers andere verk—in rezultat fun geshlept vern fun eyn lager in tsveytn.

Dos dozike bukh vert derfar geshribn loytn zikorn un iz bloyz a brukhteyl fun dem faktish-forgekumenem.

pp. 78–79:

"Bedamayikh hayyi"—"Un in dayn blut zolstu lebn"—azoy heyst dos bukh fun undzer landsman, dem opgeratevetn durkh toyznter nisim, yungn shrayber, Leyb Rokhman, velkhes mir trogn do tsu dem leyener, vi a denkmol nokh undzer shtot. Bedamayikh hayyi—der opflus fun blut vet undzer folk shtarkn un kreftikn tsu a nay lebn un tsu a banayt lebn!

p. 80:

Mir kukn aroys oyf di arumike felder—un take—alts iz tsevaksn un iberfult. Di lange zangen shvern zikh azh arop tsu der erd, ongedroln un ongeyoyrn kreftik. Eyn groys geretenish af gots erd. Der mentsh hot ir, der erd, di letse yorn gegebn azoy fil blut tsu trinken—git zi im itst ir baloyning: fete tvues zikh tsu shpayzn, nisht far eyn—nor far etlekhe yor; ...

Untn, unter der erd iz ober a bunt, a bunt fun blut, vos kon nisht farglivern, es broyzt, zidt, kokht un rayst zikh un vet nokh oysshisn biz tsu di himlen mit a vulkan, mit an erdtsiternish, erger vi in korekhs tsaytn. Di erd un der mentsh veln tsuzamen tseshtoybt vern!

p. 81:

"Shrayb a tog-bukh!" Froyman eytset mir, dos ongeshribene araynetsushikn durkh der post tsu a bakantn krist, betn er zol es nokh der milkhome ibergebn in yidishe hent. Azoy arum vel ikh mezake zayn di velt, nokh mir, mit shilderungen, mit "sensatsionel" material un efsher—mit literatur.

Moyray-veraboysay, mentshn fun nokh dem krig! Kh'veys az keyn krants af mayn keyver vet ir nisht brengen, oykh vayl beshas'n leyenen mayne shilderungen vet ir zitsn "al sir haboser" un baynakht vet ir geyn in teater, tsuriktushteln dem mut un—ir vet nit visn mayn keyver, vi ikh veys nit di kvorim fun mayn muter, shvester, bruder, un fun ale bakante, fun gantsn folk, vos mit zeyere kvorim zenen ful ale felder un gertner. Groz vakst shoyn, frukhtn blien un yunge porlekh, vos gloybn in Yezus kristus redn frekhe reyd un tuen miese maysim iber zey—iber di fargesene fun beyde veltn.

Neyn, mit aza shraybn hob ikh moyre. Kh'hob moyre, az ikh farshvekh kholile dem ondenk fun di fargesene kedoyshim, vos in tsen, oder in nokh veyniker yorn, vet kimat keyn eyn mentsh zey shoyn nisht dermonen. Nisht zey un nisht dem moyredikn kataklizm. Neyn, khaver Froyman, kh'vel es tsu keyn krist nisht ibershikn! Vet got shenken lebn, vet dos oykh zayn, un oyb, kholile—zol keyner shpeter, punkt vi fun mir, oykh fun mayne shures nisht visn. Zoln zey shpeter ruiker esn dos fleysh. Tsu vos tseshtern dem humor fun di nokh-milkhomedike porlekh—geyt beser shpeter in teater, nisht tsurik-tsubakumen mit, nor bekedey zikh tsu vayln glaykh mit der gantser velt fun nokh dem krig. Un aykh, mayne oreme shures, leyen ikh derveyl for far mayne fir mitzitsers, mit di royte hemdelekh.

pp. 82–83:

Zikher iz tishe-bov in ale yidishe shtubn in der velt! O, vi mir voltn gevolt zen khotsh a yidishe tsaytung fun dort! Vi farbitert un tsorndik muzn zayn di artiklen fun di yidishe shrayber. S'muz dokh alts dersheynen in eyn groyser shvartser ram! Tsi iz nokh bay yidn do humor? Tsi shpilt nokh yidish teater af der velt? O, brider undzere, ven ir veyst, vi mir matern zikh in itsikn moment! Ven ir kont khotsh a blik gebn tsu undz! Un ir brider un shvester undzere in erets-yisroel, mir shteln zikh for ayer shtiln tsar un ayere broyzndike yesurim! Tsu ayere shtrekn zikh undzere orems!

pp. 84–85:

Yunge shikses kleydn zikh in elegante bluzkelekh un spudnitses—ibergemakht fun taleysim; un kapelushlekh—fun sametene hitlen; in futerne kelner fun nelkene un skunsene shtraymelekh. Poyerishe tishn zenen baputst mit zilberne kidesh-bekherlekh, psomim-bikslekh, di komodes—mit etshakhaims, mit zilberne yads un shabesdike laykhter. Der vint blozt itst iber di derfer mit toyznter bletlekh fun khumoshim, gemores, meforshim, muser un khasidishe sforim, tsene-urenes, mayse-bikhlekh, yidishe klasishe un nayste literature, visnshaftlekhe un filozofishe bikher, di klozetn zenen mit zey ful. Men forkoyft makulatur in di gevelber oyfn pud, oyfn kilo. Men viklt in sheymes—spayz, khazer-fleysh un hering, di lederne tovlen vern ibergearbet oyf nutslekhe koyshlekh.

p. 86:

Tsvey teg hob ikh geshribn. Kh'bin gelegn oysgetsoygn in shtal oyf der erd, far a shpare untern fundament, un geshribn. Oybn oyf der vant hot mikh esterl fartretn un gehaltn vakh. Zi iz shoyn mid. Haynt, finf fartog, hob ikh vider gemuzt farnemen mayn postn. Ikh kuk aroys un far di oygn shvebn mir nokh alts di bilder fun yene teg.

p. 86:

"Ikh darf zey hobn epes nokhtsuzen. Kh'vel zey in etlekhe teg arum im tsurik gebn." Shoyn a shpor bisl heftn hot er dort gehat bagrobn. Shtendik, ven ikh farendik a frishn heft—gib ikh im un er bagrobt im tsuzamen mit di frierdike. Ikh dermon im keseyder, az er vet derfar amol baloynt vern.

pp. 89–90:

Plutsem iz di levaye aroys oyf an ofener gas. A shporer oylem hot zikh itst geshtupt. Feters, vayber, meydlekh— ale fun zeyer shtot. Di feters hobn nisht gedenkt di tsayt a mentsh zol zikh nemen dos lebn. Bay zey in geto, in di mesukndikste minutn, hot men dos nisht geton. Der bagleyter hot gekukt oyf di feters mit berd. In geto zenen zey shoyn geven eltere yidn. Itst iz er in zeyer elter, on a bord, a yingl. Haynt volt er shoyn oykh efsher gehat eyniklekh.

p. 90:

Plutsem hot er derzen, tif-bahaltn tvishn zayne geyendike khaverim—a noentn siluet. S'iz im bafaln an umheymlekhkeyt. Dos geyt dort tvishn zey, er aleyn, zayn mames zun. Er iz a mol tsuzamen mit yene farshvundn. Er do iz an anderer, a fremder. Er hot zikh geshrokn tsu kukn ahin, zikh tsu trefn oyg oyf oyg.

p. 91:

Der zeyde hot gefilt, s'iz der sof! Er hot gevolt betn mekhile bay Sh. Eyner fun di feters hot geshrign: "Yidn, men hot undz shoyn eyn mol oysgeshosn oyf beys-oylems. Itst iz ober umkum! Yidn, antloyft!" Ale hobn geshpant vi tsu a shekhthoyz, geshlept zikh nokhn zelbsmerder. Der bagleyter un der rov zenen nokhgegangen nokh der mite un gezogt tsidek-hadin.

Chapter 4

p. 111:

Oyfn hoyf—a mark: vert-zakhn, tayere tepikher, zilberne laykhter, a khale-tishtekh, a psomim-pushkele, makhzoyrim, sidurim—alts valgert zikh oyf der shmutsiker erd, untern tsu bloyen himl. Glaykh zey voltn keynmol keyn balebos nisht gehat, glaykh es volt keyn balebos oyf der velt nisht geven.

Les din veles dayen. Alts iz hefker, moyredik hefker.
Ven der mentsh iz oys mentsh, iz di velt oys velt.

p. 112:

. . . un itst, shraybndik di dozike shures, ze ikh im nokh alts shteyn in shotn fun blok, ongelent in a holtsernem slup, ayngeboygn iber mir. Ikh ze nokh alts zayne oygn vos hobn tsorn-flamen gevorfn oyf der arumiker velt, tsorn-flamen velkhe veln durkh mir, eybik dermonen der velt, der mentshheyt, az tsulib ir shvaygn, tsulib ir farbrekherisher glaykhgiltikeyt, iz daytshland farvandlt gevorn in a mizbeakh farn yidishn folk . . .

p. 112:

. . . modne: shraybndik di dozike shures, gloybt es zikh epes mir nisht, mir aleyn. S'dukht zikh: ikh shrayb a shrek-roman. A roman velkhn m'darf nisht leyenen baynakht, s'ken zikh nisht gloybn, az dos alts vos ikh shrayb—iz take geshen, mit mir aleyn geshen.

Un—bloyz mit tsen yor tsurik!

Chapter 5

p. 118:

Der yidisher shrayber fun amerike vert shir nisht getribn yedn tog nisht bloyz tsu a khezbm-hanefesh, nor tsum shteln zikh farn yom-hadin un tsum untertsien meslesdik a sakhakl: Vi halt ikh? Vi vayt greykht mayn vort? Vos zenen di shansn oyf an ekho? Vu iz der vald, fun vanen an ekho kon kumen?
—A. Glantz-Leyeles

p. 129:

Nisht mer vi a meshoyrer bistu,
vos iz yoytse far zikh
mit an omeyn in khor fun untergang.
Mir hobn zikh tsufil farlozt afn zikorn,
biz s'hot tropnvayz fun undz
alts oysgedenkt.
Itst zenen mir farbenkt
nokh a zemerl, nokh a gram,
nokh an oysgeveptn tam.
Arum undzere kep dreyen mir ale
a kapore-hon,
ober der gepreplter tokhn
geyt undz mer nit on.
Benkshaft-yidishkeyt iz a vig-lid far zkeynim,
vos tshkayen ayngeveykte khale.
Zoln mir tsushteln di veykhe krishkes,
di verter oysgelebte un hoyle,

mir vos hobn gekholemt
fun a nayer anshe-kneses hagdoyle?

p. 130:

Zing mir nisht keyn lidelekh fun hunger,
zog mir nisht keyn troyerdike reyd,
dertseyl mir nisht keyn moralishe mayselekh.
Zey toygn ale af toyznt kapores.
Kenstu dos gezang fun boykh-grimenish,
Fun leydike kishkes,
Dos gezang fun der farlederter tsung,
Fun dem ipeshdikn moyl,
Vos zayn eyntsik kayekhts
Iz shlingen eygn shpaykhts.
Moykhl, zing mir nisht keyn lider.

p. 136:

vos, nokh mit draysik yor tsurik, hob ikh unter di himlen dayne
getroyert tif in zikh, geklogt zikh az ikh trog mayn yidish lid
in angst, durkh dayne gasn un durkh dayne skvern,
farklamert tsvishn mayne tseyn, vi s'trogt a kats an elnte
vi di ketslekh ire, zukhndik far zey a ru-ort in a keler vu;—
az ven ikh trakht nor vegn mayne brider—yidishe poetn—
nemt zeyer goyrl vi a klamer mikh arum, un s'vilt zikh tfile ton far zey,
far zeyer mazl,—un grod demolt vern ale verter shtum.
Avade iz es mayn shuld, un nit dayn, oykh haynt, ven nokhn opgang
fun yene draysik yor tut troyern mayn harts af s'nay elegish
vos haynt, nokh mer vi ven es iz, hot s'beyze mazl
tseshlaydert ale yidishe poetn iber nay-sibirn,
un undzer flaterdike dikhter-shif faryogt in thom fun shturems,
in thom fun shturems oykh af dayne vasern, amerike

pp. 137–38:

In kiln ovnt hot der balebos
Fun boym a rayfe floym aropgerisn
In eynem mitn blat, un ayngebisn
Di toyik bloye hoyt. Hot fun zayn shlos

Der shlofediker zaft geton a gos
Mit kiln shoym. Un tsu farshlisn
Ir gantsn zaft—a tropn nit fargisn—
Hot er pamelekh, vi men trogt a kos

Mit vayn, in beyde fule hent di floym,
Gebrakht der vayb un eydl tsugetrogn
Tsu ire lipn. Hot zi mit a libn

"A dank"—fun zayne hent genumen nogn
Di floym. Biz in di hent iz im farblibn
Di hoyt, dos beyndl un tseklekter shoym.

Chapter 6

p. 145:

Ikh, vider, bin geven a literat in varshe,
vos hot gegloybt azoy vi ale
in dem nemlikhn Gete un in nokh azelkhe geniale egoistn.
Nisht gevust hob ikh, vi kleyn der mehalekh iz fun Faust biz foyst,
fun Gete's ibermentsh tsum untermentsh un tsu di hitleristn.
Vos volt geheymrat Gete geton in Hitler's tsaytn?
Volt gezesn in Vaymar un gekukt fundervaytn
vi zayne daytshn fargazn mayne milionen.
Er, vos hot geredt fun literatur mit Napoleon'en,
volt tsu Hitler'n geredt min hastam
mit a geshlifn-tifzinikn epigram.
S'volt im afile nisht a tsuk geton a brem—
Kon den a Gete mekadesh zayn dem shem?
Kon er zikh makrev zayn? Azelkhe kenen nor dikhtn,
beys di Hitlers farnikhtn.
O, di groyse egoistn, vos makhn di verter!
Eysev, vi ze ikh atsind dem farbind
tvishn dayne vort-mentshn un dayne merder!

p. 147:

Kedey tsu farshteyn dem tatn muz men farshteyn, az der farrat fun Hitlers profesorn iz geven far im a perzenlekher farrat, vos er hot gefilt. Vayl zayn studium in daytshland, dos vos er hot gebrakht mit zikh fun zayn studium in daytshland, vos er hot gevolt gebn der yidisher velt, vos er hot gemeynt az er ken zikh oyf dem forlozn, dos iz mer nit geven. Un ikh veys, az dos hot er nit gevizn azoy shtark far andere, vi far der mishpokhe . . .

Hitlers profesorn iz geven der simbol fun dem vos er hot farloyrn, tsuzamen mit zayn pkhor: di orientatsye fun a visnshaftlekhn tsugang, vos er hot a gants lebn nokh dem gepruvt vider tsuzamen-tsubrengen.

p. 147:

Az ikh hob geleynt dem briv, vos er hot gehat ongeshribn, hob ikh geshtoynt. Ershtns, afn ershtn plats— fun der elegants fun der daytsher shprakh, vos er hot geshribn. A vunderlekher literarisher daytsh, vos ale verbn zaynen gekumen ersht in dritn paragraf, mit ale heflekhkeytn un ale rikhtike stilistishe shtrikhn. Ober der inyen fun briv iz geven: "A heyser farsholtener kadokhes aykh."

pp. 151–52:

Ikh vil redn oyf der shprakh funem folk, vos di gemishpete hobn zikh farmostn oystsurotn tsuzamen mit zayn shprakh. Zol derhert vern undzer mame-loshn. Zol men derhern undzer loshn, un zol tseplatst vern Alfred Rozenberg. Zol mayn shprakh triumfirn in Nirnberg vi a simbol fun umfargeyikeyt!

pp. 152–53:

Shtelt im op a daytshl in gas
Un zogt im:—mage
Ikh inen shteln a frage?

Zogt der rayzeman:—aderage,
Mit der grester fargenage.
Makht dos daytshl ot azoy:
Hostu gezen di kuperne froy?
Git zikh der rayzeman bay der bord a glet
un zogt mit a shmeykhl: kh'makh a vet.
Avade, voden?
Avade, voden?
Alts gezan un alts gezen
Aleyn gezen di kuperne froy.
Vi ikh bin an alter goy.

p. 154:
Nor du aleyn oyf dayn blut-vursht shprakhe,
konst oysreven vi du host genumen,
daytshe, meshugene rakhe,
fun dershrokene, umbashitse, shvakhe.

p. 154:
Vi vunderlekh iz fun getlekhn mentsh
zayn muzikalisher testament,
vi durkhgenoglt mit gezang
zaynen zayne likhtike hent.
In zayn grester noyt,
Hobn baym gekraytsiktn zinger
Gelakht ale finger.
In zayn veynikstn troyer,
Hot er nokh mer vi zikh aleyn
Lib gehat dem shokhns oyer.

p. 156:
Kh'leyen nisht, liber goy,
dos davn ikh azoy.
Kh'zog tfiles, kines.
Inmitn dem tuml, dem sobvey-harmider,
davn ikh fun mayn teglekhn sider.

p. 157:
Ober du, mayn tayerer internatsionaler goy,
mitn goldenem pasport,
bistu umetum vilkomen,
in nomen fun tatn, zun un dem heylikn gayst.

p. 157:
Mit a dershrokenem pasport in keshene,
durkh di fintstere un shvindlendike fentster,
varft men mir arayn briv fun tate-mame.

p. 158:
Oykh in dem leyenen fun di moderne yidishe poetn bazunders di "Yunge" hert men dem "sing-song," hert men dos kol, oder dem nign fun dem urkvalikn un urshtamikn in der poezye —dos kol vos men hert aroys fun di lider fun primitive felker, vos viln mit zeyer monotonem tom-tom ritm, mit zeyer tsudringlekhn "sing-song" dergreykhn hipnotishe un magishe efektn.

p. 159:
Trakhtndik vegn di dozike zakhn un benkendik nokhn kol fun yidishe poetn, vos zaynen shoyn oyf eybik farshtumt gevorn, iz mir ayngefaln—farrekordirn di shtim fun yidishn poet. Iz dokh di shtim fun a poet, lekhol hadeyes, nit veyniker vikhtik far di tsukunftike doyres, vi zayne fotografyes, ven er iz geven a kind, a khosn, oder a fayer-lesher, vi Peretz.

p. 160:
Men vet efsher amol veln hern vi sheyn undzer mame-loshn hot geklungen in moyl fun di vos hobn es mit libshaft gekhovet, un getsertlt. Ober nit nor libhober un geniser fun yidishn lid, nor oykh forsher fun yidisher poetik un fonetik, voltn fun di rekordirungen gehat a sakh nutsn.

p. 162:
Dos iz beemes a freyd az s'falt arayn a dikhter vi aykh tsu kumen tsu yidishe poetn, rekordirn di shtim fun der yidisher poezye . . . dos iz nisht nor di shtim fun yidishn poet, dos iz di shtim fun yidishn dor, undzer dor, dos iz far mir aleyn a gevaldike dermutikung. Men ken af dem aleyn zeyer a sakh boyen. Ikh volt gevolt az say ir un say mir zoln dos oyfnemen nisht in gayst fun kinus, nisht in gayst fun aynzamlen . . .

p. 163:
. . . a moderne mashin vos nemt arunter dos kol, rekordirt, dos iz a blaybedike zakh, ir farshteyt. Dos zol vern a koyekh vos zol stimulirn tsu ton naye zakhn. Ikh halt az me darf fartrakhtn vi azoy dos oystsunutsn . . . tsu makhn derfun a nay kapitl fun sheferishkayt, nemen afn basis fun dem vos yidishe shraybers hobn zikh avekgezetst redn, un vos yidishe shraybers hobn geleynt zeyere lider, di lebedike antologye shpiln un nokh amol shpiln un ibershpiln, far mir iz dos groyse muzik, far mir iz dos mer muzik vi Carusos aries, nemen un shpiln un ibershpiln un oyb men zol kenen gefinen a veg tsu stimulirn un efenen a nay kapitl un ikh halt az men darf kenen gefinen a veg . . .

p. 164:
. . . un dos zol nisht zayn bloyz keyn muzey zakh, avekgebn YIVO . . . un azoy vayter untergang, shlus . . . . Neyn ikh hob gevolt say ir un say mir, az ale poetn zoln avek mitn gedank az dos iz a nay oyfn sheferishkayt.

p. 165:
*bloyz kloysterkhorn
kenen zingen azoy ruik
tsu a farkhaleshtn got
vos hot afile fargebn zayne payniker.*

p. 166:
*Di kristlekhe shtot rut,
un mayne ale umglikn drimlen umgeduldik,*

ikh kum tsurik tsu mayn eynzamer shul,
zi shteyt itst oykh ayngezuntikt in shrek.

p. 166:

Morgn veln undzere vundn
vider gevaldeven,
ober koyles fun der shtot
veln zey aribershrayen.

p. 167:

Sharfer, shnaydiker, vidershtand, vu bistu?
Yung meserdiker tselokhes
dayn dor hot dir ongeton a yarmlke
vos falt dir iber di oyern,
un hot dir oysgelernt,
tsu redn heylike dvorim beteylim

p. 168:

Mayn tayere mame, mayn klug moyl,
mayn eygn mame-loshn, vos iz azoy
tsertlekh oyfgegangen far mir
in lubliner gesheptshete farnakhtn.
Mayn mame-loshn, mit dem veksenem ponim,
Mit di yesurim-dershrokene,
Halb-farmakhte oygn.
Nokh dos muz ikh dermonen.

p. 169:

Iz gebentsht zol zayn undzer bobe yidish.
Di nit-geredte, di nit-geleynte,
In gerateveter gnize
Di nit-farumreynikte.

Mir, di pleytim fun undzere kinds-kinder,
Trogn a gedekhenish vi a bashertn yokh.
Keyn leftsn konen nisht metame zayn
Undzere yidishe reyd,
Fun shabes un der fuler vokh.

p. 172:

Ale voltn mir geshribn
A brivele iber yamen,
A brivele der mamen
Ober—
Vu iz di mame? . . .

p. 175:
Azoy lesht zikh der ben-odem, azoy muz yeder
Geyn nokh'n malekh-hamoves
Aheym tsu di oves.

pp. 176–77:
Oys beys-oylems,
oys takhrikhim, oys kadish, oys keyver-yisroel,
oys shtiler shoyder,
oys kishef-fleml, meysim-gezeml,
oys yene-veltike nign,
yene-veltike ru.
Oys bar-menens, vos lebn in fiber-nekht oyf
oyf der bashverung fun azelkhe vi du.
Keyner fun di daynike nishto—
nisht alt, nisht yung,
nisht frum, nisht umfrum, nisht rekhte, nisht linke.
Nisht keyn malekh bin ikh, nor a letster "oy"
fun a yid farbrent in Treblinke.

p. 177:
. . . ikh, dayn zun, hob gornisht
oyser verter. Tsu dem shed fun verter
bin ikh farkoyft un kh'shlep di beyze mase,
s'vil nisht kukn in mayn zayt kavyokhl,
vi kh'volt geven a makekh-toes.

p. 178:
Ikh veys: keyner darf mikh nisht af ot dem oylem,
mikh, verter-betler af dem yidishn beys-oylem.
Ver darf a lid—un nokh dertsu af yidish?

Nor bloyz dos hofnungsloze af der erd iz sheyn,
Un getlekh iz nor dos, vos muz fargeyn,
Un nor hakhnoe iz meridish.

pp. 179–80:
S'iz zuntik. s'iz may.
Porlekh un feygl oyf vashington skver.
Oykh Arn Tsaytlin iz do derbay—
Ver veys, vos mit im iz der mer.
Oykh er iz do derbay—
Vi kumt er iberhoypt aher?
A velt hot er gehat, a velt forloyrn.
Zayn veg—farhoyln.
Es tantst far im a vort,
arumgehilt mit flamen fun mord

a signal, an akord:
Poyln.

Chapter 7

p. 192:
S'yidishe vort blit af a mandlshtekn,
un yede brokhe iz batamt,
yede klole iz gegramt,
yeder vort tut shmekn,
yeder vort tut trifn,
un yeder vort iz bazaft
mit bobeshaft.
O, getraye landshaft fun amolikeyt—
in a zamdikn midber.

In a midber blit a mandlshtekn,
un af im shprotsn yidishe verter.
A vandrovnik af a keml
tsit ahin vi tsu zayn basherter.
Un arum dem shtekn vaksn
zise kraytekhtser,
un est men zey, efenen retenishn
zeyere bataytekhtser,
un ale farhoylene nishtviserayen
vern same klore farshteytzikher.
Un alts vert keday,
un alts vert haft,
alts vert ongeyornt
un ongetrunken mit freyd
fun bobeshaft.

Der vandrovnik shreyt arayn in der nakht
un tut vekn—
hoy, veygeshrign,
in der midber blit a mandlshtekn!

p. 196:
Dor fun tohu
dor vos hot gezen dem himl faln.
di zun hot fintsternish gezupt,
un afn Sinay hot men oyfgeshtelt di tome-shtaln.
Un bay dem tish ot dem tsebrokhenem, tsekrimt, tselomet,
tsind on dayn likht.
Un af der vakldiker erd shtel oyf dayn omed . . .
tsind on dayn likht.

pp. 207–8:

Nem mikh arum mit vergndiker getrayshaft,
loshn mayns, ver mir an eyferzikhtik vayb,
bind mikh tsu tsum getselt,
loz mikh vern shtum-loshn far der velt,
afile in der bester iberzetsung.
Zoln zey mikh farteyln.
Farkleyn mikh, biz nit-dershetsung,
mikh art nisht az zey veln mikh nisht tseyln.
Farshver mikh, a getrayen,
tsu dir mit goyrldiker bashertkeyt,
az s'zol mikh keyner fun dayne orems nisht bafrayen.
Emes, ikh vel nisht zayn universal,
ober az ikh vel avek,
vel ikh vern a volkn-zeyl,
a likht-shtral,
iber undzer kleynem mishkn.

Chapter 8

p. 210:

Ikh hob ober di farshvigene aleyn-geyer, ot di fun keynem nit-bamerkte batlonim un lamedvovnikes, nit gezukht tsu makhn "interesanter" durkh tsutrakhtn a shpanendike siper-hamayse, vos zoln zey tsuzamenhaltn. Ikh hob di bazundere geshtaltn un di geshikhte fun zeyer lebn tsunoyfgevebt durkhn fartunkltn shayn fun beyn-hashmoshes, vos falt oyf zey alemen glaykh, beys zey zitsn halb-fargliverte oyfn zelbn groyen hintergrunt fun zeyer hoyf un kloyz.

pp. 215–16:

Oysgeeydlte finger, farblaste, farkhaleshte, vos dreyen oyf zikh retsues yedn inderfri, bletern sforim, kushn sifrey-toyre un tunken zikh hundert mol in tog in vaser, nokhn geyn af nekies, baym vashn zikh tsum esn un baym opgisn mayim-akhroynim; veykhe finger mit pukhike kishelekh, vos gibn sholem, tseshpreytn zikh mit zeydisher libshaft af kep fun eyniklekh baym bentshn, un tseshpreytn zikh kohenish baym dukhenen; finger, vos tapn mit tsertlekher libshaft esrogim un lulovim, farshteln zikh di oygn bay krishme, haltn dem kidesh-bekher, dem havdole-kos un brekhn zikh tsuzamen baym shlogn zikh in hartsn al-khet; finger vos gibn zikh a drey mit an "i-hakha-mistabera," der pshat iz punkt farkert; geknipfte doplte finger-knekhlekh, bavaksn mit shtekhlkes, mit gedrovete hor, vos kratsn zikh mit meshene negl, knaypn oys shtiker fleysh fun eygn leyb, vi a beyzer melamed knaypt yinglekh; finger vos shlepn hor fun der bord bay a shverer sugye un krayzlen zikh di peyes; finger fargelte fun shmekn tabak un fun roykhern titun . . . di ale finger bavegn zikh, payklen in tish, redn tvishn zikh un broygesn zikh eyne oyf di andere.

pp. 216–17:

Loyt mayn meynung, hot undzer literatur biklal nit gegebn keyn tsu ekhte opshpiglung fun dayonim un moyre-horoes, vos zaynen doyres-lang geven undzere eyntsike gaystike manhigim. Oder men hot zey kharakterizirt durkhoys negativ, unter an algemeyner bitldiker batseykhenung "klekoydesh"; oder men hot zey geshildert bloyz fun droysn, di berd, di kapotes un di havayes, ober nit oysgeteylt keyn bazundere tipn, vi loyt a formule, az "ale rabonim hobn eyn ponim"; oder men hot zey ingantsn oysgeton fun zeyer guf un oyszen, kedey zey fortsushteln vi simboln fun maysim-toyvim un perzonifikatsyes fun reyne ideyen; oder zey zaynen gevorn heldn fun der legende; oder teatrale figurn, dekorative un patetishe. Ikh veys bloyz fun eyntsike oysnamen in undzer literatur, ven kreative kinstler hobn geshildert rabonim mentshlekh-real, nit tsu-himlish un nit tsu-grob erdish.

pp. 221–22:
Dos shtibl iz geven fargosn mit a tunkl-bloy likht, un in halbn shpigl ibern komod hobn ire aksl un brist geblankt vi ayz. Zi hot zikh opgerukt ahinter, kedey tsu zen ir gantse figur, nor fun vaytn iz ir layb in shpigl ayngegangen in der tif fun geshlifenem gloz, vi ir guf volt oyfgehert ekzistirn, beys zi aleyn lebt nokh. Merl hot zikh dermont vos men dertseylt in shtot vi azoy dem rovs meshugene tokhter iz aroysgeshprungen fun ir tsimer a nakete. Mistome hot oykh dem rovs tokhter shtark lib dem eyegenem kerper. Merl iz tsurik arayn in bet, ir guf hot geglit un zi hot geshoydert fun kelt un shrek; vos kumt mit ir for? Zegnt zi zikh mitn lebn? Zi hot zikh ayngehert, vi gevart oyf an entfer, un derhert fun gas dos gevoy fun vint.

p. 223:
—Ikh bin gevorn a yakhsn. Men tsolt mir skhires vi a shtotishn moyre-horoe, men git mir op koved un ale filn zikh kegn mir shuldik. Ober der emeser shuldiker bin ikh. Ikh hob nit barekhnt vifl tsores ikh vel brengen oyfn kop fun der geplogter froy davke durkh mayn heter. Di shtot zol aribergeyn oyf mayn zayt, hot zi zikh badarft makrev zayn. Ikh bin groys gevorn, a khoshev gevorn durkh ir umglik, oysgevaksn oyf ir keyver.

p. 224:
Ikh bin der dikhter vos lebt mit zikorn
Un fil oyf mayn tsung vi es vianet mayn loshn.
Alevay ken ikh zogn, az ikh bin der dorn,
Vos brent in dem midber un vert nit farloshn.

p. 225:
"Un az men vet bavilikn far dem muzey a palats anshtot di geto-tfise; un oyb afile di sovetishe melukhe zol onshteln a gantsn shtab tsu sortirn un registrirn di bikher, di sforim, di ongeshtopte pek un zek mit kartlekh fun alerley gelernte nudnikes, vos hobn zikh yortsendleker gegreyt tsu shraybn groyse verk, di greste verk—vet di oysgeshokhtene Vilne oyfshteyn tkhies-hameysim? Berg mit tseflikte bikher kenen farbaytn a shtot mit lebedike yidn?"

p. 229:
Tsurik tsum amorets!—darf zayn undzer ruf. Zol lamdones blaybn far publitsistn un maymeristn. Undzer sheyne literatur muz zayn kekhol-hagoyimdik, veltlekh un nokh a mol veltlekh! . . .

pp. 229–30:
Far undz alemen, gleyb ikh, iz dos vort "goldene keyt" nit stam a sheyner oysdruk, nor es iz a gantse program. A program in lebn un a program in der literatur, in undzer kultur-shafung. Dos vort meynt far undz: hemshekh, kultur-hemshekh on iberraysn, dos keseyderdike un eybike . . . "kibl-toyre-vem-soyre" vayter un vatyer fun dor tsu dor.

p. 231:
Undzer literatur, vos iz beys un bald nokh di yorn fun kataklizm geven epes a min khor (emes, a khor mit solos), heybt bislekhvayz on tsu kumen tsu zikh un tsurik vern, vos a literatur darf zayn—a velt

nit fun loyter tsiber un oykh nit fun shlikhe-tsiber, nor fun originel-sheferishe yekhidim, vos grobn tifer, kukn vayter un heybn zikh oyf hekher funem kohol un zayne minhogim un minhigim.

Conclusion

p. 238:

In yener tsayt hobn zikh getsoygn tsu mir, dem redaktor fun "goldene keyt," in mayn opgetsoymtn vinkl iber groye oygsgetrotene trep, tsendliker fun di antrunene, mit zeyere ksovim, vi murashkes mit eyerlekh in moyl; gebrakht farn shatskamer fun der eybikeyt zikhroynes un togbikher fun zeyere toyt-iberlebungen, beys milkhome un khurbn, vos oyb m'zol zey ale opdrukn, un ayntoyln, iz es a bibliotek fun di raykhste vundn.

p. 239:

Oykh dos vet vern fargesn, oykh dos.
Farbrent gevorn mayn folk,
Un s'vet vern fargesn oykh dos.
Vu di Nalevkes hobn geroysht —
Bloz fun vint tsvishn groz,
vint un groz.

Beymer zoyfn zaft fun lebns toyte.
Tsu a zoyne a zun
zingt a foygl a shoyte.

A koymen on a dakh,
a koymen a blinder,
shtartst fun mist vi a an alter tsilinder—
a tsilinder on a kop.

Oyf a hoyfn tsigl
vi oyf a piedestal
blaybt shteyn, glaykh
Napoleon bay di piramidn,
a groyser umetiker shtshur,
kukt on di azoygerufene natur,
a velt on got un on yidn.

Baynakht
yogt zikh a meshugener nokh vilde kets,
vert mid un zetst zikh oyf di shteyner klogn:
Vu iz meshiekh? Vu iz der kets?

pp. 240–41:

Blimeshi. Toybeshi. Rivele.
Leyenyu. Feygenyu. Perele.
Khatskele. Motele. Kivele.
Hershele. Leybele. Berele.

Shayeshi. Khayeshi. Goldeshi.
Mendelekh. Gnendelekh. Mindelekh.

Kh'tseyl in der nakht in der shloflozer
Nemen fun yidishe kinderlekh.
...

Oys un nishto mer di Heshelekh,
Heshelekh, Peshelekh, Hindelekh.
Klangen, bloyz klangen, bloyz lid-klangen —
Nemen fun yidishe kinderlekh.

Vu iz dayn fisele, Zisele?
Tsipele, vu iz dayn tsepele?
Roykh bistu, Yenteles hentele!
Ash bistu, Kopeles kepele!

NOTES

Introduction

1. *Poetishe verk*, vol. 2 (Tel Aviv: Yoyvl komitet, 1963), 33–34; trans. in *A. Sutzkever: Selected Poetry and Prose*, trans. Barbara and Benjamin Harshav (Berkeley: University of California Press, 1991), 214. Levi Yitskhok of Berditshev (1740–1808) was also known in Yiddish as "the Berditshever." Yehoash was the pen name of Solomon Blumgarten (1870–1927), a Yiddish poet, scholar, and translator of the Bible into modern Yiddish. Moyshe Kulbak (1896–1937) was a modernist poet who played a major role in creating a modern Yiddish culture in Vilna and Minsk.
2. Almost the entire run of *Yizker* books and a large portion of modern Yiddish literature are available online in full-text versions. Thanks to the National Yiddish Book Center, the New York Public Library, and other institutions, anyone with a computer can access a significant part of Yiddish print culture.
3. See Rosemary Horowitz, ed., *Memorial Books of Eastern European Jewry: Essays on the History and Meanings of Yizker Volumes* (Jefferson, NC: McFarland, 2011).
4. See David Cesarani, "Challenging the 'Myth of Silence': Postwar Responses to the Destruction of European Jewry"; Hasia R. Diner, "Origins and Meanings of the Myth of Silence"; and Eric J. Sundquist, "Silence Reconsidered: An Afterword," all in *After the Holocaust: Challenging the Myth of Silence*, ed. David Cesarani and Eric J. Sundquist (London: Routledge, 2012).
5. See the most recent books, Lara Rabinovitch, Shiri Goren, and Hannah S. Pressman, eds., *Choosing Yiddish: New Frontiers of Language and Culture* (Detroit, MI: Wayne State University Press, 2013), and Marion Aptroot, Efrat Gal-Ed, Roland Gruschka, and Simon Neuberg, eds., *Leket: Jiddistik heute* (Yiddish Studies Today/Yidishe shtudyes haynt) (Dusseldorf: Dusseldorf University Press, 2012).
6. For Yiddish works of the Jewish historians, see Mark L. Smith, "No Silence in Yiddish: Popular and Scholarly Writing about the Holocaust in the Early Postwar Years," in *After the Holocaust: Challenging the Myth of Silence*, 55–67. About Yiddish literature after the Holocaust, see Elias Schulman, *The Holocaust in Yiddish Literature* (New York: Workmen's Circle, 1983), and the 2012 overview of Yechiel Szeintuch, "Yiddish Survivors' Literature": "Focusing on the description and analysis of Yiddish literature's development, with the surviving Yiddish authors and their writings at its center, will possibly reveal new traits in the development of Yiddish literature in the twentieth century" (www.hum.huji.ac.il/units.php?cat=4621&incat=2933 [p.2], accessed April 27, 2014).
7. David G. Roskies and Naomi Diamant, *Holocaust Literature: A History and Guide* (Waltham, MA: Brandeis University Press, 2012); David Cesarani and Eric J. Sundquist, eds., *After the Holocaust: Challenging the Myth of Silence*; and Laura Jockusch, *Collect and Record! Jewish Holocaust Documentation in Early Postwar Europe* (Oxford: Oxford University Press, 2012).
8. Cecile E. Kuznitz, "Yiddish Studies," in *The Oxford Handbook of Jewish Studies*, ed. Martin

Goodman (New York: Oxford University Press, 2002), 541–71; see www.yiddishbookcenter.org/files/fckeditor/file/Kuznitz-Yiddish%20Studies.pdf
9. Roskies and Diamant, *Holocaust Literature: A History and Guide*, 9.
10. Ibid.
11. Benjamin Harshav, "The Last Days of the Jerusalem of Lithuania," in *The Polyphony of Jewish Culture* (Stanford, CA: Stanford University Press, 2007), 140–41.
12. See www.yiddishbookcenter.org/files/essentialyiddish060201.pdf (page iv).
13. Jeffrey Shandler, *Adventures in Yiddishland: Postvernacular Language and Culture* (Berkeley: University of California Press, 2006), 27: "However, this book does not strive to offer a comprehensive inventory or chronicle of Yiddish activities of the past six decades. Rather, the approach is selective, focusing on particular phenomena that best demonstrate the use and significance of Yiddish as a postvernacular language (as opposed to, say, centering the study on those examples of Yiddish culture considered to be the most popular or accomplished)."
14. See Chana Kronfeld, *On the Margins of Modernism: Decentering Literary Dynamics* (Berkeley: University of California Press, 1996), 194, and Benjamin Harshav, "The End of Language," in *The Meaning of Yiddish* (Berkeley: University of California Press, 1990), 187–95.
15. The Soviet Yiddish chapter (including the Yiddish centers in Warsaw and Moscow) is addressed in chapters 1, 2, and 5. See Gennady Estraykh, *In Harness: Yiddish Writers' Romance with Communism* (Syracuse, NY: Syracuse University Press, 2005), and *Yiddish in the Cold War* (London: Legenda, 2008); Jeffrey Veidlinger, *The Moscow State Yiddish Theater: Jewish Culture on the Soviet Stage* (Bloomington: Indiana University Press, 2000); David Shneer, *Yiddish and the Creation of Soviet Jewish Culture, 1918–1930* (New York: Cambridge University Press, 2004); Anna Shternshis, *Soviet and Kosher: Jewish Popular Culture in the Soviet Union, 1923–1939* (Bloomington: Indiana University Press, 2006); Harriet Murav, *Music from a Speeding Train: Jewish Literature in Post-Revolution Russia* (Stanford, CA: Stanford University Press, 2011); and David Shneer, *Through Soviet Jewish Eyes: Photography, War, and the Holocaust* (New Brunswick, NJ: Rutgers University Press, 2011). The studies of Murav, Shneer, and Estraykh examine Soviet Jewish culture post-1945.
16. About Yiddish in Israel, see Yael Chaver, *What Must Be Forgotten: The Survival of Yiddish in Zionist Palestine* (Syracuse, NY: Syracuse University Press, 2004); Aryeh Pilowsky, *Tsvishn yo un neyn: Yidish un yidish-literatur in Eretz-yisroel 1907–1948* (Tel Aviv: World Council for Yiddish and Jewish Culture, 1991); Shachar Pinsker, "*Yung yisroel: Tvishn heym un goles*," *Forverts*, June 29, 2007, 12–13, and "Choosing Yiddish in Israel: *Yung Yisroel* Between Home and Exile, the Center and the Margins," in *Choosing Yiddish: New Frontiers of Language and Culture*, ed. Rabinovitch, Goren, and Pressman, 277–94.
17. Yankev Glatshteyn, "*Der shverer veg*," in *In tokh genumen: Eseyen 1945–1947* (New York: Farlag matones, 1947), 426.
18. *I Keep Recalling: The Holocaust Poems of Jacob Glatstein*, trans. Barnett Zumoff (Hoboken, NJ: KTAV Publishing House, 1993), 92.
19. See Moyshe Prager, ed. *Antologye fun religieze lider un dertseylungen: Shafungen fun shrayber, umgekumene in di yorn fun yidishn khurbn in eyrope* (Anthology of Religious Poems and Stories: Works of Writers Who Perished in the Years of the Jewish Holocaust in Europe) (New York: Forshungs-institut fun religiezn yidntum, 1955).
20. Abraham Joshua Heschel, *Kotsk: In gerangl far emesdikayt*, vol. 2 (Tel Aviv: Farlag hamenoyre, 1973), 541.
21. *The Collected Stories of Isaac Bashevis Singer* (New York: Farrar, Straus and Giroux, 1982), 187.

22. William Safran, "The Jewish Diaspora in a Comparative and Theoretical Perspective," *Israel Studies* 10, no. 1 (2005): 37.

Chapter 1

1. Henryk Grynberg, *The Victory*, trans. Richard Lourie (1969; Evanston, IL: Northwestern University Press, 1993), 107.
2. Avrom Sutzkever, "*Vi azoy?*" in *Lider fun yam-hamoves: Fun vilner geto, vald, un vander: Geshribn in di yorn 1936–1967* (Tel Aviv: Farlag Bergen-Belsen, 1968), 50. Translation from *Selected Poetry and Prose*, ed. and trans. Barbara and Benjamin Harshav (Berkeley: University of California Press, 1991), 155. I have made a slight change to the Harshavs' translation: "*fargangenkeyt*" (past-in-chains).
3. "An Ambassador of the Yiddish Language," www.haaretz.com/print-edition/features/an-ambassador-of-the-yiddish-language-1.262255, accessed July 2, 2013. See also Ruth R. Wisse's personal account of her relationships with Max Weinreich and Avrom Sutzkever, "The Poet from Vilna," *Jewish Review of Books* (Summer 2010): "No official representatives of Israel's government attended Sutzkever's funeral on January 24 of this year (2010). The poet would have been hurt by the slight. But President Shimon Peres was among dozens of notables at a large public commemoration held at the end of the month of mourning, and Dan Miron . . . informs me that the mayor of Tel Aviv intends to name a street after him" (6).
4. The implementation of the Final Solution was vastly different in Vilna and in Warsaw, as summarized by Samuel David Kassow: "The Warsaw Ghetto was twenty times larger than the Vilna Ghetto and harbored a huge refugee population of 100,000 uprooted, provincial Jews. Up to the time of the Great Deportation of July 1942, the Warsaw Ghetto had experienced hunger and epidemics (which had killed 100,000 Jews) but not mass extermination. Vilna had just the opposite experience. The ghetto began only after most of the Jews of Vilna had been killed. A cyclone hit Vilna Jewry immediately after the German occupation in June 1941; by the end of that year, 75 percent of the community, including most of the prewar leadership, had been killed." See Dina Porat, "The Vilna Ghetto Diaries," and Samuel David Kassow, "Vilna and Warsaw, Two Ghetto Diaries: Herman Kruk and Emanuel Ringelblum," both in *Holocaust Chronicles: Individualizing the Holocaust Through Diaries and Other Contemporaneous Personal Accounts*, ed. Robert Moses Shapiro (Hoboken, NJ: KTAV, 1999), 160 (Porat) and 210 (Kassow).
5. Three sources are crucial for Avrom Sutzkever's work between 1944 and 1946: David E. Fishman, "Embers Plucked from the Fire: The Rescue of Jewish Cultural Treasures in Vilna," in *The Holocaust and the Book: Destruction and Preservation*, ed. Jonathan Rose (Amherst: University of Massachusetts Press, 2001), 66–78; David Roskies, "The Burden of Memory," in *Against the Apocalypse: Responses to Catastrophe in Modern Jewish Culture* (Cambridge, MA: Harvard University Press, 1984), 225–57; and Abraham Nowersztern, ed., *Abraham Sutzkever on His Seventieth Birthday*, catalogue of an exhibition at the Jewish National and University Library (in Yiddish and Hebrew) (Jerusalem: Jewish National Library, 1983).
6. Nowersztern, ed., *Abraham Sutzkever on His Seventieth Birthday*, 142.
7. Sutzkever, *Lider fun yam-hamoves*, 180. Written in the Vilna Ghetto, February 6, 1943.
8. Nowersztern, ed., *Abraham Sutzkever on His Seventieth Birthday*, 142.
9. "The Jewish Anti-Fascist Committee . . . was formed on Joseph Stalin's order in Kuibyshev

in April 1942 with the official support of the Soviet authorities. It was designed to influence international public opinion and organize political and material support for the Soviet fight against Nazi Germany, particularly from the West. In 1952, as part of the persecution of Jews in the latter part of Stalin's rule (for example, the "Doctors' plot"), most prominent members of the JAC were arrested on trumped-up spying charges, tortured, and executed by firing squad after a secret mock trial. They were officially rehabilitated in 1988." en.wikipedia.org/wiki/Jewish_Anti-Fascist_Committee, accessed July 20, 2014.
10. *The Black Book*, edited by Vasili Grossman and Ilya Ehrenburg, was published in Russian in Jerusalem in 1980. A Yiddish translation that included a section on Lithuania with a short version of Sutzkever's Holocaust memoirs was published in 1984. For the history of the book and a discussion about why it was shelved before its planned publication in 1946, see Joseph Kermish, "*Tsu der geshikhte fun ksav-yad fun 'dos shvartse bukh,'*" in *Dos shvartse bukh* (Jerusalem: Yad Vashem), xiii–xxi. See Sutzkever, "*Fun vilner geto*," 321–404.
11. Avrom Sutzkever, "*Ilya Erenburg*," in *Bam leyenen penimer: Dertseylungen, dermonungen, eseyen* (Jerusalem: Hebrew University Press, 1993), 129 (first published as "*Ilya Erenburg [a kapitl zikhroynes fun di yorn 1944–1946]*," *Di goldene keyt* 61 [1967]: 21).
12. Sutzkever, *Selected Poetry and Prose*, 22.
13. Fishman, "Embers Plucked from the Fire," 68.
14. See Rokhl Poupko-Krinsky, "*Mayn arbet in Yivo unter di daytshn*," *YIVO-Bleter* 30, no. 2 (1947): 214–23.
15. Avrom Sutzkever, "*A vort tsum zekhtsikstn yoyvl fun yivo*," in *Baym leyenen penimer: Dertseylungen, dermonungen, eseyen*, 208. The Weinreich Room was named after the renowned Yiddish scholar Max Weinreich (1894–1969), one of the founders of YIVO in Vilna.
16. See Sutzkever's statement in his interview with Yankev Pat: "The whole power and wonder of the Yiddish language . . . revealed itself to me in the Vilna Ghetto. There I truthfully could say that life and death were in the hand of the Yiddish language. My language, my poem was my magic protection on which the arrows of death were repelled. In poetry, I even became a free person in the ghetto and would under no circumstances have switched places with my torturer, the ostensibly free people." *Shmuesn mit yidishe shrayber in yisroel*, ed. Yankev Pat (New York: Der kval, 1960), 166.
17. Sutzkever, "*A vort tsum zekhtsiktstn yoyvl fun yivo*," 208.
18. Yankev Glatshteyn, *In tokh genumen: Eseyen 1945–1947* (New York: Farlag matones, 1947), 57. See also the Polish Nobel laureate Czeslaw Milosz, "Ruins and Poetry," in his *To Begin Where I Am: Selected Essays* (New York: Farrar, Straus and Giroux, 2001), 356: "some detachment, some coldness, is necessary to elaborate a form. People thrown into the middle of events that tear cries of pain from their mouths have difficulty in finding the distance necessary to transform this material artistically."
19. The best biographical source for Sutzkever's life and work is Abraham Nowersztern, ed., *Avrom Sutzkever tsum vern a benshivim: Oysshtelung* (Abraham Sutzkever on His Seventieth Birthday) (Jerusalem: Hebrew University Press, 1983); see also Nowersztern's article "Yung Vilne: The Political Dimension of Literature," in *The Jews of Poland Between Two World Wars*, ed. Yisrael Gutman, Ezra Mendelsohn, Jehuda Reinharz, and Khone Shmeruk (Hanover, NH: University Press of New England, 1989), 383–98.
20. Avrom Sutzkever, "*Penimer in zumpn*," in *Der yoyresh fun regn* (Tel Aviv: Farlag di goldene keyt, 1992), 79 (first published in *Poetishe verk*, vol. 1 [Tel Aviv: Yoyvl komitet, 1963]). Translation from *Selected Poetry and Prose*, 124–25.
21. Sutzkever, "*Penimer in zumpn*," 75.

22. Paul Celan, "Bremen Prize Speech" (1958), translated by John Felstiner in "Translating Celan's Last Poem," *American Poetry Review* (July–August 1982): 23.
23. Michael Bernard-Donals, "Beyond the Question of Authenticity: Witness and Testimony in the Fragments Controversy," *PMLA* 116, no. 5 (2001): 1312.
24. Sutzkever, *Lider fun yam-hamoves*, 32; translated in *Selected Poetry and Prose*, 149.
25. Sutzkever, *Lider fun yam-hamoves*, 35; translated in *Selected Poetry and Prose*, 149.
26. Ibid.
27. Avrom Sutzkever, *Vilner geto, 1941–1944* (New York: Ikuf farlag, 1947), 25–28. *Trial of the Major War Criminals Before the International Military Tribunal, Nuremberg, 14 November 1945–1 October 1946* (Nuremberg, 1947–1949), 3. Volume including the tribunal proceedings of February 28, 1946.
28. Sutzkever, "*Der tsirk,*" in *Di ershte nakht in geto* (Tel Aviv: Farlag di goldene keyt, 1979), 9.
29. Ibid.; translated in *Selected Poetry and Prose*, 129.
30. *Di goldene keyt* 95/96 (1979): 320.
31. These four lines stand out in the otherwise muted, metaphorical poem for their mocking reference to his Polish neighbors—"*shkheynim*" in quotation marks—as contrasted with the four times repeated word *naket* (naked), to contrast the humiliating public spectacle and the passivity of the Polish spectators:

Me tsvingt undz oystsuton zikh naket.
Naket. Naket. Naket. Un antkegn oyf di vilde
Ekldike eplbeymer zitsn mayne "shkheynim,"
Baysn epl, yogn op di fliendike funken.

They force us to undress naked.
Naked. Naked. Naked. And opposite
On the wild, disgusting apple trees my "neighbors"
Sit, and eat apples, stirring the flying sparks.
         —"*Erev mayn farbrenung,*" in *Lider fun yam-hamoves*, 379

32. For a comparison of the two poems, see Heather Valencia, "From *Der tsirk* to *Erev mayn farbrenung:* The Transformation of Experience in Two Poems by Avrom Sutzkever," in *Leket: Jiddisitik heute* (Dusseldorf: Dusseldorf University Press, 2012), 109–28; Yechiel Szeintuch, "*Di biografye fun lid 'Der tsirk,'*" in *Yikhes fun lid/Yikhuso shel shir. Lekoved Avrom Sutzkever*, ed. Dov Sadan, Khone Shmeruk, Chava Turniansky (Tel Aviv: Yoyvl-kommitet, 1983), 258–79; and Avrom Nowersztern, ed. *Abraham Sutzkever on His Seventieth Birthday*, 131–32. The quote is from Valencia, "From *Der tsirk,*" 127.
33. Avrom Sutzkever, *The Poetry of Abraham Sutzkever, the Vilna Poet, Reading in Yiddish*, Folkways Records FL-9947 (1960).
34. Sutzkever, *Lider fun yam-hamoves,* 41–42, 151–52. The poem was written in the Vilna Ghetto, January 1, 1943.
35. Sutzkever based this poem on a real event; see *Fun vilner geto*, 88, and his poem dated July 30, 1943, in *Di ershte nakht in geto*, 24–25.
36. *Trial of the Major War Criminals,* 5–6.
37. Sutzkever, "*Farbrente perl,*" in *Lider fun yam-hamoves,* 82.
38. Roskies, *Against the Apocalypse,* 24.
39. Sutzkever, "*Farfroyrene yidn,*" in *Di festung* (New York: Ikuf farlag, 1944); translated in *Selected Poetry and Prose,* 181–82.

40. Fishman, "Embers Plucked from the Fire," 74.
41. Avrom Sutzkever, *"Mayn eydes-zogn,"* in *Bam leyenen penimer,* 151.
42. Ibid., 162.
43. Avrom Sutzkever, *"Mit shloyme mikhoels,"* in *Bam leyenen penimer,* 110. See also Moyshe Knapheys, *"Di sutskever-teg in buenes ayres,"* *Di prese,* June 10, 1953. In this article a Jewish survivor of Warsaw who was present at the meeting in Moscow on April 2, 1946, gives an account about the reception of Sutzkever's presentation. In Harriet Murav's chapter on Jewish Soviet writers during and right after the war, which includes analysis and portraits of leading Yiddish writers, Sutzkever is not mentioned at all. See Murav, "In Mourning: Responding to Destruction of the Jews," in *Music from a Speeding Train: Jewish Literature in Post-Revolution Russia* (Stanford, CA: Stanford University Press, 2011), 150–99. The book's expansive view of Jewish writers in Yiddish and Russian in the Soviet Union does not include the large numbers of Eastern European Jewish writers who fled to the Soviet Union at the outbreak of the war and spent the war there until their departure between 1945 and 1947. (The most prominent Yiddish writers in this group were Chaim Grade, Rokhl Korn, Mendel Mann, Binem Heller, and Sutzkever.) See *Nisht bay di taykhn fun Bovl: Antologye fun der yidisher poezye in nokhmilkhomedikn poyln* (Not at the Rivers of Babylon: Anthology of Yiddish Poetry in Postwar Poland), ed. and intro. Magdalena Ruta (Cracow: Ksiegarnia Akademicka, 2012).
44. Sutzkever, *"Tsu poyln,"* in *Lider fun yam-hamoves,* 299.
45. Ibid., 297–307.
46. For a reading of *"Tsu Poyln"* in a Polish literary context, see Justin Cammy and Marta Figlerowicz, "Translating History into Art: The Influences of Cyprian Kamil Norwid in Abraham Sutzkever's Poetry," *Prooftexts* 3 (Fall 2007): 427–73.
47. Roskies, *Against the Apocalypse,* 250–51.
48. Avrom Sutzkever, *"Di froy fun mirml afn Per-lashez,"* in *With Everything We've Got: A Personal Anthology of Yiddish Poetry,* ed. and trans. Richard J. Fein (Austin, TX: Host Publications, 2009), 166–67.
49. Sutzkever, *"Bagleytvort tsum bukh"* (Introduction), in *Lider fun yam-hamoves,* 1.
50. Ibid., 2.
51. Ibid.
52. Avrom Sutzkever, *Lider fun togbukh* (Tel Aviv: Farlag di goldene keyt, 1977), 65; *Selected Poetry and Prose,* 37–38.
53. Neil Levi and Michael Rothberg, eds., *The Holocaust: Theoretical Readings* (New Brunswick, NJ: Rutgers University Press, 2003), 274.
54. Ruth R. Wisse, "The Poet from Vilna," 6.
55. Nowersztern, ed., *Abraham Sutzkever on His Seventieth Birthday,* 129.
56. *The Penguin Book of Modern Yiddish Verse,* ed. Irving Howe, Ruth R. Wisse, and Khone Shmeruk; trans. Cynthia Ozick (New York: Penguin, 1987), 702.

Chapter 2

1. Simkhe-Bunim Shayevitsh, *Lekh-lekho* (Lodz: Tsentraler yidisher historisher komisye, 1946), 60. The quote is from the poem *Friling 1942* (Spring 1942).
2. Shimon Redlich, *Life in Transit: Jews in Postwar Lodz, 1945–1950* (Boston: Academic Studies Press, 2011), 68.
3. Ibid., 73.

4. See Jan T. Gross, *Fear: Anti-Semitism in Poland after Auschwitz—An Essay in Historical Interpretation* (New York: Random House, 2006), and Gross, with Irena Grudzinska Gross, *Golden Harvest: Events at the Periphery of the Holocaust* (New York: Oxford University Press, 2012).
5. Shimen Dzigan, *Der koyekh fun yidishn humor* (Tel Aviv: Der gezelshaftlekher komitet tsu fayern 40 yor tetikayt fun Shimen Dzigan oyf der yidisher bine, 1974), 291–92.
6. Dan Miron, *The Image of the Shtetl and Other Studies of the Jewish Literary Imagination* (Syracuse, NY: Syracuse University Press, 2000).
7. Gabriel Finder, "Child Survivors in Jewish Collective Memory in Poland after the Holocaust: The Case of Undzere Kinder," in *Nurturing the Nation: Displaced Children, State Ideology and Social Identity in Eastern Europe and the USSR, 1918–1953*, ed. Nick Baron (Boston: Brill, forthcoming 2015), 5. See also Lawrence Langer, "*Undzere kinder:* A Yiddish Film from Poland," in *Preempting the Holocaust* (New Haven, CT: Yale University Press, 1998), 157–65; Yuri Vedenyapin, "'Doctors Prescribe Laughter': The Yiddish Stand-Up Comedy of Shimen Dzigan," BA thesis, Harvard University, 2004; John M. Efron, "From Lodz to Tel Aviv: The Yiddish Political Satire of Shimen Dzigan," *Jewish Quarterly Review* 102, no. 1 (2012): 50–79; Jim Hoberman, *Bridge of Light: Yiddish Film Between Two Worlds* (New York: Schocken Books 1991): 330–31.
8. Finder, "Child Survivors in Jewish Collective Memory in Poland after the Holocaust," 8.
9. Ibid., 26.
10. Ibid., 30.
11. Gabriel Finder makes the same assertion: "It was now no longer possible to show *Undzere Kinder* in Polish cinemas because of the film's single-minded focus on Polish Jewish fortitude as well as victimhood under Nazi rule. According to Gross, the film was screened only once in Poland before a limited audience of invited guests. Shaul Goskind (the producer of the film) smuggled a copy to Paris. Gross left Poland and arrived in Israel in 1950, followed later that year by Goskind, who brought the movie with him. After short runs in Paris and Tel Aviv in 1951, the film dissappeared from view until the original nitrate print was discovered in Paris in the early 1980s and subsequently restored by the National Center for Jewish film in Waltham, Massachussetts." Gabriel Finder, "Child Survivors in Jewish Collective Memory in Poland after the Holocaust," 8. See also Natan Gross, *Toldot hakolno'a hayehudi bepolin 1910–1959* (Jerusalem: Magnes Press/Hebrew University, 1990), 90–99.
12. Imre Kertész, *Fateless* (first published in Hungarian 1975) (Evanston, IL: Northwestern University Press, 1992), is a rare example of a novel about the author's incarceration in Auschwitz in 1944. See also Imre Kertész, *Dossier K: A Memoir* (first published in Hungarian 2006) (Brooklyn: Melville House, 2013).
13. Chava Rosenfarb, *Geto un andere lider: Oykh fragmentn fun a tog-bukh* (Ghetto and Other Poems: Also Fragments from a Diary) (Montreal: Aroysgegebn durkh H. Hershman, 1948), 86.
14. Chava Rosenfarb, "*A videh fun a mekhaber*" (Confession of a Writer; in Yiddish), *Di goldene keyt* 81 (1973): 127–41, 132.
15. Ibid., 132.
16. This is described in "*A videh fun a mekhaber.*" This essay was first presented by Rosenfarb as a lecture at the 1973 Jewish Public Library event celebrating the publication of *Der boym fun lebn*.
17. Chava Rosenfarb, "*Simkhe-Bunim Shayevitsh: Dermonungen*" (Simkhe-Bunim Shayevitsh: Reminiscences), *Di goldene keyt* 131 (1991): 9–28; translated into English as "The Last Poet

of Lodz," *Tablet Magazine*, September 13, 2012, www.tabletmag.com/jewish-arts-and-culture/books/111880/the-last-poet-of-lodz, accessed April 29, 2013 (quote appears in the Yiddish original, p. 9).
18. Rosenfarb, "*Simkhe-Bunim Shayevitsh: Dermonungen*," 10.
19. Ibid.
20. Ibid., 17. See Miriam Ulinover, *A grus fun der alter heym: Lider*, ed. and intro. Natalia Krinitska; trans. into French by Batia Baum (Paris: Medem-bibliotek, 2003), particularly regarding the Lodz Ghetto (29–34).
21. The Lodz Ghetto experienced two major waves of deportations whose destinations were largely unknown to the ghetto population. Unlike the Warsaw Ghetto, the Lodz Ghetto was almost completely sealed off from the surrounding world, including the "Aryan" side of town: "Between January and May 1942, fifty-five thousand inhabitants were transported to the death camp in Chelmno. The second phase of the deportations began on September 1, 1942, with the evacuation of the hospitals, and continued from September 5 until September 12. The ghetto was placed under general curfew during that time. In the course of this grim *Aktion*, which the ghetto Jews called the *Sperre* (an abbreviation of the German word *Gehsperre*—curfew), more than five hundred and seventy persons were murdered in the ghetto and more than fifteen thousand Jews, mostly children and the elderly, were deported from the ghetto to the Chelmno death camp." Josef Zelkowicz, *In Those Terrible Days: Notes from the Lodz Ghetto*, ed. Michal Unger (Jerusalem: Yad Vashem, 2002), 251.
22. Rosenfarb, "*Simkhe-Bunim Shayevitsh: Dermonungen*," 25
23. See Rebecca Margolis, "Chava Rosenfarb's Yiddish Montreal," *Canadian Jewish Studies/Études juives canadiennes* 18–19 (2010–11): 159–77.
24. Jewish Public Library of Montreal, "Chava Rosenfarb Evening in Honor of the Publication of Her Trilogy 'The Tree of Life' Part 1 and Part 2" (May 27, 1973), audio file, http://archive.org/detailsChavaRosenfarbEveningInHonorOfThePublicationOfHerTrilogytheTreOf_59; accessed April 29, 2013. Later published as "*A videh fun a mekhaber*," 132.
25. Yehuda Elberg was a first-rate Yiddish prose writer. See his *Unter kuperne himlen: Dersteylungen* (Buenos Aires: Tsentral-farband far poylishe yidn in argentine, 1951) and his novels from the 1970s and 1980s.
26. Jack Kugelmass and Jonathan Boyarin first introduced the concept of "substitute gravestones" in *From a Ruined Garden: The Memorial Books of Polish Jewry* (New York: Schocken Books, 1983).
27. "*Paul Celan un zayne goyrl-brider*" (Paul Celan and His Brothers of Destiny), *Di goldene keyt* 138 (1994): 56.
28. Ibid., 70.
29. Chava Rosenfarb, "Feminism and Yiddish Literature: A Personal Approach," in *Gender and Text in Modern Hebrew and Yiddish Literature*, ed. Naomi B. Sokoloff, Anne Lapidus Lerner, and Anita Norich (New York: Jewish Theological Seminary of America, 1992), 224.
30. See Goldie Morgentaler, "Land of the Postscript: Canada and the Post-Holocaust Fiction of Chava Rosenfarb," *Judaism* 49, no. 2 (2000): 168–83.
31. In an email from Goldie Morgentaler dated March 10, 2014, the choice of Rachel's family name is explained in this way: "My mother chose the name Eybeshutz [Eibeschutz] for her alter-ego Rachel, because she was always very proud of being a descendent of Reb Yonathan Eybeshutz, the great rabbi and Talmudist who tangled with Sabbatai Tsvi."
32. Rosenfarb, "*Simkhe-Bunim Shayevitsh: Dermonungen*," 13 and 9.
33. Rosenfarb, "*A videh fun a mekhaber*." Both quotes are from p. 137.

34. Chava Rosenfarb, *The Tree of Life: A Trilogy of Life in the Lodz Ghetto*, Book 3: *The Cattle Cars Are Waiting, 1942–1944*, trans. Rosenfarb, in collaboration with Goldie Morgentaler (Madison: University of Wisconsin Press, 2006), 362.
35. Chava Rosenfarb, "Feminism and Yiddish Literature: A Personal Approach," in *Gender and Text in Modern Hebrew and Yiddish Literature*, ed. Sokoloff, Lerner, and Norich, 224.
36. Rosenfarb, *The Tree of Life*, Book 3, 132.
37. The biographical origin of the image of the doll is indicated in Rosenfarb's recollection of Shayevitsh's telling her the story in 1943, a year after the events of the *Sperre*; see "*Simkhe-Bunim Shayevitsh: Dermonungen*," 25.
38. See Josef Zelkowicz, *In Those Terrible Days: Writings from the Lodz Ghetto*. Translations by Joachim Neugroschel from the Yiddish original are scattered throughout *Lodz Ghetto: Inside a Community under Siege*, ed. Alan Adelson and Robert Lapides (New York: Viking, 1989). David G. Roskies notes: "In addition to the meticulous communal record, the celebrated Polish-German *Chronicle of the Lodz Ghetto* (Dobroszycki, 1984), which was surprisingly candid about everything except the German and Jewish overlords, we also have the hidden transcripts of two professional journalists: Oskar Rosenfeld, writing in German, and Josef Zelkowicz, writing in Yiddish. Rosenfeld's and Zelkowicz's private notebooks and journalistic sketches, which each man planned to publish after the war, are unfinished masterpieces of a new literature in the making." David G. Roskies and Naomi Diamant, *Holocaust Literature: A History and Guide* (Waltham, MA: Brandeis University Press, 2012), 25. Fragments of Josef Zelkowicz's essays and reportage in Yiddish were published by Isaiah Trunk in *Lodzher geto* (The Lodz Ghetto) (New York: Yad Vashem/YIVO Institute for Jewish Research, 1962). For a biographical sketch of Zelkowicz, see Lucjan Dobroszycki, ed., *The Chronicle of the Lodz Ghetto, 1941–1944* (New Haven, CT: Yale University Press, 1984), xiv.
39. Dobroszycki, ed., *The Chronicle of the Lodz Ghetto*, xv.
40. Ibid., 255. The historian Samuel Kassow has translated and edited a volume of Zelkowicz's writings from the Lodz Ghetto which will be published in 2015 by Yale University Press.
41. Lawrence L. Langer, "Deep Memory: The Buried Self" (1991), in *The Holocaust: Theoretical Readings*, ed. Neil Levi and Michael Rothberg (New Brunswick, NJ: Rutgers University Press, 2003), 258. About the Fortunoff Video Archive for Holocaust Testimonies at Yale University, see http://www.library.yale.edu/testimonies/.
42. Hayden White, "The Modernist Event," in *Figural Realism: Studies in the Mimesis Effect* (Baltimore, MD: Johns Hopkins University Press, 1991), 66.
43. Ibid., 66.
44. Ibid., 79.
45. Ibid., 82.
46. Bogdan Wojdowski, *Bread for the Departed*, trans. Madeline G. Levine (Evanston, IL: Northwestern University Press, 1997). See also Roskies and Diamant, eds., *Holocaust Literature: A History and Guide*, 136–38 and 275–76, and Monika Adamczyk-Garbowska, "Fiddles on Willow Trees: The Missing Polish Link in the Jewish Canon," in *Arguing the Jewish Canon: Essays on Literature and Culture in Honor of Ruth R. Wisse*, ed. Justin Daniel Cammy, Dara Horn, Alyssa Quint et al. (Cambridge, MA: Harvard University Press, 2008), 627–44.
47. Rosenfarb, *Geto un andere lider: Oykh fragmentn fun a tog-bukh*, 96.
48. Rosenfarb, "The Last Poet of Lodz," 18.
49. Roskies and Diamant, eds., *Holocaust Literature: A History and Guide*, 97.

300 NOTES TO CHAPTER 3

50. Two examples include Simkhe-Bunim Shayevitsh, *Lekh-lekho* (1946), and Bernard Mark, ed., *Tvishn lebn un toyt* (Warsaw: Farlag Yidish-bukh, 1955).
51. Chava Rosenfarb, *Survivors* (Toronto: Cormorant Books, 2004), 86.
52. Rosenfarb, *Geto un andere lider: Oykh fragmentn fun a tog-bukh*, 96.
53. Rosenfarb, "*Simkhe-Bunim Shayevitsh: Dermonungen*," 22.
54. Ibid., 27.

Chapter 3

1. Leib Rochman, "*Af keyver-oves*," *Yerusholayimer almanakh* 6–7 (1976): 116.
2. Ibid.
3. In 1978, the year of his death, Rochman published a collection of stories, *Der mabl* (The Flood). The title story depicted in modernist fashion a flood engulfing the world; this might have been inspired by his visit to Sholem Aleichem's grave in Mount Carmel Cemetery, Queens, in 1976.
4. See David Roskies, "What Is Holocaust Literature?" in *Studies in Contemporary Jewry 21: Jews, Catholics and the Burden of History*, ed. Eli Lederhendler (Oxford: Oxford University Press, 2005), 172–73.
5. Mordechai Strigler, "*Tsu aykh shvester un brider bafrayte: Nokhmilkhome-problemen fun yidishn folk*" (New York: Zamoshtsher brentsh 375, Arbeter ring 8, 1945).
6. Ibid., 12. Strigler's program for Jewish renewal was informed by his Orthodox upbringing as a Hasidic *yeshive bokher* who continued to adhere to traditional Judaism while getting involved in the secular Polish Jewish world of the late 1930s. Strigler wrote for the Yiddish press and anonymously submitted an autobiography to the YIVO competition for the best youth memoir in 1939. The autobiography is located in the YIVO Institute for Jewish Research and includes a letter from Strigler to YIVO in Vilna dated February 14, 1939. In an email from March 23, 2014, Leah Strigler (his daughter), pointed out: "he was simultaneously working as an assistant rabbi to a prominent Warsaw rabbi—he had smicha from Kletsk—and writing under a pseudonym in the Yiddish press. . . . Also, for clarification, the YIVO autobiography was submitted before he began his journalistic career—he was a teenager—and is officially anonymous, although many know that the piece is identified with him."
7. Strigler's *Maydanek* was published in Hebrew in 1948, during the Israeli War of Independence. A French translation of this work was published in 1998.
8. See Felicja Karay, *Death Comes in Yellow: Skarzysko-Kamienna Slave Labor Camp* (Amsterdam: Harwood Academic Publishers, 1996), an excellent historical study of the labor camp in which Strigler was incarcerated for eighteen months. See also Christopher R. Browning, *Remembering Survival: Inside a Nazi Slave-Labor Camp* (New York: W.W. Norton & Company, 2010), a historical study of the Wierzbnik-Starachowice labor camp in the Radom district. Browning's study is to a large extent based on Jewish survivor testimonies: "Almost none involved the reflective process of writing and revising for publication. Among the survivors of the Starachowice camps, there is no Primo Levi or Elie Wiesel" (5). Strigler's Holocaust memoirs do not appear in Browning's study but are quoted extensively in Karay's study.
9. M. Strigler, *Maydanek* (Buenos Aires: Tsentral-farband fun poylishe yidn in argentine, 1947), 8 (bold in original).
10. A selection of these letters is scheduled for publication under the editorship of Professor

Yechiel Szeintuch (Hebrew University). See Strigler's letters to Shmerke Kaczerginski, "*Mordkhe Shtrigler afn sheydveg nokh Bukhnvald,*" *Forverts,* May 28, and June 4, 2004.
11. H. Leivick, *In treblinke bin ikh nit geven: Lider un poemes* (New York: CYCO-Farlag, 1945).
12. Ibid., 11.
13. H. Leivick, "*An araynfir tsu a bukhnvald-khronik,*" *Tsukunft* (August 1945): 491.
14. H. Leivick, "*Oysgeloshene likht tindn zikh vayter on,*" introduction to *Maydanek,* by Mordechai Strigler (Buenos Aires: Tsentral-farband fun poylishe yidn in Argentine, 1947); H. Leivick, introduction to Arn Tverski, *Ikh bin der korbn un der eydes* (New York: A. Tverski, 1947); H. Leivick, "*Dos folk zingt eybik,*" in *Lider fun di getos un lagern: Tekstn un melodyes gezamlt,* compiled by Shmerke Kaczerginski and edited, with an introduction, by H. Leivick (New York, CYCO Bicher Farlag, 1948), xxvii–xxxix; H. Leivick, *Mit der sheyreshapleyte: Tog-bukh fartseykhenungen fun mayn rayze iber di yidishe lagern fun der amerikaner zone in Daytshland* (New York: H. Leivick yubiley fund, durkhn CYCO farlag, 1947). See also Tamar Lewinsky, "*Un az in Treblinke bin ikh yo geven iz vos?*" in *Leket: Jiddistik heute,* ed. Marion Aptroot, Efrat Gal-Ed, Roland Gruschka, and Simon Neuberg (Dusseldorf: Dusseldorf University Press, 2012), 544–63.
15. Mordechai Strigler, "*Fun Bukhnvald: Dokumentn fun undzere teg,*" *Tsukunft* (August 1945): 495.
16. Mordechai Strigler, *In di fabrikn fun toyt* (Buenos Aires: Tsentral-farband fun poylishe yidn in argentine, 1948), 7.
17. Shmuel Niger, "*Farbrekhn un shtrof,*" *Der tog,* December 30, 1951; reprinted in *Yehuda Elberg: Eseyen vegn zayn literarishn shafn,* ed. Gershon Viner (Ramat Gan: Bar Ilan University Press, 1990), 68.
18. Y. Rapoport, *Zoymen in vint* (Buenos Aires: Argentiner opteyl fun Alveltlekhn Yidishn kultur-kongres, 1961), 484.
19. Ibid. For a similar point, see James E. Young, *Writing and Rewriting the Holocaust: Narrative and the Consequences of Interpretation* (Bloomington: Indiana University Press, 1988), 338: "This is to suggest that the events of the Holocaust are not only shaped *post factum* in their narration, but that they were initially determined as they unfolded by the schematic ways in which they were apprehended, expressed, and then acted upon."
20. Rochman's original diary is located in the Yad Vashem archive. The manuscript is legible and easy to read. It is the most important source for examining the processes of editing and rewriting that Rochman conducted during and after the war. A study of the manuscript, including a comparison with the published versions, is a desideratum.
21. I have not located the serialized work in the Yiddish newspapers, which might throw light on the editing of the work for book publication.
22. From book jacket of Leib Rochman, *The Pit and the Trap,* trans. Sheila Friedling (New York: Holocaust Library, 1983).
23. The English version leaves out some paragraphs of the original while adding other text. A particularly striking example: on the last page of the English version, a biblical reference has been included, "We had seen God's face and lived," which does not appear in the Yiddish book. Instead, the Yiddish reads "*s'geyt oyf a morgnshtern*" (a morning star rose). Thus the religious sentiment of the English translation is reinforced, replacing the image of rebirth and renewal.
24. Timothy Snyder, "Holocaust: The Ignored Reality," *New York Review of Books,* July 16, 2009, 14. Similarly, Alexandra Garbarini points to the importance of Yiddish diaries because they "may illuminate other segments of the Polish Jewish population during these years—

those who were older or were politically engaged with the Bund or were Hasidic." *Numbered Days: Diaries and the Holocaust* (New Haven, CT: Yale University Press, 2006), xii.
25. See Father Patrick Desbois, *The Holocaust by Bullets: A Priest's Journey to Uncover the Truth behind the Murder of 1.5. Million Jews* (New York: Palgrave Macmillan, 2008).
26. Yechiel Szeintuch has edited works by Yiddish writers Isaiah Shpiegl, Ka-Tzetnik, Yitskhok Katzenelson, and Aaron Zeitlin. See Yechiel Szeintuch, "The Corpus of Yiddish and Hebrew Literature from Ghettos and Concentration Camps and Its Relevance for Holocaust Studies," in *Studies in Yiddish Literature and Folklore* (Jerusalem: Hebrew University, 1986), 186–207, and "Yiddish Survivors' Literature" (2012) www.hum.huji.ac.il/units.php?cat=4621&incat=2933, accessed April 29, 2013.
27. David Roskies, "What Is Holocaust Literature?," 202.
28. Like his war diary, Rochman's critically appraised 1968 novel has been translated into Hebrew. According to Dan Miron, "Leyb Rochman (1918–1978) was perhaps the only Yiddish writer of fiction who understood the need for innovative tonality in writing on the Holocaust. His works, *Un in dayn blut zolstu lebn* (And in Your Blood You Shall Live; 1949), and *Mit blinde trit iber der erd* (With Blind Steps over the Earth; 1966), are the most rewarding texts of Yiddish prose fiction written on the unspeakable topic." *The YIVO Encyclopedia of Jews in Eastern Europe*, s.v. "Yiddish Prose." See also David Roskies, *Yiddishlands: A Memoir* (Detroit, MI: Wayne State University Press, 2008), 150: "I alone helped Leybl [Rochman] proofread the galleys of his novel *With Blind Steps over the Earth,* about survivors who journey in several simultaneous time frames, a huge work that would have changed the face of Holocaust literature if only enough people had survived in the world who still read Yiddish." A French translation by Rachel Ertel was published in 2012, *A pas aveugles de par le monde* (Paris: Denoël), with an introduction by Aharon Appelfeld.
29. *Un in dayn blut zolstu lebn (tog-bukh 1943–1944)* (Paris: Farlagkomisye bay der gezelshaft Fraynd fun Minsk-Mazovietsk in Pariz, 1949), 380. As noted earlier, the term "substitute gravestones" was first suggested by Jonathan Boyarin and Jack Kugelmass in *From a Ruined Garden: The Memorial Books of Polish Jewry* (Bloomington: Indiana University Press, 1998), 34.
30. David G. Roskies, "Dividing the Ruins: Communal Memory in Yiddish and Hebrew," in *After the Holocaust: Challenging the Myth of Silence,* ed. David Cesarani and Eric J. Sundquist (London: Routledge, 2012), 84.
31. *Un in dayn blut,* 302; *The Pit and the Trap,* 227.
32. *Un in dayn blut,* 18; *The Pit and the Trap,* 22. The hostile quip at Christianity in the second section of the quote has been removed from the English translation.
33. *Un in dayn blut,* 141; removed from the English translation.
34. *Un in dayn blut,* 223 and 224; *The Pit and the Trap,* 176.
35. Avrom Lis's review appeared in *Di goldene keyt* 7 (1951): 210–13.
36. Yitskhok Varshavski, review of *Un in dayn blut zolstu lebn, "Tsvey vikhtike bikher fun yunge yidishe shrayber"* (Two Important Books of Young Yiddish Writers), *Forverts,* October 9, 1949.
37. "Leyb Rochman," *Leksikon fun der nayer yidisher literatur,* vol. 8 (New York: Altveltlekhn yidishn kultur kongres, 1981).
38. See Garbarini, *Numbered Days: Diaries and the Holocaust:* "During the war, diaries became sites and vehicles for Jews to re-conceptualize different versions of the religious, to employ a range of cultural practices, and to cling to familial and increasingly Jewish national frameworks" (12).

39. Aharon Appelfeld, "Introduction," in *The Pit and the Trap*, 9.
40. See Wladyslaw Bartoszewski, *The Samaritans: Heroes of the Holocaust* (New York: Twayne Publishers, 1970). For a fine historical study of the Gentile rescuers of Jews during the Holocaust in the *kresy* (northeastern Poland, Volhynia, and East Galicia), see Yehuda Bauer, *The Death of the Shtetl* (New Haven, CT: Yale University Press, 2009), particularly the chapter "The Neighbors" (92–121). See also David Engel, *Historians of the Jews and the Holocaust* (Stanford, CA: Stanford University Press, 2010).
41. *Un in dayn blut*, 21–22; *The Pit and the Trap*, 25.
42. See Jan Tomasz Gross with Irena Grudzinska Gross, *Golden Harvest: Events at the Periphery of the Holocaust* (New York: Oxford University Press, 2012).
43. The member was Hersh Wasser, one of three surviving members of the Oyneg Shabes archive, quoted in Samuel David Kassow, *Who Will Write Our History? Emanuel Ringelblum, the Warsaw Ghetto, and the Oyneg Shabes Archive* (Bloomington: Indiana University Press, 2007), 13.
44. *Un in dayn blut*, 229; *The Pit and the Trap*, 182.
45. Garbarini, *Numbered Days: Diaries and the Holocaust*, 163.
46. *Un in dayn blut*, 267; *The Pit and the Trap*, 206.
47. Yitskhok Yanosovitsh, *Penimer un nemen, band tsvey: Yidishe prozaikers un zeyere verk fun nokh der tsveyter velt-milkhome* (Buenos Aires: Farlag Kiem, 1985), 299.
48. Ibid.
49. Kassow, *Who Will Write Our History?* 14.
50. Jan Gross, *Fear: Anti-Semitism in Poland After Auschwitz—An Essay in Historical Interpretation* (New York: Random House, 2006).
51. Roskies, "Dividing the Ruins," 51.
52. The *Yizker* book includes several articles by Leib Rochman.
53. Leib Rochman, *Der mabl: Dertseylungen* (The Flood: Stories) (Jerusalem: Tsur Ot, 1978), 154.
54. Ibid., 157.
55. Similarly, Sutzkever uses the twin as a metaphor in his collection of poetry *Tsviling-bruder: Lider fun togbukh, 1974–1985* (Twin-Brother: Poems from a Diary, 1974–1985) (Tel Aviv: Farlag di goldene keyt, 1986), 10.
56. Rochman, *Der mabl*, 159.

Chapter 4

1. Asher Pen, "*Naye yidishe bikher in Argentine*" (New Yiddish Book in Argentina), *Jewish Book Annual* (1946–47), *ayen khes*, Yiddish section.
2. Abraham Nowersztern, "*Dos poylishe yidntum*," *Der PaknTreger/ The Book Peddler: Magazine of the National Yiddish Book Center* (1991).
3. S. Niger, "*Tendentsn in der nayster yidisher literatur*," *Jewish Book Annual* (1955–56): 7.
4. Mark Turkov was born in Warsaw in 1904. In the interwar period he worked as a journalist for the Polish and Yiddish press in Poland, first covering sports and later the political debates in the Sejm. He was the author of three books in Polish in the 1930s. He also published books in Yiddish: *Roosevelt's America: Travel Impressions from the United States* (1937) and *In Jewish Fields: A Journey through the Jewish Colonies in Argentina* (1939). Between 1933 and 1938 he was the general director of the Anti-Hitler Committee. He immigrated to Buenos Aires in 1939. His three brothers, Jonas (1898–1988), Sigmund (1896–1970), and

Yitskhok (1906–70), were actors and directors on the Yiddish stage in Warsaw, Buenos Aires, Tel Aviv, and many other places. They survived the war and continued their Yiddish acting and writing careers. Between 1946 and 1954, Mark Turkov served as director of HIAS in South America and, from 1954, as the Argentine representative to the World Jewish Congress. He was also president of the South American Federation of Polish Jews and vice president of the World Union of Polish Jews. He died in 1983 in Buenos Aires. See M. Ravitsh, "*Di fir brider Turkov*," in *Mayn leksikon*, vol. 2 (Montreal: Aroysgegebn fun a komitet in Montreal, 1947), 230–32, and *Leksikon fun der nayer yidisher literatur*.
5. A. Pen, "*Naye yidishe bikher in Argentine*," in *Jewish Book Annual* (1946–47), *ayen khes*, Yiddish section.
6. A. Mitlberg, "*Hilf durkh kultur*," in *Spetsyele oysgabe gevidmet der bikher serye dos poylishe yidntum* 25, ed. Mark Turkov (Buenos Aires, 1947), 11.
7. Ibid., 11.
8. Nowersztern, "*Dos poylishe yidntum*," 14.
9. Z. Baker, "Yiddish Publishing after 1945," in *Yiddish after the Holocaust*, ed. J. Sherman (Oxford: Boulevard, 2004), 60, 62.
10. Ibid., 63.
11. Letter, Menashe Unger to Mark Turkov, March 1947, M. Turkov Archive, YIVO, New York.
12. Both Philip Friedman and Yankev Shatski were critical of the American Jewish community's indifference to commemorating Polish Jewry. In "*Di landsmanshaftnliteratur in di fareynikte shtatn far di letste 10 yor*," in *Jewish Book Annual* (1951–52), *fey alef*, Yiddish section, Shatski states: "It is relevant to note that this series (*Dos poylishe yidntum*) found only one subscriber in the United States and the purchase of books only reached fifty copies. The books are being sold in Argentina and a significant part of them in Israel, Europe, and South America." "*Yidish lebn in argentine*," in *Shatski-bukh*, ed. Y. Lifshits (New York: YIVO, 1958), 321.
13. For an overview of the series, see E. Schulman, "*Siyem fun tsikl Musterverk fun der yiddisher literature*," in *Jewish Book Annual* 43 (1985–86): 132–40.
14. Baker, "Yiddish Publishing after 1945," 63. For an overview of the Yidish-bukh publishing house, including an appendix with a list of Yidish-bukh publications, see Joanna Nalewajko-Kulkov, "The Last Yiddish Books Printed in Poland: Outline of the Activities of Yidish Bukh Publishing House," in *Under the Red Banner: Yiddish Culture in the Communist Countries in the Postwar Era*, Judische Kultur 20, ed. Elvira Grözinger and Magadalena Ruta (Wiesbaden: Harrassowitz Verlag, 2008), 111–45. During the 1950s an average of eighteen books yearly were published by Yidish-bukh.
15. Mark Turkov, ed., *Spetsyele oysgabe gevidmet der bikher serye dos poylishe yidntum* 25, p. 11.
16. Ibid., 12.
17. Letter, Mark Turkov to Yankev Shatski, September 21, 1949, Yankev Shatski Archive, YIVO, New York.
18. Letter, Mark Turkov to Yankev Shatski, December 19, 1950, Yankev Shatski Archive, YIVO, New York.
19. Letter, April 28, 1952, Yankev Shatski Archive, YIVO, New York.
20. For a close reading of the first volume in *Dos poylishe yidntum* and an overview of the book series, see Jennifer Cazenave and Judith Lindenberg, "*Dos Poylishe Yidntum*: Testimony and Commemoration in the Aftermath of the Destruction," in *Twentieth-Century Yiddish*

Culture in Its European Context, ed. Marion Aptroot and Jan Schwarz (Dusseldorf: Dusseldorf University Press, forthcoming 2015).
21. M. Turkov, *Malke Ovshyany dertseylt . . . Khronik fun undzer tsayt, Dos poylishe yidntum* vol. 1 (Buenos Aires: Tsentral-farband fun poylishe yidn, 1946), 5–6.
22. Ibid., title page.
23. Y. Shatski, "*Yidish lebn in Argentine*," in *Shatski-bukh*, ed. Y. Lifshits (New York and Buenos Aires: YIVO, 1958), 319.
24. Ibid., 320.
25. Ibid.
26. Mark Turkov, "The Idea of the Book Series," in *Spetsyele oysgabe gevidmet der bikher serye dos poylishe yidntum* 25, p. 2.
27. Niger, "*Tendentsn in der nayester yidisher literatur*," 6.
28. Ibid., 7.
29. For an overview of post-Holocaust Yiddish life-writing, see my *Imagining Lives: Autobiographical Fiction of Yiddish Writers* (Madison: University of Wisconsin Press, 2005), ch. 5.
30. E. Lederhendler, *New York Jews and the Decline of Urban Ethnicity 1950–1970* (Syracuse, NY: Syracuse University Press, 2001), 66.
31. The review section at the back of Chaim Grade, *Sheyn fun farloshene shtern* (1950), *Dos poylishe yidntum* vol. 66, 188.
32. The review section at the back of Rokhl Korn, *Heym un heymlozikeyt* (1948), *Dos poylishe yidntum* vol. 39, 250.
33. See Philip Friedman's scholarly biography of Shatski, "*Yankev Shatskis ort in der mizrekh eyropeisher yiddisher geshikhte-shraybung*," in *Shatski-bukh*, 11–28.
34. *Shatski-bukh*, 127.
35. For the meaning of *mentalité* in an Eastern European Jewish context, see Gershon Hundert, *Jews in Poland-Lithuania in the Eighteenth Century: A Genealogy of Modernity* (Berkeley: University of California Press, 2004), 234–35.
36. Y. Shatski, "*Problemen fun yidisher historiografye*," lecture held at a YIVO conference, January 15, 1955, published in *Shatski-bukh*, 248. The expression is derived from the final section of the lecture: "What has happened to Jews is for a Jew not an objective material that exists outside him. The history of his people is his history. A piece of his own existence. The Jew responds to history as a personal matter. As a result, the contemporary Jew is against scholarship. Therefore he is either a believer in apologetics or an antischolar. The Jew is scientifically anti-historical. A Jew can only write history 'with anger and with bias'" (248).
37. Quoted in Friedman, "*Yankev Shatskis ort in der mizrekh eyropeisher yiddisher geshikhte-shraybung*," in *Shatski-bukh*, 26.
38. Max Weinreich's brief article in *Spetsyele oysgabe gevidmet der bikher serye dos poylishe yidntum* 25, p. 14.
39. L. Lehrer, "*Vegn der yidisher khurbn-bibliografye*," in *Bibliografye fun yidishe bikher vegn khurbn un gvure*, ed. J. Gar and P. Friedman (New York: Yad Vashem/YIVO, 1962), xv.
40. Y. Robinson, in *Bibliografye fun yidishe bikher vegn khurbn un gvure*, xii.
41. Philip Friedman, "*Di landmanshaftnliteratur in di fareynikte shtatn far di letste 10 yor*," in *Jewish Book Annual* 10 (1951–52), *pey-beys*, 82, Yiddish section.
42. A. Wein, "Memorial Books as a Source for Research into the History of Jewish Communities in Europe," *Yad Vashem Studies* 9 (1973): 256.
43. Ibid., 266.

44. "Until we document the historical, social, and political context in which the memorial books were created, we will never be able to distinguish between folk history and history." J. Kugelmass and J. Boyarin, "*Yizker bikher* and the Problem of Historical Veracity: An Anthropological Approach," in *The Jews of Poland between Two World Wars*, ed. Yisrael Gutman, Ezra Mendelsohn, Jehuda Reinharz, and Khone Shmeruk (Hanover, NH: University Press of New England, 1989), 536.
45. What is needed is a thorough examination of this multivolume genre which takes into account the specific context in which the books were created, published, and received. A. Polonsky, "Introduction—The Shtetl: Myth and Reality," *POLIN* 17 (2004): 12. This examination has been begun in the recently published *Memorial Books of Eastern European Jewry: Essays on the History and Meanings of Yizkor Volumes*, ed. Rosemary Horowitz (Jefferson, NC: McFarland Press, 2011).
46. See Appendix 1 for a complete list of the 175 volumes in the *Dos poylishe yidntum* book series. Twenty volumes to date have been translated into other languages (11.1% percent of the total). Ten volumes in the book series were translated from Hebrew, Polish, or Russian into Yiddish, and eight volumes were reprints of Yiddish books first published prior to the Holocaust in Poland and in the United States.
47. A few excerpts from . . . *Un di velt hot geshvign* have been made available in English translation in Jacob Glatshteyn, Israel Knox, and Samuel Margoshes, eds., *Anthology of Holocaust Literature* (Philadelphia: Jewish Publication Society, 1968); Irving Abrahamson, ed., *Against Silence: The Voice and Vision of Elie Wiesel*, 3 vols. (New York: Holocaust Library, 1985); Elie Wiesel, *All Rivers Run to the Sea: Memoirs* (New York: Knopf, 1995); and Wiesel, Preface to the New Translation, *Night* (New York: Hill and Wang, 2006).
48. Wiesel, *All Rivers Run to the Sea*, 239–40.
49. Wiesel, "An Interview Unlike Any Other," in *A Jew Today* (New York: Random House, 1978), 15.
50. Wiesel, *All Rivers Run to the Sea*, 277.
51. Ibid., 326.
52. For an analysis of the translation of the Yiddish work into French and English, see Naomi Seidman, "Elie Wiesel and the Scandal of Jewish Rage," *Jewish Social Studies* 3/1 (1996): 1–19, and *Faithful Renderings: Jewish-Christian Difference and the Politics of Translation* (Chicago: University of Chicago Press, 2006), 199–236. See also the recent article by Alan Astro, "Revisiting Wiesel's *Night* in Yiddish, French, and English," *Partial Answers: Journal of Literature and the History of Ideas* 12, no. 1 (2014): 127–53. Astro's article is a critique of Seidman's article that presents a very different picture of the relationship between Mauriac and Wiesel, contextualized as part of the French Jewish politics and culture of the 1950s. See also *Approaches to Teaching Wiesel's Night*, ed. Alan Rosen (New York: Modern Language Association of America, 2007).
53. According to the entry for Eliezer Vizel (Elie Wiesel) in *Leksikon fun der nayer yidisher literatur* (New York: Altveltlekhn yidishn kulturkongres, 1960), 329–30. See also Yechiel Szeintuch, "*Elie Wiesel un yidish: A 'totaler' shrayber*," *Forverts*, June 10–16, 2011.
54. Alan Astro, "Revisiting Wiesel's *Night* in Yiddish, French, and English," 140.
55. Wiesel, *All Rivers Run to the Sea*, 292.
56. Wiesel's quote in the entry for Katsetnik (Ka-Tzetnik) in *Leksikon fun der nayer yidisher literature*, 121.
57. *All Rivers Run to the Sea*, 230.
58. Ibid., 320.

59. Ibid.
60. See Astro's analysis of Mauriac's homoerotic desires as expressed in his relationship with the young Wiesel in "Revisiting Wiesel's *Night* in Yiddish, French, and English," 143–48.
61. Glatshteyn, Knox, and Margoshes, eds., *Anthology of Holocaust Literature*, and David G. Roskies, ed., *The Literature of Destruction: Jewish Responses to Catastrophe* (Philadelphia: Jewish Publication Society, 1989).
62. See David G. Roskies, *Against the Apocalypse: Responses to Catastrophe in Modern Jewish Culture* (Cambridge, MA: Harvard University Press, 1984), 263–63 and 301–2. It was Naomi Seidman's 1996 article, "Elie Wiesel and the Scandal of Jewish Rage," that initiated a wide-ranging debate about the various versions of Wiesel's Holocaust memoir.
63. Naomi Diamant and David G. Roskies, *Holocaust Literature: A History and Guide* (Waltham, MA: Brandeis University Press, 2012), 242.
64. Mark Turkov, *Di letste fun a groysn dor* (1954), *Dos poylishe yidntum* vol. 100, 350.

Chapter 5

1. Published in A. Glantz-Leyeles, *Velt un vort: Literarishe un andere eseyen* (New York: Tsiko, 1958), 290.
2. Yehoshue Perle, *"Khurbn varshe,"* in *Tvishn lebn un toyt*, ed. Bernard Mark (Warsaw: Yidish-bukh, 1955), 100–141. See also Mark's study, *Di umgekumene shrayber fun getos un lagern* (Warsaw: Yidish-bukh, 1954). David Roskies's introduction to Yehoshue Perle, *Everyday Jews: Scenes from a Vanished Life* (New Haven, CT: Yale University Press, 2007), offers the best biographical introduction to the author's work in English. See also Samuel Kassow, "Shie (Yehoshua) Perle: The Accuser," in *Who Will Write Our History? Emanuel Ringelblum, the Warsaw Ghetto, and the Oyneg Shabes Archive* (Bloomington: Indiana University Press, 2007), 193–98.
3. David Roskies, "What Is Holocaust Literature?" in *Studies in Contemporary Jewry 21: Jews, Catholics, and the Burden of History*, ed. Eli Lederhendler (Oxford: Oxford University Press, 2005), 198. See Bernard Mark, "*Yudenratishe ahaves-Yisroel: An entfer afn bilbl fun H. Levick,*" *Bleter far geshikhte* 5, no. 3 (1952): 63–115. H. Leivick, "*Tsvey dokumentn,*" *Der tog*, March 17, 1952, and "*Der tog-bukh fun a kodesh,*" *Der tog*, March 31, 1952. See also H. Leivick, "*Gvure fun di getos,*" in *Eseyen un redes* (New York: Alveltlekhen Yidishn Kultur-Kongres, 1963), 411–14.
4. See Gabriel Finder, Natalia Aleksiun, Antony Polonsky, and Jan Schwarz, eds., *POLIN: Studies in Polish Jewry*, vol. 20, *Making Holocaust Memory* (Oxford: Littman Library of Jewish Civilization, 2008), particularly the articles by Finder, Aleksiun, and Boaz Cohen.
5. See Zachary Baker, "Yiddish Publishing after 1945," in *Yiddish after the Holocaust*, ed. Joseph Sherman (Oxford: Boulevard, 2004), 63.
6. See entry for "Bernard Mark," *Leksikon fun der nayer yidisher literatur* (New York: Altveltlekhn yidishn kultur-kongres, 1963), 507–10. Mark's prolific output after the Holocaust is listed in *Bibliografye fun yidishe bikher vegn khurbn un gvure*, ed. J. Gar and P. Friedman (New York: Yad Vashem/YIVO, 1962). About Mark, see also David G. Roskies and Naomi Diamant, eds., *Holocaust Literature: A History and Guide* (Waltham, MA: Brandeis University Press, 2012), 90–91.
7. Irving Howe, *A Margin of Hope: An Intellectual Autobiography* (New York: Harcourt, Brace, Jovanovich, 1982), 260–64. See also Deborah E. Lipstadt, *The Eichmann Trial* (New York: Schocken, 2011).

8. Bernard Mark, "*Dos yidishe lebn un di yidishe literatur in poyln in di yorn 1937–1957*," in *IKUF almanakh* (New York: Yidisher kultur farband, 1961), 60–86.
9. See Magdalena Ruta's introduction to *Nisht bay di taykhn fun bovl* (Not at the Rivers of Babylon) (Krakow: Ksiegarnia Akademicka, 2012), xxxiii–xlviii.
10. Yosl Rakover, "*Yosl Rakover redt tsu got*," *Di goldene keyt* 18 (1954): 102–10. Zvi Kolitz, "Yossel Rakover's Appeal to God" (a new translation, with afterword by Jeffrey V. Mallow and Franz Jozef van Beeck), *Cross Currents* (Fall 1994): 362–77. Michal Borwicz, "*Der apokrif unter nomen 'Yosl Rakover redt tsu got,'*" *Almanakh* (Paris) (1955): 193–203.
11. Melekh Ravitsh, *Di kroynung fun a yungn yidishn dikhter in amerike: Poeme* (New York: Dovid Ignatov Literatur Fond, 1953), 32 and 44.
12. Ibid., v.
13. Ibid., 69.
14. This corresponds to the Hebrew year 5714, which began on Rosh Hashanah in September 1953. The Hebrew year is what appears on the copyright page of most Yiddish books published at the time.
15. Among the titles published by Yiddish writers in the immediate post-Holocaust era were Reuven Ayzland's *Fun undzer friling: Literarishe zikhroynes un portretn* (From Our Springtime: Literary Memoirs and Portraits, 1953); Leyeles's *Kholem tvishn volknkratsers* (Dreaming Amid Skyscrapers, 1948); and I. J. Shvarts's *Yunge yorn: Poeme* (Young Years: Poem, 1952).
16. Michael P. Kramer and Hana Wirth-Nesher, *The Cambridge Companion to Jewish American Literature* (Cambridge: Cambridge University Press, 2003), 3.
17. Arthur Hertzberg, *A Jew in America: My Life and a People's Struggle for Identity* (New York: HarperCollins, 2002), 204.
18. For a discussion of Yiddish as a "culture of retrieval," see Eli Lederhendler, *New York Jews and the Decline of Urban Ethnicity* (Syracuse, NY: Syracuse University Press, 2001), 69–78.
19. New York at this point became the world's largest Yiddish literary center, publishing approximately 75 books out of an annual world total of about 140 to 150 between the years 1950 and 1960. See Lederhendler, *New York Jews and the Decline of Urban Ethnicity*, 29.
20. See Peter Novick, *The Holocaust in American Life* (New York: Houghton Mifflin Company, 2000), which, however, mostly ignores the prolific output of Yiddish material on the Holocaust in the United States. Seminal Holocaust memoirs and novels were made available in English translation in the early 1960s: Elie Wiesel's *Night* (1960), Primo Levi's *Survival in Auschwitz* (1960), and Andre Schwarz-Bart's *The Last of the Just* (1960). Moreover, as Jules Chametsky points out, "even though detailed accounts of the genocide had surfaced in America as early as 1943, in the Black Book of Polish Jewry, along with diaries and memoirs from the 1940s onward, it was not until 1961 that studies such as Raul Hilberg's *The Destruction of the European Jews* and Gerald Reitlinger's *The Final Solution* reached a wide audience" (Jules Chametsky, John Felstiner, Hilene Flanzbaum, and Kathryn Hellerstein, eds., *Jewish American Literature: A Norton Anthology* [New York: Norton, 2001], 582). See also Hasia Diner, *We Remember with Reverence and Love: American Jews and the Myth of Silence after the Holocaust, 1945–1962* (New York: New York University Press, 2009), which significantly challenges "the myth of silence." The most recent book-length discussion of this topic is David Cesarani and Eric J. Sundquist, eds., *After the Holocaust: Challenging the Myth of Silence* (London: Routledge, 2012).
21. Judd L. Teller, "Yiddish Litterateurs and American Jews: Have They Come to a Parting of the Ways?" *Commentary* 18, no. 1 (July 1954): quotes from 39–40. See also David G. Roskies,

"What Is Holocaust Literature?," 172–82, which delineates the response to the Holocaust in the Yiddish press and literature in America and elsewhere.

22. Hasia Diner, in *We Remember with Reverence and Love,* presents a variety of documentation for the importance of Holocaust commemoration among mostly non-Yiddish-speaking Jewish Americans in the 1940s and 1950s. In contrast, Holocaust commemoration was more than important for Yiddish culture in America post-1945; it was its raison d'être.

23. A. Mukdoni, "Yidishe kultur in amerike," *Di goldene keyt* 17 (1953): 184–96; *Di goldene keyt* 18 (1954): 113–25; *Di goldene keyt* 19 (1954): 172–84; and *Di goldene keyt* 20 (1954): 240–52.

24. Mukdoni, "Yidishe kultur in amerike," *Di goldene keyt* 17 (1953): 189.

25. Shaye Miller, *In di shvartse pintelekh* (New York: M. Sh. Shklarski, 1953), 12.

26. Yankev Glatshteyn, *Selected Poems of Yankev Glatshteyn,* trans. Richard J. Fein (Philadelphia: Jewish Publication Society, 1987), 139–41. I changed Fein's translation of the term "*anshe-kneses hagdoyle*" to Great Convocation. The Hebrew words refer to the ruling body of religious leaders during the Second Temple period.

27. Yankev Glatshteyn, "*Faran aza gekekhts vi hunger,*" in *Fun mayn gantser mi* (New York: Martin Press, 1956), 185.

28. Irving Howe, *A Margin of Hope,* 260, 263, 265.

29. Irving Howe and Eliezer Greenberg, eds., *A Treasury of Yiddish Stories* (New York: Viking Press, 1954), 2.

30. Ibid., 38.

31. See Jeffrey Shandler, *Adventures in Yiddishland: Postvernacular Language and Culture* (Berkeley: University of California Press, 2006), 109–10.

32. See Anita Norich, *Discovering Exile: Yiddish and Jewish American Culture during the Holocaust* (Stanford, CA: Stanford University Press, 2007), 96–121.

33. Saul Bellow, *The Adventures of Augie March* (New York: Viking, 1953), 3.

34. See my article "Second City: Jewish Culture in Chicago," in *Zutot: Perspectives on Jewish Culture,* vol. 3, ed. Shlomo Berger, Michael Brocke, and Irene Zwiep (Amsterdam: Brill, 2003), 142–49.

35. *Di goldene keyt* 17 (1953), 196.

36. *The Forward,* Jonathan Rosen's interview with Saul Bellow, October 27, 2001. Later in his career Bellow began to address the Holocaust in works such as *Mr. Sammler's Planet* (1970) and the story "Something to Remember Me By" (1990). This is acknowledged by Saul Bellow in his retrospective mea culpa in a private letter to Cynthia Ozick, from July 19, 1987: "I was too busy becoming a novelist to take note of what was happening in the Forties. I was involved with 'literature' and given over to preoccupations with art, with language, with my struggle on the American scene, with claims for recognition of my talent or, like my pals of the *Partisan Review,* with modernism, Marxism, New Criticism, with Eliot, Yeats, Proust, etc.—with anything except the terrible events in Poland. Growing slowly aware of this unspeakable evasion I didn't even know how to begin to admit it into my inner life. Not a particle of this can be denied. And can I really say—can anyone say—what was to be done, how this 'thing' ought to have been met?" (Saul Bellow, *Letters,* ed. Benjamin Taylor [New York: Viking, 2010], 439).

37. See Morris Dickstein, *Leopards in the Temple: The Transformation of American Fiction, 1945–1970* (Cambridge, MA: Harvard University Press, 2002) and idem, "The Complex Fate of the Jewish American Writers," in *A Mirror in the Roadway: Literature and the Real World,* ed. Morris Dickstein (Princeton, NJ: Princeton University Press, 2005), 168–83.

38. A. Leyeles, *Velt un vort: Literarishe un andere eseyen,* 286.

39. Leivick, "*Tsu Amerike*," in *American Yiddish Poetry: A Bilingual Anthology*, trans. Benjamin Harshav, ed. Benjamin and Barbara Harshav (Berkeley: University of California Press, 1986), 767.
40. Irving Howe, *World of Our Fathers* (New York: Harcourt, Brace, Jovanovich, 1976), 456. Roskies makes the same point in "What Is Holocaust Literature?" 62.
41. Mani Leib, "A Plum," trans. John Hollander, in *The Penguin Book of Modern Yiddish Verse*, ed. Irving Howe, Ruth R. Wisse, and Khone Shmeruk (New York: Viking, 1987), 134–35.
42. Eliezer Greenberg, "*Di yidishe literatur un di literatur af english*," *Di goldene keyt* 18 (1954): 181.
43. B. Rivkin, *Lebn un shafn* (Chicago: Farlag L. M. Shteyn, 1953).
44. Rivkin's main work, a collection of essays written from the 1930s until his death in 1945, was published posthumously in *Grunt tendentsn fun der yidisher literatur in America* (Main Trends of Yiddish Literature in America), ed. Mina Bordo-Rivkin (New York: Ikuf, 1948). The title indicates Rivkin's debt to the Danish critic Georg Brandes's work, *Main Trends in Nineteenth-Century Literature*, from 1872.
45. B. Rivkin, *Lebn un shafn*, 229.
46. Article by Mayzil in B. Rivkin, *Lebn un shafn*, 231.
47. B. Rivkin, *Grunt-tendentsn fun der yidisher literatur in amerike*, 301 and 264.
48. Dan Miron, *From Continuity to Contiguity: Toward a New Jewish Literary Thinking* (Stanford, CA: Stanford University Press, 2010), 179. For a discussion of Borekh Rivkin's critical views, see my article, "'Such a Rag-Bag': The Historical Novel as Spectacle, Neo-Hasidic Hagiography, and Pseudo-Territory," in *Joseph Opatoshu: A Yiddish Writer Between Europe and America* (Studies in Yiddish 11), ed. Sabine Koller, Gennady Estraykh, and Mikhail Krutikov (London: Legenda, 2013), 107–8. See also "Reflections on Yiddish World Literature (1938–1939)," a selection of Rivkin's critical essays, included as chapter 7 of *World Literature in Theory*, ed. David Damrosch (New York: Wiley Blackwell, 2014).
49. See Wirth-Nesher and Kramer, eds., *Cambridge Companion to Jewish American Literature*, 218: "In America of the 1950s Jews could carve out a comfortable place for themselves in the American landscape as white European children of immigrants who practiced Judaism."
50. See Avrom Sutzkever, "*Rede afn simpoziom 'Yisroel, der yiddisher shrayber, un di yidishe velt,'*" *Di goldene keyt* 19 (1954): 220.
51. Miron, *From Continuity to Contiguity: Toward a New Jewish Literary Thinking*, 257.

Chapter 6

1. Benjamin and Barbara Harshav, *American Yiddish Poetry: A Bilingual Anthology* (Berkeley: University of California Press, 1986), 53.
2. Abraham Joshua Heschel, "After Majdanek: On Aaron Zeitlin's New Poems," trans. Morris M. Faierstein, in "Abraham Joshua Heschel and the Holocaust," *Modern Judaism* 19.3 (1999): appendix 1, p. 264; Heschel essay originally published in *Yidisher kemfer* 29, no. 779 (October 1, 1948); see www.academia.edu/1327652/Abraham_Joshua_Heschel_and_the_Holocaust.
3. Ibid., 267. (The original Yiddish poem is included in Aaron Zeitlin, *Gezamlte lider*, vol. 2 [New York: Farlag matones, 1947], 472–73.)
4. Ibid., 267.
5. *I Keep Recalling: The Holocaust Poems of Jacob Glatstein*, trans. Barnett Zumoff (New York: KTAV Publishing House, 1993), 4–5.

6. Gabriel Weinreich, "Remembering Dr. Max Weinreich," in *YIVO-Bleter: Naye Serye, Band III. Khurbn-Lite* (New Series, Volume III: The Holocaust in Lithuania), ed. David E. Fishman and Avrom Nowersztern (New York: YIVO Institute for Jewish Research, 1997), 344.
7. Ibid., 346.
8. Max Weinreich, letter to Avrom Sutzkever, 1947, "*Briv fun Maks Vaynraykh tsu Avrom Sutzkever,*" *Di goldene keyt* 95/96 (1978): 171–203. See also Kalman Weiser, "Coming to America: Max Weinreich and the Emergence of YIVO's American Center," in *Choosing Yiddish: New Frontiers of Language and Culture*, ed. Lara Rabinovitch, Shiri Goren, and Hannah S. Pressman (Detroit, MI: Wayne State University Press, 2013), 253–76.
9. Max Weinreich, *Hitler's Professors: The Part of Scholarship in Germany's Crimes Against the Jewish People*, 2d ed., with an introduction by Martin Gilbert (New Haven, CT: Yale University Press, 1999), 9.
10. Ibid., 241. In the Yiddish original the phrase *muktse-makhmes-mies* refers to the religious concept that something is excluded and not permitted because it is ugly, applying the word to Nazi literature.
11. Ibid., 242.
12. Hannah Arendt, review, "*The Black Book: The Nazi Crime Against the Jewish People*; and *Hitler's Professors*, by Max Weinreich," *Commentary* (September 1946), http://www.commentarymagazine.com/article/the-black-book-the-nazi-crime-against-the-jewish-people-and-hitlers-professors-by-max-weinreich/, accessed September 6, 2014.
13. Ibid.
14. See Max Weinreich, *History of the Yiddish Language*, vol. 1 (New Haven, CT: Yale University Press, 2008), 175–246.
15. Jerold C. Frakes, "Introduction: Permeable Cultural Borders and Yiddish-German Encounters," in *Between Two Worlds: Yiddish-German Encounters*, ed. Jeremy Dauber and Jerold C. Frakes, *Studia Rosenthaliana* 41 (Amsterdam: Peeters, 2009), 8.
16. Max Weinreich, "*Vos heyst shraybn yidishlekh?*" in *Yidishe shprakh* 2, no. 4 (July–August 1942): 101.
17. Ibid., 112.
18. Avrom Sutzkever, "*Mayn eydes-zogn farn nirnberger tribunal: Togbukh-notitsn,*" in *Baym leyenen penimer: Dertseylungen. Dermonungen. Eseyen* (Jerusalem: Hebrew University Press, 1993), 151.
19. Yankev Glatshteyn, *Selected Poems of Yankev Glatshteyn*, trans. Richard J. Fein (Philadelphia: Jewish Publication Society, 1987), 85. In his translation Fein maintains the rhyme and rhythm but does not attempt to create an English equivalent to Glatshteyn's brilliant use of German and *daytshmerizm*.
20. See Janet Hadda, "German and Yiddish in the Poetry of Jacob Glatstein," *Prooftexts* 1, no.1 (1981): 197.
21. Jacob Glatstein, *I Keep Recalling: The Holocaust Poems of Jacob Glatstein*, 92.
22. Glatshteyn, *Selected Poems of Yankev Glatshteyn*, 125.
23. See "An American Yiddish Poet Visits Poland, 1934," in my *Imagining Lives: Autobiographical Fiction of Yiddish Writers* (Madison: University of Wisconsin Press, 2005), 103.
24. Glatshteyn's *Emil un Karl*, a book for young readers published in 1940, uses a realist documentary style to depict the Viennese population's anti-Semitic assault on Jews in 1938, after the Anschluss. It was translated by Jeffrey Shandler as *Emil and Karl* (New Milford, CT: Roaring Brook, 2006). See Jeffrey Shandler, "The Holocaust for Beginners: Yankev

Glatshteyn's *Emil un Karl* and Other Wartime Works for Young American Yiddish Readers," *MELUS: Multi-Ethnic Literature of the U.S.* 37, no. 2 (Summer 2012): 109–30.
25. Yankev Glatshteyn, "*Der shverer veg,*" in *In tokh genumen, eseyen 1945–1947* (New York: Matones, 1947), 427. Translated in *American Yiddish Poetry: A Bilingual Anthology,* ed. Benjamin and Barbara Harshav, 804.
26. Judd L. Teller, "Yiddish Litterateurs and American Jews: Have They Come to a Parting of the Ways?" *Commentary* 18, no. 1 (July 1954): 39–40.
27. The article is signed "The editors" (Glatshteyn, Shmuel Niger, and Hillel Rogoff). However, the style of the article makes it clear that its author was Glatshteyn. *Finf un zibetsik yor yidishe prese in Amerike, 1870–1945* (New York: Y. L. Peretz shrayber fareyn, 1945), 5–8.
28. Ibid., 5.
29. Ibid., 6.
30. Ibid.
31. The translations of the poem are mine. The poem can be found in *Shtralndike yidn* (New York: Farlag Matones, 1946), 81–88. Quotes here and in the following extracts are from pp. 84, 86.
32. Ibid.
33. The tapes are stored in the Jewish Public Library in Montreal. They include interviews and readings of V. Shtiker, Berish Vaynshteyn, Yankev Glatshteyn, H. Leivick, Eliezer Greenberg, Rokhl Korn, Naftule Gross, Melekh Ravitsh, Ephraim Auerbach, Berta Klung, A. Glants-Leyeles, Aaron Zeitlin, Kadya Molodovsky, Yosef Rolnik, Nokhem Barukh Minkoff, Itsik Manger, and Chaim Grade. Some of the interviews were published in *Der yidisher kemfer, Di tsukunft,* and *Di goldene keyt,* but, unlike Yankev Pat's *Shmuesn mit yidishe shrayber* (1954), they were never collected in book form. I have located an abridged English translation by Joseph C. Landis, "Conversation with Jacob Glatstein," *YIDDISH* 1 (1973): 40–53; A. Tabatshnik, "*A. Tabatshnik: Fun a shmues mit Arn Tseytlin,*" *Di goldene keyt* 65 (1969): 17–33; and A. Glants Leyeles, "*Mayn lid in der yidisher poezye,*" in idem, *Baym fus fun barg: Lider un poemes* (New York: CYCO Bikher farlag, 1957), 9–39. A typewritten version of Tabatshnik's interview with Rokhl Korn is located in the Yankev Glatshteyn archive in YIVO. It is possible to listen to most of the interviews in the Yiddish Book Center's Frances Brandt On-Line Yiddish Audio Library, http://archive.org/search.php?query=Tabachnick%20AND%20mediatype%3Aaudio
34. Avrom-Ber Tabatshnik (1901–70) immigrated to the United States in 1921 after attending *kheder* and a Russian *mitlshul* (gymnasia, or high school) in Mohilyev-Podolsk, Ukraine. He completed high school in 1922 and worked as a teacher in the Workmen's Circle schools in New York and Boston. Between 1936 and 1938 he was affiliated with the WPA (Works Progress Administration), working on the *Universal Jewish Encyclopedia;* from 1941, Tabatshnik was a staff member of the Jewish Telegraphic Agency. His debut as a Yiddish poet came in the journal *Proletarisher gedank* (Proletarian Thought) in 1923, following an aborted attempt at writing Russian poetry. Until his death in 1970, he published poems and critical articles in a variety of Yiddish journals and newspapers. His main contributions to Yiddish letters were his two books of poetry; a five-hundred-page collection of critical essays, *Dikhter un dikhtung* (1965); and *The Recorded Anthology: The Voice of the Yiddish* Poet (circa 1950s). Tabatshnik was affiliated with *Di yunge,* whose leading critical voice he became in the 1920s. See entry for Tabatshnik in *Leksikon fun der nayer yidisher literature* (New York: Alveltlekher yidisher kultur-kongres, 1961), 1–3.
35. Avrom Tabatshnik, *Dikhter un dikhtung* (New York: A. Tabatshnik, 1965), 417.

36. Ibid., 415.
37. Ibid., 417.
38. Ibid.
39. Ibid.
40. Ibid., 77.
41. Ibid., 403. The lecture is available in a reliable translation by Cynthia Ozick in Irving Howe and Eliezer Greenberg, eds., *Voices from the Yiddish: Essays, Memoirs, Diaries* (Ann Arbor: University of Michigan Press, 1972), 289–99. The quote is from p. 291.
42. Tabatshnik, *Dikhter un dikhtung*, 407; *Voices from the Yiddish*, 294. Tabatshnik belongs to an influential trend in Jewish literary criticism represented by Dan Miron, Gershon Shaked, and David G. Roskies in their view of Jewish poetic modernism as "conservative revolutionary" (Miron) and "revolutionary traditionalist" (Shaked). See Roskies, *A Bridge of Longing: The Lost of Art of Yiddish Storytelling* (Cambridge, MA: Harvard University Press 1995), 9.
43. Tabatshnik, *Dikhter un dikhtung*, 413; *Voices from the Yiddish*, 298.
44. A list of the poems is available at the Jewish Public Library in Montreal.
45. This final section of the interview was excluded from Landis's translation, "A Conversation with Jacob Glatstein" (1973).
46. The recording of the full interview with Glatshteyn is available in the National Yiddish Book Center's Frances Brandt Online Yiddish Audio Archive, "Jacob Glatstein interviewed by Abraham Tabatshnick, part 2." https://archive.org/details/JacobGlatstein InterviewedByAbrahamTabachnickPart2; accessed July 28, 2014. Yiddish transcription and translation of the Glatshteyn quotes from the interview are mine.
47. Ibid.
48. Ibid.
49. Landis, "A Conversation with Jacob Glatstein," 43.
50. https://archive.org/details/JacobGlatsteinInterviewedByAbrahamTabachnickPart2, accessed July 28, 2014. Yiddish transcription and translation of the Glatshteyn quotes from the interview are mine. Shachar Pinsker points out that Glatshteyn rejected the modernist manifestos by the members of Yung Yisroel because of his turn to a more commemorative poetic stance after the Holocaust: "Thus, although he clearly identified the inventiveness and originality in the poetry of Rinzler, Binyomin, and Fishman, as well as the stories of Birshtein, he could not tolerate the ideological aspects of this Israeli-modernist Yiddish literature." Shachar Pinsker, "Choosing Yiddish in Israel: *Yung Yisroel* between Home and Exile, the Center and the Margins," in *Choosing Yiddish*, ed. Rabinovitch, Goren, and Pressman, 290. For a discussion of Glatshteyn's important 1938 poem, *"A gute nakht, velt,"* and prose works from 1938 and 1940, see Anita Norich, "Yankev Glatshteyn's Ambivalent Farewell," in *Discovering Exile: Yiddish and Jewish American Culture during the Holocaust* (Stanford, CA: Stanford University Press, 2007), 42–74.
51. The poem is included in *Fun mayn gantser mi* (New York: Martin Press, 1956), 106–7. It was translated by Richard J. Fein in *With Everything We've Got: A Personal Anthology of Yiddish Poetry* (Austin, TX: Host Publications, 2009), 110–15.
52. Yankev Glatshteyn, *"A zuntik iber nuy york,"* in *With Everything We've Got: A Personal Anthology of Yiddish Poetry*, 111.
53. Ibid., 115.
54. Ibid.
55. Glatshteyn, *Selected Poems*, 124–25.

56. *Fun mayn gantser mi*, 82; my translation.
57. Landis, "A Conversation with Jacob Glatstein," 43.
58. Glatstein, *I Keep Recalling: The Holocaust Poems of Jacob Glatstein*.
59. Ibid., 286–87.
60. Christopher Hutton, "Normativism and the Notion of Authenticity in Yiddish Linguistics," in *The Field of Yiddish: Studies in Language, Folklore, and Literature*, 5th edition, ed. David Goldberg (Evanston, IL: Northwestern University Press, 1993), 47.
61. Ibid., 49.
62. Glatsteyn, *Selected Poems*, 200–201. The third line is my translation. "*Mayn kinds-kinds fargangnheyt*" (*Shtralndike yidn*, 1946). See also Richard Fein's perceptive comments in his introduction to *Selected Poems*: "Glatshteyn's was an artistic dedication maintained in the face of a cultural tragedy that even writers in totalitarian regimes do not have to confront. Glatshteyn insisted on his own standards in the face of the end. He must have also known that this was the only way the poetry could outlive its vanishing cultural context" (xxiv).
63. Glatstein, *I Keep Recalling*, xxi (italics added).
64. Exodus 17:14 and Deuteronomy 25:17, 19.
65. The Yankev Glatshteyn Archive in YIVO.
66. Irving Howe, *A Margin of Hope: An Intellectual Autobiography* (New York: Harcourt Brace, 1982), 264.
67. The letter was written as a Memo to Mr. Phil Baum, Yankev Glatshteyn Archive, YIVO.
68. See Arthur Hertzberg, *A Jew in America: My Life and a People's Struggle for Identity* (New York: HarperCollins, 2002).
69. *Di goldene keyt* 65 (1969): 33. See also Tabatshnik, "*Y. Bashevis der kritiker un Arn Tseytlin der poet*," in *Dikhter un dikhtung*, 486–97.
70. Aaron Zeitlin, *Ale lider un poemes: Lider fun khurbn un lider fun gloybn*, vol.1 (New York: Bergen-Belsen Memorial Press, 1967), 169.
71. Yechiel Szeintuch, "*Arn tseytlins ani-maamin (tsvey briv tsu shmuel niger)*," *Di goldene keyt* 112 (1983): 168. See also Aaron Zeitlin, "*Mayn foter*," in Hillel Zeitlin, *Reb nakhmen barslaver: Der zeer fun podolye* (New York: Farlag matones, 1952), 11–51.
72. Aaron Zeitlin, "*Varshe, 1912*," in *Gezamlte lider*, vol. 1, 119–20.
73. Ibid., 121. The previous three quotes from the poem "*Varshe, 1912*."
74. Ibid., 119.
75. Ibid., 120.
76. For a discussion of Peretz's centrality in Yiddish culture post-1945, see Anita Norich, "From the Politics of Culture to the Culture of Mourning," in *Discovering Exile*, 96–121.
77. Zeitlin, *Ale lider un poemes*, 42.
78. See Aaron Zeitlin, "*Perets un zayn baynakht afn altn mark*," in *Literarishe un filosofishe eseyen* (New York: Alveltlechn yidishn kultur, 1980), 15–21.
79. Zeitlin, *Ale lider un poemes*, 85. On Aaron Zeitlin's poetry, see Yechiel Szeintuch, ed., *Bereshut-harabim un bereshut-hayekhid: Arn Zeitlin un di yidishe literatur* (Jerusalem: Hebrew University Press, 2000); Emanuel S. Goldsmith, "Aaron Zeitlin (1898–1973)," in *Holocaust Literature: An Encyclopedia of Writers and Their Work*, 2 vols., ed. S. Lillian Kremer (New York: Routledge, 2003), 1352–59, and Introduction, xxxv–xxxvi. For a good literal English translation of Zeitlin's Holocaust poetry, see *Poems of the Holocaust and Poems of Faith*, ed. and trans. Morris M. Faierstein (New York: iUniverse, 2007). See also Abraham Joshua Heschel, "After Majdanek: On Aaron Zeitlin's New Poems," trans. Morris M. Faierstein, in Faierstein, "Abraham Joshua Heschel and the Holocaust," appendix 1 (see note 2, above).

80. *The Penguin Book of Modern Yiddish Verse,* trans. Howard Friend, ed. Irving Howe, Ruth R. Wisse, and Khone Shmeruk (New York: Viking, 1987), 538.
81. Hana Wirth-Nesher, *City Codes: Reading the Modern Urban Novel* (Cambridge: Cambridge University Press, 1996), 207.
82. Edward Said, *Reflections on Exile and Other Essays* (Cambridge, MA: Harvard University Press, 2000), 186.
83. Zeitlin, *Ale lider un poemes,* 49; my translation.

Chapter 7

1. Cynthia Ozick, "Envy; or, Yiddish in America" (1969), in *The Pagan Rabbi and Other Stories* (New York: Knopf, 1971), 57.
2. Yankev Glatshteyn, "*Zing ladino*" (1937) in *Fun mayn gantser mi* (New York: Martin Press, 1956), 291.
3. The audio recordings that have been made available by the 92nd Street Y include: Yankev Glatshteyn (1896–71), 1/7/1963; Isaac Bashevis Singer (1904–91), 10/27/1963; Gabriel Preil (1911–93), 2/10/1964 (Hebrew); Avrom Sutzkever (1913–2010), 2/20/1964; Kadya Molodovsky (1894–1975), 4/20/1964; Eisig Silberschlag (1903–88), 12/8/1964 (Hebrew); Eliezer Greenberg (1896–1977), 1/5/1965; Rokhl Korn (1898–1982), 1/26/1965; Joseph Rubinstein (1905–78), 3/4/1965; Aaron Zeitlin (1899–1973), 4/14/1965 (Hebrew/Yiddish); Itsik Manger (1901–69), 4/28/1965; Israel Efros (1891–1981), 4/14/ 1966 (Hebrew); Leib Feinberg (1897–1969), 5/11/1966 (Hebrew); Yankev Glatshteyn (1896–1971), 11/2/1966; I. J. Schwartz (1885–1971), 1/4/1967; Gabriel Preil (1911–93), 2/1/1967 (Hebrew/Yiddish); Dovid Einhorn (1886–1973), 11/19/1967; Chava Rosenfarb (1923–2011), 1/7/1968; Menke Katz (1906–91) and Meyer Ziml Tkatch (1894–?), 2/18/1968; Rosa Gutman-Jasny (1903–?) and Rochelle Weprinsky (1893–1981), 4/7/1968; Eliezer Greenberg (1896–1977) and Moyshe Shteingart (1912–?), 5/5/1968. Treasury of Yiddish Poetry, introduced by Irving Howe; readings in Yiddish by Glatshteyn, Greenberg, Korn, and Molodovsky; translations read by John Hollander, Carolyn Kizer, Stanley Kunitz, Cynthia Ozick, Adrienne Rich, Amand Schwerner, Marie Syrkin, and Jean Valentine, 11/2/1969.

Other recorded Yiddish poetry events at the Y: Festive Opening of the Yiddish-Hebrew Poetry Series, 11/5/1967; Jewish Motifs in Yiddish Literature, 12/14/1969; Chaim Grade (1910–82), 1/12/1975; Avrom Sutzkever with translators of his work (Ruth Whitman and Benjamin and Barbara Harshav), 5/6/1991.

Non-recorded Yiddish and Hebrew poetry readings at the 92nd Street Y: Efraim Auerbach (1892–1973), 3/11/1963; Aaron Glantz-Leyeles (1889–1966), 11/17/1964; Rachel Zychlinsky (1910–2001), 11/30/1965; Berish Weinstein (1905–67), 1/12/1966; Meyer Shtiker (1905–83), 2/16/1966; Efraim Auerbach (1893–1973), 12/7/1966; Alef Katz (1899–1969), 3/1/1967; Berish Weinstein, 4/5/1967; Israel Emiot (1909–78) and Malka Lee (1904–76), 5/3/1967; Mattes Olitsky (1915–2008) and Ruth Whitman (1922–99), 3/17/1968; Festive Opening of Yiddish Poetry Series, 11/2/1968; Yankev Glatshteyn and Meyer Shtiker, (1905–83), 12/15/1968; Saul Maltz (1906–85) and Rachel Zychlinsky (1910–2001), 1/26/1969; Gabriel Preil (1911–93) and I. J. Schwartz (1885–1971), 2/23/1969; Zelig Dorfman (1905–?) and Mordechai Rothenberg (1920–?), 3/23/1969; Aaron Berger (1889–1979) and Joseph Rubinstein (1905–78), 4/20/1969; Israel Goichberg (1893–1970) and M. M. Shafir (1909–?), 5/11/1969; American Motifs in Yiddish Literature, 1/11/1970; Social Motifs in Yiddish Literature, 2/8/1970.

4. Lawrence Rosenwald, *Multilingual America: Language and the Making of American Literature* (Cambridge: Cambridge University Press, 2008), 158. See also Alan Mintz, *Sanctuary in the Wilderness: A Critical Introduction to American Hebrew Poetry* (Stanford, CA: Stanford University Press, 2011).
5. See M. Tsanin, *Herts Grosbard* (Tel Aviv: Farlag—Di mi un der onshtreng fun M. Tsanin vi s'iz geven der vuntsh fun Herts Grosbard un zayn tsavoe, 1995).
6. Charles Bernstein, ed., *Close Listening: Poetry and the Performed Word* (New York: Oxford University Press, 1998), 22.
7. "The most common form of performance in early-twentieth-century Russian Jewish communities was the spoken-word event—poetry readings, lectures, debates, public discussions, symposia, and conventions. In the annals of performing arts, the spoken-word event has received relatively little attention, dwarfed by its more extravagant cousins of theater and opera." Jeffrey Veidlinger, *Jewish Public Culture in the Late Russian Empire* (Bloomington: Indiana University Press, 2009), 141.
8. Bernstein, *Close Listening*, 10.
9. See Werner Sollors, "Introduction: After the Culture Wars; or, From 'English Only' to 'English Plus,'" in *Multilingual America: Transnationalism, Ethnicity, and the Languages of American Literature*, ed. Werner Sollors (New York: New York University Press, 1998), 1–13.
10. See Marjorie Perloff and Craig Dworkin, "The Sound of Poetry/The Poetry of Sound: The 2006 MLA Presidential Forum," *PLMA* 123, no. 3 (2008): 749–61. PennSound (www.writing.upenn.edu/pennsound), a site founded in January 2005 by the poet Charles Bernstein and scholar Al Filreis, is devoted to assembling an increasing number of recordings of American poetry read by the poets themselves. It is an excellent example of the on-line possibilities in the dissemination of poetry for teaching and research.
11. Benjamin and Barbara Harshav, eds., *American Yiddish Poetry: A Bilingual Anthology* (Berkeley: University of California Press, 1986), 801. Aaron Leyeles, "Yiddish Literature and the World," *In Zikh* (1937).
12. The demographic outlook in terms of Yiddish speakers and cultural activities looked less gloomy as a snapshot of the year 1960. That year fewer than a million U.S. Jews, or 17 percent of the Jewish population in the United States, declared Yiddish as their mother tongue (down from 2.5 million in 1930); 22 Yiddish periodicals, with a total circulation of 231,000, were published (20 periodicals with a circulation of 775,000 were published in 1930); 75 books were published by Yiddish writers in America, 26 of them published in other countries (in 1945, 86 books by Yiddish writers were published in America); there were 98 Yiddish afternoon schools with 4,000 students (down from 146 Yiddish schools with 7,000 students in 1945); 33 Yiddish radio programs were broadcast weekly for four hours (down from 46 Yiddish radio programs broadcasting 6 hours weekly in 1956). See Shikl Fishman, "*Di sotsiologye fun yidish in amerike: 1960–1970 un vayter*" (The Sociology of Yiddish in America: 1960–1970), *Di goldene keyt* 75 (1972): 110–27.
13. See my article "Yankev Glatshteyn," in *Dictionary of Literary Biography: Yiddish Literature*, vol. 333, ed. Joseph Sherman (New York: Bruccoli Clark Layman, 2007), 45–55.
14. Yitskhok Bashevis read from his work at eleven different events at the Y from 1963 to 1985. Only at the first event in 1963 did he read in Yiddish.
15. John Felstiner, "Jews Translating Jews," in *Jewish American Poetry: Poems, Commentary, and Reflections*, ed. Jonathan N. Barron and Eric Murphy Selinger (Hanover, NH: Brandeis University Press, 2000), 342.

16. Cynthia Ozick, "A Bintel Brief for Jacob Glatstein," *Jewish Heritage* (Spring 1972): 60.
17. Ibid.
18. Ibid.
19. Sh. Margoshes: "*di tsol iz geven in di dray tsifern—aza min oylem vos di gantse tsayt hob ikh zikh gedarft bagrisn mit dem, mit yenem*" (the number was in the hundreds—such an audience in which I had to say hello to people I knew), *Der tog*, January 14, 1963.
20. Naomi M. Jackson, *Converging Movements: Modern Dance and Jewish Culture at the 92nd Street* Y (Middletown, CT: Wesleyan University Press, 2000), 21.
21. William Kolodney, "History of the Educational Department YM-YWHA," Ed.D. diss., Teachers College, Columbia University, 1950, 73.
22. Ibid.
23. *New York Times*, February 8, 1961.
24. See Brukhe Lang Kaplan, "*Zvi Scooler: Der grammayster*," *YIVO Bleter, Band IV* (New York: YIVO, 2003), 193–235.
25. Yankev Glatshteyn Poetry Reading, January 7, 1963. Transcription of the audio recording made available by the 92nd Street Y.
26. See Borukh Rivkin, "*Kmoy-teritorye—bemokem religye*" (Would-Be Territory—In Place of Religion), in *Grunt-tendentsn fun der yidisher literatur in amerike* (New York: Ikuf Farlag 1948), 145–91.
27. Maeera Y. Shreiber, *Singing in a Strange Land: A Jewish American Poetics* (Stanford, CA: Stanford University Press, 2007), 18.
28. *Selected Poems of Yankev Glatshteyn*, trans. Richard J. Fein (Philadelphia: Jewish Publication Society, 1987), 68–69.
29. For a sample of Arnold Chekow's photographs of Yiddish writers at the 92nd Street Y and other venues, see Kathryn Hellerstein, "Famous Long Ago: Yiddish in New York, 1967–1972," with photographs by Arnold Chekow, *The Book Peddler* 18 (Spring 1993): 44–57.
30. Yankev Glatshteyn, "Singer's Literary Reputation," in *Recovering the Canon: Essays on Isaac Bashevis Singer*, ed. David Neal Miller (Leiden: E.J. Brill, 1986), 145; first published in *Congress Bi-Weekly* (New York) 32, December 27, 1965), 17–19.
31. Glatshteyn, "Singer's Literary Reputation," 147.
32. Ibid., 147.
33. Yankev Glatshteyn Poetry Reading, January 7, 1963. Transcription of the audio recording made available by the 92nd Street Y.
34. Glatshteyn, "Singer's Literary Reputation," 148.
35. Schreiber, *Singing in a Strange Land*, 15.
36. An English translation of Singer's introduction to his 1963 reading at the Y is available in the I. B. Singer archive at the Harry Ransom Center, University of Texas. A transcription of part of the Yiddish version is included as an appendix to my article, "Glatshteyn, Singer, Howe and Ozick: Performing Yiddish Poetry at the 92 Street Y, 1963–1969," *Prooftexts* 30 (2010): 61–96.
37. David Roskies, "Introduction," *Prooftexts: A Journal of Jewish Literary History* 9 (1989): 4.
38. Edward Alexander, *Irving Howe: Socialist, Critic, Jew* (Bloomington: Indiana University Press, 1998), 184.
39. Singer's novel *Shotn afn Hudson* (Shadows on the Hudson), serialized in the *Forverts* from January 1957 to January 1958, which depicted a group of Holocaust survivors on the Upper West Side, was published posthumously in English translation in 1998. In the 1960s Singer

addressed the Holocaust in comedic and fantastic modalities in the short story "The Cafeteria" (1968) and the novel *Enemies: A Love Story* (serialized in the *Forverts* in 1966 and published in English in 1972).
40. Kadya Molodovsky, *Likht fun dornboym* (Buenos Aires: Kiem, 1965), 143–44; my translation.
41. Kadya Molodovsky, "*Tsu der banayung fun der 'svive'*" (To the Renewal of *Svive*), *Svive*, (November 1960): back page.
42. Moyshe Shtarkman, "*Mishkn fun yidisher vort-kunst,*" *Svive* (September 1966): 44–51.
43. Kadya Molodovsky, "*Mendeles boyd in yugnt-tsenter af der 92ter gas,*" *Svive* (December 1964): 13. Although the downward turn in American Yiddish culture was evident, the 1960s still witnessed a variety of Yiddish cultural activities and a sizeable demographic base for continued development. In an article, the sociolinguist Joshua Fishman praised the multicultural and multilingual character of America, and mentioned that 10 percent of the population declared a mother tongue other than English in 1960. Nonetheless, the open American society and the push toward English-only education were inhospitable to the maintenance of Yiddish among first- and second-generation Jewish Americans. Shikl (Joshua) Fishman, "*Di sotsiologye fun yidish in amerike: 1960-1970 un vayter,*" *Di goldene keyt* 110/111 (1983): 75. New York, however, remained unique. As Eli Lederhendler points out, the city's special status set the city apart in terms of its numbers of Yiddish speakers and the depth and breadth of Yiddish cultural life: "New York was home to a much greater concentration of recent Jewish immigrants and their children than were other American communities." Lederhendler, *New York Jews and the Decline of Urban Ethnicity*, 105.
44. Eliezer Greenberg Poetry Reading, January 5, 1965. Transcription of the audio recording made available by the 92nd Street Y.
45. Festive Opening of the Yiddish-Hebrew Poetry Series, various artists, November 5, 1967. Transcription of audio recording made available by the 92nd Street Y.
46. Letter from Irving Howe to Galen Williams, July 20, 1969, 92nd Street Y archive.
47. Letter from Galen Williams to Irving Howe, November 13, 1969, 92nd Street Y archive. In another letter from Williams to Howe on March 28, 1969, he writes: "It would be very nice if we could include some of the Yiddish poets in person, although many have already read here. For instance Stanley Moss was amazed to learn that Joseph Rubenstein is alive and lives on FDR Drive! Adrienne was astonished to know that Kadya Molodowsky lives in New York City!" The reference to Stanley Kunitz appears in the same letter.
48. Letter from Galen Williams to Irving Howe, July 10, 1969, 92nd Street Y archive.
49. Anita Norich quoted in Eli Lederhendler, *New York Jews*, 70. The quote is from Anita Norich, *The Homeless Imagination in the Fiction of Israel Joshua Singer* (Bloomington: Indiana University Press, 1991), 8.
50. Ibid., 69.
51. Eliyahu Shulman, "*Iz meglekh a yidishe literatur af a nit-yidishe shprakh?*" (1971), in *Portretn un etyudn* (New York: Tsiko, 1979), 490.
52. Ozick, "A Bintel Brief for Jacob Glatstein," 60.
53. Ozick, "Envy," 97.
54. Cynthia Ozick, "America: Toward Yavneh," *Judaism* 19 (Summer 1970): 264–82; reprinted in *What Is Jewish Literature?* ed. Hana Wirth-Nesher (Philadelphia: Jewish Publication Society, 1994), 20–34. The essay was first delivered as a lecture at the Weizmann Institute in Rehovot, Israel, in the summer of 1970.
55. Irving Howe, *A Margin of Hope* (San Diego: Harcourt Brace Jovanovich, 1982), 267.

56. Ozick, "Envy," 62.
57. Jeffrey Shandler, *Adventures in Yiddishland: Postvernacular Language and Culture* (Berkeley: University of California Press, 2006), 116.
58. Ozick, "America: Toward Yavneh," 30.
59. Ibid., 31.
60. Morris Dickstein, "The Complex Fate of the Jewish Writer," in *A Mirror in the Roadway: Literature and the Real World* (Princeton, NJ: Princeton University Press, 2005), 181.
61. Naomi Seidman, *Faithful Renderings: Jewish-Christian Difference and the Politics of Translation* (Chicago: University of Chicago Press, 2006), 255.
62. Not until the year after Glatshteyn's death in 1971 was his poetry published in book form in English translation, in *The Selected Poems of Jacob Glatstein*, ed. and trans. Ruth Whitman (New York: October House, 1972).
63. *Selected Poems of Yankev Glatshteyn*, trans. Richard Fein, 58–59.
64. Cynthia Ozick, "America: Toward Yavneh," 20–34.
65. Ruth Wisse, "Language as Fate," *Studies in Contemporary Jewry* 12 (1996): 143.

Chapter 8

1. Chaim Grade, "Introduction," *Der shtumer minyen* (The Silent Quorum) (New York: Farlag Brider Shulzinger, 1976), not paginated.
2. Quoted in Donald R. Noble, "Isaac Bashevis Singer: Nobel Prize-Winning Novelist," in *Isaac Bashevis Singer: Conversations*, ed. Grace Farrell (Jackson: University Press of Mississippi, 1992), 166.
3. Alana Newhouse, "Dissent Greets Isaac Bashevis Singer Centennial," *New York Times*, June 17, 2004, section E, 1. In this article, Professor Alan Nadler (Drew University), who studied with Grade as a graduate student at Harvard University in the late 1970s, is quoted as saying: "Every fiber of Grade's being and everything he did—every line of poetry, every work of fiction—was animated by a sense of responsibility to the Jews: to their history, to the culture, to the people. None of those commitments resonate in my reading of Singer." See also Nadler's autobiographical piece about Grade, "Whoppers: A Former Student Remembers a Seminar with Chaim Grade and How It Changed His Life," *Tablet Magazine*, June 2, 2010, www.tabletmag.com/jewish-arts-and-culture/books/35006/whoppers; accessed July 30, 2014. See also Rabbi Emanuel Rackman (Bar Ilan University) and Stephen Wagner (Bar Ilan University), "Philo-Semitism in the Work of the Polish Nobel Laureate Czeslaw Milosz: He Pays Tribute to Jewish Literature," *Congressional Records*, October 11, 2001; and Czeslaw Milosz's entry about Grade in *Milosz's ABC* (New York: Farrar, Straus and Giroux, 2001.
4. Elie Wiesel, review of *The Agunah*, *New York Times*, September 1, 1974 (ProQuest Historical Newspapers: *The New York Times* [1851–2003]), 209. For a critical view of Grade's work see Ruth Wisse, "Religious Imperatives and Mortal Desires," *New York Times*, November 14, 1982 (ProQuest Historical Newspapers: *The New York Times* [1851–2003]), BR3, and "In Praise of Chaim Grade," *Commentary* (April 1977): 70–73.
5. Khayim Bez, "*Yitskhok Bashevis-Zingers kinstlerishe proze: Fragmentn fun a kritishn analiz*," in *Oyf di vegn fun der yidisher literatur* (On the Paths of Yiddish Literature) (Tel Aviv: Y. L. Peretz Farlag, 1980), 569.
6. Morris Dickstein, "The Jewish American Writer," in *A Mirror in the Roadway: Literature and the Real World* (Princeton, NJ: Princeton University Press, 2005), 170.

7. Chaim Grade, *The Well*, trans. Ruth Wisse (Philadelphia: Jewish Publication Society, 1967), 94.
8. Grade, *The Well*, 189, and *Der brunem*, in *Der shulhoyf: Dray dertseylungen* (New York: Yidish natsionaler arbeter-farband, 1958), 161.
9. *The Well*, 190, and *Der shulhoyf*, 161.
10. *The Well*, 191, and *Der shulhoyf*, 162.
11. *The Well*, 193, and *Der shulhoyf*, 164.
12. *The Well*, 194, and *Der shulfhoyf*, 164.
13. Chaim Grade's introduction to *Di agune* (New York: CYCO bikher farlag, 1961), 5.
14. See David G. Roskies, "Rabbis, Rebbes and Other Humanists: The Search for a Usable Past in Modern Yiddish Literature," *Studies in Contemporary Jewry* 12 (1996): 71–73.
15. *The Well*, 202, and *Der shulhoyf*, 172.
16. *The Well*, 203, and *Der shulhoyf*, 174.
17. *Doyres* (Generations), 1945; *Farvoksene vegn* (Overgrown Paths), 1947; *Pleytim* (Refugees), 1947; *Oyf di khurves* (On the Ruins), 1947; *Der mames tsvoe* (My Mother's Will), 1949; *Sheyn fun farloshene shtern* (Light of Extinguished Stars), 1950.
18. See Yechiel Szeintuch, "Khayim Grade bal-pe: Di vikhtikeyt fun intonatsye un lebedikn vort af yidish," *Forverts* (New York), September 21, 2012, 22–23.
19. Harold U. Ribalow, "A Conversation with Chaim Grade," *Congress Monthly*, February 21, 1975, 16.
20. David Fishman, "The Musar Movement in Interwar Poland," in *The Jews of Poland Between Two World Wars*, ed. Yisrael Gutman, Ezra Mendelsohn, Jehuda Reinharz, and Khone Shmeruk (Hanover, NH: University Press of New England, 1989), 250.
21. Ibid., 249.
22. Lucy Davidowicz, *From That Place and Time: A Memoir 1938–1947* (New York: Norton, 1989), 126, 130.
23. On Jonah Rosenfeld, see "The Trials of a Yiddish Writer" in my *Imagining Lives: Autobiographical Fiction of Yiddish Writers* (Madison: University of Wisconsin Press, 2005), 79–98.
24. Chaim Grade, *The Agunah*, trans. Curt Leviant (New York: Twayne Publishers, 1974), 197, and *Di agune*, 236.
25. See Janet Hadda, *Passionate Women, Passive Men: Suicide in Yiddish Literature* (Albany: State University of New York Press, 1988).
26. *The Agunah*, 263; *Di agune*, 322.
27. "Der oysgebrenter dorn," in *Der mentsh fun fayer* (The Man of Fire) (New York: CYCO bikher farlag, 1962), 35.
28. R. Avraham Karelitz—the Hazon Ish—was a Talmudic luminary of the first half of the twentieth century. In *The Yeshiva* he is called Abraham Kassover. See Yechiel Szeintuch, "Khayim Grade un der Hazon Ish," *Di tsukunft* (New York), vol. 114 (August 2012): 38–45.
29. The novel was serialized in weekly installments in *Forverts*, from March 25, 1979, to June 27, 1982. Chaim Grade died suddenly of a heart attack on June 8, 1982.
30. *Fun unter der erd*, *Forverts*, March 25, 1979.
31. Avrom Tabatshnik, tape recorded interview with Chaim Grade in the early 1950s, Jewish Public Library, Montreal. They are available in the Yiddish Book Center Multimedia Library: Part 1: https://archive.org/details/ChaimGradeReadsFromHisWorkAndIsInterviewedByAbrahamTabachnickPart1_636; Part 2: https://archive.org/details/ChaimGradeReadsFromHisWorkAndIsInterviewedByAbrahamTabachnickPart2
32. Ribalow, "A Conversation with Chaim Grade," 17.

33. Cynthia Ozick, "Tradition and (or versus) the Jewish Writer," in *The Din in the Head: Essays* (New York: Houghton Mifflin, 2006), 125–26; italics in original.
34. Dickstein, "The Jewish American Writer," 170.
35. I. B. Singer, *Der sotn in goray: A mayse fun fartsaytns un andere dertseylungen* (New York: Farlag matones, 1943).
36. Like the German Jewish Kabbalah scholar Gershom Scholem (1897–1982), Singer turned Sabbatai Zevi into the prototype of his times. Scholem's first published essay about Sabbatai Zevi, "Redemption through Sin," appeared in 1937. Later, in his magisterial study *Sabbatai Zevi: The Mystical Messiah* (1973), Scholem would acknowledge Singer's stories as one of the most vivid expressions of Polish kabbalism in its "unique fascination with the sphere of evil" (quoted in Scholem, *Major Trends in Jewish Mysticism* [New York: Schocken, 1974], 299).
37. Correspondence between Alfred A. Knopf and Singer, 1948–1949, Isaac Bashevis Singer Papers, Harry Ransom Center, University of Texas at Austin, file 104:3.
38. I started such an examination in my article "Such a Rag-Bag": The Historical Novel as Spectacle, Neo-Hasidic Hagiography, and Pseudo-Territory," in *Joseph Opatoshu: A Yiddish Writer Between Europe and America* (Studies in Yiddish 11), ed. Sabine Koller, Gennady Estraykh, and Mikhail Krutikov (London: Legenda, 2013), 97–111. I am currently working on a monograph about I. B. Singer, where I plan to explore the genre of the Yiddish historical novel in greater detail.
39. The story was published in *Partisan Review* (May–June 1953): 300–313. First published as "*Gimpl tam,*" *Yidisher kemfer,* March 30, 1945, 17–20.
40. *Der lebediker* [Khayim Gutman], "*Lamdn un amorets in der yidisher literature,*" *Di goldene keyt* 6 (1950): 141.
41. Ibid., 142.
42. Avrom Golomb, "*Lo zeh haderekh,*" *Di goldene keyt* 7 (1951): 192.
43. Ibid., 195.
44. See Irving Howe, *A Margin of Hope: An Intellectual Autobiography* (San Diego: Harcourt Brace Jovanovich, 1982), 269–75.
45. The title of Irving Howe's 1976 book about Jewish life in New York.
46. For a selection of Singer's prolific output as an interviewee, see *Isaac Bashevis Singer: Conversations,* ed. Grace Farrell (Jackson: University Press of Mississippi, 1992).
47. Shmuel Niger, "*Tendentsn in der nayster yidisher literatur,*" *Jewish Book Annual* (1955–56): 8 (Yiddish section).
48. See Dan Miron, "Passivity and Narration: The Spell of Bashevis Singer," *Judaism* 1 (Winter 1992): 6–17, and Harold Bloom, "Revisiting Isaac Bashevis Singer," *New York Review of Books,* October 28, 2010, 45.
49. Seth L. Wolitz and Joseph Sherman, "Bashevis Singer as a Regionalist of Lublin Province," in *The Hidden Isaac Bashevis Singer,* ed. Seth L. Wolitz (Austin: University of Texas Press, 2001), 224.
50. For a close reading of this work, see my *Imagining Lives: Autobiographical Fiction of Yiddish Writers,* 142–52.
51. For a close reading of "The Cafeteria," see my article "'Death Is the Only Messiah': Three Supernatural Stories by Yitskhok Bashevis," in *The Hidden Isaac Bashevis Singer,* 107–18.
52. Isaac Bashevis Singer, *Shadows on the Hudson,* trans. Joseph Sherman (New York: Farrar, Straus and Giroux, 1998), 198.
53. Morris Dickstein, in "The Achievement of Isaac Bashevis Singer: A Roundtable Discus-

sion," in *Isaac Bashevis Singer: An Album,* ed. Ilan Stavans (New York: Library of America, 2004), 118.

54. See Joseph Sherman's article about his conflicts with the publisher Farrar, Straus and Giroux about how to translate Singer into English, "Translating *'Shotns baym hodson'* (Shadows on the Hudson), Directly Encountering Isaac Bashevis Singer's Authorial Dualism," in *Isaac Bashevis Singer: His Work and His World,* ed. Hugh Denman (Leiden: Brill 2002), 49–80.

55. Richard Bernstein, "'Shadows on the Hudson': Dark Side of Isaac Bashevis Singer," *New York Times,* December 31, 1997, www.nytimes.com/books/97/12/28/daily/singer-book-review.html?module=Search&mabReward=relbias%3Ar%2C{%221%22%3A%22RI%3A8%22}; accessed July 30, 2014.

56. Ibid.

57. Lee Siegel, "West Side Story," *New York Times,* January 25, 1998, www.nytimes.com/books/98/01/25/reviews/980125.25siegelt.html?module=Search&mabReward=relbias%3Ar%2C{%221%22%3A%22RI%3A8%22}, accessed April 27, 2012.

58. Chava Rosenfarb, "*Yitskhok Bashevis un Sholem Ash (a pruv fun a farglaykh),*" *Di goldene keyt* 133 (1992): 76.

59. Ibid., 104.

60. The Yiddish and Hebrew poet Aaron Zeitlin displayed a similar self-deprecating, self-destructive view in his post-Holocaust poetry. See his *Poems of the Holocaust and Poems of Faith,* ed. and trans. Morris M. Faierstein (New York: iUniverse, 2007). The quote is from Singer's author's note in *Enemies: A Love Story* (New York: Farrar, Straus and Giroux, 1972).

61. "He emphasizes many times his negativity, and with such passion, that it becomes clear that the opposite is the case. And if he would not have sought any light, he would have been consistent and committed literary suicide, stopped writing, because every form of creativity regardless of its despair is in itself a way of saying yes to life and to man." Rosenfarb, "*Yitskhok Bashevis un Sholem Ash (a pruv fun a farglaykh),*" 102.

62. I. B. Singer, *Collected Stories: A Friend of Kafka to Passions,* ed. Ilan Stavans (New York: Library of America, 2004), 758. "My Adventures as an Idealist" was published in English translation in *The Saturday Evening Post,* November 18, 1967; it was first published in Yiddish, under the name Yitskhok Bashevis, in *Forverts,* October 8, 9, 15, 1965, p. 2 (signed Bashevis).

63. Stavans, ed., *Isaac Bashevis Singer: An Album,* 63–64.

64. "'You're Isaac Bashevis Singer?': To the 15th *Yortseit* of One of Our Greatest Yiddish Writers, Who Died On July 24, 1991," *Algemeyner zhurnal* (2006), www.algemeiner.com/generic.asp?print-true&id=1984; accessed July 30, 2014.

65. See Ozick's, Foer's, and Rothenberg's appreciations in Stavans, ed., *Isaac Bashevis Singer: An Album.*

Conclusion

1. Avrom Sutzkever, "*Zunroyzn*" (Sunflowers, 1987), in *Di nevue fun shvartsaplen: Dertseylungen* (The Prophecy of the Pupils: Stories) (Jerusalem: Hebrew University Press, 1989), 159.

2. The term "late style," reconceived by Edward Said from Theodor Adorno's essay "Beethoven's Late Style," can be usefully applied to Yiddish culture and individual careers of Yiddish writers after 1945. Late style designates the final years of a writer's oeuvre, characterized by unresolved conflicts: "In Adorno's account of late style there is violence,

experimental energy and, most important, a refusal to accept any idea of a healing, inclusive restfulness that comes at the end of a fruitful career" (Edward W. Said, *Music at the Limits* [New York: Columbia University Press, 2008], 302). Beethoven's final years, between 1817 and 1827, are a paradigm of "late style," demonstrating a radical new conception of musical aesthetics based on the composer's rethinking of fundamental issues of philosophical, musicological, and historical ideas during early Romanticism: "The masterpieces of Beethoven's final decade are late to the extent that they are beyond their own time, ahead of it in terms of daring and startling newness, later than it in that they describe a return or homecoming to realms forgotten or left behind by the relentless forward march of history" (Said, *Music at the Limits*, 300). As a result of his increasing deafness, which became complete in 1818, Beethoven became isolated from society, turning inward in a quest to fully express his musical vision based on "such central concepts of Romanticism as the infinite, yearning, nostalgia, and inwardness" (Maynard Solomon, *Late Beethoven: Music, Thought, Imagination* [Berkeley: University of California Press, 2003], 7).

3. Aaron Zeitlin, "*A kholem fun nokh Maydanek*," in *Gezamlte lider*, vol. 1 (New York: Farlag matones, 1947), 77–78; translation from *Poems of the Holocaust and Poems of Faith*, ed. and trans. Morris M. Faierstein (New York: iUniverse, 2007), 67–68.
4. "*A kholem fun nokh Maydanek*," in *Gezamlte lider*, 83; Faierstein, *Poems of the Holocaust and Poems of Faith*, 72.
5. The rise of the internet in the 1990s greatly enhanced and contributed to the expansion of Yiddish culture as a global, virtual reality.
6. Samuel Kassow, *Who Will Write Our History? Emanuel Ringelblum, the Warsaw Ghetto, and the Oyneg Shabes Archive* (Bloomington: Indiana University Press, 2007), 14.
7. Benedict Anderson, *Imagined Communities: The Origins and Spread of Nationalism* (London: Verso, 2006).
8. On Yiddish culture in the Soviet Union and Israel, see notes 15 and 16 in the Introduction. For a study of Montreal as Yiddish center, see Rebecca Margolis, *Jewish Roots, Canadian Soil: Yiddish Culture in Montreal, 1905–1945* (Montreal: McGill-Queen's University Press, 2011). On Yiddish culture in Paris post-1945, see Simon Perego, "Remembering in Yiddish: World War Two Jewish Commemorations in Paris between 1945 and 1967," and Constance Paris de Bollardiere, "The Jewish Labor Committee's Actions for the Continuation of Yiddish Culture in France 1945–1950," in *Twentieth-Century Yiddish Culture in Its European Context*, ed. Marion Aptroot and Jan Schwarz (Dusseldorf: Dusseldorf University Press, forthcoming 2015).
9. David Cesarani, "Introduction," in *After the Holocaust: Challenging the Myth of Silence*, ed. David Cesarani and Eric J. Sundquist (London: Routledge, 2012), 11.
10. Very little has been translated into English from the Yiddish press (newspapers and journals), a central part of Yiddish print culture. Only a few samples of Yiddish audio recordings of cultural events and performances, a small part of which has been made available online, have been translated into English.
11. Cecile E. Kuznitz, "Yiddish Studies," in *The Oxford Handbook of Jewish Studies*, ed. Martin Goodman (New York: Oxford University Press, 2002), 560. See also Dara Horn, "The Future of Yiddish—in English: Field Notes from the New Ashkenaz," *Jewish Quarterly Review* 96, no. 4 (2006): 471–80; and Janet Hadda, "Imagining Yiddish: A Future for the Soul of Ashkenaz," *Pakn Treger* (Spring 2003): 10–19, and "Transmitting Ashkenaz," *Shofar: An Interdisciplinary Journal of Jewish Studies* 25, no. 1 (2006): 114–26.
12. Lara Rabinovitch, Shiri Goren, and Hannah S. Pressman, "Introduction," in *Choosing*

Yiddish: New Frontiers of Language and Culture, ed. Lara Rabinovitch, Shiri Goren, and Hannah S. Pressman (Detroit, MI: Wayne State University Press, 2013), 4.

13. Anita Norich, *Writing in Tongues: Translating Yiddish in the Twentieth Century* (Seattle: University of Washington Press, 2014); idem, "From the Politics of Culture to the Culture of Mourning," in *Discovering Exile: Yiddish and Jewish American Culture during the Holocaust* (Stanford, CA: Stanford University Press, 2007), 96–121.

14. See the list of Holocaust works in English published in the 1940s and early 1950s in Eric Sundquist, "Silence Reconsidered: An Afterword," in *After the Holocaust: Challenging the Myth of Silence*, 207–8.

15. Similar to Kirshenblatt-Gimblett's point that "a field organized around the idea of Ashkenaz would, by definition, be more holistic because it would encompass the totality of the languages (not only Yiddish) and cultural expressions of Jews within the historically defined Ashkenazi culture area and its diasporic extension." Kirshenblatt-Gimblett, "Foreword—Yiddish Studies: Toward a Twenty-First-Century Mandate," in *Choosing Yiddish*, ed. Rabinovitch, Goren, and Pressman, xiii.

16. Dan Miron's concept of contiguity in Jewish literary history is particularly useful in the development of a global view of Jewish literary production after 1945. See his *From Continuity to Contiguity: Toward a New Jewish Literary Thinking* (Stanford, CA: Stanford University Press, 2010).

17. See Jeffrey Shandler, *Adventures in Yiddishland: Postvernacular Language and Culture* (Berkeley: University of California Press, 2006), 1: "at the turn of the twenty-first century estimates are sometimes well under 1,000,000."

BIBLIOGRAPHY

Primary Sources

1943
Bashevis, Yitskhok. *Der sotn in goray: A mayse fun fartsaytns un andere dertseylungen.* (Satan in Goray: A Tale from the Past and Other Stories). New York: Farlag matones.

Glatshteyn, Yankev. *Gedenklider* (Poems of Remembrance). New York: Yidisher kemfer.

1944
Sutzkever, Avrom. *Di festung.* New York: Ikuf farlag.

1945
Bashevis, Yitskhok. "*Gimpl tam*" (Gimpel the Fool). *Yidisher kemfer* 24 (March 30): 17–20. Translated as "Gimpel the Fool." Trans. Saul Bellow. *Partisan Review* (May–June 1953): 300–313.

Heschel, Abraham Joshua. "*Di mizrekh eyropeisher tkufe in der yidisher geshikhte.*" Lecture at the YIVO Institute for Jewish Research, January 1945. Published in *YIVO Bleter* 25, no. 2 (March–April 1945): 163–183. Translated into English as *The Earth Is the Lord's: The Inner World of the Jew in East Europe.* New York: H. Schuman, 1950.

Leivick, H. *In treblinke bin ikh nit geven: Lider un poemes* (In Treblinka I Was Not: Poems). New York: CYCO Farlag.

Strigler, Mordechai. "*Tsu aykh shvester un brider bafrayte: Nokhmilkhome-problemen fun yidishn folk*" (To You Liberated Sisters and Brothers: Postwar Problems of the Jewish People). New York: Zamoshtsher brentsh 375, Arbeter ring 8.

1946
Glatshteyn, Yankev. *Shtralndike yidn* (Illuminated Jews). New York: Farlag matones.

Kolitz, Zvi. "*Yosl Rakover vendung tsu got*" (Yosl Rakover's Appeal to God). *Di yidishe tsaytung* (Buenos Aires), September 25. Reprinted in *Di goldene keyt* 18 (1954): 102–10, with the title "*Yosl Rakover redt tsu got*" (Yosl Rakover Speaks to God). Translated as *Yosl Rakover Talks to God.* Afterword by Emanuel Levinas and Leon Wieseltier. New York: Pantheon Books, 1999.

Shayevitsh, Simkhe-Bunem. *Lekh-lekho* (Get Up and Go). Lodz: Tsentraler yidisher historisher komisye.

Sutzkever, Avrom. *Vilner geto, 1941–1944* (Vilna Ghetto, 1941–1944). Moscow: Melukhe-farlag "Der emes."

Weinreich, Max. *Hitler's Professors: The Part of Scholarship in Germany's Crimes Against the Jewish People.* New York: Yiddish Scientific Institute-YIVO. 2d ed. published with an introduction by Martin Gilbert. New Haven, CT: Yale University Press, 1999.

1947
Auerbach, Rachel. *Oyf di felder fun Treblinke: Reportzsh.* Warsaw: Tsentraler Yidisher historisher komisye.

Bergelson, Dovid. *Naye dertseylungen* (New Stories). Moscow: Emes Farlag.

Glatshteyn, Yankev. *In tokh genumen: Eseyen 1945–1947* (The Heart of the Matter: Essays 1945–1947). New York: Farlag matones.

Strigler, Mordechai. *Maydanek. Dos poylishe yidntum* 20. Buenos Aires: Tsentral-farband fun poylishe yidn in argentine.

Zeitlin, Aaron. *Gezamlte lider* (Collected Poems). 2 vols. New York: Farlag matones. Translated in *Poems of the Holocaust and Poems of Faith,* ed. and trans. Morris M. Faierstein. New York: iUniverse, 2007.

1948

Kaczerginski, Shmerke. *Lider fun di getos un lagern: Tekstn un melodyes gezamlt* (Songs from the Ghettos and the Camps: Collected Texts and Melodies). Ed. H. Leivick. New York: CYCO Farlag.

Katsenelson, Yitskhok. *Dos lid funem oysgehargetn yidishn folk* (The Song of the Murdered Jewish People). Brooklyn: Ha-Kibuts ha-Meuchad. Reprinted as *The Song of the Murdered Jewish People.* Bilingual edition (Yiddish and English). Tel Aviv: Hakibbutz Hameuchad, 1980.

Niger, Shmuel, ed. *Kidush hashem* (The Sanctification of the Name). New York: CYCO Farlag.

Rosenfarb, Chava. *Geto un andere lider: Oykh fragmentn fun a tog-bukh* (Ghetto and Other Poems: Also Fragments from a Diary). Montreal: Aroysgegebn durkh H. Hershman.

Strigler, Mordechai. *In di fabrikn fun toyt* (In the Factories of Death). *Dos poylishe yidntum* 32. Buenos Aires: Tsentral-farband far poylishe yidn in argentine.

Turkov, Jonas. *Azoy iz es geven: Khurbn varshe* (So It Was: The Destruction of Warsaw). *Dos poylishe yidntum* 27. Buenos Aires: Tsentral-farband far poylishe yidn in argentine.

1949

Rochman, Leib. *Un in dayn blut zolstu lebn (togbukh 1943–1944)* (And In Your Blood Shall You Live [Diary, 1943–1944]). Paris: Fraynd fun Minsk Mazowieck. Translated as *The Pit and the Trap: A Chronicle of Survival.* New York: Holocaust Library, 1983.

Turkov, Jonas. *In kamf farn lebn* (In Struggle for Life). *Dos poylishe yidntum* 53. Buenos Aires: Tsentral-farband fun poylishe yidn in argentine.

1950

Strigler, Mordechai. *Verk "Tse"* (Work "C"). In *Dos poylishe yidntum* 64–65. Buenos Aires: Tsentral-farband fun poylishe yidn in argentine.

1951

Elberg, Yehuda. *Unter kuperne himlen: Dersteylungen* (Under Copper Skies). *Dos poylishe yidntum* 73. Buenos Aires: Tsentral-farband fun poylishe yidn in argentine.

1952

Bryks, Rakhmiel. *Oyf kidesh ha-shem un andere dertseylungen* (Sanctification of the Name and Other Stories). New York: Y. Briks bukh-komitet. Translated as *Kiddush hashem.* New York: Behrman House, 1977.

Shpiegl, Isaiah. *Likht funem opgrunt: Geto-noveln* (Light from the Abyss: Ghetto-Stories). New York: CYCO Farlag. Translated as *Ghetto Kingdom: Tales of the Lodz Ghetto.* Evanston, IL: Northwestern University Press, 1998.

Strigler, Mordechai. *Goyroles* (Destinies). *Dos poylishe yidntum* 85–86. Buenos Aires: Tsentral-farband fun poylishe yidn in argentine.

1953

Miller, Shaye. *In di shvartse pintelekh* (In the Writings). New York: M. Sh. Shklarski.

Turkov, Jonas. *Farloshene shtern* (Extinguished Stars). In *Dos poylishe yidntum* 95–96. Buenos Aires: Tsentral farband fun poylishe yidn in argentine.

1953–54

Grade, Chaim. "My Quarrel with Hersh Rasseyner." In *A Treasury of Yiddish Stories*, ed. Irving Howe and Eliezer Greenberg. New York: Viking Press.

Howe, Irving, and Eliezer Greenberg, eds. *A Treasury of Yiddish Stories*. New York: Viking Press.

Ravitsh, Melekh. *Di kroynung fun a yungn yidishn dikhter in amerike: Poeme*. New York: Dovid Ignatov Literatur Fond.

Sutzkever, Avrom. *Griner akvarium: Dertseylungen* (Green Aquarium: Stories). *Di goldene keyt* 16–20 (1953–54). Repr. in *Ode tsu der toyb*. Tel Aviv: Di goldene keyt, 1955, 75–129. Repr. *Griner akvarium: Dertseylungen*. Jerusalem: Hebrew University Press, 1975.

1955

Grade, Chaim. *Der mames shabosim* (My Mother's Sabbath Days). Chicago: L. M. Stein. Translated as *My Mother's Sabbath Days: A Memoir*. Northvale, NJ: J. Aronson, 1997.

Ka-Tzetnik. *Dos hoyz fun di lyalkes* (House of the Dolls). In *Dos poylishe yidntum* 115. Buenos Aires: Tsentral farband fun poylishe yidn in argentine. Translated as *House of Dolls*. New York: Simon and Schuster, 1955.

Mark, Bernard, ed. *Tvishn lebn un toyt* (Between Life and Death). Warsaw: Yidish-bukh.

Prager, Moyshe ed. *Antologye fun religieze lider un dertseylungen: Shafungen fun shrayber, umgekumene in di yorn fun yidishn khurbn in eyrope* (Anthology of Religious Poems and Stories: Works of Writers Who Perished in the Years of the Jewish Holocaust in Europe). New York: Forshungs-institut fun religiezn yidntum.

1956

Bashevis, Yitskhok. *Mayn tatns bezdn shtub*. New York: Der Kval.

Glatshteyn, Yankev. *Fun mayn gantser mi* (From All My Labors). New York: Martin Press.

Wiesel, Eliezer. . . . *Un di velt hot geshvign* (And the World Was Silent). In *Dos poylishe yidntum* 117. Buenos Aires: Tsentral-farband fun poylishe yidn in argentine. Translated as *Night*. New York: Hill and Wang, 1961.

1957

Nister, Der. *Dertseylungen un eseyen: 1940–1948* (Stories and Essays: 1940–1948). New York: Ikuf-Farlag.

1957–58

Singer, Isaac Bashevis. *Shotns baym Hodson* (Shadows on the Hudson). Serialized twice weekly in *Forverts* between January 1957 and January 1958. Translated as *Shadows on the Hudson*. New York: Farrar, Straus and Giroux, 1998.

1958

Grade, Chaim. *Der shulhoyf: Dray dertseylungen* (The Synagogue Courtyard). New York: Yidish natsionaler arbeter-farband.

1959

Turkov, Jonas. *Nokh der bafrayung: Zikhroynes* (After the Liberation: Memoirs). In *Dos poylishe yidntum* 145. Buenos Aires: Tsentral farband fun poylishe yidn in argentine.

1961

Grade, Chaim. *Di agune*. New York: CYCO bikher farlag. *The Agunah*, trans. Curt Leviant. New York: Twayne Publishers, 1974.

1962
Molodovsky, Kadya, ed. *Lider fun khurbn: Antologye* (Holocaust Poems: Anthology). Tel Aviv: I. L. Peretz farlag.

1964
Man, Mendel. *Di milkhome trilogye: Bay di toyern fun Moskve; Bay der veisl; Dos faln fun Berlin* (War Trilogy: At the Gates of Moscow; At the Vistula; The Downfall of Berlin). Paris: Noimanfond far yidishe literatur. First volume translated as *At the Gates of Moscow: A Novel*. New York: St. Martin's Press, 1963.

1967
Glatshteyn, Yankev. *Ikh tu dermonen* (I Keep Recalling). New York: Farlag Bergen-Belsen.
Zeitlin, Aaron. *Ale lider un poemes: Lider fun khurbn un lider fun gloybn* (All Poems: Poems of the Holocaust and Poems of Faith). 2 vols. New York and Tel Aviv: Farlag Bergen-Belsen, 1967–70.

1968
Glatshteyn, Yankev, Israel Knox, Samuel Margoshes, eds. *Anthology of Holocaust Literature*. Philadelphia: Jewish Publication Society of America.
Grade, Chaim. *Tsemakh Atlas: Di yeshive* (Tsemakh Atlas: The Yeshiva). New York: CYCO. Translated as *The Yeshiva*. 2 vols. Trans. Curt Leviant. New York: Menorah 1976, 1979.
Rochman, Leib. *Mit blinde trit iber der erd* (With Blind Steps over the Earth). Tel Aviv: Menorah.
Sutzkever, Avrom. *Lider fun yam-hamoves, fun vilner geto, vald un vander: Geshribn in di yorn 1936-1967* (Poems from the Sea of Death, from Vilna Ghetto, the Woods, and Wanderings: Written in the Years 1936–1967). Tel Aviv: Farlag Bergen-Belsen. See translations in *A. Sutzkever: Selected Poetry and Prose*. Berkeley: University of California Press, 1991.
———. *Lider fun yam hamoves: Fun vilner geto, vald un vander* (Poems from the Sea of Death: From Vilna Ghetto, the Woods and Wandering). Tel Aviv: Remembrance Award Library.

1972
Rosenfarb, Chava. *Der boym fun lebn: Trilogye* (The Tree of Life: Trilogy). Tel Aviv: Ha-Menorah. Translated as *The Tree of Life:* Book 1. *On the Brink of the Precipice, 1939*; Book 2. *From the Depths I Call You, 1940–1942*; Book 3. *The Cattle Cars Are Waiting, 1942–1944*. Madison: University of Wisconsin Press, 2004–2006.
Singer, Isaac Bashevis. *Enemies: A Love Story*. New York: Farrar, Straus and Giroux.

1973
Heschel, Abraham Joshua. *Kotsk: In gerangl far emesdikayt* (Kotsk: In the Struggle for Truth). 2 vols. Tel Aviv: Farlag hamenoyre.

1974
Auerbach, Rachel. *Varshever tshvoes* (Warsaw Testimonies). Tel Aviv: Yisroel-bukh.

1977
Grade, Chaim, *Der shtumer minyen* (The Silent Quorum). New York: Farlag Brider Shulzinger.
Sutzkever, Avrom, *Lider fun togbukh*. Tel Aviv: Farlag di goldene keyt.

1978
Rochman, Leib. *Der mabl: Dertseylungen* (The Flood: Stories). Jerusalem: Tsur Ot.

1979
Sutzkever, Avrom. *Di ershte nakht in geto* (The First Night in the Ghetto). Tel Aviv: Farlag di goldene keyt.

1983
Schekhtman, Eli. *Erev: Roman* (On the Eve: Novel). 7 vols. Tel Aviv: Yisroel Bukh.

1986
Sutzkever, Avrom. *Lider fun togbukh, 1974–1985* (Twin-Brother: Poems from a Diary, 1974–1985). Tel Aviv: Farlag di goldene keyt.

1987
Howe, Irving, Ruth R. Wisse, and Khone Shmeruk, eds. *The Penguin Book of Modern Yiddish Verse*. New York: Penguin

1989
Roskies, David, ed. *Literature of Destruction: Jewish Responses to Catastrophe*. Philadelphia: Jewish Publication Society.
Sutzkever, Avrom. *Di nevue fun shvartsaplen: Dertseylungen* (The Prophecy of the Pupils: Stories). Jerusalem: Hebrew University Press.

1992
Sutzkever, Avrom. *Der yoyresh fun regn*. Tel Aviv: Farlag di goldene keyt.

1993
Glatshteyn, Yankev. *I Keep Recalling: The Holocaust Poems of Jacob Glatstein*. Trans. Barnett Zumoff. Hoboken, NJ: KTAV Publishing House.
Sutzkever, Avrom. *Bam leyenen penimer: Dertseylungen, dermonungen, eseyen* (By Reading Faces: Stories, Recollections, Essays). Jerusalem: Hebrew University Press.

1999
Molodowsky [Molodovsky], Kadya. *Paper Bridges: Selected Poems of Kadya Molodowsky*. Detroit, MI: Wayne State University Press.

2004
Rosenfarb, Chava. *Survivors: Seven Short Stories*. Toronto: Comorant Books.
Singer, Isaac Bashevis. *Collected Works*. 3 vols. Ed. Ilan Stavans. New York: Library of America.

Secondary Sources and Critical Works
Adelson, Alan, and Robert Lapides, eds. *Lodz Ghetto: Inside a Community under Siege*. New York: Viking, 1989.
Anderson, Benedict. *Imagined Communities: The Origins and Spread of Nationalism*. London: Verso 2006.
Aptroot, Marion, Efrat Gal-Ed, Roland Gruschka, and Simon Neuberg, eds. *Leket: Jiddistik heute* (Yiddish Studies Today/Yidishe shtudyes haynt). Dusseldorf: Dusseldorf University Press, 2012.
Arendt, Hannah. "*The Black Book: The Nazi Crime Against the Jewish People*, and *Hitler's Professors*, by Max Weinreich." *Commentary* (September 1946).

Astro, Alan. "Revisiting Wiesel's *Night* in Yiddish, French, and English." *Partial Answers: Journal of Literature and the History of Ideas* 12, no. 1 (January 2014): 127–53.
Barron, Jonathan N., and Eric Murphy Selinger, eds. *Jewish American Poetry: Poems, Commentary, and Reflections*. Hanover, NH: Brandeis University Press, 2000.
Bartoszewski, Wladyslaw. *The Samaritans: Heroes of the Holocaust*. New York: Twayne Publishers, 1970.
Bauer, Yehuda. *The Death of the Shtetl*. New Haven, CT: Yale University Press, 2009.
Bellow, Saul. *Letters*. Ed. Benjamin Taylor. New York: Viking, 2010.
Bernard-Donals, Michael. "Beyond the Question of Authenticity: Witness and Testimony in the Fragments Controversy." *PMLA* 116, no. 5 (2001).
Bernstein, Charles, ed. *Close Listening: Poetry and the Performed Word*. New York: Oxford University Press, 1998.
Bez, Khayim. *Oyf di vegn fun der yidisher literatur* (On the Paths of Yiddish Literature). Tel Aviv: Y. L. Peretz Farlag, 1980.
Bloom, Harold. "Revisiting Isaac Bashevis Singer." *New York Review of Books*, October 28, 2010, 45.
Browning, Christopher R. *Remembering Survival: Inside a Nazi Slave-Labor Camp*. New York: W.W. Norton & Company, 2010.
Cammy, Justin Daniel, Dara Horn, Alyssa Quint et al., eds. *Arguing the Jewish Canon: Essays on Literature and Culture in Honor of Ruth R. Wisse*. Cambridge, MA: Harvard University Press, 2008.
Cammy, Justin, and Marta Figlerowicz. "Translating History into Art: The Influences of Cyprian Kamil Norwid in Abraham Sutzkever's Poetry." *Prooftexts* 3 (Fall 2007): 427–73.
Cesarani, David, and Eric J. Sundquist. *After the Holocaust: Challenging the Myth of Silence*. London: Routledge, 2012.
Chametsky, Jules, John Felstiner, Hilena Flanzbaum, and Kathryn Hellerstein, eds. *Jewish American Literature: A Norton Anthology*. New York: Norton, 2001.
Chaver, Yael. *What Must Be Forgotten: The Survival of Yiddish in Zionist Palestine*. Syracuse, NY: Syracuse University Press, 2004.
Chinski, Malena. "A Catalogue in Memory of Polish Jewry: *Dos poylishe yidntum* Collection, Buenos Aires, 1946–1966." In *Marginados y consagrados: Nuevos estudios sobre la vida judía en Argentina*, ed. E. Kahan, L. Schenquer, D. Setton, and A. Dujovne, 213–38. Buenos Aires: Lumiere, 2011 (Spanish).
———. "Illustrating Memory: The Book Covers of *Dos poylishe yidntum* [Polish Jewry] Collection, Buenos Aires, 1946–1966." *Estudios Interdisciplinarios de América Latina y el Caribe* 23.1 (2012): 11–33 (Spanish). Retrievable from www1.tau.ac.il/eial/images/v23n1/chinski-v23n1.pdf
Damrosch, David, ed. *World Literature in Theory*. New York: Wiley Blackwell, 2014.
Dauber, Jeremy, and Jerold C. Frakes, eds. *Between Two Worlds: Yiddish-German Encounters*. Studia Rosenthaliana 41. Amsterdam: Peeters, 2009.
Davidowicz, Lucy. *From That Place and Time: A Memoir, 1938–1947*. New York: Norton, 1989.
Desbois, Father Patrick. *The Holocaust by Bullets: A Priest's Journey to Uncover the Truth behind the Murder of 1.5 Million Jews*. New York: Palgrave Macmillan, 2008.
Dickstein, Morris. *Leopards in the Temple: The Transformation of American Fiction, 1945–1970*. Cambridge, MA: Harvard University Press, 2002.
———, ed. *A Mirror in the Roadway: Literature and the Real World*. Princeton, NJ: Princeton University Press, 2005.
Diner, Hasia. *We Remember with Reverence and Love: American Jews and the Myth of Silence after the Holocaust, 1945–1962*. New York: New York University Press, 2009.

Dobroszycki, Lucjan, ed. *The Chronicle of the Lodz Ghetto, 1941–1944*. New Haven, CT: Yale University Press, 1984.

Dzigan, Shimen. *Der koyekh fun yidishn humor* (The Power of Jewish Humor). Tel Aviv: Der gezelshaft-lekher komitet tsu fayern 40 yor tetikayt fun Shimen Dzigan oyf der yidisher bine, 1974.

Efron, John M. "From Lodz to Tel Aviv: The Yiddish Political Satire of Shimen Dzigan." *Jewish Quarterly Review* 102, no.1 (2012): 50–79.

Ehrenburg, Ilya, Vasily Grossman, and Binem Heller, eds. *Dos shvartse bukh*. Jerusalem: Yad Vashem 1984.

Elberg, Yehuda. *Eseyen vegn zayn literarishn shafn*. Ed. Gershon Viner. Ramat Gan: Bar Ilan University Press, 1990.

Engel, David. *Historians of the Jews and the Holocaust*. Stanford, CA: Stanford University Press, 2010.

Estraykh, Gennady. *In Harness: Yiddish Writers' Romance with Communism*. Syracuse, NY: Syracuse University Press, 2005.

———. *Yiddish in the Cold War*. London: Legenda, 2008.

Farrell, Grace, ed. *Isaac Bashevis Singer: Conversations*. Jackson: University Press of Mississippi, 1992.

Fein, Richard J., ed. and trans. *With Everything We've Got: A Personal Anthology of Yiddish Poetry*. Austin, TX: Host Publications, 2009.

Felstiner, John. "Translating Celan's Last Poem." *American Poetry Review* (July–August 1982). Includes a translation of Paul Celan's "Bremen Prize Speech" (1958).

Finder, Gabriel. "Child Survivors in Jewish Collective Memory in Poland after the Holocaust: The Case of Undzere Kinder." In *Nurturing the Nation: Displaced Children, State Ideology and Social Identity in Eastern Europe and the USSR, 1918–1953*, ed. Nick Baron. Boston: Brill, forthcoming 2015.

Finder, Gabriel, Natalia Aleksiun, Antony Polonsky, and Jan Schwarz, eds. *POLIN: Studies in Polish Jewry*, vol. 20, *Making Holocaust Memory*. Oxford: Littman Library of Jewish Civilization, 2008.

Fishman, David E. *The Rise of Modern Yiddish Culture*. Pittsburgh, PA: University of Pittsburgh Press, 2005.

———, and Avrom Nowersztern, eds. *YIVO-Bleter: Naye Serye, Band III. Khurbn-Lite* (New Series, Volume III: The Holocaust in Lithuania). New York: YIVO Institute for Jewish Research, 1997.

Fishman, Shikl. "Di sotsiologye fun yidish in amerike: 1960–1970 un vayter" (The Sociology of Yiddish in America: 1960–1970). *Di goldene keyt* 75 (1972): 110–27.

Friedlaender, Saul. *Nazi Germany and the Jews, 1939–45, vol. 2: The Years of Extermination*. New York: HarperCollins, 2007.

Friedman, Philip. "*Di landmanshaftnliteratur in di fareynikte shtatn far di letste 10 yor*." In *Jewish Book Annual* 10 (1951–52), Yiddish section.

Garbarini, Alexandra. *Numbered Days: Diaries and the Holocaust*. New Haven, CT: Yale University Press, 2006.

Glatshteyn, Yankev. *Selected Poems of Yankev Glatshteyn*. Trans. Richard J. Fein. Philadelphia: Jewish Publication Society, 1987.

Glatshteyn, Yankev, Shmuel Niger, and Hillel Rogoff, eds. "*75 yor yidishe prese in amerike*." In *Finf un zibetsik yor yidishe prese in amerike, 1870–1945*. New York: Y. L. Peretz shrayber fareyn, 1945.

Golomb, Avrom. "*Lo zeh haderekh*." *Di goldene keyt* 7 (1951).

Grade, Chaim. *Der mentsh fun fayer* (The Man of Fire). New York: CYCO bikher farlag, 1962.

———. *The Well*. Trans. Ruth Wisse. Philadelphia: Jewish Publication Society, 1967.

Greenberg, Eliezer. "*Di yidishe literatur un di literatur af English*." *Di goldene keyt* 18 (1954).

Greenberg, Eliezer, and Irving Howe, eds. *A Treasury of Yiddish Stories*. New York: Viking Press, 1954.

———. *Voices from the Yiddish: Essays, Memoirs, Diaries.* Ann Arbor: University of Michigan Press, 1972.

Gross, Jan T. *Fear: Anti-Semitism in Poland After Auschwitz—An Essay in Historical Interpretation.* New York: Random House, 2006.

———, with Irena Grudzinska Gross. *Golden Harvest: Events at the Periphery of the Holocaust.* New York: Oxford University Press, 2012.

Gross, Natan. *Toldot hakolno'a hayehudi bepolin 1910–1959.* Jerusalem: Magnes Press/Hebrew University, 1990.

Grözinger, Elvira, and Magdalena Ruta, eds. *Under the Red Banner: Yiddish Culture in the Communist Countries in the Postwar Era.* Judische Kultur 20. Wiesbaden: Harrassowitz Verlag, 2008.

Grynberg, Henryk. *The Victory* (1969). Trans. Richard Lourie. Repr. Evanston, IL: Northwestern University Press, 1993.

Gutman, Khayim (Der lebediker). "*Lamdn un amorets in der yidisher literature.*" *Di goldene keyt* 6 (1950).

Gutman, Yisrael, Ezra Mendelsohn, Jehuda Reinharz, and Khone Shmeruk, eds. *The Jews of Poland Between Two World Wars.* Hanover, NH: University Press of New England, 1989.

Hadda, Janet. *Yankev Glatshteyn.* Boston: Twayne Publishers, 1980.

———. "German and Yiddish in the Poetry of Jacob Glatstein." *Prooftexts* 1, no.1 (1981).

———. *Passionate Women, Passive Men: Suicide in Yiddish Literature.* Albany: State University of New York Press, 1988.

———. *Isaac Bashevis Singer: A Life.* New York: Oxford University Press, 1997.

———. "Transmitting Ashkenaz." *Shofar: An Interdisciplinary Journal of Jewish Studies* 25, no. 1 (2006): 114–26.

Harshav, Benjamin. *The Meaning of Yiddish.* Berkeley: University of California Press, 1990.

———. *The Polyphony of Jewish Culture.* Stanford: Stanford University Press, 2007.

Harshav, Benjamin, and Barbara Harshav, eds. *American Yiddish Poetry: A Bilingual Anthology.* Berkeley: University of California Press, 1986.

Hellerstein, Kathryn. "Famous Long Ago: Yiddish in New York, 1967–1972." With photographs by Arnold Chekow. *The Book Peddler* 18 (Spring 1993): 44–57.

Hertzberg, Arthur. *A Jew in America: My Life and a People's Struggle for Identity.* New York: HarperCollins, 2002.

Heschel, Abraham Joshua. "After Majdanek: On Aaron Zeitlin's New Poems." *Yidisher kemfer* 29, no. 779 (October 1, 1948). Translated by Morris M. Faierstein in "Abraham Joshua Heschel and the Holocaust." *Modern Judaism* 19.3 (1999): Appendix 1.

Hoberman, Jim. *Bridge of Light: Yiddish Film Between Two Worlds.* New York: Schocken Books, 1991.

Horn, Dara. "The Future of Yiddish—in English: Field Notes from the New Ashkenaz." *Jewish Quarterly Review* 96, no. 4 (2006).

Horowitz, Rosemary, ed. *Memorial Books of Eastern European Jewry: Essays on the History and Meanings of Yizker Volumes.* Jefferson, NC: McFarland Press, 2011.

Howe, Irving. *World of Our Fathers.* New York: Harcourt, Brace, Jovanovich, 1976.

———. *A Margin of Hope: An Intellectual Autobiography.* New York: Harcourt, Brace, Jovanovich, 1982.

Hundert, Gershon. *Jews in Poland-Lithuania in the Eighteenth Century: A Genealogy of Modernity.* Berkeley: University of California Press, 2004.

Hutton, Christopher. "Normativism and the Notion of Authenticity in Yiddish Linguistics." In *The Field of Yiddish: Studies in Language, Folklore, and Literature*, ed. David Goldberg. 5th ed. Evanston, IL: Northwestern University Press, 1993.

Jackson, Naomi M. *Converging Movements: Modern Dance and Jewish Culture at the 92nd Street Y.* Middletown, CT: Wesleyan University Press, 2000.
Jockusch, Laura. *Collect and Record! Jewish Holocaust Documentation in Early Postwar Europe.* Oxford: Oxford University Press, 2012.
Karay, Felicja. *Death Comes in Yellow: Skarzysko-Kamienna Slave Labor Camp.* Amsterdam: Harwood Academic Publishers, 1996.
Kassow, Samuel D. *Who Will Write Our History? Emanuel Ringelblum, the Warsaw Ghetto, and the Oyneg Shabes Archive.* Bloomington: Indiana University Press, 2007.
Knapheys, Moyshe. "*Di sutskever-teg in buenes ayres.*" *Di prese*, June 10, 1953.
Kolitz, Zvi. "Yossel Rakover's Appeal to God." A new translation with afterword by Jeffrey V. Mallow and Franz Jozef van Beeck. *Cross Currents* (Fall 1994): 362–77.
Koller, Sabine, Gennady Estraykh, and Mikhail Krutikov, eds. *Joseph Opatoshu: A Yiddish Writer Between Europe and America.* Studies in Yiddish 11. London: Legenda, 2013.
Kramer, Michael P., and Hana Wirth-Nesher. *The Cambridge Companion to Jewish American Literature.* Cambridge: Cambridge University Press, 2003.
Kremer, S. Lillian, ed. *Holocaust Literature: An Encyclopedia of Writers and Their Work*, 2 vols. New York: Routledge, 2003.
Kronfeld, Chana. *On the Margins of Modernism: Decentering Literary Dynamics.* Berkeley: University of California Press, 1996.
Krutikov, Mikhail. *From Kabbalah to Class Struggle: Expressionism, Marxism, and Yiddish Literature in the Life and Work of Meir Wiener.* Stanford, CA: Stanford University Press, 2011.
Kugelmass, Jack, and Jonathan Boyarin. *From A Ruined Garden: The Memorial Books of Polish Jewry.* New York: Schocken Books, 1983.
Kuznitz, Cecile E. "Yiddish Studies." In *The Oxford Handbook of Jewish Studies*, ed. Martin Goodman. New York: Oxford University Press, 2002, 541–71. www.yiddishbookcenter.org/files/fckeditor/file/Kuznitz-Yiddish%20Studies.pdf.
Landis, Joseph C. "Conversation with Jacob Glatstein." *YIDDISH* 1 (1973): 40–53.
Lang Kaplan, Brukhe. "Zvi Scooler: Der grammayster." *YIVO Bleter, Band IV.* New York: YIVO, 2003.
Langer, Lawrence. "Deep Memory: The Buried Self" (1991). In *The Holocaust: Theoretical Readings*, ed. Neil Levi and Michael Rothberg. New Brunswick, NJ: Rutgers University Press, 2003.
———. "*Undzere kinder:* A Yiddish Film from Poland." In *Preempting the Holocaust.* New Haven, CT: Yale University Press, 1998, 157–65.
Lederhendler, Eli. *New York Jews and the Decline of Urban Ethnicity, 1950–1970.* Syracuse, NY: Syracuse University Press, 2001.
Leivick, H. "*An araynfir tsu a bukhnvald-khronik.*" *Tsukunft* (August 1945): 491.
———. *Mit der sheyres-hapleyte: Tog-bukh fartseykhenungen fun mayn rayze iber di yidishe lagern fun der amerikaner zone in Daytshland.* New York: H. Leivick yubiley fund, durkhn CYCO farlag, 1947.
———. "*Tsvey dokumentn.*" *Der tog*, March 17, 1952. And "*Der tog-bukh fun a kodesh.*" *Der tog*, March 31, 1952.
———. "*Gvure fun di getos.*" In *Eseyen un redes.* New York: Alveltlekhen Yidishn Kultur-Kongres, 1963, 411–14.
Levi, Neil, and Michael Rothberg, eds. *The Holocaust: Theoretical Readings.* New Brunswick, NJ: Rutgers University Press, 2003.
Leyeles, A. Glants. *Baym fus fun barg: Lider un poemes* (At the Foot of the Mountain: Poems and Epic Poems). New York: CYCO Bikher farlag, 1957.

———. "*Mayn lid in der yidisher poezye.*" In A. Glants Leyeles, *Baym fus fun barg: Lider un poems.* New York: CYCO Bikher farlag, 1957, 9–39.

———. *Velt un vort: Literarishe un andere eseyen* (World and Word: Literary and Other Essays). New York: Tsiko, 1958.

Lifshits, Y., ed. *Shatski-bukh: Opshatsungen vegn dr. Yankev Shatski* (Shatski-Book: Appreciations of Dr. Yankev Shatski). New York and Buenos Aires: YIVO, 1958.

Lipstadt, Deborah E. *The Eichmann Trial.* New York: Schocken, 2011.

Margolis, Rebecca. "Chava Rosenfarb's Yiddish Montreal." *Canadian Jewish Studies Études juives canadiennes* 18–19 (2010–11): 159–77.

———. *Jewish Roots, Canadian Soil: Yiddish Culture in Montreal, 1905–1945.* Montreal: McGill-Queen's University Press, 2011.

Mark, Bernard. "*Yudenratishe ahaves-yisroel: An entfer afn bilbl fun H. Levick.*" *Bleter far geshikhte* 5, no. 3 (1952): 63–115.

———. *Di umgekumene shrayber fun getos un lagern.* Warsaw: Yidish-bukh, 1954.

———. "*Dos yidishe lebn un di yidishe literatur in poyln in di yorn 1937–1957*" (The Jewish Life and Yiddish Literature in Poland in the Years 1937–1957). In *IKUF almanakh.* New York: Yidisher kultur farband, 1961, 60–86.

Miller, David Neal, ed. *Recovering the Canon: Essays on Isaac Bashevis Singer.* Leiden: E.J. Brill, 1986.

Milosz, Czeslaw. *Milosz's ABC.* New York: Farrar, Straus and Giroux, 2001.

———. "Ruins and Poetry." In *To Begin Where I Am: Selected Essays.* New York: Farrar, Straus and Giroux, 2001.

Mintz, Alan. *Popular Culture and the Shaping of Holocaust Memory in America.* Seattle: University of Washington Press, 2001.

———. *Sanctuary in the Wilderness: A Critical Introduction to American Hebrew Poetry.* Stanford, CA: Stanford University Press, 2011.

Miron, Dan. "Passivity and Narration: The Spell of Bashevis Singer." *Judaism* 1 (Winter 1992): 6–17.

———. *The Image of the Shtetl and Other Studies of the Jewish Literary Imagination.* Syracuse, NY: Syracuse University Press, 2000.

———. *From Continuity to Contiguity: Toward a New Jewish Literary Thinking.* Stanford, CA: Stanford University Press, 2010.

Morgentaler, Goldie. "Land of the Postscript: Canada and the Post-Holocaust Fiction of Chava Rosenfarb." *Judaism* 49, no. 2 (2000): 168–83.

Mukdoni, A. "*Yidishe kultur in amerike.*" *Di goldene keyt* 17 (1953): 184–96; *Di goldene keyt* 18 (1954): 113–25; *Di goldene keyt* 19 (1954): 172–84; and *Di goldene keyt* 20 (1954): 240–52.

Murav, Harriet. *Music from a Speeding Train: Jewish Literature in Post-Revolution Russia.* Stanford, CA: Stanford University Press, 2011.

Niger, Shmuel. "*Tendentsn in der nayster yidisher literatur*" (Trends in Contemporary Yiddish Literature). *Jewish Book Annual* (1955–56): 3–8.

Norich, Anita. *Discovering Exile: Yiddish and Jewish American Culture during the Holocaust.* Stanford, CA: Stanford University Press, 2007.

———. *Writing in Tongues: Translating Yiddish in the Twentieth Century.* Seattle: University of Washington Press, 2014.

Novick, Peter. *The Holocaust in American Life.* New York: Houghton Mifflin Company, 2000.

Nowersztern, Abraham, ed. *Abraham Sutzkever on His Seventieth Birthday.* Catalogue of an exhibition at the Jewish National and University Library. In Yiddish and Hebrew. Jerusalem: Jewish National Library, 1983.

———. "*Dos poylishe yidntum.*" *Der PaknTreger/The Book Peddler: Magazine of the National Yiddish Book Centre.* 1991.
Ozick, Cynthia. *The Pagan Rabbi and Other Stories.* New York: Knopf, 1983.
———. "Tradition and (or versus) the Jewish Writer." In *The Din in the Head: Essays.* New York: Houghton Mifflin, 2006.
Pat, Yankev. *Shmuesn mit yidishe shrayber* (Conversations with Yiddish Writers). New York: CYCO and Workmen's Circle, 1954.
———. *Shmuesn mit yidishe shrayber in yisroel* (Conversations with Yiddish Writers in Israel). New York: Der kval, 1960.
Perle, Yehoshue. *Everyday Jews: Scenes from a Vanished Life.* New Haven, CT: Yale University Press, 2007.
Pilowsky, Aryeh. *Tsvishn yo un neyn: Yidish un yidish-literatur in Eretz-yisroel 1907–1948* (Between Yes and No: Yiddish and Yiddish Literature in Israel). Tel Aviv: World Council for Yiddish and Jewish Culture, 1991.
Pinsker, Shachar. "*Yung yisroel: Tvishn heym un goles*" (Young Israel: Between Home and Diaspora). *Forverts,* June 29, 2007, 12–13.
———. "Choosing Yiddish in Israel: *Yung Yisroel* between Home and Exile, the Center and the Margins." In *Choosing Yiddish: New Frontiers of Language and Culture,* ed. Lara Rabinovitch, Shiri Goren, and Hannah S. Pressman, 277–94. Detroit, MI: Wayne State University Press, 2013.
Polonsky, Antony. "Introduction—The Shtetl: Myth and Reality." *POLIN* 17 (2004).
Poupko-Krinsky, Rokhl. "*Mayn arbet in Yivo unter di daytshn.*" *YIVO-Bleter* 30, no. 2 (1947): 214–23.
Rabinovitch, Lara, Shiri Goren, and Hannah S. Pressman, eds. *Choosing Yiddish: New Frontiers of Language and Culture.* Detroit, MI: Wayne State University Press, 2013.
Rapoport, Y. *Zoymen in vint.* Buenos Aires: Argentiner opteyl fun Alveltlekhn Yidishn kultur-kongres, 1961.
Redlich, Shimon. *Life in Transit: Jews in Postwar Lodz, 1945–1950.* Boston: Academic Studies Press, 2011.
Ribalow, Harold U. "A Conversation with Chaim Grade." *Congress Monthly,* February 21, 1975.
Rivkin, Borekh. *Grunt tendentsn fun der yidisher literatur in America* (Main Trends of Yiddish Literature in America). New York: IKUF farlag, 1948.
———. *Lebn un shafn.* Chicago: Farlag L.M. Shteyn, 1953.
Rochman, Leib. "*Af keyver-oves: Bay di kvorim fun Sholem-Aleichem un fun andere yidishe shrayber in New York*" (Visiting the Ancestors' Graves: At the Graves of Sholem Aleichem and Other Yiddish Writers in New York). *Yerushalayimer almanakh* 6–7 (1976): 113–16.
Rose, Jonathan, ed. *The Holocaust and the Book: Destruction and Preservation.* Amherst: University of Massachusetts Press, 2001.
Rosen, Alan, ed. *Approaches to Teaching Wiesel's Night.* New York: Modern Language Association of America, 2007.
Rosenwald, Lawrence. *Multilingual America: Language and the Making of American Literature.* Cambridge: Cambridge University Press, 2008.
Roskies, David. *Against the Apocalypse: Responses to Catastrophe in Modern Jewish Culture.* Cambridge, MA: Harvard University Press, 1984.
———. *A Bridge of Longing: The Lost Art of Yiddish Storytelling.* Cambridge, MA: Harvard University Press, 1995.

———. "Rabbis, Rebbes and Other Humanists: The Search for a Usable Past in Modern Yiddish Literature." *Studies in Contemporary Jewry* 12 (1996).

———. "What Is Holocaust Literature?" *Studies in Contemporary Jewry 21: Jews, Catholics and the Burden of History*, ed. Eli Lederhendler. Oxford: Oxford University Press, 2005.

———. *Yiddishlands: A Memoir*. Detroit, MI: Wayne State University Press, 2008.

———. "Dividing the Ruins: Communal Memory in Yiddish and Hebrew." In *After the Holocaust: Challenging the Myth of Silence*, ed. Cesarani and Sundquist. London: Routledge, 2012, 67–82.

———, ed. *The Literature of Destruction: Jewish Responses to Catastrophe*. Philadelphia: Jewish Publication Society, 1989.

Roskies, David, and Naomi Diamant. *Holocaust Literature: A History and Guide*. Waltham, MA: Brandeis University Press, 2012.

Rozenfarb, Chava. "*A videh fun a mekhaber*" (Confession of a Writer). *Di goldene keyt* 81 (1973): 127–41. (In Yiddish.)

———. "*Simkhe-Bunim Shayevitsh: Dermonungen*" (Simkhe-Bunim Shayevitsh: Reminiscences). *Di goldene keyt* 131 (1991): 9–28.

———. "Feminism and Yiddish Literature: A Personal Approach." In *Gender and Text in Modern Hebrew and Yiddish Literature*, ed. Naomi B. Sokoloff, Anne Lapidus Lerner, and Anita Norich. New York: Jewish Theological Seminary of America, 1992.

———. "*Yitskhok Bashevis un Sholem Ash (a pruv fun a farglaykh)*" (Yitskhok Bashevis and Sholem Asch [An Attempt of a Comparison]). *Di goldene keyt* 133 (1992): 75–105.

———. "*Pol Tselan un zayne goyrl-brider*" (Paul Celan and His Brothers of Destiny). *Di goldene keyt* 138 (1994).

Ruta, Magdalena, ed. *Nisht bay di taykhn fun Bovl: Antologye fun der yidisher poezye in nokhmilkhomedikn poyln* (Not at the Rivers of Babylon: Anthology of Yiddish Poetry in Postwar Poland). Ed. and with an introduction by Magdalena Ruta. Cracow: Ksiegarnia Akademicka, 2012.

Safran, William. "The Jewish Diaspora in a Comparative and Theoretical Perspective." *Israel Studies* 10, no. 1 (2005): 36–60.

Said, Edward. *Reflections on Exile and Other Essays*. Cambridge, MA: Harvard University Press, 2000.

Schulman, Elias. *The Holocaust in Yiddish Literature*. New York: Workmen's Circle, 1983.

———. "*Siyem fun tsikl Musterverk fun der yiddisher literature*." *Jewish Book Annual* 43 (1985–86): 132–40.

Schwarz, Jan. *Imagining Lives: Autobiographical Fiction of Yiddish Writers*. Madison: University of Wisconsin Press, 2005.

Seidman, Naomi. "Elie Wiesel and the Scandal of Jewish Rage." *Jewish Social Studies* 3/1 (1996): 1–19.

———. *Faithful Renderings: Jewish-Christian Difference and the Politics of Translation*. Chicago: University of Chicago Press, 2006.

Shandler, Jeffrey. *Adventures in Yiddishland: Postvernacular Language and Culture*. Berkeley: University of California Press, 2006.

———. "The Holocaust for Beginners: Yankev Glatshteyn's *Emil un Karl* and Other Wartime Works for Young American Yiddish Readers." *MELUS: Multi-Ethnic Literature of the U.S.* 37, no. 2 (Summer 2012): 109–30.

Shapiro, Robert Moses, ed. *Holocaust Chronicles: Individualizing the Holocaust Through Diaries and Other Contemporaneous Personal Accounts*. Hoboken, NJ: KTAV Publishing House, 1999.

Sherman, Joseph. "Translating '*Shotns baym hodson*' (Shadows on the Hudson), Directly Encountering Isaac Bashevis Singer's Authorial Dualism." In *Isaac Bashevis Singer: His Work and His World*, ed. Hugh Denman. Leiden: Brill, 2002, 49–80.

———. *Dictionary of Literary Biography: Yiddish Literature*, vol. 333. New York: Bruccoli Clark Layman, 2007.

———, ed. *Yiddish after the Holocaust*. Oxford: Boulevard, 2004.

Shneer, David. *Yiddish and the Creation of Soviet Jewish Culture, 1918–1930*. New York: Cambridge University Press, 2004.

———. *Through Soviet Jewish Eyes: Photography, War, and the Holocaust*. New Brunswick, NJ: Rutgers University Press, 2011.

Shreiber, Maeera Y. *Singing in a Strange Land: A Jewish American Poetics*. Stanford, CA: Stanford University Press, 2007.

Shternshis, Anna. *Soviet and Kosher: Jewish Popular Culture in the Soviet Union, 1923–1939*. Bloomington: Indiana University Press, 2006.

Singer, Isaac Bashevis. *The Collected Stories of Isaac Bashevis Singer*. New York: Farrar, Straus and Giroux, 1982.

———. *Collected Stories: A Friend of Kafka to Passions*. Ed. Ilan Stavans. New York: Library of America, 2004.

Sollors, Werner, ed. *Multilingual America: Transnationalism, Ethnicity, and the Languages of American Literature*. New York: New York University Press, 1998.

Stavans, Ilan. *Singer's Typewriter and Mine: Reflections on Jewish Culture*. Lincoln: University of Nebraska Press, 2012.

———, ed. *Isaac Bashevis Singer: An Album*. New York: Library of America, 2004.

Strigler, Mordechai. "*Fun Bukhnvald: Dokumentn fun undzere teg.*" *Tsukunft* (August 1945): 495.

Sutzkever, Avrom. *Poetishe verk*, vols. 1 and 2. Tel Aviv: Yoyvl komitet, 1963.

Szeintuch, Yechiel. "*Arn tseytlins ani-maamin (tsvey briv tsu shmuel niger).*" *Di goldene keyt* 112 (1983).

———. "*Di biografye fun lid 'Der tsirk.*'" In *Yikhes fun lid/Yikhuso shel shir: Lekoved Avrom Sutzkever*, ed. Dov Sadan, Khone Shmeruk, and Chava Turniansky. Tel Aviv: Yoyvl-kommitet, 1983, 258–79.

———. "The Corpus of Yiddish and Hebrew Literature from Ghettos and Concentration Camps and Its Relevance for Holocaust Studies." In *Studies in Yiddish Literature and Folklore*. Jerusalem: Hebrew University, 1986, 186–207.

———. "*Mordkhe Shtrigler afn sheydveg nokh Bukhnvald.*" *Forverts*, May 28, and June 4, 2004.

———. "*Khayim Grade bal-pe: Di vikhtikeyt fun intonatsye un lebedikn vort af yidish.*" *Forverts* (New York), September 21, 2012, 22–23.

———. "Yiddish Survivors' Literature." Jerusalem: Hebrew University of Jerusalem, 2012. http://www.hum.huji.ac.il/units.php?cat=4621&incat=2933

———, ed. *Bereshut-harabim un bereshut-hayekhid: Arn Zeitlin un di yidishe literatur* (Public and Private: Aaron Zeitlin and Yiddish Literature). Jerusalem: Hebrew University Press, 2000.

Tabatshnik, Avrom. *Dikhter un dikhtung* (Poet and Poetry). New York: A. Tabatshnik, 1965.

———. "*A. Tabatshnik: Fun a shmues mit Arn Tseytlin.*" *Di goldene keyt* 65 (1969): 17–33.

Teller, Judd L. "Yiddish Litterateurs and American Jews: Have They Come to a Parting of the Ways?" *Commentary* 18, no. 1 (July 1954).

Trunk, Isaiah. *Lodzher geto* (The Lodz Ghetto). New York: Yad Vashem/YIVO Institute for Jewish Research, 1962.

Turkov, Mark, ed. *Spetsyele oysgabe gevidmet der bikher serye dos poylishe yidntum* 25. Buenos Aires, 1947.

Tverski, Arn. *Ikh bin der korbn un der eydes*. New York: A. Tverski, 1947.

Ulinover, Miriam. *A grus fun der alter heym: Lider*. Ed. and intro. Natalia Krinitska; trans. into French by Batia Baum. Paris: Medem-bibliotek, 2003.

Valencia, Heather. "From *Der tsirk to Erev mayn farbrenung:* The Transformation of Experience in Two Poems by Avrom Sutzkever." In *Leket: Jiddisitik heute*. Dusseldorf: Dusseldorf University Press, 2012, 109–28.
Vedenyapin, Yuri. "'Doctors Prescribe Laughter': The Yiddish Stand-Up Comedy of Shimen Dzigan." BA thesis, Harvard University, 2004.
Veidlinger, Jeffrey. *The Moscow State Yiddish Theater: Jewish Culture on the Soviet Stage*. Bloomington: Indiana University Press, 2000.
———. *In the Shadow of the Shtetl: Small-Town Jewish Life in Soviet Ukraine*. Bloomington: Indiana University Press, 2013.
Wein, A. "Memorial Books as a Source for Research into the History of Jewish Communities in Europe." *Yad Vashem Studies* 9 (1973).
Weinreich, Max. "*Briv fun Maks Vaynraykh tsu Avrom Sutzkever*." *Di goldene keyt* 95/96 (1978): 171–203.
———. "*Vos heyst shraybn yidishlekh?*" *Yidishe shprakh* 2, no. 4 (July–August 1942).
———. *History of the Yiddish Language*, 2 vols. New Haven, CT: Yale University Press, 2008.
White, Hayden. *Figural Realism: Studies in the Mimesis Effect*. Baltimore, MD: Johns Hopkins University Press, 1991.
Wiesel, Elie. *All Rivers Run to the Sea: Memoirs*. New York: Knopf, 1995.
———. *Night*. New York: Hill and Wang, 2006.
Wirth-Nesher, Hana. *City Codes: Reading the Modern Urban Novel*. Cambridge: Cambridge University Press, 1996.
Wisse, Ruth. "In Praise of Chaim Grade." *Commentary* (April 1977): 70–73.
———. "The Poet from Vilna." *Jewish Review of Books* (Summer 2010): 10–15.
Wojdowski, Bogdan. *Bread for the Departed*. Trans. Madeline G. Levine. Evanston, IL: Northwestern University Press, 1997.
Wolitz, Seth. L., ed. *The Hidden Isaac Bashevis Singer*. Austin: University of Texas Press, 2001.
Yanosovitsh, Yitskhok. *Penimer un nemen, band tsvey: Yidishe prozaikers un zeyere verk fun nokh der tsveyter velt-milkhome*. Buenos Aires: Farlag Kiem, 1985.
Young, James E. *Writing and Rewriting the Holocaust: Narrative and the Consequences of Interpretation*. Bloomington: Indiana University Press, 1988.
Zeitlin, Aaron. "*Mayn foter*." In Hillel Zeitlin, *Reb nakhmen barslaver: Der zeer fun podolye*. New York: Farlag matones, 1952.
———. *Literarishe un filosofishe eseyen*. New York: Alveltlekher yidisher kultur-kongres, 1980.
———. *Poems of the Holocaust and Poems of Faith*. Ed. and trans. Morris M. Faierstein. New York: iUniverse, 2007.
Zelkowicz, Josef. *In Those Terrible Days: Notes from the Lodz Ghetto*. Ed. Michal Unger. Jerusalem: Yad Vashem, 2002.

Bibliographies

Bibliografye fun yidishe bikher vegn khurbn un gvure (Bibliography of Yiddish Books about the Holocaust and Heroism). Ed. Josef Gar and Philip Friedman. New York: Yad Vashem/YIVO Institute for Jewish Research, 1962.
Essential Yiddish Books: 1000 Great Works from the Collection of the National Yiddish Book Center. Ed. Zachary M. Baker. Amherst, MA: National Yiddish Book Center, 2004.
Leksikon fun der nayer yidisher literatur. Ed. Shmuel Niger and Yankev Shatski. New York: Altveltlekhn yidishn kultur-kongres, 1956–81.
Leksikon fun yidish-shraybers. Ed. Berl Cahan. New York: Illman-Cahan, 1986.

INDEX

Page numbers in italics refer to photographs.

Abramovitsh, Sholem Yankev, 217
Adorno, Theodor, 41–42, 322–23n2
Ahad Ha'am, 139, 229
akeyde (binding of Isaac), 20
Aleichem, Sholem. *See* Sholem Aleichem
Algemeyner zhurnal, 237
Amalek, 27–28, 29, 31, 170
Der amerikaner (periodical), 107
Anglo-Jewish writers and writing, 124, 126, 186, 187, 202
anokhi (biblical "I am here"), 31
An-Ski, *Der dybbuk* (1913–1917), 217, 221
Anthology of Holocaust Literature (1968), 113–14
Appelfeld, Aharon, 75, 84
Arendt, Hannah, 149–50, 230; *Eichmann in Jerusalem* (1962), 120
Argentina. *See* Buenos Aires, Yiddish literature in; *poylishe yidntum*
Asch, Sholem, 114, 124, 133, 194, 259; *Farn mabl* trilogy (Before the Deluge, 1949), 99, 258
Ashkenazi civilization, 250, 324n15. *See also* Yiddish culture after the Holocaust; calls for return to religious *Yiddishkeit* of, 145; continuity after WWII, 244; Hebrew-Yiddish bilingualism of, 9; radical transformation after 1945, vii, 142; rejection of Yiddish and Ashkenazi civilization by majority of Jews, 17–18, 124–25, 148, 203, 243, 247; Yiddish and other languages embodying, 3, 6, 250; Yiddish writers endeavoring to memorialize, 10–12, 142, 244–45; *Yizker* books memorializing, 12, 242, 250
Astro, Alan, 107, 306n52, 307n60
Auden, W. H., 184
Auerbach, Ephraim, 312n33, 315n3
Auerbach, Rachel, 243
Auschwitz, 32, 50, 57–58, 65, 76, 108, 128, 243
aynzamlen (collecting), 163

Ayzland, Reuven, *Fun undzer friling* (From Our Springtime, 1953), 308n15

Bak, Samuel, *ii*, x, *35*
Baker, Zachary M., *Essential Yiddish Books* (2004), 6
Bal Shem Tov, 130, 198
Balaban, Mayer, 99, 254
Banco Israelita del Rio de La Plata, Argentina, 94
Bashevis, Yitskhok. *See* Singer, I. B.
Beethoven, late style of, 322–23n2
Bellow, Saul, *53*, 131–35, 229, 236, 237, 251; *The Adventures of Augie March* (1953), 133–35; *Mr. Sammler's Planet* (1970), 309n36; "Something to Remember Me By" (1990), 309n36
Belzec, 76
Berezovski, Shaul, 45
Bergelson, Dovid, 8, 133, 207
Bergen-Belsen, 51–52, 58, 65
Berger, Aaron, 315n3
Berkowitz, William, 237
Bernard-Donals, Michael, 27
Bernstein, Charles, 184–85, 316n10
Bez, Khayim, 212
Bialik, Haym Nahman, "*In shkhite-shtot*" (In the City of Slaughter, 1904), 39
Bintl briv column, *Forverts*, 172–73
Blumenfeld, Diana, *101*, 265, 266
Blument[h]al, Nakhmen (Nachman), 4, 243, 264, 267, 268
Blumgarten, Solomon (Yehoash), 3, 199, 291n1
Bokher, Eliohu, *Bove Bukh*, 25
Borges, Jorge Luis, "The Other" (1975), 90
Borwicz, Michal: *Arishe papirn* (Aryan Papers, 1955), *110*, 262; *Yosl Rakover* controversy and, 122
Brandes, Georg, 310n44

339

the Bratslaver (Nachman of Bratslav), 130, 155, 160, 232, 237
"*A brivele der mamen*" (popular song), 172, 174
Browning, Christopher R., 300n8
Buchenwald, 69, 70, 72
Buenos Aires, Yiddish literature in, 4, 12, 13, 49, 68, 75, 78, 94–95, 114, 126. See also *poylishe yidntum*
Bund, 54, 57, 96, 97, 302n24

Caruth, Cathy, 27
Celan, Paul, 27, 54
Central Jewish Historical Commission, Poland, 23, 95
Central Union of Polish Jews, Argentina, 38, 94, 96
Chagall, Marc, 25
Chametsky, Jules, 308n20
Charney, Daniel, *Vilne: Memuarn* (Vilna: Memoirs, 1951), *102*, 260
Chekow, Arnold, 193, 317n29
Chelmno, 57, 298n21
children's trauma in *Undzere kinder* (film, 1948), 45–50
Choosing Yiddish: New Frontiers of Language and Culture (2013), 246
Chopin, Frederick, 38
The Chronicle of the Lodz Ghetto, 59, 299n38
collaboration, Jewish, 118–21
comedy, Jewish/Yiddish, 45–50, 83, 134, 135, 186, 195, 203, 218
Commentary (periodical), 126
communal memory: Ashkenazi civilization, Yiddish writers endeavoring to memorialize, 10–12, 142, 244–45; in Glatshteyn's and Zeitlin's poetry, 144, 154–58, 169–71, 176–80, 247–48; in Grade's portrayal of *litvak* culture, 210–17, 223–26; New York Yiddish literary world, elegiac aspects of, 135–39, 141–42; past-orientation in Yiddish literature, vii, 125; in *Dos poylishe yidntum* series, 100; realist style and, 245, 249; religious imagery, secular writers adopting, 8–9, 24, 37–38, 40, 54, 79, 137–39, 175, 189–90; in Rochman's *Un in dayn blut zolstu lebn*, 80–83, 87; Singer's stories moving beyond, 135; in Sutzkever's poetry, 15; traumatic memory and testimony, relationship between, 27
communism. See Soviet sphere, Yiddish culture in

Dawidowicz, Lucy, 219–20
daytshmerism, 152, 156, 158, 311n19
derekh hashas (Way of the Shas/the Mishna), Yiddish viewed as, 150, 151, 168
Diamant, Naomi, 116
Dickstein, Morris, 206, 213, 226
Diner, Hasia, 309n22
Dinur, Yekhiel. See Ka-Tzetnik
Dluznowsky, Moyshe, *204*
Dorfman, Zelig, 315n3
Dostoyevsky, Fyodor, 213, 225
Dworzecki, Mark, 4
Dzigan, Shimen: *Der koyekh fun yidishn humor* (The Power of Jewish Humor, 1974), 46; *Undzere kinder* (film, 1948), 45–50

East European versus West European Jews, 76, 132–33
Edelshtat, Dovid, 123, 159
Efros, Israel, 254n12, 315n3
Ehrenburg, Ilya, 20, 22, 35, 151; *The Black Book* (with Vasili Grossman, 1946/1980), 22, 149, 294n10, 308n20
Eichmann trial (1961), 5, 88, 114, 120, 230, 249
Einhorn, Dovid, 135, 315n3; "*Geshtorbn der letster bal-tfile*" (The Last Prayer Leader Died), *204*
Elberg, Yehuda, 54, 99, 100, 298n25; *Unter kuperne himlen* (Under Copper Skies, 1951), 74, 259
Eliot, T. S., 126, 198, 309n36
Ellison, Ralph, *The Invisible Man* (1952), 134–35
Emiot, Israel, 266, 315n3
English translations. See translations from Yiddish
Enlightenment, 144, 145, 146, 237
ets khayim (Tree of Life), 40
European literature and history, Yiddish turn from, 145–46, 150–51, 155
Eybeshutz, Reb Yonathan, 298n31

Farlag, L. M. Shteyn, 139
Fein, Richard, 191, 251, 314n62

Feinberg, Leib, 315n3
Fiddler on the Roof (musical, 1965), 18, 47, 186, 251
Filreis, Al, 316n10
Finder, Gabriel, 48, 49, 297b11
Finkelstein, Leo, *Megiles poyln* (Scrolls of Poland, 1947), 94, 255
Fishman, David E., 34
Fishman, Gele, 67
Fishman, Joshua, 67, 318n43
Foer, Jonathan Safran, 237
Forverts (New York daily), 13, 78, 83, 107, 125, 172, 224, 228, 229, 231, 232, 234, 236, 237, 247
Frakes, Jerold C., 150
Frank, Anne, *Diary* (1947), 75, 76
Frank, Jacob, 211
Friedman, Philip, 4, 45, 94, 105, 243, 304n12; *Oshvyentshim* (Auschwitz, 1950), 95, 258
Friedman, Yankov, 67

Garbarini, Alexandra, 301–2n24, 302n38
Gary, Romain, 54
gender: in Grade's works, 220–21; poetry and prose in Yiddish literature, gendered division between, 50, 55–56, 194–95
genres employed in Yiddish post-Holocaust literature, 249
German: Glatshteyn and, 152–58; Weinreich and, 146–52
Germany: as Amalek, 27–28, 29, 31, 170; *Institut zur Erforschung der Judenfrage*, 23; migration of Jewish displaced persons from, 8; rage against, in Yiddish culture, 5, 30–31, 112, 144–48, 151–52, 153–54, 170, 249
Ginsberg, Allen, 189
Glants-Leyeles, Aaron. *See* Leyeles, Aaron Glants
Glatshteyn, Yankev, 153–71, *191*, *199*; boundaries of linguistic medium and, 207–8, 319n62; Grade compared, 167, 225; modernism and, 164, 166, 169, 249, 313n50; new Yiddish writers immigrating to America and, 124; 92nd Street Y poetry readings and, 14, 181–83, 184, 186, 187, 189, 190–95, *191*, 198, *199*, 200–201, 206, 315n3; Ozick and, 187, 188, 202, 206; in Pat's *Shmuesn mit yidishe shrayber*, 135; performative style of, 249; from rage to communal memory in poetry of, 144, 151, 153–58, 169–71, 247–48, 249; religious imagery used by, 137; Singer and, 135, 187, 193–95, 196; Sutzkever compared, 18, 131, 167; on Sutzkever's ghetto poems, 25; on Tabatshnik, 160; Tabatshnik recording of, 144, 162–65, 167, 312n33; on Yiddish culture's long-term viability, 248
Glatshteyn, Yankev, works: "*Bratslaver*" (1946), 130; *Dem tatns shotn* (My Father's Shadow, 1953), 128–31, 165, 167; *Emil un Karl* (1940), 311n24; "*Faran aza gekekhts vi hunger*" (Such a Dish as Hunger Exists, 1946), 130–31; *Di freyd fun yidishn vort* (The Joy of the Yiddish Word, 1961), 162, 169; *Fun mayn gantser mi* (From All My Toil, 1956), 170; "*Gebentsht zol zayn*" (May It Be Blessed), 169–70; *Gedenklider* (Poems of Remembrance, 1943), 130, 143, 152, 190; "*A gute nakht, velt*" (Good Night, World, 1938), 146, 200–201, 207, 247; "*Ikh davn a yidish blat in sobvey*" (I Pray from a Yiddish Newspaper in the Subway), 156–58; "*Ikh tu dermonen*" (I Keep Recalling), 167–68; "*In tokh genumen*" (The Heart of the Matter) weekly column, 186; *Khurbn* poems (1943), 130, 131; "*Lider fun shtilkeyt*" (Poems of Silence), 167; "*Mayn getselt*" (My Tent, 1956), 207–8; "*Motsart*," 154–55, 166–67; "*Nisht di meysim loybn got*" (The Dead Don't Praise God), 8–9; "*Der rayzeman*" (The Traveling Man), 152–53; *Shtralndike yidn* (Illuminated Jews, 1946), 130, 154, 156, 167; "Sing Ladino," 181–83; "Singer's Literary Reputation" (1965), 193–95; "*S'yidishe vort*" (The Yiddish Word), 190–93, 207; "*Undzer tsikhtik loshn*" (Our Neat and Tidy Language), 152, 153–54; *Ven yash iz geforn* (1938), 155; *Ven Yash iz*

Glatshteyn, Yankev, works (*continued*) *geforn* (When Yash Set Out, 1957), 99, 263; *Yankev Glatshteyn* (1921), 128, 162; "Yidishkeyt" (1953), 128–30; *Yidishtaytshn* (Yiddishmeanings, 1936), 128, 130, 208; *Yosl Loksh fun Khelm* (Yosl Loksh of Chelm, 1936), 130; "*A zuntik iber nyu york*" (A Sunday over New York), 165–66
Globus (journal)
Goethe, Johann Wolfgang von, 145–46, 151
Goichberg, Israel, 315n3

Di goldene keyt (The Golden Chain; periodical), 17, 23, 31, 64, 83, 94, 99, 122, 130, 133, 139, 171, 229–30, 231–32, 238, 243

Goldfaden, Avrom, 47, 48; *Di tsvey Kuni-Lemls,* 47

Golomb, Avrom, "*Lo zeh haderekh*" (That Is Not the Way), 229–30

Goskind, Shaul, 48

Grade, Chaim, 210–26, *211;* artistic multiplicity and multiculturalism of, 244; authenticity of work in portrayal of *litvak* culture, 210–17, 223–26, 319n93; gender in works of, 220–22; Glatshteyn compared, 167, 225; Hebrew-Yiddish bilingualism and, 9; in Howe and Greenberg, ed., *A Treasury of Yiddish Stories* (1954), 133; immigration to New York, 124; in Lodz, 45; migration from Germany as Jewish displaced person, 8, 212; at 92nd Street Y poetry readings, 184, 209, 315n3; personal and professional life, 212, 218–20, 222; in *Dos poylishe yidntum* series, 99, 100, 255, 259; Ravitsh's "*Di kroynung fun a yungn yidishn dikhter in amerike*" and, 123; realism of, 245, 249; Rochman compared, 76, 78; Singer and, 135, 211, 217, 221, 222, 225, 226–27, 232, 234, 319n3; in Soviet Union, 296n439; survivor guilt in work of, 222–23; Tabatshnik recording of, 162, 225, 312n33; Vilna and, 214, 215, 218, 219, 220, 223–26; Wiesel influenced by, 114; Yiddish culture and work of, 142

Grade, Chaim, works: *The Agunah* (The Abandoned Wife, 1961), 212, 216–17, 219–23; *Der brunem* (The Well, 1958), 213–18, 219–21; *Fun unter der erd* (From under the Earth, 1979–82), 224–25; "*Di kloyz un di gas*" (The Synagogue and the Street, 1974; in English as *Rabbis and Wives,* 1983), 214; *Der mames shabosim* (My Mother's Sabbath Days, 1955), 28, 220, 224, 225; "*Mayn krig mit Hersh Rasseyner*" ("My Quarrel with Hersh Rasseyner," 1953), 11, 127, 218, 219, 224; "*Di musernikes*" (1939), 218; "*Der oysgebrenter dorn*" (The Extinguished Bush), 223–24; *Pleytim* (Refugees, 1947), 99, 255; *Shayn fun farloshene shtern* (Light of Extinguished Stars, 1950), 99, 259; *Der shtumer minyen* (The Silent Minyan, 1976), 210; *Tsemakh Atlas: Di yeshive* (The Yeshiva, 1967–68), 224; *Yo* (1936), 220

Grade, Vela (mother), 220, 224

graves and gravestones, in Yiddish post-Holocaust writing, 38–39, 54, 67–68, 70, 78, 81–82, 85, 177, 178

Greenberg, Eliezer, 184, 198, 200, 312n33, 315n3; *A Treasury of Yiddish Poetry* (with Irving Howe, 1969), 186, 187, 188, 200, *201,* 202, 204, 248, 315n3; *A Treasury of Yiddish Stories* (with Irving Howe, 1954), 131–33, 141, 186, 187, 248; "*Di yidishe literatur un di literatur af english*" (1954), 139

Greenberg, Uri Zvi, 123

Gris, Noakh, 103

Grosbard, Herts, *vort-kontsertn* (word concerts) of, 184

Gross, Jan, 88

Gross, Naftule, 312n33

Gross, Natan, 45, 48, 50, 297n11

Grossman, David, *See: Under Love* (1986), 64

Grossman, Vasili: *The Black Book* (with Ilya Ehrenburg, 1946/1980), 22, 149, 294n10, 308n20; *Treblinke* (with Y. Viernik, 1946), *109,* 253

Gros-Zimerman, M., 141

Gruss, Noah, ed., *Kinder-martirologye: Zamlung fun dokumentn* (Children Martyrology: Collection of Documents, 1947), *109,* 255

Grynberg, Henryk, 48; *The Victory* (1969), 15

Gutman, Khayim *(Der lebediker),* 229–30

Gutman-Jasny, Rosa, 184, 315n3

Haaretz (Israeli newspaper), 17

Hadda, Janet, 153

Halkin, Shmuel, 35

Halpern, Moyshe Leib, 126, 200

Hamelitz (Hebrew journal), 229

Hamsun, Knut, 231

Harshav, Barbara, 143, 208, 261, 315n3

Harshav, Benjamin, 5, 143, 208, 251, 315n3

Hashomer Hatzair, 19

Hasidism: Bal Shem Tov, 130, 198; Glatshteyn and, 130, 146, 155; homiletic style of, 9; Kolitz, Zvi, "*Yosl Rakover redt tsu got*" (Yosl Rakover Speaks to God, 1946),

122; *misnagdim* (opponents of Hasidim) in Grade's works, 213, 215, 217; Nachman of Bratslav (the Bratslaver), 130, 155, 160, 232, 237; Peretz and, 160; *Dos poylishe yidntum* and, 100, 107; Rochman and, 77, 85; in Singer's work, 196, 211, 217, 221, 237; Strigler and, 300n6; in Zeitlin's poetry, 174, 175

Haskalah (Jewish Enlightenment), 144, 145, 146, 237

Hazlitt, William, "On the Conversation of Authors," 158

the Hazon Ish (R. Avraham Karelitz), 224, 320n28

Hebrew alphabet: Kotzker Rebbe on, 9–10, 11; in Singer's *"Mayse Tishevitz,"* 10–11

Hebrew-Yiddish bilingualism of Ashkenazi civilization, 9

Helenowek orphanage, 45, 46, 48

Heller, Binem, 45, 48, 296n43

Hersey, John, *The Wall* (1950), 64

Hertzberg, Arthur, 124–25

Herzl, Theodor, 122

Herzog, Elizabeth, and Mark Zborowski, *Life Is with People* (1952), 132

Heschel, Abraham Joshua, 132, 144–46, 148, 244, 248; biography of Kotzker Rebbe, 9–10; *"Di mizrekh eyropeisher tkufe in der yidisher geshikhte"* (The Eastern European Period in Jewish History, in English as *The Earth Is the Lord's,* 1950), 132, 145, 248

Hilberg, Raul, *The Destruction of the European Jews* (1961), 243

Hirsch, Baron Maurice de, 97

Hirshoyt, Yekhiel (Julian), 101, 257, 261

Histadrut, 17, 93

Hollander, John, 186, 200, 251, 315n3

Holocaust: destruction of European Jewry in, 18–19, 76; as *der driter khurbn* (the third destruction), 1, 23, 25, 32, 44, 54, 117, 144, 151, 152, 196, 198, 242; East European versus West European Jews in, 76; as focus of 1953–1954 Yiddish culture, 126–31; Glatshteyn on, 164; *Institut zur Erforschung der Judenfrage* (Germany), 23; Jewish collaboration in, 118–21; Lodz and Lodz Ghetto, 44–45, 50, 52–53, 56–60, 63, 298n21; Minsk-Mazowiecki, Rochman in hiding in, 74–75, 77, 83–84; as modernist event, 60–61; Rosenfarb's experience of, 50–53, 56–58; *sheyres hapleyte* (saved remnants) from, 12, 44, 64, 69–70, 72, 73, *115,* 234, 237; Singer and, 230, 231, 233, 234–35, 317–18n39; Strigler's program for resurrection of Jewish culture following, 69–70, 300n6; survivor guilt, 222–23, 234–35; survivors versus those not experiencing, 44; Vilna and Vilna Ghetto, 15, 17, 18–22, 32, 131, 293n4; Warsaw Ghetto, 47–48, 60, 61, 76, 87, 98, 101, 103, *110,* 118–19, 122, 243, 293n4; Yiddish world not ended by, 244, 246–47

Holocaust literature, 238–42; difficulty of adequately writing about Holocaust, 59–63; emotional histories, 105; importance of Yiddish texts to, 113–14; memorialization of Ashkenazi civilization in, 10–12; myth of silence/existence before Eichmann trial, 114, 244, 245, 249, 308n20, 309n22; at 92nd Street Y poetry readings, 196; *Dos poylishe yidntum* and, 69, 98, 99, 100–103, *102,* 105; problem of creating art about Holocaust, 41–42, 74; Sutzkever's distinctive poetic response, 39–43; testimonial or survivor literature, 44–45, 50, 55, 57, 59–60, 63, 68–69, 76; works of those who died in Holocaust, 62–63

Holocaust studies and Yiddish culture, 4–6, 74, 243

Horn, Dara, 237

Howe, Irving: on Glatshteyn's use of religious imagery, 137; *A Margin of Hope* (1983), 131; 92nd Street Y poetry readings and, 183, 187, 196, 199–200, 315n3; *Penguin Book of Modern Yiddish Verse* (with Ruth Wisse and Khone Shmeruk, 1987), 200; transmission of Yiddish culture and, 202, 230, 251; *A Treasury of Yiddish Poetry* (with Eliezer Greenberg, 1969), 186, 187, 188, 200, *201,* 202, 204, 248; *A Treasury of Yiddish Stories* (with Eliezer Greenberg, 1954), 186, 187, 188, 200, *201,* 202, 204, 248, 315n3

Hugo, Victor, 58

humor, Jewish/Yiddish, 45–50, 83, 134, 135, 186, 195, 203, 218

Hurwitz, Yosef, 218

Hutton, Christopher, 168

I. L. Peretz Shrayber Fareyn (I. L. Peretz Writers Union), New York, *Finf un zibetsik yor yidishe prese in Amerike, 1870–1945* (Seventy-five Years Yiddish Press in America, 1870–1945), 155–56, 158
Ianansovich, Isaac, 45
ideological and cultural clashes (1953–1954), 118–42; aging generation of Yiddish writers, 123, 126, 135–36; Holocaust as focus of, 126–31; language, translation, and addressing Jewish-American public, 131–35, 139, 140–42; modernism, 124, 125, 126, 128, 130, 142; mythologization of Jewish victims versus historical realism, 118–22; past-orientation, elegiac approach, and use of religious imagery, 135–39, 141–42; Peretz's literary legacy and, 123, 128, 130, 133, 139, 140, 142; Rivkin's literary criticism, 139–40, 142; younger Yiddish writers immigrating to America and, 122–26
Ignatoff, David, 135
immigration: to America, 78, 101, 122–26, 132, 173, 212; Germany, migration of Jewish displaced persons from, 8; to Palestine/Israel, 7, 17, 18
Institut zur Erforschung der Judenfrage (Germany), 23
Inzikhistn (Introspectivists), 25, 34, 128, 143, 162, 186
Isaac, Abraham's sacrifice of, 20
Israel. *See* Palestine/Israel, Yiddish culture and letters in
Itsik Manger Prize, 50, 78
Izban, Shmuel (Samuel): *Familye Karp: Roman* (The Family Karp: Novel, 1949), 257; *"Umlegale" yidn shpaltn yamen* ("Illegal" Jews Split the Seas, 1948), *115*, 256

Jackson, Naomi, 189
James, Henry, 187
Jewish Anti-Fascist Committee (Soviet Union), 22, 36, 293–94n9
Jewish collaboration, 118–21
Jewish Public Library, Montreal, 51, *53*, 54, 56, 248
Jewish State. *See* Palestine/Israel
Joyce, James, 126, 198

Judenforschung ohne Juden (Jewish Research Without Jews), 23

Kabbalah, 321n36
Kaczerginski, Shmerke, 19, 23, 34, 45, 72, 76, 224; *Partizaner geyen!* (Partisans March! 1947), 98, *110*, 255
Kaddish, 46, 66, 68
Kaminska, Ida, 45
Karelitz, R. Avraham (the Hazon Ish), 224, 320n28
Katz, Alef, 315n3
Katz, Menke, 209, 315n3
Katz, Mickey, 195
Ka-Tzetnik (Yekhiel Dinur), 55, 76, 114, 262, 302n26; *The Clock: Stories of the Holocaust* (1960), 108; *Dos hoyz fun di lyalkes* (The House of Dolls, 1955), 108, 262; *Salamandra* (1946), 108
kemoy-teritorye (quasi-territory), 140, 142, 190, 243, 244
Kermish, Joseph, 4, 45, 243; *Der oyfshtand in varshever geto* (The Warsaw Ghetto Uprising, 1948), 98, *110*, 256
Kerouac, Jack, *On the Road* (1956), 134–35
Kertész, Imre, *Fateless* (1975), 297n12
Kielce pogrom, Poland (1946), 36, 46, 88, 156
kinus (ingathering), 12, 93, 100, 104, 116, 163
Kirshenblatt-Gimblett, Barbara, 324n15
Kishinev pogroms (1904), 39
Kizer, Carolyn, 315n3
di klasikers, vii, 7, 165–66, 247
kloles (curses), 30–31
Klung, Berta, 312n33
Knopf, Alfred A., 228
Kobrin, Leon, 95
Kolitz, Zvi, "*Yosl Rakover redt tsu got*" (Yosl Rakover Speaks to God, 1946), 122
Kolodney, William, 14, 189
Konrad, Guta, *101*
Korach's rebellion against Moses and Aaron, 80
Korn, Rachel (Rokhl), 45, *53*, 99, 100, 162, 184, 186, 196, 200, *201*, 296n43, 312n33, 315n3; *Heym un heymlozikeyt* (Home and Homelessness, 1948), 98, 257
Kosinski, Jerzy, 54
Kotzker Rebbe, 9–10, 11

Kovner, Abba, 19
Kramer, Michael P., 124, 310n49
Krauss, Nicole, 237
Kressyn, Miriam, 199
Kruk, Herman, 34
Kulbak, Moyshe, 3, 207, 291n1
Kunitz, Stanley, 200, 315n3, 318n47
Kuznitz, Cecile, 4

Lamm, Norman, 211, 212, 225
Landau, Zishe, 199
landsmanshaftn, 4, 12, 13, 68, 69, 75, 79, 88, 94, 96, 98, 105–6, 191. *See also* Yizker books
Langer, Lawrence, 60
Laocoön (Roman poet), 66
late style, concept of, 233, 238, 322–23n2
Der lebediker (Khayim Gutman), 229–30, 231–32
Lederhendler, Eli, 100, 201, 318n43
Lee, Malka, 315n3
Leib, Mani, 135, 200; *A floym* (A Plum), 137–39
Leivick, H., 120; elegiac view of, 136–37, 248; Jewish collaboration debate with Mark, 118–21, 132; new Yiddish writers immigrating to America and, 124; 92nd Street Y poetry readings and, 198, 199; in Pat's *Shmuesn mit yidishe shrayber*, 135–36; Siberia, escape from, 71; Strigler and, 70, 71–72, 135; Tabachnik recording of, 312n33
Leivick, H., works: *In treblinke bin ikh nit geven (1940–1945)* (I Was Not in Treblinka, 1945), 71–72; "*Treblinke kandidat*" (Candidate for Treblinka, 1945), 72; "*Tsu Amerike*" (To America, 1954), 136–37; "*Tsvey dokumentn*" (Two Documents), 118–19; *Yidishe poetn* (Yiddish Poets, 1932–40), 136–37
Leneman, Leon, 45, 264
Lessing, Johann Gottfried, 151
Lestschinsky, Yankev: *Erev khurbn* (On the Eve of Destruction, 1951), 98, 260; *Oyfn rand fun opgrunt* (On the Edge of the Abyss, 1947), 98, 255
Levi, Primo, 50, 54, 222; *If This Is a Man*, 76; *Survival in Auschwitz* (1960), 57, 308n20
Leyeles, Aaron Glants, 17, 18, 118, 124, 135, 143, 162, 185, 312n33, 315n3; *Kholem tvishn volknkratsers* (Dreaming Amid Skyscrapers, 1948), 308n15
Lifshitz, Joseph, 95
Lindon, Jerome, 107
Lis, Avrom, 83
Literarishe bleter (journal), 139, 228
The Literature of Destruction: Jewish Responses to Catastrophe (1989), 113–14
Lithuania. *See* Vilna
litvaks, 211, 213, 217, 223, 224, 225, 226
Lodz: Grynberg on, 15; as post–WWII Jewish cultural center, 45, 49; Rochman in, 77, 88; Rosenfarb in Lodz and Lodz Ghetto, 44–45, 50, 52–53, 56–60, 63, 298n21

magical realism or supernaturalism, Yiddish, 245, 249
Mailer, Norman, 189, 203
Majdanek, 55, 69, 70, 71–72, 74, 76, 109, 230, 238, 240
Makhshoves, Bal, 139
Malamud, Bernard, 236, 237
Maltz, Saul, 315n3
mame-loshn (Yiddish as mother-tongue), viii, 152, 168, 191, 242, 251
Man, Mendel, 212
Manger, Itsik, 18, 50, 78, 135, 159, 162, 184, 198, 312n33, 315n3
Mann, Mendel, 296n43
Mann, Thomas, 213; *The Magic Mountain* (1929–30), 231, 236
Manor, Dory, 17–18
Margoshes, Shmuel (Samuel), 187, 198, 317n19
Mark, Bernard, 4, 45, 118–21, 119–20, 121, 132, 243; "Jewish Life and Yiddish Literature in Poland, 1937–1957" (1957), 121–22; *Tvishn lebn un toyt* (Between Life and Death, 1955), 121; "*Yudenratishe ahaves-Yisroel: An entfer afn bilbl fun H. Leivick*" (*Judenrat* Love of Israel: An Answer to a False Accusation of H. Leivick, 1953), 119
Markish, Peretz, 35, 123; "*Di kupe*" (The Heap, 1922), 39
Maskilim, 153
Mauriac, François, 107, 113, 306n52, 307n60
Mayzil, Nakhmen, 139–40
memory. *See* communal memory

memory studies, as academic discipline, 6
menakhem av, 10
Mendele Moykher Sforim, 150, 151, 156, 184, 198
Mickiewicz, Adam, 37
Mikhoels, Shloyme, 22, 35, 36
Miller, Shaye: *In di shvartse pintelekh* (In the World of Letters, 1953), 127; "Reb Odem" (Mr. Adam, 1953), 127–28, 131
Milosz, Czeslaw, 294n18, 319n3; *Native Realm* (1968), 132
Minkoff, Nokhem Barukh, 312n33
Minsk-Mazowiecki: Rochman in hiding in, 74–75, 77, 83–84; *Seyfer Minsk-Mazowiecki* (The Book of Minsk-Mazowiecki, 1977), 88
minyan, 57, 198, 210
Miron, Dan, 140–41, 293n3, 302n28, 313n42, 324n16
misnagdim (opponents of Hasidim) in Grade's works, 213, 215, 217
Mitlberg, Abraham, 95–96, 116
Mlotek, Joseph, *199*
modernism: distortion and rejection of Yiddish modernism, 18; Glatshteyn and, 164, 166, 169, 249, 313n50; Grade and, 213, 226; Holocaust as modernist event, 60–61; 92nd Street Y poetry readings and, 187, 198, 208; of Peretz, 159, 175; religious imagery used by, 8–9; Singer and, 226, 232; Tabatshnik and, 159, 160; year 1953–1954, ideological and cultural clashes in, 124, 125, 126, 128, 130, 142; Zeitlin and, 143, 175
Molodovsky, Kadya, *197;* as editor of *Svive,* 197–98; immigration to New York, 124; at 92nd Street Y poetry readings, 184, 186, 196–98, 200, 209, 315n3; religious imagery, use of, 137; religious imagery used by, 8–9; Rich, Adrienne, and, 318n47; Singer compared, 135; Tabatshnik recording of, 162, 312n33
Molodovsky, Kadya, works: *Likht fun dornboym* (Light of the Thornbush, 1965), 196, 197; "*Mendeles boyd in yugnt-tsenter af der 92ter gas*" (Mendele's Covered Wagon at the 92nd Street Y, 1964), 198; "*Tsind on mayn likht*" (Kindle My Light, 1964), 196–97
Montreal, Yiddish culture in, 4, 13, 51, 54, 64–65, 78, 114, 126, 248
Moore, Marianne, 184

Morgentaler, Goldie, 58, 298n31
Morgn-Frayhayt (New York daily), 125
Morgn-Zhurnal (New York daily), 125
Moss, Stanley, 318n47
Mukdoni, A., 127, 133, 258, 259, 262
multilingualism: in America, 183, 184, 185, 318n43; Ashkenazi civilization, Hebrew-Yiddish bilingualism of, 9
Murer (German Commandant), 33
muser movement, 11, 128, 213, 218–19, 224
Musterverk (Masterpieces) series, 94–95
"myth of silence," 114, 244, 245, 308n20, 309n22

Nachman of Bratslav (the Bratslaver), 130, 155, 160, 232, 237
Nadler, Alan, 319n3
Nahtomi, Abraham, *In shotn fun doyres: Kindheyt* (In the Shadow of Generations: Childhood, 1948), 102, 256
National Yiddish Book Center (NYBC), viii, 245
Dos naye lebn (Lodz newspaper), 77, 88
neologisms, Yiddish, 15, 166, 190–91
New York Times, 189, 225, 233–34
New York, Yiddish culture and letters in, 8–9, 13–14. *See also* ideological and cultural clashes (1953–54); 92nd Street Y poetry readings; *specific writers;* elegiac aspects of, 135–39, 141–42; graves of Yiddish writers in New York visited, 67–68; Heschel's portrayal of, 144–46; immigration to America, 78, 101, 122–26, 132, 173, 212; number of Yiddish books published, 308n19; *Dos poylishe yidntum* series, inability to replicate, 94, 304n12; Strigler and, 73
New Yorker, 230
Niger, Shmuel, 74, 83, 92, 99–100, 135, 139, 174, 176, 178, 231–32
92nd Street Y poetry readings, 14, 181–210, 248. *See also specific writers;* audio recordings of, 315n3; dates, participants, performance style, and purpose of, 183–89, 248; historical approach of 1969 event, 199–201; Kolodney founding, 14, 189; Ozick's "Envy" and, 181, 183, 187–88, 202–6; Poetry Center, 92nd Street Y, 189; religious service, equated with, 189–90;

A Treasury of Yiddish Poetry (Howe and Greenberg, 1969) and, 186, 187, 188, 200, *201*, 202, 204, 315n3
Nister, Der, 8
Norich, Anita, 200, 247
normalization of Yiddish, 187, 195
Norwid, Cyprian, 37
Nowersztern, Abraham, 20, 42, 92, 93
Nudelman, M., *Gelekhter durkh trern* (Laughter through Tears, 1947), 49, 254
Nuremberg Tribunal: Sutzkever's testimony before, 16, 17, 19, 29, 33, 35–36, 151–52; Weinreich's *"Hitlers profesorn"* and, 148, 149
NYBC (National Yiddish Book Center), viii, 245

Olitsky, Mattes, 315n3
Opatoshu, Yosef, 124, 135
Operation Reinhard, 76
orality in Yiddish/Jewish culture, 184–85, 248, 316n7
Oyerbakh, Rokhl, 48
Oyneg Shabes archive, Warsaw Ghetto, 48, 60, 85–86, 87, 103, 119, 120, 122, 303n43
Ozick, Cynthia, 183, 186, 187–88, 200–206, *201*, 237, 251, 315n3; "America: Toward Yavneh" (1970), 202, 203, 205–6; "Envy; or, Yiddish in America" (1969), 181, 183, 187–88, 202–6, 232, 247; *The Messiah of Stockholm* (1987), 64; *The Pagan Rabbi and Other Stories*, 202; translations for *A Treasury of Yiddish Poetry* (Howe and Greenberg, 1969), 204; *Trust* (1966), 187

Palestine/Israel, Yiddish culture and letters in, 8, 141; establishment of Jewish State and, 1–3; focus of American Jews on, 125; immigration to Palestine/Israel, 7, 17, 18; Rochman in, 78, 79, 88; Sutzkever in, 1–3, 17, 19, 36–37, 39; Yung Yisroel, 8, 39, 165, 313n50
Paper Brigade, Vilna, 19, 23–24
Paris Cemetery of Bagneux, Jewish memorial in, 78
Paris, Yiddish writers in, 7, 8, 39–40, 68, 71, 114
Partisan Review, 134, 230, 309n26
Pat, Yankev (Jacob): *Henekh* (1948), 256; *Shmuesn mit yidishe shrayber* (Conversations with Yiddish Writers, 1954), 135–36
Pen, Asher, 92
PennSound, 316n10
Peres, Shimon, 293n3
Peretz, I. L.: Glatshteyn's "Yidishkeyt" and, 128, 130; *Di goldene keyt* (The Golden Chain) and, 37; literary legacy of, 123, 128, 130, 133, 139, 140, 142, 176; Miller's "Reb Odem" and, 128; portrayal of rabbis in work of, 217; *Dos poylishe yidntum* books about, 99, 253; in Ravitsh's *"Di kroynung fun a yungn yidishn dikhter in amerike,"* 123; readings by, 184; religious and secular modalities fused by, 175, 190; Singer and, 227, 228, 232; as Yiddish culture hero, 247; Zeitlin influenced by, 174–79
Peretz, I. L., works: *Bay nakht afn altn mark* (A Night in the Old Marketplace), 176; *"Dray matones"* (Three Gifts), 128, 227; in Howe and Greenberg, ed., *A Treasury of Yiddish Stories* (1954), 133; *"Der kishefmakher"* (The Magician), 174–75; *"Mekubolim"* (Cabbalists), 159; *"Monish"* (1888), 222, 227, 228; *Ohel* (grave monument), Jewish Cemetery, Warsaw, 37
Perle, Yehoshue: *"Khurbn varshe"* (The Destruction of Warsaw, 1942/1952), 118–19; *Yidn fun a gants yor* (Ordinary Jews, 1951), 99, 259–60
Pinsker, Leo, "Autoemanzipation" (1882), 150
Pinsker, Shachar, 313n50
Pinski, Dovid, 141
Poalei Zion, 96, 98
Poetry Center, 92nd Street Y, 189
Pohl, Johannes, 23
Poland. *See also* Lodz; Minsk-Mazowiecki: anti-Semitism in, 36–37, 84, 88; Central Jewish Historical Commission in, 23, 95; Kielce pogrom (1946), 36, 46, 88, 156; Rochman's *Un in dayn blut zolstu lebn*, Polish helpers and peasant society in, 79, 84, 85, 86–87; Warsaw Ghetto, 47–48, 60, 61, 76, 87, 98, 101, 103, *110*, 118–19, 122, 243, 293n4; Yidish-bukh publishing house, Warsaw, 95, 243
Polonsky, Antony, 106
Ponar, 20, 33, 36, 42–43, 131
Porat, Dina, 18

post-vernacular Yiddish culture, vii, 7, 205, 245–46, 249, 251
Pound, Ezra, 126, 198
Dos poylishe yidntum, 92–117, 243. *See also specific authors;* Argentine Jewish community's support for, 93, 94, 95–98; Ashkenazi civilization, Yiddish writers memorializing, 12; book covers, *102–3, 109–10, 115;* books and authors published by, 98–105, 253–68; commercial versus reputational success of, 95–96; Holocaust literature in, 69, 98, 99, 100–103, *102,* 105; profits used for Jewish relief work, 97; publication rate, distribution, and raison d'etre, 92–94, 96–97, 101, 116; Rosenfarb's *Der boym fun lebn* and, 54; Strigler's output for, 55, 69, 70–71, 99, 100, 255, 256, 259, 260, 262; translations of texts in, 106, 106n46; Turkov and, 94, 95, 101, 107, 108, 114, 116; Wiesel's work in, 99, 106–16, 262; Yiddish cultural rebirth signified by, 99, 116–17; *Yizker* books and, 100, 105–6, 260
Pravda (Moscow newspaper), 22
Preil, Gabriel, 209, 315n3
Proust, Marcel, 56, 174, 309n36

Rahv, Philip, 230
Rapoport, Yehoshua, 74, 130
Rashi, 151
Rasseyner, Hersh, 11
Ravitsh, Melekh, 127, 261, 266, 267, 312n33; "*Di kroynung fun a yungn yidishn dikhter in amerike*" (The Coronation of a Young Yiddish Poet in America, 1953), 122–23; *Mayn leksikon* (My Encyclopedia, 1945), 176
Rawicz, Piotr, 54
realism in Yiddish literature, 59–61, 66, 75, 87, 104, 122, 134–35, 213, 216–18, 226, 249, 311n24
Redlich, Shimen, 48
Reisen, Avrom, 135
religious imagery, secular writers using, 8–9, 24, 37–38, 40, 54, 79, 137–39, 175, 189–90, 197
religious Yiddish writers, 9–10
remembrance. *See* communal memory
Rich, Adrienne, 186, 200, *201,* 251, 315n3, 318n47
Ringelblum, Emanuel, 48, 60, 64, 69, 85–86, 87, 99, 100, 103, 104, 119, *121,* 121–22, 242, 261
Rivkin, Borekh, 139–40, 142, 190, 310n44

Robinson, Y., 105
Rochman, Esther (wife), 67, 74, 76, *77,* 79, 86
Rochman, Leib, 13, 67–69, 74–91, *77, 89;* artistic multiplicity and multiculturalism of, 244; at graves of Yiddish writers in New York, 67–68, 300n3; in group of young adult Holocaust survivor writers, 76–78; Hebrew-Yiddish bilingualism and, 9; as Holocaust survivor, 44, 68–69; in Israel, 78, 79, 88; life and experience of, 77–78; magical realism or supernaturalism of, 245; migration from Germany as Jewish displaced person, 8; Minsk-Mazowiecki, in hiding in, 74–75, 77, 83–84; Rosenfarb compared, 55, 76, 78; Singer compared, 232; Sutzkever compared, 76, 303n55
Rochman, Leib, *Un in dayn blut zolstu lebn* (And in Your Blood Shall You Live, 1949; translated as *The Pit and the Trap*), 13, 74–88; blood as literary trope in, 79–80; communal memory in, 80–83, 87; consciousness of readership in, 82–83, 86–87; different versions, translations, and titles, 75, 79, 88, 301n23; on eradication of Jewish culture and heritage, 79, 83, 84–86; lack of visibility outside Yiddish world, 75–77; original diary, 75, 301n20; Polish helpers and peasant society in, 79, 84, 85, 86–87; post-war life informing, 77–78, 87–88; realism of, 249; structure and phases of, 77–78; as *Yizker* book, 75, 78–79, 85, 88
Rochman, Leib, works: "*Af keyver-oves*" (Visiting the Ancestors' Graves, 1976), 67; "*Di levaye*" (The Funeral, 1978), 67, 88–91; *Der mabl* (The Flood, 1978), 238, 300n3; *Mit blinde trit iber der erd* (1968), 78, 302n28
Rolland, Roman, 58
Rolnik, Yosef, 312n33
Romm's Press, Vilna, 37–38
Rosenberg, Alfred, 23, 152
Rosenfarb, Chava, 13, 44–45, 50–66, *53;* artistic multiplicity and multiculturalism of, 244; in Bergen-Belsen, 51–52; difficulty of adequately writing about Holocaust and, 59–63; in Lodz and Lodz Ghetto, 44–45, 50, 52–53, 56–60, 63, 298n21; in Montreal,

51, 54, 64–65; at 92nd Street Y poetry readings, 184, 196, 209, 315n3; post-1945 cultural and political landscape, navigating, 63–64; realism of, 59–61, 66, 245, 249; Rochman compared, 55, 76, 78; Shayevitsh and, 52–53, 56, 57, 60–66, 299n37; Singer and, 232, 234, 322n61; Sutzkever compared, 40, 50, 55, 57; as woman author of major Yiddish prose work, 50, 55–56; Yiddish cultural milieu supporting, 54–55

Rosenfarb, Chava, works: "Bats fly by the window," 51–52; *Der boym fun lebn* (The Tree of Life, 1972), 50, 51, 52, 54, 55–59, 60–61, 65–66; *Briv tsu Abrashn* (Letters to Abrasha, 1992), 57–58; "Edgia's Revenge," 64–65; *Fragments of a Diary* (1945), 51–52, 55, 61–62, 65, 66; "*Paul Celan un zayne goyrl brider*" (Paul Celan and His Brothers of Destiny, 1989), 54; "*Simkhe-Bunim Shayevitsh: Dermonungen*" (Simkhe-Bunim Shayevitsh: Reminiscences; in English as "The Last Poet of Lodz"), 52, 66; *Survivors* (2004), 64–65, 238

Rosenfeld, Isaac, 141
Rosenfeld, Jonah, 220; "Competitors," 133
Rosenfeld, Morris, 159
Rosenfeld, Oskar, 299n38
Rosenwald, Lawrence, 184
Roskies, David G., 4, 5, 34, 88, 119, 298n38, 302n28, 313n42
Roth, Philip, 203, 236
Rothenberg, Jerome, 237
Rothenberg, Mordechai, 315n3
Rousseau, Jean-Jacques, 151
Royzenblatt, H., 135
Rozenfeld, M., 199
Rozhanski, Shmuel, 94, 97
"*Rozhinkes mit mandlen*" (Raisins and Almonds), 1
Rubenstein, Joseph, 196, 315n3, 318n47
Rudnitsky, Adolf, 54
Rumkowski, Chaim, 56, 57, 59, 64

Sabbatai Zevi, 211, 321n36
sacred text, Yiddish literature as, 54, 106
Said, Edward, 179, 322–23n2
Salanter, Israel, 218

Salinger, J. D., *Catcher in the Rye* (1951), 134–35
Sasel, 58, 65
Schechtman, Eli, 232
Scholem, Gershom, 321n36
Schreiber, Maeera, 190
Schulz, Bruno, 64
Schumacher, Yisroel, 45–50
Schwartz, I. J. (Y. Y.), 135, 315n3
Schwarz-Bart, Andre, *The Last of the Just* (1960), 308n20
Schwerner, Amand, 315n3
Scooler, Zvi, 189–90, 198
Segalovicz, Zusman: *Gebrente trit* (Burned Steps, 1947), 99, 255; *Der letster lodzher roman* (The Last Lodz Novel, 1951), 102, 260; *Mayne zibn yor in Tel-Aviv* (My Seven Years in Tel-Aviv, 1949), 257; *Tlomatske 13: Fun farbrentn nekhtn* (Tlomatske 13: From an Extinguished Past, 1946), 254
Seidman, Hillel, *Togbukh fun varshever geto* (Diary from the Warsaw Ghetto, 1947), 98, 254–55
Seidman, Naomi, 306n52, 307n62
self-criticism and self-hatred, 28–29, 69, 130, 202
Sem-Sandberg, Steve, *The Emperor of Lies* (2009), 64
Shafir, M. M., 315n3
Shaked, Gershon, 313n43
Shakespeare, William, *Sonnets*, Yiddish translation of (1953), 138
Shandler, Jeffrey, 7, 205, 292n13, 324n17
Shatski, Yankev, 94, 95, 97–100, 103–4, 114, 261, 304n12, 305n36; "The Confessions of a Jewish Historian" (1954), 104; *Kulturgeshikhte fun der haskole in lite* (Cultural History of the Enlightenment in Lithuania, 1950), 259; *In shotn fun over* (In the Shadow of the Past, 1947), 98, 254
Shayevitsh, Simkhe-Bunim: *Friling 1942* (Spring 1942), 44, 52; *Lekh Lekho* (Go Forth), 52; Rosenfarb and, 52–53, 56, 57, 60–66, 299n37
Shema, 83
Sherman, Joseph, 233, 322n54

sheyres hapleyte (saved remnants), 12, 44, 64, 69–70, 72, 73, *115*, 234, 237

Shivkhey HaRan, 237

Shmeruk, Khone, Ruth Wisse, and Irving Howe, eds., *Penguin Book of Modern Yiddish Verse* (1987), 200

Shoah. *See* Holocaust; Holocaust literature

Sholem Aleichem, 30, 48, 49–50, 57, 67–68, 133, 135, 141, 184, 194, 300n3; *Navenad* (Refugee), 49; *Nokhn mabl* (After the Flood), 49; *A sreyfe in Kasrilevke* (A Fire in Kasrilevke), 45, 47, 49; *Tevye der milkhiger* (Tevye the Dairyman), 47, 49, 186, 251

Shoshkes, Henry: *Poyln—1946: Ayndrukn fun a rayze* (Poland—1946: Impressions from a Journey, 1946), *115*, 254; *A velt vos iz farbay: Kapitlekh zikhroynes* (A World That Is Over: Chapters of Memoirs, 1949), 257

Shpiegl, Isaiah, 44, 50, 76, 128, 135, 242, 302n26; *Likht funem opgrunt* (Light from the Abyss, 1952), 56; *Shtern ibern geto* (Stars over the Ghetto, 1947), 56

Shtarkman, Moyshe, 198

Shtaynvaks, Pinkhes: *Yidishe mames tsum gedenken* (Jewish Mothers to Remember, 1959), 265; *Yidn tsum gedenken* (Jews to Remember, 1955), *102*, 262

Shteingart, Moyshe, 315n3

Shtiker, Meyer, 315n3

Shtiker, V., 312n33

Shulman, Eliyahu, "*Iz meglekh a yidishe literatur af a nit-yidisher shprakh?*" (Is a Jewish Literature Possible in a Non-Jewish Language? 1971), 202

Shvarts, I. J., *Yunge yorn: Poeme* (Young Years: Poem, 1952), 308n15

Silberschlag, Eisig, 315n3

Singer, I. B. (Yitskhok Bashevis), 213, 226–37, *235*; artistic multiplicity and multiculturalism of, 244; Bez on, 212; Glatshteyn and, 135, 187, 193–95, 196; Grade and, 135, 211, 217, 221, 222, 225, 226–27, 232, 234, 319n3; Hasidism in works of, 196, 211, 217, 221, 237; Hebrew-Yiddish bilingualism and, 9; Holocaust and, 230, 231, 233, 234–35, 317–18n39; immigration to New York, 123–24; *kloles* and, 30; *Der lebediker* controversy and, 229–30, 231–32; literary stature of, 232–33, 236, 237, 247; magical realism or supernaturalism of, 245, 249; 92nd Street Y poetry readings and, 184, 187, 193–96, 205, 209, 315n3, 316n14, 317n36; Ozick's "Envy" and, 187, 203, 204, 205, 206, 232, 247; Peretz and, 227, 228, 232; personal and professional life, 228, 230–32, 233; on Rochman's *Un in dayn blut zolstu lebn* (as Yitskhok Varshavski), 83; Sholem Aleichem' stories used by, 135; Soviet communism, antagonism toward, 8; Sutzkever compared, 18; translatability and wide appeal of work of, 131–33, 134–35, 186, 194, 206–7, 226–27, 228, 231, 232, 236, 237, 247, 248; Wiesel compared, 114; *yeytser-hore* (the Evil Inclination) and, 226–28; Yiddish culture and work of, 142; Zeitlin and, 135, 171, 172, 176, 178, 234, 322n60

Singer, I. B. (Yitskhok Bashevis), works: "*Arum der yidisher literatur in Poyln*" (On Yiddish Literature in Poland, 1943), 176; "The Cafeteria" (1968), 231, 318n39; Conversations (1992), 210; *The Death of Methuselah and Other Stories* (1988), 232; *Enemies: A Love Story* (1972), 64, 231, 233, 234, 318n39; *The Family Moskhat* (1950), 134, 228, 229, 233; *Gimpel the Fool and Other Stories* (1957), 232; "*Gimpl tam*" (Gimpel the Fool, 1945/1953), 131–32, 133, 134–35, 228, 229, 230, 232, 251; "*Der khurbn fun Kreshev*" (The Destruction of Kreshev), 227–28; "*Kleyn un groys*" (Big and Little), 195–96; *Love and Exile* (1976–82), 230; *Mayn tatns bezdnshtub* (My Father's Court), 233; "*Mayse Tishevitz*" (The Last Demon, 1959), 10–11; *Der mekhaber* (The Author, 1965; in English as "My Adventures as an Idealist," 1967), 236–37; *Satan in Goray* (1935), 134, 221, 226, 227, 228; *Shotn afn Hudson* (Shadows on the Hudson, 1957–58/1991), 64, 228, 233–34, 238, 317n39; *Der shpigl* (The Mirror), 222; *The Sinful Messiah* (1936), 228

Singer, I. J. (brother), 132, 228, 231; *Di brider ashkenazi* (The Brothers Ashkenazi, 1936), 57, 134, 228

Skarzysko-Kamienna, 70, 74

Slowacki, Juliusz, "*Smutno mi, Boze,*" 37

INDEX 351

Smirnov, Colonel L. N., 35
Snyder, Timothy, 76
Sobibor, 76
socialism. *See* Soviet sphere, Yiddish culture in
sonnet form, 138–39
Sovetish heymland (journal), 243, 250
Soviet sphere, Yiddish culture in, 7–8, 249–50; Jewish Anti-Fascist Committee, 22, 36, 293–94n9; Leivick's escape from Siberia, 71; Mark and, 119–22; Stalin, Joseph, and Stalinist era, 7, 22, 35, 123, 125, 293–94n9; Sutzkever in Moscow and post-war Vilna, 7, 17, 22–25, 34–36, 296n43; Sutzkever's childhood in Siberia, 17; Sutzkever's prediction of end of political oppression, 141
Sperre, Lodz Ghetto, 53, 58, 59–60, 298n21
Stalin, Joseph, and Stalinist era, 7, 22, 35, 123, 125, 293–94n9
Steiner, George, 203
Stern, Steve, 237
Strigler, Mordechai, 69–74; as Holocaust survivor, 44, 69; immigration to New York, 124; Leivick and, 70, 71–72, 135; memoirs of, 70–71, 249; migration from Germany as Jewish displaced person, 8, 69–70; in Miller's "Reb Odem," 128; in *Dos poylishe yidntum* series, 55, 69, 70–71, 99, 100, 255, 256, 259, 260, 262; program for resurrection of Jewish culture following Holocaust, 69–70, 300n6; realism of, 245, 249; Rochman compared, 76; Wiesel influenced by, 114
Strigler, Mordechai, works: autobiography, 300n6; *In di fabrikn fun toyt* (In the Factories of Death, 1948), 71, 256; *Georemt mit vint* (Embraced by Wind, 1955), 72, 262; *Goyroles* (Destinies, 1952), 72, 260; "*Der letster yid in geto*" (The Last Jew in the Ghetto, 1945), 71, 73; *Maydanek* (1947), 71–72, 74, *109*, 255, 300n7; *Oysgebrente likht* cycle, 73–74; "*Tsu aykh shvester un brider bafrayte: Nokhmilkhome-problemen fun yidishn folk*" (To You Liberated Sisters and Brothers: Post-War Problems of the Jewish People, 1945), 69–70; *Verk "Tse"* (Work "C," 1950), 71–72, 259

suicide, 55, 65, 89–91, 222–23, 227, 322n61
surrealism, 9, 43, 89, 166, 249
survivor guilt, 222–23, 234–35
Sutzkever, Avrom, 15–43, *35*; artistic multiplicity and multiculturalism of, 244; Ashkenazi civilization memorialized by, 11; Bez on, 212; boundaries of linguistic medium and, 207; Glatshteyn compared, 18, 131, 167; as *Di goldene keyt* editor, 17, 23, 31, 93–94, 99, 122, 238; on Grade, 225;
Sutzkever, Avrom (*continued*) Holocaust, distinctive poetic response to, 39–43; Leivick on, 135; in Lodz, 45; migration from Germany as Jewish displaced person, 8; Miller's "Reb Odem" and, 128, 131; in Moscow and post-war Vilna, 7, 17, 22–25, 34–36, 296n43; at 92nd Street Y poetry readings, 184, 196, 209, 315n3; at Nuremberg Tribunal, 16, 17, 19, 29, 33, 35–36, 150–51; in Palestine/Israel, 1–3, 17, 19, 36–37, 39; in Paper Brigade, Vilna, 19, 23–24; in Paris, 8, 39–40; as partisan, 17, 21; politics of Yiddishism and, 250; in pre-war Vilna and Vilna Ghetto, 15, 17, 18–22, 23, 32, 131; rage against Germany in poetry of, 151; Ravitsh's "*Di kroynung fun a yungn yidishn dikhter in amerike*" and, 123; religious imagery used by, 9, 24, 37–38, 40; Rivkin compared, 140; Rochman compared, 76, 303n55; Rosenfarb compared, 40, 50, 55, 57; Siberia, childhood in, 17; Singer compared, 135; Soviet communism, antagonism toward, 8; speech of 1985, 24; surrealism/magical realism of, 9, 43, 166, 245, 249; at symposium on Jewish writers (1954), 140; Weinreich and, 148; Wiesel influenced by, 114; *Yasl Rakover* controversy and, 122; Yiddish culture and work of, 142, 207
Sutzkever, Avrom, works: "*Di blayene platn fun roms drukeray*" (The Lead Plates at Romm's Press, 1943), 37–38; *Dortn vu es nekhtikn di shtern* (Where the Stars Spend the Night, 1975–77), 9; "*Erev mayn farbrenung*" (Before My Burning), 31–32, 295n31; *Di ershte nakht in geto* (The First Night in Ghetto, 1979), 29–32, 39; "*Farbrente perl*" (Burned Pearls, 1943), 33; "*Farfroyrene yidn*" (Frozen Jews, 1944), 34, 249; *Di festung* (The Fortress, 1945),

19, 34; *"Di froy fun mirml afn Per-lashez"* (The Woman of Marble in Pere Lachaise, 1947), 38–39; *"Fun beymer makht men vunderlekh papir"* (Trees Are Made into Wonderful Paper), 40–41; *Fun vilner geto* (From the Vilna Ghetto, 1945), 19, 27–28, 29–30; *"Geheymshtot"* (Clandestine City, 1945–47), 36, 57; ghetto poems of, 19, 23–34, 39–40, 42, 294n16; *"A grezl fun Ponar"* (A Blade of Grass from Ponar, 1981), 42–43; *"Griner akvarium"* (Green Aquarium, 1953–54), 9, 43, 57, 131; *Di karsh fun dermonung* (The Cherry of Remembrance, 1949), 31; *"Kol Nidre, dertseylt fun a geblibenem"* (Kol Nidre, Told by a Survivor, 1943), 20–22; *"Di lererin Mire"* (The Teacher Mire), 31; *Lider fun yam-hamoves* (Poems from the Sea of Death, 1968), 31, 39–40; *Lider* (Poems, 1937), 25; *"Mayn eydes-zogn farn nirnberger tribunal"* (My Testimony at the Nuremberg Tribunal, 1966), 35–36, 151–52; *"Mayn mame"* (My Mother, 1942), 28–29; *Nevue fun shvartsaplen*, 238; *Di nevue fun shvartsaplen* (The Prophecy of the Pupils, 1975–89), 9; *"Penimer in zumpn"* (Faces in the Swamps), 25–27; *Poems from a Diary*, 42; *"Der tsirk"* (The Circus, 1941), 29, 30–32; *"Tsu Poyln"* (To Poland, 1946), 17, 36–37; *Tsviling-bruder* (Twin-Brother, 1986), 303n55; *Valdiks* (Of the Forest, 1940), 25; *"Vi azoy?"* (How?, 1943), 15–16; *"A vogn shikh"* (A Wagon of Shoes), 31–32; *"Yiddish"* (1948), 1–3, 18; *"Zunroyzn"* (Sunflowers, 1987), 238
Sutzkever, Freydke (wife), 17, 21, 22
Svive (literary quarterly), 197–98, 232

Tabatshnik, Avrom, *161*; personal and professional life, 312n34; school of literary criticism of, 313n42; *"Traditsye un revolt in der yidisher poezye"* (Tradition and Revolt in Yiddish Poetry, 1950), 160–61
Tabatshnik, Avrom, *"Di rekodirte antologye: Di shtim fun yidishn poet"* (Recorded Anthology: The Voice of the Yiddish Poet, mid to late 1950s), 13, 158–60, 250; Glatshteyn interview, 144, 162–65, 167; Grade interview, 162, 225, 312n33; 92nd Street Y poetry readings compared, 184; Zeitlin interview, 144, 170, 171–72, 174

Teitelbaum, Abraham, *Varshever heyf: Mentshn un gesheenishn* (Warsaw Courtyards: People and Happenings, 1947), *103*, 255
Tel Aviv, Yiddish literary culture in, 4, 13, 78, 114, 126
Teller, Judd L., 126, 155, 248
Tisha B'Av, 10, 66, 83
Tkatch, Meyer Ziml, 315n3
Tkhies hameysim (Resurrection of the Dead; first DP journal), 69
Tlomatske 13 (Yiddish Writers Union, Warsaw), 8, 99, 175, 176
Der tog (New York daily), 75, 83, 94, 118, 125, 187
Tolstoy, Leo, 213
translations from Yiddish: different solutions to problem of, 247–48; increased interest in Yiddish literature and, 186; reconceptualization of works in, 9–10, 106–7, 111–16; of Singer's works, 131–33, 134–35, 186, 194, 206–7, 226–27, 228, 231, 232, 236, 237, 247, 248; survival of Yiddish culture in, 245–46, 250–51; year 1953–1954, Yiddish culture in, 131–35, 139, 140–42
transliteration of Yiddish texts using YIVO system, 269–89
transnational infrastructure of Yiddish post-Holocaust culture, 6–7, 12, 14, 18, 44, 95, 141, 242–45
trauma theory, 27
Treblinka, 71–72, 76, *109*, 177
Trunk, Y. Y., 124, 135, 259, 262; *Poyln* (1944–53), 176; *Di yidishe proze in poyln* (Yiddish Prose in Poland), 100, 258
Tsivion, 135
Di tsukunft (periodical), 70, 71, 72, 73, 134, 176, 232
Turkov, Jonas (brother), *101*, 101–3, 303–4n4; *Azoy iz es geven: Khurbn Varshe* (So It Was: The Destruction of Warsaw, 1948), 98, 256; *Farloshene shtern* (Extinguished Stars, 1953), 101, 261; *In kamf farn lebn* (In Struggle for Life, 1949), 258; *Mayne zikhroynes . . .* (My Memoirs . . . , 1953), 261; *Nokh der bafrayung: Zikhroynes* (After Liberation: Memoirs, 1959), 265
Turkov, Mark, *101*; personal and professional life, 303–4n4; politics of Yiddishism and,

250; *Dos poylishe yidntum* and, 94, 95, 101, 107, 108, 114, 116
Turkov, Mark, works: "The Idea of the Book Series" (1948), 98; *Di letste fun a groysn dor* (The Last of a Great Generation, 1954), 93, 100, 261; *Malke Ovshyany dertseylt* (Malke Ovshyany Tells Her Tale, 1946), 96, 253; *Oyf yidishe felder* (In Jewish Fields, 1939), 97, 303n4; *Roosevelt's America* (1937), 303n4
Turkov, Roza (sister-in-law), *101*
Turkov, Shura (sister-in-law), *101*
Turkov, Yitskhok (brother), *101*, 303–4n4
Turkov, Zygmunt (brother), *101*, 259, 263, 266, 303–4n4
Twain, Mark, *Huckleberry Finn*, 133

Ukraine, post-WWI pogroms in, 39
Ulinover, Miriam, 52, 63
Undzer vort (Paris Zionist weekly), 72
Undzere kinder (film, 1948), 45–50, 287n11
Unger, Menashe, 94, 257
United States Holocaust Memorial Museum (USHMM), 4

Valencia, Heather, 31–32
Valentine, Jean, 315n3
Varshavski, Yitskhok. *See* Singer, I. B.
Vaynshteyn, Berish, 312n33
Veidlinger, Jeffrey, 316n7
Verk C, 70, 71–72
Viernik, Yankel, and Vasili Grossman, *Treblinke* (1946), *109*
Vilna: Charney, Daniel, *Vilne: Memuarn* (Vilna: Memoirs, 1951), *102*, 260; Grade and, 214, 215, 218, 219, 220, 223–26; Sutzkever in Moscow and post-war Vilna, 7, 17, 22–25, 34–36; Sutzkever in pre-war Vilna and Vilna Ghetto, 15, 17, 18–22, 23, 32, 131; Warsaw Ghetto compared to Vilna Ghetto, 293n4; Yung-Vilne, 7, 25, 132
Vilner, Chaim, 11
Vintshevski, Morris, 159

Warsaw Ghetto, 47–48, 60, 61, 76, 87, 98, 101, 103, *110*, 118–19, 122, 243, 293n4
Warsaw Ghetto Uprising, 98, *110*, 243
Wasser, Hersh, 303n43
Weinreich, Gabriel (son), 146–48

Weinreich, Max, 146–52; Holocaust studies and, 243; politics of Yiddishism and, 250; *Dos poylishe yidntum* series and, 99, 100, 104–5, 262; rage against Germany, 146–48,
Weinreich, Max (*continued*)
151–52, 249; reinvigoration of YIVO in New York, 148, 152; Weinreich Room, YIVO, Vilna, 24, 294n15; on Yiddish language, 150–51
Weinreich, Max, works: *Fun beyde zaytn ployt* (From Both Sides of the Fence, 1955), 262; *"Hitlers profesorn"* (Hitler's Professors, 1946), 146, 147, 148–50, 151, 152, 248, 249; *Der veg tsu undzer yugnt* (The Road to Our Youth, 1936), 149; "*Vos heyst shraybn yidishlekh?*" (What Does It Mean to Write in a Jewish Manner? 1942), 150–51
Weinreich, Uriel (son), 146
Weinstein, Berish, 315n3
Weissenberg, Isaac Meir, 132
Weprinsky, Rochelle, 184, 315n3
White, Hayden, 60–61
Whitman, Ruth, 315n3
Whitman, Walt, 136–37
Wierzbnik-Starachowice labor camp, 300n8
Wiesel, Elie, 106–16; on advisory board of Holocaust Library, 75; artistic multiplicity and multiculturalism of, 244; childhood of, 107–8; on Grade, 212, 225; on Ka-Tzetnik, 108; Rosenfarb compared, 50, 55; switch from Yiddish to French and English, 247; Yiddish writers influencing, 114
Wiesel, Elie, works: *All Rivers Run to the Sea: Memoirs* (1995), 107, 108; "*A bagegenish*" (An Encounter, 1947), 107; "An Interview Unlike Any Other" (1978), 107; in *Dos poylishe yidntum* series, 99, 106–16, 262; *Shtile heldn* (Quiet Heroes), 107; *Un di velt hot geshvign* (And the World Was Silent, 1956; in French and English as *La Nuit/Night*, 1958/1960), 57, 76, 106–7, 108, 111–16, 262, 306n47, 308n20
Wilkomirski affair (1990s), 122
Williams, Galen, 200, 318n47
Wirth-Nesher, Hana, 124, 178, 310n49
Wisse, Ruth, Irving Howe, and Khone Shmeruk, eds., *Penguin Book of Modern Yiddish Verse* (1987), 200
Wisse, Ruth R., 41–42

Wojdowski, Bogdan, *Bread for the Departed* (1971), 61
Workmen's Circle, 54, 67, 69, 91, 199, 312n34

Yad Vashem archive, 13, 48, 75, 301n20; *Bibliography of Yiddish Books about Destruction and Heroism* (1962), 105
Yale video interviews of Holocaust survivors, 60
Yanosovitsh, Yitskhok, 87
Yediot Ahronot (Israeli newspaper), 107
Yehoash (Solomon Blumgarten), 3, 199, 291n1
yeytser-hore (the Evil Inclination), 226–28
Yiddish culture after the Holocaust, vii–viii, 1–14, 238–51. *See also specific Yiddish writers*; academic study of, 245–51; decline after 1960s, 209, 245, 318n43; establishment of Jewish State and, 1–3; European literature and history, turn from, 145–46; genres employed, 249; Holocaust literature in, 238–42 (*See also* Holocaust; Holocaust literature); Holocaust studies and, 4–6, 74, 243; *mame-loshn* (Yiddish as mother-tongue), viii, 152, 168, 191, 242, 251; memorialization of Ashkenazi civilization, 10–12 (*See also* Ashkenazi civilization; communal memory); navigating post-1945 cultural and political landscape, 63–64; in New York, 8–9, 13–14 (*See also* New York, Yiddish culture and letters in); number of current speakers of Yiddish, 250, 324n17; orality of, 184–85, 248, 316n7; in Palestine/Israel, 8, 141 (*See also* Palestine/Israel, Yiddish culture and letters in); periodization of, 249–50; as post-vernacular, vii, 7, 205, 245–46, 249, 251; rage against Germany, 5, 30–31, 112, 144–48, 151–52, 153–54, 170, 249; rejection of Yiddish and Ashkenazi civilization by majority of Jews, 17–18, 124–25, 148, 203, 243, 247; religious Yiddish writers, 9–10; as "silver age," 3–4, 6–14, 68, 85, 142, 212, 245, 248; in Soviet sphere, 7–8, 249–50 (*See also* Soviet sphere, Yiddish culture in); statistical snapshot (1960), 316n12; Strigler's program for resurrection of, 69–70; survivors versus non-survivors in, 44; translation, survival in, 245–46, 250–51 (*See also* translations from Yiddish); transnational infrastructure of, 6–7, 12, 14, 18, 44, 95, 141, 242–45

Yiddish culture hero, 247
Yiddish PEN Club, 99, 160, 175, 196
Yiddish theater, 45–50, 101–3, 159, 199
Yiddishkeit, 17, 24, 128, 145, 167, 190, 195, 200, 248
Yidish-bukh publishing house, Warsaw, 95, 243
Di yidishe tsaytung (Buenos Aires daily), 75, 122
Der yidisher kemfer (Labor Zionist journal), 186
Yinglish, 183, 195, 203
"Yisroel, der yidisher shrayber, un di yidishe velt" (Israel, the Jewish Writer, and the Jewish World; symposium, 1954), 141
Yitskhok Bashevis. *See* Singer, I. B.
YIVO Institute for Jewish Research: in Argentina, 94, 97; Heschel and, 145, 146; historical style associated with, 104; *kinus* and *aynzamlen* as used by, 163; reinvigoration by Weinreich in New York, 148, 152; Strigler and, 300n6; Sutzkever and, 19, 22, 23–24, 35, 294n15; transliteration of Yiddish texts using YIVO system, 269–89; Yiddish normalization efforts, 195
Yizker books: Ashkenazi civilization, memorializing, 12, 242, 250; goals of, 96–97; as Holocaust literature, 69; New York Yiddish culture and, 127; online availability, 291n2; *Dos poylishe yidntum* series and, 100, 105–6, 260; Rochman's *Un in dayn blut zolstu lebn* framed as, 75, 78–79, 85, 88; Rosenfarb's *Der boym fun lebn* and, 54; *Seyfer Minsk-Mazowiecki* (The Book of Minsk-Mazowiecki, 1977), 88; in USHMM library, 4; Yiddish writers adapting format of, 13
Yom Kippur, 21
Young, James E., 301n19
Yung Yisroel, 8, 39, 165, 313n50
Di yunge, 137, 158–59, 160–61
Yung-Vilne, 7, 25, 132

Zachor: Holocaust Remembrance Foundation, 75
Zborowski, Mark, and Elizabeth Herzog, *Life Is with People* (1952), 132
Zeitlin, Aaron, 171–80, *173*; artistic multiplicity and multiculturalism of, 244; Ashkenazi civilization memorialized by, 11; communal memory in poetry of, 144, 176–80; in Cuba, 143; Hebrew-Yiddish bilingualism and, 9; Heschel on poetry of, 144–46; immigration

to New York, 124; at 92nd Street Y poetry readings, 184, 196, 315n3; Peretz influencing, 174–79; rage against Germany and, 144–46, 149, 151; religious imagery used by, 8–9, 175; Singer and, 135, 171, 172, 176, 178, 234, 322n60; Sutzkever compared, 18, 40; Tabatshnik recording of, 144, 162, 170, 171–72, 174, 312n33; Yiddish culture and work of, 142

Zeitlin, Aaron, works: "*A Bintl Varshe-lider*" (A Bundle of Warsaw Poems), 172; *Gezamlte lider* (Collected Poems, 1947), 143–80, 144, 172; "*Gornisht oyser verter*" (Nothing Remains but Words), 177; *"A kholem fun nokh Maydanek"* (A Dream from after Majdanek, 1946), 238–42; *Lider fun khurbn un lider fun gloybn* (Poems of the Holocaust and Poems of Faith, 1967), 143–80; "*Mayn foter*" (My Father), 177; "*Nokh a kleyne poeme, geshribn 1946: Vegn frau Hilde un Her von Goethe*" (Yet Another Small Poem: About Mrs Hilde and Herr von Goethe, 1946), 145; "*Nokhklang tsu 'bay nakht afn altn mark*" (Echo of "A Night in the Old Marketplace," 1943), 176–77; *Poems of the Holocaust and Poems of Faith* (2007), 322n60; "*Varshe, 1912*" (Warsaw, 1912), 172–75, 178–79; "*Zeks shures*" (Six Lines), 178; "*Zuntik af Vashington skver*" (Sunday in Washington Square, 1942), 179–80

Zeitlin, Elkhonon (brother), *In a literarisher shtub* (In a Literary Home, 1946), 100, 176, 254

Zeitlin, Hillel (father), 100, 174

Zelkowicz, Josef, *In yene koshmarne teg* (In Those Terrible Days), 59–60, 63, 298n21, 299n38

Zerubavel, Fryda, *Na venad: Fartseykhenungen fun a pleyte* (Homeless: Notes of a Refugee, 1947), *115*, 255

Zionism, 19, 36, 76, 122, 141

Zychlinsky, Rachel, 315n3

www.ingramcontent.com/pod-product-compliance
Lightning Source LLC
Chambersburg PA
CBHW031425230426
43668CB00007B/439